The Rude, the Bad and the Bawdy

Essays in honour of
Professor Geert Jan van Gelder

edited by

Adam Talib, Marlé Hammond
and Arie Schippers

Gibb Memorial Trust
2014

Published by

The E. J. W. Gibb Memorial Trust

Hardcover Edition ISBN 978-1-909724-33-4
Digital Edition 978-1-909724-34-1

A CIP record for this book is available from the British Library

Further details of the E. J. Gibb Memorial Trust and its publications
are available at the Trust's website

www.gibbtrust.org

Printed in Great Britain by
Berforts Information Press

Contents

Tabula Gratulatoria

قَائِمَة آلمُهَنِّئِين

Wolfhart Heinrichs†
Harvard University

Margaret Larkin
University of California, Berkeley

Andras Hamori
Princeton University

Christopher Melchert
University of Oxford

Hilary Kilpatrick
Lausanne

Robin Ostle
University of Oxford

Willem Stoetzer
University of Leiden

James E. Montgomery
University of Cambridge

Emilie Savage-Smith, FBA
University of Oxford

Remke Kruk
Leiden University

Everett Rowson
New York University

Matthew S. Gordon
Miami University

Chase F. Robinson
The Graduate Center
The City University of New York

Wen-Chin Ouyang
SOAS

Michael Beard
University of North Dakota

Renate Jacobi
Freie Universität Berlin

Wim Raven
University of Marburg

Clifford Edmund Bosworth
University of Exeter

Mohamed-Salah Omri
University of Oxford

Harry Munt
University of Oxford

Anna Livia Beelaert
University of Leiden

Stefan Sperl
SOAS

Martin Stokes
University of Oxford

Ronald E. Kon
Leiden University

István Kristó-Nagy
University of Exeter

Nadia Jamil
University of Oxford

Kristina Richardson
Queens College
The City University of New York

Ulrich Marzolph
Enzyklopädie des Märchens, Gottingen

Robert Hoyland
University of Oxford

Gregor Schoeler
University of Basel

Pieter Smoor
University of Amsterdam

Ewald Wagner
University of Giessen

Gert Borg
University of Nijmegen

Jan Schmidt
University of Leiden

Roger Allen
University of Pennsylvania

Julia Bray
University of Oxford

John Nawas

Antonella Ghersetti
Ca' Foscari University, Venice

Th. Emil Homerin
University of Rochester

Sir Michael Scholar
former President, St John's College, Oxford

Emily Selove
University of Manchester

Jeremy Johns
University of Oxford

Adam Talib
The American University in Cairo

Shawkat Toorawa
Cornell University

Sinan Antoon
New York University

Petra Sijpesteijn
University of Leiden

Humphrey Davies
The American University in Cairo

Thomas Bauer
University of Münster

Jaakko Hämeen-Anttila
University of Helsinki

Nefeli Papoutsakis
University of Münster

Richard van Leeuwen
University of Amsterdam

Clive Holes, FBA
University of Oxford

Monica Balda-Tillier
IFAO (Cairo)

Laurent Mignon
University of Oxford

Monique Bernards

Muhsin al-Musawi
Columbia University

Denis McAuley
United Nations, New York

Beatrice Gruendler
Yale University

Frédéric Lagrange
Université Paris-Sorbonne (Paris IV)

Marlé Hammond
SOAS

Arie Schippers
University of Amsterdam

Philip Kennedy
New York University

Dominic Brookshaw
University of Oxford

Geert Jan van Gelder
A Biographical Sketch

The celebrant of this volume retired from full-time teaching duties in 2012, an occasion we mark with the publication of this collection of essays, but his active work as a researcher, supervisor, translator, and teacher shows no signs of abating. Indeed in the last year alone, Geert Jan van Gelder has given us a major study of the formal aspects of classical Arabic poetry (*Sound and Sense in Classical Arabic Poetry*) and an anthology of classical Arabic texts in translation (*Classical Arabic Literature: a Library of Arabic Literature anthology*). In addition, Prof. van Gelder has recently embarked on major projects including translations and editions of Abū l-ʿAlāʾ al-Maʿarrī's *Risālat al-Ghufrān* with Prof. Gregor Schoeler, of *Ḥikāyat Abī al-Qāsim al-Baghdādī* with Emily Selove, and Ibn Abī Uṣaybiʿah's *ʿUyūn al-anbāʾ fī ṭabaqāt al-aṭibbāʾ* with Profs Simon Swain, Emilie Savage-Smith, and others. The reader should therefore be aware that any summary of Prof. van Gelder's intellectual contributions to date is premature and will soon be rendered obsolete by the honouree's indefatigable commitment to scholarship.

Gerard Jan Henk van Gelder (known to most as Geert Jan) was born on 10 June 1947 in post-war Amsterdam to Gerard Jan van Gelder, a bank employee, and Hendrika Venmans, a widely read polyglot and music lover. His parents were areligious, though their ethics and frugality were owed somewhat to a Calvinist cultural background as well as to the aftermath of the Second World War. Geert Jan inherited his father's name, but it was his mother's passions – languages and music – which were to become his own. In addition to a lifelong interest in music as a performer, singer, and aficionado, Geert Jan studied several languages throughout his schooling and his adult life. His only sister, Molly, is also a linguist, and she works as an English-Dutch translator in Amsterdam. At his Dutch Gymnasium, students studied Greek, Latin, English, French, German, and even some Russian. Geert Jan and his schoolfriends invented their own secret language and he precociously bought himself *Teach Yourself Arabic* before he had even begun his university course. Geert Jan and his English wife Dr Sheila M. Ottway raised their two daughters, Caroline (b. 1977) and Fiona (b. 1981), who happen also to share their father's interest in music, in an entirely bilingual Dutch-English household.

It was no surprise then that Geert Jan chose to study Arabic and Semitic Languages first at the University of Amsterdam and then at Leiden. He received his Doctoraal (combined bachelor's and master's degree) in 1972 and began working as a librarian at the Institute for Modern Near Eastern Studies in 1973. At the time, he was also teaching Arabic and Dutch language classes to adults in Zaandam. It was in one of his Dutch classes that Geert Jan first met Sheila Ottway who had moved to the Netherlands to work for a scientific publisher after completing a degree in Zoology in the U.K. Geert Jan took Sheila on holiday to Cairo, where he had spent a year studying as an undergraduate, and they were married in Winchester in England in 1973. A couple of years later in 1975, the couple moved from Amsterdam to Haren, a large village five miles outside of Groningen, where Geert Jan took up a position as lecturer in Arabic. Sheila continued to work as an academic editor and translator, a job that she could perform from home, especially fortunate since childcare facilities in the Netherlands were highly inadequate at the time. Many years later, Sheila would complete a Ph.D. at the University of Groningen on 17th-century autobiographical writings by English women. For his part, Geert Jan had already begun his doctoral research at Leiden under the supervision of Prof. Jan Brugman, a fellow music lover, when he was appointed lecturer in Arabic at Groningen.

Alongside his teaching, Geert Jan wrote the doctoral thesis that was to become his first book *Beyond the Line: Classical Arabic Literary Critics on the Coherence and Unity of the Poem* (published in Leiden by Brill in 1982). The book went against the mainstream 'unitarian' trend in classical Arabic poetry that was prevalent at the time and was, perhaps for that reason, not reviewed in the pages of the *Journal of Arabic Literature* for more than a decade. Mild controversy stalked Geert Jan in his employment, as well. Before he had finished his Ph.D., his tenure was blocked, but with the support of his colleagues, he won the case at tribunal. This aside, Geert Jan and his family spent many happy years in Groningen, where he usually worked from home and cycled to work even in the snow. Geert Jan also went on book-buying expeditions to Cairo every few years until relatively recently when he discovered he no longer had any more shelf space in the house. He published widely on topics in classical Arabic literature including invective poetry, incest, food, bathhouses, and countless other subjects, though he has focussed primarily on the history of classical Arabic poetic stylistics and literary criticism and theory.

Geert Jan would soon become one of the most prolific scholars in the field, publishing countless articles, encyclopaedia entries, and book reviews as well as nineteen monographs and edited collections in both English and Dutch. This would not have been possible had Geert Jan not benefited from Sheila's energy, generosity, and skill in their life at home as well as in his scholarship. Not everyone knows that Sheila has always been the first person to read Geert Jan's writings and that she has edited all his English publications, a priceless gift for any of us whether or not English is our mother tongue. Beginning with his first book, Geert Jan's publications have always reflected an erudition and breadth of reading unique among Arabists and he has been heard to exhort students to 'pickle themselves in texts'. Geert Jan also served as executive editor of *Middle Eastern Literatures* from 1999–2011 and chair of the editorial board of the Oxford Oriental Monographs Series from 2001–2012. He continues as chair of the advisory board of the *Encyclopedia of Islam, Third Edition*, a position he has held since 2003, and as a member of the Gibb Memorial Trust. His impressive research profile won him election to the Koninklijke Nederlandse Akademie van Wetenschappen (Royal Netherlands Academy of Arts and Science) in 1997, an honour that came as a surprise as it was usually unheard of for lecturers. A year later in 1998, Geert Jan was elected to succeed Wilferd Madelung as Laudian Professor of Arabic in the University of Oxford and his election to the British Academy followed soon thereafter.

The move to Oxford was challenging in certain respects, but it afforded Geert Jan and

Sheila a range of new opportunities. She completed a master's in garden history at the University of Bristol, which she supplemented with a diploma in architectural history, and subsequently began teaching courses on these subjects in the University of Oxford's Department for Continuing Education in 2005. Geert Jan, on the other hand, enjoyed Oxford's rich musical life as well as his fellowship and governing body membership at St John's College. Noteworthy in this respect were the piano duets that he performed with Sir Michael Scholar, President of St John's, in the 'Concerts in the Lodgings' series that Sir Michael hosted in his official residence. Geert Jan furthermore relished the university's holdings in Arabic literature, and the opportunity to supervise graduate theses (though he had already been doing this as 'second supervisor' in the Netherlands). He has also continued to share his specialist knowledge with the wider community through print and broadcast media and in public lectures; a practice he continues with his translations for the Library of Arabic Literature Series (edited by Philip Kennedy and published by NYU Press). Geert Jan retired from most of his teaching duties in 2012 at the age of sixty-five in part to escape the burdens of marking and administration, and also to make more time for his scholarship and the two newest members of his family: his grandchildren, Luca James (Fiona's son) and Robin Julia (Caroline's daughter), born within two weeks of each other in Groningen in July 2012. The editors and contributors join Geert Jan's students, colleagues, and friends in wishing him the long and productive retirement he so richly deserves.

Notes on the Contributors

Roger Allen is Professor Emeritus of Arabic and Comparative Literature at the University of Pennsylvania, having retired in 2011. He is the author, among other works, of *The Arabic Novel*, 2nd ed., Syracuse University Press, 1995; and *The Arabic Literary Heritage*, Cambridge University Press, 1998. In addition to publishing a number of articles on the Arabic literary tradition and particularly its fiction, he has translated over 20 novels into English. He currently serves as co-editor of the journal *Middle Eastern Literatures* and as sub-editor of the *Encyclopaedia of Islam*, 3rd ed.

Monica Balda-Tillier is a specialist in classical Arabic literature. She is currently a research fellow at the French Institute for Oriental Archaeology (IFAO) in Cairo and will assume a teaching position at Grenoble Stendhal 3 in September 2013. There are two strands to her research activities: she investigates 'courtly' love prose and the theory of profane love on the one hand and 'neglected' literature on the other. Her interests focus, in particular, on non-classical aspects of Arabic literature and on the Mamluk and Ottoman periods of Arabic literature that have long been considered an age of 'decadence'.

Thomas Bauer (Ph.D. /Habilitation, Erlangen 1989/1997) is Professor of Arabic and Islamic Studies at the University of Münster. His main research areas are Arabic literature, rhetoric and cultural history from ancient times (*Altarabische Dichtkunst*, 1992) and the Abbasid period (*Liebe und Liebesdichtung in der arabischen Welt des 9. und 10. Jahrhunderts*, 1998) up until the Ottoman era. His recent studies have focused on the Arabic literature of the Mamluk period, especially on the work of Ibn Nubāta al-Miṣrī and the popular poet al-Miʿmār. In the field of cultural anthropology of the pre-modern Arabic world Bauer has treated subjects such as love and sexuality, death, strangeness, and tolerance of ambiguity (*Die Kultur der Ambiguität*, 2011). He was appointed member of the North Rhine-Westphalian Academy of Sciences, Humanities and the Arts in 2012 and was awarded the Gottfried Wilhelm Leibniz Prize in 2013.

Jaakko Hämeen-Anttila (Ph.D. 1994), Professor of Arabic and Islamic Studies at the University of Helsinki (since 2000), has published widely in English and Finnish on Classical Arabic literature, Classical Persian literature, and Mediaeval Arabic-Islamic cultural history. His books include *Maqama: A History of a Genre* (2002), *Islamin käsikirja* (Handbook of Islam, 2004), and *The Last Pagans of Iraq: Ibn Wahshiyya and his Nabatean Agriculture* (2006). He has also translated numerous works from Arabic and Persian into Finnish, including the Qur'an (Koraani, 1994).

Marlé Hammond is Lecturer in Arabic Popular Literature and Culture at SOAS, University of London. After earning her Ph.D. under Magda Al-Nowaihi at Columbia University, she was appointed Research Centre Fellow in the Programme of Arabic Poetry and Comparative Poetics at St John's College, Oxford (2002–2006) and then as British Academy Postdoctoral Fellow at the Oriental Institute, Oxford (2007–2010). She is the author of *Beyond Elegy: Classical Arabic Women's Poetry in Context* (2010) and the co-editor (with Professor van Gelder) of Takhyīl*: the Imaginary in Classical Arabic Poetics* (2009).

Clive Holes has been Khalid bin Abdullah Al Saud Professor for the Study of the Contemporary Arab World at the University of Oxford since 1997, having previously been a Lecturer and Reader in Arabic at the University of Cambridge. He served for many years in the Middle East and North Africa as a cultural diplomat. His research and writing range widely over the Arabic language, in particular its regional forms, and he has also published extensively on Arabic dialectal poetry from Arabia, the Gulf, Jordan, Iraq and Egypt. He is a Fellow of the British Academy.

Frédéric Lagrange, born 1964, is a Professor of Arabic language and literature at Université Paris-Sorbonne and a translator of classical prose (Tawḥīdī's *Maṯālib al-Wazīrayn*) and contemporary fiction (Hudā Barakāt, Ḫayrī Šalabī, 'Abduh Ḫāl). His research mainly focuses on (1) linguistics in literature and pop culture productions: representation and stylization of diglossia (2) gender constitution and gender transgression in Arabic literary lore (3) sociology of music and musicians in the modern and contemporary Middle-East. He is presently working on a new monograph entitled 'Portraits of debauchery' (in French).

Richard van Leeuwen (Ph.D. 1992) is lecturer in Islamic Studies at the University of Amsterdam. His research interests focus on Middle Eastern history, Arabic Literature and Islam in the modern world. His scholarly publications include *The Thousand and One Nights: Space, Travel and Transformation* (2007), *Waqfs and Urban Structures: the Case of Ottoman Damascus* (1999), and *Notables and Clergy in Mount Lebanon: the Khāzin Sheiks and the Maronite Church (1736–1840)* (1994). He also serves as a translator of Arabic literature.

Denis McAuley was Beeston Scholar at St John's College, Oxford. His doctoral thesis on the poetry of Ibn ʿArabī was co-supervised by Professor van Gelder, who brought a welcome dose of levity to that ponderous subject. McAuley is the author of *Ibn 'Arabī's Mystical Poetics* and several related articles, and his research interests include Sufi poetry and classical Arabic poetics more generally. He now works as a translator at United Nations Headquarters in New York.

Wen-chin Ouyang is Professor of Arabic and Comparative Literature at SOAS, University of London. She is the author of *Politics of Nostalgia in the Arabic Novel* (2013), *Poetics of Love in the Arabic Novel* (2012), and *Literary Criticism in Medieval Arabic Islamic Culture* (1997), editor of *New Perspectives on the Arabian Nights* (2005) and co-editor (with Stephen Hart) of *A Companion to Magical Realism* (2005). She currently serves as executive editor of the journal *Middle Eastern Literatures*.

Nefeli Papoutsakis earned her doctorate under Professor van Gelder at Oxford University (D.Phil. 2008) and was subsequently appointed British Academy Postdoctoral Fellow (2009–2012) at the Oriental Institute, Oxford. She is presently senior research fellow of the Gerda-Henkel Stiftung at the University of Münster. Her monograph, *Desert Travel as a form of Boasting: a Study of* D̲ū *r-Rumma's Poetry*, was published in 2009.

Arie Schippers, born in Voorburg, Netherlands (near The Hague) 1947, studied Semitic and Romance Languages (Arabic, Hebrew, Italian, Spanish) at Leiden University, where he passed his 'doctoraal' examination in Arabic in 1973 and in Italian in 1974. He received his Ph.D. degree in Literature in 1988 at Amsterdam University with his dissertation *Arabic Tradition and Hebrew Innovation: Arabic Themes in Hebrew Andalusian Poetry*. He was a researcher at Leiden University from 1974–1976, taught Hebrew at Nijmegen University in 1976–1977, and taught Arabic at Amsterdam University from 1977–2012. He is now a guest researcher Semitic and Romance languages at the same university. His research is concentrated on Arabic and Hebrew medieval poetry in Muslim Spain (al-Andalus) in connection and comparison with the medieval Romance literatures of Southern Europe (Spain, Provence and Italy).

Jan Schmidt is Lecturer in Turkish at Leiden University. His main field of interest is Ottoman history and literature. He wrote a dissertation on Mustafa Âli Efendi's famous late sixteenth-century history *Künhü l-ahbar* and books and articles on the diplomatic and economic relations between the Ottoman Empire and the Netherlands. His substantial publications include a four-volume catalogue of Turkish manuscripts in Dutch libraries and museums.

Gregor Schoeler, born 1944, is Professor Emeritus in Islamic studies at the University of Basel. He obtained his Ph.D. in 1972 at the University of Giessen (Germany) and his Habilitation in 1981 at the same university. From 1982 to 2009 he held the Chair of Islamic Studies at the University of Basel (Switzerland). In 2000 he lectured at the Ecole pratique des Hautes Etudes at the Sorbonne in Paris; in 2010 he was Messenger Lecturer at Cornell University. His books include *The Oral and the Written in Early Islam* (2006), *The Biography of Muhammad* (2011) (winner of Iran's World Prize for the best book of the year, 2012) and an edition of Part 4 (*al-Ghazaliyyāt*) of the *Dīwān* of Abū Nuwās (2nd ed. 2003). Together with Geert Jan van Gelder, he edited and translated the *Epistle of Forgiveness* by Abū l-ʿAlāʾ al-Maʿarrī.

Emily Selove is a research associate at the University of Manchester, where she is part of the Arabic Commentaries on the Hippocratic Aphorisms project. She received her Ph.D. from UCLA's department of Near Eastern Languages and Cultures in 2012, where her dissertation, The Hikaya of Abu al-Qasim: The Comic Banquet in Greek, Latin, and Arabic, focused on an 11th-century text about a Baghdadi party-crasher crashing a party in Isfahan. Her research interests include medieval Arabic satire, banquet literature, and medieval medicine, especially as it pertains to quackery, the obscene, and erotological literature. She is also a translator of medieval Arabic literature, and her illustrated translation, *Selections from the Art of Party-Crashing in Medieval Iraq*, was published in 2012.

Pieter Smoor was born in Bandung, the Dutch East Indies (now Indonesia) in 1939 and studied Arabic and Islam at Leiden University. From 1966–2004 he taught Arabic Literature at the University of Amsterdam. He has produced studies on Abū l-ʿAlā al-Maʿarrī, Ibn al-Rūmī, Ibn Qalāqis and ʿUmāra al-Yamanī . His publications include 'Enigmatic allusion and double meaning in Maʿarrī's newly-discovered Letter of a horse and a mule', *Journal of Arabic Literature* 12 (1981) and 13 (1982); *Kings and Bedouins in the Palace of Aleppo as reflected in Maʿarrī's Works* (1985); 'Ibn al-Rūmī, Elegies and Mock Elegies for Friends and Foes', *Quaderni di Studi Arabi* 15 (1997); 'ʿUmāra's Elegies and the Lamp of Loyalty', *Annales Islamologiques* 34 (2000); and *Wazāra: the Killer of Many Husbands* (2007). He has also conducted scholarly travels to ancient libraries in Istanbul, Damascus, Tunis and Cairo.

Adam Talib teaches classical Arabic literature at the American University in Cairo and is a literary translator. His research is concerned primarily with the history of Arabic poetry, especially in the poorly studied period, 1200–1800. Adam wrote his doctoral thesis on Arabic epigram anthologies at Oxford under Geert Jan van Gelder's supervision and indeed it was to study with Prof. van Gelder that Adam moved to the U.K. He counts this as one of the best decisions he has ever made and Prof. van Gelder remains his most important mentor.

Ewald Wagner was born in Hamburg in 1927 and studied Semitic languages, Islamic studies and phonetics at the University of Hamburg. He worked as a librarian at the University of Mainz (1955–64) before his appointment as Professor for Semitic Languages and Islamic Studies (1964–93) at the University of Giessen. His publications include two works which have featured prominently as essential sources for many of the chapters in this volume: his study of Abū Nūwās, *Abū Nuwās: eine Studie zur arabischen Literatur den frühen 'Abbāsidenzeit* (1965), and his scholarly edition of Abū Nuwās' collected poetry, *Dīwān Abī Nuwās* (*Der Dīwān des Abū Nuwās* 1958–2006).

Introduction

In the summer of 2012, Geert Jan van Gelder retired from the post of Laudian Professor of Arabic at the University of Oxford and also celebrated his sixty-fifth birthday. In the light of Professor van Gelder's distinguished career and collegial generosity, his doctoral student Adam Talib, his post-doctoral mentee Marlé Hammond, and his esteemed colleague Professor Arie Schippers, wrote to a number of friends and associates proposing to produce a Festschrift in honour of Professor van Gelder's legacy. In an effort to lend coherence to the proposed volume, and as tribute to the celebratee's sustained interest in humour and irreverence, they invited potential contributors to compose essays on *mujūn*, broadly understood as literary expressions of indecency, encompassing the obscene, the profane, the impudent, and the taboo. Contributors were encouraged to tackle the subject from a wide variety of perspectives beyond the merely prurient and to produce studies detailing the ways in which indecency has been signified, signalled, evaluated, and preserved. They were furthermore invited to contribute translations and commentaries of exemplarily audacious texts. *The Rude, the Bad, and the Bawdy*, whose title echoes that of Professor van Gelder's own book on Arabic satire (*The Bad and the Ugly*), was thus conceived.

We open our volume with a playful exploration of the rather unstable temporal and cultural dimensions of the semantic field of *mujūn*, often translated simply as 'obscenity' and intimately associated with both poetic imagery and the lifestyles of poets. **Wen-chin Ouyang**'s *Mujūn, Junūn, Funūn*, an essay whose titular paronomasia aptly describes the intersection of debauchery, madness and art, as matters of conduct, reason and expression, considers the ambiguity of the term's usage in Abbasid anecdotal literature where the practitioners of *mujūn* are represented as engaged in clever banter rather than any kind of sexual impropriety. This non-judgmental portraiture is contrasted with the moralistically disapproving stances of early twentieth-century scholars, who, in a process of cultural 'othering', were rather keen to distance the Arabic tradition from the origins of the 'obscene' genre and to view it as emanating from the Persians. Through this juxtaposition, the various ways (*funūn*) in which discussions of *mujūn* and *junūn* tend to intersect with, for example, *zandaqa*, point to the broader discourses on community and the ways in which this community is imagined as one whose members' conduct has consequences for social harmony. The literary arts (*adab*) clearly have an important role, but should they be subject to communal control? Or do discourses on *mujūn* and *junūn* carve out multifarious trajectories (*funūn*) of transgression on which art thrives and is legitimated? These questions about terminology lead us to the second chapter, **Jaakko Hämeen-Anttila**'s *What is Obscene? Obscenity in Classical Arabic Literature*, which also questions the limits of the term as it is culturally defined. What is considered obscene in one culture need not be so in another. In Classical Arabic literature the reception of obscenity is rarely discussed, yet it is an important aspect in assessing not only the *mujūn*, a term often reserved for texts deemed obscene, but also a variety of other genres, from anecdotes about sexual mores to love poetry. The article discusses various forms of erotic literature and their reception in mediaeval Arab-Islamic culture, as well as the attitude towards the use of sexual vocabulary. The material is taken from erotic manuals, poetry and anecdotes, as well as from prefaces to *adab* compilations and learned literature.

Enter the Abbasid poet Abū Nuwās (199 AH/814 CE), the *mājin* par excellence, and the central figure of Chapters 3–6. As a transition from the interrogation of terminology to the treatment of the images, themes and poetic devices of this particular poet, as well as others composing within his tradition, we begin this section of the volume with **Pieter Smoor**'s *A Suspicion of Excessive Frankness*, which enumerates the language and imagery of sex and their often irreverent cloaking in religious expressions. The distinguishing mark of *mujūn*, Smoor argues, is a style of poetry which is in its wording quite unashamed and open and whose allusions to sexual intercourse are both transparent and intertwined with serious and religious discourse. Abū Nuwās, for example, applies the metaphoric images of the whale of Jonas and the staff of Moses frequently, and these images derive, of course, from the Quranic stories concerning the prophets. A few generations after him, Ibn al-Rūmī draws the attention of his contemporary public with *mujūn* of lesser gravity; the poet's equally uninhibited descriptions of scandalous varieties of intercourse are often inserted into fiercely satirical poems rather than draped in religious symbolism.

Chapter 4, **Gregor Schoeler**'s *Abū Nuwās' Poem to the Zoroastrian Boy Bihrūz: An Arabic 'sawgand-nāma' with a Persian 'kharja'*, analyses an unusual poem by Abū Nuwas in which the poet addresses a Zorastrian youth with a view to seducing him. Very interesting are the scores of oaths the poet swears in order to play up to the young man and to bring him to heel: he swears by the Zoroastrian religion, fire temples, the elements, etc. The poem contains a great number of Persian words, and what is most noteworthy in this regard is that the last verse of the poem is made up of an entire sentence in the Persian language – something like a 'final *taḍmīn*' and in a way a precursor of the *kharja* of the Andalusian *muwashshaḥ*. The contribution is divided in three parts: translation, philological commentary and interpretation of the poem. This linking of the poet's legacy with the cultural production of al-Andalus paves the way for Chapter 5, **Arie Schippers**' *The Mujūn Genre by Abū Nuwās and by Ibn Quzmān: a comparison*. It is often said that the poetic themes of Abū Nuwās' *mujūn* poems as well as his wine poems (*khamriyyāt*) influenced all later themes in *mujūn* and *khamr* poetry. Schippers contests this notion, however, arguing that the famous *mujūn zajal* poem (no. 91) by the Arabic Andalusian poet Ibn Quzmān (1078–1160) has a totally different inspiration.

From a notoriously bawdy poet and the dimensions of his corpus we move on to some famously bawdy works by other authors. Chapter 6, **Nefeli Papoutsakis**' *The The Ayrīyāt of Abū Ḥukayma (d. 240/854): A preliminary study*, discusses the motifs and structures of a series of poems known as the *ayriyyāt* – or penis odes – in which the rather obscure Abbasid poet Abū Ḥukayma laments his impotence. This is followed by two essays about the Ḥikāyat Abī l-Qāsim, a prosimetrical narrative work composed in the tenth or eleventh century and ascribed to Abū l-Muṭahhar al-Azdī featuring the antihero and *mājin* Abu l-Qāsim, who crashes a party and challenges a guest to a game of chess, reciting a baffling speech or poem with each move. In Chapter 7, **Monica Balda-Tillier**'s *ʿUdhrī Love and Mujūn: Opposites and parallels*, the language and themes of Abū l-Qasim's utterances are compared with those of the exemplary 'platonic' ʿUdhrī love poets, as they are cited in a variety of love treatises and *adab* compilations. Though this comparison, Balda-Tillier illustrates how the theory of profane love influenced the 'code' of *mujūn* and how these two models are not only built on opposition, but also on imitation and complementarity. Then, in Chapter 8, **Emily Selove**'s *Mujūn is a Crazy Game* examines the function of chess and Abū l-Qāsim's nonsensical speeches in the narrative as a microcosm of the world of *mujūn*, often characterized not only by the inversion of the rules of everyday life, but also by the establishment of an alternative and temporary topsy-turvy set of rules. The chapter offers some theories on the philosophical and metaphorical significance of the game of chess, while attempting to describe the game played in the *Ḥikāya* move by move.

Thomas Bauer's contribution, *Dignity at Stake: Mujūn epigrams by Ibn Nubāta (686–768/1287–1366) and his contemporaries*, which forms Chapter 9, also explores and contextualises the obscene corpus of a particular poet, Ibn Nubāta. Bauer's tribute to Geert Jan van Gelder stands out in this collection in that it is the only piece which models itself on its primary sources. Like a Mamluk anthology dedicated to poems on a particular theme, the essay approaches its subject matter in the form of a syllogism; the 'premises' are comprised of studies on the topic, and the 'conclusion' consists of poetic citations. In Bauer's first premise, he offers the reader an overview of Mamlūk *mujūn* verse; in the second he focuses on the corpus of four particular poets; and in his conclusion he presents 21 epigrams by Ibn Nubāta.

From an exploration of concepts of obscenity as they apply to Arabic poetic culture, to investigations of particular poems and poets featuring sexual indiscreet imagery, we move on to two chapters that dwell on less 'adult' matters and enter into the realm of scatological humour. Chapter 10, **Ewald Wagner**'s *Lyrics on a Fart*, discusses a variety of satirical verses inspired by the legendary Abbasid breaker-of-wind Wahb b. Sulayman, a postmaster whose newsworthy if inadvertent gaseous emission at the assembly of a vizier became proverbial for fast-spreading fame. Particular attention is paid in this piece to the lyrics of Ibn al-Rūmī (d. 896) on the subject. Following on from Ewald Wagner, in Chapter 11, *Two fart jokes in Ibn ʿArabī's* Muḥāḍarat al-abrār, **Denis McAuley** returns to the subject of the fart, more specifically the inclusion of fart jokes in an *adab* compilation by Ibn ʿArabī (1165–1240), a writer known for his metaphysical works. Their inclusion, argues McAuley, seems to be for the sole purpose of entertainment and disproves to a certain extent the idea that the author was concerned with either a moralising or didactic purpose.

After our brief foray into the scatological we return to the sexual, this time dwelling not on sexual poetry but rather sexuality in narrative, narratives which are modern and contemporary but very much imprinted with and responding to old erotic paradigms. We begin with what might be termed phantasmagoric encounters between people and genies. Chapter 12, **Richard van Leeuwen**'s *Love or Lust: Sexual relationships between humans and jinns in the Thousand and One Nights and The Djinn in the Nightingale's Eye*, compares the psychological and narratalogical aspects of the jinn figure in a story by the British author A.S. Byatt as well as in the tale of 'Sayf al-Mulūk and Badīʿ al-Jamāl' in the *Thousand and One Nights* and argues that the jinn functions psychologically as a release of repressed desire and structurally as a disruption of the narrative. The next two chapters also address a kind of disruption, but this time it is not necessarily internal to the narrative but rather relates to the disjuncture between the playfulness of expressions of *mujūn* in the classical Arabic tradition versus the gravity that often characterizes explicit or graphic sexuality in modern prose narratives. In Chapter 13, *The Obscenity of Sexual Torture*, **Roger Allen** suggests that obscenity in these texts often evokes squeamishness rather than laughter. After considering the theme of sexual torture in modern Arabic literature in general and in prison literature more specifically, he then discusses its exemplification in BenSalim Himmich's *Muʿadhdhibatī* (*My Torturess*, 2010), a novel featuring a ghoulishly sexual female interrogator. Chapter 14, **Frédéric Lagrange**'s *Modern Arabic Literature and the Disappearance of Mujūn: Same-sex rape as a case study* similarly notes this shift away from traditional expressions of *mujūn* (or ribaldry) and contemplates its noticeable disappearance from contemporary Arabic fiction, at a time when sexuality is no longer a discursive taboo. Sexuality is obviously much less linked to laughter and humour in modern literature than it was in medieval *adab*. However, things may not be as straightforward as they seem. One humorous script common in pre-modern *mujūn* literature revolves around the scenarized rape of a male adolescent in his sleep. Deemed a frivolous but immensely amusing subject at the time, this act is hardly considered a matter for laughter nowadays and forces us to a closer examination of the rapist's laugh and the victim's shame. The analysis is based on Ibn al-Manẓūr's *Akhbār Abī Nuwās* and al-Iṣfahānī's *Kitāb al-Aghānī;* these texts are contrasted with modern Arabic works of fiction, particularly ʿAbduh Khāl's *Tarmī bi-sharar* (2009) and ʿAbdallāh Bin Bakhīt's *Shāriʿ al-ʿAṭāyif* (2009). Together these three chapters reflect on representations of sexuality in modern literature and how they are both entangled with and distinct from their pre-modern precedents.

Thereafter we have a cluster of chapters with three aspects in common; 1) they each engage with elements of folklore or 'popular culture', 2) they each explore women's verse, and 3) they each feature, more specifically, women's satire, or lampooning of men. Chapter 15, **Marlé Hammond**'s *The Foul-Mouthed Faḥla: Obscenity and amplification in early women's invective*, analyses the spousal invectives of Ḥumayda, daughter of al-Nuʿmān b. Bashīr (d. 684 CE) and the patterns of escalation in their 'indecent' scatological and sexual images. The patterns, Hammond argues, are characteristic of folkloric literature and, as the anecdotes in question become increasingly historicised the patterns within them become somewhat obscured, and the perspective rooted in female sexuality becomes somewhat muted, undermining to some extent Ḥumayda's sexual and poetic 'prowess'. We then move from the seventh century, C.E., to the twenty-first, and the case of a less personal and intimate but no less 'damaging' invective is the subject of Chapter 16, **Clive Holes**' *A Saudi 'Housewife' Goes to War: الفتاوي الشريرة or 'the evil* fatwas'. In March 2010, a colloquial (so-called nabaṭī) poem by a Saudi woman, Ḥiṣṣa Hilāl, entitled الفتاوي الشريرة or 'the evil *fatwas*' was awarded third prize in the final of the fourth season of the popular colloquial poetry talent show 'Poet in a Million', produced and broadcast by Abu Dhabi TV. The poem takes issue with the tendency of Saudi clerics to issue *fatwas* in line with their own particular interpretations of Islam, and the intolerant fanaticism that often lies behind them. It has been interpreted by some as a personal attack on one particular cleric, the blind seventy-seven year-old Sheikh Abdurraḥmān bin Nāṣir al-Barrāk, who had issued a *fatwa* condemning the mixing of the sexes in public places two weeks earlier. Ḥiṣṣa Hilāl has repeatedly denied that her poem was ever intended as a personal attack on Sheikh Abdurraḥmān, but this has not prevented death threats being issued against her. Following age-old nabaṭī tradition, her poem has attracted a number of poetic rebuttals, attacking her poem and position, and defending the *status quo*. Alongside the originals, the chapter provides versified English translations and explanations of both Ḥiṣṣa Hilāl's poem and the most high-profile of the rebuttals. The vehicle of format television for the satirizing of a male authority then leads into an essay on the lyrics of popular music with Chapter 17, **Adam Talib**'s *Caricature and Obscenity in Mujūn Poetry and African-American Women's Hip-Hop*. Talib argues that there is a particular rhetorical facet of Arabic poetry that is analogous to camp, and he explores one such example of this tendency in poetic discourse – what he describes as caricatured obscenity – through a comparison of pre-modern Arabic *mujūn* poetry and contemporary hip-hop by female rappers, some of whom have decided to redeploy masterfully the so-called vulgar discourse of 'gangsta rap' to exaggerate and caricature stereotypical depictions of hyper-masculinity (or machismo) in hip-hop culture.

We close the volume with a piece which in many ways stands on its own and yet returns to some of the issues raised in the first chapter by Wen-chin Ouyang. Chapter 18, **Jan Schmidt**'s *Love and Sex among the Ottomans (1500–1800)*, is singular in a few respects: first, it is a review article, making scholarship its subject matter; second, it surveys homoeroticism rather than rudeness, obscenity, and bawdiness; and third, it encompasses a Turkish dimension. Schmidt discusses the recurring theme of the infatuation of men for young boys in Ottoman literary works, a topic which has become a focus for scholarly interest from the 1980s onward. Schmidt charts the phenomenon through a discussion of three books: 1) *The Age of the Beloveds: Love and the Beloved in Early-Modern Ottoman and European Culture and Society* by Walter Andrews and Mehmet Kapaklı (2005); (2) *Before Homosexuality in the Arab-Islamic World, 1500–1800* by Khaled el-Rouayheb (2005); and (3) *Producing Desire: Changing Sexual Discourse in the Ottoman Middle East, 1500–1900* by Dror Ze'evi (2006). Like Ouyang, Schmidt considers the conceptual framework through which representations of sexuality are filtered by scholars, but whereas Ouyang captures a scholarly moment at the beginning of the twentieth century when Arab scholars, writing in Arabic, were reinterpreting their literary legacy in the light of emergent nationalisms as well as orientalist influences, Schmidt considers scholarship produced nearly a century later by academics publishing in English. Both reveal the volatile and contested nature of the reception of sexual representation in literary discourse.

Together these chapters cover a range of interrelated and complex issues on sexuality, gender, language, and poetics from an array of perspectives and with a variety of approaches reflecting the interests and methodologies of several generations of scholars across numerous specialisations within the field of Middle Eastern and Islamic literary studies. Collectively the essays have historical depth and geographical breadth, investigating correspondences and incompatibilities between textual production and textual reception. One intriguing area of investigation that has emerged is the question of what becomes of *mujūn* in the modern era and how it transforms and mutates across space, time, and genre. But many other questions arise from the ways in which the chapters complement each other in their interrogation of boundaries, broadly construed – be they historic turning points or gradual evolutions, cultural dichotomies and fusions, the so-called gender gap, or the dividing line between the erotic and the pornographic.

It hardly bears recapitulating, but the highlights of Professor van Gelder's career are undeniably impressive. His monographs include: *Beyond the Line: classical Arabic literary critics on the coherence and unity of the poem* (1982), *The Bad and the Ugly: attitudes toward invective poetry (*Hijāʾ*) in classical Arabic literature* (1988), *Of Dishes and Discourse: classical Arabic literary representations of food* (2000), *Close Relationships: incest and inbreeding in classical Arabic literature* (2005), and *Sound and Sense in Classical Arabic Poetry* (2012). And that is to say nothing of his numerous journal articles and book chapters, two anthologies of literary translations – one in Dutch, *Een Arabische Tuin: klassieke Arabische poëzie* (2000), and one in English, *Classical Arabic Literature: a literary anthology* (2013) – a translation of al-Maʿarrī's *Risālat al-ghufrān*, The Epistle of Forgiveness (co-authored with Professor Gregor Schoeler, 2013), an important textual edition – *Two Arabic treatises on stylistics: al-Marghīnānī's* al-Maḥāsin fī 'l-naẓm wa-'l-nathr, *and Ibn Aflaḥ's* Muqaddima, *formerly ascribed to al-Marghīnānī* (1987) – and a number of important edited volumes. In addition, Professor van Gelder, who is a fellow of both the Royal Netherlands Academy of Arts and Sciences and the British Academy, served for many years on the editorial board of the *Journal of Arabic Literature* and was a founder and – until 2012, chief editor – of the journal *Middle Eastern Literatures.* (An exhaustive list of his publications appears at the end of this volume.) It is hoped that *The Rude, the Bad and the Bawdy*, inspired as it is by Geert Jan's interests, ideas, and occasionally irreverent erudition, will be considered a small but diverting component of his vast and monumental legacy.

The editors would like to thank a number of individuals for their material, logistical, and moral support. Roger Allen, Clive Holes and Frédéric Lagrange all submitted their contributions within weeks of our invitation letter, enabling us to secure a publishing contract at an early stage. We are furthermore indebted to the E.J.W. Gibb Memorial Trust for accepting our book proposal and, more particularly, to Trustees James Montgomery and Hugh Kennedy and to Secretary Robin Bligh for their helpful and discrete interventions ahead of the meeting of the Trustees (the celebrant among them) at St John's College in May 2012. Sheila Ottway was instrumental in getting this project off the ground, and we are very grateful for her assistance and enthusiasm. We would also like to thank the staff at Oxbow Books, and especially Val Lamb and Tara Evans, for their careful attention to the manuscript. Alasdair Watson of the Bodleian Library, Oxford and Professor Bernard O'Kane of the American University in Cairo provided their expert advice and sample images for the cover art. Finally, we would like to acknowledge all those colleagues and friends who voiced their support for the Festschrift; we have added your names to the Tabula Gratulatoria.

A NOTE ON TRANSLITERATION

Although it was originally our intention as editors to follow one system of transliteration from the Arabic throughout the entire volume, in the end we decided to allow the contributors some leeway in their chosen method, and we have aimed instead to ensure consistency within the individual essays.

1

Mujūn, Junūn, Funūn

Wen-chin Ouyang

> I imagine that the form in which *mujūn* and wine poetry developed in the second century, as well as love poetry addressed to boys, must have been an echo of ancient Persian poetry accessible to and read by poets towards the end of the first century and during the second. It is inconceivable that these poets would have dared to deal openly with the subject [in their poetic expressions] simply because these phenomena [wine-drinking and homosexuality] had become widespread in society due to Persian influence. If this had been the case, they would have been met with disdain according to public taste and prevalent conventions. However, the existence of the expressions of these subjects in ancient Persian poetry, the availability of these to the reading public, and their familiarity with them made it easy for poets to tackle these subjects boldly, without embarrassment or fear of societal disapproval.
>
> Muḥammad Muṣṭafā Haddāra[1]

The Arab twentieth century saw a cultural revivalist and revisionist movement that was both massive and stupendous. It took it upon itself the task of reviving and revising Arabic cultural heritage in its entirety and of writing sizable, multi-volume histories of Muslim civilisation and Arabic literature as part of the project of modernisation that was begun by the first generation of modernists and modernisers in the nineteenth century. The contributions of the twentieth century modernists and modernisers are, however, marked by an easily detectable but to-date unexplained difference, even though what they wrote and published were, one may argue, equally imitative of and responsive to 'Orientalist' discourses on Islam, the Middle East and the Arabic speaking 'world'. This difference may be glimpsed in the discussions of *mujūn*, as a feature of both society and poetry in the period known in Arabic as the first Abbasid era (usually referring to the ninth and tenth centuries of the common calendar). The appearance and ascendance of *mujūn* in the writings of key architects of modernisation of the twentieth century signalled a departure from the classical genres in which the nineteenth century modernists and modernisers wrote, such as *riḥla*, *khiṭaṭ*, *ṭabaqāt*, and a turn to civilisational and literary history through

[1] Muḥammad Muṣṭafā Haddāra, *Ittijāhāt al-shiʿr al-ʿarabī fī l-qarn al-thānī l-hijrī*, 2nd ed. (Cairo: Dār al-Maʿārif, 1970), 93–94.

which they would, as their predecessors did, produce their discourses on Europe, Islamic reform, cultural renaissance and, above all, their civilisational vision and mission articulated as lessons learnt not only from the West but also the past, coloured, as it were, by Arab nationalism that swept through the Arab world at the time.

Muḥammad Muṣṭafā Haddāra, writing before 1969, explains in the passage I quoted above that *mujūn* was of Persian origin both socially and literarily and its spread was precipitated and bolstered by the dominance of Persian cultural and social practices in the trend-making upper classes of Abbasid society. Haddāra was not alone in blaming the Persians for the moral decay of the Abbasids. The hint of condemnation of *mujūn* here, as well as in the writings of his contemporaries in the second half of the twentieth century, such Shawqī Ḍayf[2] and Muṣṭafā al-Shakʿa,[3] was already explicit in the writings of Aḥmad Amīn (1886–1954)[4] and Jurjī Zaydān (1861–1914)[5] and rather vociferous in Ṭāhā Ḥusayn (1989–1973)[6] in the first half of the same century. The social influence of the Persians was now universally acknowledged and condemned. Haddāra here adds ancient Persian poetry as an important source of moral corruption and target of censure. Beyond the purview of this passage, Haddāra, like al-Shakʿa and Ḍayf, juxtaposes the 'decadence' of the Persians to the 'purity' of the Arabs (*ṭahārat al-ʿarab*) as evidenced by the expressions of another group of poets known as the *ʿudhrī*s, considered the heirs to the poetry of mad love, *junūn*, of the Umayyad era when Arab culture was dominant, and gives coherence in an indirectly totalising narrative to the ideas with which Ṭāhā Ḥusayn only flirted. More importantly, he links *mujūn* to *shuʿūbiyya*, *shuʿūbiyya* now seen as racialised movements driven by *zandaqa*, here, understood clearly as Manichaeism.

The narratives of Arab cultural and literary historians in the second half of the twentieth century were clearly responsive to multiple sets of discourses 'East' and 'West' identifiable only in part through the works they cite explicitly in their texts, notes and bibliographies. Haddāra, for one example, refers to classical Arabic as well as 'Orientalist' sources available in Arabic translation. A quick survey of these quoted sources yielded no precedent of the kind of 'othering' on the basis of language and ethnicity so prevalent in these twentieth century narratives. It may be possible to assume that linguistic and ethnic othering was an integral part of the articulation of cultural difference in modern nationalist discourses surrounding these narratives; however, it is impossible to trace the origins of the explicit moral condemnation of *mujūn* to any particular classical Arabic source or any specific

---

[2] See *Al-ʿaṣr al-ʿabbāsī l-awwal* (Cairo: Dār al-Maʿārif, n.d.), 44–88 and 201–289; and *Al-ʿaṣr al-ʿabbāsī l-thānī*, 2nd ed. (Cairo: Dār al-Maʿārif, 1970), 53–114.

[3] See *Al-shiʿr wa l-shuʿarāʾ fī l-ʿaṣr al-ʿabbāsī* (Beirut: Dār al-ʿIlm li l-Malāyīn, 1973), 171–224.

[4] See *Ḍuḥā l-islām*, vols. 1 and 2 (Cairo: Lajnat al-Taʾlīf wa l-Tarjama wa l-Nashr, 1938).

[5] See *Tārīkh al-tamaddun al-islāmī* (1901–1906), vol. 5 (Cairo: Dār al-Hilāl, 1905); and *Tārīkh ādāb al-lugha al-ʿarabiyya* (1910–1913) vol. 2, ed. Shawqī Ḍayf (Cairo: Dār al-Hilāl, n.d.), 12–106.

[6] See *Ḥadith al-arbiʿāʾ*, a collection in three volumes of a series of essays Ḥusayn published in the nineteen twenties and thirties on literary criticism (vol. 1 [Cairo: al-Maktaba al-Tijāriyya al-Kubrā, 1925], vol. 2 [Cairo: Dār al-Kutub, 1926], vol 3 [Cairo: Dār al-Maʿārif, n.d.]), which were republished in a three-volume *Min tārīkh al-adab al-ʿarabī* (Beirut: Dār al-ʿIlm li l-Malāyīn, 1979), of which the 'introduction' made up of lectures Ḥusayn gave at the University of Cairo in 1941 and 1942 (7–107) is interesting in that its condemnation of the Persian influence is even harsher than his original *Ḥadīth al- arbiʿāʾ* essays.

'Orientalist' discourse. An explanation of this moralising turn in Arabic narratives of the past in the twentieth century, and its particular trajectory, here, of othering, would require a massive collaborative project that would read and analyse closely cultural and literary discourses identifiable in conventional texts (civilisational and literary histories not to mention writings of all kinds) as well as mass media (newspapers, magazines, journals, radio and television broadcasts) in at least a three-way comparison between past and present, East and West. How daunting! And where is the fun in this kind of investigation that utterly devoid of humour that is so much part of *mujūn* in classical Arabic sources?

If *mujūn* in modern Arabic is singularly associated with moral depravity conveyed in the Arabic words most frequently used to describe the phenomenon, *khalāʿa* (licentiousness), *tahattuk* (shamelessness) and *fuḥsh* (obscenity and indecency often in relation to adultery), *fisq* (moral depravity), and *fujūr* (debauchery), its semantic field in classical Arabic is both wider and more ambivalent. Hans Wehr (1909–1981) seems to have picked up some of its nuances, defining *mujūn* as 'buffoonery, clowning; shamelessness, impudence', *mujūnī* as 'brazen sarcast, cynic', and *mājin* pl. *mujjān* as 'impudent, shameless, brazen, insolent, saucy, joker, jester, wag, buffoon', making innocuous the two contradictory meanings in *Lisān al-ʿarab* and *Tāj al-ʿarūs*. '*Al-mājin* among the Arabs is one who commits ugly deeds that may lead to death and causes scandals that may lead to shame, and who is not affected by reproach or rebuke' (*al-mājin ʿind al-ʿarab alladhī yartakib al-maqābiḥ al-murdiya wa l-faḍā'iḥ al-mukhziya wa la yamuḍḍuhu ʿadhl ʿādhilihi wa la taqrīʿ man yaqraʿahu'*). *Al-mājin* is someone who pays no heed to what he says or what is said to him, as if his face became thick and hard. *Mujūn*, therefore, is disregard for the consequences of his actions (*An-lā yubālī l-insān bima ṣanaʿ*) and, interestingly, mixing seriousness with frivolity (*khalṭ al-jidd bi l-hazl*). *Al-majjān* is also *al-bāṭil* (invalid, false, etc.). Ibn Manẓūr (1233–1311) and al-Zabīdī (1731–1790) are relative latecomers to the arena of *mujūn*. Before them, Ibn al-Jawzī (508–597/1114–1200) in *Akhbār al-ẓirāf wa l-mutamājinīn*[7] treats *mujūn* as synonymous with *ẓarf*, and defines them as a combination of good looks, lightness of figure, elegance in dress, eloquence in speech, quickness in wit, keen sense of humour, and generosity in a person (4). In his preface to the anecdotes he tells of the witty repartees of men, women and youth from among prophets, companions of the Prophet Muhammad, religious scholars (*ʿulamā'*) and philosophers (*ḥukamā'*), Arabs and common folk (9) he situates his collection in the tradition of mixing seriousness with frivolity in classical Arabic writings and scholarly assemblies, 'Since the soul (*al-nafs*) gets bored of seriousness there is no harm in letting it go free in jesting' (1). One of these anecdotes concerns Muṭīʿ Ibn Iyās, Yaḥyā Ibn Ziyād and Ḥammād ʿAjrad, three famous *mujūn* figures in the classical sources (118–119). The story goes:

> Isḥāq Ibn Ibrāhīm al-Mawṣilī said: Muṭīʿ Ibn Iyās and Yaḥyā Ibn Ziyād went to visit Ḥammād Ibn ʿAjrad (al-Rāwiya in *Kitāb al-aghānī* [6: 83]).[8] They found that he had raised his lamp on three reed pipes, having held them together and firm with mud. Yaḥyā turned to Ḥammād and said, 'you are truly extravagant!'. Muṭīʿ chipped in, 'will you sell it and buy something cheaper so you can spend the rest on us?' Yaḥyā retorted,

[7] References are made to *Akhbār al-ẓirāf wa l-mutamājinīn*, ed. al-Sayyid Muḥammad Baḥr al-ʿUlūm (Najaf: al-Maktaba al-Ḥaydariyya, 1967).

[8] References are made to *Kitāb al-aghānī*, in 27 volumes, ed. ʿAbdallāh ʿAli Muhannā and Samīr Jābir, 2nd ed. (Beirut: Dār al-Kutub al-ʿIlmiyya, 1992).

> 'you think too well of him. How can he afford such a lighthouse? Is it something someone has entrusted to you, or did you borrow it?' Muṭīᶜ answered, 'it must be an important item of trust then'. Yaḥyā quipped, 'If it is of such importance, then whoever let it leave his house and entrusted it to someone else must be a fool'. Muṭīᶜ came back, 'I don't think it is something entrusted or lent to him. I'm sure it is mortgaged to him for a good sum of money, otherwise who would let something like this be taken out of his house?' Ḥammād finally replied, 'only the devil would let you two into his house!'

There is nothing indecent, obscene or shameless in this anecdote, nor is there any moral censure in Ibn al-Jawzī's account of the playful repartee between Muṭīᶜ Ibn Iyās and Yaḥyā Ibn Ziyād, and between them and Ḥammād ᶜAjrad, or of the three '*mutamājinīn*'.

This is not to say that classical sources quoted by twentieth century cultural and literary historians are entirely judgment free. After all, the modern narratives do derive their material from these sources. There is, however, a marked difference between classical sources and modern narratives. The anecdotal quality of the classical sources makes it difficult for readers to arrive at a totalising vision of their 'authors'. Ibn al-Muᶜtazz (861–908), who may serve as an exemplar of ninth- and tenth-century authors who dealt with *mujūn* in poetry and society, writes in *Ṭabaqāt al-shuᶜarā*[9] that, for example,

> Ḥammād ᶜAjrad was *mawlā* of Banū Suwāᶜa Ibn ᶜĀmir Ibn Ṣaᶜṣaᶜa. He was a teacher then became known for poetry and praised kings. There were three Ḥammāds in Kufa: Ḥammād ᶜAjrad, Ḥammād Ibn al-Zibirqān, and Ḥammād al-Rāwiya. They were close drinking companions, who recited poetry together, and lived a beautiful companionable life, as if they were one person.[10] They were all accused of zandaqa and if anyone should see one of them they would say, '*zindīq*, kill him!' (69).

Another example is found in Wāliba Ibn al-Ḥubāb, who taught Abū Nuwās poetry (87), composed poetry on *mujūn*, *fatk* and *khalāᶜa* in a way no one had done before (88), even though people attributed his poetry to Abū Nuwās out of ignorance (89), as they would all poetry in which Laylā is mentioned to Majnūn (89). Wāliba, according to al-Yazīdī and Abū Sahlab (a poet) was '*mājin khalī*', who did not worry (*mā yubālī*) about what he said or did' (89). Muṭīᶜ Ibn Iyās and Yaḥyā Ibn Ziyād were, like the three Ḥammāds, close friends until they fell out (95). Abū Nuwās, a disciple of Wāliba and Khalaf al-Aḥmar, was a talented poet and learned scholar but he was also a *khalīᶜ*, *mājin* and *fatan shāṭir*, and more importantly, he was handsome, witty (*ẓarīf*)[11] and generous, and people were enchanted by him (195).

What emerges in these disparate anecdotes, especially when they are read together, is a network of poets, scholars and members of the elite, including the caliphs, princes and

---

[9] References are made to *Ṭabaqāt al-shuᶜarā*ʾ, ed. ᶜAbd al-Sattār Aḥmad Farrāj (Cairo: Dār al-Maᶜārif, 1956).

[10] Repeated in Ibn Qutayba (828–885), *Al-shiʿr wa l-shuᶜarā*ʾ, ed. Aḥmad Muḥammad Shākir, 3rd ed. (Cairo: Dār al-Turāth al-ᶜArabī, 1977), 2: 783, and al-Ṣūlī (88–946), *Kitāb al-awrāq*, Section on Contemporary Poets, ed. J. Heyworth Dunne (London: Luzac & Co., 1934), 10. Al-Ṣūlī adds the following names to the network of *mujūn* poets in the section on Abbān Ibn ᶜAbd al-Ḥamīd al-Lāḥiqī: Yunis Ibn Hārūn, ᶜAlī Ibn al-Khalīl, Yazīd Ibn al-Fayḍ, ᶜUbāda, Jamīl Ibn Maḥfūẓ, Qāsim, Muṭīᶜ, Wāliba Ibn al-Ḥubāb, Abbān Ibn ᶜAbd al-Ḥamīd, and ᶜUmāra Ibn Ḥarbiyya.

[11] This is also al-Marzubānī's (d. 984) description of Muṭīᶜ Ibn Iyās; see *Muᶜjam al- shuᶜarā*ʾ, ed. F. Krenkow (Cairo: Maktabat al-Quds, 1354 AH), 480.

viziers, who made up the 'gay' society of the eighth and ninth centuries and who made the golden triangle of Kufa (led by Muṭīᶜ Ibn Iyās and his circle, including Wāliba), Basra (led by Bashshār Ibn Burd) and Baghdad (led by Abū Nuwās, Abū al-ᶜAtāhiya and al-Ḥusayn Ibn al-Ḍahhāk) their playing field (118–119), regardless of their ethnic origin, sectarian inclination and, perhaps unsurprisingly, gender. Their 'gay' lifestyle is confirmed by their poetic expressions and by the anecdotes strewn about the anthologised poems. They were, as Jurjī Zaydān notes in *Tārīkh al-tamaddun al-islāmī* (4: 129–131), a sign of the freedom of belief, and as Ṭāhā Ḥusayn reluctantly acknowledges in *Min tārīkh al-adab al-ᶜarabī*, a feature of freedom of expression (2: 248), rather in contradiction to his own severe moral condemnation of this very society elsewhere. It is clear that these bon-vivant poets flouted all norms of propriety in their poetry and even amorous behaviour, as many anecdotes attest, but it is not entirely obvious that the classical authors condemned their literary expression or social conduct in the similar vein as the twentieth century cultural and literary historians, or blaming the Abbasid 'age of decadence' on the Persians or their influence.

Al-Iṣfahānī's (897–967) entry on Muṭīᶜ Ibn Iyās in *Kitāb al-aghānī* (13: 300–362), in which as many as possible of the anecdotes included in the short entries in earlier and even contemporary oral and written sources (e.g., Ibn al-Muᶜtazz, Ibn Qutayba, al-Ṣūlī and al-Marzubānī) are brought together in one expanded entry, presents a lively portrait of a multi-cultural, libertine, elite social group who lived their life to the full, competing with each other for princely and sexual favours (among men or women), mocking, making fun of, bickering with and attacking each other, and laughing through it all. Muṭīᶜ, an Arab accused of *zandaqa*, was at the centre of this group,[12] as his name crops up everywhere in, for example, al-Iṣfahānī's similarly extended entries on Ḥammād ᶜAjrad (14: 313–375) and Ḥammād al-Rāwiya (6: 79–104). In all these entries, the two most famous *mujūn* poets, Bashshār Ibn Burd and Abū Nuwās, figure prominently. Where relevant, the same anecdotes are repeated in these entries, and quite often *Kitāb al-aghānī* reads like *The Thousand and One Nights* in that 'archetypal' characters and 'stock' motifs recur in such a way that stories resemble each other in the *Nights* and 'biographies' follow a similar trajectory, intersecting and overlapping frequently. If the earlier and other contemporary sources provide isolated anecdotes, al-Iṣfahānī uses these as vignettes and weaves them into canvases of individual lives only to present each as a small tableau of an expansive and colourful tapestry of a society out on an extended holiday at the carnival.

It is interestingly possible to trace the transformation of the *mujūn* poets into what Hans Wehr identifies in *mujūnī* or *mājin* as 'impudent, shameless, brazen, insolent, saucy, joker, jester, wag, buffoon' to *Kitāb al-aghānī*. The life of Muṭīᶜ, for examples, is an all-consuming wine party played out against a background of music and song made up of escapades with patrons, friends, lovers and little else. At this party, he is shameless, insolent and a clown. The carnivalesque in *Kitāb al-aghānī* is easily noticeable when the entries are read against

[12] The only discussion of Muṭīᶜ and his poetry in English I have been able to find is by G.E. von Grunebaum, 'Three Arabic Poets of the Early Abbasid Age: Muṭīᶜ b. Iyās, Salm al-Ḫāsir and Abū 'š-Šamaqmaq', *Orientalia* 17, 19, 22 (Rome 1948, 50, 53), 260–304, 53–80, 262–283, republished in *Themes in Medieval Arabic Literature* (London: Variorum Reprints, 1981), XII.

al-Iṣfahānī's sources available to us today. Carnivalisation is subversion but not necessarily moralisation, especially not the kind prevalent in modern narratives of the past, in which *Kitāb al-aghānī* is omnipresent; it is the single most quoted source. The modern cultural and literary historians seemed to have completely misread *Kitāb al-aghānī*. What is afoot here?

I will not go on my usual theoretical tirade on the autonomy of text and its unique worldliness, or on ideology and genre ideology that shape the textual world, or on the production of meaning locatable in the dialogism between writerly and readerly texts, or on misreading as an integral part of reading. I have yet to prepare the ground for this. I will refrain too from pontificating on the ways in which the portability and mobility of *khabar* in classical Arabic writings challenges us to locate the production of meaning not in the text but in the relationship between 'text' and a metanarrative inherent in the act of compilation. Here, I merely wish to draw attention to the multifarious *funūn* ways in which authors, whether classical compilers of anecdotes or their modern interpreters, have artfully organised these same anecdotes each in a particular configuration to produce meanings which, if one were to think them through a single epistemological system, one would go mad, in the Arabic sense of *junūn*, madness being not simply possessed by a genie but also transgressing boundaries of reason, *ʿaql*. This madness is precisely the pleasure of classical Arabic literature.

WORKS CITED

Aḥmad Amīn, *Ḍuḥā l-islām*, vols. 1 and 2 (Cairo: Lajnat al-Taʾlīf wa l-Tarjama wa l-Nashr, 1938).

Shawqī Ḍayf, *Tārīkh al-adab al-ʿarabī: al-ʿaṣr al-ʿabbāsī l-awwal* (Cairo: Dār al-Maʿārif, n.d.).

Shawqī Ḍayf, *Tārīkh al-adab al-ʿarabī: al-ʿaṣr al-ʿabbāsī l-thānī*, 2nd ed. (Cairo: Dār al-Maʿārif, 1970).

G.E. von Grunebaum, 'Three Arabic Poets of the Early Abbasid Age: Muṭīʿ b. Iyās, Salm al-Ḫāsir and Abū 'š-Šamaqmaq', *Orientalia* 17, 19, 22 (Rome 1948, 50, 53), 260–304, 53–80, 262–283, republished in *Themes in Medieval Arabic Literature* (London: Variorum Reprints, 1981), XII.

Muḥammad Muṣṭafā Haddāra, *Ittijāhāt al-shiʿr al-ʿarabī fī l-qarn al-thānī l-hijrī*, 2nd ed. (Cairo: Dār al-Maʿārif, 1970).

Ṭāhā Ḥusayn, *Ḥadith al-arbiʿāʾ*, vol. 1 (Cairo: al-Maktaba al-Tijāriyya al-Kubrā, 1925), vol. 2 (Cairo: Dār al-Kutub, 1926), and vol. 3 (Cairo: Dār al-Maʿārif, n.d.).

Ṭāhā Ḥusayn, *Min tārīkh al-adab al-ʿarabī* (Beirut: Dār al-ʿIlm li l-Malāyīn, 1979).

Ibn al-Jawzī, *Akhbār al-ẓirāf wa l-mutamājinīn*, ed. al-Sayyid Muḥammad Baḥr al-ʿUlūm (Najaf: al-Maktaba al-Ḥaydariyya, 1967).

Ibn al-Muʿtazz, *Ṭabaqāt al-shuʿarāʾ*, ed. ʿAbd al-Sattār Aḥmad Farrāj (Cairo: Dār al-Maʿārif, 1956).

Ibn Qutayba, *Al-shiʿr wa l-shuʿarāʾ*, ed. Aḥmad Muḥammad Shākir, 3rd ed. (Cairo: Dār al-Turāth al-ʿArabī, 1977).

Al-Iṣfahānī, *Kitāb al-aghānī*, in 27 volumes, ed. ʿAbdallāh ʿAli Muhannā and Samīr Jābir, 2nd ed. (Beirut: Dār al-Kutub al-ʿIlmiyya, 1992).

al-Marzubānī, *Muʿjam al-shuʿarāʾ*, ed. F. Krenkow (Cairo: Maktabat al-Quds, 1354 AH).

Muṣṭafā al-Shakʿa, *Al-shiʿr wa l- shuʿarāʾ fī l-ʿaṣr al-ʿabbāsī* (Beirut: Dār al-ʿIlm li l-Malāyīn, 1973).

al-Ṣūlī, *Kitāb al-awrāq*, Section on Contemporary Poets, ed. J. Heyworth Dunne (London: Luzac & Co., 1934).

Jurjī Zaydān, *Tārīkh ādāb al-lugha al-ʿarabiyya* (1910–1913), vol. 2, ed. Shawqī Ḍayf (Cairo: Dār al-Hilāl, n.d.).

Jurjī Zaydān, *Tārīkh al-tamaddun al-islāmī* (1901–1906), vol. 5 (Cairo: Dār al-Hilāl, 1905).

2

What is obscene? Obscenity in Classical Arabic literature

Jaakko Hämeen-Anttila

Obscenity is a culturally defined term. What is considered obscene in one culture need not be so in another. In classical Arabic literature the definition of obscenity is rarely discussed, G.J. van Gelder's *The Bad and the Ugly* (1988), being one of the rare studies seriously tackling the question of obscenity in Arabic literature, especially in *hijā'*. Yet it is an important aspect in assessing not only the *mujūn*, a term for texts often considered obscene, but also other genres, from anecdotes to love poetry.

Thus, for example, many mainstream homoerotic *ghazals* in Arabic, Persian or Turkish courtly literature would have been considered scandalous in Victorian England, where homosexuality was considered not only obscene but even criminal. Several translations of Arabic books in the period were made anonymously and published giving false places of publication and under the name of fake publishing houses. Thus, when the famous publisher of erotic works, Charles Carrington (1867–1921) published a year after the Wilde trial in 1896 his translation of pseudo al-Suyūṭī's *Kitāb al-Īḍāḥ fī ʿilm al-nikāḥ*, he did so anonymously (the translator is identified on the title page as 'An English Bohemian') and the place of publication was marked as Paris.

Many 19th-century authors considered the East a voluptuous paradise of uninhibited eroticism. This fallacy might, at first sight, seem credible when one looks at mediaeval Arabic or Persian literature, which contains much material that would have made a Victorian blush. Lexicographers list terms for genitals seemingly without embarrassment and a scholar such as al-Suyūṭī seems quite at ease in his erotic monographs. A *nādira* may be built on words that one would find less than polite, like the famous one involving the learned Bedouin Suwayd ibn ʿAlqama (or Ghafala)[1] whom the Caliph ʿAbdalmalik asks to mention ten human body parts beginning with 'k'. After listing nine (*kaff*, *kūʿ*, *kursūʿ*, *katif*, *kāhil*, *kabid*, *kulya*, *karish* – not being a *human* body part, this is rejected by the Caliph – *kafal*, *kaʿb*), he has a momentary block, asks to be excused to go to the toilet and returns triumphantly, pants still down (*maḥlūl al-sarāwīl*) and shouts: '*al-kamara* (glans penis), *al-*

[1] Suwayd is probably to be identified with Suwayd ibn Ghafala, cf. Friedmann (1992): 160, note 555. He was a *muʿammar*, so at the time of the anecdote he would have been a dotard.

kamara, now there's full ten!' (al-Tīfāshī, *Nuzha*, p. 47). Such stories are also told in respectable, learned sources. Likewise, manuals of Islamic law seem to discuss sexual behaviour as dispassionately as any other subject.

Erotic themes were discussed in the Islamic world with an ease that could not have been thought of in the West until the 20th century. A frequently repeated story of a *mufākhara* between Southern and Northern Arabs lets the late Umayyad, early Abbasid orator Khālid ibn Ṣafwān condemn his Southern Arab opponent in a devastatingly brief formula: 'How can he boast to Muḍar of people who ride asses, weave clothes, train monkeys and tan hides?' In translation, the phrase seems rather innocent, but the Arabic is more revealing, using for 'ass' the word *ʿard*, which also means 'erect penis'. That the obscene allusion was not lost to near-contemporaries is shown by a (certainly unhistorical) linguistic joke at the end of the story, where Khālid refers to the Yemeni Arabic equivalent for *liḥya*, namely *zubb*, playing with an allusion to Q 20: 94. In Ibn al-Faqīh's version (*Mukhtaṣar*, pp. 39–41), there is an additional claim that head, *ra's*, is in Yemeni Arabic *faqḥa*. This play on words could not have been lost even on the dullest, yet it was repeated in dozens of quite respectable books, including al-Balādhurī, *Ansāb* VII/1, 77–79.[2]

Such outspoken stories are found in literature that cannot, by any standard, be considered marginal or underground. The borderline between decent and indecent was drawn very liberally. Often the genre defines this limit. Hence in love poetry, for example, the *ghazals* for women (*mu'annathāt*) are clearly more reserved than those for young men (*mudhakkarāt*) in which coarser language was more acceptable, as a study of the poems by Abū Nuwās seems to confirm.[3] Perhaps the most conspicuous genre for 'accepted obscenity' is the *hijā'*, where the invective was ritualized and in the wake of this ritualization expressions were accepted which would otherwise have been considered obscene.[4] This regulated tolerance of obscenity may at least partly be due to the history of the genre, which, I would argue, retained its roughness as a conscious, nostalgic imitation of 'uncouth' Bedouin ancestors. There may be nostalgia even in obscenity.

Be that as it may, the *hijā'* poems provide us with a wide selection of sexual invective and their obvious aim is to comment upon and to exaggerate the sexually deviant behaviour of their target and his mainly female relatives. Their aim is to provoke and hence their sexual content would in other genres have been considered offensive. There is no point in describing merely acceptable sexual habits in an invective.

This genre sheds some light as to what was considered obscene. Among features that are blamed in an invective one finds homosexual feelings towards grown-up men. Such a passion was obviously considered uncouth and reprehensible, and a man's passive role in a homosexual relationship was considered unbecoming and its description offensive. Another case of obscenity is connected with female sexual needs. It is always acceptable for a man to desire women, from slave girls to married ladies, and desire for beardless

---

[2] For full references, see Hämeen-Anttila (forthcoming).

[3] See Hämeen-Anttila (2005). Note that in the case of Abū Nuwās the Mediaeval editors of his *Dīwān* made the classification as to which of his poems went into the section of *mu'annathāt* or *mudhakkarāt*, which to the *mujūn*, so that we are not left on our own in labelling the poems.

[4] For the genre, see van Gelder (1988).

boys is also acceptable, but for a woman to be sexually active was a threat to her social integrity. To respond to the feelings of a desert lover was within the limits of propriety, but all other female sexual instincts were suspect. Perhaps the most common form of inappropriate behaviour is the widespread – if we believe our sources – passion of women for donkeys and other equine lovers.

This brings us to a further characteristic of obscenity. In Western literature, defining obscenity may be simpler, but in Arabic and Persian literature the obscene was also found in respectable literature. Thus, e.g., the mystical poet Rūmī (d. 1273) finds an applicable exemplum in a story (*Mathnawī* V, 1333–1429; transl. V, 82–87) about a lady and her donkey lover, whom a servant girl tries to emulate, forgetting how deep a donkey may penetrate when not checked. The story is told in the mystic story collection used by generations of pious, religiously-minded Muslims and often called 'the Persian Qur'ān'.

Mujūn is the genre most often mentioned in connection with obscenity.[5] This poetic genre, however, contains much that is not obscene by any standard and should be considered more provocative than obscene, as topics such as atheism also belong to this genre. The Arabic etymology of the word, from *majana* 'to jest', also supports this interpretation and a look at the *dīwān*s where such a chapter is found further confirms that obscenity, as such, is not at the heart of *mujūn*. Most *mujūn* poems by, for example, Abū Nuwās, disappoint the scholar who searches for erotic materials.

This, however, is not the whole story, for Arabs had their scruples, too. When writing his introduction to the *ʿUyūn al-akhbār*, Ibn Qutayba felt it necessary (I, 44–45) to defend himself for using explicit vocabulary, which shows that he, a learned scholar and the author of several books on the Qur'ān and the *Ḥadīth*, had a reputation to defend and that he thought that even the rather inoffensive tales of his book might still offend some.

Likewise, his older contemporary, al-Jāḥiẓ, took up the question of obscenity in many of his books. In his *Mufākharat al-jawārī wa'l-ghilmān* he criticizes (II, 92) those who hypocritically shirk from words they consider inappropriate (*wa-baʿḍ man yuẓhiru l-nusk wa'l-taqashshuf idhā dhukira l-ḥir wa'l-ayr wa'l-nayk taqazzaza wa-nqabaḍa*). On the following pages, al-Jāḥiẓ collects such words from pious sayings, including *ayr* and *baẓr*, and later (II, 95) labels them *min alfāẓi l-mujjān*, which in this context shows his approval of the words: even though some may consider them obscene, they were used by pious ancestors.[6]

In Arabic discourse, obscenity was very much related to the use of certain lexical items. Thus it is what both al-Jāḥiẓ and Ibn Qutayba take up in their respective books. As each part of the human body has a God-given name,[7] it follows that the use of these nouns cannot be sinful in itself, but, on the contrary, avoiding them is in a certain sense disrespectful towards the Creator of these words.

---

[5] For this genre, see Rowson (1998).

[6] Cf. al-Jāḥiẓ, *Ḥayawān*, III, 40–43. For al-Jāḥiẓ's views on obscenity, see also van Gelder (1988): 44–47.

[7] In her study on *Kitāb al-Bayān wa'l-tabyīn*, Lale Behzadi (2009) shows (especially on pp. 107–127) how all words, including those that denote unworthy objects, are of value for al-Jāḥiẓ (cf. also p. 126, note 262 "Zur Notwendigkeit des Minderwertigen", from *Bayān* I, 145). Cf. also van Gelder (1988): 79. Already in Q 2: 31 God is seen as the origin of language and, most appropriately, of all nouns.

Very often the author-compilers of *adab* anthologies made much of defending light-hearted, comic stories as a necessary counterweight to serious study. This juxtaposition of *jidd* and *hazl* has been expertly studied by van Gelder (1992) and one finds among *ḥadīth* collections works of *arbaʿīna muḍḥika*, which prove to a pious Muslim beyond doubt that not everything must be deadly serious.[8]

In many anthologies this discussion of the legitimacy of light reading has a proper place. In erotic manuals, though, it seems that at least some authors have endeavoured to use this discourse mainly to muddy the waters and hide the real problem. If God created obscene words, fair enough. There is no reason not to use them appropriately, but why write about sex – often in appreciative tones – and focus the attention of readers on obscenity? And if comic literature is a necessary counterweight to serious study, why not laugh – like the Prophet did – at innocent good-humoured jokes? What has laughter to do with obscenity? For al-Tīfāshī, *Nuzha*, pp. 45–50, proving the legitimacy of laughter is a way to avoid the real question. The faulty deduction of al-Tīfāshī goes: entertainment is permitted. (Some) obscene stories entertain us. *Ergo*, obscene stories are permitted, as they entertain (some of) us. Whether the author himself realized the invalidity of his reasoning cannot, of course, be proven, but I would think he made his mistake on purpose. For a casual reader his preface is satisfactory in proving that the perusal of the book is by no means a sin, but closer to a religious deed, emulating the Prophet who laughed at light-hearted things, which give us strength to get on with serious things.

Al-Tīfāshī's preface deserves some close reading. In the very beginning of the book (p. 43), in the Qur'ānically flavoured evocation, God is praised for giving us civilized jokes (*mulaḥ al-ādāb*) as a way to clear the mind from rust. The next sentence is crucial for understanding where al-Tīfāshī actually stands: 'He (God) made the people of virtue[9] love them (the *mulaḥ al-ādāb*) in privacy as well as in company. Among the élite (*khawāṣṣ*) he set them as good deeds whereas among the general public (*ʿawāmm*) he set them as bad deeds'. The sentence shows the elitism of al-Tīfāshī. Jokes, and here he must be thinking about the uncouth ones in his book, suit the élite but not the *vulgus*, or whatever he here means with *ʿawāmm*, which is a very elastic term.

This is put more explicitly on p. 49 of the preface, where al-Tīfāshī admonishes the reader not to be too relaxed among uncultured people (*maʿa ghayr ahl al-adab*). This, he explains, is injurious to one's reputation. What is merely elegance for civilized people is folly (*sukhf*) for rough common people.[10]

After the evocation, the very first sentence of the preface proper (p. 45) gives us a *ḥadīth*, proving that the Prophet used to joke (*mazaḥa*), which makes joking a *sunna*, hence

---

[8] Many prefaces to *adab* anthologies take up the same discussion of whether it is permissible for a believer to read stories that are made to be laughed at. The contrary position was taken by those who leaned on the Qur'ānic injunctions against *khurāfāt*. Ibn al-Nadīm, in his famous comment on the *Alf Layla wa-Layla* (*Fihrist*, p. 363), was perhaps not so much indignant for any religious reasons, but for him the tales of this story collection were not of sufficient quality. For him, they were just dull.

[9] The translation of *muruwwa* as "virtue", though, may be misleading, as the Arabic word refers to manly qualities, whereas the English word carries Christian overtones.

[10] For the term *sukhf*, see van Gelder (1988): 16, and Index, s.v.

giving the highest authority for joking. But this, in fact, does not address the question whether the indelicacies in the book should be accepted or not. In another story (p. 46), ʿAlī's use of outspoken vocabulary in his saying *man ṭāla ayru abīhi tamanṭaqa bihi* is labelled *duʿāba* 'jesting', a word which does not contain sexual overtones. The use of this innocent word supports the confusion created by al-Tīfāshī: jesting is acceptable following the Prophet's example, using words such as *ayr* is merely jesting and, hence, this vocabulary has religious sanction. Al-Tīfāshī also quotes al-ʿUtbī (p. 46) to the effect that overstretching a joke is *mujūn*, whereas a suitable amount of jesting is elegance (*ẓarf*) and its lack is to be pitied (*nadāma*). In the author's opinion, of course, his own book falls nice and squarely into the elegant middle way.[11]

Al-Tīfāshī also relates in the preface the story of Suwayd's ten 'k' words to show that early authorities, in this case the Caliph ʿAbd al-Malik, did not frown at words which denote private parts. The graphic story even tells us that the overexcited Bedouin did not stop to button his trousers before reappearing before the Caliph, who does not take offence at this.

Al-Tijānī's thick volume of mildly erotic stories and verses, *Tuḥfat al-ʿarūs wa-mutʿat al-nufūs*, is camouflaged as a learned book and partly, indeed, is such.[12] In the preface (p. 24), the author takes up the old idea of his book both educating and entertaining the reader (*tajmaʿu bayna ifādat al-ʿilm wa-imtāʿ al-nufūs*). In order to make his point clear, the author ends his preface by directly stating that his book is not, though it might so seem, a book of entertainment (*kitāb samar*) but a book of science and critical study (*kitāb ʿilm wa-naẓar*), which, however, is an obvious exaggeration of its contents, for they are rather meagre from a scholarly point of view.

Al-Nafzāwī's *al-Rawḍ al-ʿāṭir* is rather more outspoken. The author, with all his religious credentials given before his name (*al-shaykh al-imām al-ʿallāma*), starts with an evocation of God (p. 36): 'Praise be to God who has set the greatest enjoyment for men in women's cunts and for women in men's pricks. A cunt will not find peace and rest until a prick enters it, neither does the prick except by cunts,' etc. The beginning is daring and it would seem that the author is writing in a quite unrestrained manner, but the following explanation of the book's genesis (p. 37) tells a slightly different story. Here the author informs us how a shorter book of his, titled *Tanwīʿ al-wiqāʿ fī asrār al-jimāʿ*, had drawn the attention of the Vizier of Tunis. When the Vizier mentioned this book and asked whether it was, indeed, by al-Nafzāwī, the latter blushed and it took some effort on the Vizier's side to calm him down and to tell him to write a longer one in the same vein. The Vizier calls erotica a branch of science (*ʿilm*).

The story is there not just to tell us how the book came to be written. It is also a justification for the book, which was ordered by the Vizier and hence was not compiled completely on al-Nafzāwī's initiative. Whether the story is historical or not need not concern us – it is a topos that the author wrote his book only after a friend or a patron

---

[11] Al-Tīfāshī also quotes (p. 46) al-Jāḥiẓ's comment *al-qawl al-sakhīf fī amākinihi ka'l-qawl al-sadīd fī mawāṭinihi.*

[12] Al-Suyūṭī, *Wishāḥ*, p. 34, extols it as the best book in the field and quotes it in several of his erotic works (e.g., *Wishāḥ*, p. 245ff., *Shaqā'iq*, pp. 68, 91, 99, 100, etc.).

had asked him to do so – but its message is clear. There was, after all, something shameful in writing about erotica, but, ultimately, the author only complies with the wishes of his patron.

Most authors of erotic manuals seem to have tried to sweep aside the erotic content of their books and to discuss their work in terms of comic entertainment, instead of obscenity. There are, though, some exceptions. Pseudo al-Suyūṭī, in his *Īḍāḥ*, seems to set out to shock his reader. Shocking is a rather necessary part of pornography, which takes its delight in openly defying the sexual norms of society.

The *Īḍāḥ* is one of the rare pre-modern Arabic texts which have been published[13] and which I would call partly pornographic. Contrary to al-Tīfāshī's preface, pseudo al-Suyūṭī seems to be aiming at maximizing the shock value of his book. Reading the first pages only, one might expect rather explicit material to follow. But the preface is deceptive. After the initial pages, the book turns out to be a rather dull and conventional collection of stories which sometimes titillate, but more often make one yawn, being quite familiar from earlier literature. The preface, thus, falsely advertises it as pornography.

The abrupt beginning of the book makes one expect a certain kind of book. Already the initial evocation (p. 122) verges on obscenity: 'Praise be to Him who has embellished the chests of virgins with breasts and has set women's thighs as benches for the wild asses of pricks and who has made the prick-spears stand erect, ready to push in cunts, not chests,' etc. After this, there follows an imaginary discussion preceded by an openly fictitious *isnād*, narrated by an anonymous friend, who has sex with his neighbours through a breach in the wall (*ḥukiya ʿan baʿḍ al-aṣdiqāʾ wa'l-khullān wa-nayyākī l-jīrān min shuqūq al-ḥīṭān*). The story involves, among other characters, Cunt, Cock and Reverend (literally *ḥājj*) Balls (pp. 122–123).[14] Instead of a fully-fledged Cock and Bull story, though, we only have a brief Cock and Balls dialogue.

To make sure the reader understands we are treading in dangerous territory, pseudo al-Suyūṭī defines all girls over fourteen as old hags (*ʿajūz fī ʿābirīn*) that have to be avoided. Both ideas – the preference for young girls and the avoidance of old women – are present in many respectable books that discuss whom a man should marry, but the outrageous way of defining who is an old hag must be there to provoke even the pre-modern reader of the time. Even more outrageous are the mock *ḥadīths* narrated on the authority of Iblīs (p. 124) and the listing (p. 125) of whores bearing names that make Rushdie's *Satanic Verses* sound innocent: Umm al-Khayr, Khadīja, Ḥalīma, Fāṭima, and Bilqīs.

In the preface to his *Rujūʿ al-shaykh ilā ṣibāhu* (pp. 8–9), Ibn Kamāl-pāshā (d. 941/1535)[15] openly lists sexual excitement as one of the motives, or uses, of his book (*naqaltu ʿanhunna fī amr al-bāh mimmā yuḥarriku shahwat al-sāmiʿ lahā*). The book had royal patronage and Ḥājjī Khalīfa, *Kashf* (p. 835), tells that it was written on the orders of Sulṭān Selim himself. The

[13] Libraries contain many erotic manuscripts that would deserve our attention. In many cases, the published books will be found under various titles and names of author and many seemingly new books turn out to be old friends and *vice versa*. Unfortunately, the published books are usually very inferior editions that cannot be relied on. The history of Arabic erotic literature still waits to be written.

[14] In Carrington's translation: Madame Slit, Mr. Tool and Al Hajj Eggs.

[15] See GAL II: 452, no. 103.

author emphasizes in his preface that his book aims at helping the reader enjoy his lawful share of enjoyment (by exciting him, but also by giving hints as how to cure impotence), not at helping one towards sin. Basically, Ibn Kamāl-pāshā tells us that his book is not reprehensible as its reader is supposed to use it with lawful partners. How the distinction is supposed to work in practice is not discussed: what happens if an excited reader turns to an illegal partner? Ibn Kamāl-pāshā is not concerned with this possibility but leaves it to the reader's conscience. Whether this is only a fiction to help him defend his book against imagined accusations or whether he really thought this to be the case cannot be known. At least we know that his book, both in its Turkish and Arabic forms, was well received and eagerly read, being in the East *the* Turkish/Arabic erotic book, a position taken in the West by al-Nafzāwī's *Perfumed Garden*, thanks to Burton's translation.[16]

The shocking effect is, I think, also there in al-Kātib al-Qazwīnī's *Jawāmiʿ al-ladhdha*, a rather famous erotic manual in its time.[17] It seems to draw on lost sources, still known to Ibn al-Nadīm, and it may have connections to Indian erotic manuals. Even though the edition of the text[18] starts abruptly without a preface, it is clear that the author does not wish to appear respectable. His descriptions of anal and oral sex, to take an example, go far beyond what, e.g., al-Tijānī would have cared to share with his readers. However, al-Qazwīnī's work is a curious mixture of the serious and the obscene. He also quotes respectable authors – though until we check these quotations we remain uncertain whether all of them are real. Some, in any case, are genuine quotations from respected authors.

In general, it seems that quoting obscenities from well-known religious or philological authorities purged the texts of obscenity in a similar way as using Latin did in modern vernacular literatures in Europe or in Victorian translations of Arabic and Persian texts. When al-Qālī quotes in his *Amālī* (II, 105–106) the three verses by the three unmarried daughters of the Bedouin Humām ibn Murra, there is not the slightest hint that he would be venturing into the realms of the obscene, even though the last verse reads: "Oh Humām ibn Murra, I long / for a cock to stick into where I pee from" (*ilā ʿardin asuddu bihī mabālī*). There is nothing reprehensible in quoting this verse, though, as it is Bedouin folklore.[19] Likewise, the occasional indelicacies in Ibn Ṭayfūr's *Balāghāt al-nisā'* are hidden amidst a sometimes forbidding mass of extremely complex and archaic verbosity.

The real al-Suyūṭī tackled erotic topics in several of his books, including a set of three works, *al-Wishāḥ fī fawā'id al-nikāḥ*, *Shaqā'iq al-utrunj fī raqā'iq al-ghunj*, and *Nawāḍir al-ayk fī maʿrifat al-nayk*.[20] In especially the first two, the erotic content is hidden behind a learned

---

[16] The book has been translated through Burton's free version into many European languages, but there is also a direct – and more reliable – German translation by Ulrich Marzolph.

[17] For the author, see GAL S I: 946, l. 1. Al-Suyūṭī quotes this book several times in his *Nawāḍir al-ayk*, usually calling it *Jāmiʿ al-ladhdha* but without naming its author. Cf., e.g., *Nawāḍir*, p. 123, which is a rather free paraphrase of *Jawāmiʿ*, pp. 150–151.

[18] I have not been able to use the manuscripts.

[19] The story was a favourite of writers of erotica and it can be found in, e.g., al-Tijānī, *Tuḥfa*, pp. 416–417, al-Suyūṭī, *Wishāḥ*, pp. 233–234, and al-Suyūṭī, *Nawāḍir*, p. 121 (only the first verse).

[20] For all these works, see GAL II: 153, nos. 207–209. Brockelmann accepts the *Īḍāḥ* as genuine (no. 210), but the attribution is dubious and some manuscripts give ʿAbd al-Raḥmān ibn Naṣr al-Shīrāzī as the author. Al-Suyūṭī himself reviews his erotic works in the preface to *Wishāḥ*, pp. 34–35.

and antiquarian attitude. Al-Suyūṭī cites the best Classical sources, quoting early poetry and giving *isnāds*, thus giving a very respectable form to his books. The *Wishāḥ* is, according to al-Suyūṭī himself (*Wishāḥ*, pp. 34–35), an abbreviation of a large book of his, *Mabāsim al-milāḥ wa-manāsim al-ṣibāḥ fī mawāsim al-nikāḥ*, which proved to be too long and does not seem to have been put into circulation. In this work, al-Suyūṭī proceeds as a well-educated *adab* author, quoting the Qur'ān, *ḥadīths* and respectable authors, including *adab* authors, lexicographers, philosophers and doctors. He gives lexical lists (pp. 91–196) for expressions meaning coition, penis, vagina and its parts, and movement during coition. When he finally (p. 393)[21] comes to sexual positions, he mentions that there are long lists of these in *Jawāmiʿ al-ladhdha* (about twenty different positions), *Rujūʿ al-shaykh ilā ṣibāhu* (45 positions),[22] and other sources, so that the sum total comes to over 100, though he only gives some examples of these. All the positions, al-Suyūṭī says, are described in the larger version of his book, the *Mabāsim*. The learned discussion must have exhausted the *ʿawāmm* well before coming to this passage. Only the *khawāṣṣ* would have read the learned book to its end.

Al-Suyūṭī's *Shaqā'iq* is similar to his *Wishāḥ*, though more restricted in scope, discussing only making noises during coition. The book proceeds in the usual erudite mode, discussing sexual habits in a scholarly fashion. At the end (p. 108), al-Suyūṭī quotes a saying by al-Qāsim ibn Muḥammad ibn Abī Bakr, an authoritative early Muslim, to the effect that – in modern terms – whatever happens between two consenting adults is their private concern (*idh khalawtum fa-fʿalū mā shi'tum*).[23] This also seems to be al-Suyūṭī's position on the question of erotica. At least he, a religious scholar, wrote freely on sex.

Al-Suyūṭī's third book, *Nawādir al-ayk*, is more explicit and less academic. In the preface (p. 31), he informs us that the book is a *dhayl* to his *Wishāḥ*. The stylistic difference between the more respectable *nikāḥ* in the full title of the *Wishāḥ* versus *nayk* in the full title of this book seems deliberately chosen. Although this book, too, is learned and provides quotations from respectable sources, it is much less so than al-Suyūṭī's other books. The number of titles he gives as his sources is smaller and the material is more explicit, al-Suyūṭī, e.g., copying a long passage (pp. 129–142) from *Rujūʿ al-shaykh* on sexual positions and quoting poems that go straight to the point (e.g., the long one on pp. 166–168, beginning: *khudh rijlahā wa-rmi ʿalā ẓahrihā / wa-ḥakkik-i l-zubba ʿalā shufrihā*). This book comes close to pornography and shows that, even though the *Īḍāḥ* were by pseudo al-Suyūṭī, the real al-Suyūṭī could also write in a very uninhibited way.

Al-Suyūṭī's books give us different views on his relation with erotica. His and other authors' *adab* books seem to fall into two different categories, although some of the material is common to both. On the one hand, we have books on erotic topics that discuss their material in the usual *adab* style, quoting religious and lexicographical sources, giving

Only the *Shaqā'iq* is mentioned in al-Suyūṭī's autobiography *Kitāb al-taḥadduth bi-niʿmat Allāh* (II, 123, no. 24).

[21] He had, though, already in passing discussed sexual positions on pp. 361–362 and in some of the anecdotes.

[22] There are two books by this title, one by al-Tīfāshī (for whom, see GAL I, 495) and another by Ibn Kamāl-pāshā (see GAL II, 452, no. 103). The latter author died in 941/1535, so the references in this and other books by al-Suyūṭī seem to be to al-Tīfāshī's book.

[23] For a similar saying, see al-Jāḥiẓ, *Mufākhara* II, 94.

(short) *isnāds* and mentioning their written sources by their titles. The other category does not do away with all indications of sources, but the works belonging to it mention these much more rarely, usually only giving the name of the poet, but not the immediate source of the verses. In this category, more explicit material is preferred, with sexual positions, indecent anecdotes and pornographic verses having a large share of the book. However, there is no clear indication that books in this category would have been considered injurious to their authors' reputation.[24] Writing obscenities for a learned audience was not condemnable as long as it was done in a scholarly fashion.

The boundary between the groups is by no means clear, but especially in the case of the *Īḍāḥ* we can observe that the preface, instead of toning down the erotic aspects of the book, actually suggests more than the book actually provides. It is the attitude of the author that makes a book respectable or indecent.

The preface is, for these authors at least, the instrument with which to define their books. For those authors of erotica who aim at respectability, erotic material is slyly renamed joking, and joking and jesting are acknowledged to have been practices accepted even by the Prophet himself. This attitude has to be differentiated from that of authors such as al-Jāḥiẓ and Ibn Qutayba, who did not discuss solely erotica, but only defended themselves against possible accusations of indecency in books that were not, *prima facie*, erotic tomes but books that were, indeed, more entertaining than erotic. The works of both authors do contain verses and stories that do not suit the nursery, but neither – in the case of al-Jāḥiẓ speaking only of his preserved works – dedicated much room for the obscene in their works, even though it was not completely lacking either.

The openly erotic or even pornographic authors, on the other hand, also used their prefaces to define their works. Pseudo al-Suyūṭī tried to advertise his book as highly indecent, even though his imagination failed him after the preface and he had to content himself with culling old anthologies to find lamely erotic tales to insert into his book. One wonders whether the author has deliberately concealed his identity which, obviously, was often done for purely financial reasons, the name of al-Suyūṭī selling better than that of some obscure author.

The prefaces show us how authors wanted their readers to read their books, but what about the readership? We know next to nothing about who, in fact, read these erotic books. Al-Samaw'al al-Maghribī dedicates a chapter of his *Nuzhat al-aṣḥāb fī muʿāsharat al-aḥbāb* (pp. 86–92) to the coition etiquette for women, but it is dubious whether there, in fact, were very many women who read his book.

Thus, we have little evidence as to how these manuals were received. Compared with modern, or even 19th-century erotica, the most conspicuous difference is that mediaeval Arabic erotic manuals remained within the sphere of court literature and were written by competent authors and read by cultured readers. Reading Victorian erotica one cannot fail to notice the often poor style of the text, the repetitiveness of the incidents and the almost total lack of intertextual connection with the literary heritage respected at the

[24] Not mentioning the more explicit works in his autobiography may yet be taken as an indication that al-Suyūṭī was not quite comfortable with them. On the other hand, their attribution to al-Suyūṭī is not certain nor do we know whether they were written before or after the autobiography.

time. In Arabic erotic manuals, on the contrary, the material is largely shared with other, quite respectable collections of *adab* and they often contain cumbersome verses and archaic vocabulary that presuppose a learned reader.

How the interaction between blatantly erotic material and learned literature worked is hard to say. One cannot quite see the erotic materials having been read for sexual arousal, but it is equally difficult to imagine the pre-modern reader of many of these texts fully absorbed only in the literary value of these stories and verses.

What, then, was considered obscene in Classical Arabic literature? It is not easy to answer this question, but we might tentatively draw a line between books that do their best to appear scholarly and those that do not. Qur'ānic quotations, *ḥadīths*, lexicographical lists and Classical sources seem to indicate that the book was not aimed at being obscene, whereas the lack of these indications shows that the erotic material was laid bare to the audience and would probably have shocked the more conservative reader in a way lexical lists of the names for private parts and the like did not.

When it comes to an individual item without its context, on the other hand, we can hardly say whether it is obscene or not. Extremely respectable scholarly and religious works contain discussions of the most varied kinds of sexual topics and the same anecdotes are to be found in outspoken erotic manuals and in polite anthologies. The difference lies in the context. What is obscene is that which is served to us as an obscenity.

BIBLIOGRAPHY

al-Balādhurī, *Ansāb al-ashrāf*. VII/1. Ed. Ramzī Baᶜlabakkī. Bibliotheca Islamica 28i. 1997.

Behzadi, Lale (2009), *Sprache und Verstehen. Al-Ǧāḥiẓ über die Vollkommenheit des Ausdrucks*, Diskurse der Arabistik 14, Wiesbaden: Harrassowitz.

Friedmann, Yohanan (1992), *The History of al-Ṭabarī*. XII: *The Battle of al-Qādisiyyah and the Conquest of Syria and Palestine*. Bibliotheca Persica. Albany: State University of New York Press.

GAL = Carl Brockelmann: *Geschichte der arabischen Literatur*. I–II + Supplementbände I–III. Leiden 1936–1944.

van Gelder, Geert Jan (1988) *The Bad and the Ugly. Attitudes towards Invective Poetry (Hijā') in Classical Arabic Literature*. Publication of the "De Goeje Fund" XXVI. Leiden/New York/Koebenhavn/Köln: Brill.

van Gelder, Geert Jan (1992), "Mixtures of Jest and Earnest in Classical Arabic Literature". *Journal of Arabic Literature* 23: 83–108, 169–190.

Ḥājjī Khalīfa, *Kashf al-ẓunūn ᶜan asāmī l-kutub wa'l-funūn*. I–II. Ed. Serefettin Yaltkaya–Rifat Bilge [Maarif matbaasi 1941], repr. Bayrūt: Dār al-Kutub al-ᶜilmiyya 1413/1992.

Hämeen-Anttila, Jaakko (2005), "Abū Nuwās and Ghazal as a Genre". In: Thomas Bauer–Angelika Neuwirth (eds.): *Ghazal as World Literature* I: *Transformations of a Literary Genre*. Beiruter Texte und Studien 89: 87–105.

Hämeen-Anttila, Jaakko (forthcoming), "Khālid ibn Ṣafwān: An Orator in Umayyad and ᶜAbbāsid Courts".

Ibn al-Faqīh, *Mukhataṣar K. al-Buldān* = M.J. de Goeje (ed.), *Ibn al-Fakīh al-Hamadhānī, Compendium libri Kitāb al-Boldān*. Bibliotheca Geographorum Arabicorum V. Lugduni Batavorum (1885), repr. Beyrūt: Dār Ṣādir 1967.

Ibn Kamāl-pāshā, *Kitāb Rujūᶜ al-shaykh ilā ṣibāhu*. In: *al-Jins ᶜinda l-ᶜarab. Nuṣūṣ mukhtāra* II. Manshūrāt al-Jamal: Köln 1997, pp. 7–182.

Ibn an-Nadīm, *Kitāb al-Fihrist* . Ed. Riḍā Tajaddud. Intishārāt-e asāṭīr 348. 1381 A.H.Sh.
Ibn Qutayba, *ᶜUyūn al-akhbār*. Ed. Yūsuf ᶜAlī Ṭawīl. I–IV. Bayrūt: Dār al-kutub al-ᶜilmiyya 1406/1986.
Ibn Ṭayfūr, *Kitāb Balāghāt al-nisā'*. Bayrūt: Dār al-Nahḍa al-ḥadīthiyya 1972.
al-Jāḥiẓ, *al-Bayān wa'l-tabyīn*. Ed. ᶜAbdassalām Muḥammad Hārūn. I–IV. al-Qāhira 1968. Repr. Bayrūt: Dār al-Jīl s.a.
al-Jāḥiẓ, *Kitāb al-Ḥayawān*. Ed. ᶜAbdallāh Muḥammad Hārūn. 2nd edition. I–VIII. Al-Qāhira: al-Bābī al-Ḥalabī wa-awlādihi 1384–1387/1965–1969.
al-Jāḥiẓ, *Mufākharat al-jawārī wa'l-ghilmān*. In: al-Jāḥiẓ, *Rasā'il*, I–II. Ed. ᶜAbdassalām Muḥammad Hārūn, al-Qāhira: Maktabat al-Khānjī 1384/1964, II: 91–137.
al-Nafzāwī, *al-Rawḍ al-ᶜāṭir fī nuzhat al-khāṭir*. Ed. Jamāl Jumᶜa. 2nd edition. London-Cyprus: Riad El-Rayyes Books 1993; transl. Sir Richard Burton, *The Perfumed Garden of the Shaykh Nefzawi*. Ed. Alan Hull Walton London: Grafton Books 1963; German transl. Ulrich Marzolph, *Nafzâwî: Der duftende Garten. Ein arabisches Liebeshandbuch*. München: Beck 2002.
al-Qālī, *Kitāb al-Amālī*. I–II. s.l. s.a.
al-Kātib al-Qazwīnī, *Jawāmiᶜ al-ladhdha*. Ed. Khālid ᶜAṭiyya. Sūriyā: Dār al-Kitāb al-ᶜarabī s.a.
Rowson, E.K. (1998), art. "mujūn". In Julie Scott Meisami–Paul Starkey (eds.), *Encyclopedia of Arabic Literature*. I–II. London/New York: Routledge, II, 546–548.
Rūmī, *Mathnawī* = Reynold A. Nicholson (ed. and transl.), *The Mathnawí of Jalálu'ddín Rúmí*. I–VI. "E.J.W. Gibb Memorial" Series. New Series IV, 1–6, Repr. Cambridge The Trustees of the "E.J.W. Gibb Memorial" 1982.
al-Samaw'al al-Maghribī, *Nuzhat al-aṣḥāb fī muᶜāsharat al-aḥbāb*. Ed. Sayyid Kisrawī Ḥasan. Bayrūt: Dār al-Kutub al-ᶜilmiyya 2008.
al-Suyūṭī, *Kitāb al-Taḥadduth* = E.M. Sartain, *Jalāl al-dīn al-Suyūṭī*. I–II. University of Cambridge Oriental Publications. Cambridge: Cambridge University Press 1975.
al-Suyūṭī, *Nawāḍir al-ayk fī maᶜrifat al-nayk*. Ed. Ṭalᶜat Ḥasan ᶜAbdalqawī. Sūriyā: Dār al-kitāb al-ᶜarabī s.a.
al-Suyūṭī, *Shaqā'iq al-utrujj fī raqā'iq al-ghunj*. Ed. Muḥammad Sayyid al-Rifāᶜī. Sūriyā: Dār al-kitāb al-ᶜarabī s.a.
al-Suyūṭī, *al-Wishāḥ fī fawā'id al-nikāḥ*. Ed. Ṭalᶜat Ḥasan ᶜAbdalqawī. Sūriyā: Dār al-kitāb al-ᶜarabī s.a.
Ps.-al-Suyūtī, *al-Īḍāḥ fī ᶜilm al-nikāḥ*. In *al-Jins ᶜinda l-ᶜarab. Nuṣūṣ mukhtāra* I. Manshūrāt al-Jamal: Köln 1997, pp. 121–146; transl. *The Secrets of Oriental Sexuology. The Book of Exposition (Kitab al-Izah fi'Ilm al-Nikah b-it-Tamam w-al-Kamal)*, literally translated from the Arabic by An English Bohemian. Paris 1896. (repr. Darf Publishers: London 1987).
al-Tīfāshī, *Nuzhat al-albāb fīmā lā yūjad fī kitāb*. Ed. Jamāl Jumᶜa. London/Cyprus: Riad El-Rayyes Books 1992.
al-Tijānī, *Tuḥfat al-ᶜarūs wa-mutᶜat al-nufūs*. Ed. Jalīl al-ᶜAṭiyya. London/Cyprus: Riad el-Rayyes Books 1992.

3

A Suspicion of Excessive Frankness

Pieter Smoor

The genre of *mujūn* employs an unexpected frankness about sexual matters, both the physical act itself, in its many varieties, and the specific naming of the body parts involved. The genre does not aim to titillate or shock the reader. It simply uses words and expressions which were part of the natural language of a certain class at the time when the poetry was written. This usage is no longer in vogue among many readers in today's world.

The genre of *mujūn* was already known at the time of early Islam. It occurs in the works of Abū Nuwās, as we can see in the fifth volume of his Diwan, as well as in poetry by other writers.

Abū Nuwās was a friend of the highly-placed al-Amīn, one of the first Abbasid Caliphs who was himself a firm friend of the eunuchs at the caliphal court. This is illustrated by a short poem of Abū Nuwās in the *rajaz* metre:

1. Exhibit your love while you are openly speaking of beardless youngsters and eunuchs.
2. Leave the people who come in the morning talking rubbish about women.[1]

Due to their influence, *mujūn* poetry embodies a natural openness concerning the private parts of the human body, for clearly there was no reticence in these matters on the part of the eunuchs.

The modern reader will be forgiven for being amazed by some of the poet's allusions – such as how the *penis* 'erupts', and how the *vulva* 'roars' and 'swallows' – where there seems to be absolutely no attempt by the writer to cloak his descriptions in decency or mystery.[2]

However, despite his unexpectedly frank language, Abū Nuwās sometimes mixes into his text metaphors which have their origins in Quranic stories – an odd admixture of sacred and secular, where the poet derives his elevated style from the acclaimed superiority of the Quran.

Another writer, Rāghib al-Iṣbahānī, employs delicious but scandalous anecdotes to depict strange excesses of sexual behaviour in his *Muḥāḍarāt*, and refers in particular to

[1] Dīwan Abī Nuwās V, p. 99, no. 114.
[2] Rāghib al-Iṣbahānī, Muḥāḍarāt II, 261.

the *mujūn* poets and their genre as an example of such excesses, mentioning some of them by name, including Abū Nuwās, Ibn al-Rūmī, and Ibn al-Ḥajjāj.

A poet whom we will discuss later in this article is Ibn al-Rūmī, who was actually two generations younger than Abū Nuwās. A tenuous connection between the two poets seems to lie through ʿAbbās, the father of Ibn al-Rūmī, who once met Abū Nuwās at the house of another literary man. When he encountered Abū Nuwās, who was by then famous for his love of wine and *mujūn*, ʿAbbās must have been impressed by the unusually risqué allusions that Abū Nuwās had introduced into his poetry. He would have noticed how the vulva was changed into 'Jonah's whale', and how the penis became 'a loaded ship', or the reason for 'springs gushing out from the rock'. In fact, Abū Nuwās cleverly enhanced his poetry by taking respectable images from Quranic verse and subtly diverting them into his description of the all too human activities of those around him.

We do not know what ʿAbbās said to his son years later about listening to Abū Nuwās' poetry. He may have been shocked, surprised or filled with admiration at his cleverness.

In any event, some time after that his own son found himself working in the same genre. Abū Nuwās had described himself as a 'jester of black comedy'. Ibn al-Rūmī in his own poetry tried to improve on the genre, and his works show less reserve than that of Abū Nuwās.

It is fascinating to observe the poets' serendipitous style as they skim across various instances of intercourse between different – or indeed, not so different – sexes in the Arab world. Extreme behaviour is not bypassed by circumlocution. In some instances particular words for fornication, depilation, pederasty and masturbation are used without any misgivings at all.

The Quran itself permits only a very tiny amount of such unfettered shamelessness: Allah, it seems, does allow *lamam*, that is 'inadvertence' on the part of a believer. At least one prose author refers to the concept of *lamam*, which occurs in the Quran in Surat al-Najm, verse 32: {Those who avoid heinous crimes and indecencies, **unless by inadvertence** (*illā l-lamam*); verily thy Lord is wide in forgiveness; He knoweth you well, when He produced you from the earth.}[3]

In his *Muḥāḍarāt*, Rāghib al-Iṣbahānī makes use of this Quranic verse when he acknowledges its application to the question 'that the penis and its sperm is to be screened off by the thighs (*mufākhadha*)'. He points out that this practice is connived at: 'Someone among the interpreters of the Quran has declared that Allah's Word *illā l-lamam* can be applied to the *mufākhadha*.'[4]

In the introduction to the text of several poems in Abū Nuwās' *Dīwān* which are summarised under the title *mujūn*, we encounter a description of the contents as follows:

> To this subject belongs what comes here to pass, namely poems in an open-hearted style, which is not passed on by every one person. This is so, because it concerns firstly the unveiling of names for the private parts (*sawʾāt*), and secondly the declaring in public of openings in the human body (*fajarāt*) causing feelings of shamefulness. Some elements of this occur in the text incidentally (*taʿrīḍan*) as they are a slip of the tongue.

---

[3] Surat al-Najm (LIII, 32), see Arberry, p. 245; Dawood, p. 115–116. **Bold** characters are the author's.

[4] *Muḥāḍarāt* II, 250.

> Every class passes this on to the people, for instance when describing the private parts of man and woman (*al-saw'atayn*).[5]

In this volume of the *mujūn* poems, Abū Nuwās immediately indicates which sexual acts or which genital parts are of such interest to him, saying that he will describe them within a conventional context. These poems of his are certainly somewhat offensive in their shamelessness; at least, to a religious-minded or squeamish reader. In the example of *mujūn* style quoted, we also find an example of intimate discourse between Abū Nuwās and his friend, a *warrāq* called ʿAmr, who earned his livelihood by making paper, or copying documents onto paper. In this short poem to be quoted, the poet describes without much restraint the genital parts, as for instance the *penis* and what lies near to it, namely the *anus*. At the same time he refers to the presence of the *vulva*, which is suggested as a possible saddle to assist a second *penis*. This is indeed a very frank and uninhibited description of things; it is almost as if it were written as part of a sexological or anatomical study.[6]

> 1. As for ʿAmr, who belongs to my devoted circle of acquaintances and to those people whom I love, I have presented him with a gift of the noblest subtlety.
> 2. I encountered him when he walked on his feet, then I set him up high on the mount which runs alongside him.
> 3. He is deaf and blind and bald, with a split opening at the crown of his head: a most perverse ending,
> 4. And it is compact. I said: "Look there and ride upon him. This is one of the most elegant of presents."
> 5. Just like the wind, he runs at one moment beneath his mount, but then again he rears up at a forced pace.
> 6. A saddle and reins he does not need to have; no bag holding wheat grains must be bound beneath his mouth for him to munch from.
> 7. Then ʿAmr spoke: By Allah, through this I have attained the highest degree of happiness.
> 8. However, this [*penis*] is for my Mother; so fetch me another for myself! I will then ride mounted upon it at the feast of my departure.
> 9. I said: 'I do not own another mount apart from this; you yourself must therefore be the leading rider (*imām*) standing in front, and you must tell her to sit behind.'

The comment on the passage quoted above enlightens us as to the relationship of the paper merchant to his mother, as seen by the poet Abū Nuwās.[7]

> This ʿAmr al-Warrāq was his companion in striving after the style of *mujūn*. This which is now going to be quoted is a saying of the latter when he looked at the huge penis (*thayl*) of an elephant when its elephant driver (*ḥizāmī*) was standing nigh.
>
> The friend said to the mahout: 'Now, do describe to us the state of this genital part.'
>
> Thereupon the mahout said in doggerel:
>
> When he came into a visible ambiance,
> He was like a roasting spit in his semblance,
> Or the quiver of a Turkish man with a pennant
> Waving in its walking or ambulating stance.

---

[5] See *Dīwān Abī Nuwās* V, p. 2.

[6] *Dīwān Abī Nuwās* V, p. 3, No. 2.

[7] *Dīwān Abī Nuwās* V, p. 3.

But Abū Nuwās criticised him: 'I say, you committed a rhyming error in this line.'

Thereupon he answered: 'Then it should be you who must give us a verse on this subject.'

Thereupon Abū Nuwās said in the *rajaz* metre:

1. I describe a *penis* as the spout at the top of a wineskin
2. Making ready for a forward leap, it appears
3. To resemble a great number; the penis of several asses gathered together in one saltation.'

Despite this preoccupation with the *penis*, we have a different text by Abū Nuwās where, in a complete *volte face*, he confirms how much he is in love with girls and women, as if he really likes them.[8]

In general, irrespective of whether a man or a girl was intended, there was one sure way of attracting the notice of eventual lovers. It was usual practice to send an apple with the centre filled with a sweet-smelling substance, musk for instance, or some other fragrant material. The human lover sent the apple as if it were a messenger, by a real messenger – some woman or girl – who paraded in her capacity as a *rasūl* (bearer of a message) in front of the person intended to be the beloved.

Indeed, this beloved can accept with goodwill the fruit presented. He can keep it as a cherished item to be remembered when he meditates in his hall during the daytime, or even in bed at night. The receiver of the apple will realise that someone who is in love with him must be responsible for the sending of the apple. In the poem it is suggested that the critical outsiders and acquaintances of the beloved one are not conscious of the sly inference of the sender of the apple. This means that the critics and outsiders do not understand the extra value of the apple sent, it being a mere symbol of love for the person intended as receiver of the apple. Sometimes the critics are aware of what happens, then they show jealousy and start sniping and backbiting.

In the *Dīwān Abī Nuwās*, the author refers to backbiters who make comments about the gift to be received by the beloved one. Although the woman who comes with the apple is mostly a mere messenger, the yearning lover who is at the receiving end is sometimes so hungry for sex that he does not hesitate to consummate the relationship as if the messenger is equal to the beloved person. He then forgets that the apple is not meant to be eaten, but only to be symbolic in order to enhance the meditation on love throughout the sleepless nights. The messenger should not be violated, neither should the apple be eaten.[9] In the *Dīwān Abī Nuwās*, we have the following poem concerning the apple from the lover who is sending this special item of fruit. This poem is under the heading of *Bāb al-mudhakkarāt*, or 'chapter on masculine subjects', and the metre is *sarīᶜ*:

1. Oh you who describe the house and the person who built it and the wind which is blowing in every direction!
2. By the footprints left behind in the region by the season of spring when the inhabitants have moved away, and by the stars which he did not cease to gaze upon at night, I swear:

---

[8] *Dīwān Abī Nuwās* IV, p. 1.

[9] *Dīwān Abī Nuwās* IV, p. 2–8.

3. 'More beautiful than the constellation, the harbinger of rain (*naw*ʾ), and more beautiful than a well-trodden track to someone crossing the desert
4. Is the beloved: she who now greets you by this red apple from which she has already bitten,
5. Or he, the young gazelle who has already munched it.' Then the messenger continues: 'You should desire it with your eyes alone.'
6. I say: 'That is indeed my aim; who will help me to obtain it? I am afraid that the beloved one will wound me with it.'
7. He says: 'Take it and conceal its secret. Do not betray the one who gave you the apple.'
8. I say: 'Oh, it is welcome here,' whilst I kiss it, and offer myself as a surety.
9. Mark my words, this is not love for an apple but for its owner.
10. It was he who selected it from his own orchard; and then he filled its interior with sweet musk.
11. Feeling cheerful, I spent the night with it. The memory of him who carried it filled me with contentment.
12. It heals the sickness of the soul, which had been sorrowful, an apple which I cuddle through the night.
13. Knowing nothing of it, my companion chides me when he sees I cannot be parted from it.
14. Alas poor apple, tortured by injustice and by lusting lovers.
15. If it could speak, it would be sorry for itself, giving vent to curses against those who do it harm.
16. Beware, lest he who eats the apple should harbour contempt for the one who offered it.
17. If only the eater of the apple could become a surety when disasters threaten! [10]

There is at least one other poem which is of interest here. It is the only *qaṣīda* in *Dīwān Abī Nuwās* under the heading 'Of the *mujūn* of Abū Nuwās in praise of women, and the ugliness of beardless boys' which appears in the chapter on the subject of women. The poem is in the metre *munsariḥ* and runs as follows:[11]

1. Many a poet does not awaken from the glow of his idle talk; by his ignorance he is led astray.
2. In his poems he gives precedence to beardless youths (*murd*); I am astounded by his poetry and by anyone like him.
3. He asserts that any young man is filled to the brim with coquettishness, but safeguarded from menstruation (*tamth*) and pregnancy.
4. Hey you; you abandon beautiful women and find satisfaction in a beardless youth who looks like someone else as he gets going
5. Just like the people of Lot (*Lūṭ*); but when smart gazelles (*khushf*) lured him into losing his way, Allah brought his people to perdition.
6. No cunning artist, plunged into homosexuality (*liwāṭ*) and led astray because of his haughtiness
7. Is equal to someone in the pangs of love and captivated by women; terror-stricken, he never awakens from his love (*min ghazalih*).
8. A youth whom you once loved is not the same as that Full Moon when it has descended into his cloak.
9. Only when the moment arrives and you have him in your hands, are you annoyed by his procrastination and his alleged excuses.

---

[10] *Dīwān Abī Nuwās* IV, p. 6–7, No. 7.

[11] *Dīwān Abī Nuwās* V, p. 104–105, No. 121.

10. And then a tangled beard appears on his face which prevents his lovers from kissing him.
11. Such a youth does not resemble a young girl, whose nether half consists of a hillock of smoothly curving sands, while her upper half is a tender twig sweeping in its motion.
12. Above her girdle, long strands of hair quiver as they hang in clusters of curls.
13. Does the youth (*al-ghulām*) with whom you are in love, possess anything like her cheeks when he approaches with embarrassment?
14. Or is he the owner of the locks at both sides of her face, with another curly lock in front of it, and of a belly confined by a waist, which fits proudly over her buttocks?
15. The love for these beautiful girls is something which belongs to 'correct behaviour' (*al-rashād*) even though this almost causes the lover to come to his own last moment.
16. Joseph was tempted by beauty; and the same happened to David, to such an extent that he also succumbed to cravings of love, despite his servant Uriah,
17. Him whom he had murdered in order to acquire his unique ewe; he allowed himself to fall in love [with Bath-sheba] even as he had him [Uriah] transferred (to the forefront of the battle).
18. And as for Moses, he who was addressed by the Godhead, a cloud of love appeared to him despite his fear (*maʿa wajalih*).
19. The "Friend" [Abraham, The Friend of Allah, Khalīl Allah] caused Hagar to depart with him for a desert upon whose tracks the people lose their way.
20. And Zaynab turned our Muhammad into a slave, addicted to love; when Zayd left, the latter took his place.
21. When Allah formed Adam, the latter lusted after a beautiful woman, for women were the only hope he had.
22. Allah then set about creating a woman for our sakes; thus the desire for women was the result of an act of His.
23. A camel stallion wants sexual intercourse with the mares in his herd, but you do not see him bending over a male camel.
24. When you are in the midst of ill fortune, you should refuse to become an imitator of Iblīs [the Devil] because one of his wiles is *liwāṭ* (homosexual activity).

Despite his remark in the above poem to the effect that intercourse is better with a woman than a man, and that homosexuality is connected with the Devil, in another of his poems Abū Nuwās seems to take the opposite point of view. In his *Dīwān* volume V, Abū Nuwās admonishes a young woman and tells her to go away from his presence and find a young man, for him to hire for intercourse and companionship. He appears to think this is a normal course of events – and adds that the girl herself should seek other amusement, and perhaps work as a prostitute. In the metre *khafīf* to rhyme *wa-maṭlabī*, Abū Nuwās is alleged to have written:

1. My ambition, my questions and my desires are all concerned with a young man (*ghulām*).
2. A tender girl felt a desire for me; but many a one who is hopeful will suffer disappointment.
3. When I saw her, I said: 'Be gone, my sister; disappear.
4. Find someone for me who is for hire, make yourself scarce, become a whore!
5. As long as I live, I shall never allow my finger to enter the hole of a scorpion.'[12]

From the lines attributed to him, one must deduce that Abū Nuwās preferred young boys

[12] *Dīwān Abī Nuwās* V, p. 7, No. 8.

to girls; and in this connection he explains his preference as follows: intercourse with a girl is risky because she might conceive a child; once that new life has announced itself, it will be hard to stop it.

Although the poet makes no mention of the pre-Islamic custom of the *mawʾūda* (the killing of newly-born baby girls by burying them alive) we are informed that at all costs, sin must be avoided. Therefore, since bringing a new life into the world will give rise to more sin, it is advisable not to run the risk of starting a new life in the first place.

Abū Nuwās's reasoning is explained in the comment on the poem which is quoted below. The poet says that intercourse with women is inadvisable because of women's impurity, due to menstruation, and also because of the likelihood that they will become pregnant. In his opinion, intercourse with a man is the preferred option.

> This *qaṣīda* is based by Abū Nuwās upon the delivered tradition (*riwāya*) deriving from the Christians on the authority of their Christian scholars. I encountered this line of thought at the beginning of an extended message written by one Abū l-ʿAnbas al-Ṣaymarī addressed to al-Mutawakkil. He entitled his book with the words Excellence of the Buttocks (*al-satihīn*) over the Vaginas (*al-ḥariḥīn*); and Excellence of the Homosexuals (*al-lāṭa*) over the Barbers who shave the hairs off one's *pudendum* with *nūra*, a depilatory [usually applied by the *jammāshīn*]. I inform you here about this *qaṣīda* so that hereby you will understand the explanation that is in the poem.
>
> Abū l-ʿAnbas said the following:
>
> The Christians inform us on the authority of St Paul (*Fawlus*) that he said the following concerning this: 'Do not have sexual intercourse with women, because sinners will come forth from your loins who will be disobedient to Allah, instead, you should pay attention to the thighs'. The Christians inform us also on the authority of Bar Ṣawmā from Naṣīb that he said: 'Do not have sexual intercourse with women in order to prevent sinners from coming forth from their bellies, who then will be disobedient towards Allah with the result that their sins will be a charge upon you; but use the inside (*buṭūn*, also meaning: "bellies") of the thighs as a shield screening off your male organs. But if that is not possible, then you must use saliva which you will leave flowing upon the palm of your hands, then you will rub the penis over it little by little until it ejaculates what is inside. Then you will be relaxed and if it is possible for you to act reciprocally (*al-mubādala*), do so for in that practice is repose for the soul and composure for the heart and exclusive devotion to worship. Are you then not aware that a human when his penis is standing, is occupied thereby and unable to worship Allah (may He be elevated and majestic); and take the Messiah (*al-masīḥ*) as an example as he did not approach women and did not shed blood.'
>
> And he said:
>
> And since the monks are fond of travelling through the lands (*al-siyāḥa*) you almost never encounter a monk unless he has a companion with him who accompanies him to give reciprocal assistance (*yurāfiquhu li l-mubādala*).
>
> He said:
>
>> I saw once a sheikh from among the monks who was alone without a companion and it was necessary for him to pierce a melon (*biṭṭīkha*) and to cause his penis to penetrate into the hole. He raised his voice (*ʿaqīratahu*) and cried: 'I'll screw and screw, until I ejaculate in this melon!'

[Up till here is the wording of the explanation of the *qaṣīda*.]

After this he said:

> The following words were said to Siyāh: 'What is the more sensual pleasure in life?'

He answered: 'Something well-cooked, yellow wine, and a youth with piercing glance.'

He said:

I heard the Supreme Qāḍī and Judge Yaḥyā ibn Aktham speak, reciting [lines in the metre *ramal*]:

> 1. This World only consists of food, wine, and a youth (*ghulām*);
> 2. But when all these have gone, then say goodbye to the World.

He said:

> I say: This youth is easier to sustain and of more assistance to you, while you are safeguarded from his uncleanness and from his pregnancy; and you need not fear any punishment by cutting (*ḥadd*) and stoning (*rajm*) if you are arrested when you are with him. When you feel isolated he is family; and when you are with drinkers he is a fellow drinker; and on the road he is a companion. (...)[13]

Now follows the poem, whose explanation we considered above.
About ʿAbdīshūʿ he said a poem in metre *wāfir* and on rhyme *al-ʿadhārā* as follows:[14]

> 1. Let the rains take turns with their pourings over the deserted places; turn around from there and turn into the road to the Convent of the Virgins (*al-ʿadhārā*).
> 2. Avoid describing a girl like Arwā or Lubaynā, while ʿAbdīshūʿ is here. And leave the girl Nawār alone.
> 3. This is because of a gazelle of the Christians (a young christian man), who resembles a crescent moon, whose delicate features will make you abstain from the virgins.
> 4. Because of him, I gave up the company of beautiful girls with their eyes in black and white; all this was due to my heart being occupied by love for him as their substitute.
> 5. After I had turned my love from the girls, they became confused as I kept my distance from them. Then they started to speak:
> 6. 'According to what argument, or in consequence of which opinion have you strayed from the pious Muslim in the direction of the Christians?'
> 7. I said: 'This happened because of Bar Ṣawmā from Naṣīb, who has openly declared that their thighs are to be permitted as an acceptable place.
> 8. He is used to observing that marriage with a girl is a sinful trend, for fear that these maidens would produce wicked descendants.
> 9. He considers the upper part of the legs as a shield preventing any penis from entering whether he is standing upright in the night or in the daytime,
> 10. While he resembles a caller to prayer, anouncing *ṣalāt* on a cloudy day, who never ceases from looking out, both right and left.
> 11. But if no one is found, he takes his repose in the palms of both his hands; then he will not be fearful of sin and shame.'
> 12. In ancient times St Paul was also of the opinion that the begetting of mortals is a perilous adventure.
> 13. He said: 'Do you not see on any day when his penis comes into a state of motion and tumult

---

[13] *Dīwān Abī Nuwās* V, p. 155–157.

[14] *Dīwān Abī Nuwās* V, p. 154–155, No. 153 ; and see E. Wagner, *Abū Nuwās*, p. 202–203.

14. That it will then distract him from his pious worship?' Measure this in the way of analogy alongside the words I have already said before; and consider Jesus
15. As your guideline! For neither did he ever shed blood on any given day, nor did he loosen a girl's girdle.
16. However, take instead your guidance from the monks. When travelling around the World and starting upon a jouney, no one among them is ever observed
17. While he is all alone, without a comrade who accompanies him in order to exchange intercourse, either in public or in private;
18. But while he is busy by himself, this lascivious young friend of mine will procure a melon (*biṭṭīkha*) and lean over it
19. And exclaim: 'It's time for me to screw and screw!' – words which he repeats several times until the juice flows in abundance.
20. For this reason, oh women, I have avoided you on your way, and taken instead the path to the Christians; for these are folk who feel no shame in honest fucking.

Note that in his poetry Abū Nuwās confesses that he has harboured doubts as to what is obligatory and what is strictly forbidden in his own religion of Islam.

He prefers the *mujūn* and fully expects that because of his own excesses with regard both to drinking and to sex, he may well have to look forward to an alternative garden of Paradise. The poet seems to think that since Man was formed from clay and since wine that is stored for a long time turns yeasty, when the wine is mixed with the clay a delectable vintage (the wine of Musṭār) will result, and this is what will be flowing in the river of the alternative Paradise aimed specifically at oenophiles.

Could such a Paradise really exist? In one of his poems, Abū Nuwās reflects on this very topic:

'This belongs to the *mujūn* of Abū Nuwās concerning his opposition against those men or women, who criticised him and his open shamelessness in his perseverance in the committing of sins and in his contempt for their warnings of imminent judgment.' [15] The text of the poem, which is in the metre *kāmil* and falls within the chapter on wine poems, appears below with the redactor's commentary interpolated in italics:

1. Many a woman who constantly criticises, seems to think that because of her blame I shall abandon the company of intelligent men.
2. In the morning she presents herself with the intention of increasing my concept of correct behaviour (*al-rashād*), as if I would ever be led by the advice of the pious!
3. She says: "Woe unto you, you are no longer young, for you are an adult. Time has thrown a heap of excuses upon you.
The meaning of this is, that Time offers its excuse to someone. As he has become old and hoary, his pleasure in the affairs of love has now diminished, namely after the passing-by of so many years.
4. For how much longer will you continue to fall in love and be addicted to love, whilst you go spinning round the courtyard like a voyeur?
5. Do you not realise that morning and evening compete against each other to see who will be the one to end a person's life by means of a shot from Perdition's brow, by an arrow from its bow?
6. I answered her by saying that I was well aware of my behaviour; thereafter I applied my mind to banishing her accusations.
7. 'Take your words of complaint away, you disgruntled woman; for I have already harkened

[15] *Dīwān Abī Nuwās* V, p. 224–227, No. 225.

to mine own error, and I have chucked all the words of blame I received over the wall.'
8. I consider a preference for lust and love and pleasure as something which is bound up with the perfume of this place.
9. As for my suspicion that what is reported to be taking place is mere guesswork, cobbled together from reports (*akhbār*), that suspicion is more accurate and more definite than any anticipation of the moment of my death.
10. I am only concerned with whatever you see before you on this very day; however because of certain traditions (*āthār*), we are aware retrospectively of certain things which happened long ago.
11. No one has ever come to me to make a report to the effect that since the hour of his decease he has been resident in Paradise or in Hell.
12. Leave behind the complaints against me regarding the ascending path to self-sufficiency; and leave behind the prognostications concerning fate's decision.
13. As for restraint, its moment has not yet come; that will only happen when both my cheeks are covered in grey hair.
14. Suppose my destiny were to make an appearance – which would be helpful – only then should you contemplate my state of restraint and dignity.
The meaning of this is, that no opinion is offered and no intelligence is available for the lover, but everything about him has been decided.
15. But I love the *mujūn*; and in the middle of everything which I find pleasurable, I am desirous for the veils to be torn off.
16. But how can restraint exist in respect of a gazelle who looks with a piercing eye and thereby prolongs the moment of death?
17. From time to time he practices the *mujūn*; he is someone whose beautiful features are perfect, someone towards whom people's glances are drawn, as if pulled by strings.
18. He offers light full of brilliance from his shining face, just like the shining Full Moon when it illuminates the traveller's path.
19. The two tapestries of his cheeks compete with each other like two arrows below the curving brow of Perdition while they both find their targets in the eyes of all who gaze upon him.
20. The mere mentioning of his majesty plays havoc with the speech of those who wish to fuck him. Therefore he will only be fucked in a spiritual sense.
21. If my desire to kiss him is achieved, I shall attain eternity in the Garden of Paradise.
22. Many a man who has curled his side-whiskers up like scorpions will find that his glance can penetrate all secret matters.
23. He possesses a flat belly, is gifted with a melodious voice, sparkles and has a beautiful shape; he is thus one of the Banū ʿAmmār.
24. I competed with him for a well-filled glass of wine; Nizār (the cupbearer) had mixed its contents.
25. As for that wine, when it is mixed with Adam's clay it becomes a grey-haired old woman concealed within her pitcher, hidden behind a veil.
26. And when at last Time has departed, having banished all blame from her, and when she has been purified and turned into the essence of a very fine wine (*al-musṭār*),
27. Then she changes back into such a colourful array that an entire horoscope of heavenly lights can be found in the wineglass.[16]

In the above poem Abū Nuwās seems to be proposing an alternative view of Paradise which is in complete contrast to the traditional concept of the hereafter. He appears to envisage a landscape where wine is constantly offered by beardless youths, the *murd* he so often

[16] *Dīwān Abī Nuwās* V, p. 224–227, No. 225.

adduces in his poems. This poses incidentally the question whether these youths are so important that they will be allowed to live in eternity. [Of course, they could be constantly replaced as an outfit of Paradise.]

In this alternative Garden, as believers arrive, they are allowed to enjoy the company that is already present.

Compare this with the Quran, Surat al-Insān (LXXVI, 14):[17]

> {11. So Allah hath preserved them from the evil of that day, and hath caused them to meet cheerfulness and joy;
> 12. And hath recompensed them for the endurance they have shown with a Garden and silk;
> 13. Reclining therein on the couches, they see not therein sun or cold;
> 14. Near over them are its shades, and its fruit-clusters are let lowly down.
> 15. Round amongst them are passed vessels of silver and goblets made of glass,
> 16. Glasses of silver, which they have determined by measure.
> 17. In which they are given to drink a cup the admixture of which is ginger.
> 18. A spring therein the name of which is Salsabīl.
> 19. Round amongst them go boys of perpetual youth, whom when one sees, he thinks them pearls unstrung.
> 20. When one sees, then one sees delight, and a great kingdom.
> 21. There cover them green garments of satin, and brocade, and they have been adorned with bracelets of silver, and their Lord hath given them to drink a pure draught.}

Although Abū Nuwās frequently opposes the role normally played by women in sexual relationships, and although he makes use of a certain brutal frankness when referring to human reproductive organs, he is certainly not alone in taking this stance. It is now time, therefore, to consider the *mujūn* of other poets who favoured the same genre.

Abū Nuwās ibn Hāniʾ al-Ḥakamī lived some two generations before Abu l-Ḥasan ʿAlī ibn al-ʿAbbās Ibn Jurayj al-Rūmī, a client of the Abbasids. The former had died in around 199 H, while the latter was born some twenty years later, because Ibn al-Rūmī lived from 221 H until about 282 H.

While the two poets themselves could not have met each other, it is believed that Ibn al-Rūmī's father met Abū Nuwās at the house of a literary friend in Baghdad, and it may well be that Ibn al-Rūmī's father boasted of this in later life, which is why his son felt called to take up poetry-writing. Certainly, Ibn al-Rūmī used expressions deriving from the Quran in exactly the same way that Abū Nuwās had done, and certainly both men admired the style of *mujūn*.

There exists a commentary upon the poetry of Abū Nuwās. The first topic referred to is passive pederasty, and because it is a shameful topic, the act is mentioned with a degree of circumlocution.

> His friend answered him, and he said in metre *ṭawīl* as follows:
>
> > The buttocks are a surface suitable for walking on at night; but is there another way of crossing over places of horror than by way of the surface?[18]

---

[17] Compare translations by Arberry p. 315; and Dawood p. 18.

[18] The word *ẓahr* has two meanings: 'surface'; and 'backside' or 'buttocks.'

The commentator then starts off again, saying:

> There are 30 stories which I have transferred from the start of this series of chapters to this final chapter. In the meantime other stories came to my mind, for which I deemed this chapter appropriate.
>
> On the authority of Ibn al-Rūmī the poet, on the authority of his father al-ʿAbbās Jūrjīs, a person with literary connections has delivered the following report:
>
>> When he was still a young child, al-ʿAbbās had been taken as prisoner from among the Byzantines, together with his father. Thereupon he came at last to the house of ʿUbayd Allah ibn ʿĪsā ibn Jaʿfar ibn Abī Jaʿfar al-Manṣūr. Thereafter he used to study together with the children of ʿUbayd Allah and he said:
>>
>> ʿUbayd Allah sent me on a certain day to al-Sindī ibn Ṣadaqah ibn Dādawayhi. Ṣadaqah was someone from the inhabitants of Isfahan, afterwards he settled in Baghdad. The Sindī taught his son every branch of the profession of literature. Later on, I was with him at his house when a man entered who had a colourful complexion, a beautiful face, a perfect posture, a well-filled body, a black beard and with white patches (*nubadh*) on his cheeks. He was wearing a beautiful cloak (*bizzah*) and his feet were shod with fine sandals. When the Sindī's eyes fell upon him, he got to his feet. The person who had entered, in front of whom he was going to be seated, recited for him the following poem in metre *wāfir* and said [a couple of lines describing some intricate sexual relationship]:
>
> 1. When she had been broken laying on top of him, you turned towards me from below. If she rises, you are "the raven of Noah."[19]
>
> [Meaning: you shudder away from her oceanic void. Compare al-Kisāʾī, *Qiṣaṣ al-anbiyāʾ*:
>
> Thereafter Noah sent the pigeon and he said to her, Look how much of the water has remained on the surface of the earth. Thereupon she flew off to the East and the West and returned quickly because Noah had called out to her, Quickly! She [the pigeon] said: Oh Prophet of Allah, the earth and the trees have perished except the olive tree, for she has grown green just as she was before. Noah had already sent the raven (*al-ghurāb*) before that, but it shuddered away from him; and therefore Noah sent the pigeon.[20]
>
> The poem continues:]
>
> 2. When we came to you, because we wished to drink; you appeared in front of us, rigid and upon a rearing mount.
>
> Thereupon the man from Sind said: 'With all respect, I say if you do not cease adding to this, I will do to you so-and-so-something wicked.' Thereupon he (Abū Nuwās) ceased speaking in that manner. And the Sindī asked him about the report concerning his name, and it was the season of the Old Woman [the season of Wine which is long preserved]. Thereupon Abū Nuwās started reciting and said:
>
> 1. On many a day during the 'days of the Old Woman', as if they were the faces of drinking companions against whom snow is being blown,
> 2. We performed the *ṣalāt* upon the palms of our hands which were flaming hot; and they caused our bellies to be aflame, so the skins began to leak through. [meaning: we practiced masturbation.]

[19] *Dīwān Abī Nuwās* V, p. 507, Bāb 15, No. 22, 23.

[20] *Qiṣaṣ al-anbiyā'* I, p. 98.

> Thereupon the man from Sind turned towards me [scilicet, ʿAbbās Abu l-Faḍl, Ibn al-Rūmī's father] and said: 'Oh Abu l-Faḍl, here is Abū Nuwās, the chief among the people of literature, the best among those who are decorated for their literature (*adab*), who deliver that *adab*. Therefore, rise up before him!' I hurried towards him, and kissed his hand, and I remained that day with him. After that I returned from him, having received useful knowledge concerning many matters, about which I had previously never heard.[21]

Having seen the examples from Abū Nuwās, we find in the poems of the later poet, Ibn al-Rūmī, a similarly large amount of text which tends to be in the style of *mujūn*. This poet's cavalier attitude towards the mentioning of the names of the private parts is even more pronounced than that of Abū Nuwās. But in Ibn al-Rūmī's poems we find quite frequently that *mujūn* passages are inserted within satirical poems, in the style of *hijāʾ*. Here the poet tends to have a sort of *poésie parlante*, a story of conversation and description.

In particular we must be aware of the poet's preference for very rough descriptions of certain female singers, with whom he had come into conflict for some strange reason. One wonders whether he simply did not like their music, or whether they had upset him in some way. The poet refers to specific women by name: Summāna, Kunayza and Shunṭuf; and then he stresses their individual faults. In the case of the unfortunate Shunṭuf, he complains that she suffers from bad breath [her mouth stinks, or her hole has a foul odour]; when she cries out, she croaks [possibly a reference to the noise during sex]; she stumbles about; she stoops; she suffers from diarrhoea; she is attracted to rough types. And as for her bodily parts: her *vulva* gapes widely in order to give access to a great multitude of *penises*. It is as large as a great plain in front of a fortress. Apart from the above, Ibn al-Rūmī refers to Shunṭuf's *clitoris*. He does not see it as contrasting with the male organ, but rather notes its similarities; in his phantastic imagery it can even compete with its counterpart in length; and from this point he is able to allude to female circumcision.

As if this was not enough, Ibn al-Rūmī then moves on to other fascinating happenings in the region around the *penis*, including masturbation by means of a melon (*biṭṭīkha*), just as Abū Nuwās did before him; and in the case of the arsenic-seller's grandson he also appears to suggest stimulation by means of a sadistic sexual beating.

Here now follows a short epigrammatic poem by Ibn al-Rūmī. In the commentary it is introduced thus:

> Here follows the poem about Ismāʿīl ibn Bulbul in metre *rajaz* and to rhyme *ṣarīkhi*, where Ibn al-Rūmī says the following:
>
> 1. Is it possible for me to utter a scream against the days?
> 2. Does someone hear me, giving ear to my complaint?
> 3. When the days appear to be deaf to my reproach.
> 4. Are they then enamoured with numbing cold?
> 5. I refer to the son of the arsenic seller's daughter (*ibn binti bāʾiʿi l-zirnīkhi*),
> 6. She who is famous for her proud behaviour (*bi l-takmīkhi*).

[21] See *Dīwān Abī Nuwās* V, p. 507–508, in Bāb 15, No. 23. The Sindī, who instantly recognised Abū Nuwās, was one of the gypsies who must have migrated from the Sind valley in India through the Persian regions of Fārs and Ahwāz to the Marshes north of Basra, as far as the reed-land all around al-Baṭīḥa. See Charles Pellat, *Le milieu Basrien et la formation de Ǧāḥiẓ*, Paris 1953, p. 37–40. For a recent description, see Wilfred Thesiger, *The Marsh Arabs*, Penguin, Harmondsworth 1967.

7. After he is slapped about the neck and beaten (*bi l-taklīkhi*) –
8. Often with the bald penis and a melon (*bi l-biṭṭīkhi*) –
9. He changes into ʿUṭārid (the planet Mercury) and seeks shelter with Mirrīkh (the fiery red planet Mars).[22]

The Old Man – and here, we do not know whether the poet means himself, or another specific old man, or simply old men in general – is complaining against the trials of old age and remembering the days when he was able to find sexual satisfaction in the company of a handsome youth. Now, when he is left alone he accepts that he will have to exercise his bald penis and to commit masturbation with the help of a melon. Of course, this is just like the practice described by Abū Nuwās in the earlier-mentioned poem, where Abū Nuwās wrote of the practices of a lone monk crossing the desert who had been unable to find a travelling companion and was obliged to satisfy himself. Finally, the man in the poem is named by Ibn al-Rūmī. Having become sadder and wiser with the years, he now appears in the guise of ʿUṭārid, the heavenly figure of an old man or scribe who himself seeks solace with Mirrīkh, the symbol of fiery Martian youth. At this stage in his life, the old man has no companion to travel with, and continues his journey in the company of the jinn in the hereafter, where he finds himself transcended to another condition in an alternative world resembling the conjunction of the two luminary bodies Mercury and Mars. At this point our wandering planet, an elderly and passive pederast finds himself in the company of another wanderer, his fiery friend Mars.[23]

Here follows Ibn al-Rūmī's poem in metre *majzūʾ al-khafīf* and on rhyme *shunṭufu*:

Concerning Shunṭuf he said the following:

1. Cursing all the time, Shunṭuf slipped and lost her footing, her feet being encircled by bangles.
2. After that, she moved at a crouch and continued to fart; standing still did not prevent it.
3. It was a gust of wind which caused the peal of thunder to be silent, for her fart crackled in confusion.
4. After that, she started to rise, just as she was; she pretended to be in pain, but her gestures were too rough.
5. They said: 'Get up and go back to the high road, for you are only pretending.
6. How can there be a pretence of elegance, given the situation in which you are?
7. How is one to be deeply moved by sweetness, whilst your excrement is flowing?'
8. She continued walking and directed herself towards the high road, but she was full of shame.
9. The hem of her garment slithered around her feet.
10. Hands stretched out to steady her, but she was full of pride.
11. A slap from somebody's [hand, penis] landed upon her head as she took turns to run and walk.

---

[22] *Dīwān Ibn al-Rūmī*, Muhannā II, 106–107, No. 440; Naṣṣār Cairo 1974, II, 580, No. 440.

[23] See for instance Anna Caiozzo, *Images du ciel d'Orient au Moyen Âge*, Paris-Sorbonne 2003, p. 399 (Mercure), p. 402 (Mars) and Index. The planet Mercury, personified in ʿUṭārid, descends from its heavenly sphere in order to speak to the human ʿUṭārid, whose dwelling is upon the earth, see Jāḥiẓ, *Kitāb al-tarbīʿ wa-l-tadwīr*, ed. Charles Pellat, Damascus 1955, p. 29 = No. 45; p. 44. Compare the metamorphosis from a voluptuous woman into the planet Venus (Zuhara); and the change from a tax collector (*ʿashshār*) in Yemen into Canopus (Suhayl), the second brightest star in the southern sky. See Jāḥiẓ, *Kitāb al-tarbīʿ*, p. 39 and 46; Jāḥiẓ, *Kitāb al-ḥayawān*, 2nd printing Cairo 1950, vol. VI, 198 and vol. I, 297.

12. So her show of sorrow ended, and her proud attitude ceased.
13. She is an ape, who pretends not to be in need of anyone, though she always follows on last behind the others.
14. She is a whore who rides on top of the penises, while unseemly behaviour lies within her.
15. In the minds of the nobility there is no desire for her.
16. She owns a hole where clitorises are bruised for ever and ever.
17. It swallows up the elephant, and also the camel who groans with pain.
18. It resembles the staff of the Man-with-the-Staff, who is elevated above all these acts of swallowing-up.[24]

There is a Quranic text about a staff which swallowed up all the other staffs owned by the magicians of Pharaoh. However, it did not swallow any liquid.[25]

19. The penis is tasting a fig which has in the meantime been overtaken by an illness which attacks figs (*taḥashshuf*).
20. You desire me to fuck you, although I am of the opinion that I should refrain from that.
21. I say: Alas, that is the way it is, otherwise I should have to go begging on behalf of my penis.
22. Any intercourse is forbidden; it is only allowed when the place of urination is well-smelling and clean.
23. Who is about to pass away, and yet no one sorrows on his behalf?
24. And as for the fucking of a coloured woman who resembles darkness as it falls, thickly woven,
25. And whose ornaments consist of grey old age, no crowns make her elegant and sparkling,
26. There is *karafs* (a kitchen vegetable, meaning celery) upon her face, and *kursuf* (cotton wool) on the top of her head.
27. The sight does not please the eye, although it is unusual.
28. There was once Joseph renowned for his beauty; but she is also a Joseph, but renowned for her unsightliness.
29. Her ugliness forces them to lessen their ranting, for she would be raised in notoriety to match their raving.
30. She rejects Allah her Lord, for her devotions are dedicated to the penis.
31. She busies herself with wiping the white scum from her eyes and she also hunts for maggots in datestones.
32. She is a silly cunt who continually seeks glorification by behaving outrageously.
33. If she were a Kaᶜba (the Holy House) then circumambulation would never have been permitted.
34. Her intentions are always twisted; they have sharp edges on both sides.

---

[24] *Dīwān Ibn al-Rūmī*, Muhannā IV, p. 256–258, No. 1240; Naṣṣār, Cairo 1978, IV, p. 1616–1619, No. 1240. Compare *Dīwān Ibn al-Rūmī*, Muhannā I, p. 96, No. 61; Naṣṣār, Cairo 1973, p. 112, No. 61.

[25] Quran, Surat al-Shuᶜarāʾ (XXVI, 41):

{41. So when the magicians came, they said to Pharaoh: "Is there then for us a reward, if it is we who are the victors?"
Said he: "Yes, and in that case ye will be of those brought near."
Moses said to them: "Throw down what ye are going to throw."
So they threw down their ropes and their staves, and said: "By the might of Pharaoh, it is we who are the victors."
Then Moses threw down his staff, and there it was, swallowing what they were faking.}

35. It is obvious that she has grown old because she drags herself along clad in the chains of old age.
36. Oh Abu l-Qāsim, in whose courtyard the guest is regaled,
37. And whose command over the heights shall never cease,
38. And whose majesty does not end and whose essence is subtle,
39. Having spent the winter, how many times will we pass the summer? May the days of summer last forever!
40. Protect us from the cold of this female ape who pretends to be sorrowful but practises mockery.[26]

In another place in the *Dīwān* of Ibn al-Rūmī we find a further description of a staff and its ability to conjure up an immense fertile flood. This is the staff of Moses which was noted for its ability to produce huge quantities of water; when it was struck against a rock, twelve springs suddenly gushed forth.

In the minds of readers of the Bible who study this story, there is no possible connection between the rod of Moses and a penis. In the mind of Ibn al-Rūmī, however the association between the imagery of the staff and the imagery of the penis is a point of poetic style and an elevation in the way of expression.

On another occasion Ibn al-Rūmī addresses someone who possesses a staff similar to that of Moses and states that his ability to produce water is so potent that he should consider himself as a godhead. However, knowing Ibn al-Rūmī's delight in producing salacious texts, one wonders whether water is really intended, or whether the poet and his readers might actually have been thinking of semen.

Compare that with Ibn al-Rūmī's poem in rhyme *bi-sayrik* as follows:

1. Mount upon the backs of all the people, and snort like a stallion as you race along!
2. You are a godhead for all the people; they serve no one but you.
3. They differ in their sentiments; some people among them fear your malevolence, whilst others long for your goodness.
4. Moses through his staff acquired less than whatever you will acquire through your penis.[27]

And compare it with Quran, Surat al-Aʿrāf (VII, 160–163):[28]

{160. We suggested to Moses, when his people asked him to give them drink: **'Strike the rock with thy staff"; then there gushed out from it twelve springs;**
All the people already knew their drinking places; and We caused the thick cloud to shade them, and sent down upon them the manna and the quails; 'Eat the good things which We have provided for you.' They did not wrong Us, but themselves were they wronging.
161. (Recall) when it was said to them: 'Inhabit this town, and eat from wheresoever ye please of it, and say: "ḥiṭṭa" and enter the gate prostrating yourselves; We shall forgive

[26] *Dīwān Ibn al-Rūmī*, Muhannā IV, p. 256–258, No. 1240; Naṣṣār, Cairo 1978, IV, p. 1616–1619, No. 1240.

[27] Poem in the rhyme *bi-sayrik*, *Dīwān Ibn al-Rūmī*, Muhannā V, p. 62, No. 1424; Naṣṣār V, p. 1872–1873, No. 1424.

[28] Compare the translations by Arberry p. 190: *ḥiṭṭa* meaning, 'Unburdening'; Dawood p. 259: *ḥiṭṭa* meaning, 'Pray for forgiveness'; Sale p. 160: *ḥiṭṭa* meaning, 'Forgiveness!'; Irving p. 85: *ḥiṭṭa* meaning 'Relieve [us]!'; and Muhammad Ali, p. 363 and cf. p. 34 note 93: *ḥiṭṭa* meaning 'Put down from us our heavy burdens.'

you your sins; We shall increase those who do well.'
162. But those of them who did wrong substituted a different word for that which had been said to them, so We sent upon them wrath from the heaven, for the wrong they were doing.
163. Ask them about the town close on the sea when they transgressed in the matter of the sabbath whose fish came to them on the day of their sabbath right to the shore, but on the day when they did not keep sabbath, they did not come to them. Thus do We afflict them for the impiety they have been committing.}

Here follows a very strange comment by Ibn al-Rūmī. He seems to be making an attempt to be humorous by adapting a Quranic text, his aim being to remind – and possibly criticise – his friends for failing to keep an appointment.[29]

1. Why did our fish avoid us? Why did the visitors disappoint those who were awaiting them?
2. We prevented them from having an excuse to offer when we turned their Sabbath (Saturday) into *Jumʿa* (Friday). So what gave them cause to cancel?
3. Their visits used to occur on Saturdays, therefore we kept to the same day to suit them.
4. We turned it into a celebration, as if we were Jews, or similar to Jews.

From the above it would appear that in Ibn al-Rūmī's day there was room for confusion if friends from different religions agreed to meet. An appointment for 'next week, on the Sabbath' could mean Friday (to a Muslim) Saturday (to a Jew) or Sunday (to a Christian).

The reference to the fish is explained in the various explanations of the Quranic text quoted above, and here we need not go further into this.

It was common practice among poets to take a poem by an earlier writer and elaborate upon it. Below follows an example of a short epigrammatic poem by Abū Nuwās which was re-worked by Ibn al-Rūmī many years after the former's death. The reader should note that Ibn al-Rūmī inserts words from the Quran just as Abū Nuwās had done before him.

Abū Nuwās said the following:

1. How many a singer causes his drinking companion to inherit something which consists of a chill and a headache.
2. If he were to roll in a fire, then it would bring coolth (coolness) and peace.[30]

It should be noted that the phrase 'coolth and peace' comes directly from the Quran , Surat al-Anbiyāʾ (XXI, 69): {Said We: "O fire, be coolth and peace to Abraham."}

Another of the little poems of Abū Nuwās which was later used by Ibn al-Rūmī as a source is written in metre *sarīʿ*. Abū Nuwās wrote:

1. Speak to Summāna, the pair of you – and may her name not be hallowed – saying, 'Praise be to Him Who has widened your belly!'
2. As if a revelation were given to her womb: A voice came: 'Oh earth, swallow up thy water!'

---

[29] The poem is dedicated to Ibn Bishr al-Marthadī. *Dīwān Ibn al-Rūmī*, Muhannā V, p. 299 No. 1617; Naṣṣār V, p. 2119–2120, No. 1617; also *Dhayl zahr al-ādāb*, p. 239. Compare also *Dīwān Ibn al-Rūmī*, Muhannā V, p. 6–7; Naṣṣār V, p. 1810, No. 1360. He said this poem concerning Ibn Bishr al-Marthadī.

[30] *Dīwān Abī Nuwās* V, p. 251, No. 265; and compare *Dīwān Ibn al-Rūmī*, vol. I, p. 114, No. 75, poem to rhyme *aḥshā-ki.*

The words 'a voice came' are found in the Quran in the story of Noah and his Ark.

In the *Dīwān* of Ibn al-Rūmī, the above poem is found in a more extended form in metre *mutaqārib* with the title, 'About Khālid's wife':

1. You two, speak to Summāna, that chasm of fornication, and say to her: Praise to Him Who enlarged your belly!
2. The sperm of men, all of it, vanishes into your insides; and your winding coils are not to be straightened out.
3. By Allah, Oh earth! Have you been burdened with her vastness, ever since you began to be burdened with your own loads?
4. As if a revelation had been given to her womb, a voice came: 'Oh earth, swallow up thy water!'[31]

This is in the Quran, Surat Hūd (XI, 40–44):[32]

{40. Until when Our affair came and the oven boiled, We said: "Put on board of it pairs, two of each kind, and thy household – except him upon whom sentence has already passed – and whoever has believed"; but there had not believed with him more than a few.
41. He said: "Embark ye therein; in the name of Allah its course and its harbourage! verily my Lord is forgiving, compassionate."
42. It was running with them among waves like mountains, and Noah called to his son, who was in a place apart: "O my son, embark with us, and be not with the unbelievers."
43. He said: "I shall betake myself to a mountain which will defend me from the water"; he said: "There is no defender to-day from the affair of Allah, except (for) him upon whom He has mercy." The waves came between them and he was among the drowned.
44. A voice came: "Oh earth, swallow up thy water, and cease, oh sky"; and the water subsided, the affair was finished, and it stood firm on al-Jūdī; a voice came: "Away with the wrong-doing people!"}

The metaphorical comparison implies that the water which was to be swallowed is sperm, a large quantity of it, coming from a great number of penises. And all of it must disappear into Summāna's vast vagina. The vagina now takes on its own identity and no further details of Summāna are given. Returning to the metaphor, we find the flood has ended because suddenly a voice is heard which calls out to the whole earth saying 'Oh earth, swallow up thy water, and cease oh sky.' At other moments the water disappearing resembles a deep well or a vortex with its circling waters. The intruding item, the penis, will be drowned and is on the point of dying, and the fear is overwhelming.

When another lady presents her *vulva*, a doubt arises; for is not the neighbouring region of the human body more attractive? In the case of Shunṭuf's *vulva* the choice seems to be simple, the poet chooses its neighbour, the *anus*, because of its depth, for when there is a pressing need, the *penis* has no alternative but to break into the nearest treasure house. This difficult choice is explained in the poem to be quoted, where we again encounter Shunṭuf (in particular the description in line 14 further on, referring to her 'nose' and her 'dormer window').

Here she is experiencing difficulties with her voice because she has caught a cold. Her

[31] *Dīwān Ibn al-Rūmī*, Muhannā vol. I, p. 114, No. 75; Naṣṣār I, p. 127, No. 75; 'About Khālid's wife, Ibn al-Rūmī said...'

[32] Arberry p. 244; Dawood p. 136.

master (someone called Abū l-Ḥasan) is being addressed and it is possible that he is actually satisfied with her services – but it is equally possible that the poet is making fun of him. This is relayed in the *Dīwān* of Ibn al-Rūmī in the poem with the rhyme *wa l-khulṭah*:

> Concerning Shunṭuf he said as follows:
>
> 1. Oh you whose surname is also my surname, did you not pay heed to love and discourse?
> 2. You upset my ears in the presence of a person who is shaking, aggressive, degenerate and bald.
> 3. When she starts singing, people are left discomforted, and happiness deserts them.
> 4. In her voice, huskiness is constantly present, which gives the impression that she has a cold in the head.
> 5. Her melodic line is that of someone suffering from a headache after mucus has gathered in her nose.
> 6. In my opinion she has no right to speak when she comes moaning and crying, unless I say to her: 'how suffocating is this sobbing!'
> 7. Hit her on the head, and through the impact she will make prosternation on the ground, and hit her on the forehead on the patch where she makes contact with the ground.
> 8. 'Because of her I passed a piercingly cold night with great difficulty and what a terrible thing it was!'
> 9. When I was informed that you had been in touch with her, I said: 'Because of this false step of hers, may success remain out of her reach.'
> 10. Whatever does he see in this woman's face when she is in the grip of consumption? May Allah be unwilling to raise her up after her fall.
> 11. Like a scorpion she is greenish with a yellow tinge; and patchy like a black and white speckled snake.
> 12. She has a wide mouth full of fat flies; everyone desires it if they are accustomed to living shamelessly.
> 13. Whoever is tested by Allah, and is kissed by such a one, will soon die an unexpected death while still young.
> 14. Just as she shows a nose on her face, so she owns a dormer window (*rawshan*, Persian) in the gable over her door; is the chief of police not aware of this?
> 15. I have sworn an oath: 'If I were to own a nose such as hers, then I would be obliged to cut a small slice off its trunk.'
> 16. It is as if Thou hast created it as an act of revenge, preceded by the fiercest fury.
> 17. How contemptible she is! But she is even more ancient than the smell of balm in this underworld.
> 18. Beneath her, the detritus of the world is always found; somebody's droppings or someone's refuse.
> 19. She has a slender body, but is in love with someone uncouth who slaps her roughly.
> 20. Her two caves are wide and open, as if she is a whore well pleased by pushings and piercings.
> 21. As soon as she spies a swollen penis (*fayshalatan ḍakhmatan*), she throws herself flat crying *ḥiṭṭa* !
> 22. It is as if because of her generosity with her anus, she offers to each penis through her anus a *khiṭṭa* (highway).
> 23. She wishes that the penis in her vagina (*anna l-ayra fī farji-hā*) could stretch even longer than her own body.
> 24. She bids her fornicating partner to sniff the scent of her armpit. The discharge from it really stinks!

25. Her mouth reeks and sets the nostrils of the youngster ablaze, as if it were cutting inside his nose.
26. Truly, anyone who is strong enough to screw her must have the power to withstand the pressure of the narrow grave.
[Pressure is put upon the dead as they lie in the grave due to the avenging angels Munkar and Nakīr.]
27. A man who tries to buy her as a piece of low-class rubbish is no different from someone who thinks of her as a catch: they've both ended up with shit.
28. Is there anything at all in her apart from a piece of crap or a gust of wind?
29. Women with whopping clitorises will be told of her fall into an abyss. And could anyone fall further?[33]

Note: Verse 21 is an allusion to the Quranic story in which Moses is advised to persuade his people to put their trust in God. When they enter a certain town, they must kneel down as they approach the gate and utter the word *ḥiṭṭa* as a sort of magical password.

Compare with Quran, Surat al-Baqara (II, 58):[34]

> {When We said: 'Enter this town, and eat comfortably from it wherever ye please; enter the gate doing obeisance, and say "ḥiṭṭa" and We shall forgive you your transgressions and increase those who do well.'}

And compare with Quran, Surat al-Aʿrāf (VII, 161):[35]

> {(Recall) when it was said to them: 'Inhabit this town, and eat from wheresoever ye please of it, and say: "ḥiṭṭa" and enter the gate prostrating yourselves; We shall forgive you your sins; We shall increase those who do well.'}

If the reader has recovered from the shock of learning about Shunṭuf and Summāna then it is now time to summon up another woman of ill repute – in this instance, Kunayza. The following poem from *Dīwān Ibn al-Rūmī* rhymes in *tattasiʿu* and is dedicated to Kunayza the singing girl.

About Kunayza he said the following:
1. The earth is missing at her fringes, but Kunayza is wide, stretching as far as time.
2. She owns a broad vagina (*ḥirun wāsiʿun*), which nothing causes to be sated, just like the whale of Jonah which wished to swallow whatever it desired.
3. She has a crap, in order that the stench of her mouth be cut off us when she has to perform singing, but it is not cut off.
4. I swear by the existence of Allah: in that crap a portion of each smell is found, but as to her business it is yet horrible.[36]

In the case of another *vulva*, we find an allusion to the contemporary view of the world, the earth is flat and its fringes fall off in the void, but nevertheless the surface of the earth

---

[33] *Dīwān Ibn al-Rūmī*, Muhannā IV, p. 65, No. 1090; Naṣṣār, Cairo 1978, IV, p. 1422–1424; 'he said concerning Shunṭuf' the poem to rhyme *wa-l-khulṭah*.

[34] Compare the translations by Arberry p. 35: ḥiṭṭa meaning, 'Unburdening'; and Dawood p. 338: ḥiṭṭa meaning, 'We repent.'

[35] Compare Arberry p. 190; and Dawood p. 259.

[36] *Dīwān Ibn al-Rūmī*, Muhannā IV, p. 105, No. 1120; Naṣṣār IV, p. 1463–1464, No. 1120.

is enormous. This is metaphoric for the *vulva* of Kunayza who is another singing lady who is the object of Ibn al-Rūmī's satire. The poet fosters again some sort of vengeance against her, is her singing not as satisfying as Shunṭuf's singing? In the meantime this vulva is a dangerous place where one encounters again the whale which once swallowed Jonah. But her stinking mouth is overwhelmed by other stenches which are horrible.

The ocean of the *vulva* is huge, wide and deep, to such an extent that it will hide the whale for a very long time and Jonah's hope of deliverance is (proportional to this) very slight. When Jonah has lost his game of chance aboard of the ship he is thrown overboard and carried by the whale into the deep region of shadows, something reminding us of the nether world. His condition will only end when the dead shall be resurrected on the Day of Judgment. The poem about this was dedicated to Kunayza the singing girl. Its connection is of course to Quran, Surat al-Ṣāffāt (XXXVII, 139–146):[37]

> {139. Verily Jonah too is among the envoys;
> 140. When he ran away to the loaded ship;
> 141. He cast lots, but was one of those who drew blank.
> 142. So the whale swallowed him, he being to blame.
> 143. And had it not been that he was one of those who give glory,
> 144. He would have remained in its belly until the day of their being raised up.
> 145. We cast him upon a desert, ill,
> 146. And caused to grow up over him a tree, a gourd.}

The poet refers to Jonah in another short, light-hearted poem which is also an example of *mujūn*, though in this poem the importance of Jonah is reduced. In this instance there is no prayer for deliverance from the depths, for the deep ocean has changed into wide open courts, and the water has changed into the sweet waters of a river. Perhaps it is an alternative version of Paradise? But once again a doubt arises: something is hidden in this *vagina*, and it stinks as though the wide open courts have suddenly metamorphosed into a tomb.

Here follows the poem in the metre *khafīf* and with the rhyme *safīnu:*[38]

> In order to satirise a singing girl he said the following:
>
> 1. Say to her, and may death strike her down (*akharrat-hā*) when she is far away from you: My ship shall not float in your sea.
> 2. Among humans I am the fierest of stallions except when I am with you, when I am impotent and kept at bay.
> 3. I do not follow the religion of Jonah so I do not need to ask for rescue after the whale has retired into the shadow.
> 4. Oh woman, do not desire anything from that fucking of yours; it never happened, and it never will come to pass.
> 5. That fanny of yours (*fī hin-ki*) has two characteristics like Paradise; it's very cold (just as Paradise is cold) and it stretches a long way (just like the courts of Paradise).
> 6. Except that the coolness of Paradise comes with a good smell, but in you there is no fragrance, except that a sickness is buried inside you (*bal fīki dāʾun dafīnu*).

There is another poem about Shunṭuf, so clearly Ibn al-Rūmī must have been involved

---

[37] Compare Arberry p. 155; Dawood p. 173.

[38] *Dīwān Ibn al-Rūmī*, Muhannā VI, p. 326, No. 1944; Naṣṣār p. 2587–2588, No. 1466.

with her more than once. In this poem there appears to be some cause for fear and terror, even though the huge whale has disappeared. But the woman's vagina has become totally independant as an agent of destruction: it is now a dangerous vortex into which the penis will entirely vanish, having completed a lengthy sea voyage. The threat becomes more terrifying when one contrasts the black colour of Shunṭuf's skin (which by itself would be a favourable sign) with the white of other hidden parts of her skin where a leprous condition has been diagnosed. In spite of earlier mentions of Paradise, the poet now seems to have travelled a long way in the opposite direction. The poem, from *Dīwān Ibn al-Rūmī*, rhymes with *muṭṭaliʿ*:

> In order to satirise Shunṭuf he said the following lines:
> 1. Your face, oh Shunṭuf, is a source of terror for anyone who looks at it.
> 2. It grips me with disquiet and fear.
> 3. When it arrives, disaster appears alongside it.
> 4. Woe to your clothes should they perchance be stolen
> 5. For when they are pulled from your body, leprosy and patches of white will appear.
> 6. As for the head, it has mere tufts of hair, for it is balding
> 7. As for the vagina (*wa l-farju*), it resembles a vortex and swallows whatever you wish.[39]

We have so far considered the works of two poets of *mujūn*: Abū Nuwās with his measured, sometimes serious poetry, and Ibn al-Rūmī with his humour as he practises the genre of satire (*hijāʾ*). Abū Nuwās sometimes describes the love of youngsters who are not fortunate enough to enter Paradise. Beneath the thin veil of Abū Nuwās's jokes there is another stratum where we find him very serious in his intentions. There is, for instance the passage from *Dīwān Abī Nuwās* V, 507:

> This *adīb* also told me on the authority of Ibn al-Rūmī on the authority of his father and also of ʿUbayd Allah ibn ʿĪsā, that on a certain day he was present with Caliph al-Rashīd after Abū Nuwās had already entered. When al-Rashīd saw him, he said: 'Are you the one who recited the following line of poetry: "May the wine be kept in its wine skin, until it resembles my religion in its subtlety"?' He answered: 'Yes indeed oh Prince of the Believers, and I am the one who uttered the following words: "How huge a fire has been lit by the one who started the blaze! How black a comedy has been attained by the joker"!'

Ibn al-Rūmī, on the other hand, seems fascinated by badness: bad girls – singing girls – and their bad health, and the bad qualities of their musical voice. He discusses genital parts with unwholesome frankness, and refers to the *clitoris* and its characteristics, and even to the question as to whether it should be circumcised or whether it could be elongated like an elephant's trunk.

In one poem, however, Ibn al-Rūmī leaves the topic of dubious *chanteuses* behind and seems to speak in earnest when he compares the body of a healthy young girl with that of a young man and ponders which would enchant him more. The poem is related in *Dīwān Ibn al-Rūmī*:

---

[39] *Dīwān Ibn al-Rūmī*, Muhannā IV, p. 187, No. 1186; Naṣṣār IV, p. 1546, No. 1186; metre *rajaz*.

He said the following, and I consider this poem as merely ascribed to him, as if it were put in his mouth. The metre is *wāfir* as follows:

1. Suppose that on a certain day I was obliged to give judgment, and I was entrusted with both prosecuting and defending,
2. Then the eye of someone feeling love for girls had found consolation, but I condemn him who loves a young man (*ghulām*) to be punished.
3. I might ask you: what would be the most painful thing to talk about? and what would it be best to do when he embraces him?
4. Is it a sensitive girl with perfectly rounded buttocks, who causes your love to increase even beyond the love that you already have?
5. Or is it a beardless youth (*amradu*) whose armpit is hollow and whose penis, when it is raised, is equal to yours?
6. He wishes your money in Dirhams, not anything else. But the girl is dissolving into tears of love and pain.[40]

This ending is too simple and straightforward to be an example of *mujūn* style. Usually in Ibn al-Rūmī's poetry, the act of sexual intercourse is described more roughly, and body parts are described with an excess of frankness.

One such poem of Ibn al-Rūmī's will now be quoted. In this poem Ibn al-Rūmī strikes out in a slightly different direction. Although he is still with a female partner, he has dispensed with *vulva*, *vagina* and *clitoris* and moved on to the relative safety of *anal* intercourse. Now intercourse may be enjoyed without worries over periods, pregnancy or progeny. The poem is in the *rajaz* metre:

About ᶜAbīd ibn al-ᶜAbbās he said the following:

1. There is an *anus* (*faqha*) which resembles a fish in the way it swallows.
2. The treasure chest is not sufficient to satisfy its hunger
3. For highly strung penises, nor can it nurture it
4. With the sperm of many men, such that it is sated.
5. ᶜUbayd Allah roars with rage because of being caught up in a cloak
6. Which is torn open too far for it to be mended.
7. This is so because the earth is only one among its (the *anus*'s) many regions.
8. Suppose a survey of that region were conducted, it would be found too unyielding for the surveyor's fold-out gauges.
9. This is because its dimensions are too large for parcellation.
10. It might well be that his eyes are as deep
11. As his *anus*, which possesses a large-scale surface as well as a bottomless depth.[41]

In the meantime the Quranic fishes did not arrive on Saturday, nor had they arrived on Friday; and as we have seen, Ibn al-Rūmī was greatly disappointed that his human visitors (denoted by his metaphoric fish) failed to visit him, especially after he had taken trouble to prepare a meal for them.

We now have to consider a similar occasion in the paradisaical universe of Ibn al-Rūmī.[42]

---

[40] *Dīwān Ibn al-Rūmī*, Muhannā VI, p. 170–171, No. 1779; Naṣṣār p. 2418, No. 1301; poem to rhyme *wa l-khiṣāmā*.

[41] *Dīwān Ibn al-Rūmī*, Muhannā IV, p. 154, No. 1165; Naṣṣār IV, p. 1515–1516, No. 1165; poem to rhyme *btilāᶜi-hā*.

[42] Ibn al-Rūmī's poem is in metre *kāmil* and on rhyme *al-zuwwāri*. See *Dīwān Ibn al-Rūmī*, Muhannā III, p. 79–80, No. 730; Naṣṣār III, p. 980, No. 730; cf. *Muḥāḍarāt* I, 614. For heads of sheep, see A. Raymond

Here the scene reveals the dwellers of Paradise who are still visible beyond the flaming oven of Hell. This is not a case of two parallel worlds, but a collation where two universes overlap:

> About sheep's heads and pancakes Ibn al-Rūmī said:
>
> 1. If you are told that the food which we have prepared for unexpected visitors is now ready, what will you think?
> 2. It seems as though the two ingredients of a well-prepared meal produce a resemblance to both pious people and to committed sinners.
> 3. Sheep's heads and clear sumptuous pancakes, both extracted from a fiercely boiling hell,
> 4. Are equal to the smiling faces of those who dwell in Paradise; the latter look at us but they are conjoined to those who dwell in Hell.

The idea of a shared meal occurs in the works of several poets of the *mujūniyyāt*, including Ibn al-Rūmī and Abū Nuwās. In the case of Ibn al-Rūmī, the meal is merely alluded to, as we shall see later. In the case of Abū Nuwās, the poem below represents the beloved in an unusual light: he is like a good meal – the very best of meals, in fact – and in such circumstances how could the writer refrain from sampling the dish?

The poet continues with the image of food when justifying his attempt to take advantage of his young guest or victim by saying (in modern imagery): If you lock someone who likes deer meat in an animal sanctuary with a herd of gazelles, you must expect him to be tempted. And after the act of violation (the *dabīb*, a cringing and crouching during the night towards the victim) has occurred, and *semen* has been spilled upon the skin of the youth, the poet, still with food on his mind, describes it as looking like a patch of spilled brain potage. But the youth appears angry, and one is not sure whether the anger is feigned or real.

In the years to come, after Abū Nuwās' own generation had passed away, the theme of a meal continued to be explored by poets of *mujūn*, who prepared their own favourite dishes in the context of the *mujūniyyāt*. Consider the following poem with the rhyme *ṣanami* in the *wāfir* metre:

> 1. *Mujūn* has been poured into the statue of an idol (*ṣanam*), whose sickening glance is due to an unwholesome passion. [Because of his glance, he causes those who look at him to be sick.]
> 2. He looks as if Beauty has been poured into him, from the crown of his head to the soles of his feet.
> 3. Obscured by the darkness he took a draught of the white wine, which absorbed his powers of rationality.
> 4. He then retracted his head into an abyss; I passed the night without falling asleep.
> 5. If you consider my friend as a single meal (*rizma*), which is superior to all other meals (*rizam*),
> 6. Then how will my pen perform when it penetrates the encircling line of the letter *kāf* which lies upon his vellum?
> 7. If you observe someone who regularly eats within a hallowed precinct;
> 8. If the wild gazelle then awakens and becomes aware of something resembling a spillage of brains upon a human skin;
> 9. If he says: 'I used to believe you could do no harm, yet now you have done this!'

---

and G. Wiet, *Les marchés du Caire traduction annotée du texte de Maqrizi*, IFAO du Caire, 1979, p. 150–151, "Souq du khān des marchands de têtes de mouton (*sūq al-Rawwāsīn*)."

> 10. Then I shall answer him: 'Did you ever see a Wolf who could be trusted in the presence of Sheep?'
> 11. Thereupon, in order to frighten me, with his cheeks coloured red as blood, he pronounced the sentence:
> 12. 'Your noble servant is now entitled to take as much revenge as will surpass the usual ways of taking vengeance.'[43]

The reader will recall that we have already mentioned two meals in this group of *mujūn* poems: first was the meal which Ibn al-Rūmī prepared for guests who did not turn up, which caused the poet to exclaim: 'Why did our fish avoid us? Why did the visitors disappoint those who were awaiting them?' [See page 40 above]

And second, the meal which consisted of sheep's heads and clear sumptuous pancakes – the former recalling the grinning faces in Hell, and the latter the shining faces of those in Paradise, which inspired the poet to describe it in a pair of poetical lines saying:

> 3. Sheep's heads and clear sumptuous pancakes, both extracted from a fiercely boiling hell,
> 4. Are equal to the smiling faces of those who dwell in Paradise; the latter look at us but they are conjoined to those who dwell in Hell. [See page 47 above.]

Now we come to a third meal, in this case the so-called *kozab*, or in Arabic, *jūdhāba*, which is a porridge consisting of rice, meat and sugar.

The poet in this instance is Ḥusayn ibn Aḥmad ibn Muḥammad ibn Jaᶜfar ibn Muḥammad ibn al-Ḥajjāj, Abū ᶜAbd Allah who died 391 H, in the village Nīl close to Baghdad. According to Aybak al-Ṣafadī, Ibn al-Ḥajjāj was a poet who followed the tradition of Abū Nuwās in his *mujūniyyāt*. In his literary encyclopaedia, al-Ṣafadī says about him the following:

> He is the Chancellor (*kātib*) and poet; man of *mujūn*; of impudent behaviour and scornful in his poems. He was unique in his time and in his class; a precursor of poetry in its varieties; the first who opened up the gate was Abū Nuwās. Ibn al-Ḥajjāj came after him with the entire *ṭimm* and *rimm* (everything in perfection) and he accomplished many things and enhanced these things in beauty, he added perfect handiwork and continued it. I consider him as someone who belongs to those who deserve that the name of poet be applied to them. For he was excellent in eulogy, satire and elegy, as well as love poetry, description and literary style – in short all manner of poetry. However, as far as the *mujūn* is concerned, he was the master (*imām*).[44]

Ibn al-Ḥajjāj arrived on the scene some one hundred years after Ibn al-Rūmī's death, and his poetry is just as licentious as that of Ibn al-Rūmī, although an essential difference between the two poets seems to be that Ibn al-Ḥajjāj moved in circles closer to the lower end of the social spectrum in Baghdad. At any rate, although his images are sometimes founded on Quranic styles and formulas, as far as their contents are concerned, they are frank, vulgar and frequently shameless.

As for his treatment of the body, Ibn al-Ḥajjāj prefers to personify the private parts, and takes particular care to describe the various positions of *penis*, *clitoris* and *vulva*, and pays close attention to the anal region, both male and female. He also poses questions as

[43] *Dīwān Abī Nuwās*, p. 52, No. 70.
[44] See al-Ṣafadī, *al-Wāfī* XII, p. 331, No. 312.

to who is longer, or deeper, and other topics of a similar titillating nature. We will refer first to a poem which describes a certain day when the poet makes a vow to maintain the erection of his penis for the equivalent of a thousand months:

> In another poem with the rhyme *nasri* and in the *mukhallaʿ al-basīṭ* metre, Ibn al-Ḥajjāj said the following:
>
> 1. Oh Ibn ʿAmru, may Allah extend your span of life as far as the lives of thirty thousand eagles.
> 2. Your face in the morning is my Sun; in the night you are my Full Moon.
> 3. Oh my master, in my opinion: Today, on a day of good fortune which looks down on more than a thousand months,
> 4. I make a vow: When, having already drunk earlier, we meet at a drinking session which will last all evening,
> 5. Accompanied by a slave girl who desires none but me, as she approaches me (*tajīnī*) without inhibition;
> 6. While my penis, though long in its reach, lacks the stretch of her clitoris by one span;
> 7. While the wool of the hair around her anus contains the pigment to impart colour (*midād*) and her urine dissolves it into ink (*ḥibr*).
> 8. Asserting that: Whatever you may say, this (penis of mine) produces an erection so perfect as to fulfil my vow.[45]

Another undoubtedly vulgar poem by Ibn al-Ḥajjāj is dedicated to an administrator, a head clerk called Abū l-Faḍl al-Shīrāzī. However Ibn al-Ḥajjāj also mentions a second name, which incidentally occurs in the text of the poem, namely that of Shīrāzī's former colleague Abū l-Faraj ibn Fasānaḥs. Ibn al-Ḥajjāj's poem is to the rhyme *shamsu* in metre *mukhallaʿ al-basīṭ*, and it says the following:

> 1. Your portion of fortune (*saʿd*) signifies misfortune (*naḥs*) for the jealous people, for they are the darkness whilst you are the Sun.
> 2. Have compassion upon them, for they will not return until Yesterday returns;
> 3. But as for You, you exert yourself under the cloak of darkness; as for him, he emits a noiseless fart under the covers (*taḥta l-liḥāfi yafsū*).[46]

The literary historian al-Thaʿālibī continues this story about the poet Ibn al-Ḥajjāj as he quotes another poem in the same vein as if it belonged to the stream of vulgarity already embarked upon:

> On one certain day, he (the poet) was seated beside the throne podium (*dast*) inside the Palace of Abū l-Faraj Fasānaḥs; but of necessity it crossed his mind that he had to go to the lavatory; thereupon he swiftly ran to it and returned. The people asked him, why the hurry? And he gave them answer, saying the following lines of a poem in rhyme *qadharī* in metre *majzūʾ al-rajaz*:
>
> 1. Oh you who ask for a report about me: my impurity was jostling inside my belly.
> 2. I nearly shitted upon the throne of the chief of the clerks, al-Ṭabarī;
> 3. Thereupon I ran barefooted as I kept my eyes down, not seeing
> 4. Until I had passed a turd as large as a pile of debris left in a butcher's shop;

---

45 See al-Thaʿālibī al-Nīsābūrī, *Yatīmat al-dahr fī maḥāsin ahl al-ʿaṣr*, edition Dār al-Fikr, Beirut no date III, p. 73–74.

46 Idem, III, p. 40.

5. That turd was of such an enormous size that it was as large as the stomach of my [golden] calf.[47]

There is another reference to Chancellor al-Ṭabarī in *Yatīmat al-dahr*. It appears that he died of a disease which caused him terrible diarrhoea, and that the disease was such that his bodily remains would be transported to Hell. The explanation now follows:

Concerning a certain person, al-Ṭabarī [from Ṭabaristān] who had died from the illness of *qūlanj* (he suffered from diarrhoea), Ibn al-Ḥajjāj said a poem to rhyme *al-ṭabarī* in metre *majzūʾ al-rajaz* as follows:

1. Oh you, Final Suffocation of Death, open your mouth wide to let the spirit of al-Ṭabarī pass
2. That you may spit her out into Hell, because of her deficiencies!
3. Oh you who are now at rest and who once equated success with being able to have a bowel movement.
4. It was because of a day like this, that the proverb arose: 'Whoever shits is no longer ill.'[48]

This poem satirises al-Ṭabarī who was a tax collector and an enemy of the benefactor of Ibn al-Ḥajjāj, the famous Vizier al-Muhallabī. Ibn al-Ḥajjāj, as eulogiser, was always loyal to his benefactor and would have enjoyed an opportunity to get back at al-Ṭabarī. In the year 339 AH when the poet's friend came to be installed as Vizier al-Muhallabī in the function of the Vizierate by the Buyid prince Muʿizz al-Dawla, al-Ṭabarī – who was already a tax collector of some importance – tried to pre-empt him by offering a huge sum of money in order to buy the identical lucrative position. But Abū ʿAlī al-Ṭabarī (al-Ḥasan ibn Muḥammad) did not succeed, although he had been encouraged by the elevated Buyid prince Muʿizz to pay his first instalment on behalf of his nomination. Though al-Muʿizz had received the instalment in due order, he suddenly appointed Abū l-Faḍl al-Muhallabī instead, even though the latter was relatively poor and modest. Ibn al-Ḥajjāj must have rejoiced in this appointment; for he was accustomed to praise (the new Vizier) al-Muhallabī as long as the praised one lived. Unfortunately, however, this was not very long, for al-Muhallabī died some twelve years later, in 352 AH.

The poem quoted is a satire, because of the huge amounts of money which were available to the previous tax collector and aspiring Vizier, al-Ṭabarī. He had given the amount in vain to the Buyid prince, and moreover the unlucky man had to repay much more than this from the money he had collected in taxes, for as soon as the new Vizier took over, the Būyid prince (Muʿizz al-Dawla) decided to confiscate all of Ṭabarī's 'silent and speaking possessions' – all of his goods, chattels and livestock. As we will notice, the poet Ibn al-Ḥajjāj was more involved with the politics of his day than Ibn al-Rūmī and Abū Nuwās had been.

In his youth, Ibn al-Ḥajjāj became acquainted with the tenants of the lower classes in his neighbourhood, and he observed how some old houses were transformed into a simple hostelry or inn where poor people without a house could stay. Those who came to live in these *khān*-s were poor beggars and people who had sunk so low that they had undergone self-imposed mutilations in order to attract more sympathy and obtain more

[47] Idem, III, p. 40–41.
[48] The reference to Chancellor al-Ṭabarī, in *Yatīmat al-dahr* III, p. 41.

alms. The father of Ḥusayn ibn Aḥmad Ibn al-Ḥajjāj was a person who rendered his services to these simple folk, and this would have enabled Ibn al-Ḥajjāj to penetrate further into this environment than would normally have been possible for people of his education in society. Ibn al-Ḥajjāj said:

> I was supported in my method (*madhhab*) by the fact that my father caused his profits connected with houses acquired by him, to be sold to building managers who broke down and converted these private houses into *khān*-s. They caused beggars and strangers of the lower classes to dwell and live there, next to those who acquired their income by begging and showing off their infirmities, and those who were always postponing payment of their debts and those who had suffered amputations like the people from al-Khuld and al-Rabīdiyya. Thereupon I was accustomed to listen patiently to them, in particular during the summer nights; and to hear how they scoffed at each other, both men against men, and men against their women, while they were high up on their roof gardens or terraces. Then I used to be seated with my pen box and writing paper. I wrote down whatever I heard and then I wrote the expressions down literally when I was aware of something occurring in front of me that I could not understand. I immediately caused the people to come in front of me, those from whom I had heard those expressions. I was acquainted with their languages as they are of my neighbourhood. Then I asked such a person the explanation and I wrote that down. For a long time I did not cease to be **the Aṣmaʿī of the desert steppe**.[49]

Thus we can form an image of this remarkable author and artist, Ibn al-Ḥajjāj, and note his interest in language and his painstaking attention to detail. Of course he was also significantly influenced by the style of poets such as Abū Nuwās and Ibn al-Rūmī, whom we have already discussed. This is particularly apparent in Ibn al-Ḥajjāj's practical application of some of their concepts, such as a person's feelings of guilt or his attempts to seek forgiveness.

We need to consider Ibn al-Ḥajjāj's quotation from the tale of David and Bath-sheba which appears in both the Bible and the Quran, and his quotation from the parallel case of Muhammad and his love for Zaynab as it is described in the Quran. We need to ask what happened to the two women's first husbands: Uriah and Zayd respectively. Uriah was

49 Ṣafadī, *al-Wāfī* XII, p. 334. Ibn al-Ḥajjāj's proud comparison of himself to 'the Aṣmaʿī of the desert steppe' is a reference to an incidental meeting between the literary scholar al-Aṣmaʿī (a contemporary of the Abbasid Caliph Hārūn al-Rashīd) and an unknown Bedouin woman. Somewhere in the desert, she is standing in front of someone's grave when al-Aṣmaʿī meets her and hears her reciting a poem of 14 lines, starting with the introduction: 'Does the grave ever inform those who never cease asking it? or, does it grant coolness to the eyes of those who have come to visit? / Or is it then, that you suspect it will know whose body is hidden inside?' When, in spite of the poem's message, al-Aṣmaʿī asks the woman after the identity of the grave's occupant, she answers in the negative. She considers al-Aṣmaʿī's question foolish to such an extent, that when asked to do so, she refuses to recite the poem once again. Nevertheless, al-Aṣmaʿī himself is capable of performing a faultless repetition of the poem to the utter amazement of the Bedouin woman. Thereupon she concludes, 'You are perhaps the Aṣmaʿī, about whose fame we are already informed?' [Al-Aṣmaʿī :] 'I said "Yes indeed" – and departed.' Thus according to Abū ʿUbayd Allah Muḥammad ibn ʿImrān al-Marzubānī, his compilation of Abū l-Maḥāsin Yūsuf ibn Aḥmad ibn Maḥmūd al-Ḥāfiẓ al-Yaghmūrī, *Kitāb nūr al-qabas al-mukhtaṣar min al-Muqtabas fī akhbār al-nuḥāt wa l-udabāʾ wa l-shuʿarāʾ wa l-ʿulamāʾ* (Die Gelehrtenbiographien, Teil I: text); edition Rudolf Sellheim, Wiesbaden 1964, p. 162, No. 31.

killed quite soon after David first began to lust after Uriah's wife; for David, as King, had the power to arrange for Uriah to be transferred to the battlefront, where he was almost immediately killed beneath the walls of a beleaguered city. Zayd was killed during an expedition directed against the enemies who did not acknowledge the prophet Muhammad. We need to refer to the meaning of the Quran , Surat al-Aḥzāb (XXXIII, 37–38) where the injunction of Allah to His prophet was clear and simple: he had to keep his newly wedded wife Zaynab and he should not return her to his adopted son Zayd.

With reference to this Quranic text, Muqātil ibn Sulaymān then explains as follows:

> The custom or Sunna of Allah has been shown in those who have passed away aforetime: In this manner was the custom of Allah (*sunnatu llah*) in connection with those who have existed before Muhammad, namely Dāwūd (may Allah be contented with him) when he fell in love with the woman by whom he had been seduced. She was the wife of Uriyāʾ ibn Ḥanān. Thereupon Allah caused Dāwūd and the woman with whom he had fallen in love to be united with each other. Even so Allah (Most Powerful and Exalted) caused Muhammad (may Allah bless and guard him) and Zaynab when he fell in love with her, to be united with each other, just as He did with Dāwūd (may Allah be contented with him).
>
> {-**the command of Allah is a settled decree**-}
>
> 'Thus it is that Allah (Most Powerful and Exalted) destined the marriages of Dāwūd and of Muhammad to occur.

The above is a quotation from Ibn Muqātil's *Tafsīr*.[50] What is surprising is that this quite usual practice concerning the forgiveness of sin recurs in a short poem by Ibn al-Ḥajjāj. According to al-Thaᶜālibī, Ibn al-Ḥajjāj composed the following poem (on rhyme *jahilā* and in metre *basīṭ*) concerning Uriah and Zayd:

> 1. Oh you who wage war against passion (*hawā*), though you know nothing of its impact, for it never ceases to oppose a manly man as long as he remains ignorant regarding religion.
> 2. Were you then not aware of how passion overwhelmed the prophets by its charm; of how it thereby led the messengers into error?
> 3. If you are in doubt, ask Zayd about his story, and ask Uriah (Uriyā); the two of them will then speak true if they are questioned.
> 4. Why did one of them break the bond with his wife by divorcing her? And what about the other in the battle of the Ark of the Covenant (*al-tābūt*)? Why were the two of them killed?[51]

In his poem Ibn al-Ḥajjāj refers indirectly to the custom of Allah – His *sunna*, we might say – and the poet describes how passion came to overwhelm the Prophet, or some of the prophets, and how they came to wander away from the path prescribed to them. Why was one of their henchmen a victim who fell outside the walls of a beleaguered city and why was the other killed on the battlefield while combatting the enemies of Muhammad? Although there is no answer to either of these questions in the poem by Ibn al-Ḥajjāj quoted above, we can still see that the poet finds consolation for his own errors in passionate love when he asserts that Allah will certainly forgive him if he ever commits a sin. Elsewhere

[50] Compare *Tafsīr Muqātil ibn Sulaymān*, edition ᶜAbd Allah Maḥmūd Shaḥātah, Cairo 1984, III, p. 466–467; W.M. Watt, *Muhammad at Medina*, p. 331; and Régis Blachère, *Le problème de Mahomet*, p. 109.

[51] Al-Thaᶜālibī, *Yatīmat al-dahr* III, 48–49.

al-Thaʿālibī reports:

> In another poem to the rhyme *mawjūdu* and in metre *sarīʿ*, the poet says:
> 1. Oh, my Master, You are the One to whom the saying refers: it is possible to discover everything, except someone who is equal to you.
> 2. I may indeed have sinned because of my ignorance; but David (Dāwūd) also sinned and asked for forgiveness.[52]

By the above, the poet implies that Allah is generous in his willingness to forgive sins.

It is now time to look in an unbiassed way at several incidents which happened in the vicinity of Ibn al-Ḥajjāj which clearly made a deep impression upon him and contributed to his unique poetic imagery, especially within the area of the *mujūn*. On one occasion a woman accidentally fell from her roof terrace. Ibn al-Ḥajjāj begins by describing her interment and mentions how sad it was. But then he gives a very strange reason for her falling off the roof – and here we move into the etiology of phantasy: the fall from the roof is explained as the effect of the imagined appearance of a spickled snake which the unlucky woman mistook for a giant penis, for which she felt an overpowering desire: she stooped looking at it, lost concentration, and fell from the roof. Al-Thaʿālibī relates:

> Concerning a man whose wife fell off a roof terrace whereupon she died, he said a poem (to rhyme *mughayyabi* in metre *ṭawīl*) as follows:
>
> 1. May Allah forgive her! On the day that she was laid in the earth, she was most majestic to us, now lost and hidden under the earth.
> 2. Had she been sick, her accident would have been borne more lightly by the saddened and tortured heart.
> 3. But it was an adder, which she had observed wriggling on the ground, which was equal in size to the penis of an aroused donkey.
> 4. She assumed that it was a penis; but a guess can be deceptive when it informs us on good authority of a source blinded and hidden away.
> 5. This caused her to fall from a height, the measurement from the roof to the ground being eighty arm's lengths.
> 6. Her story became a tale which spread to a variety of people; some consider it true, having fathomed its depths; others declare it a lie.
> 7. Destructive desire hurried towards her, in order to present her with a quick death. Anyone paying heed to the demands of desire will come to perdition.
> 8. Oh sire, may Allah be your Lord and hers. The punishment of childlessness is even greater than that which concerns the affair of Ashʿab's sheep.
>
> Note: Ashʿab was once asked: 'Have you ever seen anyone more greedy than yourself?' He answered: 'Yes, a sheep which I kept on a roof terrace. For when it saw a rainbow and thought it was a bundle of *qat* plants, it leant forward and jumped. Thereupon it fell from the roof and broke its neck.'[53]

The scene on the roof may find its origin in an actual incident which happened at a house in or nearby the swamps and reed islands north of Basra. We find the report in Ibn al-Athīr, al-Kāmil, sub anno 372 AH:

> In this year al-Ḥusayn ibn ʿImrān ibn Shāhīn, Lord of al-Baṭīḥa [name of a fortress

[52] Idem, *Yatīmat al-dahr* III, 49.

[53] *Yatīmat al-dahr*, III, p. 46.

> in the Tigris delta, a maze of shallow waterways and reedbeds close to Basra] was murdered. His brother, called Abū l-Faraj, killed him and became master over al-Baṭīḥa. The reason for this murder is the fact that he was jealous of Ḥusayn's governorship and the fact that Ḥusayn was so much beloved by the ordinary people. How did this happen? It happened that a sister to each of the two brothers got ill. Thereupon Abū l-Faraj informed his brother Ḥusayn and said: 'Our sister has lain down and is on the point of dying; is it not preferable for you to visit her?' The brother decided to pay a visit, and he travelled towards her.
>
> But Abū l-Faraj positioned in the house several persons who were meant to give assistance in order to murder Ḥusayn who came to visit. When al-Ḥusayn had entered the house his comrades remained waiting outside, while they left him to enter alone. Thus Abū l-Faraj entered the house together with Ḥusayn, while holding the sword in his hand; when he was alone with him, he killed him. The cry of alarm was raised, upon which he ascended within the house as far as possible, high up to the roof terrace. Then he caused the soldiers who were waiting below, standing on the ground, to be informed that it was himself who had killed the other. But when he promised to treat them well, they refrained, remaining quietly in silence. He donated them money upon which they accepted his authority over them. Then he wrote letters to the authorities in Baghdad to show his obedience, asking them to confirm him in his governorship. He was pigheaded (*mutawahhiran*) and ignorant.[54]

This horrible incident has been described in a dry, matter-of-fact manner. However the poet also moves towards the extremes of phantasy. Ibn al-Ḥajjāj does not describe how someone had applied depilatory cream (*nūra*) to the woman's anus to remove the hair; quite the contrary: he describes hair as thick as that of a sheep. Even the name of the wool store is mentioned – it belonged to the Banū l-Ṣulḥī.

Extra exciting for the poet was perhaps the fact that the woman had not removed her hair in the customary manner, and so it became quite visible to the bystanders. But then one is forced to ask whether the hair was in fact the thick beard of someone kneeling on the roof. Here an introductory rhetorical question is suggested (an element of style frequently found in poems of the time), namely: is this really her pubic hair, or is it the woolly hair of a thick beard which belongs to a tyrant like Pharaoh? As usual he is accompanied by his Vizier, the Quranic Haman.

The link between what happened in the reed-land, and in the marsh fortress of Baṭīḥa, with the next poem by Ibn al-Ḥajjāj to be quoted below, is suggested by its opening line: 'Suppose you were Shāhīn, the daughter of the slavegirl of [her master] al-Faḍl; and suppose that the women's chamber were your home'. As we have already seen, the historian mentions the same name 'Shāhīn'. He applies it to a member of the clan who is overlord of the fortress of Baṭīḥa, and was called ʿImrān ibn Shāhīn. After murdering his brother, the surviving brother (the murderer) speaks from the roof as if he were that ancient Pharaoh who had also been known for his murderous inclination. We are of course acquainted with this from the Quranic text which tells us twice about a scene on the roof of Pharaoh's Palace (which is, however, situated in Egypt):

---

54 Ibn al-Athīr, *al-Kāmil*, vol. 9, p. 23–24, sub anno 372 AH: 'Report of the murder perpetrated on al-Ḥusayn ibn ʿImrān ibn Shāhīn.'

1) {Pharaoh said: "O nobles, I know no god for you except myself; so light for me, O Haman, a fire upon clay, and make me a tower; mayhap I shall mount up and see the God of Moses; verily I think him one of those who speak falsely."} (Quran, Surat al-Qaṣaṣ [XXVIII, 38])
2) {Pharaoh said: "O Haman, build me a tower, mayhap I may reach the ways of access, The ways of access to the heavens, and look upon the God of Moses, for I think he is speaking falsely." Thus was the evil of what he did made attractive to Pharaoh, and he was turned aside from the way; the craft of Pharaoh led only to ruin.} (Quran, Surat Ghāfir [XL, 36–37])

The poem by Ibn al-Ḥajjāj is very short. It first mentions the attractive aspect of Shāhīn, but then is extended in another poem which includes the anus and its woolly surroundings.

> 1. Suppose you were Shāhīn, the daughter of the slavegirl of [her master] al-Faḍl; and suppose that the women's chamber were your home;
> 2. Then I would have to bite into the pubic bone which forms a window high up in the roof vaults of the gallery of your vagina.[55]

But this passage is completed by the following lines from another short poem:

> 1. I saw her when she was seated on her terrace just at the edge of the roof,
> 2. Her anus was full with black and white hair, like the goats' wool which is crammed into the storehouse of the Banū l-Ṣulḥī.
> 3. By way of a joke – may my life be a ransom for her – while she was persevering in her refusal of such jokes, I said:
> 4. 'Is that an anus there on the roof, surrounded by hair? Or is it the beard grown by Pharaoh on the Palace above?'

Ibn al-Ḥajjāj was extreme in his description of the private parts, but he could do so because he felt protected by his Shīʿite adherence. As we will see in the following poem (to the rhyme *al-makāni*) he felt quite safe because he believed in the 'Protection of the Five', that is, of the five holy personalities, namely Muḥammad, Fāṭima, ʿAlī, Ḥasan, Ḥusayn, who all came together, and once united swore an oath with the angel Gabriel supporting them; in early pristine Islam theirs was a dangerous formula with which they attacked their unbelieving opponents.

In the poem we do not find the roof terrace, but there is the meal of *ḥūdāba*, sweetened rice with meat – also known in Persian as *kozab*. Pharaoh arrives at the meal in the company of his Vizier. Ibn al-Ḥajjāj describes himself as being seriously addicted to drinking wine in vast quantities, and relates how he spent days on end doing nothing but drinking or sleeping off the effects of the drink, such that he appeared to be living continuously in the month of Ramaḍān. To someone who is fasting, Ramaḍān is a time when no wine is allowed during the day, and people who desire alcohol spend the night drinking.

The following is from a selection of Ibn al-Ḥajjāj's wine poems,[56]

[55] Al-Ṣafadī, *al-Wāfī bi l-wafayāt* III, p. 335, quoting Ibn al-Ḥajjāj.
[56] *Yatīmat al-dahr* III, p. 65–66.

A poem by Ibn al-Ḥajjāj to the rhyme *al-makāni* and in metre *khafīf*:

1. One of the conditions of the morning drink at a time of festivity is little to do, combined with a lonely place.
2. And it is the presence of food even before the sun is rising; and cold food from yesterday should be available in all its different varieties.
3. And the bride should be introduced, and she should be worth the weighty amount paid for her, and clad in a cloak coloured purple.
4. They make a label for the wineskin in clay which is still moist, marking it with the name of 'Khosraw Anū Sharwān'.
5. You observe the iris flowers of the beakers, in which a cloth of red anemones has been draped.
6. Then you become aware of the pounding of the drum, beating between the songs; then came the vibrations of the snares of the lute.
7. To listen to music alone is somewhat tedious to one's ears, for people desire only to listen to a songster.
8. Each vocal part belongs to the propositions of Isḥāq al-Mawṣilī, which belong to the voice parts which embellish the Book of Songs.
9. If you set the morning drink at a time after the summons to prayer, then I do not count the morning drink, but rather I reckon it to be the drink of evening.
10. Oh my two friends! I am already thirsty for wine, feeling the thirst of someone who, dried-out, is full of desiring.
11. Give me then to drink a pure draught from that which the Quran describes as deserving to be forbidden.
12. As far as the explanation of this is concerned, there is no School of Law (*madhhab*) except that it teaches obedience to Satan.
13. Come with me and turn off towards her, whose powers are capable of the destruction of Fire and the smothering of Smoke;
14. I am fearful of each thing which is tainted with the fires!
15. Oh you, the two of you, neither of you should fear my slim waist, for I am confident that manly men will jump on me!
16. In the meanwhile you should allow me to drink from amongst the wineskins until the moment when you find I have turned into a wineskin.
17. And so I have changed into an invalid, after a brief period of being upright; and now I am reduced to silence, having ceased to pour out a babble of rubbish.
18. One bout of drunkenness following hours of drinking will suffice to confirm my reputation among the lame and the blind.
19. Give me a drink on the day of jubilation, even though five nights of Ramaḍān still remain.
20. Give me a drink, since I have with my very own eyes gazed into the depths of Hell, where my place is to be.
21. I am *ḥudhāba* and my brains (*dhihnī*) are nothing but the moisture of Hell (*ṣadīd*) beneath Pharaoh's balls, or beneath those of Hāmān (his Vizier).
22. Everything which you donated to me is capital money seeking shelter in Perdition.
23. This is so, except my preference for the people of the *ḥawāmīm*, and of the resurrection (*ḥashr*), and of Ṭā Hā, and of Sūrat al-Raḥmān.

Here in line 23 of his poem to rhyme *al-makāni*, Ibn al-Ḥajjāj has encoded a strange confession of heresy: he does not at all refer to the Quranic text, but rather, makes a sexual play on words; *ḥawāmīm* is a play on words which refers to the 'anus' of a 'woman' (*ḥawāʾ*

signifying Eve, and the letter *mīm*, written in the middle position, indicating an opening).[57]

The use of the word *ḥashr*, meaning the resurrection, refers to Ibn al-Ḥajjāj's belief in the Dahriyya, a school of thought which does not acknowledge the importance of the Resurrection. See for evidence the poetical lines of Abū Nuwās,[58] who was Ibn al-Ḥajjāj's acclaimed predecessor in the *mujūn* in combination with Abū Nuwās' lines quoted elsewhere,[59] where we find an epigrammatic poem which informs us about Abū Nuwās' denial of the Resurrection:

> (1) Oh you woman, who accuse me of foolishness blaming me all the time; listen to what I'm going to tell you:
> (2) My tongue informs you of its well-hidden secret, namely that I believe in the concept of Dahr.
> (3) I have various friends dwelling throughout the gardens of happiness, who confess their disbelief in the day of the Reckoning and in the Resurrection (*al-ḥashr*).
> (4) Being absolutely sure of someone's decease, they deny it when people talk to us of a severe confinement inside the grave.
> (5) Thus after someone's decease no serious offence can exist, for Death is nothing but a Non-fertile Egg (*bayḍatu l-ʿuqr*).[60]

Here ends the quotation from Abū Nuwās, informing us of his concealed criticism of *ḥashr*.

Also in Ibn al-Ḥajjāj's line 23, immediately after his note on the Resurrection, we find a wordplay on *ṭa-hā* which (not referring to the Quran , but rather to the genre of *mujūn*) signifies the imperative form of the verb *waṭaʾa* which means 'penetrate'! This is to be combined with the circular form of the arabic letter *hāʾ*, because it can then mean 'penetrate into the centre of the anus'. Finally we can see, line 23, how Ibn al-Ḥajjāj refers to the Quran, Surat al-Raḥmān (LV, 65 and 68–69), where the Quran admonishes the company of jinn and men, and where its hallowed text describes the two gardens:

> {65. In them are (damsels) of restrained glance, whom deflowered before them has neither man nor jinn} and {68. In which too are fruit and palms and pomegranates. 69. Which then of the benefits of your Lord will ye twain count false?}.[61]

After the above discussion of line 23, it is time to look at the final passage from Ibn al-Ḥajjāj's poem to the rhyme *al-makāni*:

> 24. But when my fear intensifies, there are the Five, my love of whom signifies my trust, as well as my salvation close to my Creator.
> 25. I am assured that they will hand me over from Mālik (the guardian angel of Paradise) to the hands of Riḍwān (the angel admitting people to Paradise).
> 26. Because of them, I am protected from any fear that I might return from Death; and because of this Vizier, I am protected from any fear regarding my life time:

---

[57] The word *ḥawāmīm* occurs earlier in a poem by Ibn al-Rūmī. See *Dīwān Ibn al-Rūmī*, Muhannā, VI, p. 78, No. 1696; Naṣṣār, VI, p. 2316, No. 1218; poem by Ibn al-Rūmī: 'he said in the *mujūn*'.

[58] *Dīwān Abī Nuwās*, V, p. 459.

[59] Wagner, *Nebenüberlieferung*, p. 120–121.

[60] *Dīwān Abī Nuwās*, V, p. 459; Wagner, *Nebenüberlieferung*, p. 120–121.

[61] Compare Wagner, *Überlieferung*, p. 118–119: Abu Nuwās' poem No. 248.

27. Oh Abū Ṭāhir! if you had not existed, no one over the whole earth would have come second to you excepting only the Full Moon.

Abū Ṭāhir, whose name is mentioned in line 27 is of course the same person as the Vizier Ibn Baqīya.

28. Oh Sire! the prayers of the Breaking of the Fast, of the Day of Sacrifice, of the Day of New Year, and of the Day of Jubilation are all dedicated to you.[62]

Note: Abū Ṭāhir ibn Baqīya had been appointed to the Vizierate by another Buwayhid prince, ᶜIzz al-Dawla (Bakhtiyār). Immediately before he obtained his high position, Abū Ṭāhir ibn Baqīya had been an important cook in the entourage of the chief clerk Abu l-Faḍl ᶜAbbās al-Shīrāzī. As part of his work he was involved in the presentation of meals, and wore a piece of cloth (*mandīl*) thrown over his shoulder when offering food. When he received the high title of Vizier, he received the honorific title of Lord Counsellor (*al-Nāṣiḥ*). His appointment was in 362 H, but after four years in 366 H, Bakhtiyār had him blinded as a punitive measure because of his chaotic administration, and later in the same year he was trampled under the feet of one or more elephants, at the orders of yet another Buwayhid prince, ᶜAḍud al-Dawla (Fanā-khosraw).[63]

The remarkable meal described by the poet may have been a reference to the simple background of Vizier Abū Ṭāhir, whom the poet had much appreciated in his dedicative praise poems. Certainly, we again find the depiction of a meal of *ḥudhāba* offered in another poem by Ibn al-Ḥajjāj. In this instance, the poet describes his own drinking bouts which are followed by his pleasure-filled sessions in bed, when he would have sexual intercourse with any type of lover he might desire. In Ibn al-Ḥajjāj's poem to rhyme *al-fityāni*, metre *khafīf*, we read the following:

1. Woe unto you, you elderly people, or you who are middle-aged, or you who are youngsters.
2. Drink the wine which the people of the ᶜAqūl monastery have concocted for their Holy Supper while it is red;
3. Drink it in beakers as if they are chalices of the wild rose (*nisrīn*), filled inside with red anemones (*shaqāʾiq al-nuᶜmān*).
4. Drink it up! And when you've guzzled it all, every sin will be weighed in the balance in ounces and held against you.
5. If they plunge into my anus in the course of every night, I will arrive bang in the middle of the month of Ramaḍān.
6. I am Iblīs: Drink it up and sing the song 'To men you appear in the image of Satan'
7. I am *jūdhāba* and my balm (*dihnī*) is my putrid drink from Hell (*ṣadīd*) from beneath Pharaoh's balls; and the balls of Hāmān, his Vizier.[64]

Although *ḥūdhāba* or *jūdhāba* is a delicious dish when included in a normal meal, it is easy to imagine that in the mind of Ibn al-Ḥajjāj, something more sinister – or indeed sexual – will have been added to the ingredients of the dish on this occasion. The porridge was almost certainly sweetened with sperm, possibly from Iblīs himself. The choice vocabulary

[62] See *Yatīmat al-dahr* III, p. 65–66.
[63] See *Dhuyūl Tārīkh al-Ṭabarī*, p. 429–430, 457.
[64] See *al-Wāfī* XII, p. 337 (7 lines); cf. *Muᶜjam al-udabāʾ* III, p. 107 (5 lines).

has further ramifications: the person referred to as 'I' in the poem is almost certainly dead and has gone to Hell; *dhihn*, of course, means brains; *dihn* however refers to the balm applied to a dead body.

There is another delicacy which occurs in Ibn al-Ḥajjāj's prose and poetry: a sheep's head. Again the poet employs a degree of ambiguity and it is therefore not always certain if he is referring to a physical head present on the table at a feast, or a functional head such as the Head of the Administration or the Head of the Clerks – or even, indeed, the head of the penis.

Ibn al-Ḥajjāj certainly felt great animosity against the Head of the Clerks and would have enjoyed the opportunity to poke fun at a senior clerk. The target of his particular hatred was al-Ṭabarī the tax collector whose assets had been confiscated by Muʿizz. Al-Ṭabarī himself harboured antagonism against Ibn al-Ḥajjāj's beloved friend the Vizier and patron, the Vizier al-Muhallabī.

Now follows the poem with the rhyme *al-nāsi* and the *mujtathth* metre:

> 1. Many people say: 'He is the Head of the collectors of taxes from among the people.'
> 2. But even if the Head is not advantageous to you, it will be of advantage to someone who owns a shop offering sheep's heads for sale (*al-rawwās*).
> 3. This is the truth, and whenever the truth is maintained, nothing can be wrong.'[65]

We saw earlier how Ibn al-Rūmī compared Heaven to Hell, the one with the shining faces of pancakes, the other with grinning sheep's heads boiling over a fiery stove. In another context, this time in prose, we again find a reference to grinning sheep's heads – and in view of our interest in *mujūn*, it is necessary to examine them in more detail.

In the *Risāla Baghdādiyya*, Abū Ḥayyān al-Tawḥīdī describes a strange and rather jocular conversation which takes place in a literary salon, *majlis*, due to the presence of an intelligent but drunken personality who is very insistently giving expression to his weird sense of humour. The regular members of the salon had tried in vain to make him very drunk so that he would fall into a silent stupor, but they had not yet succeeded and the reader therefore has to put up with the foolish ramblings of the intruder:

> Someone among the people of the salon laughed, but this [uninvited] person became aware of him and addressed him saying: 'The adder laughs in the water jar, like a bear laughs amongst a pack of dogs. The sheep's heads keep grinning in front of the man who is preparing heads of sheep, just as an ass laughs above its bit even though he cannot move his lips. This way of laughing, which sounds like the creaking of a water wheel, is exactly like the laughter of a whore.'[66]

Certainly the grinning sheep's head occurs in Ibn al-Rūmī's poetry, but interestingly Ibn al-Ḥajjāj is even more involved with it. There is one interesting example of a sheep, *al-shāh*, where the word seems to refer to a woman who is very passive in sexual intercourse.

---

[65] *Yatīmat al-dahr* III, p. 50–51.

[66] Abū Ḥayyān ʿAlī ibn Muḥammad al-Tawḥīdī, died in 414 AH, *Risāla Baghdādiyya*, p. 349.

There was a Khān al-Rawwāsīn in al-Qāhira during the fifth century AH, a market where sheep's heads were offered for sale; see Pieter Smoor, *Wazāra The Killer of Many Husbands*, IFAO, Cairo 2007, p. 308.

There is also a dildo involved, a *murdī*, but the reason that it is present in the scene with the woman – or sheep – seems to be that the male partner is either impotent, or absent.

The passive woman however, is not the main focus of the poet's interest. Rather, it is the butchered sheep which is depicted by the metaphorical image of a languid woman with no will of her own. This woman is menstruating and therefore she is experiencing intercourse *per anum*, or so the poet would have us believe. The ambiguity which arises when we read the Arabic, forces us to ask: is it a sheep, or is it a woman? Are we looking at a sheep hanging from a hook or a woman hanging onto a dildo? And as for the hair involved, is it sheep's wool or part of the woman's anatomy? It may be that the sight of a sheep hanging in a butcher's shop with a hook through its backside has reminded the dirty-minded poet of a woman being penetrated from the rear with a dildo.

'According to Quranic law, entrance from behind was permitted.' This is asserted by Rāghib al-Iṣbahānī in his *Muḥāḍarāt*, on the basis of the Quranic text and its application by Anas ibn Mālik and the latter's Mālikī School of Law (*madhhab*). Compare on this Quran, Surat al-Baqara (II, 223):

> {"**Your women are to you (as) cultivated land; come then to your cultivated land as ye wish [*faʾtū ḥartha-kum annā shiʾtum*], but send forward something for yourselves, and act piously towards Allah, and know that you are going to meet Him.**"}[67]

However, it is not only the Quran which comments on this matter. We also have the testimony from Ibn al-Ḥajjāj who explains how he once presumed to enter a (menstruating) woman from the backside, which was contrary to what was expected of him. Thereupon he was expected to accept and pay compensation (*diya*) for his offensive act which he had committed through his penis coming at the backside, by which he wandered off the right path, the prescribed way of intercourse, namely an honest entry at the front; his penis then entered not the vulva, but the anus in an immediate and spontaneous action, absolutely not premeditated, not *ʿamdan*. In other words, the poet committed his deed by inadvertence, being under the impression of the flow of blood at the front.

And in this manner the poet's offence fell within the category of people committing the grave sin of entering at the wrong side, though it occurred by *lamam* (negligence or inadvertence).

This aspect of negligence because of the offender's penetrating the wrong place is suggested in the poem ('But I immediately jumped upon her in her anus'). The act is not premeditated, but it is either spontaneous or by mistake (*khaṭaʾan*); and it is not found as a case in the casuistry of the *Muwaṭṭaʾ* lawbook by Mālik ibn Anas, however the effect of unpremeditation is agreed upon. The blood money (*diya*) to be paid for accidental injury or even accidental murder is less than the amount of the full price, and can be divided into instalments over three or four years. Under this condition financial assistance can be

---

[67] *Muḥāḍarāt* II, p. 267. The tradition, 'He said: come to your cultivated land as ye wish' (*qāla iʾti ḥartha-ka annā shiʾta*) is found in Abū Dāwud, *Sunan*, kitāb al-nikāḥ, bāb 41, according to *Concordance tradition musulmane* I, 139, 1. Compare translation by Sale p. 31: *annā shiʾtum*, meaning: 'in what manner soever ye will' adding in a note 'It has been imagined that these words allow that preposterous lust, which the commentators say is forbidden by the preceding; but I question whether this can be proved.' And translation by Muhammad Ali p. 102: *annā shiʾtum*, meaning: 'when you like' or 'how you like.'

offered by members of the poet's clan, his family members, who will contribute by paying part of the blood money. So the adagio of the *diya ʿalā l-ʿāqila* is fulfilled. And the poet will be aware of a gradual diminishing of his individual burden of the *diya*:

> 1. While she had her period for a long stretch of time, she was arrogant with her backside (*isti-hā*).
> 2. But I immediately jumped upon her in her *anus* (*surmi-hā*). The blood money for the way I screwed her is due to be paid by the members of my family (*wa-diyatu l-nayki ʿalā l-ʿāqilah*).[68]

Rāghib al-Iṣbahānī interprets the will of Allah in the same sense, equally severe but in a different style:

> The prohibition to come to her in her anus (*fī duburi-hā*)
>
> The prophet, may Allah bless him and guard him, did not permit them to come to her in her 'fireplace' (*fī maḥāshshi-hinna*), where she is stoked up with a poker (*miḥashsh*). He was asked: 'In which one of the two openings?' He answered and said: 'As regards the front side, it is yes; as regards the backside, it is no.' And he said: {'**but Allah is not ashamed of the truth**.'} 'Do not come to the women in their anuses (*lā taʾtū l-nisāʾa fī adbāri-hinna*)!'[69]

Indeed, it is as if a war is going on between the *vulva* and the *anus*, with dire consequences. About the enmity between *anus* and *vulva*, there is an illustrative anecdote in *Muḥāḍarāt* II, 267:

> Mazyad said: 'Allow me to come to you in your *anus*.' She answered: 'I will not permit that the one concubine, the anus, will compete with the other concubine, namely 'she' who is the vulva (*lā ajʿalu istī ḍarratan li-ḥirī*); though it's true that the former is at a short distance from the latter, just around the corner.
>
> They asked Abū Ḥafṣ about coming to a woman at her backside. Thereupon he answered: Quran , Surat al-Baqara (II, 223): {'**Your women are to you (as) cultivated land**'} and the anus is for her a sowing-land. To whomsoever the village is allowed, to him also the sowing-land will be allowed.'[70]

However, compare this to Quran, Surat al-Aḥzāb (XXXIII, 53): {'**but Allah is not ashamed of the truth. When ye ask them for any article, ask them from behind**'}. Of course the Quranic verse is not complete here, as the sentence continues: {'**a curtain**; that is purer for your hearts and for theirs. It is not for you to insult the messenger of Allah, or ever to marry his wives after him; verily that has become in Allah's eyes important.'}[71]

To return for a moment to the 'grinning sheep' which Ibn al-Ḥajjāj depicts in his poetry:

---

[68] *Muḥāḍarāt* II, p. 268. The blood money (*diya*) for his way of screwing is now due to be paid by "the offender's family members" (*ʿalā l-ʿāqila*); his crime being unpremeditated, his family is legally permitted to assist him in paying a smaller amount. See the casuistry in Mālik ibn Anas, *al-Muwaṭṭaʾ*, in 'Kitāb al-ʿUqūl', chapter about 'Whatever necessitates the paying of blood money due to be paid by a male person' (*Bāb mā yūjibu l-ʿaqla ʿalā l-rajul*) and following chapters, pp. 865–876. Also *Al-Muwatta of Imam Malik ibn Anas*, translation by Aisha Abdurrahman Bewley, London 1989, Index.

[69] *Muḥāḍarāt* II, p. 267. Quran, Surat al-Aḥzāb (XXXIII, 53), supplemented by a tradition: *lā taʾtū l-nisāʾa fī adbāri-hinna*. See reference in *Concordance tradition musulmane* VI, 439, 2.

[70] Quran, Surat al-Baqara (II, 223) supplemented by a tradition, and see *Muḥāḍarāt* II, p. 267.

[71] Quran, Surat al-Aḥzāb (XXXIII, 53).

it is interesting to see how pre-occupied the poet was by this imagery. Ultimately the word *shāh* does not represent here the idea of the Shāh as a chesspiece, although sexual intercourse is frequently discussed in the salon of a company of chess players; nor is it representing the *shāh* as the young boy who is described as being a Shāh, an overlord at playing chess; but what is really intended is the *shāh* as a sheep that has already been slaughtered and hung wrong side up for sale in the market street. In the latter situation the sheep is hooked by a ringlet of hair, or an iron or wooden fetter.

That sheep is comparable to a woman in a resigned condition; the woman is then penetrated by a *murdī*, meaning a dildo. The poem is ambiguous, for *murdī* can also mean, something 'causing destruction'.

Al-Thaʿālibī, *Yatīmat al-dahr*, reports:

> Part of the proverbs of Ibn al-Ḥajjāj concerning seriousness and humorous approach, consists of jocular stories (*mulaḥ*) which belong exactly to various trades or crafts (*funūn*) within his anecdotes, as for example in his poem to rhyme *fustuqa*, in metre *majzūʾ al-rajaz* as follows:
>
> 1. All that I possess is a wedding gift (*ṣadaqa*) designed to break open a pistachio nut (*fustuqa*).
> 2. So let the amount of your kisses be as great as your desire to blether, oh you outcast whore of Sind!
> 3. The anvil (*al-sindān*) must stay strong beneath the blows of the hammer.
> 4. I must empty the head of my penis into the melting pot of the goldsmith (*būtaqa*).
> 5. I have to plunge the wooden pole (*murdī*) into the gap of the peep-hole (*daraqa*).
> 6. I must insert the colouring pencil (*mīl*, collyrium stick) into the black pupil of the eye.
> 7. You desire me to abandon the meat and slurp up the gravy (*maraqa*).
> 8. The broth (*al-tharīd*) is no worse for my impotence than a hearty meal, well-prepared (*mulabbaqa*).
> 9. All I desire is the minced flesh from around the anus of my beloved.
> 10. You sweet girl, I am pleased that you aren't afraid. Please don't give way to an attack of fear.
> 11. Tomorrow, every sheep will be hung by its feet.
> 12. The lock of hair must fit into the hole of the anus (*al-ḥalaqa*).[72]

In the first instance we do not necessarily recognise the sexual connotations of the poem, because the poet has depicted simply what he noticed in the butcher's shop – which was probably situated in the Darb al-Rawwāsīn (Alley of Sheep's Head Sellers). Once the reader has appreciated the extensive use of double entendre and innuendo, by Ibn al-Ḥajjāj, we can return to Ibn al-Rūmī who depicts the same variety of sexual intercourse, but in a more philosophical manner. The *vulva*, Ibn al-Rūmī claims, is a Great Swallower or a Great Sewer (meaning, an underground conduit of some kind), which resembles the mouth of a fish, and roars with its mouth open wide. Ibn al-Rūmī also describes the cucumber (*khiyār*) which, he thinks, should not be subjected to the ignoble job of functioning as a dildo, but should be valued simply as a vegetable in its own right. Now follow three examples found in Ibn al-Rūmī's meditative poems. As for the first meditation, in its opening line, Chess serves as a Great Swallower, and in the closing line the discussion concerns a Cucumber

---

72 *Yatīmat al-dahr* III, p. 49.

functioning as a Dildo. Ibn al-Rūmī says:

1. I steadfastly observed a game of Chess until I understood it; so, if my conclusion is correct, that game functions like an underground pipe, swallowing Reason.
2. As people make their way to watch the game, Reason diminishes while its purity is sullied by horrible rubbish and all sorts of jokes.
3. This is not due to a fault of the game of Chess, for a huge amount of energy is expended if we strive to achieve the correct balance.
4. And since for a young person, chess is a means of removing from Reason the trappings of ignorance, the question arises as to whether it is really worth the effort.
5. But certainly, to cleanse one's drink of impurities is a profitable thing, and it is equally meritorious to rid the Cucumber of ignominy (*takhlīṣ al-khiyāri mina l-radhli*).[73]

As regards the third example, Ibn al-Rūmī composed a meditative poem, in which he dwells on the concept of Motion. He considers the fish which swallowed Jonah, and which was later allowed to continue swimmingly after Jonah had interceded with God on its behalf. Ibn al-Rūmī says:

1. Praise be to Allah,
   Who rescued the fish
   from floating hooks and nets.
2. Through his prayer of 'Glory Be to Thee' (*min tasbīḥi-hi*)
   Jonah taught it a lesson
   which left it free on its way.
3. Thus it was safeguarded from the fisherman;
   and kept safely
   for as long as I continued to desire it (namely, its gaping mouth).
4. I am a huge blessing
   upon him (Jonah),
   so let him pray for a blessing on my behalf
   and may Motion (*al-ḥaraka*) continue its friendship with it.[74]

Jonah's prayer of *subḥāna-ka* (Glory Be to Thee) has just saved the whale which keeps swimming along its path with its mouth agape.[75]

According to Rāghib al-Iṣbahānī in his *Muḥāḍarāt*, Quṭrub, a teacher at the Abbasid court in Baghdad, was once asked: 'Which of the two is faster at splitting open (*mubāḍaʿa*), a woman's vagina or a penis?' Thereupon he was answered in a poem:

---

[73] Poem on rhyme *al-ʿaqli*, metre *ṭawīl*. See *Dīwān Ibn al-Rūmī*, Muhannā V, p. 119, No. 1501; Naṣṣār V, p. 1934, No. 1501.

[74] Poem on rhyme *wa l-shabak*, metre *rajaz*. *Dīwān Ibn al-Rūmī*, Muhannā V, p. 7, No. 1361; Naṣṣār V, p. 1811, No. 1361.

[75] The poet's phrase, *min tasbīḥi-hi*, has two different meanings; first it signifies: 'his prayer of Glory Be to Thee'; but the alternative meaning signifies 'thereby causing it to swim'. For Jonah's prayer, see the text on page 44, above; and see Surat al-Anbiyāʾ (XXI, 87–88): {And him of the fish – when he went off at cross purposes and thought that We would not have power over him; then he called in the darkness: "There is no god but Thou; glory be to Thee! Verily I have been one of the wrong-doers." So We answered him and delivered him from the worry; so do We deliver the believers.}

> 1. By Allah, I am upright and yet I do not know whether it is the penis or the vagina which is closer to sin.
> 2. For, given free rein, the former gallops while the latter progresses roaring through his gaping mouth.[76]

To give Abū Nuwās the last word on the subject of gaping mouths.[77] In *Dīwān Abī Nuwās*, in the poem on rhyme *al-ḥiru* and in metre *ṭawīl*, he says:

> 1. By Allah, I know it not and I must ask: is it the penis (*al-zubbu*) which is more delicious for humans, or is it the vagina (*al-ḥiru*)?
> 2. While the former one strides along with his scabbard trailing behind him, the latter progresses braying through his gaping mouth,
> 3. Then the first enters into the belly of the second, with his mind fully made up, as if he were about to be strangled (*ka-dhi l-khanaq*), as he sees his own death looking at him,
> 4. The second with his jaws bent and frozen into a grin (*kāliḥan*) makes the first descend; then the first retreats with his bowed head dripping.

THE END

BIBLIOGRAPHY

Abū Nuwās, *Der Dīwān des Abū Nuwās (Dīwān Abī Nuwās al-Ḥasan ibn Hāniʾ al-Ḥakamī)*, vol. IV, ed. Gregor Schoeler (Wiesbaden: Franz Steiner, 1982).

Abū Nuwās, *Der Dīwān des Abū Nuwās (Dīwān Abī Nuwās al-Ḥasan ibn Hāniʾ al-Ḥakamī)*, vol. V, ed. Ewald Wagner (Beirut: Resalah, 2003).

Maulvi Muhammad Ali, *The Holy Qur-an containing the Arabic text with English translation and commentary* (Woking: Islamic Review Office, 1917).

Arthur J. Arberry, *The Koran Interpreted*, by Arthur J. Arberry (London: Allen & Unwin, 1980).

Richard Bell, *The Qurʾān Translated, with a critical re-arrangement of the Surahs*, 2 vols. (Edinburgh: T. & T. Clark, 1960).

Marc Bergé, *Pour un humanisme vécu: Abū Ḥayyān al-Tawḥīdī* (Damascus: French Institute, 1979).

Régis Blachère, *Le problème de Mahomet* (Paris: Presses universitaires de France, 1952).

Said Boustany, *Ibn ar-Rūmī sa vie et son oeuvre (I. Ibn ar-Rūmī dans son milieu)* (Beirut: Imprimerie catholique, 1967).

Anna Caiozzo, *Images du ciel d'Orient au Moyen Age* (Paris: Paris-Sorbonne, 2003).

N.J. Dawood, *The Koran, a translation by N.J. Dawood* (London: Allen Lane, 1978).

Ibn al-Athīr, *al-Kāmil fi l-tārīkh*, vol. 8 (Beirut: Dār Ṣādir, 1966).

Ibn al-Rūmī, *Dīwān Ibn al-Rūmī*, ed. ʿAbd al-Amīr ʿAlī Muhannā, 6 vols. (Beirut: Dār wa-maktabat al-Hilāl, 1991).

Ibn al-Rūmī, *Dīwān Ibn al-Rūmī Abi l-Ḥasan ʿAlī ibn al-ʿAbbās ibn Jurayj*, ed. Ḥusayn Naṣṣār, 6 vols. (Cairo: al-Hay'a al-Miṣriyya l-ʿĀmma li-l-Kitāb, 1973–1981).

[76] *Muḥāḍarāt* II, 261. Quṭrub (Muḥammad ibn al-Mustanīr), a scholar of Arabic grammar, was one of the teachers of the sons of al-Amīn. See E. Wagner, *Abū Nuwās*, p. 64; Charles Pellat, *Le milieu Basrien et la formation de Ǧāḥiẓ*, Paris 1953, p. 61–62: al-Jāḥiẓ considers Quṭrub as one of the schoolmasters (*muʿallimūn*) well qualified for teaching the children of the elite.

[77] *Dīwān Abī Nuwās* V, p. 29, No. 40.

Muqātil ibn Sulaymān, *Tafsīr al-Qurʾān*, ed. ʿAbd Allah Maḥmūd Shaḥāta (Cairo: al-Hay'a al-Miṣriyya l-ʿĀmma li-l-Kitāb, 1984).
Muḥammad Abu l-Faḍl Ibrāhīm (ed.), *Dhuyūl Tārīkh al-Ṭabarī* (Cairo: Dār al-Maʿārif, 1982).
T.B. Irving, *The Qur'an The first American version* (Brattleboro, Vt: Amana, 1985).
Abu l-Qāsim Ḥusayn ibn Muḥammad al-Rāghib al-Iṣbahānī, *Muḥāḍarāt al-udabāʾ wa-muḥāwarāt al-shuʿarāʾ wa l-bulaghāʾ*, pts. I–IV, in 2 vols. (n.p, n.d).
Abū ʿUthmān ʿAmru ibn Baḥr al-Jāḥiẓ, *Kitāb al-ḥayawān*, ed. ʿAbd al-Salām Muḥammad Hārūn (Cairo: Muṣṭafā l-Bābī l-Ḥalabī, 1949–1950).
Muḥammad ibn ʿAbdallah al-Kisāʾī, *Qiṣaṣ al-anbiyāʾ* (*Vita prophetarum auctore al-Kisāʾī*), ed. Isaac Eisenberg (Leiden: Brill, 1922).
Mālik ibn Anas, *al-Muwaṭṭaʾ*, ed. Muḥammad Fuʾād ʿAbd al-Bāqī, 2 vols. (Cairo: Dār Iḥyāʾ al-Kutub al-ʿArabiyya, 1951).
Mālik ibn Anas, *Al-Muwatta of Imam Malik ibn Anas : The First Formulation of Islamic Law*, trans. Aisha Abdurrahman Bewley (London/New York Kegan Paul, 1989).
Abu ʿUbayd Allah Muḥammad ibn ʿImrān al-Marzubānī, his compilation of Abu l-Maḥāsin Yūsuf ibn Aḥmad ibn Maḥmūd al-Ḥāfiẓ al-Yaghmūrī, *Kitāb Nūr al-qabas al-mukhtaṣar min al-Muqtabas fī akhbār al-nuḥāt wa l-udabāʾ wa l-shuʿarāʾ wa l-ʿulamāʾ* (*Die Gelehrtenbiographien*, Teil I: text.), ed. Rudolf Sellheim (Wiesbaden: Franz Steiner, 1964).
Charles Pellat, *Le kitāb at-tarbīʿ wa-t-tadwīr de Gāḥiẓ* (Damascus: French Institute, 1955).
Charles Pellat, *Le milieu Baṣrien et la formation de Gāḥiẓ* (Paris, 1953).
A. Raymond and G. Wiet, *Les marchés du Caire traduction annotée du texte de Maqrizi* (Cairo: IFAO, 1979).
Khalīl ibn Aybak al-Ṣafadī, *Kitāb al-Wāfī bi l-Wafayāt (Das biographische Lexikon des Ṣalāḥaddīn Khalīl ibn Aibak aṣ-Ṣafadī)*, vol. 12, ed. Ramaḍān ʿAbd al-Tawwāb (Wiesbaden: Franz Steiner, 1979).
George Sale, *The Koran translated into English from the original Arabic* (London, n.d).
Pieter Smoor, *Wazāra: The Killer of Many Husbands* (Cairo: IFAO, 2007).
A. Sprenger, *Das leben und die lehre des Mohammad*, reprint (Hildesheim: Georg Olms, 2003).
Abū Ḥayyān ʿAlī ibn Muḥammad al-Tawḥīdī, *al-Risāla al-Baghdādiyya*, ed. ʿAbbūd al-Shāljī (Beirut: Maṭbaʿat Dār al-Kutub, 1980).
Abū Manṣūr ʿAbd al-Malik ibn Muḥammad ibn Ismāʿīl al-Thaʿālibī al-Nīsābūrī, *Yatīmat al-dahr fī maḥāsin ahl al-ʿaṣr*, ed. Muḥammad Muḥyi l-Dīn ʿAbd al-Ḥamīd (Beirut 1947). See vol. III, pp. 30–99: '*al-bāb al-sābiʿ nadhkuru fīhi maḥāsina Abī ʿAbd Allah al-Ḥasan ibn Aḥmad ibn al-Ḥajjāj wa-gharāʾibuh*'.
E. Wagner, *Abū Nuwās: eine studie zur arabischen literatur der frühen ʿabbasidenzeit* (Wiesbaden: Franz Steiner, 1965).
E. Wagner, *Abū Nuwās in der Nebenüberlieferung: Dem Dichter zugeschriebene Gedichte und Verse*, Arabische Studien 2 (Wiesbaden: Harrassowitz, 2008).
W.M. Watt, *Muhammad at Medina* (Oxford, 1956).
A.J. Wensinck and J. Brugman, *Concordance et indices de la tradition musulmane: les six livres, le Musnad d' al-Dārimī, le Muwattaʾ de Mālik, le Musnad de Ahmad ibn Hanbal* (Leiden: Brill, 1936–1988) (Istanbul, 1986–1988.)
Abū ʿAbd Allah Yāqūt ibn ʿAbd Allah al-Rūmī al-Ḥamawī, *Muʿjam al-udabāʾ aw Irshād al-arīb ilā maʿrifati l-adīb* (Beirut: Dār al-kutub al-ʿilmiyya, 1991). See vol. III, p. 101 ff., no. 342: 'al-Ḥusayn ibn Aḥmad ibn Muḥammad [Ibn al-Ḥajjāj]'.

4

Abū Nuwās' poem to the Zoroastrian boy Bihrūz: An Arabic '*sawgand-nāma*' with a Persian '*kharja*'

Gregor Schoeler

In a masterly article, the honoree treated a long stanzaic poem by a 10th century poet, Mudrik al-Shaybānī, on a Christian boy. In this poem 'the sacred and the profane, the human and the divine [...] are closely intermingled.'[1] Geert Jan devoted his particular attention in this regard to 'the extensive use of Christian oaths.'[2] The object of concern is a long series of oaths: the poet swears by the Trinity, Jesus, Mary, the evangelists and numerous other Christian saints, prophets, and other persons, and by things and phenomena of significance for Christians. The honoree then asserts that Mudrik al-Shaybānī may have taken over this peculiarity – oaths on religious phenomena – from Abū Nuwās (d. ca. 815). Abū Nuwās, the most important poet of the early Abbasid period, had composed a similar oath-poem on a Christian youth.[3] In the *Dīwān* of Abū Nuwās there are a total of eleven love poems on Christian boys (*suryāniyyāt*), four of which contain a series of such oaths.[4]

As it turns out, however, Abū Nuwās is found also to have written commensurate oath poems, three in total,[5] on Zoroastrian boys (*fārisiyyāt*). They warrant our interest just as much as those on Christian boys. I would like in the following to treat the first and indeed most interesting of the 'Zoroastrian' oath-poems of Abū Nuwās.[6]

---

[1] Geert Jan van Gelder, 'Mudrik al-Shaybānī's Poem on a Christian Boy: Bad Taste or Harmless Wit?' (quotation on p. 50). I would like to thank Dr Bertram Thompson for his excellent translation and Dr Anna Livia Beelaert for important bibliographical references. Dr Mohsen Zakeri was kind enough to give me the manuscript of an unpublished paper ('A Middle Persian poem by Abū Nuwās? Or yet another Fārisīya?'), which he read on the occasion of the 4th SIE Conference in Paris 1999. I profited from his treatment in my investigation.

[2] Ibid., p. 56.

[3] Abū Nuwās, *Dīwān* V, pp. 148–153 (no. 151). Partially translated in van Gelder, 'Mudrik', p. 57, and Wagner, *Abū Nuwās*, p. 200.

[4] Abū Nuwās, *Dīwān* V, pp. 148–162 (no. 151–161). Oaths are contained in nos. 151, 154, 155, 156. No. 153 has only a few oaths. For these poems, see Wagner, *Abū Nuwās*, pp. 195–204.

[5] P. 139ff. (no. 147, 148, 150). Another poem, consisting of only two verses, from this group (p. 146, no. 149) contains no oaths. On these poems, see Wagner, *Abū Nuwās*, pp. 190–195.

[6] *Dīwān* V, pp. 139–142, no. 147.

1. *yā ghāsila l-ṭarjahārī*	1. O you, who washes the flask (or: jug)
2. *lil-khandarīsi l-ʿuqārī*	2. for the old wine!
3. *bi-ḥaqqi bayti l-nārī*	3. By the truth of the fire temple,
4. *wal-dīni wal-zīnahārī*	4. of the faith and protection,
5. *wa-ḥurmati l-nūbahārī*	5. and by the sanctity (or: reverence) of the Nūbahār [fire temple]
6. *wa-kanki l-raftārī*	6. and the fallen (?) city of Kank
7. *wa-ghurrati l-anwārī*	7. and the 'blaze' (i.e. sparkle) of the lights!
8. *wa-bi-nṣidāʿi l-nahārī*	8. and by the day as it breaks
9. *wa-wathbatī l-karbikārī (?)*	9. and by the springing of the pious one (?) (from bed) (?)
10. *fī sāʿati l-isḥārī*	10. at the morning hour!
11. *wa-bil-riyāḥi l-dhawārī*	11. By the winds that sweep away (dust)
12. *wa-hawlihā fī l-majārī*	12. and their ferocity (or: their terror) on the byways (or: waterways)!
13. *wa-bil-nujūmi l-darārī*	13. By the sparkling stars,
14. *idhā badat fī l-kanārī*	14. when they appear at the 'edge' (i.e. horizon)!
15. *wa-shamsihā l-shahriyārī*	15. By their sun, the king,
16. *wa-māhihā l-kāmakārī*	16. and their powerful moon!
17. *wal-mihrajāni l-mudārī*	17. By the Mihrajān festival that proceeds
18. *li-waqtihi l-karrārī*	18. at its ever returning time!
19. *wal-nawkarūzi l-kubārī*	19. By the great New Year's Day festival
20. *wa-jashni kāhanbārī*	20. and the Gāhānbār festival,
21. *wa-ābasāli l-wahārī*	21. by the spring festival of year's begin!
22. *wa-khurrah īrānshārī*	22. By the majesty of Iran,
(22.* *wal-bāmi wal-ayyārī*)	(22*. and dawn and the month of May!)
23. *bi-maʿqidi l-zunnārī*	23. By the knot of your Zoroastrian waist-belt, wrapped around
24. *min ḥaqwika l-khawwārī*	24. your soft loins:
25. *lammā qabilta -ʿtidhārī*	25. (I beseech you:) accept my apology
26. *min hafwatī wa -ʿithārī*	26. for my sin and lapse.
27. *fa-lastu bil-ṣabbārī*	27. I can stand it no longer
28. *ʿan wajhika l-saḥḥārī*	28. without your enchanting face
29. *wa-ridfika l-marmārī*	29. and your quivering buttocks.
30. *bal man li-ṭūli -ddikārī*	30. Alas, who can help me against my long thinking (about you)
31. *wa-ḥurqati wa-ntiḥārī*	31. and my torment and my suicide
32. *ʿalā layāli qiṣārī*	32. in short nights
33. *qad bittu fīhā shiʿārī*	33. I spent, whereby my underclothing
34. *min dūni kulli dithārī*	34. was without any covering!
35. *yaqillu ʿanka -ṣṭibārī*	35. My patience, to be without you, is ebbing.
36. *yā ṣūrata l-dīnārī*	36. O you with the face of a dinar
37. *fī rāḥati l-qusṭārī*	37. in the hand of a moneychanger!
38. *arāka/arāhu dūna l-kibārī*	38. I see that you are/it is not too big
39. *naʿam wa-fawqa l-ṣiġārī*	39. nor too small.
40. *yaqillu ʿan miqdārī*	40. a) He (the boy), however, is inferior to my 'measure', b) He (the boy), however, is too small for my 'measure',
41. *idhā -stawā bil-qarārī*	41.a) when he stands upright in his place. b) when it (my member) stands erect in its place.
42. *yā narjisī wa-bahārī*	42. O my narcissus and ox-eye daisy:
43. *bi-dih marā yak bārī*	43. 'Give me an audience'![7]

[7] Another possible translation would be: 'Give me yourself just once', or 'Give it to me just once!' (see below, commentary on l. 43!).

The poem is extant in two recensions of the *dīwān* of Abū Nuwās: Abū Bakr al-Ṣūlī (d. ca. 946) cites it in his recension in the chapter of love poems about young men (*al-mudhakkarāt*), and Ḥamza al-Iṣfahānī (d. 961 or 971) features it as the first poem of a sub-chapter (*fann*) of the chapter containing licentious verse (*al-mujūniyyāt*).[8] The text of the poem is not the same in the two recensions, however. Suffice it to say the most significant difference between al-Ṣūlī's and Ḥamza's versions for our immediate interest here is that some of the lines with Persian words that we find in Ḥamza's recension (ll. 20–22) are absent in al-Ṣūlī's; occasionally, passages in Ḥamza containing Persian words are found reformulated in al-Ṣūlī's version such that these words no longer figure in the text (e.g. in ll. 15 and 16).

Ḥamza's sub-chapter contains fifteen poems, which (according to the title) deal with Abū Nuwās' '(outrageous) pastimes with as yet beardless Zoroastrians and Christians';[9] the first four are addressed to Zoroastrians. Ḥamza says that the young 'Magian' to whom the composition is addressed was called Bihrūz b. Rūzbih. Three other poems are also addressed to him.

The poem to be treated here is in many respects one which is unusual and particularly interesting. It is unusual simply because of the many Persian words it contains. In this regard, however, it is no different than most of the other four *fārisiyyāt* (poems with numerous Persian words)[10] in this sub-chapter. In order to shed light on the pronounced significance of the Persian components of these and other *fārisiyyāt* for the history of the Persian language, the fact should be noted that New Persian at the time of Abū Nuwās (around 800) had not yet been committed to writing. These words thus provide us with very early testimonies of New Persian. What, however, makes our poem unique among the *fārisiyyāt* is that here, and only here, Abū Nuwās formulates a complete sentence in Persian. This sentence ends the poem: who is not reminded – by this foreign-language closing – of the Romance *kharja*s of the Spanish *muwashshaḥ*s?[11]

This *fārisiyya* is also unusual, however, by virtue of a formal characteristic: its rhyme scheme. The continuous (mono-)rhyme in this poem – composed in the *mujtathth* meter – is not – as prescribed by rhyme-technical rules – restricted to the first two and every second hemistich; rather, in this poem every hemistich rhymes, which is otherwise only the case in *rajaz* poetry. (For the sake of simplicity, I will henceforth speak not of 'hemistichs' but of 'lines'.)

A peculiarity of the content in this poem (as well as in three other *fārisiyyāt*) is the lengthy series of oaths on religious and cultic items as mentioned above. One is reminded not only of koranic oaths,[12] but also of a genre that arose later in Persian poetry, the

---

[8] Abū Nuwās, *Dīwān* V, p. 139.

[9] Ibid., p. 139–162.

[10] Ḥamza devoted a special (sub-)chapter (*Dīwān* V, 272–281), entitled *mā qālahū min al-fārisiyya fī athnāʾ shiʿrihi* ('What he said in Persian in his poetry'), to the verses containing Persian words and expressions found in the entire Dīwān (ib. p. 278–281). The relevant verses (lines) in our poem are found on p. 280.

[11] See Wagner, *Abū Nuwās*, p. 214f.

[12] See in this regard Watt, *Bell's Introduction*, p. 79, p. 194–195, fn. 4.

sawgand-nāma (oath poetry).[13] In the poems concerning young Zoroastrians, things and phenomena sacred to 'Magians' are sworn upon: their religion, their temples, their festivals, etc. The like holds for the poems on young Christians, in which Abū Nuwās swears by the Gospels, the Messiah, John the Baptist, Old Testament prophets, apostles, evangelists, Christian festivals, sacraments, etc.[14]

Finally, our poem – and the *fārisiyyāt* and *suryāniyyāt* taken as a whole – are of interest for the history of culture and morality. They provide insight into what particular knowledge Muslims – learned yet uninterested in the history of religion – had of minority religions in the early Abbasid period in Baghdad.[15] Moreover, they show a specific aspect of coexistence and interaction between members of different religious communities in this period.

The relevant difficulties and peculiarities of the poem, especially the Persian words, require comment before we move on to the actual interpretation. The Persian components in the *mujūniyya* attracted the attention of Iranian scholars beginning in the second half of the 20th century, long before Ewald Wagner's critically edited text of the poem (published in 2003) became available. After Sayyid Ḥasan Taqīzāda (Hassan Taqizadeh) had already treated nine lines from the poem in his book *Gah-šumārī* ('Timekeeping'),[16] and after Mujtabā Mīnuvī (Mojtaba Minovi) in his essay (published in 1954) 'Yakī az fārsiyyāt-i Abū Nuvās'[17] had likewise treated these lines and interpreted some words,[18] a researcher by the name of ᶜAbd ul-Raḥmān ᶜImādī had in his article 'Surūd-i fārsī-yi Abū Nuvās-i Ahvāzī' asserted, based on Taqīzāda's quotations, that these lines represented a Middle Persian or early New Persian poem which had been preserved by Abū Nuwās (which is of course completely wrong.) In his standard work *Abū Nuwās: Eine Studie zur arabischen Literatur der frühen ᶜAbbāsidenzeit*, Wagner did make some empirically sound statements about the poem long before the critical edition was published.[19] There he translated lines 5, 13, 14, 17, 18, 19, 20, 21 and treated the relevant Persian words, whereby he in turn occasionally referred to the interpretations of Mīnuvī and others. My explanations are based extensively on Wagner's study.

---

[13] See in this regard A.L. Beelaert, 'The *Saugand-nāma*' in particular pp. 57–60. The late Prof. Benedikt Reinert of Zurich University was of the opinion that Abū Nuwās and the poets of the later Persian *sawgand-nāmas* drew on an old Iranian tradition (personal communication). I would rather assume that the models for Abū Nuwās as well as for the Persian *sawgand-nāma* poets (Rūḥānī, Khāqānī, Kamāl al-Dīn Iṣfahānī, ᶜUrfī, et al.; see in this regard A.L. Beelaert, 'The *Saugand-nāma*') were the Quranic oaths. This does not exclude that the first *sawgand-nāma* poet (cf. ibid., p. 58, fn. 13) had been familiar with the 'Zoroastrian' oath poems of Abū Nuwās and had possibly been inspired to emulation by some of the oaths.

[14] See in this regard Wagner, *Abū Nuwās*, pp. 190–202 (with numerous translations).

[15] Ibid., p. 188 f.

[16] Taqīzāda, *Gah-šumārī*, p. 292, fn.

[17] In this essay, Mīnuvī focused on a poem other than the present one, namely, Abū Nuwās, *Dīwān* V, pp. 143–146, no. 148.

[18] Mīnuvī, 'Yakī az fārsiyyāt', pp. 74–75.

[19] Wagner, *Abū Nuwās*, pp. 190–194.

COMMENTARY

In lines 1 and 2, the addressee is evidently a young cup-bearer who is preparing to pour out the wine. The word *ṭarjahār* is probably of Persian origin; according to Dozy, *Supplément*, s.v. *Ṭarjahāra*, it stems from the Persian *tarkihār*, which means 'cup, goblet or flacon'. According to Steingass, *Dictionary*, s.v. *Tarkihār*, this word originally designates a vessel for condensing sour milk. It is tantalizing to take it here as designating 'jug'. Because jugs were stored in the wine cellar they were often dusty or even covered with spider webs, and therefore needed to be cleaned before the wine was poured.[20] But the meaning 'washing *the wine flask'* makes of course also good sense here. The word *khandarīs* (most frequent meaning: 'old wine') is treated by al-Jawālīqī (d. 1144)[21] in his dictionary of Arabicized loan words. He cites the lexicographer Ibn Durayd (d. 933) who says the word is of Byzantine origin. According to other authorities quoted by al-Jawālīqī, however, the word is of Persian origin. In addition to 'old wine', it can also mean 'old wheat'; some assume 'old' to be the basic meaning of the word. Western researchers generally agree with the Byzantine-Greek etymology and derive it from the Greek *chondros* (triticum romanum); cf. Dozy, *Supplément*, s.v. *Khandarūs*; Lane, *Lexicon*, s.v. *Khandarīs*. This confirms the view of S. Fraenkel, who likewise derives it from *chondros*, taken to mean 'grain of pearl barley', 'gruel (made of pearl barley)'. Accordingly, the word 'would have become, through a metaphor, a name for wine.'[22] According to those who suggest a Persian origin, it would derive from the Persian *khanda rīsh*, 'having a laughing beard' or 'one whose beard is laughed at' (cf. Lane, l.c.). The explanation proffered by al-Jawālīqī certainly makes no sense: 'He who drinks it, rips out his beard because his senses have dwindled.'[23]

In lines 3 and 4 begin the numerous oaths that occur up to lines 24–25. A word still common in Persian today is *zīnhār*, an 'appeal for safety, protection, refuge' (see Wolff, *Glossar*, s.v. *Z.*). Like many other Persian words in this poem, following the rules of Arabic grammar, it carries the Arabic definite article because it is definite.

Lines 5–6: Ḥamza says that Nūbahār was a fire temple (*bayt nār*) in Balkh. It is mentioned by Abū Nuwās another time in a praise poem.[24] At this sanctuary the ancestors of the Barmakid family of viziers were engaged as high priests. In reality, however, Nūbahār was a Buddhist temple, not a fire temple and the Barmakids were Buddhist priests, not Zoroastrians. It was not until later that they were declared to be Zoroastrian. As the lines of Abū Nuwās demonstrate, this tradition arose already very early.[25] *Kank* (New Persian *ganj*, 'treasure [chamber]') is, according to Ḥamza, the city Kankār in the 'east' (Turān), which according to legend was built by the Kayanian Siyāvush b. Kāʾūs. In the *Shāhnāma* it is called Gangdiž (see Wolff, s.v. *G.*). Firdawsī relates the history of its construction.[26] *Raftār*, 'going', 'moving off' (see Steingass, s.v. *R.*); here perhaps meaning 'transitory', 'transient', 'extinct'.

---

20 E.g. Abū Nuwās, *Dīwān* III, no. 243, p. 285, l. 8; cf. Bencheikh, 'Poésie bachiques', p. 24.
21 al-Jawālīqī, *al-Muʿarrab*, p. 172f.
22 Fraenkel, *Die aramäischen Fremdwörter*, p. 163f.
23 al-Jawālīqī, *al-Muʿarrab*, p. 173.
24 Abū Nuwās, *Dīwān* Vol. I^2, p. 232, l. 15, and f.
25 Cf. Wagner, *Abū Nuwās*, p. 140, fn. 7.
26 Firdousī, *Shāhnāme*. Ed. E. Bertels et al., vol. III, p. 104ff.

Lines 7 and 8: Lights (*anwār*). Here perhaps metonymic for 'fire', which, as everybody knows, is sacred to Zoroastrians.

Lines 9 and 10: The *rasm* (lettering) of *al-karbikār* (variants include *karnikār, kīdikār, kandikār, kūbikār*; see in the critical apparatus to the edition[27]) cannot be confidently read and interpreted. A plausible interpretation has been suggested by Mohsen Zakeri. He derives *karbikār* from the Middle Persian *kirpak-kār*, 'a person who does good deeds', 'one who is pious'; from *kirpak*, 'good deed, virtue'.[28] The line would thus be translated as follows: 'By the springing of the pious one (out of bed) at the morning hour!'[29] The writer of a marginal gloss in a manuscript belonging to the al-Ṣūlī recension apparently reads the word as *al-kīdikār* and explains it as 'rooster' (*al-dīk*). Should this be accurate, it could pertain to the 'cosmic cock', the cosmic caller to prayer.[30] The terrestrial rooster, however, could be a candidate as well: 'the cock served as rouser to prayer already in the Avesta (Vidêvdāt 18, 14–29)'.[31] In Arabic and Persian wisdom literature, the cock is 'the devil's most hated bird.' '... [W]hen the cock of God's throne praises God, the earthly cocks imitated it, whereupon the devils fled and their cunning was destroyed.'[32] According to Vīdêvdāt 18, 14–29, 'at night the fire wakes the Sraôša, the Sraôša the cock and the cock the people so that they pray, revile the demons and observe the fire rites.'[33] However, since the reading and explanation of the *rasm* as 'cock' is by no means certain, further speculations along these lines are not possible.

Line 14: The writer of a gloss in a manuscript belonging to the Ḥamza al-Iṣfahānī recension explains the Persian word *kanār* (also: *kinār*), meaning 'edge', 'border', 'side', as 'horizon', which is certainly correct. This meaning, however, is not found in the conventional dictionaries. Since the poet needs words ending with *-ārī*, he also uses, when feasible, metonyms.

Lines 15–16: The translation of both lines is based on the text of the Ḥamza al-Iṣfahānī recension; the manuscripts of the al-Ṣūli recension feature a highly divergent text which contains no Persian words. *Shahriyār* is a word for 'king' frequently evidenced in the *Shāhnāma* (s. Wolff, *Glossar,* s.v. *Sh.*). The sun is here termed 'the king', *scil.* of the stars, or, perhaps, of the seven climes (cf. Steingass, s.v. *Shahr-yār*). Whereas 'sun' is expressed with the Arabic word *shams*, the Persian word *māh* is used for 'moon'. *Kāmakār*, for *kāmgār*: 'successful', 'happy', 'powerful' (s. Wolff, *Glossar,* s.v. *K.*, and Steingass, *Dictionary*, s.v. *K.*).

Lines 17–18: The Mihrajān festival, celebrated on the day of the autumnal equinox, is the autumnal pendant of the New Year's festival (Nawrūz) (s. below, on line 19).[34] Like the Christian festivals, both Old Iranian festivals were celebrated at the time of Abū Nuwās, and still for a long time thereafter, by the entire population regardless of any difference

27 Abū Nuwās, *Dīwān* V, p. 140.

28 Nyberg, *Hilfsbuch*, p. 129.

29 Personal communication by Dr Mohsen Zakeri.

30 Meier, 'Niẓāmī und die mythologie des hahns', p. 996ff.

31 Ibid., p. 1006.

32 Ibid., p. 1008.

33 Ibid., p. 1011.

34 Christensen, *L'Iran,* p. 168; EI^2, s.v. Mihragān.

of religion.[35] The relative clause is certainly intended to express that the Mihrajān, unlike the Islamic festivals, remains unchanged within the seasons.[36]

Line 19: Nawrūz, the New Year's festival, is the most well known Old Iranian festival and is still celebrated today. It is observed at the vernal equinox.[37] In his address to the Zoroastrian, Abū Nuwās employs a form of the term related to Middle Persian (*nawkarūz;* Middle Persian *nôghrôz*) although by his time the New Persian Nawrūz (including its Arabicized variant Nayrūz) was common.[38]

Lines 20–22 are found only in the Ḥamza recension; in the al-Ṣūlī recension they are absent, i.e., they have been replaced by line 22*.

Line 20: Gāhānbār: The Persian calendar has five or six festivals of this name; each lasted for five days. The last one (celebrated from 15–20 March) became the Gāhānbār festival *kat' exochen.*[39]

Lines 21–22: Ābasāl al-wahār (or Vahārjashn) which is dealt with here is likewise a spring festival, celebrated on 1 Ādhar; *vahār* corresponds to the New Persian *bahār* ('spring'). Given for *ābasāl* by Mīnuvī[40] (ibid.) is an explanation going back to the Iranist Walter B. Henning: the Old Iranian form of this word would evidently be *upasard*, in the sense of 'that which signals the start of the year'.

Line 22a is found only in the al-Ṣūlī recension, which, in turn, lacks lines 20–22. The first word is to be read in most of the manuscripts as *al-bām* (however, there is also a variant *al-yām*). *Bām* is the Persian word for 'dawn'. The name of the month, al-Ayyār (May), is Aramaic.

Line 23: *zunnār* is the belt which free non-Muslim subjects, who paid taxes for their freedom and toleration in a Muslim polity, were obliged to wear.[41]

Line 25: *lammā* is here synonymous with *illā* introducing the apodosis (main clause) of an oath.[42] This meaning arises compellingly from the sense of that which follows.

Lines 25–26: These two lines contain the imploration of the poet, which the many preceding oaths comprising 22 lines have been sworn for. He asks the 'beloved' to forgive him his sin. It is not too difficult to imagine what led to this situation.

Lines 33–34: *Shiʿār* is 'the garment that is next to the body' (Lane, *Lexicon*, s.v. *Š.*); *dithār* is 'a garment which one wears for warmth above the garment that is next the body' (Lane, *Lexicon*, s.v. *D*). There is a saying which reads: *hum al-shiʿār dūna l-dithār*; it means 'they are mutually close as regards love' (ibid.) The meaning in our line is likely commensurate; perhaps: 'whereby as regards love, I was very close to him'.

Lines 36–37 contain the poet's address to the young Zoroastrian. One should assume that such an address would introduce a new section rather than close a previous one. Only

---

35 Mez, *Renaissance*, p. 394ff., esp. pp. 400–402.

36 Wagner, *Abū Nuwās* 191, with fn. 4.

37 Christensen, *L'Iran*, p. 166f.; EI², s.v. Nawrūz.

38 Wagner, *Abū Nuwās*, p. 190.

39 Christensen, *L'Iran*, p. 164f.; Wagner, *Abū Nuwās*, p. 191.

40 Mīnuvī, 'Fārsiyyāt', p. 75.

41 See EI² and Lane, *Lexicon*, s.v. *Zunnār*; A. Mez, *Renaissance*, p. 45.

42 Wright, *Grammar* I, p. 294 A; II, 340A; Reckendorf, *Syntax*, p. 512, § 262, 12; Fischer, *Grammatik*, §334, 1.

in the al-Ṣūlī recension, however, does the address allow itself to be perceived as a prelude to an address ('O you, the you...! I see that you ...'). In the Ḥamza recension this is hardly possible because following the address, the pronoun switches from the 2nd to the 3rd person ('O you, the you...! I see that he ...'). One thus has to assume despite everything that the address to the young man closes the previous section here.

In line 36, the young Zoroastrian is addressed as '*dīnār*-face(d)' (*ṣūrat al-dīnār*); *ṣūra*, which in modern Persian is the most common word for 'face', can already have this meaning in classical Arabic (s. Lane, *Lexicon*, s.v. Ṣ.). Consequently, in this line, too, *ṣūra* would certainly denote 'face'. The metaphor 'dīnār' as '(light) face of the beloved' is encountered frequently with Abū Nuwās.[43]

Line 37: *qusṭār* (or *qisṭār*) means – according to dictionaries,[44] a commentary of Ḥamza, and glosses in two manuscripts of the al-Ṣūlī recension – 'moneychanger'. Indigenous scholars generally explain the word to be of Byzantine origin; at any rate, all agree that it is not of Arabic origin. *Qusṭār* (or *qisṭār*) is also supposed to be related to the koranic word *qisṭās* 'balance' (17:35; 26:182).[45] The supplement '(*dīnār*) *in the hand of a moneychanger*' is probably intended to denote an especially shiny coin that the moneychanger has polished.

Line 37 provisionally ends Abū Nuwās' address to his 'beloved', according to the Ḥamza recension (line 38 begins with 'I see *him* ...'), and is followed by four lines (38–41) comprising the poet's 'inner monologue'. The al-Ṣūlī recension, however, has the address going further ('I see *you* ...'); according to *one* manuscript, up to the end of the poem (see the critical apparatus to the edition!). Both versions make sense. The continuous al-Ṣūlī version seems to read more smoothly. The Ḥamza version, however, could be the *lectio difficilior* and therefore preferable. Moreover an 'inner monologue' here makes good sense because the poet remarks on the physical features and suitability of the coveted person for intercourse (roughly: 'he has just the right size, but...'), which the latter is certainly not supposed to hear. A secure decision as to the superiority of any one version is not possible. I base my interpretation (see below) on the Ḥamza version.

Lines 40–41 have a double meaning: one harmless, the other obscene. It depends on the interpretation of the words *miqdār* and *qarār*. *Miqdār* (literally 'dimension') can refer to the physical size of the young man mentioned in the previous line and *qarār* ('abode', 'resting place') to his position on the ground. The meaning of the line is then: 'He is smaller than I when he is standing upright on the ground'. The two words can, however, refer to the member of the speaker; the meaning is then: 'He (the young man) is too small for the size of my member (i.e. not yet penetrable, or only with difficulty), when it is erect in its place'. That the obscene meaning is intended can be taken for certain; the scribes of the marginal glosses of two Ṣūli manuscripts are also of this opinion. One of them, however, suggests the double meaning in his explanation of line 41: 'That is to say: when he (the young man) stands upright on the ground (*idhā -stawā qāʾiman ʿalā wajh al-arḍ*)', but then

[43] E.g. *Dīwān* III, p. 128, l. 7; III, p. 173, l. 2; V, p. 73, l. 2, V, p. 307, l. 5). My thanks to Professor Wagner for the supporting pieces of evidence!

[44] See e.g. al-Jawālīqī, *al-Muʿarrab*, p. 311.

[45] Ibid., p. 299.

adds, '"When he/it stands upright in his/its place' is a concealed allusion (*kināya*)[46] to something unsaid; he (the poet) means in this regard: 'my thing' (*matāʿī*).' The line thus means: 'when my private part is able to find its place inside you.' The ideal age of a beloved youth, which was rather regarded as a lower age limit, was 15 years.[47] When a boy was still too young for anal intercourse, the *lūṭī* (the one assuming the role of penetrator)[48] should be satisfied with intercrural sex (*tafkhīdh*).[49] But pederasts like Abū Nuwās appreciated the tightness of the anus of a boy as opposed to the breadth of the vagina.[50]

Line 42: the address to the young man, by two flower-names, is resumed; it ends in the following line with the end of the poem. *narjis*, a Greek word originally which entered Arabic via Persian, is the fragrant white narcissus of the poets (see Lane, s.r. *r-ğ-s*); *bahār* (which is supposed to be identical to *ʿarār*), possibly of Persian origin, can refer to different flowers: the yellow ox-eye daisy which grows in spring (buphtalmum; a composite) (Lane, s.v. *bahār*); but also, mainly in the West, a type of narcissus (narcissus tagetta) (see Dozy, s.v. *B.*).

In line 43, the poem's last line and its climax, Abū Nuwās formulates a complete sentence in Persian: *bi-dih marā yak bārī*. Commensurate with the ambiguity of the word *bār* (1. 'a time, turn' [*yak bārī* = 'one time', 'once'] 2. an audience), the sentence can be perceived and translated differently. The first possibility is 'Give to me once'. This interpretation is suggested by the scribe of the marginal gloss of a al-Ṣūlī manuscript. One wonders however *what* exactly it is that is to be given: 'Give me yourself' (?), or perhaps 'Give me a glass of wine' (referring back to l. 1) (?). The second possibility 'Give me an audience', 'Receive me', expressed less formally would mean 'Let me come to you', 'Pay attention to me', (or perhaps 'Let me in[side]'). I consider the second possibility as the more probable. With this foreign-language closing, Abū Nuwās set out to do exactly what Andalusian poets intended with Romance *kharja*s of Andalusian *muwashshāḥ*s, namely, to close the poem with a 'contentual climax comprising pathos and agudeza' (H. Lausberg).[51] As a difference, it can be pointed out that the typical *kharja*s (often citations from songs or proverbs) are *quotations* put by the poet into the mouth of others (but sometimes also in his own!),[52] whereas our line seems to be a sentence freely formulated by the poet himself. Perhaps

---

46 Precise definitions for *kināya* (like 'periphrastic expression') do not come about until relatively late. With the early rhetoricians the expression can simply denote 'innuendo' (E. Wagner, *Abū Nuwās*, p. 418f.) According to Ibn al-Athīr (d. 1239), '*kināya* describes a word or a group of words which [...] are used to replace other words which are to be rejected, sometimes simply for considerations of style, sometimes out of respect for decency, avoiding the use of words likely to shock or judged to be of bad omen' (EI², s.v. *K.* [Ch. Pellat]). The case is one of *kināya* in the terms of the later rhetoricians, if, e.g., in a verse, the main issue which is central to the affair is concealed and only a minor detail or a result is mentioned, the audience or reader must then guess the meaning by thought combinations (Wagner, *Abū Nuwās*, p. 418f.; see also W. Heinrichs in EAL II, s.v. 'Rhetorical figures', p. 661). Here the *kināya* arises rather through the ambiguous formulation.

47 See in this regard Bauer, *Liebe*, p. 170.

48 Ibid., p. 166.

49 Cf. in this regard recently Wagner, 'Schrift', p. 350, fn. 42.

50 Abū Nuwās, *Dīwān* V, p. 101, l. 14; no. 118 ; cf. Wagner, *Abū Nuwās*, p. 175ff.

51 Lausberg, 'Review of P. le Gentil, *Le Virelai et le villancico*', pp. 208–9.

52 But by no means are all Andalusian *kharja*s authentic quotations!

the case here concerns something like a common saying, whereby one could thus speak of a quasi-quotation.[53] It remains to be noted that Abū Nuwās also authored numerous poems ending in genuine quotations (including citations from songs and proverbs); these were certainly not in a foreign language.

It is a credit to Ewald Wagner that he not only recognized the significance of Abū Nuwās' song and proverb quotations, but likewise that of the closing Persian line in the present poem as precursors of Andalusian *kharjas*.[54] Later on, Alan Jones compiled and commented on these quotations in an essay entitled 'Final Taḍmīn in the Poems of Abū Nuwās'.[55] Jones relied for his corpus of final *taḍmīn* on the incomplete and uncritical edition of Abū Nuwās' *Dīwān* by Aḥmad ʿAbd al-Majīd al-Ghaz(z)ālī,[56] although Wagner's and my critical edition of the *khamriyyāt* and *ghazaliyyāt*, which contain the most examples of final *taḍmīn* by far, was already available by the time this essay was published. The Persian line was completely unknown to Jones, although he could have found it in Wagner's monograph on Abū Nuwās.[57] Even if this line, as noted, is probably not a quotation (but perhaps something like a common saying), it should at least have been mentioned by Jones – at the point in his essay where he treats an example of *taḍmīn*,[58] which, according to the wording of the preceding line, is a Persian proverb (*mathal*) translated into Arabic.[59]

INTERPRETATION

The poem can be divided into four parts:

I. Address to a young Zoroastrian, followed by a long series of oaths. At the end of this section, the poet beseeches the boy to accept his apology (it is for this that the many oaths are sworn) (ll. 1–26).
II. Lament of love, closes with a second address to the boy (ll. 27–37).
III. Interruption of the address and 'inner monologue' of the poet. Speculation on the correct age and the (questionable) physical 'suitability' of the youth for intercourse (ll. 38–41).
IV. Third address and poet's request that the boy 'receive' him (ll. 42–43).

With respect to genre, our *fārisiyya* stands between love poetry 'in the masculine' (*ghazal mudhakkar*) and licentious poetry (*mujūniyya*); this intermediate position is also evidenced

---

53 The expression comes from Jones, 'Final Taḍmīn', p. 66.

54 Wagner, *Abū Nuwās*, pp. 428–30, with fn. 2, and pp. 214–15.

55 See in bibliography.

56 Abū Nuwās, *Dīwān*, Cairo, 1953.

57 Wagner, *Abū Nuwās*, pp. 214–15.

58 Jones, 'Final Taḍmīn', p. 67.

59 *fa -btasamat thumma arsalat mathalan yaʿrifuhu l-ʿujmu laysa bil-kadhibī: lā tuʿṭiyanna l-ṣabīya wāḥidatan, yaṭlubu ukhrā bi-aʿnafi l-ṭalabī* (She smiled and uttered a well-known saying which the Persians know to be no lie: 'Don't give the young man one [kiss]; [if you do so] he will press you very hard for another.' (Jones' translation). Abū Nuwās, *Dīwān* IV, p. 25, Nr. 30, cf. Wagner, *Abū Nuwās*, p. 429.

in Ḥamza's and al-Ṣūlī's differing arrangement. Leaving aside the oaths, which are an exception, many characteristic motifs of Abbasid love poetry are encountered in the 'lament of love' section (II) (see below!). The poet's 'inner monologue' (ll. 38–41), especially its two last lines (ll. 40–41), is a *mujūn* passage.

As for metre, the poem is distinguished by short dimeter lines. They are particularly well suited for the long series of short oaths. An oath is generally confined to one line. Two oaths in succession occasionally exhibit a parallel construction (*muwāzana*) (full *muwāzana:* ll. 15–16). The short lines, however, are likewise suited to the addresses, which can be accompanied by a short adverbial determinant in the line following (ll. 1–2, 36–37, 42); likewise the explanations consisting of brief thoughts often follow each other associatively (ll. 27–35).

Phonetically, the poem is characterized by the rich rhyme *-ārī*. Since all of the lines (technically, hemistiches) rhyme, the rhyme appears twice as often as in a normal *qarīḍ* poem. Since the lines are short, the rhyme reaches the listener's ear in short intervals over and over again during recitation.

The poet first addresses the youthful Zoroastrian cup-bearer, who is in the act of cleaning the wine flask (or jug) (see above, commentary on ll. 1–2). Following this address he swears a number of oaths the reason behind which remains unknown to the listener for a long time. The long series of Zoroastrian items in the oaths are supposed to create an atmosphere familiar to the 'beloved' and to prove the poet's familiarity with and respect for the former's non-Islamic religion – upon the 'truth' of which he even swears! Concealed behind this is of course nothing other than the endeavor to win the young man over and make him submit to the poet's wishes. Thus, the oaths are actually pure rhetoric. Abū Nuwās initially swears by Zoroastrian sanctuaries and the Zoroastrian religion and likewise by things closely associated therewith; then by elements sacred to Zoroastrians, including, naturally, 'light' (i.e. 'fire'); furthermore by times of day and natural forces, the celestial bodies, Zoroastrian festivals; near the end, and in a clear enhancement, by the majesty (*khurra*, Old Persian *khvarᵉnā*, New Persian *farr*) of Iran, and immediately thereafter, all the way at the end, by a part of the body of particular interest to the coveter. The connection to the previously named Zoroastrian objects and phenomena facilitates mention of the waist-belt of the Zoroastrians (*zunnār*), which is knotted at this place on the body. The transition from the Glory of Iran to this body part nonetheless feels like a big leap, but this is exactly what the poet intends; at any rate, this is how he gets down to his actual point.

The subsequent lament of love (ll. 27–35) contains several *ghazal* motifs current in Abbasid poetry: the declaration of being overwhelmed by love,[60] the sadness, sorrow, yearning and pain of the lover,[61] especially sleeplessness and 'burning'.[62] It likewise includes a brief lauding description of the corporal charms of the coveted (significantly face and buttocks!) (ll. 28–29).

The second address (line 36) exhibits a stylistic enhancement with respect to the first one in that it expresses a feature of the boy's beauty through a striking metaphor (light

[60] Bauer, *Liebe*, p. 344ff.
[61] Ibid., p. 361ff.
[62] Ibid., p. 376ff.

face by means of *dīnār*) – a procedure employed by the poet in the third address as well, where two flower metaphors are used for the loved one.

The 'inner monologue', which could be distinguished from the presentation of the rest of the text through the reciter's 'aside', has the effect, superficially, of a break in style. The obscene thoughts (*mujūn* motifs), especially those in the last two lines, do not seem to fit at all with the love lament (*ghazal* motifs) of the previous section. The obscenity is attenuated, however, in that it is not directly, or not clearly, expressed; rather, it is merely implied through the stylistic device of the *kināya*. As a matter of fact, however, this 'break in style' is an express and consciously applied artistic device. The *ghazal* lines, like the oaths, are largely purely rhetorical; what is true is only that the poet covets the boy as a sexual object. Abū Nuwās says the whole truth – although it comes in the form of a *kināya* – only in the 'inner monologue'. It turns out that his apology (l. 25–26) was also insincere because what he is planning to do with the boy is exactly what he had asked him to forgive him for.

The subsequent lines, the final ones, in which the poet again addresses the 'beloved' directly and in which he returns to the imagery and motifs characteristic of the *ghazal*, bring the closing climax of the poem. The prelude is formed by the (third) address to the young man with the names of two fragrant flowers. They are 'markedly' implemented 'striking' metaphors and the names of the flowers are 'naturally' Persian. The 'contentual climax comprising pathos and agudeza' (H. Lausberg) is the last line, which is all in Persian. Summarized there, as it were, are the many Persian words used in the poem; here the poet not only utilizes individual words from the native language of the 'beloved', he even addresses him in a complete sentence in his native tongue. This sentence, 'Give me an audience', contains in all succinctness precisely what the poet had sworn oaths and expressed affirmations of love for, and what he was ultimately out to get. What Abū Nuwās meant by 'audience' certainly exceeds what is normally understood under the term.

Surely this poem is outrightly immoral, but let us not forget that we are dealing with a *mujūniyya*, (an appropriate, but 'weak' translation of the term would be 'jesting' poem', or 'buffoonery'[63]). That a real incident is portrayed cannot be ruled out, but it is more probable that Abū Nuwās, here, as in the poems where he tells of how he summoned Iblīs (Satan) to assist him in matters of love,[64] is presenting his listeners with something invented – a kind of fiction the great theorist of literature Ḥāzim al-Qarṭājannī (d. 1285) would describe as an 'invention of possibility'.[65] The case here is certainly not, like in the Iblīs poems, one of playful Satanism, 'ritual clownery',[66] but perhaps it is something similar. The oaths on kinky Zoroastrian things and the many non-Arabic words, the – surely unintelligible to many listeners and readers without commentary – Persian sentence at

[63] See EI^2, s.v. "Mudjūn" (Ch. Pellat).

[64] Schoeler, "Iblīs", p. 56.

[65] Ḥāzim al-Qarṭājannī makes a distinction between 'invention of possibility' (*al-ikhtilāq al-imkānī*), and 'invention of impossibility' (*al-ikhtilāq al-imtināʿī*); (see *Minhāj*, pp. 77–78; cf. Heinrichs, *Arabische Dichtung*, p. 45f.). Ḥazim explains 'invention of possibility' by means of examples as follows: 'What I mean (thereby) is that someone asserts that he is in love, and speaks of a loved one who has enslaved him, though this is not the case in fact.'

[66] Hamori, *On the Art*, p. 53; Schoeler, 'Iblīs', p. 56.

the end, and of course the section whose obscure obscene dimension becomes apparent only after reflection – all of this was already able to impress and amuse an audience, and even more to the point, an audience which had little familiarity with things Persian.

This can perhaps be gleaned from an anecdote noted by Ḥamza about the poem:[67]

> When Abū Nuwās, on his way to Egypt, entered Damascus, the people of the city gathered around him and asked him to recite some of his poetry. Thereupon he recited to them, 'O you who washes the flask.' They then said to him, 'Recite more to us!' whereupon he countered, 'I don't think you deserve any more than that (*lā arākum tastaḥiqqūna akthar minhā*)!'

WORKS CITED

Abū Nuwās, al-Ḥasan b. Hāniʾ, *Dīwān*. Ed. E. Wagner (vol. IV: ed. G. Schoeler). 5 vols. + Index, 2 vols. Cairo, Wiesbaden, Beirut, Stuttgart, Berlin, 1958–2006 (vol. I: 2nd ed. Beirut, Berlin, 2001.) (Bibliotheca Islamica 20a–f).

Th. Bauer, *Liebe und Liebesdichtung in der arabischen Welt des 9. und 10. Jahrhunderts*. Wiesbaden, 1998.

A.L. Beelaert, 'The *Saugand-nāma* (or *Qasamīya*), a Genre in Classical Persian Poetry'. In *Iran. Questions et Connaissances: Actes du IVe Congrès Européen des Études Iraniennes*. Vol. II: *Périodes Médiévale et Moderne*. Ed. Maria Szuppe. Paris 2002, p. 55–73. (Studia Iranica, Cahiers 26).

J.E. Bencheikh, 'Poésie bachiques d'Abū Nuwās: thèmes et personnages'. In: *Bulletin des Etudes Orientales* 18 (1963–64), p. 7– 84.

A. Christensen, *L'Iran sous les Sasanides*. Copenhagen, 1936.

R. Dozy, *Supplément aux Dictionnaires Arabes*. 2 vols. Leiden, 1881 (reprint Beirut 1968).

EAL = J. Scott Meisami and P. Starkey (eds.), *Encyclopedia of Arabic Literature*. 2 vols. London/New York, 1998.

EI^2 = *The Encyclopaedia of Islam*. New Ed., 12 vols. Leiden, 1960–2004.

Firdousī, *Shāhnāme*. Ed. E. Bertels et al. 9 vols. Moscow, 1963–71.

W. Fischer, *Grammatik des klassischen Arabisch*. 2nd ed. Wiesbaden, 1987.

S. Fraenkel, *Die aramäischen Fremdwörter im Arabischen*. Leiden, 1886.

G.J. van Gelder, 'Mudrik al-Shaybānī's Poem on a Christian Boy. Bad Taste or Harmless Wit?'. In *Representations of the Divine in Arabic Poetry*. Ed. by G. Borg and Ed de Moor. Amsterdam/Atlanta, 2001.

A. Hamori, *On the Art of Medieval Arabic Literature*. Princeton, 1974.

W. Heinrichs, *Arabische Dichtung und griechische Poetik. Ḥāzim al-Qarṭāǧannīs Grundlegung der Poetik mit Hilfe aristotelischer Begriffe*, Beirut, 1969 (Beiruter Texte und Studien, vol. 8).

al-Jawālīqī, Mawhūb b. Aḥmad, *al-Muʿarrab min kalām al-ʿajamī ʿalā ḥurūf al-muʿjam*. Ed. A. M Shākir. Cairo, 1969.

A. Jones, 'Final Taḍmīn in the Poems of Abū Nuwās.' In A. Jones (ed.), *Arabicus Felix: Luminosus Britannicus*. Essays in Honour of A.F.L. Beeston on his Eightieth Birthday. Oxford, 1991.

E. Lane, *An Arabic-English Lexicon*. 8 parts. London 1863–93.

H. Lausberg, '[Review of] P. le Gentil, *Le Virelai et le villancico*'. In *Archiv für das Studium der neueren Sprachen* CXCII [1955], p. 208–9.

F. Meier, 'Niẓāmī und die mythologie des hahns'. In id., *Bausteine* I-III. *Ausgewählte Aufsätze zur Islamwissenschaft*. Ed. E. Glassen and G. Schubert. Istanbul, Stuttgart 1992. Vol. II, p. 996–1056 (Beiruter Texte und Studien, vol. 53a–c).

[67] Abū Nuwās, *Dīwān* V, p. 142.

A. Mez, *Die Renaissance des Islâms.* Heidelberg 1922.
M. Mīnuvī, 'Yakī az fārsiyyāt-i Abū Nuwās'. In: *Majalla-i Dānishkada-i Adabiyyāt,* year 1, no. 3 1333 H.Sh. [= 1954], p. 62–77.
H.S. Nyberg, *Hilfsbuch des Pehlevi.* 2 vols. Uppsala 1928–31.
al-Qarṭājannī, Ḥāzim b. Muḥammad, *Minhāj al-bulaġā wa-sirāj al-udabāʾ.* Ed. M. Ḥ. Ibn al-Ḫūja (Belkhodja). Tunis, 1966.
H. Reckendorf, *Arabische Syntax,* Heidelberg 1921.
G. Schoeler, 'Iblīs in the Poems of Abū Nuwās'. In *Zeitschrift der Deutschen Morgenländischen Gesellschaft* 151 (2001), p. 43–62.
F. Steingass, *A Comprehensive Persian-English Dictionary.* 1st ed. 1892 (new impression 1970).
E. Wagner, *Abū Nuwās. Eine Studie zur arabischen Literatur der frühen ʿAbbāsidenzeit,* Wiesbaden, 1965.
E. Wagner, 'Schrift, Schreiben und Schreiber bei Abū Nuwās'. In Th. Bauer and U. Stehli-Wehrbeck (eds), *Alltagsleben und materielle Kultur in der arabischen Sprache und Literatur.* Festschrift für H. Grotzfeld zum 70. Geburtstag. Wiesbaden, 2005, p. 341–356.
W.M. Watt, *Bell's introduction to the Qurʾān.* Edinburgh, 1970. (Edinburgh University Press.)
F. Wolff, *Glossar zu Firdosis Schahname.* Berlin 1935 (reprinted Hildesheim, 1965).
W. Wright, *A Grammar of the Arabic Language. Translated from the German of Caspari and edited with numerous additions and corrections.* 2 vols. Reprinted, Cambridge, 1967.

5

The *Mujūn* Genre by Abū Nuwās and by Ibn Quzmān: a comparison

Arie Schippers

The *mujūn* genre in Arabic literature has two well-known representatives: one is the famous wine poet from the east of the Arabic world – Abū Nuwās al-Ḥasan ibn Hāniʾ (d. 199/814),[1] who lived in the time of the Abbasid caliphs, such as al-Amīn and al-Rashīd – and the other is Ibn Quzmān (d. 555/1160),[2] who lived in Muslim Spain, the west of the Muslim world, in the time of the Almoravid caliphs, such as Yūsuf ibn Tashufīn. Both poets practised the *mujūn* genre, a kind of obscene poetry, while professing to lead a dissolute life with much wine drinking and other extravagancies. Here, I will present an analysis of the similarities and differences between their poetic productions.

The *Dīwān* of Abū Nuwās has a special chapter devoted to *mujūniyyāt* that contains the kind of poetry written by the poet as a debauchee, with his sins of unlawful love making and wine drinking. Although he did not edit his *Dīwān*, he must have suggested its arrangement into chapters.[3] However, the problem of the authenticity of his poetry remains, since the popularity of his poetry and poetic themes made other poets imitate his work. Ewald Wagner recently published a whole volume of poetic fragments ascribed to Abū Nuwās that are probably largely, if not entirely spurious.[4] While this poetry is not by Abū Nuwās himself, it is at least Abū Nuwāsian.

In the following, I present a survey of Abū Nuwās's *mujūniyyāt* in the twelfth chapter of his *Dīwān*,[5] and deal with its main characteristics. The chapter of his *mujūniyyāt* starts with an alphabetical section according to the rhymes of the poems (pp. 5–59). Then follow subchapters dealing with the poet's laughing at and mocking of the mischievous swindlers (*ahl al-shaṭārah*), about the abominable attitudes of women and the praiseworthy behaviour of the beardless lads, about the praiseworthy attitudes of women and the loathsome behaviour of beardless lads, about mocking the beardless lads of the offices (*dawāwīn*),

[1] Wagner (1965), Kennedy (2005), Kennedy (1997).

[2] Colin (1971).

[3] Schoeler (2010/2011), especially 25–30.

[4] Wagner (2008).

[5] Abū Nuwās, 1958–2006, Volume V.

about laughing at the beardless lads in the mosques, about laughing at beardless Mazdeans and Christians, and about weeping upon the remnants of the encampment in pre-Islamic style, that is, describing the dung heaps and traces that are left there.

Moreover, other subchapters deal with the poet's testaments for the people of debauchery (*ahl al-khalāʿah*); his dislike of the month of Ramaḍān; his dispute with the male and female censors who criticize his sinful behaviour and his contempt of threats of punishment for sins; playing jokes with the language and metrical Qurʾānic phrases; proverbs that are spread by his poetry; what is said in the Persian language or riddles with precious and humorous words; beautiful *badīʿ* style and what he said with mockery and exaggerated imagery, transgressing the usual boundaries; what he said in one-liners and two-liners of poetry fragments; what he said according to the language of the whisperers; in the style of merchants and in his own testaments about ludicrous behaviour (*khalāʿah*). He also has a section on the debauchery genre in prose with some poetry inserted, and on debauchery in correspondence and in poetic recital. Many of his *mujūniyyāt* also figure in his poems about boys or girls (*mudhakkarāt* or *muʾannathāt*). And some of his *mujūniyyāt* are also wine poems (*khamriyyāt*).

As far as Ibn Quzmān is concerned, at first sight he differs from Abū Nuwās, not only in lifestyle but also in poetic production: his main genre is not Classical Arabic poetry, but strophic poetry in stylized Andalusi Arabic dialect, the *zajal*. He was even called the 'leader of the *zajal* makers'.[6] Ibn Quzmān lived under the dynasty of the Almoravids, who were not very interested in poetry. They came to power when, after the fall of Toledo (478/1085) and the battle of al-Zallāqah [Sagrajas] (479/1086), in 489/1096 Yūsuf Ibn Tashufīn deposed the last of the 'party kings' with their luxurious courts and their entourages of paid poets.[7] Yūsuf and his entourage are said not even to have spoken Arabic, let alone understand the subtleties of Arabic poetry. Thus the only audience to which the poets could turn were their own administrative class, which consisted of local authorities such as the chief *qāḍī* Abū Jaʿfar Ibn Ḥamdīn (d. 548/1153). Although Ibn Quzmān was not a wandering poet, he was sometimes obliged to seek the patronage of other dignitaries outside his native town, Cordoba. He often went to Seville and Granada, where he had his famous discussion and poetic exchange with the poetess Nazhūn (fl. 545/1150). His anecdote about Nazhūn already demonstrates his *mujūn* lifestyle.

This anecdote about Ibn Quzmān can be found in the *al-Ṭāliʿ al-saʿīd* by Ibn Saʿīd, from which the *Iḥāṭah* derives a passage.[8] It is about Ibn Quzmān during his visit to Granada, when he met several other poets in one of the gardens of the Banū Saʿīd in the little village of La Zubia [Zāwiya] near Granada.

> When the poetess Nazhūn saw him dressed in yellow, in the manner of the *faqīhs*, she exclaimed: 'How nicely dressed you are, golden calf of the Israelites! Only you do not make happy the people who look at you!' Ibn Quzmān replied: 'Perhaps I do not delight the people who see me, but in any case I will delight the people who hear me; it is your task to please the people that see you, whore!' Then inebriety came over Ibn Quzmān. The long and the short of it was that people, including lbn Quzmān, began to push one

[6] Colin (1971).

[7] Schippers (2008).

[8] Ibn al-Khatib, II, 504–5; Schippers (1993).

another away in the direction of the pond. Finally they threw Ibn Quzmān into the pond.

He came out in sopping wet clothes, and had swallowed a large quantity of water. He then said: 'Listen, o vizier!' and he recited:

1. ʾIh Abā Bakrin wa-lā ḥawla lī/ bi-dafʿi aʿyānin wa-andhāli//

Listen Abu Bakr, I have no force/ to push away prominent or insignificant people//.

2. Wa-dhāti jurḥin wāsiʿin dāfiqin/ bi-l-māʾi yaḥkī ʿāla adhyālī//

By the woman who possesses that wide vagina, which overflows/ with fluid, and resembles the tails of my garment!//,

3. Gharraqta-nī fi-l-māʾi ya sayyidī/ kaffir-hu bi-l-taghrīqi fi-l-māli//

You plunged me in water, o lord, pay for this by plunging me in your money.

The vizier ordered Ibn Quzmān to be stripped of his clothes and gave him fresh garments and presents, which suited him.

As a poet, Ibn Quzmān 'derided courtly love and portrayed himself as a bohemian, a reckless toper, a whoremonger and a sodomite (*khalīʿ*, *zānī*, *lawwāṭ*).'[9] His great enemies were the *faqīhs* (Islamic juridical functionaries), who were powerful dignitaries during the reign of the Almoravids, or better: his attitude is dubious because the person entitled *faqīh* can sometimes be the praised person, the dignitary, from whom he receives money, but at other times it is the moralist preacher who reproaches the poet for his lifestyle as a debauchee. Because of his frequent wine drinking, Ibn Quzmān was condemned to death by flogging, but he was saved by an Almoravid dignitary.

Most of his nearly 150 *azjāl* usually have between five and nine strophes, although some have as many as 40 or 42. The panegyric poems often have a light love or wine introduction, which replaces the old *nasīb* of traditional Classical Arabic poems; the second part is usually the proper laudatory part (*madīḥ*). Between the two there is a brief transition (*dukhūl*, *khurūj*, *takhalluṣ*).[10] Some have a more developed structure, such as poem no. 90, which includes the testament of a drinker who wants to be buried between grape vines (0–7); it then tells of a sexual liaison between the poet and a Berber girl, a section that also includes some realistic details (8–13), a quarrel between the poet and the girl's family (14–15), a *khurūj* (16–17) and a short laudatory passage (18–22). We will deal with this poem later.

Ibn Quzmān's *azjāl* do not contain *kharja*s or *marākiz* in Romance, but there are three occasions when he takes over *kharja*s in vernacular Arabic from the *muwashshaḥāt* of his contemporary, Ibn Bāqī (d. 545/1151). On the other hand, his *azjāl* contain many Romance words by themselves. His only *muwashshaḥ* is Allen Jones no. 579 from al-Ḥillī's *al-ʿĀṭil al-ḥālī*, which contains a *kharja* with some Romance words.[11]

In order to compare the *mujūn* motifs used by Abū Nuwās and Ibn Quzmān, respectively, I will discuss some characteristic poetic fragments by each of them more in detail, starting with Abū Nuwās. After that, I will draw some conclusions and make some comparisons.

One of the *mujūn* poems about a *ghulāmiyyah* – a shorthaired girl in male dress or tunic,

[9] Colin (1971).
[10] Nykl (1946), 266–301.
[11] Jones (1993), 194–195.

who looks like a *ghulām* or male servant – has already been partly translated by Ewald Wagner into German,[12] and by myself into Dutch.[13] In her paper on 'Arabic *mujūn* poetry' presented at the UEAI Congress at Utrecht University in 1990, Julie Scott Meisami partly quoted the poem in Arabic transcription and English translation.[14] I have picked some points from the translation by Julie Scott Meisami into English, in giving here the translation of the whole poem into English. This poem is to be found in Ghazzālī's edition of Abū Nuwās's *Dīwān*.[15] In the more recent edition by Wagner of Volume V of the *Dīwān*, the poem is to be found as *mujūniyyāt* no. 118.[16] This version has two extra lines at the end, lines 14 and 16. Line 3 in the new version has *kawākib* (stars) instead of *kawāʿib* (those with breasts).

Some readers may of course prefer the ancient reading *kawāʿib*, because the poet says that women ('those with breasts') are not his affair. This expression fits wonderfully in the context, because the poem belongs to the third subchapter of Abū Nuwās's *mujūniyyāt* devoted to the 'abominable attitudes of women and the praiseworthy behaviour of the beardless lads.' But it may be too easy to prefer the *lectio facilior*. However, the reading *kawākib* may suggest the real meaning *kawāʿib*. I will quote here from the poem from Wagner's edition (metre: *Ṭawīl*):

1. Wa-nāhidati th-thadyayni min khadami l-qaṣri/ muzarfanati -l-aṣdāghi maṭmūmati sh-shaʿri//
2. Ghulāmiyyatun fī zayyi-hā Barmakiyyatun / manāṭiqu-hā qad ghibna fī luṭufi-l-khaṣri //

A maiden with thrusting breasts, a servant in the palace,/ adorned with curled hair locks covering the temples and short-cropped hair//
A boy-like person, Barmakid[17] in her dress,/ her belts were invisible because of the thinness of her waist//

3. Kaliftu bi-mā abṣartu min ḥusni wajhi-hi/zamānan wa-mā ḥubbu-l-kawākibi min amri//
4. Fa-mā ziltu bi-l-ashʿāri fi kulli mash'hadin/ ulayyinu-hā wa-l-shiʿru min ʿuqadi -l-siḥri//

I was infatuated with her because of the beauty of her face that I saw. / Already sometime [I was in love with her], although love for the ones who have breasts is not my affair//
I made poem after poem on every occasion/ speaking kindly to her, because poetry is one of the magic arts//

5. Ilā an ajābat li-l-wiṣāli wa-aqbalat/ ʿalā ghayri mīʿādin ilayya maʿa-l-ʿaṣri//
6. Fa-qultu la-hā 'ʾahlan' wa-dārat kuʾūsu-nā / bi-mashmūlatin ka-l-warsi aw shuʿila-l-jamru//

Finally she answered my urgings to meet her and came/ unannounced to me on a late afternoon//
I said to her: 'Welcome' when the cups with wine cooled by the northern wind went around yellow-red as *wars* plants or burning coals that are lighted.//

---

[12] Wagner (1965), 175–176 and 177.

[13] Schippers (1990).

[14] Meisami (1993).

[15] Abū Nuwās, 1982, 264; Kennedy (2005), 47.

[16] Abū Nuwās, 1958–2006, V, 101–102.

[17] Barmakids or Barmecides, Persian-descended vizier family from Khorasan, so the meaning here is fatuous and pompous.

7. Fa-qālat '*asā-hā-l-khamru? Innī barī'atun / ilā –l-Lāhi min waṣli-l-rijāli maʿa-l-khamri'//
8. Fa-qultu ' -shrabī in kāna hādhā muḥarraman/ fa-fī ʿunuqī, yā rīmu, wizru-ki maʿ wizrī'//

She said: 'Is that perhaps wine? I am for God free from meeting men with wine.'/ I said: 'Drink. When it is forbidden, o little gazelle, may your fault as well as my fault come upon my neck.'

9. Fa-ṭālabtu-hā shayʾan fa-qālat bi-ʿabratin/ amūtu idhan min-hū wa-damʿatu-hā- tajrī//
10. fa-mā ziltu fī rifqin wa-nafsī taqūlu lī / juwayriyyatun bikrun ! fa-dhā jazaʿu-l-bikri//

Then I demanded something of her, and she said tearfully/ 'I shall die of it then!' as her tears flowed.//
I continued to be kind, because I said to myself: 'She is still a young girl, a virgin, this is the grief of a virgin.'

11. Fa-lammā tawāṣalnā tawassaṭtu lujjatan/ ghariqtu bi-hā, yā qawmu, min lujaji-l-baḥri//
12. Fa-siḥtu 'aʿin-nī, yā ghulāmu' fa-jāʾa-nī/ wa-qad zaliqat rijlī wa-lajjajtu fī-l-ghamri//

But when we had intercourse, I found myself in the midst of a bottomless sea, in which I drowned, o men, a sea of the deep seas.//
So I cried 'Help me, o boy', and there he came to me when my foot already slipped away, and I entered the full sea in its very depth.

13. Fa-law-lā siyāḥī bi-l-ghulāmi wa-anna-hū/ tadāraka-nī bi-l-ḥabli ṣirtu ilā l-qaʿri//
14. wa-ʿŪjiltu fī-hi bi-l-mamāti wa-khiltu-nī/ sa-albathu fī-hī ṭūla dahrī ilā-l-ḥashri//

And were it not for my cry to the boy, and his reaching me with the rope,/ I would surely have ended up in the depths.//
I would therein be given the death without respite and I imagined myself already/ that I had to stay there all my time left until the Resurrection on the Last Day.

15. Fa-ālaytu al-lā arkaba l-baḥra ghāziyan/ ḥayātī wa-lā sāfartu illā ʿalā ẓ-ẓahri//
16. ʿAjibtu li-man yaznī wa-fī-l-nāsi amradun/wa-qad dhāqa ṭaʿmu-l-bardi shiddata ḥarri//

Therefore I swore never again in my life to ride the seas when being on expedition,/and to travel only on the back//
I wonder about persons who commit fornication with women, as long as there exist beardless young men among mankind, especially when the sensation of coolness [of the kissing of these young men] tasted the heavy warmth//.

This poem is characteristic of Abū Nuwās on the following points. The drinking scene normally features several persons, among whom we find the pourer of the wine – a young male or female servant for whom the poet professes love. The accent is on love for young people. Male and female are sometimes interchangeable as symbolized by the *ghulāmiyyah*. In some poetry, the masculine grammatical forms can even be used when referring to a female. We see here the typical Abū Nuwāsian motif that he prefers men to women, sometimes expressed as preferring the back to the belly, or the images 'travelling over the sea' and 'travelling over the land' to indicate sexual intercourse with women and with men, respectively.

Another interesting poem in the same subchapter is no. 107 which has another important theme of the *mujūniyyāt*: namely the censor or censurer who reproaches the drinking and loving habits of the debauched poet and condemns his *mujūn* lifestyle (metre: Wāfir):[18]

---

[18] All the further references are from Abū Nuwās, 1958–2006, V.

1. A-ʿādhilu mā-shtafayta min-al-malāmi/ wa-lā tukthir malāmata mustahāmi//
2. A-ʿādhilu mā hajartu-l-kaʾsa yawman/ wa-lā qaṣṣartu fī ṭalabi-l-ḥarāmi//
3. Wa-lā –stabṭaʾtu nafsī ʿan mujūnin/ wa-lā ʿaṭṭaltu samʿī ʿan malāmī//

O censor! Are you not yet recovered from your reproaches? Do not multiply your reproaches of passionate lovers//
O censor! I never separate from my cup, even for one day!/ And I never fall short in my search for forbidden things!//
And I do not slow myself down in debauchery/ nor do I switch off my hearing from a reproach.

This poem expresses the poet's attitude, namely that he does not care about the censor's reproaches. He divides the world into 'good guys' [*kirām*], who have his sympathy [*ṣafāʾī*], and 'bad guys' [*liʾām*]. You can apparently immediately see that he is a 'good guy', as we see in line 6:

6. Matā mā talqa-nī yawman tajid-nī/ khalīʿan fī-l-majānati wa-l-ʿurāmi//

Whenever you meet me one day you will find me/ as a debauchee in shamelessness and ill-nature.//

In the rest of the poem there is an interesting portrait of a girl who is excellent at imitating the behaviour of a young, beardless male debauchee, but does not manage to hide the fact that she has a vagina. The passage begins as follows:

7. wa-shāṭiratin tatīhu bi ḥusni wajhin/ ka-ḍawʾi-l-barqi fi junḥi-l-ẓalāmi//
8. Raʾat ziyya-l-ghulāmi atamma ḥusnan/ wa-adnā li-l-fusūqi wa-li-l-athāmi//

And a mischievous girl,[19] who was proud of the beauty of her face/ which was as the light of lightning in the dark wing of the night//
Considered the dress of a young lad as more perfect in beauty/ and nearer to immoral life and sins.

In other poems the poet says explicitly that he is in love not with women, but with men. The pilgrimage to Mecca was always related to love affairs with women. He says in the last lines of the poem (metre: Khafīf):[20]

8. Lastu mimman/ yaṭūfu fī// ʿArafātin wa-lā Minā //.

I am not of those who make *ṭawāf* [the ceremonial procession] in ʿArafāt or Minā,

9. Arkabu-l-murda fī-l-diyā//ri wa-fī-l-mudni wa-l-qurā//

I ride the beardless young lads in the lands and the cities and the villages.

10. Fa-idhā-mā tamannaʿū// wa-'aṣaw, abdhulu –l-rushā //

And when they try to refuse and are rebellious, I will spend bribes [to try to get them to cooperate].

The theme of masculine love is overwhelmingly present in the *mujūn* poems by our poet. For instance, the poet starts poem no. 6 as follows (metre: Sarīʿ):

---

[19] Wagner (1965), 177–78, 'street girl'; see Wagner (1965), 212.
[20] Abū Nuwās, 1958–2006, Volume V , no. 4 [p. 5, 6].

1. Mā-stakmala – l-ladhdhatī illā fatan// yashrabu wa-l-murdu nadāmā-hu//

The joys are not complete without a lad who drinks while the beardless are his boon companions.

Wine drinking and love for boys are the poet's ideal, often uttered in a enumerative aphorism, such as in poem no. 7 (metre: Khafīf):[21]

1. Innamā himmatī ghazālun wa-ṣahbāʾu ka-l-dhahab//

My wish is only a gazelle, and red wine like gold//

2. Innamā-l-ʿayshu, ya akhī,// nayku khushfin mina-l-ʿarab//

Life, my friend, is only fucking a gazelle of the Arabs//

3. Aw sharīfin mina-l-ʿajam// wa-ẓarīfin la-hu adab//

Or a honourable person of the Persians, or a civilized person with manners//

Poem 8 (metre: Khafīf; p. 7, 8) also starts with an 'enumerative aphorism', which ends rather negatively for women:

1. Innamā himmatī ghulāmun wa-suʿlī wa-maṭlabī//

My wish, my demand and my pursuit is only a lad.

2. Ṭamiʿat fiyya khawdatun rubba rājin mukhayyabi//

A ripe woman was longing for me, but many a hoping person is frustrated!

3. Qultu lammā raʾaytu-hā: 'idhhabī, ukhtu, wa-ghrubī'//.

I said when I saw her: 'Go away sister, and depart'.

4. 'Uṭlubī lī muʾājiran wa-dhhabī anti qaḥḥibī'

'Find me a servant and go away, make yourself a prostitute.'

5. Lastu mā ʿishtu mudhkhilan iṣbaʿī ḥujra ʿaqrabi//

As long as I live I will not put my finger in the hole of a scorpion.

The poet also speaks about his female reproachers: in poem no. 9 [metre: *Wāfir*; p. 8]:

1. Dakhalna ʿawādhilī min kulli bābi Wa-lumna ʿalā –t-taladhdhudhi wa-t-taṣābī//

My female censors entered from every door, they reproached [me] because of [my] hedonist and childish behaviour;

2. wa-lastu bi-tārikin abadan hawāʾī wa-in aktharna jahlan min ʿitābī//

I shall never abandon my love even if they increase in the ignorance of reproaching me//

3. Hawāʾī tābiʿun fatkī wa-lahwī wa-kullu –l-lahwi fi sharkhi –sh-shabābi//

My love is following my greediness and my pleasure, and all the pleasures are in the bloom of youth.

And also in poem 16 we have the reproach: the poet tells us that he was reproached by a woman for preferring good looking lads and not having trysts with beautiful women. The poet answers (metre: Wāfir, line 3 sqq.):

[21] Curtius (1948), 499.

3. Fa-qultu la-hā: Jahilti fa-laysa mithlī yukhādiᶜ nafsa-hu bi-t-turrahāti.//

I said to her: You are ignorant, because a person like me is not deceiving himself with trifles.

4. A-akhtāru –l- biḥāra ᶜalā –l-barārī wa-ḥitānan ᶜalā ẓabyi-l-falāti//

Should I prefer seas over lands and fishes over the gazelle of the desert?

5. Daᶜī-nī lā talūmī-nī fa-innī ᶜalā mā takrahīna ilā-l-mamāti//

Let me do and do not blame me, but I will be like that until my death, whether you like it or not.

6. Bi-dhā awṣā Kitābu-l-Lāhi fi-nā bi-tafḍīli l-banīna ᶜalā-l-banāti//

This has the Book of God already ordered upon us, namely to give preference to the sons over the daughters.

The people who blame the poet always ask the poet to repent, but the poet refuses to repent in poem no. 17 (metre: Hazaj):

1. Yaqūlu l-nāsu: 'qad tubta', wa-lā wa-l-Lāhi mā tubtu//

People say: 'you have repented,' but no, by God, I did not repent;

2. wa-lā atruku taqbīla khudūdi-l-murdi mā ᶜishtu//

I will not cease kissing the cheeks of beardless lads as long as I live.

3. Arā –l-murda yamīlūna ilay-yā ḥaythumā miltu//

I see the beardless lads incline to me to where I incline.

4. wa-arjū baᶜdu yā rabbā-hu ghufrāna-ka in mittu//

I still hope for Your forgiveness when I die, o Lord!

The poet also describes his sexual liaisons with boys and how he seduces them, as we see in poems no. 14 and 15.

The descriptions of the lad in no. 14 (metre: *Sarīᶜ*; rhyme: – *tihi*; p. 13) are very conventional: the lad has a proud walk, looking like a stick in his slenderness; his teeth are pearls in his laughing mouth, musk is his smell. The poet struggles with him over a wine, cooled by the north wind and sparkling like lightning in its dazzling. He mixes the rest of the wine for the poet from what is left. Kisses, plucked from his cheek, are identified with the *nuql,* delicious dried fruits, which are eaten with wine. The poet wants the wine party to finally lead to sexual intercourse with the lad.

A kiss is also involved in Poem 15 (metre: *Wāfir*; rhyme: -*tihi*; pp. 13–14), using the lad's inadvertence at a certain moment. When he became drunk, the poet rose to undo the cord of the lad's trousers. 'Woe to me with him when he recovered from the abundant waves of his drunkenness. I see how he will kill me with one of the swords of the harshness [of his glances], especially now that I have changed the knot of the tie of his trouser cord.' Another sexual liaison with beardless young men in which the poet/lover unties their trouser cords is to be found in, for instance, poem 28 (pp. 22–24; *munsariḥ*; rhyme *du*) which has been translated by Philip F. Kennedy.[22]

[22] Kennedy (2005), 40–42.

Other motifs that occur in the *mujūn* poetry by Abū Nuwās are obscene pieces in which the poet describes the size or the behaviour of his penis. For example, in poem 10 (metre: *Ramal*; rhyme *-buh*, p. 9):

1. Inna li ayran khabīthan, lastu adrī mā ʿiqābu-h//
I have a wicked penis, I do not know what its punishment will be//

2. Kullamā abṣaru wajhan ḥasanan, sāla luʿābu-h//
Every time I see a beautiful face, its drivel flows.//

In poems 21 and 22 the poet describes the size of his penis in a hyperbolic way. This is an example from poem no. 21 (metre: *Rajaz*; p. 18):

1. Qultu li-ayrī idh abā an yarqudā//:
I said to my penis, when it refused to sleep:

2. 'Mā la-ka? Qad qumta qiyāman sarmadā'//
'What ails thee? Thou rose up with an eternal uprising.'

3. Anʿaẓa ḥattā qultu: jāza-l-Farqadā//
It rose up in such a way that I said: it passed the Pole Star

4. Aw yabtaghī ʿinda bni Naʿshin maqʿadan. //
If it did not want right away a seat at the stars of the Great Bear

5. Aw waʿada-l-jawzāʾa thamma mawʿidan//
Or make an appointment with the Gemini stars there

6. Tarā-hu fi-r-rakbi idhā asʿadā//.
I wonder how it is in riding when it makes a journey,

7. Niṣfan Tihāmiyyan wa- niṣfan munjidā//
half Tihāmī [at sea level] and half going up to the Nejd.

In the comment on this poem, we read: 'His (= the penis's) head reaches the Nejd while his lowest part of it is in Tihāma'. Both refer to places on the Arabian Peninsula.

Other motifs in Abu Nuwās's poetry are his pact with Iblīs (the devil), his debunking of the fasting month Ramaḍān, and the testaments or *waṣiyyah*s given to the debauched people by the poet.[23] We have a special article about Iblīs by Gregor Schoeler;[24] poems denigrating Ramaḍān and praising Shawwāl are a whole genre in Arabic literature and Geert Jan van Gelder recently published an article about it.[25]

To give an example of the Iblīs genre: in poem 11 (pp. 9–10; lines 16 sqq.; metre: *Sarīʿ*), he seduces the boy while drinking wine with the help of Iblīs, the devil who was originally punished because he behaved with too much haughtiness before Adam, the first man:

19. Sarat ḥumayyā-l-kaʾsi fī raʾsi-hi wa-dabbat-i-l-khamratu fī wajnati-h//
The wine of the cup travelled in his head, and while the red wine crept in his cheek ...

---

[23] Abū Nuwās (1958–2006) V: 199 ff.
[24] Schoeler (2001); Kennedy (2005) 43–47; Wagner (2012), 143–160 (*mujuniyyāt*).
[25] Van Gelder (2010/2011).

20. Mallaka-nī ḥalla sarāwīli-hi idh shaghalat-hu-l-kaʾsu ʿan tikkati-h//

He gave me the possibility of loosening his trousers, because the cup distracted him from his trouser cord ..

21. Fa-ṣāra lā yadfaʿu ʿan nafsi-hi wa-kāna lā yaʾdhanu fi qublati-h//

So that he no longer defended himself, whereas he used not to allow any kiss.

22. Dabba la-hu Iblīsu fa-qtāda-hu wa-sh-shaykhu naffāʿun ʿalā laʿnati-h//

Iblīs [the devil] crept for him and seduced him so that the old man was very useful in spite of his being cursed.

23. ʿAjibtu min Iblīsa fī tīhi-hi wa-ʿuẓmi mā aẓhara min nakhwati-h//

I was astonished by Iblīs because of his haughtiness and the size of what he showed [us] from his pride.

24. Tāha ʿalā Ādama fī sajdatin wa-ṣāra qawwādan li-dhurriyyati-h//

He was too proud to bow down before Adam and became the seducer of his offspring.[26]

The descriptions of these liaisons and sometimes the outer qualities of the boy, such as the nasal voice and effeminate speech, are characteristic.[27]

The obscene poems by Abu Nuwās lead to the conclusion that this poet prefers love for males above love for females, although he sometimes has an affair with a woman. An important element of his love poetry is the drinking scene. The drinking scene is also important in the work of the later Andalusian obscene poet Ibn Quzmān, but in his love affairs women are important as the object of love.

The poetry of Ibn Quzmān is composed for a large part in Andalusi Arabic dialect, especially the strophic poems or *azjāl* in his *Dīwān*[28]. My point of departure is his famous *zajal* no. 90, which has been translated by Monroe into English[29] and by García Gómez[30] and Corriente[31] into Spanish. I will analyse this poem and to sum up its characteristics and its *mujūn* inspiration.

The poem is to be found in the St Petersburg manuscript of the *Dīwān* that was published in facsimile at the end of the nineteenth century.[32] This is a unique manuscript. Only some fragments of the poem can be found in Arabic anthologies such as the one by a member of the Banū Saʿīd family, who were acquainted with the poet.[33]

Poem no. 90 contains some striking characteristics that we also find in the poetry of Abū Nuwās, but a great difference is the absence of the motif of preferring male lovers to female lovers. On the other hand, it has some striking resemblances in the flaunting of his *mujūn* lifestyle. Just like Abū Nuwās, the poet says that his lifestyle is *mujūn* by drinking wine and making love, and that he will never repent. He also comes up with a *waṣiyyah*

[26] Cf. Schoeler (2001), 45.

[27] Abū Nuwās (1958–2006), vol. V no. 18: 2; Wagner (1965) 182–183.

[28] For the Spanish Arabic dialect (andalusí): Corriente (1977), Corriente (1997a), Corriente (1997b).

[29] Monroe (1974) 260–273.

[30] Ibn Quzmān (1972), vol. 1: 464–471.

[31] Ibn Quzmān (1989), 181–184; Ibn Quzmān (1980), 598–609; Ibn Quzmān (1995), 284–290.

[32] Ibn Quzmān 1896.

[33] Ibn Saʿīd (1978), I, 167–177.

(testament) in connection with his drinking habits. Another difference from Abū Nuwās is, of course, Ibn Quzmān's strophic form and his dialectal language and the insertion of Romance words. But let us not forget that Abū Nuwās is seen by some as the forerunner of strophic poetry;[34] Abū Nuwās also has poems with insertions of foreign, e.g. Persian, words.[35] It is important that the metre of the *azjāl* must sometimes be reconstructed, which means that the long and short syllables must be determined each time in establishing the metrical shape of the verses. We occasionally used the Ibn Saᶜīd anthology to establish a better version of the verse than in the *Dīwān*.

The most interesting pieces at the beginning of the poem are about wine drinking. Poem 90 starts with the poet's statement about his life as a *mujūn* poet. He is and will remain a libertine who drinks wine and who does not want to repent [strophes 0 and 1]. The repeated word in Spanish 'bino bino' ('wine wine') is the expression for his sin. In the second strophe the poet stresses his oath to liberate his servant and to give his money to pious foundations, whenever he leaves the bottle aside. This is also stressed with the Spanish word *jarron*, which means 'big jar' and is a combination of Arabic *jarr* followed by a Romance 'augmentative' ending with '-on'. The third strophe also tells us about the poet's intention to drink from the early morning onwards. In the fourth strophe the poet wants his money to be spent on wine drinking. His clothes must be divided among the prostitutes, if he does not spend his money on wine drinking.

In the fifth strophe, he says that when he dies he wants to have an appropriate funeral and to be laid to rest in a vineyard between the grapevines with the leaves wrapping him as a winding sheet and a turban of vines around his head. In the sixth strophe, he hopes that a friend in evil and all his lovers stand up to keep the remembrance of him alive 'in sitting and standing'. Strophe 7 is another exhortation to have a drink from the greatest pitcher and to drink it in one go. The tone for the *khalāᶜah* and *mujūn* is set here. The poet does not have to repent, and at the end he professes his wine drinking with a *waṣiyyah* (testament).

90. And he also said – may God pardon him! – (metre: *khafīf*; XSLL/XLSL/LSL//):

0. nafni ᶜumrī/ fa'l-khankarah/ wa-l-mujūn//
Yā bayāḍi/ khalīᶜ badīt/ an nakūn//

I pass my life in dissoluteness and doing nothing.
What a lucky life for me. My endeavour was always to be dissolute.

1. innamā an/ natūba-'nā/ fa-muḥāl//
Wa-baqāʾī/ bi-lā shuray/bah ḍalāl//
Bīnu bīnu/ wa-daᶜ-nī mim/mā yuqāl//
Inna tark al-/khalāᶜah ᶜin/dī junūn//
That I would ever show repentance is unthinkable
Staying without a sip of wine would be a grave error for me.
Wine, wine! Let me in peace of whatever they say!
Because leaving my picaresque way of life, is foolishness for me.

2. Khādimī ḥur/ra māli li-l/-aḥbās//

[34] García Gómez (1956).

[35] Abū Nuwās, 1958–2006, V, 278 ff.

An-nahāra-l/-ladhī nuᶜaṭ/ṭal-al-kās//
Wa-ana-sqayt/ bi-ᶜullal aw/ jullās [khammās]//
An nuṣṣayyit/ illā ḥalqī/ la-l-jarrūn//

May my slave girl be freed, and my money paid to the pious foundations
On the day that I leave the cup in peace
And when no drinks are offered anymore to me in two- or five-fold fust
Because my throat can only be satisfied with the jar.

3. Ayya-alṭam/ bi-nā bi-dhā-l/-aqdāḥ//
Sukra sukra/ ay maᶜnā fi-/nā ṣiḥāḥ//
Wa-matā a/radtum u-l/-istibāḥ//
Anbahū-nī/ min awwali –l-/falaqūn//

O what I am thirsty for the wine cups
Drunkenness, drunkenness, what meaning has being sober for us?
And when you want to drink the morning drink,
Please, wake me before the morning watch.

4. Khudhu mālī/ wa-baddaduh/ fī sharāb//
Wa-thiyābī/ fa-faṣṣalū/ li-l-qiḥāb//
Wa-ḥlifū li /bi-anna rā/yī ṣawāb//
Lam nakun qaṭ/ fi dha-l-ᶜamal/ maghbūn//

You can take my money and spend it on drinks,
And take my clothes and distribute them to the whores
And you must swear to me that my view is just;
I was never deceived in doing so.

5. wa-idha mut/tu madhhabi/ fa-l-dafan//
Inni narqud/ fī karma bay/na-l-jafan//
Wa-tatammu-l/-waraq ᶜalay/ya kafan//
Wa-fi rāsī/ ᶜimāma min/ zarajūn//

When I die, my last will for the burial will be
To rest in a vineyard between the grapevines
And that the leafs wrap me like a winding sheet
And around my head a turban of vines.

6. wa-yuqīm ṣā/ḥī saw thumma/ kull wadūd//
Wa-dhkurū-nī/ ᶜalayh qiyām/ wa-qaᶜūd//
Wa-l-ᶜinab kul/li man akal/ ᶜunqūd//
Fa-yagharras/ fī qabriya l-/ ᶜarjūn//

May a friend in evil stand up and may stand up all [my] lovers
Keep the remembrance of me alive in sitting and standing,
And the grapes, everyone who eats a bunch of them,
Has to plant the vine tendril on my grave.

7. sirra-ka-l-ᶜā/lī ba-l-kabīr/ nasqīh/
khudh qaṭīᶜa-k/ wa-rfaᶜ li-fawq/ wa-mḥi-h//
Wa-niᶜam sir/ri mā tafaḍ/ḍalta bih//
Kullamā taḥ/kum at, ᶜalay/ya yakūn/

To your good health! Let us pour the greatest pitcher
Take your portion, raise your cup, and drink it in one go

Amenities of my health are what you are so kind to offer me.
Everything you decide, I will have to do.

The next passage deals with a liaison with a woman. *Mujūn* is also meant here. The passage ends with 'the day after', which forms a kind of *khurūj* (transitional passage) to the final part of the poem in praise of his patron. The anecdote about the Berber woman starts in strophe 8, in a kind of dialogue with someone: 'By God! Why for a change shouldn't we talk about a chick!' This encounter is described from strophes 9–10.

A dialogue format continues: 'We sat there, and I saw – by God! – coming with a diadem on top! A Berber woman! What a beautiful basket! Well, let us go there! She is not a basket with thistles'; 'Do not attack her harshly because she is not a sweetie.' This is continued in strophe 10 with a dialogue with the woman herself: 'Tell me, little girl, are you from fine flour or what are you made of?' 'I go home in order to sleep'; 'By God you were right in doing so.' Thereupon the poet says, supposedly to his penis: 'You stand up first.' It answers: 'No, you first' and the protagonist concludes: 'We will put the horns on her husband.'

Strophe 11 describes how the beautiful thighs of the woman arouse his sexual feelings. Strophe 12 describes the sexual act, as does strophe 13: 'I had already started – by God – with the job', followed by: 'I pushed something so sweet, so sweet as honey, and my spirit descended between her two hot legs.'

In strophes 14 and 15, the following morning is described: our protagonist is attacked by the people of the house, also with invectives and spoken language: 'It would have been good, had they not begun to quarrel during the day.' And after that they started to be riotous and argue: 'Take your hands off my beard, donkey!' 'Keep your hands off the pan of the toasts.' Strophe 15 describes the consternation as follows: 'One pulls out an eye and another slaps. One tears my clothes to pieces from me, the other seizes them, from the place to which I throw an unripe quince, nothing else but a stick comes towards my head.'

In the next two strophes (16 and 17), the protagonist realizes that the inhabitants of the house lack hospitality: 'These people are not my sort. This only leads to my humiliation. By God!, gentlemen, and by Sahli [his patron]! A similar humiliation is not a pleasure for me. My opinion is: when they look at you in a humiliating manner, there is no room for you in this city! This is not the manner of someone like Ibn Quzmān. For me such a place is no option.' It appears from the last strophes [18–22] that the only salvation comes from the Maecenas.

9. Naḥnu wa-l-Lāh/ julūs wa-jāt-/nā bi-tāj//
Fa-barbariy/[ya] wa-ayyi ḥusn/ min qināj//
Arra baᶜad/ las shayra min/ qirtāsh
Wa-l*a* tahjam/fa-lassi igh/rannūn//

We sat there, and I saw – by God! – coming with a diadem on top!
A Berber woman! What a beautiful basket!
Well let us go there! She is not a basket with thistles
Do not attack her harshly because she is not a sweetie

10. 'mawlatī, qul[36] /, darmak at aw/ eshant?'
'li-l-mabīt jayt'/, 'wal-Lāh la-qad/ aḥsant'//
Qultu: 'Qum ant'/, Qāl: 'Lā wa-l-Lāh/, illā ant'.
'Najᶜalū la-r/-rājil matā/-hā qurūn'//

'Tell me, little girl, are you from fine flour or what are you made of?'
'I go home in order to sleep' – 'By God you were right to do so.'
Thereupon I said [to my penis]: 'You stand up first'. He said: 'No, you first'.
'We will put the horns on her husband.'

11. Innamā-hu/ mā rayt [dhaka-t-/taḥti] sāq//[37]
Wa-dhika-l-ᶜay/nayna-l-milā/ḥ-ar-rishāq//
Wa-rafaᶜ ay/rī fi-s-sarā/wīl riwāq//
Wa-ᶜamal fi-th/-thiyāb bi-ḥāl/ qayṭūn//

Immediately after having seen her beautiful thigh
And those beautiful and handsome eyes,
My prick set up a tent in my trousers
And made my vestment a kind of pavilion.

12. fa-ka-mā rayt/ abnādaman/ mafrūsh
Arāda-l-farkh/ an yanṭamir/ fi-l-ᶜūsh
Ay tajī zay/gha bi-hādhi/ka-l-bulūsh
Ahnā in/sān yaqul liyya: 'ā-mujūn'

And when I saw that the creature was lying in the bed,
My chicken wanted to jump into the nest;
Where would be deviation with such vaginal hair?
Here a man says: 'this is *mujūn*'.

13. Ana wa-llah/ qad abtadayt fi-l-ᶜamal//
Awwadhā qad/ kharaj wa-hu/ qad dakhal
[*Variant*: Awadhaykā/ zalaq li-sā/ᶜat dakhal]//
Wa-na nadfaᶜ/ ḥuluw ḥuluw/ ka-l-ᶜasal//
Wa-kharaj rū/ḥi bayn saqay-/ha sukhūn//

I had already started – by God – with the job
It just came out and oh, it had entered already
[Variant: See, it slipped the moment it entered]
I pushed something so sweet, so sweet as honey,
And my spirit descended between her two hot legs.

14. Jid hu lawlā/ mā shātamū/ ban-nahār//
Thumma qāmū/ la-l-ᶜarbadhah/ wa-l-niqār//
Khalli yadda-k/ min laḥyatī/ yā ḥimār!/
Irmi inta –l-/ṭābiq matā –ṭ-/ṭushtūn//

It would have been good, had they not begun to quarrel during the day
And after that they started to be riotous and argue:
'Take your hands off my beard, donkey!'
'Keep you your hands off from the pan of the toasts'

---

36 Andalusi has no feminine for the second person singular.

37 I add from Ibn Saᶜīd, I, 175–176 the passage between brackets to make the metre plausible.

15. Hādha yaqlaᶜ/ jafan wa-dhā/ yalṭam//
Dhā yaqaṭṭaᶜ/ thiyāb wa-dhā/ yarzim//
Ay ma armī/ safarjalan/ ḥaṣram//
Lam yajī-nī/ <> li-rās*i*- <ghayr>/ bashṭūn//

One pulls out an eye and another slaps
One tears my clothes to pieces from me, the other seizes them
To the place where I throw an unripe quince
Nothing else but a stick comes towards my head.

16. hādha ᶜālam/lassan-hu min/shaklī//
Wa-kadhā yab/lugh ila ay/ dhullī//
Ana bAllāh/ yā qawm! wa-bas/-Sahli//
Las anā ᶜin/da dhāk bi-hā/dhā-l-hūn!//

These people are not my sort
This only leads to my humiliation
By God!, gentlemen, and by Sahli!
A similar humiliation is not a pleasure for me!

17. Inna rāyī/ yunẓar bi-ᶜay/ni-l-hawān//
Las yasaᶜ-kum/ fi dhī-l-madī/nah makān//
Ay ṭarīqah/ wa-mithla b*an*/ Quzmān//
Las yakūn ᶜin/dī mithl hadhā-l/-makīn//

My opinion is: when they look at you in a humiliating manner
Then a place for you in this city is not great!
This is not the manner of someone like Ibn Quzmān
For me there is no place for such a thing!

Especially in the description of the liaison with the woman lies the difference from motifs of Abū Nuwās. Here we have the poet's preference for women; there is no trace of Abū Nuwās's preference for young men. Ibn Quzmān stresses his sexual relation with a woman: his description is very explicit.

Let me mention some striking points from the other *azjāl* by Ibn Quzmān in the following. Just like Abū Nuwās, the Andalusī poet stresses that he does not want to repent for his *mujūn* behaviour. Ibn Quzmān reacts negatively in his poem no. 148 (metre: *majzūʾ al-ramal;* LSLL/ LSLL), a wine and love poem, when he is invited to repent by the *faqīh*, the Islamic preacher. The poem starts:

0. Asmaᶜ ash qal/-li –l-faqī: 'tub'// inna dhā fu/ḍūli aḥmaq//
Kif natūb wa-r-/rawḍa ḍaḥkah// wa-n-nasīm kal/-miski yaᶜbaq//

Hear how the *faqīh* says: 'You have to repent'. What a stupid intruder!
Why repent when the garden laughs and the wind is fragrant like musk?

The poem continues with a garden description and the poet's wish to drink wine, which here too is called by its Romance word, *bino.* In the sixth and last strophe he drops his own name Ibn Quzmān as a kind of self-praise with a magic explanation of his name as a form of *qasam* ['oath, asseveration, magic formula'] with its variant *qazma.*

The poet also does not want his dissolute colleagues to repent, as he reveals in poem no. 143 (metre: *madīd mabtūr*; LSLL/LL), which is a *mujūn* poem without known addressee.

0. Ḥaqqa khullāᶜ/ tubtum? Allah kān yak/fī-kum//
Sataraw dhā-n-/nawwār// ay sharāb yas/qī-kum//

Is it really true, drunken people, that you have shown repentance? May God help you.
You will see the 'flowers'[38] what a wine they will pour you!

There are, however, ascetic poems [*zuhdiyyāt*] in Ibn Quzmān's *Dīwān* in which the poet feigns to show repentance such as poem no. 147 [metre: *Basīṭ al-maqṭūᶜ*; XLSL/ LL/XLSL/L//], which has a kind of 'abandoned campsite' introduction, with following *ubi sunt* or *où sont les neiges d'antan* motif.[39]

0. Dār-al-ḥabīb/ mudh bān/ mahdūm la-l-/qāᶜ//
[LLSL/LL/LLL/L//]
ᶜalā ḥafī/r-ad-dār/ li-waddu narjaᶜ//
[SLSL/LL/SLSL/L//]

The house of the beloved, since he left, is destroyed to the bottom]
To the remnants of the house, because of my longing for him, I will return

1. Raḥal ᶜan-a-l/-mawṭan// man ḥān raḥī/lu-h//
Wa-d-dār qāᶜan/ ṣafṣaf// ka-dhā faṣī/lu-h//
Yarthī fi-hā-l/-qumrī/ 'alā hadī/lu-h//
Man faraq-al/-khillān// fayy khayra yaṭ/maᶜ//
Bal yanduba –l/-āthār/ mawḍiᶜ fi maw/ḍiᶜ//

The one whose time had arrived, went away from the dwelling place
The house is a deserted plain just as its enclosure
There the dove is lamenting his young
Who is left by his friends for which good he can desire?
He has to complain the remnants, place for place.

He then speaks about his own sufferings because of his lost world in strophe 4 and repents in strophe 5:

3. Ayn darba Ban/ Zaydūn// wayn-iḥtifā/luh//
Ayn ḥawmata-l/-jāmiᶜ// wayn jamā/luh//
ḥummil min al/-makrūh// fawq iḥtimā/luh//
Aqrub tara-h/ faddān// yuḥrath wa-yur/zaᶜ//
Wa-l-bāqiy-ash/tīpar/ li-l-qāma yuq/ṭaᶜ//

Where is the street of Ibn Zaydūn, that people frequently visited?
Where is the quarter of the mosque, where is its beauty?
It had to support more disgracefulness than it could bear.
Come nearer and you will see it has become land ploughed and cast with seeds
and the rest is steppe (*estepar*) high as the stature of a man.

4. ka-anni lam/ naḥḍur / dhīkal-majā/lis//
Māᶜ kulla mus/taẓraf/ malīḥ muwā/nis//

[38] The servants pouring the wine had apparently been nicknamed after flowers.
[39] The traditional elegiac motif of the deserted campsite of the tribe of the beloved is used here to express the motif of 'Ubi sunt qui ante nos fuere?' (where are the people who lived before in former times?), which also occurs in a poem by the medieval poet François Villon (where are the snows of former times?).

Yā fī ḥusna -z-/zīnah/ min-al-malā/bis//
Wa-n-naqri ba-l-/ʿīdān/ yufʿal wa-yuṣ/naʿ//
Wa-ṣawlata-l- /mizmār/ min barra tus/maʿ//

It is as if I was never present at these gatherings
With all the distinguished, beautiful and amiable people
What beautiful adornments of the garments!
When the sound of the lutes was made and produced.
And you could hear the noise of the flutes from outside.

5. Qad tāb Aban/ Quzmān// tubā-lu, in dām//
Qad kānat ay/yāmu-h/ aʿyād f-al-ay/yām//

Baʿda-ṭ-ṭabal/ wa-d-duff// wa-fatl al-ak/mām//
Min ṣumʿat al-/ādhān// yahbaṭ wa-yaṭ/laʿ//
Imām fi mas/jad ṣār// yasjud wa-yar/kaʿ//

Now Ibn Quzmān has repented himself, blessings for him, I just hope it will last
His days were feasts among the days!
Leaving behind drums and tambourine and the rolling back of the sleeves (in order to be ready to go to the dance)
From the minaret of the call to prayer he goes down and up
He has become an Imam in a mosque.

The poet feigns now to become as pious as an Islamic preacher or imam under the influence of the elegiac *Ubi sunt* motif. However, this is not his normal behaviour. He normally does not want to repent, and prefers a *mujūn* life, also in his taste for women.

The poet's love of women is clear from poem no. 145 (metre: *majzūʾ al-mutaqārib* SLX/SLX/SL//): the poet praises brown-skinned women:

0. Nirīd an/ naqūl lak/ khabar// ḥalāwah/ fi hawla-s-/sumar//

I want to say you one thing: sweet are those brown-skinned ladies

The poet says: brown is a noble colour, brown has some white and some black, like the breaking through of light at dawn; the poet is seduced by that colour of old wine; he is seduced by its shamelessness and its passion, which leads to death:

5. Futintu/ bi-amra –l/-mujūn//
Wa-ʿishqi/ bi-ḥāl-al-Manūn/
Wa-mā qad/dar al-Lāh/ yakūn/
Nafadh fiy/ya siḥra-l/-jufūn/
Nufūdh al-/qaḍā wa-l-/qadar/

I was seduced for the sake of shamelessness...
When my love passion was in the situation of Death
But what God decides, will happen.
The charm of the eyelids had an effect upon me
An effect like Fate and Predestination.

He finally mentions a lady called Umm Saʿd, and describes her haughtiness and his torment. There is furthermore no specific panegyric in this poem.

Poem 94 (metre: *khafīf*; XSLL/XLSL/LSL) is a poem of debauchery with the mention of Iblīs, the devil. The first lines go as follows:

0. Las hu ᶜandak/ qawām wa-lā hu falāḥ//
Ghayri shurb ash/-sharāb wa-ᶜish/q al-milāḥ//

For you it does not seem correct or useful/.....
... To do other things than drinking wine or loving beautiful women

1. Qad dakhal dhā-sh/-shahar wa-yā/ qad kharaj//
Wa-na ᶜāṭil?/ Laqad anā/ mundamaj!//
Min ghadā –n sha –l/-Lāh nabtadī/ fa-l-'iwaj//
ṭariq al-jid/di ghayr ṭuruq/ al-muzāḥ//

This month has started and has finished/
Why I was doing nothing of this kind of wrongdoing? I am disturbed in my mind!
From this morning, God willing, I will start with the wrongdoing.
The way of being earnest is different from the jest.

2. Narḍi Iblīs,/ ilā matā dhā-l-'uqūq?
Fa-hu shaykh saw,/ wa-law ᶜalay/ya ḥuqūq//
Wa-sh-shuraybah/ miftāḥ li-kul/li fusūq//
Fī lisānī/ narbaṭ dhak al/-miftāḥ//

I will satisfy Iblīs: until when this disobedience of him?
Because he is the old man of evil and has his rights on me
The little drink is the key to every sin;
I will tie this tongue with this key.

3. Ayyuha-n-nās/ waṣiyya hī la-l-jamīᶜ//
ṣīru khullāᶜ/ fa-inniya-l-/yawm khalīᶜ//
Wa-la tamshū/ illā bi-kās aw qaṭīᶜ//
wa-sukārā/ ayyā-k la tam/shū ṣiḥāḥ//

To you all people, I will give this order:
You have to become debauchees, as I am today
Do not go on your way without bottle or cask ...
And be drunk, it is no use to be sober.

Here the old man or the devil is apparently the one who encourages the poet to indulge in drinking. There is also an order or testament that gives directives for the way of life of the poet. The antagonist of the devil in these situations is the *faqīh*, the Islamic preacher or juridical authority. Even a lawyer and juridical specialist such as the famous al-Ghazzālī could not keep him away from the wine, as he says in poem no. 22 (metre: *mujtathth*; XLSL/XSLL/XSL//):

4.Yakhshā-l-faqīh/ kulli man lā /yadrub//
Ana nawaq/qar faqīh aw /nahrub//
Jaqjaqtu um/m alladhī lā /yashrub//
Law kān ᶜalā/ rāsiya-l-Ghaz/zālī//

Only the inexpert is afraid of the preacher
I have no respect for a *faqīh* nor do I try to escape him
I would throw shit over the mother of the one who does not drink
Even if al-Ghazāli [the super *faqīh*] was standing before me.

In poem no. 23 (metre: *Ṭawīl* SLL/SLLL/SLL/SLSL//), which is about wine drinking and dissolute life, the poet wishes to be vintner and an Islamic preacher at the same time, after having said that he does not like preachers at all:

4. Ay ma kān/ wazīr bi-qur/bu naqrub//
Wa-in rayt/ faqīh, naqūm/ wa-nahrub//
Wa-kulli/ jamāʿatan/ la tashrub//
Las naqrub/ anā dhik-al/-jamāʿah//

I come near to a vizier wherever I find him,
But from the preacher I stand up and run away
Because all the people who do not drink,
I do not approach this kind of people.

5. Faqī an/ khammār min rū/ḥī naʿmal//
Fa-las kit/takūn ʿimā/ma ashkal//
In lam al/qa qālis al/qa juljal//
Tara-h am/si dīk wa-l-yawm/ qubāʿah//

I want to make of myself a wine-selling preacher.
I would not bear the most elegant turban
When I do not find a cap, I will find in any case bells hung on my neck.
You see it (the red cap) yesterday as a cock and today as (the feathers of a) hedgehog.

So apparently when he does not find the gown and cap of a judge, he at least does not hesitate to look like a clown.

Many anecdotes about Abū Nuwās and Ibn Quzmān point at their lives as debauchees. Both were thrown into jail because of their behaviour. The censor plays a significant role in the poetry of both men. Both poets generally manifest no repentance, although they sometimes say they hope for the Lord's forgiveness. In Ibn Quzmān's *Dīwān* we find an ascetic poem with the motif of repentance. Here, the poet abandons his role for a while, but how long does it last? Ibn Quzmān's *Dīwān* contains so many *mujūn* motifs that it remains comparable with Abū Nuwās's *mujūniyyāt*. Both have poems, sometimes starting with enumerative aphorisms, mentioning love objects and wine when professing their debauched desires.

What is different, however, is the outspoken affirmation by the poet Abū Nuwās with regard to his predilection for male love with lads described by some outer qualities, such as a nasal voice and effeminate speech. There are descriptions of the poet untying his lad's trouser cord and other descriptions of liaisons with boys, which in a way stand for his *mujūn* lifestyle, but are different from Ibn Quzmān's *mujūn* behaviour. Abū Nuwās also likes descriptions of penises and their hyperbolic dimensions. His penis 'reaching to the stars' is far more of an exaggeration than Ibn Quzmān's dialogue with his penis in poem no. 90.

Abū Nuwās several times uses the expression 'travelling over sea' or 'going over land' for female and male sexual intercourse, respectively. In his wine scene there is often a role for the female pourer in the drinking scene who wants to behave like a male (a *ghulāmiyyah*). In Abū Nuwās's poetry, there are even women who reproach him for his love of males. Abū Nuwās is negative towards love during the pilgrimage to Mecca, since love affairs during the pilgrimage are normally with women. In Ibn Quzmān's poetry is there is no special propaganda for love of males; instead, he extolls *mujūn* [sexual liaisons] with women, such as in poem no. 90, and his preference for brown ladies in another poem. Particular to Ibn Quzmān is, of course, his strophic form; the insertion of romance words, and the fact that he coins his own dialectal Arabic as his poetic language. However, he remains in the framework of reference of classical Arabic literature. Abu Nuwās and other Classical Arabic poets are sometimes even mentioned as literary references.

Both poets feign the same kind of relationship with Iblīs, the devil, who supports the poets in their evil. In Ibn Quzmān's poem no. 143, the poet speaks about the devil as the 'old evildoer' whom the poet invokes as a patron protector of the dissolute people. See also poem 90 (strophe 6) for this concept, and poem 94 (strophe 2). The theme of Shawwāl and Ramaḍān, a whole genre in Abū Nuwās' poetry, also plays a role in Ibn Quzmān's poetry. In poem no. 13, a poem dedicated to Abū Yūnus ibn Mughīth, also called Washqī, it is said that the new moon of Shawwāl, which concludes the fasting month Ramaḍān, made someone exclaim 'Allahu Akbar' when he saw it.

The *waṣiyyah* genre does occur in both poetries: Abū Nuwās's ninth subchapter of his *mujūniyyāt* (poem 191 sqq.; pp. 199 ff) is dedicated exclusively to *waṣāyā* giving advice about a life of debauchery, mostly in the form of imperatives. The *waṣiyyah* par excellence by Ibn Quzmān is, of course, the testament of the poet as a wine drinker in poem no. 90, but occasionally he gives advice in the form of *waṣiyyah* in his other poems.

The fact remains that although Ibn Quzmān sometimes mentions Abū Nuwās in passing in his poems, he has other inspirations and predilections in his practices of *mujūn* in lifestyle and in composing *mujūn* poems.

BIBLIOGRAPHY

Abū Nuwās (1982), *Dīwān*. Ed. A.A. Ghazzālī, Beirut.

Abū Nuwās (1958–2006), *Dīwān* [*Dīwān Abī Nuwās*], vols. I–V, eds. Ewald Wagner and Gregor Schoeler, Wiesbaden/ Beirut/ Berlin: Franz Steiner, and Klaus Schwarz.

G.S. Colin, (1971), 'Ibn Kuzmān', EI2, III, 849–852.

Federico Corriente, (1977), *A Grammatical Sketch of the Spanish Arabic Dialect Bundle*, Madrid: Instituto hispano-àrabe de cultura.

Federico Corriente, (1997a), *A Dictionary of Andalusi Arabic*, Handbuch der Orientalistik 29, Leiden/ New York: Brill.

Federico Corriente, (1997b), *Poesía dialectal árabe y Romance en Alandalús*, Madrid : Gredos.

Ernst Robert Curtius, (1948), *Europäische Literatur und lateinisches Mittelalter*, Bern: Francke.

EI2= *Encyclopaedia of Islam* (1960–2005), Leiden, etc.: Brill (1960 2005).

G.J. van Gelder, (2010–2011), 'Poets against Ramadan', *Quaderni di Studi Arabi*, nuova serie 5–6, 103–119.

E. García Gómez, (1956), 'Una "pre-muwaššaḥa" atribuída a Abū Nuwās', *Al-Andalus* 21, 406–414.

Lisān al-Dīn Ibn al-Khaṭīb, (1974), *al-Iḥāṭah fī Akhbār Gharnāṭah*, Ed. Muh. Abd. 'Inan, Cairo: Khanji.
Ibn Quzmān (1972), *Todo Ben Quzman*, ed. Emilio García Gómez, I–II–III, Madrid: Gredos.
Ibn Quzmān (1989), *Cancionero andalusí*, trad. Federico Corriente, Madrid: Hiperión.
Ibn Quzmān (1995), *Dīwān* [ibn Quzmān al-Qurtubi]= *Iṣābat al-Aghrād fī Dhikr al-Aʿrād*, ed. Federico Corriente, Cairo: Arabic Language Academy.
Ibn Quzmān (1980), *Dīwān*, ed. Federico Corriente, Gramática, Métrica y texto del cancionero hispanoárabe de Aban Quzman, Madrid: Instituto hispanoàrabe de cultura.
Ibn Quzmān (1896), *Dīwān*, Éd. Günzburg, baron David, *Le divan d'Ibn Guzman; texts, traduction, commentaire, enrichi de considérations historiques, philologiques et littéraires sur les poèmes d'Ibn Guzman, sa vie, son temps, sa langue et sa métrique ainsi que d'une étude sur l'Arabe parlé en Espagne au VIe s. de l'Hégire dans ses rapports avec les dialects Arabes en usage aujourd'hui et avec les idiomes de la péninsule Ibérienne*, édition facsimile, Berlin: S. Calvary & Co.
Ibn Saʿīd (1978), *al-Mughrib fī ḥulā al-maghrib*, ed. Shawqi Ḍayf, Cairo.
Alan Jones, (1993), 'Index of Andalusian Arabic Muwaššaḥāt', *Studies on the Muwaššaḥ and the Kharja*, eds., Alan Jones and Richard Hitchcock, Reading: Ithaca Press.
Philip F. Kennedy, (2005), *Abu Nuwas: A Genius of Poetry*, Oxford: Oneworld.
Philip F. Kennedy, (1997), *The Wine Song in Classical Arabic Poetry: Abū Nuwās and the Literary Tradition*, Oxford: Clarendon Press.
Julie Scott Meisami, (1993), 'Arabic *Mujūn* Poetry', *Verse and the Fair Sex: Studies in Arabic Poetry and the Representation of Women in Arabic Literature*, ed. Frederick de Jong, Utrecht: Houtsma Stichting, 8–30.
James T. Monroe, (1974), *Hispano-Arabic Poetry: A Student Anthology*, Berkeley.
A.R. Nykl, (1946), *Hispano-Arabic Poetry and its relations with the Old Provençal Troubadours*, Baltimore.
E.K. Rowson, (1998), '*Mujūn*', *Encyclopedia of Arabic Literature*, eds. Julie Scott Meisami and Paul Starkey, London–New York: Routledge, II, 546–548.
Arie Schippers, (1990), '"On-islamitische" uitingen in de Klassiek Arabische literatuur', *Sharqiyyāt* 2, 4, 324–351.
Arie Schippers, (1993), 'The Role of Women in Medieval Andalusian Arabic Story-Telling', *Verse and the Fair Sex: Studies in Arabic Poetry and the Representation of Women in Arabic Literature*, ed. Frederick de Jong, Utrecht: Houtsma Stichting, 139–152.
Arie Schippers, (2008), 'The Role of Heroes in Medieval Historical Narrative: New Light on the Battle of al-Zallâqah', *Continuity and change in the realms of Islam: studies in honour of Professor Urbain Vermeulen*, eds. K. D'hulster and J. van Steenbergen (Orientalia lovaniensia analecta, 171), Leuven: Peeters, 567–582.
Gregor Schoeler, (2001), 'Iblīs in the poems of Abū Nuwās', ZDMG 151: 1, 42–62.
Gregor Schoeler, (2010/2011), 'The Genres of Classical Arabic Poetry: Classifications of Poetic Themes and Poems by Pre-Modern Critics and Redactors of Diwans', *Quaderni di Studi Arabi*, nuova serie 5–6, 1– 48, especially 25–30.
Ewald Wagner, (2012), *Abū Nuwās in Übersetzung: eine Stellensammlung zu Abū Nuwās -Übersetzungen vornehmlich in europäische Sprachen*, Wiesbaden: Harrassowitz.
Ewald Wagner, (1965), *Abū Nuwās: Eine Studie zur arabischen Literatur der frühen 'Abbasidenzeit*, Wiesbaden, Franz Steiner.
Ewald Wagner, (2008), *Abū Nuwās in der Nebenüberlieferung: dem Dichter zugeschriebene Gedichte und Verse*, Arabische Studien Bd 2, ISBN 9783447058025. Wiesbaden: Harrassowitz.

6

The *Ayrīyāt* of Abū Ḥukayma (d. 240/854): A preliminary study

Nefeli Papoutsakis

Abū Muḥammad Rāshid b. Isḥāq b. Rāshid al-Kātib, known as Abū Ḥukayma,[1] was an Abbasid secretary and amateur poet who flourished in the first half of the 9th century. His fame rests on a series of poems, the *ayrīyāt* (poems on the *ayr* = penis), in which he laments his impotence. Due to their subject-matter the *ayrīyāt* have so far been shunned by most Arabists with the exception of two Arab scholars, Najjār and Aʿrajī, who edited them and offered useful introductions to the poet and his surviving work. Certainly, the primary intent of this humorous poetry was to amuse and draw a laugh, but its intense parody of traditional poetic themes and conventions suggests that it was also meant to satirize the repertoire and pomposity of contemporary court poetry and perhaps also to comment on the status of non-professional poets.

THE POET AND HIS DĪWĀN

Information about Abū Ḥukayma is sparse.[2] He was probably born at Kūfa – hence the *nisba* al-Kūfī, found in some sources[3] – and presumably was of non-Arab origin, for there is no mention of his being descended or affiliated to any Arab tribe. As can be gathered

---

[1] *Pace* Sezgin (*GAS* 2:577–8), Najjār (*ŠAM* 3:299–309, 5:23–84) and Weipert (*CAPP* 166), who vocalize Ḥakīma, the correct vocalization is the one adopted by Aʿrajī, the *Dīwān*'s editor, i.e. Ḥukayma – on the evidence of Ibn Aydamir's autograph of *al-Durr al-farīd* (1:185v) as well as Ṣafadī (*al-Wāfī bi-l-wafayāt*, 14:59, where he expressly says: *bi-ḍammi l-ḥāʾ*) and Kutubī (*ʿUyūn al-tawārīkh*, 269; *Fawāt al-wafayāt*, 2:15), who copies Ṣafadī. Brockelman (*GAL* S1:123) vocalized both Ḥakīma and Ḥukayma and even allowed Ḥalīma, a corrupted form found in some sources. No explanation is given for this sobriquet.

[2] See Aʿrajī's introduction to the *Dīwān*, 17–20 (all references are to Aʿrajī's third edition).

[3] cf. *Dīwān*, 18, note 1. Ṣafadī (ibid.) and Kutubī (ibid.) give the *nisba* al-Anbārī. Aʿrajī speculates that his family may have originally been from Anbār and subsequently moved to Kūfa. In his *al-Shiʿr fī l-Kūfa mundhu awāsiṭ al-qarn al-thānī ḥattā nihāyat al-qarn al-thālith*, *passim*, he presents Abū Ḥukayma as a Kufan poet representative of the literary tradition of that city.

from a poem in which he grieves over the atrocities of the civil war between al-Amīn and al-Maʾmūn, he was at Baghdad during that period (196–8/812–3). He subsequently served for a time as secretary to al-Maʾmūn's general ʿAbdallāh b. Ṭāhir, whom he seems to have followed to Egypt (211/826–7) and then to Khurāsān.[4] During al-Maʾmūn's reign he repeatedly lampooned the caliph's advisor and great *qāḍī* Yaḥyā b. al-Aktham (*qāḍī l-quḍāt* of Baghdad from 202/817–8 to 218/833), whom he accused of pederasty and corrupting public mores.[5] Towards the end of al-Maʾmūn's reign (217–8/832–3?) we find him in the entourage of the future vizier Muḥammad b. ʿAbdalmalik b. al-Zayyāt, with whom he reportedly was closely befriended.[6] Most likely he spent the rest of his life either at Baghdad or at Samarrāʾ employed as a state secretary.

Even less is known about his personal life. A romantic story about his love for Jullanār, a slave-girl and poetess owned by his sister, is recounted by Abū l-Faraj al-Iṣbahānī. After some hesitation Abū Ḥukayma eventually bought the girl, relinquishing his share of an estate inherited from his father, and they lived happily ever after.[7] Abū Ḥukayma is said to have died after a short illness on his way to perform the pilgrimage to Mecca in 240/854.[8]

The overtly humorous tone of the *ayrīyāt* suggests that he was not impotent (not that it matters, of course). According to Ibn al-Muʿtazz, he was one of those poets who presented themselves as the exact opposite of what they actually were: although he claimed to be impotent, in reality even a billy-goat would fall short of his sexual stamina.[9] Regarding the origins of the *ayrīyāt*, we are told that Abū Ḥukayma started composing them while in the service of ʿAbdallāh b. Ṭāhir, so as to rebut the latter's suspicions that he was having an affair with a *ghulām* of his.[10] But, as Aʿrajī rightly objects, if this were the case, a few poems would have sufficed to convince Ibn Ṭāhir. Their large number suggests that, whatever his reasons for initiating the series, they met with great success and this induced him to subsequently devote most of his work to this subject.[11] Thus, we hear for instance that he

4 This assumption is based on a *khabar* regarding the origins of the *ayrīyāt* and on Abū Ḥukayma's poems dispraising Egypt (see below).

5 Masʿūdī, *Murūj al-dhahab*, 4:318–9. On Ibn al-Aktham, who was again appointed to that post under al-Mutawakkil during the years 237–40/851–5, see C.E. Bosworth's article in *EI2*.

6 See *Ṭabaqāt al-shuʿarāʾ*, 389–90, on an exchange of verses between the two men after Ibn al-Zayyāt's return from the pilgrimage. cf. Yāqūt, *Irshād al-arīb*, 4:203–4.

7 *al-Imāʾ al-shawāʿir*, 211–2. The *khabar* makes clear that the girl predeceased the poet.

8 *Irshād*, 4:204 (no date given); *ʿUyūn al-tawārīkh*, 269 (his death dated in 240 H.); *Fawāt al-wafayāt*, 2:19 reads *baʿda l-arbaʿīn wa-miʾatayn.*

9 *Ṭabaqāt*, 308 (on the authority of Ibn Abī ʿAwn al-Madīnī, a certain *faqīh*); cf. another version of this *khabar* in Ibn Khallikān, *Wafayāt al-aʿyān*, 3:79. A third version, on the authority of Mubarrad, is found in Ḥamza al-Iṣbahānī's recension of Abū Nuwas's *Dīwān* 4:7–8. For a second *khabar* to the same effect (sexually overactive, Abū Ḥukayma supposedly left a caliphal slave-girl pregnant), see *al-Durr al-farīd*, 1:185v.

10 On the authority of Ibn al-Marzubān: *Irshād* 4:203; *ʿUyūn al-tawārīkh*, 269; *Fawāt al-wafayāt*, 2:15. Thaʿālibī (*Thimār al-qulūb*, 226) names Isḥāq b. Ibrāhīm al-Muṣʿabī (chief of Baghdad police, 213–35/828–49) instead of ʿAbdallāh b. Ṭāhir.

11 Aʿrajī (*Dīwān*, 20–2) suggests that Abū Ḥukayma developed this theme because he could not compete with poets such as Abū Tammām and Buḥturī in the domains of 'serious poetry' (*sabīl al-jidd*).

once recited an *ayrīya* to the literate general Abū Dulaf al-ʿIjlī,[12] whereas another *ayrīya* was addressed to an unnamed caliph. Still during the life-time of Abū Tammām (i.e. prior to 845–6), Abū Ḥukayma reportedly discontinued this practice and vowed never to compose an *ayrīya* again, although until then he had regarded the theme as his private preserve. This was because Aḥmad b. Abī Ṭāhir Ṭayfūr recited to him an ode he had composed on the same subject, which Abū Ḥukayma obviously deemed could not be surpassed in poetic excellence. Henceforth Abū Tammām used to greet Ibn Abī Ṭāhir as 'the one who made Abū Ḥukayma repent from his misery' (*fa-kāna Abū Tammām yaqūlu baʿda dhālika: 'Yā mutawwibi Abī Ḥukaymata min shaqāʾihī kayfa ḥāluka?'*), a statement which, as Aʿrajī suggests, may well betray Abū Tammām's jealousy of the success and popularity of Abū Ḥukayma's *ayrīyāt*.[13]

In his *Thimār al-qulūb* dealing with proverbial phrases, Thaʿālibī included an entry on *ayr Abī Ḥukayma*, which expression, he says, had become proverbial, the poet's penis being as infamous as the *ṭaylasān* of Ibn Ḥarb, the fart of Wahb [b. Sulaymān b. Wahb], the donkey of Ṭayyāb and the ewe of Saʿīd – all of which were just as paroemial and had been the subject of similar series of defamatory poems.[14] As attested by Kushājim's quatrain quoted by Thaʿālibī in that same entry, the above-mentioned *khabar* on Ibn Abī Ṭāhir and the numerous pieces on impotence preserved in the much latter work *Maʿāhid at-tanṣīṣ*, Abū Ḥukayma found numerous imitators.[15]

The *ayrīyāt* make up the bulk of Abū Ḥukayma's *dīwān*, which survives only partially in a *unicum* manuscript first published by Ibrāhīm Najjār in his *Shuʿarāʾ ʿAbbāsīyūn mansīyūn* (partial edition) and then by Muḥammad Ḥusayn al-Aʿrajī (third corrected edition, 2007).[16]

---

[12] Ibn Ṭabāṭabā, *ʿIyār al-shiʿr*, 124; Marzubānī, *Muwashshaḥ*, 238: in both works the incident serves as an example of unseemly or inauspicious openings. Abū Dulaf, supposedly offended by the poem's opening line (*a-lā dhahaba l-ayru lladhī kunta taʿrifu*), retorted: *ummuka kānat taʿrifu*. But in reality this is not the opening line, but the second hemistich of v. 7 of poem 26 (p. 99), addressing a mock-railer.

[13] *Ṭabaqāt*, 416; *Dīwān*, 22–3. For a translation and discussion of this passage see Sh. Toorawa, *Ibn Abī Ṭāhir Ṭayfūr*, 36–7.

[14] *Thimār al-qulūb*, 225–7, 361, 602; cf. *Yatīma*, 3:3. The series of epigrams on the *ṭaylasān* of Ibn Ḥarb and the ewe of Saʿīd are by the 9th-century Basran poet al-Ḥamdawī (on him see J. van Ess, *Der Ṭailasān des Ibn Ḥarb*; A. Arazi, 'Thèmes et style d'al-Ḥamdawī'). The poems on Ṭayyāb's frail donkey are by the otherwise unknown poet Abū Ghalāla al-Makhzūmī (*ŠAM* 4:273–7; *Thimār* 366–9). Poems on the fart of Wahb were composed by several poets, including Buḥturī and Ibn al-Rūmī (*Thimār* 206–9; R. McKinney, *The Case of Rhyme Versus Reason*, 150, note 78; see also E. Wagner's contribution to the present volume).

Indeed, in *Zahr al-ādāb*, 2:176, Ḥuṣrī uses most of these expressions in a series starting with *ajmaʿu li-l-ʿuyūbi min...* to describe a boring person (*thaqīl*).

[15] al-ʿAbbāsī, *Maʿāhid*, 3:195–7. It is interesting to note, however, that al-ʿAbbāsī, who mentions these pieces on impotence in his note on Ibn al-Ḥajjāj, quotes only an excerpt from an *ayrīya* by Abū Ḥukayma (ibid., 3:197) without even mentioning his name. See, further, two poems in *Yatīma*, 2:334–5 (by al-Mufajjaʿ al-Baṣrī) and 4:382–3 (by ʿAbdallāh b. Ismāʿīl al-Mīkālī), and three pieces by Ṣafī d-Dīn al-Ḥillī in his *Dīwān* (ed. Damascus 1880), 570–2. The references given here are not exhaustive; they only aim at showing the subsequent growth of the theme.

[16] Aʿrajī refers to Najjār's first edition of *ŠAM* (Manshūrāt Kullīyat al-Ādāb, al-Jāmiʿa al-Tūnisīya, 1990, unavailable to me). His own first edition (Damascus: Dār Wahrān) was published in 1993, and the second (Köln: Al-Kamel Verlag) in 1997.

Aʿrajī's complete edition comprises sixty-six poems, forty of which are *ayrīyāt*[17] (no *ayrīya* is found in the *Dhayl*, which contains seventeen more poems and fragments culled from *adab* works). Apart from another three *mujūnīyāt*, the remaining poems include five lampoons on Ibn al-Aktham, six *ghazal*-poems, three pieces dispraising Egypt, two *marthiyas* and a few poems on other subjects;[18] worth special mention are his humorous lampoons on his servant (no. 55, pp. 131–2, and *Dhayl*, nos. 1, 14, pp. 145, 154–5).

THE AYRĪYĀT

Classical Arab authors view the *ayrīyāt* as *marthiyas* on the poet's *ayr* and typically say of Abū Ḥukayma that 'he bewails his thing' (*yarthī matāʿahū*). Najjār published them in the fifth volume of his thematically arranged *Shuʿarāʾ ʿAbbāsīyūn mansīyūn*, which is devoted to elegies. The volume documents the many new uses which the elegy was put to, whether jocular and parodistic, as in the case of the *ayrīyāt* and at least some of the laments over animals, or serious, as in the case of laments over cities. In fact, the poet himself describes his poems as *marāthī* (see especially 2/1–6/46–7[19]). This is not to say that his intent was to parody the elegy. His irony was rather directed at a whole range of themes and conventions of traditional Arabic poetry and in this respect he clearly followed in the footsteps of Abū Nuwās and the earlier Kufan poets.[20]

The *ayrīyāt* are rather freely built and vary in length and structure. There are sixteen short pieces, up to eight verses long, the remaining twenty-four poems ranging between eleven and fifty lines.[21] Broadly considered, they fall into two types: a) declamatory or non-narrative poems, which is the largest group, and b) narrative poems, which are few in number and cannot be viewed as *marthiyas*.

Let us first look at the former type. Non-narrative *ayrīyāt* normally combine two kinds of utterances: a) lament or complaint of the present sad predicament of the penis and

---

According to Aʿrajī's calculations, the surviving corpus represents around a third of the poet's output (according to the *Fihrist*, his *dīwān* was seventy folios long). The manuscript is much damaged by moisture and worms and many verses are difficult to read.

[17] I have excluded from this series no. 31 (pp. 105–6), a four-liner in praise of the poet's penis and virility, which as such sticks out of the group. This poem is also attributed to Bashshār b. Burd and is most probably his (see Abū Ḥukayma's *Dīwān*, 105, note 5). Despite their name, Abū Ḥukayma's *ayrīyāt* are about impotence, not about the *ayr* in general.

[18] The *Dhayl* contains seven more *ghazal*-poems, a few lampoons and some occasional pieces.

[19] In references to Abū Ḥukayma's *dīwān* the first number indicates the no. of the poem, the second the verse/s in that poem and the third the page/s where the poem/passage is found (the numbering of poems and verses is mine).

[20] On Kufan poets and their licentious poetry, see C.A. Nallino, *La littérature arabe*, 221–32; Y. Khulayyif, *Ḥayāt al-shiʿr fī l-Kūfa*, *passim* (on *mujūn*: 591–642) and the study of Aʿrajī mentioned above, note 3.

On parody in Abū Nuwās, see J. S. Meisami, 'Abū Nuwās and the Rhetoric of Parody'.

[21] Twelve poems are 2–5 verses long; five pieces are 6–8 lines long; nine poems are 11–15 lines long; 16- to 20-lines-long: four poems; 22- to 30-lines-long: four poems; 31- to 38-lines-long: four poems; one 50-liner. Average poem length: 13 verses.

dispraise of it and b) recollection and praise of its former prowess and potency. As a rule the poem opens with the lament, which is of varying length and is followed by the recollection, which also varies in length.[22] Very often a second mostly brief lament[23] and/or a couple of mock-gnomic verses on the vicissitudes of Time conclude the poem. In the short pieces, however, the recollection of happy times is regularly omitted altogether or confined to one or two verses at the poem's end.

Very rarely (in only five poems) a few introductory verses precede the lament. In 1/1–8/41–2 and 19/1–5/78–9, Abū Ḥukayma complains about the vicissitudes of Time, in whose destructive effects he sees the signs and warnings of God; in 18/1–4/72–3 and 20/1–7/83 he urges himself not to cry over those departed nor over the remnants of deserted abodes, but rather on the sad state of his penis; whereas in 26/1–7/98–9 he recounts an exchange with a mock-*ʿādhil* who blamed him not for indulging in amorous adventures and licentious activities but, on the contrary, for abandoning and shunning them (*yalūmu ʿalā rafḍi l-ṣibā wa-yuʿannifū*).

The following poem (no. 5, *Dīwān*, pp. 54–6), often quoted in *adab* works, was presumably one of Abū Ḥukayma's hits. It starts with the dispraise of the penis (vv. 1–6), followed by the recollection of its past glory (vv. 7–10), which is put into the mouth of Sulaymā. Sulaymā or Salmā stands for the wife or a lover of the poet and appears in several *ayrīyāt* either in the context of the lament or of the recollection: she complains or wonders at the penis's languidness that thwarts all her attempts to arouse it and she remembers (or is reminded by the poet of) her past happiness and the penis's exploits. In this poem after recalling the past, in her turn Sulaymā bemoans the present state of the penis and blames it on the mishaps of Time (vv. 11–13).

1. When every cock's valour is lauded, my cock's cowardice refuses to let it be praised.
2. At a league's distance it flees wary of the army; how much more when the army draws near!
3. It slugs betwixt beautiful women, shirking from what consummates the revel of the brethren of joy.
4. It sleeps on the palm of the young woman's[24] hand; and when it [infrequently] moves, the hand fails to perceive it.
5. Like a two-day-old chick that raises its head to its parents but is instantly overtaken by weakness (variant: but weakness instantly makes it to fall).
6. It coils over the testicles like a rope wound up at the top of a well.
7. When decay affected it and the days' vicissitudes hit it, said Sulaymā:
8. If it's now thin and flaccid, its grip was once hard in its taker's hand,
9. on the morning when it'd hasten to strike with a head out of stone, with no lesions or horns.[25]
10. When I so wished, it met me with straightened surface and pointed head like a sharp-edged spear-head.

[22] The recollection precedes the lament in only two poems (no. 8, pp. 59–61, and no. 17, p. 72).

[23] Rarely, however, the second lament is longer than the first, as, e.g., in 2/17–29/48.

[24] *Fatāh* can also mean 'slave-girl'.

[25] This is of course very ironic and implies that due to his impotence the poet has now become a cuckold.

11. Why do I now see it plummeted[26] like one drunk whom unmixed wine has caused to recline?
12. It finds it hard to rise to [satisfy] a need and even if it rose, neither limb nor flank would obey [*lit.* follow] it.
13. Ever since I saw it bowed, my life has turned turbid. All things limpid are turned turbid by Time's mishaps.

The first two verses, on the *ayr*'s lack of courage and valour, its cowardice and eschewal of battle, evidently refer to sexual intercourse, as does v. 3. Both in the lament and in the recollection, but mostly in the latter, sex is routinely referred to as war (*ḥarb, waghā, waqʿa, qitāl, liqāʾ, ṭiʿān*). As we shall see, recalling the past, the poet praises the penis's former martial prowess, its many conquests of well-fortified places and its intrepid nightly attacks (*tabyīt*) and predatory raids (*ghārāt*) on lovers/adversaries (*aqrān*) who willingly succumbed, prostrating themselves to their faces. A fleeting reference to this theme is found here in Sulaymā's monologue (vv. 9–10) where the healthy roused penis is, as usual, compared to a powerful weapon – its glans, stone-hard, resembled a spear-head. On the contrary, in the lament the penis is said to cowardly shirk from fight (e.g., 6/5/57, 8/6–7/60, 13/6/66, 15/10/69, 22/18/90 *jubn*), be routed and shamefully flee away from beautiful women (e.g., 22/8/89 *tuwallī l-ghāniyāti qafā laʾīmin talīqu bihī l-hazīmatu wa-l-firārū*; cf. 1/21–24/44; 2/20–21/48; 22/10–13/89 avoiding Sulaymā). Alternatively, as in 5/3, it is said to shun pleasures and fun, to abandon delights and debauchery, to part company from the bands of joy and to desert the places of revel (e.g., 1/15/43, 3/10/50, 4/9/52, 15/12/69, 19/18/81).

As in 5/4, the poet very often alludes to the vain attempts of his lover/s to arouse him with caresses and kisses (e.g., 2/27/48, 9/6/61, 15/13/69, 18/7–9/73, 19/20/81, 20/7/83, 20/12/84, 22/3/88), which frustrate and embarrass them both. Sloth, sluggishness, languor and lifelessness are frequently attributed to the penis (*kaslān* 24/4/94; *mayt* 20/14/85, 24/4/94; *ṣubba ʿalayhi kaslun dāʾimun* 4/8/52), which sometimes, as in 5/11, is said to be as if drunk, dizzy or 'stoned' (17/4/72, 22/5/88). But sleep (*nawm*) is what is mostly imputed to it. Hence the quasi-formulaic openings of many poems: *ayyuhā l-ayru tanabbah...* (nos. 9, 10, 61), *tanabbah ayyuhā l-ayru l-naʾūmū...* (no. 13) / *l-mudallā...* (no. 22). The poet is exasperated by the penis's long sleep (e.g., 9/4/61, 10/1/63, 19/14/80, 22/1/88), which he thinks is abjectness and ignominy (3/1/49 *dhullun wa-hūnun*), disaster (4/4/51 *iḥdā l-muṣībāt*), incurable disease (20/11/84 *dāʾun lā dawāʾa lahū*), remissness and baseness (13/3/66 *fashalun wa-lūmū*) that brings shame on him (9/7/62 *ʿār*; 22/1/88).

In this poem Abū Ḥukayma concentrates on the penis's inability to rise and its imperceptibly faint movements (cf., e.g., 11/5/64, 14/2/67, 22/7/89; *lā ḥarāka bihī*: 18/4/73, 19/5/79, 20/7/83), which he illustrates by means of the chick comparison. This theme is taken up again by Sulaymā in 5/12, where, as is often the case, the penis is personified: even if it wished to rise, its body would fail it.

The comparison of the penis to a well-rope (*rishāʾ*), as in 5/6, is quite common (3/19/50, 15/14/69, 26/14/100); the image of the coiled rope seeks to specifically convey how it lies

[26] *Ḍāribān bi-jirānihī*. The expression *alqā jirānahū bi-l-arḍi* is typically applied to exhausted camels that stretch out their necks upon the ground out of extreme fatigue.

bent and inert upon the testicles. The somnolent member that dozes on its balls (14/3/67 *tawassada iḥdā bayḍatayhi wa-nāmā*; cf. 6/2/56) or is glued on them (36/3/110 *mulṣiqun jildata ḫuṣyayhi ilā farwati ra'sih*; cf. 8/7/60) is elsewhere likened to a tired courier from Damascus [on his way to ʿIrāq] resting over his saddle-bags (17/5/72), to an old man sitting on his saddle-bags (8/11/61; cf. 1/17/43 a traveller), or simply an old man weighed down by age (18/11/73).

It is worth pausing here, to look at some of the faults typically ascribed to the *ayr* in the lament – as the poet himself repeatedly says, it is impossible to enumerate all its blemishes. The list of items which the flaccid penis is compared to is long – suffice it to mention a few: the wetted thong of a water-skin (20/12/84 *sayru l-idāwati lammā massahū l-balalū*; cf. 35/5/109); a piece of skin soaked by the rain (18/5/73 *jildatun qad massahā l-maṭarū*; cf. 7/5/58); a wet rag squeezed of its water (42/4/116 *khirqatun ʿuṣirat bi-mā'ī*) or a loosely hanging hem (9/11/62 *ka-l-hudbi l-mudallā*). It is lax like the unstringed bow of a carder (19/11/80 *qawsu naddāfin bi-lā watarī*; cf. 18/8/73) and bent like a polo-stick (3/20/51, 26/17/100 *ṣawlajān*), a curved cucumber or the handle of a ewer (27/7/102 *quththātun muʿaqqafatun aw ʿurwatun rukkibat fī ra'si ibrīqī*), the letters *nūn* (1/13/43, 3/20/51) and *dāl* (4/7/51, 23/9/93), or a hag bent with age (19/10/80 *mithla l-ʿajūzi ḥanāhā shiddatu l-kibarī*). It became thin (5/8/55, 29/4/104 *daqqa*) like the string of a whirligig (27/6/101 *zīqun yulaffu ʿalā duwwāmati l-zīqī*), yielding and soft like tender leguminous plants (24/3/94 *baqla*). Another such graphic and much quoted piece is the following couplet (no. 33, p. 107):

1. So thin of grip, it is as if my penis were a sac (*kharīṭa*) emptied of books,
2. Or a lean coiled snake that has placed its head on its tail.

The penis's shrinkage is such that it is often said to have almost vanished and become invisible, as in 16/1–6/70–1 where the poet discusses its disappearance with Sulaymā (cf. 18/12–13/74, 19/17/81, 21/1/87). It is no more visible than an effaced letter (19/7/79 *yakhfā ʿani l-ʿayni ḥattā mā ushabbihuhū illā bi-khaṭṭi kitābin dārisi l-atharī*). Once it would fill up the palm of a young woman's hand, now it can pass through a ring (30/11/105). Time destroyed it piecemeal (4/25/53) leaving nothing but what resembles erased remnants of Bedouin encampments, obliterated marks and traces (16/8/71 *wa-lam yubqi minhū l-dahru illā maʿāliman balīna kamā tablā l-rusūmu l-dawāthiru*; 4/27/53 *mithlu baqāyā ṭalalin dārisin dāthiri aʿlāmin wa-āyātī*; cf. 13/5/66, 19/8/79, 20/13/84).

Along with the many picturesque similes, there are simple, factual descriptions of the *ayr*'s decadent state: it is weak, slack and its nerves are worn out (24/2/94 *ḍaʿīfu l-matni raththu l-quwā*; 24/7/95 *mustarkhiyan*; cf. 4/2–3/51; 19/10/80 *taʿaqqafa wa-starkhat mafāṣiluhū*; 18/4/73, 16/3/70). Time reduced it to a tiny bald head amidst wilted skins and veins (4/26/53 *fa-lam tadaʿ minhu siwā ṣalʿatin bayna ʿurūqin wa-julaydātī*; 19/6/79).

Abū Ḥukayma often refers generally to the *ayr*'s innumerable faults (24/6/95 *kam min ʿuyūbin fīhi lam uḥṣihā*; cf. 19/16/81, 22/19/80, 23/10/93, 28/6/103) and ignominies (3/21/51 *khazāyāka*), as well as to its present uselessness (12/1/65 *ayyuhā l-ayru l-qalīlu l-manfaʿah*, 11/1/64 *qalla nafʿuhū*, 6/1/56 *laysa yanfaʿu*; cf. 6/4/57, 10/2/63), and declares that, were it not for urination, he would gladly cut it off (42/5/116); whereas in 8/12/61 he expresses the wish – were this possible – to buy a new penis at any cost. He practically has no penis

(35/2/109 *laysa lī ayrū*), as he confesses to a group of women who scold him for ignoring them. His penis is living-dead (e.g., 3/4/49, 20/14/85, 22/21–22/90, 39/1–2/112) and no resurrection is hoped for (32/7/106). The poet tried to keep its faults secret, but in vain – all secrets are eventually disclosed (2/30/48 *katamtu ʿuyūbaka ḥattā maliltu wa-kam yustaru l-ʿaybu aw yankatim*; 22/20/90). Dispraised and eschewed by people (2/10/47; 13/1/66 *madhmūmun malūmū*; 11/1/64 *kam tudhammu wa-kam tushkā*), his *ayr* has become a story (30/1/104 *ṣirta uḥdūthatan*). Once a paragon of nobleness (1/9/42 *ʿuḍwan ilayhī tanāhat ghāyatu l-karamī*), it has shifted from its virtuous mores and qualities (1/15/43 *ḥāla ʿan ṣāliḥi l-akhlāqi wa-l-shiyamī*) to the lowliness of the wronged (2/7/47 *ʿalayka stikānatu man qad ẓulim*).

On the whole, Abū Ḥukayma's attitude towards the *ayr* varies considerably through the corpus. At times he expresses sympathy for it (3/2–3/49 *...inna hammī bi-hammihī maqrūnū...*; 39/3/112), recognizes that the fault is not its own but rather Time's (3/5/49 *ayyuhā l-ayru lam takhunnī wa-lākin khānanī fīka raybu dahrin khaʾūnū*) and seeks to acquit it. Hence, in 16/11–13/71 or 19/24/82 he defends it against Sulaymā who belittles it, the typical excuse adduced in its favour being that everybody succumbs to Time (e.g., 2/9/47, 2/31–32/48–9, 5/13/56). On the other hand, he sometimes is so dismissive of it and his dispraise is so fierce that it verges on lampoon; nos. 37, 40 and 42 (pp. 110, 114 and 115–6), in which Abū Ḥukayma gives vent to his anger for the penis's shaming him, are genuine invectives.

On the contrary, in the recollection the penis is presented in all its past glory. Hard and solid, as if out of iron or stone (5/9/55, 9/16/62, 19/21/81), it stood like a lighthouse (3/6/49, 4/21/53, 9/15/62 *manāra*) or a minaret (12/4/65 *ṣawmaʿa*[27]), admired by all (3/6/49 *tasmū ilayhi l-ʿuyūnū*). It protruded beneath the poet's clothes like a peg (4/23/53 *taḥta thawbī watadun nātī*; cf. 24/3/94, 30/8/105), so that, had you seen him walking, you would think he had recently been circumcised (3/7/50 *rubba yawmin rafaʿta fīhi qamīṣī fa-kaʾannī fī mishyatī makhtūnū*). Sometimes the penis is likened to a mallet (4/23/53 *mirzabba*), a pillar supporting the pulley of a well (27/10/102 *baʿḍu ajdhāʿi l-zarānīqī*), a pole or column that the poet could hardly bear (24/9/95 *athqaltanī kaʾannanī aḥmilu baʿḍa l-ʿamad*). But most typically it is compared to weapons: a cudgel (18/14/74 *hirāwa*) or a big, smooth and straight club (24/11/95 *ʿaṣan ḍakhmatun malsāʾu mā fī qaddihā min awad*; cf. 27/11/102); an iron mace or rod (26/13/100 *ʿamūdu ḥadīdin*), a spear (18/14/74, 22/15/90 *rumḥ*), a javelin (24/15/96, 24/19/96 *ḥarba*; cf. 27/11/102 *amḍā ʿalā l-ṭaʿni min baʿḍi l-mazārīqī*: referring to the glans), or a polished and sharpened sword (26/10/99 *maṣqūlu l-dhubābayni murhafū*; cf. 30/10/105 stronger in battle than a lion and more penetrative than a sharpened sword).

This is because, as said above, the central theme of the recollection is the penis's sexual exploits, which are always presented as grand-scale military encounters and conquests[28] – in fact in some cases, as in 20/25–6/86, you get the impression that what Abū Ḥukayma is describing is an orgy. In these lively battle-scenes the penis advances proudly, boldly

[27] *Ṣawmaʿa* normally means a monk's cell or the pointed roof thereof, or the pointed hillock on top of the *tharīd*. But it can also denote a minaret.

[28] Very seldom is sex presented as a ride: in 17/1–2/72 and, in warring context, in 20/23–24/86 and the *mujūnīya* no. 25 (pp. 96–8). The recollection of quatrain 61 (p. 139) praises the penis's prowess in attacking drinking-companions after their having fallen asleep, i.e. in a symposial context.

and unswervingly, displaying indomitable courage and stamina and wreaking havoc on the lovers/foes. The following passage, which forms part of the recollection of poem 4 (pp. 51–3), is perhaps as good a specimen of such war memories as any (p. 52):[29]

10. It shuns war as if it had not been a champion of nightly attacks and predatory raids;
11. As if – in time past – it had not blindly plunged into glorious battle-fields,
12. Battle-fields whose folk knew it for its sense of duty (*muḥāmāh*) and strength (*ṣidq*),
13. Bravely and proudly attacking the peer on the morning of battle,
14. Prostrating on their chins [foes] that fell down obediently, of their own accord;
15. They did not complain of their wounds nor feared death.
16. You heard from beneath it the longing of voices and breaths;
17. You would liken it to a rancorous avenger retaliating upon heinous crooks.
18. Once it was easy for it to storm castles well-fortified
19. And fortresses that could only be reached after ventures and perils.

As in 4/10–13, the grandiose scale of the encounter is conveyed by means of traditional clichés used in descriptions of devastating wars, such as 'when a stubborn war was kindled among armed warriors' (3/11/50 *idhā mā saʿarat bi-l-kumāti ḥarbun zabūnū*), or 'on how many a brave fighter have your grinding mill-stones not revolved in the rigours of battle?!' (3/13/50 *kam ṣadūqi l-liqāʾi dārat ʿalayhī fī ghimāri l-waghā raḥāka l-ṭaḥūnū*), or 'you have long brought brave warriors down' (12/5/65 *ṭāla mā jaddalta fursāna l-waghā*). The penis is adorned with all the typical attributes of a fighter: it is courageous (18/33/76 *shujāʿ*; cf. 36/5/110), vigorous and valiant (2/11/47 *dhī najdatin*; 16/9/71 *najdan ʿinda l-ḥarbi*), a boldly advancing and victorious hero (8/6/60 *miqdāman ʿalā l-ḥarbi*; 19/28/82 *miqdāmatan baṭalan muʾayyadan fī l-waghā bi-l-naṣri wa-l-ẓafarī*), reckless and stubborn in battle (12/2/65 *jamūḥan fī l-waghā*; 8/5/60 *lā yazdādu illā ṣuʿūbatan*), reliable and penetrative in its affairs (19/26/82 *takashshafu l-ḥarbu minhu ʿan akhī thiqatin māḍī l-ʿazīmati ʿinda l-wirdi wa-l-ṣadarī*), awe-inspiring and much dreaded (27/8/102; 36/5/110 *yuttaqā waqʿu mirāsih*) – the verb routinely used for its advances being *taqaḥḥama* or *iqtaḥama* (e.g., 2/11/47, 6/9/57, 8/3/60; 12/5/65). It fearlessly plunged into the dreads of the heart of the battle at a time when the terrified coward shunned it (6/6/57 *a-lam tarkabi l-ahwāla fī ḥawmati l-waghā idhā mā taḥāmāhā l-jabānu l-murawwaʿū*; cf. 20/18–20/85, 20/25/86, 26/9/99); it rose and encountered all alone, brave and resolved, a whole army of fucking (8/2/59 *yathūru fa-yalqā ʿaskara l-nayki waḥdahū liqāʾa ṣadūqi l-baʾsi mujtamaʿi l-qalbī*). With its help the poet used to indiscriminately assault warriors, attendants and servants (1/28/45 *yā rubba ʿaskari aqrānin aghartu bihī ʿalā l-akābiri wa-l-atbāʿi wa-l-khadamī*). As in 4/17, because of the ferociousness of its attacks it is frequently likened to an avenger, the objection normally being made that its victims were guiltless (2/12/47 *tashuddu ʿalā ghayri dhī iḥnatin fa-tasṭū bihī saṭwata l-muntaqim*; 2/14/47 *ṣarīʿin tuṭālibuhū bi-t-tirāti wa-lam yajni dhanban wa-lam yajtarim*; cf. 8/4/60).

The wounds it inflicted on prostrated lovers were often unhealable (2/15/47 *kulūman ʿalā l-dahri lam taltaʾim*; 1/33/46 *wa-bayna fakhdhayhi jurḥun ghayru multaʾimī*). Nonetheless, once they overcame their initial fears and gave up resistance, lovers enjoyed and ended up loving the act (3/16–17/50), whereas some of them, fearless right from the start, did

[29] Compare, e.g., 1/27–36/45–6, 2/11–16/47–8, 3/11–17/50, 6/6–10/57, 8/1–5/59–60, 20/15–26/85–6, 24/15–19/96, 26/9–12/99–100.

not feel any pain (2/16/48) nor did they complain (4/15). The lovers – as implied, both boys and women – were typically difficult to access, jealously defending and keeping their private parts safe (3/15/50 *wa-ṣarīʿin abaḥta minhu makānan kāna yaḥmīhi marratan wa-yaṣūnū*; 8/5/60 *kullu mumtaniʿin ṣaʿbī*). They were noble, even royals (27/12/103 *min kulli biṭrīqatin minhum wa-biṭrīqī*; 20/23/86 *wa-markabin min nitāji l-mulki ghādarahū baʿda l-ṣiyānati wa-l-ikrāmi yubtadhalū*), surrounded by guards and attendants (20/22/86 *dhī sharafin mumannaʿin ḥawlahū l-anṣāru wa-l-khawalū*), but occasionally also by nannies who wished they could ransom them (1/33/46 *khallaytahū tatafaddāhū khawāḍinuhū*). As in 4/18–19, the penis often had to storm inaccessible strongholds and forts (3/14/50, 6/9/57, 18/27–28/75), but it also went down *wādīs* and dungeons of pleasure (12/5/65 *wa-taqaḥḥamta maṭāmīra l-hawā fa-ʿarafta l-ḍīqa minhā wa-l-saʿah*; 19/27/82). Obviously all these places stand for the lovers' private parts, *wādīs* and dungeons for female genitals in particular.

Representations of sexual intercourse in terms of a battle or conquest are common in world literature and derive from the much broader and common idea of love as war.[30] But Abū Ḥukayma's obsession and elaborate treatment of the theme calls for an explanation – all the more so as the metaphor of love as war was not all that common in Arabic poetry; far more widespread was the idea of the beloved as killer.[31] Abū Ḥukayma's obvious irony and parody of the conventions of earlier as well as contemporary heroic poetry suggest that he shared the anti-war sentiments occasionally voiced in the work of early Abbasid poets. Ewald Wagner has long ago drawn attention to the anti-war poetry of Abū Nuwās,[32] whose influence on Abū Ḥukayma is noticeable in other domains as well. In a similar vein Abū Nuwās presented the revelling party as a campaigning host and depicted their alternative, pacifist warfare, which consisted in shelling and bombarding each other with flowers and fruits, using their hands as bows, and slaying and then bringing back to life by means of excellent wine. Most famous in this respect is his *mujūnīya* no. 167 (*Dīwān* 5:168–9), which has been translated and discussed repeatedly.[33] But there are numerous other poems and excerpts in the relevant *mujūnīyāt* subsection[34] bringing out his anti-war feelings (e.g., nos. 165, 169, 176, 181–3) or in which he depicts his carousals as battles (in

---

[30] For sex as war in ancient Greek literature, see J. Henderson, *The Maculate Muse: Obscene Language in Attic Comedy*, 169–73; in Greek and Latin literatures, K. Preston, *Studies in the Diction of the Sermo Amatorius in Roman Comedy*, 50–52. Generally on love as war: A. Spies, *Militat omnis amans: Ein Beitrag zur Bildersprache der antiken Erotik*, *passim* (on sex, in particular: 36–8, 73–8; see also Spies's pertinent remarks on the popularity of the metaphor of love as war in Augustan times, 72–3); E. Kohler, *Liebeskrieg: Zur Bildersprache der hoffischen Dichtung des Mittelalters*, *passim*.

[31] For instance, al-Aʿshā calls his beloved Qatla or Qutayla (see his *Dīwān*, index), whereas al-Farazdaq warns his own beloved that his sons will retaliate upon her for his being slain by her and will not accept blood-money instead (see his ode 111, ed. Boucher). Hence especially in Abbasid *ghazal*-poems the beloved was often described as possessing an array of deadly weapons. On the beloved's cruelty cf. T. Bauer, *Liebe und Liebesdichtung*, 450–1; on the beloved's weaponry in Persian poetic imagery, see H. Ritter, *Das Meer der Seele*, 368.

[32] E. Wagner, *Abū Nuwās: Eine Studie zur arabischen Literatur der frühen ʿAbbāsidenzeit*, 134–5.

[33] See the many references in E. Wagner, *Abū Nuwās in Übersetzung*, 151.

[34] Ḥamza al-Iṣbahānī grouped Abū Nuwās's anti-war poetry in the same subsection of the *mujūnīyat* in which he placed pieces ridiculing traditional poetic themes such as the lament over the deserted encampment etc.: see Abū Nuwās's *Dīwān* 5:163–98.

addition to no. 167, see nos. 168, 173–5, 177). In *mujūnīya* no. 211, from a different *mujūnīyāt* subsection, using the persona of a dissolute religious scholar, Abū Nuwās recommended making peace with the infidels and pronounced instead making love to their boys and girls as the most effective way to fight them and indeed a most holy war. An anti-war stance had previously been adopted by the Kufan poet Abū Dulāma (d. *ca.* 778), the jester-poet of as-Saffāḥ, al-Manṣūr and al-Mahdī, who was eager to evade partaking in military campaigns. Various versions survive of a *khabar* narrating how he managed to avoid fighting a belligerent Khārijī when he was prompted to do so by a military commander.[35] To judge by the many odes lamenting the atrocities committed in the civil war between al-Amīn and al-Maʾmūn, one of which, as said above, is by Abū Ḥukayma (no. 52, pp. 126–8), anti-war poetry seems to have gained momentum during that period.[36] It is thus conceivable that one of the strands of thought that went into the creation of the series of the *ayrīyāt* was the wish to criticize the militarism of the Empire and especially ridicule the pompous celebration of war in contemporary court poetry.

Many non-narrative *ayrīyāt* are composed as apostrophes to the penis. Ten out of the sixteen short pieces and five longer poems apostrophize the penis throughout; in two more cases (nos. 3 and 24, pp. 49–51 and 94–6) the apostrophe takes up most of the poem but is preceded by a few verses that do not address the penis.[37] The following piece (no. 9, pp. 61–3), which apostrophizes the penis throughout, was obviously well-liked by Ibn al-Muʿtazz who quoted it in his note on Abū Ḥukayma in the *Ṭabaqāt*. The emphasis here is on the shame it brings on the poet and the disappointment it causes to his lovers.

1. O cock, wake up! The young gazelle has taken off its [his/her?] clothes!
2. How shall I excuse myself now that you lie with it [him/her?] skin to skin!
3. Information about incited cocks is revealed at encounters.
4. O you heavy-headed one that slumbers all night and all day,
5. Using the skin of its testicles as a wrapper against the cold![38]
6. [You] who won't move aught to benefit its stirrer!

[35] See the various versions of the account in M. Ben Cheneb, *Abū Dolāma*, 20–22, 47–55, 105–6. In one version the commander is Marwān b. Muḥammad, the last Umayyad caliph, and the poet is said to have shamefully fled the battle-field. In the other, more elaborate versions, the commander is Rawḥ b. Ḥātim al-Muhallabī, governor of Basra under al-Mahdī; thanks to his humour and wit the poet manages to come to terms with the Khārijī and/or the commander.

[36] The poems have been collected and published by Najjār in *ŠAM* 5:127–70, 177–82.

[37] Apostrophe is also used in nos. 27 and 36. No. 27 (pp. 101–3), a 13–liner, apostrophizes a woman throughout: the poet prompts her to betray lovers, warns her not to be duped by his flirting and explains how things stand with his penis. No. 36 (pp. 109–10), a 5–liner, opens with an apostrophe to *maʿshar al-nās*. Two poems, nos. 16 and 35 (pp. 70–1 and 109), are pseudo-dialogical in form; they open with the précis of a question (16/1–2/70) or reproof (35/1) addressed to the poet (in 16/1–2 Sulaymā enquires about the penis's disappearance, in 35/1 a group of women blame the poet for neglecting them); his reply, in the usual way of moan and recollection, takes up the rest of the poem.

[38] Similarly, in 4/5/51, the penis lies chilled in the summer like one who freezes on a cold winter night (cf. 22/6/89); in 10/4–5/63 it is likened to an old woman plagued by cold weather. On the contrary, in his recollection (24/10/95) Abū Ḥukayma praises the heat of the penis's glans that could warm up the palm of the hand of one freezing with cold.

7. Verily the cock's sleep is abjectness! Beware of abjectness and the shame it brings!
8. Beautiful women seldom like a cock's forbearance and gravity.
9. They do not want it when they know it is languid.
10. They only keep to it when they test and find it praiseworthy.
11. You have become like a loosely-hanging hem after prosperity and glam.
12. No visitor of yours finds favour with you when he visits.
13. No, nor do you profit aught the neighbor whom love has brought next to you.
14. Where is your past briskness, where the fervor?
15. I remember the time when you stood like a light-house.
16. People thought you were made out of iron or stone.
17. A mere sign with the eye or a hint was enough for you [to get you hard-on].
18. You embarked upon perils and run at the hippodromes of perdition (*fī mayādīni l-ḫasārah*)
19. Dragging the trail of wantonness (*mujūn*) in midst of mischief (*fatk*) and unruliness (*shaṭāra*).
20. Every peer dreaded your attack and predatory raid.
21. You were a commander in fucking – your command has now come to an end.
22. You are absent from the places [of pleasure] after frequenting and abiding in them.
23. Borrowed robes of might have been taken off from you.
24. Time made bitterness follow the sweet part of your life.

Noteworthy here are the images of the closing verses (18–24). Boasting about wantonness and waywardness is common in licentious poetry, both among the Kufans and in Abū Nuwās and later poets such as Ibn al-Ḥajjāj, and in a way it is reminiscent of the brigands' (*ṣaʿālīk*) vaunting about their crimes and unruliness.[39] *Fatk* (man-slaughter and more generally mischief) apparently refers to the slaying of lovers in the sex-war. In 10/6–7/63, comparing the present to the past state of the penis, Abū Ḥukayma notes that, although it is harmless now, one was never safe from its violence and crimes in the past (*ṣirta baʿda l-fatki mimman lā yakhāfu l-nāsu sharrah/ wa-la-ʿahdī bika dahran ghayra maʾmūni l-maʿarrah*). While admitting that past adventures were *khasāra* (error, perdition), he complacently avows that, were it able, his penis would relapse into its scandalous ways and repeatedly blames it for feigning asceticism and piousness (12/3/65 *tazahhadta ʿalā ghayri tuqan*; 4/28–30/53; 11/2/64, 11/4/64), which smacks of an attack on fake ascetics and perhaps, more generally, against ostentatious display of piety.[40]

The devastating effects of the turns of Time routinely form the theme of the closing verses of the *ayrīyāt*, but they are also frequently decried throughout the poems. The mishaps of Time were a recurrent theme in *marthiyas* and *taʿziyas* meant to provide consolation. The capriciousness of fortune also featured as a warning and proof of the deceptiveness of this world in ascetic poetry, which probably was the butt of the poet's irony rather than the elegy or the consolatory poem. On the other hand, it is important to stress that the adversities of Time were held solely responsible for the failing of the poet's penis. His impotence was not blamed on old age. On the contrary, on several occasions

39 cf. Meisami, 'Abū Nuwās and the Rhetoric of Parody', 248–52.

40 Worthy of notice in this respect is poem 12 in the *Dhayl* (pp. 152–3), where in a Nuwasian vein Abū Ḥukayma celebrates his alternative *ḥajj*, the *ḥajj* of lovers, and its rites that he performed when others set out for the pilgrimage to Mecca.

we are told that it befell him while he was still young (1/19/44 *harimta qabla awāni l-shaybi wa-l-haramī*; 2/19/48; 23/6/92; cf. 37/3/110). His impotence then corresponds to the altered state and the untimely hoariness of the pre-Islamic and early Islamic hero-poet, conditions which often caused the beloved's consternation, triggering disapproving comments, and which were blamed on worries and calamities – the buffets of Time. As we shall see, the antecedents of the impotence theme confirm this interpretation.

But before looking into this matter, we should turn to the less typical *ayrīyāt*, most of which, as said above, are narrative in structure and present accounts of failed sexual encounters. Poem 39 (pp. 112–4) is exceptional as it is a request-poem addressed to an unnamed caliph. After lamenting his quasi-dead penis (39/1–6), Abū Ḥukayma apostrophizes himself (39/7 *yā rāthiya l-ayri*) declaring that pleasure can only be attained with beautiful young women. He thus prompts himself to petition the caliph for a pretty slave-girl whom he goes on to describe, suggesting that this will most probably cure his penis (39/9–13). The last line is a direct appeal to the caliph and praise of his generosity (39/14).

In poems 7 and 15 the lover is attractive but the penis fails. No. 7 (pp. 58–9) is about failing a dark-eyed young gazelle of royal descent (*duʿīta ilā shādinin adʿajī ... min nitāji l-mulūki...* – it is unclear whether the gazelle is a boy or a girl). In poem 15 (pp. 68–70) Abū Ḥukayma narrates how he once excused himself to his servant (*khādim*) who had been flirting with him, blaming the condition of his penis; were it functioning, he added, his wife would have been worthier of it than the youth/girl, as she had long been neglected.

Poems 23 and 29 are about over-age, unattractive lovers. No. 23 (pp. 91–4) recounts how the poet repelled the salacious advances of a crone (*ʿajūz*), partly blaming his impotence, partly the woman's lack of appeal. A shortened version of this poem is attributed to both Abū Nuwās and Abū Ḥukayma in Abū Nuwās's *Dīwān* (5:102), but given the many similarities in diction and motifs between the longer version and the *ayrīyāt*, I believe that it can safely be attributed to Abū Ḥukayma.[41] *Vetula*-Skoptik, i.e. ridicule of crones who despite their old age are lecherous and keen on men and sex, is a recurrent theme in ancient Greek and Latin literatures, at times found in connection with the theme of impotence as in Horace and the *Priapea*.[42] In Classical Arabic, poems dispraising old women are less common and

[41] Ph. Kennedy translated part of the poem in *Abu Nuwas*, 48, without noting its dubious authenticity. Another poem attributed to both Abū Ḥukayma and Abū Nuwās is no. 38 (pp. 111–2 = Abū Nuwās *mujūnīya* 50, *Dīwān* 5:37–8). In this case however all three redactors of Abū Nuwās's *Dīwān* are unanimous in ascribing the poem to him. What perhaps speaks for Abū Ḥukayma's authorship is that he treated similar themes in his *mujūnīyāt* 25 and 41.

[42] The crone (Latin *vetula*), already appearing in the Old Comedy, survived throughout late antiquity in the epigrams of the Greek Anthology and in Latin poetry, where she repeatedly appears in connection with the theme of impotence: see H.G. Oeri, *Der Typ der komischen Alten in der griechischen Komödie, passim* and especially 19–21; A. Richlin, *The Garden of Priapus: Sexuality and Aggression in Roman Humor*, 67–8, 109–16, 122–3; on the *Priapea*, in particular: N. Holzberg, 'Impotence? It Happened to the Best of Them! A Linear Reading of the *Corpus Priapeorum*'. On impotence as a theme of Greek and Latin literatures, see Richlin, *ibid*, 116–20; J.M. McMahon, *Paralysin Cave: Impotence, Perception, and Text in the Satyrica of Petronius*, 19–48.

tend to focus on their ugliness and sterility.[43] Abū Ḥukayma's emphasis on the woman's salaciousness may have influenced Ibn al-Ḥajjāj who composed several pieces on lustful hags.[44]

Although not narrative in structure, quatrain 29 is also untypical: the poet presents himself and his wife as an old couple, the problem being not that he is impotent but that he cannot make love to her daily as she wishes. If genuine, the piece sticks out of the series insofar as it puts the failing down to aging.

Finally, no. 51 (pp. 124–6), translated below as an example of narrative *ayrīyāt*, is an invective on the poet's own wife. Poems against one's wife are not uncommon in classical Arabic literature, but they typically concentrate on the woman's ugliness, silliness, spendthriftiness and/or bossiness.[45] Shifting attention to her lecherousness and the deceptiveness of her beauty and wit and using a narrative frame, however, poem 51 follows the Nuwasian tradition of self-victimizing and self-mocking narratives of failed sexual adventures, as do the few other narrative *ayrīyāt* too. No. 51 in particular is modelled on Abū Nuwās's well-known piece on the *ghulāmīya* (*Dīwān* 5:101–2),[46] to which the poem makes direct reference. In that poem Abū Nuwās narrates how he had managed to lure the girl to have sex with him. Only that, contrary to his expectations and fantasies, she was not a virgin. Were it not for his servant who came to his rescue dragging him out, he would have drowned in her large vagina – a *lujja* (fathomless depth). His bad experience with the promiscuous girl only strengthened his preference for boys. A similarly traumatic experience with an enthrallingly beautiful woman whom he was duped into marrying is what causes Abū Ḥukayma's impotence in the following:

1. One who kills with her eyes and enchants with her glances but whose good looks you scorn when you know her well,
2. One who hunts with her eyes the hearts and enslaves whom she sets out to win with her talk,

---

[43] See, e.g., the few short pieces preserved in Ibn Qutayba's *ʿUyūn al-akhbār* (*Kitāb al-nisāʾ*, *Bāb al-ʿujuz wa-l-mashāyikh*), 4:43–53, where however there are also two pieces in praise of old spouses and some poems dispraising old men. cf. *Muḥāḍarāt al-udabāʾ*, 2:223–4; *Aghānī* 2:418–9 (a poem by Ibn ʿAbdal on marrying a crone); see also poems nos. 8–9 translated by van Gelder in his article cited below, note 46.

[44] See Aṣṭurlābī's anthology of Ibn al-Ḥajjāj's poetry, *Durrat al-tāj*, 381–8 (due to the nature of this anthology the pieces quoted here are excerpts of poems), and the partial edition of his *Dīwān*, no. 95 (on spending the night with a Nabatean hag); no. 96 (on marrying a crone); cf. 6/25–40 on his feculent old neighbor at Wāsiṭ, 50/25–31 on his feculent old *qahramāna* at Wāsiṭ.

[45] See G.J. van Gelder, 'Against Women and Other Pleasantries: The Last Chapter of Abū Tammām's *Ḥamāsa*', 65, especially note 17, 67–71 (translations of nos. 1–11 and 16 from the section of the *Ḥamāsa* entitled *Madhammat al-nisāʾ* – as van Gelder notes, some more lampoons against one's own wife are found in other sections of the work). Other famous poems are by Jirān al-ʿAwd (see his *Dīwān*, no. 1); Ismāʿīl b. ʿAmmār (*ŠAM* 4:199); Ibn ʿAbdal (see note 44); among other things, ʿAmmār Dhū Kināz accused his aging wife of being bibulous and lecherous: *Aghānī* 24:223–6 (for this poet see below); petitioning for a slave-girl Abū Dulāma described his wife as an old and ugly shrew (*Aghānī* 10:262–3).

[46] *Ghulāmīya* is a slave-girl cutting her hair short and dressing up like a boy (see Wagner, *Abū Nuwās*, 176–9). cf. Meisami's analysis of the poem in 'Arabic *Mujūn* Poetry: The Literary Dimension', 18–9.

3. [Leaving victims] deceived by the skill of her tongue and exposed to perdition,
4. Like a shinny green pumpkin whose colour you like but you know it doesn't taste good –
5. Her pretty face got me to marry her not knowing the warnings hiding under her clothes.
6. When I hoped to relish being alone with her and said to myself: Soul, rejoice! You've gotten the day!
7. I encountered the rampart of Gog and Magog all around her and a ravine obstructed with thistle and trees;[47]
8. [A ravine] you could only traverse on a narrow path, crawling as if upon knives' edges and spikes;
9. [One that leads to] a fathomless depth, next to which a sea swelling with waves seems too small.
10. ['Twas a place] of mishaps, terrifying. When I entered it, I thought it's the end.
11. Many men have gone down it before me and perished without a trace.
12. If eyes could see it, they'd witness things monstrous, never seen nor heard of before.
13. I turned back fleeing swiftly and chided her, for such women make fear and caution fill a man's heart,
14. Just as soldiers flee from the mangonels when the lookouts shout: Mind the stones! The stones!
15. My cock lies now wounded, its head full of injures like those inflicted by Turks and Khazars.[48]
16. When beautiful women's hands disapprove of its stupor, it bemoans her mistreatment to them and excuses itself.
17. Let no lover be beguiled by her after me! In our story is a warning for those who take admonition.

ᶜAMMĀR DHŪ KINĀZ, THE FORERUNNER

Despite the abundance of earlier Arabic licentious poetry, including bold references and descriptions of male and female genitals, impotence was a sensitive topic that was eschewed in poetry prior to Abū Ḥukayma. Nevertheless, as pointed out by Aᶜrajī, Abū Ḥukayma did have a predecessor: ᶜAmmār Dhū Kināz,[49] a little-known bibulous Kufan poet who flourished in the first half of the 8th century and was friendly with Ḥammād al-Rāwiya and Muṭīᶜ b. Iyās.[50] Because of his poor sight, he reportedly never left Kūfa, but he praised local notables and his poems circulated widely. We are told that Ḥammād once recited ᶜAmmār's poetry to the caliph al-Walīd b. Yazīd at Ruṣāfa, receiving thirty thousand dirhams for his services.

[47] The rampart should refer to the clitoris, cf. a verse by Ibn al-Ḥajjāj in *Yatīma*, 3:63: *...wa fī ḥirihā khandaqu bawlin wa-baẓruhā sūrū*. The woman's monstrously large genitals obviously stand for her salaciousness and unquenchable lust. Neglect of depilation (ravine obstructed with thistle and trees) is normally 'a feature of prostitutes in the Islamic world': see Monroe's remarks in J.T. Monroe and M.F. Pettigrew, 'The Decline of Courtly Patronage and the Appearance of New Genres in Arabic Literature', 148, note 11. The following description of the woman's genitals is modelled on similar depictions by Abū Nuwās: see Wagner, ibid., 175–6.

[48] Note that the similes in verses 14–15 derive from the sphere of warfare.

[49] *Dīwān*, 25–30. I have also been unable to find any other antecedents of the theme of impotence.

[50] *GAS* 2:341. The following account is based on *Aghānī* 24:219–35.
How close his relationship to Muṭīᶜ b. Iyās was is hard to tell, for there seems to have been considerable age difference between the two, but they certainly could have met.

Another ten thousand dirhams were given to him to forward to ʿAmmār. Ḥammād also succeeded in persuading the caliph to issue a writ prohibiting Kufan authorities from arresting and punishing ʿAmmār if they found him drunk (and urging them instead to punish those who denounced him for drunkenness). The poet, who received both gifts with great gratitude, died before wholly consuming that sum, i.e. most probably before the fall of the Umayyads. Among the few poems by ʿAmmār preserved in the *Aghānī*, there are two pieces addressed to Khālid b. ʿAbdallāh al-Qasrī (governor of ʿIrāq in 105–20/724–38) in which the poet refers to the predicament of his penis.

ʿAmmār came to Khālid to collect his stipend (*ʿaṭāʾ*) but the governor refused to give it to him lest he spend it on wine and debauchery. ʿAmmār strongly denied any such intention: 'Not in the least!' – he said – 'How can I still long for such things? Am I not the one who said':

1. ʿAmmār's cock has today become slack and lethargic –
2. Is this due to an ailment or due to his worries and grief?
3. Or is it bewitched? Bewitchment can be cured with a charm.
4. If today it is bowed or if age has gnawed it,
5. In the past it attained its pleasure to the full.
6. [Then] I did have erections and always my penis stood up.
7. But today, had a houri lain by me, it would fail to expand.
8. It is bent with its head stooping over the testicles.
9. Whenever I task it to rise to a slot (*kuwwa*), it stumbles and falls.

Thereupon Khālid laughed and let ʿAmmār cash in his stipend. After paying off his debts and putting his condition to rights, the poet composed some more verses in the same metre and rhyme:

1. Today ʿAmmār's cock has risen and stretched itself.
2. It received its allowance, became brisk and stood up filled with pride.
3. Today it's erect and exulting, resembling the peg at the loop of a provision-bag.
4. It leaves the peer prostrated at the battle-field and does not become languid.
5. It wields its rod to thrust (*ṭiʿān*) at a time when a weakling would quit.
6. O Salmā! What a pleasant bed-fellow you are on a chilly night! [...]

There follow five verses praising Salmā.[51] Unfortunately we are not told whether ʿAmmār recited the latter poem to the governor. At any rate, his influence on Abū Ḥukayma can be seen in the many common motifs used in their depictions of the changes in the penis's state.[52] Abū Ḥukayma, however, never produced a poem like ʿAmmār's second piece, even though he used its motifs to depict the penis's past. On the contrary, he persisted in lamenting his impotence, expanding and elaborating on this subject and thus creating his own *madhhab*, to use Ḥuṣrī's expression.[53]

The importance of ʿAmmār's poems and of the accompanying *khabar* lies, not least, in

[51] *Aghānī*, 24:227–8.

[52] As pointed out by Aʿrajī, Sulaymā/Salmā, the name of the poet's partner in Abū Ḥukayma's *ayrīyāt*, most probably refers to ʿAmmār's Salmā. Aʿrajī also drew attention to the fact that ʿAmmār too composed poems against his wife (see note 46 above), but those poems are very different from Abū Ḥukayma's lampoon of his own wife, which is obviously fictitious.

[53] *Zahr al-ādāb*, 3:91.

that they clarify the original intent of the *ayrīyāt*, which, I believe, was clear to Abū Ḥukayma too. In other words, ʿAmmār's first piece was in fact a begging-poem – that is, a poem in which the poet protests his poverty, depicting himself in dire need and exaggerating the effects of his indigence, with a view to arousing the patron's compassion. Such poems hardly ever lack a humorous tint, drolleries and self-mockery serving to mitigate the discomfiture and importunacy of begging.[54] A further begging-poem was reportedly again recited by ʿAmmār to Khālid al-Qasrī in the context of their argument about whether the poet was entitled to a stipend or not. In this more elaborate version of the story the governor refused to pay the poet his stipend because ʿAmmār did not do military service nor did he finance a substitute-soldier (*badīl*) to serve in his stead. Thereupon ʿAmmār offered such a vivid description of his penury, his empty house and hungry children that Khālid purportedly burst into tears and gave him the money.[55]

In this context it is worth pointing out the penis's great semiotic value in ancient and mediaeval Greek and classical Arabic dream interpretation. As shown by Oberhelman, in these interpretative traditions, 'the penis is judged as a man's reputation, power and children'; 'a penis that is powerful and erect symbolizes a dreamer's domination over his enemies and strength in all his activities [...] If you dream that your penis is erect, this means that you will acquire honor and children'. On the other hand, 'the flaccid penis denotes powerlessness, defeat and humiliation' and 'a lack of strength in all [one']s actions'; 'if [the dreamer] dreams that his penis is small and withered, he will fall from honor and become a beggar, while his children will have disease and lack of power. [...] If someone dreams that his penis is cut off, he will be severely punished and become poor'.[56] ʿAmmār's use of the penis as a symbol for his personal condition is thus readily understood and justified, all the more so as he himself gave ample hints to clarify his poems' import. It was because of his (financial) worries (*humūm*)[57] and grief (*ḍajar*) that his penis grew languid and it was thanks to the stipend (*rizq*) that he eventually became potent again.

No doubt Abū Ḥukayma was well aware of this aspect of the poetry of his predecessor. By developing the pictorial and the humorous aspects of the theme of impotence he moved away from the central idea of ʿAmmār's *ayrīyāt*, which he however may have assumed to be present in his audience's minds. It was perhaps to counterbalance this shift that he complained so emphatically of the treacherous turns of Time, the counterpart of the earlier poet's *humūm*. Like his predecessor, he thereby probably meant to suggest that he himself was hit and brought down by the mishaps of Fate. Be this as it may, it is worth noting that Abū Ḥukayma modernized ʿAmmār's claim as to the causes of his impotence adapting it to the conventions of his own times. For in his own era negative comments about Time specifically implying dissatisfaction with one's financial circumstances or the precariousness thereof gained recurrence and gradually displaced the earlier *humūm* motif as a token of pecuniary worries.

---

[54] I hope to elaborate on this point in a forthcoming study.

[55] *Aghānī*, 24:229–31.

[56] See S.M. Oberhelman, 'Hierarchies of Gender, Ideology, and Power in Ancient and Medieval Greek and Arabic Dream Literature', *passim* and especially 61, 73–74.

[57] On the *humūm* motif in early Arabic poetry, cf. my *Desert Travel as a Form of Boasting*, 28–9, where I should have stressed even more its financial implications.

In this connection, it should be added that the original import of the *ayrīyāt* resurfaced in a poem by the 10th-century literate *amīr* (i.e. municipal head) of Nishapur ʿAbdallāh b. Ismāʿīl al-Mīkālī (d. 379/989–90).[58] This suggests that it was not wholly forgotten. Quoting the poem in the *Yatīma* (4:382–3), Thaʿālibī comments that it refers to the overthrow suffered by ʿAbdallāh in his old age (*qawluhū fī l-nakbati llatī ʿaraḍat lahū fī ākhiri ayyāmih*).[59] Significantly, the first verse reads:

> When Time betrayed me, my cock did so too; it treated me as harshly as my brethren did.[60]

ʿAbdallāh complains that his beloved abandoned him once he became impotent (vv. 2–4) and goes on to deplore the condition of his penis:

> 5. No hope that it wake up from its sleep or that it manifest desire when beautiful women are mentioned!
> 6. Previously it used to listen, obey and assist me; now it treats me disrespectfully and harshly.
> 7. Nay, rather it saw me stripped of my wealth [*lit.* having my wealth confiscated: *muṣādaran*] and brought low (*mustakīnan*) and pitied me for the sudden reversal of Fortune (*min-i nqilābi l-zamānī*),
> 8. and bowed its neck and became soft and pliable like a rattan twig.
> 9. It does not reply to my calling for help in the gloom of the night or to the call of the fair-faced ones.
> 10. [Even though] I have not tasked it to take upon itself a heavy debt – no! Nor to ward off a calamity that befell me.
> 11. The debt and the damage affect [only] my wealth. What does it care about what betided me?
> 12. Have you ever heard of an iron staff that has melted for fear of the Sultan?
> 13. Would that it returned to obeying my wish and distracted me from the plague of my sorrows!

In the last four verses of his poem (14–17) ʿAbdallāh addresses the two railers (*al-ʿādhilāni*) asking them to pity him and abstain from blaming him and declares that, in the face of his brethren' treacherous behaviour, he places his confidence in God. In this *ayrīya* the poet's feigned surprise and indignation at the penis's failure – considering that it was not directly affected by the *nakba* as his wealth was – playfully underscores the connection between his overthrow and his impotence and brings out, once again, the relationship between potency and status/prosperity.

In contrast, Abū Ḥukayma's protest of the buffets of Time is too general and stylized and therefore it is rather unlikely that it referred to concrete financial problems or an abrupt reversal of his condition and status. But one could perhaps speculate that by

---

[58] On ʿAbdallāh b. Ismāʿīl and the Mīkālī family see C.E. Bosworth's article 'Mīkālīs' in *EI2*.

[59] *Nakba* (calamity, disaster) typically denotes a dramatic overthrow of one's career and status such as often befell high-ranking Abbasid officials.

[60] Complains about one's friends – especially their failure to assist one in the face of adversities – grew very common in the 10th century, related as they were to plaints about one's times and contemporaries.

comically exaggerating his complain he meant to comment on his status as an amateur poet, although admittedly this is a daring hypothesis.

On the other hand, it is well possible that, as said above, through his parody of the motifs of heroic war poetry he aimed at criticizing the militarism of the Abbasid Empire, as well as poking fun at those professional poets who pompously celebrated and propagated that ideology.[61] Referring to Ibn al-Ḥajjāj's phenomenally obscene and scurrilous poems and the popularity they enjoyed, J.S. Meisami suggested that 'their parody [may be] directed in part at the type of poetry exemplified, for instance, by al-Mutanabbī's panegyrics for Sayf al-Dawla'.[62] It seems to me that there should be no doubt about that and that this was also true of earlier *mujūn* poetry; it too was apparently in part directed at the grandeur, pomposity and stylization of contemporary court poetry. Likewise, Abū Nuwās's irony and parody of traditional poetic conventions targeted not the early poetry itself but the inopportune use of its motifs by his contemporaries. Very telling in this respect is the well-known story about Abū l-ᶜAnbas al-Ṣaymarī's improvised scurrilous burlesque of one of Buḥturī's panegyrics on Mutawakkil immediately after the latter poet's recital of his ode in the caliph's presence. Notably the amused caliph gave Abū l-ᶜAnbas the reward he had ready for Buḥturī, who left the scene humiliated and enraged to the extent that he contemplated leaving Samarrāᵓ for good.[63] This story brings out not only the tensions and rivalry between competing poets, especially those who endorsed completely different attitudes and views of poetry (Abū l-ᶜAnbas was an amateur poet), but also shows how ceremonial poetry could irk and weary its very patrons and dedicatees – not to speak of the wider audiences.

After all, through its very themes, *mujūn* poetry was in a sense the antipode of official court poetry and the mockery of traditional poetic genres and conventions was one of its most prominent and amusing features. Again, as Meisami rightly pointed out, to really understand and relish it we have to recognize and appreciate its humour and entertaining qualities, which indeed supplied the typical excuses for tolerating it.[64] Aside from all possible covert criticism or complaint, Abū Ḥukayma's *ayrīyāt* were obviously meant to amuse and draw a laugh.

---

[61] Abū Tammām's masterpiece, the Amorium ode, with all its dramatic imagery and symbolisms (e.g. the celebration of the captive women's rape as a token of domination and subjection of the enemy), is a particularly good example.

[62] 'Arabic *mujūn* poetry', 29–30.

[63] Ṣūlī, *Aḫbār Buḥturī*, 87–9; Buḥturī's *Dīwān*, 3:1992–5. On Abū l-ᶜAnbas al-Ṣaymarī, see Pellat's article in *EI2*.

[64] Ibid., 13–5 and *passim*.

BIBLIOGRAPHY

Abbreviations

CAPP: Reinhard Weipert, *Classical Arabic Philology and Poetry: A Bibliographical Handbook of Important Editions from 1960 to 2000*. Handbuch der Orientalistik, Erste Abteilung, Nahe und der Mittlere Osten: 63 (Leiden: Brill, 2002).
EI2: Peri J. Bearman [et al.], ed. *Encyclopaedia of Islam*. New Edition, 12 vols & Index (Leiden: Brill, 1954–2002).
GAL: Carl Brockelmann, *Geschichte der arabischen Litteratur*. 5 vols. (Leiden: Brill, 1937–49).
GAS: Fuat Sezgin, *Geschichte des arabischen Schrifttums*, vol. I–XI. (Leiden: Brill, 1967–84).
JAL: *Journal of Arabic Literature*.
ŠAM: Ibrāhīm an-Najjār, *Shuʿarāʾ ʿAbbāsīyūn mansīyūn*. 7 vols. (Beirut: Dār al-Gharb al-Islāmī, 1997).

Works Cited

ʿAbdarraḥīm b. ʿAbdarraḥmān al-ʿAbbāsī, *Maʿāhid al-tanṣīṣ ʿalā shawāhid al-Talkhīṣ*. 4 vols. (Cairo: Maṭbaʿat al-Saʿāda, 1947–8).
Abū Ḥukayma, *Dīwān Abī Ḥukayma*, ed. Muḥammad Ḥusayn al-Aʿrajī. 3rd revised ed. (Köln/ Baghdad: Al-Kamel Verlag, 2007).
al-Ḥasan b. Hāniʾ Abū Nuwās, *Dīwān Abī Nuwās al-Ḥasan b. Hāniʾ al-Ḥakamī*, ed. Ewald Wagner and Gregor Schoeler, 7 vols. (Beirut-Berlin: [various publishers], 2001–2006).
Muḥammad Ḥusayn al-Aʿrajī, *al-Shiʿr fī l-Kūfa mundhu awāsiṭ al-qarn al-thānī ḥattā nihāyat al-qarn al-thālith* (Köln/Baghdad: Al-Kamel Verlag, 2007).
Albert Arazi, 'Thèmes et style d'al-Ḥamdawī: Un poète chansonnier du III/Ixe s', *Journal Asiatique* 267 (1979): 261–307.
al-Aʿshā, *Dīwān al-Aʿshā al-kabīr*, ed. Muḥammad Muḥammad Ḥusayn (Beirut: Muʾassasat al-Risāla,⁷1983).
Hibatallāh al-Aṣṭurlābī, *Durrat al-tāj min shiʿr Ibn al-Ḥajjāj*: Ikhtiyār Hibatallāh Badīʿ al-Zamān al-Aṣṭurlābī, ed. ʿAlī Jawād al-Ṭāhir (Köln: Al-Kamel Verlag, 2009).
Thomas Bauer, *Liebe und Liebesdichtung in der arabischen Welt des 9. und 10. Jahrhunderts: Eine literatur- und mentalitätsgeschichtliche Studie des arabischen Ġazal* (Wiesbaden: Harrassowitz, 1998).
Mohammed Ben Cheneb, *Abū Dolāma, Poète bouffon de la cour des premiers caliphes abbassides*, (Alger: Typographie Jules Carbonel, 1922).
Abū ʿUbāda al-Walīd b. ʿUbayd al-Buḥturī, *Dīwān al-Buḥturī*, ed. Ḥusayn Kāmil al-Ṣayrafī, 5 vols., 2nd ed. (Cairo: Dār al-Maʿārif, 1972–78).
Josef van Ess, *Der Ṭailasān des Ibn Ḥarb: "Mantelgedichte" in arabischer Sprache*, SBHAW, Phil.-hist. Kl. 1979/4. (Heidelberg: Winter, 1979).
al-Farazdaq, *Divan de Férazdaq: Récits de Mohammed-Ben-Habib d'après Ibn-el-Arabi, publié sur le manuscrit de Sainte-Sophie de Constantinople, avec une traduction française par R. Boucher*. 2 vols. (Paris: A. Labitte, 1870–5).
Geert Jan van Gelder, 'Against Women and Other Pleasantries: The Last Chapter of Abū Tammām's *Ḥamāsa*', *JAL* 16 (1985): 61–72.
Jeffrey Henderson, *The Maculate Muse: Obscene Language in Attic Comedy*, 2nd ed. (New York/ Oxford: Oxford University Press, 1991).
Ṣafī l-Dīn al-Ḥillī, *Kitāb dīwān Ṣafī l-Dīn Abī l-Mahāsin ʿAbd al-ʿAzīz b. Sarāyā al-Ḥillī* (Damascus: Maṭbaʿat Ḥabīb Afandī Khālid, 1880).
Niklas Holzberg, 'Impotence? It Happened to the Best of Them! A Linear Reading of the *Corpus Priapeorum*,' *Hermes* 133/3 (2005): 368–81.

Yūsuf Khulayyif, *Ḥayāt al-shiʿr fī l-Kūfa ilā nihāyat al-qarn al-thānī li-l-hijra* (Cairo: Dār al-Kātib al-ʿArabī, 1968).
Ibrāhīm b. ʿAlī al-Ḥuṣrī, *Zahr al-ādāb wa-thamar al-albāb*, ed. Ṣalāḥ al-Dīn Hawwārī, 4 vols. (Beirut: al-Maktaba al-ʿAṣrīya, 2001).
Muḥammad b. Sayf ad-Dīn Ibn Aydamir, *Kitāb al-durr al-farīd wa-bayt al-qaṣīd*, ed. Fuat Sezgin et al., 7 vols., facsim. (Frankfurt: Institut für Geschichte der Arabisch-Islamischen Wissenschaften, 1988–97).
Ibn al-Ḥajjāj, *Der Dīwān des Ibn al-Haǧǧāǧ: Teilausgabe der Reimbuchstabe nūn*, ed. Abdelghafur A.A. el-Aswad (Giessen, 1977).
Ibn Khallikān, *Wafayāt al-aʿyān wa-anbāʾ abnāʾ al-zamān*, ed. Iḥsān ʿAbbās, 8 vols. (Beirut: Dār Ṣadir, 1977).
Ibn al-Muʿtazz, *Ṭabaqāt al-shuʿarāʾ li-Bni-l-Muʿtazz*, ed. ʿAbdassattār Aḥmad Farrāj, 2nd printing (Cairo: Dār al-Maʿārif, 1968).
Ibn Qutayba, ʿAbdallāh b. Muslim, *Kitāb ʿuyūn al-akhbār*, 4 vols. (Cairo: Dār al-Kutub al-Miṣrīya, 1925–30).
Ibn Ṭabāṭabā, Muḥammad b. Aḥmad, *ʿIyār al-shiʿr*, eds. Ṭāhā Ḥājirī & Muḥammad Zaghlūl Sallām (Cairo: Maktabat al-Tijārīya al-Kubrā, 1956).
Abū l-Faraj al-Iṣbahānī, *Kitāb al-aghānī*, 24 vols. (Cairo: Dār al-Kutub/al-Hayʾa al-Miṣrīya al-ʿĀmma, 1927–74).
Abū l-Faraj al-Iṣbahānī, *al-Imāʾ al-shawāʿir*, ed. Jalīl ʿAṭīya (Beirut: Dār al-Niḍāl, 1984).
Jirān al-ʿAwd, *Dīwān Jirān al-ʿAwd al-Numayrī*, ed. Nūrī Ḥammūdī al-Qaysī (Baghdad: Wizārat al-Thaqāfa wa-l-Iʿlām, 1982).
Philip F. Kennedy, *Abu Nuwas: A Genius of Poetry* (Oxford: One World, 2005).
Muḥammad b. Shākir al-Kutubī, *ʿUyūn al-tawārīkh: wa fīhi min sanat 219 H. ilā 250 H.*, ed. ʿAfīf Nāyif Ḥaṭūm (Beirut: Dār al-Thaqāfa, 1996).
Muḥammad b. Shākir al-Kutubī, *Fawāt al-wafayāt wa-l-dhayl ʿalayhā*, ed. Iḥsān ʿAbbās, 5 vols. (Beirut: Dār Ṣādir, 1973–4).
Muḥammad b. ʿImrān al-Marzubānī, *al-Muwashshaḥ fī maʾākhidh al-ʿulamāʾ wa-l-shuʿarāʾ* (Miṣr: al-Maṭbaʿa al-Salafīya, 1924).
al-Masʿūdī, *Murūj al-dhahab wa-maʿādin al-jawhar*, ed. Charles Pellat, 7 vols. (Beirut: Manshūrāt al-Jāmiʿa al-Lubnānīya, 1966–79).
Robert McKinney, *The Case of Rhyme Versus Reason: Ibn al-Rūmī and His Poetics in Context* (Leiden: Brill, 2004).
John M. McMahon, *Paralysin Cave: Impotence, Perception, and Text in the Satyrica of Petronius* (Leiden: Brill 1998).
Julie Scott Meisami, 'Arabic *Mujūn* Poetry: The Literary Dimension,' in Frederick De Jong (ed.), *Verse and the Fair Sex: Studies in Arabic Poetry and the Representation of Women in Arabic Literature* (Utrecht: M.T. Houtsma Stichting, 1993), 8–30.
Julie Scott Meisami, 'Abū Nuwās and the Rhetoric of Parody', in Wolfhart P. Heinrichs and Gregor Schoeler (eds.) *Festschrift Ewald Wagner zum 65. Geburtstag* (Stuttgart: Franz Steiner Verlag, 1994), 2:246–57.
James T. Monroe, and Mark F. Pettigrew, 'The Decline of Courtly Patronage and the Appearance of New Genres in Arabic Literature: The Case of the *Zajal*, the *Maqāma*, and the Shadow Play,' *JAL* 34 (2003), 138–77.
Carlo Alfonso Nallino, *La littérature arabe dés origines à l' époque de la dynastie umayyade*, trans. Ch. Pellat (Paris: G.P. Maisonneuve, 1950).
Steven M. Oberhelman, 'Hierarchies of Gender, Ideology, and Power on Ancient and Medieval Greek and Arabic Dream Literature', in Jerry W. Wright and Everett K. Rowson (eds.) *Homoeroticism in Classical Arabic Literature* (New York: Columbia University Press, 1997), 55–93.

Hans Georg Oeri, *Der Typ der komischen Alten in der griechischen Komödie* (Basel: B. Schwabe, 1948).
Nefeli Papoutsakis, *Desert Travel as a Form of Boasting: A Study of Ḏū r-Rumma's Poetry* (Wiesbaden: Harrassowitz, 2009).
Keith Preston, *Studies in the Diction of the Sermo Amatorius in Roman Comedy* (Menasha: Private ed., 1916).
Abū l-Qāsim al-Ḥusayn b. Muḥammad al-Rāghib al-Iṣbahānī, *Muḥāḍarāt al-udabāʾ wa-muḥāwarāt al-shuʿarāʾ wa-l-bulaghāʾ*, ed. ʿUmar al-Ṭabbāʿ, 2 vols. (Beirut: Dār al-Arqam, 1999).
Amy Richlin, *The Garden of Priapus: Sexuality and Aggression in Roman Humor* (New Haven/London: Yale University Press, 1983).
Hellmut Ritter, *Das Meer der Seele: Mensch, Welt und Gott in den Geschichten des Farīduddīn ʿAṭṭār* (Leiden: Brill 1955).
Khalīl b. Aybak al-Ṣafadī, *Kitāb al-wāfī bi-l-wafayāt*, ed. Sven Dedering et al., 30 vols. ([various places]: Deutsche Morgenländische Gesellschaft, 1931 to date).
Abū Bakr Muḥammad b. Yaḥyā al-Ṣūlī, *Akhbār al-Buḥturī*, ed. Ṣāliḥ Ashṭar (Damascus: n.p., 1958).
ʿAbdalmalik b. Muḥammad al-Thaʿālibī, *Yatīmat al-dahr fī maḥāsin ahl al-ʿaṣr*, 4 vols. (Cairo: Maṭbaʿat al-Ṣāwī, 1934).
ʿAbdalmalik b. Muḥammad al-Thaʿālibī, *Thimār al-qulūb fī l-muḍāf wa-l-mansūb*, ed. Muḥammad Abū l-Faḍl Ibrāhīm (Cairo: Dār al-Maʿārif, 1985).
Shawkat M. Toorawa, *Ibn Abī Ṭāhir Ṭayfūr and Arabic Writerly Culture: a Ninth-Century Bookman in Baghdad* (New York: Routledge Curzon 2005).
Ewald Wagner, *Abū Nuwās: Eine Studie zur arabischen Literatur der frühen ʿAbbāsidenzeit* (Wiesbaden: Harrassowitz, 1965).
Ewald Wagner, *Abū Nuwās in Übersetzung: Eine Stellensammlung zu Abū Nuwās-Übersetzungen vornehmlich in europäischen Sprachen* (Wiesbaden: Harrassowitz, 2012).
Yaqūt b. ʿAbdallāh al-Ḥamawī, *The Irshád al-Aríb ilá Maʿrifat al-Adíb: or, Dictionary of Learned Men of Yáqút*, ed. D.S. Margoliouth, 7 vols., 2nd ed. (London: Luzac, 1923–31).

7

ᶜ*Udhrī* Love and *Mujūn*: Opposites and Parallels

Monica Balda-Tillier

Mujūn is one of those Arabic words that discourage any attempt at translation. More than a simple word, it comprises an entire concept of civilisation and a complete literary genre that has no equivalent in European languages. Moreover, *mujūn* has a multiplicity of meanings. Arabic authors' definitions of this term cover a wide range of meanings. In his book *Akhbār al-ẓirāf wa-mutamājinīn*, Ibn al-Jawzī defines it as a way to divert an expression from its primary meaning to another one. It reveals the ready wit of the person who makes use of it.[1] For Ibn al-Jawzī, *mujūn* is just a linguistic device. This is its weakest sense, one that' approximates to *hazl* (jest) as opposed to *jidd* (seriousness) and corresponds in an appreciable degree to frivolity'.[2]

Lisān al-ᶜarab defines *mujūn* as the stiffness and the thickness of a thought. The term *mājin* derived from the same root and, when used to refer to a man, indicates a hard-faced shameless person. According to Ibn Manẓūr, the *mājin* is also a person who does not care whether his acts and sayings are good or bad.[3] Arabic literary texts show that the semantic field of *mujūn* can be extended further to mean the most shameless debauchery, libertinage, obscenity, and everything that may provoke coarse laughter, such as scatological humour.[4] In *Ḥikāyat Abī l-Qāsim al-Baghdādī*, all of the wide range of meanings from the 'softer' (*mujūn* as a jest) to the strongest (*mujūn* as obscenity) coexist, and that is why I have chosen to use this extremely rich text to serve as model for *mujūn* literature.

---

[1] Ibn al-Jawzī, *Akhbār al-ẓirāf wa-l-mutāmajinīn*, p. 41.

[2] Ch. Pellat, 'Mudjūn', *EI²*, VII, p. 304ab.

[3] Ibn Manẓūr, *Lisān al-ᶜarab*, 'majana'.

[4] Ch. Pellat, 'Mudjūn', VII, p. 304ab.

The *Ḥikāyat Abī l-Qāsim al-Baghdādī* by Abū Muṭahhar al-Azdī,[5] known also as *al-Risāla al-Baghdādiyya* attributed to Abū Ḥayyān al-Tawḥīdī (d. 413/1023),[6] is a text unique in Arabic literature.[7] The book recalls one day of Abū l-Qāsim's life as he enters an assembly (*majlis*) in Isfahan uninvited and discharges his fearsome eloquence on the people present. As the author explains in his introduction, he met his character in Baghdad and witnessed his speeches, both laudable and shameful. The *Ḥikāya* is supposed to be reporting Abū l-Qāsim's behaviour and words, as a model of the costumes and the lifestyle of all Baghdadis.[8] Abū al-Muṭahhar[9] plays on the double meaning of Arabic term *ḥākā* (to imitate) and *ḥikāya* (story) to invoke an imitation of reality.

In seemingly total opposition to *mujūn* stands the genre of Arabic love poetry called *ghazal*, especially the kind called *ʿUdhrī* in opposition to the *ʿUmarī ghazal*[10] as well as the prose works about passionate love (*ʿishq*) and lovers (*ʿushshāq*).[11] This kind of literature recalls the stories of lovers who fall in love with somebody who is or becomes forbidden for them to reach, and pursue this hopeless, chaste love all their life until they waste away and finally die. In Medieval Arabic literature, passionate and chaste love is a very common topic in poetry from the pre-Islamic period. Starting from the third/ninth century, prose relating lovers' stories as well as the theory of profane love also begins to develop. There are approximately fifteen books dealing exclusively with these topics in the history of Arabic literature. These books share some characters and themes such as an explanation of the real nature of passionate love (*māhiyyat al-ʿishq*), its forms, its causes, and its effect on lovers; this is why they can be set apart in the literary genre of

---

[5] According to the *Encyclopaedia of Islam*, none of the known biographical sources speaks about this author. All we know about him must be taken from his only existing work, the *Ḥikāya*. Historical references in the *Ḥikāya* show that he lived in the fifth/eleventh century. F. Gabrieli, 'Abū al-Muṭahhar al-Azdī', *EI*², I, p. 31a.

On the question of the authorship of this work see: M. Balda, 'Marginalité et éloquence contestataire : le personage d'Abū l-Qāsim dans la *Ḥikāyat Abī l-Qāsim d'Abū al-Muṭahhar al-Azdī*', p. 371.

[6] Abū Ḥayyān al-Tawḥīdī was a man of letters and a philosopher who lived in the fifth/eleventh century. The *Ḥikāya* has been attributed to him, because it has some similarities with his pamphlet *Mathālib al-wazīrayn* in which he draws a negative portrait of the two viziers Abū l-Fatḥ and Ibn ʿAbbād. S. M. Stern, 'ʿAbū Ḥayyān al-Tawḥīdī', *EI*², I, pp. 130a–131a.

[7] The two existing editions of this text (Abū l-Muṭahhar al-Azdī, *Ḥikāyat Abī l-Qāsim*, Mez, A. (ed.), Heidelberg, 1902 and Abū Ḥayyān al-Tawḥīdī, *al-Risāla al-Baghdādiyya*, al-Shālijī 'A. (ed.), Köln, 1997) are both based on the same manuscript, Br. Mus. 1127.

[8] Abū Ḥayyān al-Tawḥīdī, *al-Risāla al-Baghdādiyya*, pp. 42–43.

[9] I choose to follow the traditional attribution of the *Ḥikāya* to Abū l-Muṭahhar, because the more recent one, attributing the work to al-Tawḥīdī, cannot be proved.

[10] While *ʿUmarī* 'poets devoted their attention to wellborn Arab ladies [...] and were inspired by the chase, [...]*ʿUdhrī* poets fell desperately in love with a single lady and remained attached to her exclusively all their lives, even though she was chaste and forbidden to them in marriage.' R. Farrin, *Abundance from the Desert, Classical Arabic Poetry*, p. 96.

[11] R. Farrin, *Abundance from the Desert*, p. 96.

love treatises.[12] They equally seem to me to be the most representative texts about *ʿUdhrī* love theory in classical Arabic literature.

Mujūn poetry is an innovation of the Abbasid period.[13] However, no literary phenomenon is completely sui generis and devoid of an ancestry. In this paper, I will try to understand how *mujūn* was born and how it is rooted in previous literary expressions. In order to do this, I will compare different aspects of the *Ḥikāya* (which, as I said, I consider to be the *mujūn* text *par excellence*) with *ghazal* poetry and love prose.

I will first focus on the comparison between the characters described in the *Ḥikāya* and the image of the perfect and refined lovers (*ẓurafāʾ*) as it appears in particular in the *Kitāb al-Muwashshā* by al-Washshāʾ (d. 325/937).[14] I will then analyse the vocabulary, themes, and images in the *mujūn* poetry of the *Ḥikāya*, comparing them to *ghazal* poetry.

ẒARĪF VS MĀJIN

Portrait of the ẓarīf

The *Kitāb al-Muwashshā*, written in the fourth/tenth century by al-Washshāʾ (d. 325/937),[15] stands apart as a unique text even though it belongs to the literary genre of love treatises. The book is not only a code of refinement and courtly love but also a guide for social conventions and elegance.[16] The author declares in the opening that the main purpose of his book is to explain the concept of refinement (*ẓarf*),[17] the rules of masculinity (*murūʾa*),[18] and the definition of good manners (*adab*).[19] For this reason, I

---

[12] On the literary genre of love treatises in Arabic literature see: M. Balda, 'Genèse et essor d'un genre littéraire: les traités d'amour dans la littérature arabo-islamique médiéval (IIe/VIIIe–VIIIe/XIVe siècle)', pp. 121–30.

[13] B. Gruendler, 'Motif vs. Genre. Reflections on the *Dīwān al-Maʿānī* of Abū Hilāl al-ʿAskarī', p. 67.

[14] *Ẓurafāʾ* would be the transposition of *ʿudhrī* bedouin lovers in an urban context. Th. Bauer, *Liebe und Liebesdichtung in der arabischen Welt des 9. und 10. Jahrhunderts*, p. 65.

[15] Al-Washshāʾ is a literary man from Baghdad who was also a specialist of grammar, lexicography and an authority in good manners. W. Raven, 'al-Washshāʾ', *EI²*, XI, pp. 175b-176a.

[16] M.F. Ghazi, 'Un groupe social: 'Les raffinés' (*ẓurafāʾ*)', p. 50.

[17] In the social and literary life of the Middle Ages, the *ẓarīf* is a person who possesses *ẓarf* 'elegance' or 'refinement'. We can also translate the term as 'dandy'. The *taẓarruf* is generally regarded as the intensification of some intellectual, literary, social, and personal traits of the literary man. J.E. Montgomery, 'ẓarīf', *EI²*, XI, pp. 497b–498b.

[18] The meaning of the term *murūʾa* is not precisely defined. It is probable that it designated at first the physical characteristics of a man and then, by abstraction and spiritualization, his moral qualities. In the period of the first four caliphs, the *murūʾa* consisted in being chaste, having a good nature and observing Koranic law. With the Umayyad caliphs, it drew on politics, diplomacy, work, dignity, and compassion. During the Abbassid caliphate, it involved the possession of merit and it was the opposite of baseness. B. Farès (ed.), 'Murūʾa', *EI²*, VII, pp. 636a–638a.

[19] Al-Washshāʾ, *Kitāb al-Muwashshā*, p. 3. As for *adab*, it is also a difficult word to define precisely. This explanation of the word by K. Zakharia seems to me the most accurate description of the meaning of this word: 'mêlant l'art du bien vivre et du bien écrire, l'*adab* éclot dans le microcosme de l'élite citadine (khāṣṣa), comme une réflexion à la fois déontologique (sur le métier de secrétaire),

consider *Kitāb al-Muwashshā* to be, out of all the love treatises, the most helpful in defining the figure of the perfect lover[20].

According to al-Washshā', a passionate lover can be recognized by the marks listed in the following paragraph. They are so clear and visible they make it impossible for him to hide his feelings:[21]

The thinness of the body[22] (نحول الجسم); the never-ending illness (طول السقم); the yellowish colour (اصفرار اللون); insomnia (قلة النوم); the timid look (خشوع النظر); being always occupied by his thoughts (إدمان الفكر); the easy crying (سرعة الدموع); showing humility (إظهار الخشوع); the continuous lamentations (كثرة الأنين); showing nostalgia (إعلان الحنين); the abundant shedding of tears (انسكاب العبرات); the repeated sighs (تتابع الزفرات).

The following verses give also a description of the lover's face:[23]

وجه الذي يعشق معروف لأنه أصفر منحوف

The table in Appendix 1 shows some of the rules that al-Washshā' recommended the following in order to be considered as a *ẓarīf*. The *ẓarīf* has to wear cotton tunics of delicate colours[24] and to be perfumed.[25] He has to follow rules when eating. For instance, he won't eat more than one plate during the day and will not laugh or speak too much while at table.[26]

Description of Abū l-Qāsim

The main character of the *Ḥikāya*, who is called Abū l-Qāsim, can be defined as a *ṭufaylī* (party-crasher or parasite), a picaresque character recognisable by his peculiar costumes and behaviour.[27] In the introduction to his *Kitāb al-Tafṭīl*, al-Khaṭīb al-Baghdādī presents

---

éthique (définition des valeurs et vertus), comportementale (l'exercice du pouvoir et les relations des hommes de cour au prince, à leurs pairs et au commun et 'anthropologique', ou identitaire (reconnaître les membres de son groupe et se faire connaître par eux)'. K. Zakharia, 'Genèse et évolution de la prose littéraire: du *kātib* à l'*adīb*', p. 317.

[20] Thomas Bauer defines the *ẓurafā'* as an elitist group whose 'nobility' is not to be found in blood, but rather following a strict code of behaviour. Th. Bauer, *Liebe und Liebesdichtung in der arabischen Welt des 9. und 10. Jahrhunderts*, p. 65.

[21] Al-Washshā', *Kitāb al-Muwashshā*, p. 61.

[22] In his study *Of Dishes and Discourse*, Geert Jan van Gelder points out that 'the Bedouin hero should disdain food, neither partaking of it nor depicting it lovingly'. See *Of dishes and discourse, Classical Arabic Literary Representation of food*, p. 109.

[23] *You can recognize a lover from his yellow and thin face*. Al-Washshā', *Kitāb al-Muwashshā*, p. 63.

[24] Al- Washshā', *Kitāb al- Muwashshā*, p. 160.

[25] Al- Washshā' devotes an entire chapter to the scents the *ẓurafā'* are allowed or not to be perfumed with. Al- Washshā', *Kitāb al- Muwashshā*, pp. 162–163.

[26] Al- Washshā', *Kitāb al- Muwashshā*, p. 169.

[27] According to Antonella Ghersetti's study, the image of the *ṭufaylī* is well known in Arabic narrative texts and has its own well defined features. See A. Ghersetti, 'En quête de nourriture : étude des thèmes liés aux pique-assiettes (*ṭufayliyyūn*) dans la littérature arabe', p. 433.

the reader with a philological discussion of the term *ṭufaylī*. The word is explained as indicating someone who comes in uninvited or 'as a *nisba* (adjective describing the origin or the derivation of a thing or a person) to Ṭufayl, a man from Kūfa who attended receptions without an invitation'.[28] But Abū l-Qāsim is a very special kind of *ṭufaylī* whose most noticeable characteristic is his extraordinary verve in insulting and attacking people and things verbally. First of all, let us see some of the main physical and moral features with which he is described.

The *Ḥikāya* opens with a description of its main character's distinguishing physical features followed by a long list of adjectives and attributes portraying him.[29]

> كان هذا الرجل [...] يعرف بأبي القاسم [...] شيخًا بلحية بيضاء تلمع في حمرة وجه يكاد يقطر منه الخمر الصرف وله عينان كأنه ينظر بها من زجاج أخضر تبصران كأنهما تدران على زئبق.[30]

In the following paragraph are reported some of the most significant terms used to describe Abū l-Qāsim, classified by the semantic field to which they belong:

> *Rebel, bolshy, bawling (عيّار، نعّار، زعّاق، شهّاق); parasite, insistent (in demanding), greedy*[31] *(طفيلي، رصّاف، قصّاف); exceptional literary man (أديب عجيب), praising (مدّاح), blaming (قدّاح) mocking(طنّاز) , slanderer*[32] *(همّاز، همزة), malicious (لمزة), insulting (سبّاب), blaming (عيّاب), condemning (مندّد), sincere (مصادق), hypocritical (مماذق); refined (ظريف), filthy (سخيف); magician (بابلي); sagacious (نبيه، حديد),*[33] *stupid (سفيه); close (قريب), distant (بعيد); dignified (وقور); good companion in the evening (مسامر); playing hazard games (مقامر); homosexual*[34] *(لوطي ، حلقي), bawdy (شكّاز); malignant (غمّاز), quarrelsome (معربد); pious, irreligious (صدّيق ، زنديق), ascetic, debauched (ناسك ، فاتك); pimp (قوّاد), adventurer (كروك).*

Abū l-Qāsim is also said to be more foul-smelling than fishers' mud (*أشر من طين السماكين*) and to stink more than the lingering odour of tanners (*أنتن من ريح الدباغين*).[35] He is compared to a bag of faults (*عيبة العيوب*), to a pail of sins (*ذنب الذنوب*), and to garbage in a dustbin (*كبة على مزبلة*). He is filthier than the flame-tender's sooty hands (*قضبة من كف*

[28] F. Malti-Douglas, 'Structure and Organisation in a Monographic Adab Work: *al-tafṭīl* of al-Khaṭīb al-Baghdādī', p. 229.

[29] This list is too long to be quoted entirely and it is made of a great number of synonyms that I choose to translate with one word only. Abū l-Muṭahhar, *Ḥikāya*, pp. 3–4.

[30] 'This old man known as Abū l-Qāsim had a white beard shining with the redness of his face which was almost exuding drops of wine. His never-resting eyes were like green crystal which seemed to be turning around on mercury'. Abū l-Muṭahhar, *Ḥikāya*, p. 3.

[31] I translate here with 'insistent' both the terms *raṣṣāf* and *qaṣṣāf* which literary meaning is respectively 'paving' and 'bombing'.

[32] I translate with 'slander'; both *hammāz* and *hamaza* which derive from the same root *HMZ*.

[33] I translate with 'sagacious' both *nabīh* and *ḥadīd*.

[34] I translate with 'homosexual' both *lūṭī* and *ḥalaqī*, knowing that the *lūṭī* is the active partner in a homosexual intercourse and *ḥalaqī* is the passive one. E.K. Rowson, "The Effeminates of Early Medina", p. 686.

[35] Abū l-Muṭahhar, *Ḥikāya*, p. 3.

الوقاد), more impure than the urethra (أخرق من خرق البول), as noxious as old rotten cheese (أضر من الجبن العتيق), more destructive than a rat (أفسد من الجرذان)[36] and older than the Prophet's mantle (أعتق من البردة).[37]

The few poems that follow this list of 'qualities' underline the propensity of Abū l-Qāsim to practice any kind of sexual activity all the time and with all sorts of people.[38]

The members of the assembly

Abū l-Qāsim is not the only character described in the *Ḥikāya.* After installing himself in the assembly and reciting a few prayers, our character starts pouring his foul-mouthed eloquence on the members of the assembly. The following cast list details how members of the assembly appear to the merciless look of Abū l-Qāsim:

A literary man (*adīb*) called Abū Bishr:

He is debauched, dirty, ignorant, and stupid. He is good-looking on the outside, but completely rotten inside. He looks like a dog. (*Ḥikāya*, pp. 6–7)

A secretary (*kātib*) very close to the general director of the chancellery (*ṣāḥib al-dīwān*) and who is said to be a refined man (*ẓarīf*):

He is ugly. He takes advantage of his power. He farts all the time. His hands are dirty, he is stinky, and he looks like a catamite. (*Ḥikāya*, pp. 7–9)

A person with a big turban on his head:

He is self-important and vain. (*Ḥikāya*, p. 9)

A notable person:

He pretends to think about big political issues. He takes everything he can reach, but he never gives anything. He is an extremely greedy parasite looking all the time for food and young men. He is compared to a rooster whose life consists of eating, drinking, and fornicating. (*Ḥikāya*, pp. 9–11)

A guitar player (*ṭunbūrī*):

He is so greedy he could eat an elephant and drink the Nile. He cannot sing. He is extremely ugly. (Ḥikāya, p. 11)

Another guest (*nadīm*):

---

[36] Abū l-Muṭahhar, *Ḥikāya*, p. 3.

[37] The *burda* is a piece of wool, which was used in the pre-Islamic era as a coat during the day and as a blanket in the night. The *burda* of the Prophet became famous. R. Basset, 'Burda', *EI*², I, pp. 1354b–1355a.

[38] Abū l-Muṭahhar, *Ḥikāya*, p. 4.

He so ugly that, if his picture were hung on the bathroom door, all the cockroaches would flee. (*Ḥikāya*, p. 12)

A man who likes making jokes and having good time:

He is dirty, ugly and ill-smelling. He is so vain that he would starve rather than sell his clothes. He will never go out without his young servant. (*Ḥikāya*, pp. 12–15)

The supervisor of the house (*wakīl*) who is in charge of the guests' food, drink and entertainment:

He is a pimp and the exact opposite of what he pretends to be. (*Ḥikāya*, pp. 15–17)

The master of the house:

He is just like the others because you can judge a person from his company. (*Ḥikāya*, pp. 17–18)

The distorting mirror

Both *Kitāb al-Muwashshā* and *Ḥikāyat Abī l-Qāsim* portray the members of a culture's urban aristocracy[39] who gather to eat and drink and discuss literature, politics, theology, and philosophy. The members of these chosen groups have to follow some specific rules that distinguish them from the other 'ordinary' people and allow them access to this restricted high society. However, while *Kitāb al-Muwashshā* represents a practical guide-book which teaches the refined man how to behave in society, in the *Ḥikāyat Abī l-Qāsim* this code of behaviour is just the underlying starting point for building a *mujūn* text based on a social satire. This is clear if we compare the refined man of the *Muwashshā* and the characters described in the *Ḥikāya*.

The data collected in the table in Appendix 2 shows an almost perfect symmetry of opposites between the 'good' merits of the *ẓarīf* and the demerits of the *mājin*. The base of Abū l-Qāsim's eloquence in describing the image of the people present in the assembly he enters is the code of *ẓarf*. A clear parallelism can easy be seen between the description of the refined lover and the image that Abū l-Qāsim gives of the *mājin*. His eloquence acts as a mirror that returns distorted images.

One can certainly object that some of the (rare) positive qualities Abū l-Qāsim is described with, like *ẓarīf* or *adīb ʿajīb*, have not been mentioned in the table in Appendix 2 and that they can therefore distort the symmetry. On the contrary: I think that they consolidate the parallels between *mājin* and the *ẓarīf* because they have the double function of being ironic and showing how the main character of the *Ḥikāya* has perfectly mastered the code of refinement. It is precisely his knowledge of all these rules of behaviour that allows him to reverse them so completely.

---

[39] *Khāṣṣa* and *ʿāmma* are two antithetical terms that generally designate the elite and the common people, the notables and the plebs, the aristocracy and the masses even if the exact composition of these two elements of the population is extremely difficult to identify more precisely. M.A.J. Beg, 'al-Khāṣṣa wa-l-ʿāmma', *EI*², IV, pp. 1128b–1130b.

GHAZAL VS. *MUJŪN* POETRY

> '*Ghazal*' is a text that intertextually refers to the tradition of independent love poems, as formed during the seventh, eighth, and ninth centuries. For the fully developed *ghazal* of the ninth and tenth centuries [...] holds that nearly all its themes and motifs can be subsumed under five categories, namely: 1) *praise* of the beloved beauty; 2) a *complaint* made by the lover, who cannot (or cannot yet, or can no longer) attain a union with the beloved; 3) a *declaration* of passionate, unsurpassable, and unavoidable love; 4) a *reproach* directed against the beloved [...]; 5) a *portrayal*, i.e. the description of successful or unsuccessful encounters.[40]

We have already mentioned some definitions of *mujūn.*

A qayna from Baghdad

In the *Ḥikāya,* several pages are devoted to the description of singing girls and young men respectively. Abū l-Qāsim starts evoking the usual themes of *ghazal* when he describes *qiyān* (singing girls) and *ghilmān* (young men) from his native town, then turns suddenly to *mujūn* to give an image of the same category of people in Isfahan. In his description of a singer from Baghdad, Abū l-Qāsim follows exactly the five categories of motifs that *ghazal* usually deals with, starting from the first one, (the *praise* of the beloved beauty), and describing the *qayna*'s beauty and power of seduction. He quotes *ghazal* poetry and recalls images and themes common to this kind of poetry. Some of these are evoked below.

(1) Abū l-Qāsim starts his praise of a Baghdadi *qayna* reciting a verse by Dhū l-Rumma (d. around 117/735–6)[41] that compares the young girl standing up to a raised flagpole and to the undulating horizon of the hills shivering in the wind:

ترى خلفها نفصًا قناة قويمة   ونفصًا نقا يرتجّ أو يتمرمر[42]

(2) In a subsequent poem, he recalls the common theme of the killing power of ladies'eyelids:

أقاتلتني بانعكاس الجفون   ومستوفرين على معصر[43]

---

[40] Th. Bauer and A. Neuwirth, *Ghazal as World Literature*, 18.

[41] Very little is known about the life of Dhū al-Rumma, whose nickname was given to him because of an amulet he always wore around his neck as a pendant. The existing narratives about him deal mainly with his love affairs and his relationship with his contemporary poets, patrons and other literati. Love poetry is the dominant theme of Dhū al-Rumma's *dīwān*. Most of his poems are lyrical odes that start with the description of the deserted camp, followed by motifs on the beloved woman (named Mayya), and end with the description of the female camel and the narration of the poet's journey on the back of his mount. R. Blachère, 'D͟hū al-Rumma', *EI*[2], II, pp. 252a–253 and N. Papoutsakis, *Desert travel as a form of boasting*, p. 1 and p. 8.

[42] Abū l-Muṭahhar, *Ḥikāya*, p. 51 and Dhū l-Rumma, *Dīwān*, p. 109.

[43] Abū l-Muṭahhar, *Ḥikāya*, p. 51.

The verse can be compared, among others, with this verse whose author is not mentioned:

يا عين أنت قتلتن وجعلت ذنبك من ذنوبي[44]

(3) He compares pomegranates and women's breasts:

كأنما رمانتا صدرها حسنًا وطيبًا حقتًا عطر[45]

This comparison is quite common in *ghazal* poetry. Al-ʿAbbās b. al-Aḥnaf (d. 192/808),[46] for instance, recited this verse:

جال الوشّاح على قضيب زانه رمان صدر ليس يقطف ناهد[47]

The expression *rummān al-ṣadr* ou *al-ṣudūr* is also a common one.[48]

(4) Comparing the fragrance of the lady's breath with ambergris and her teeth with pearls is a classical theme:

نكهتها عنبر وغالية وثغرها لؤلؤ وكافور[49]

In the *Tazyīn al-aswāq*, Dāwūd al-Anṭākī reports this verse, which he attributes to Ibn al-Raʾīs:

لئن كان من لؤلؤ ثغرها فأنّ له صدفًا عن عقيق[50]

A verse from an anonymous poem says:

وكأنّ نكهتها إذا هي صفقت مسك يخالط عنبرًا وقرنفلًا[51]

(5) In a verse that Abū l-Qāsim quoted from ʿUmar Ibn Abī Rabīʿa (d. 93/712 or 103/721),[52] a singing girl of Baghdad is said to be as white as silver:

---

[44] Al-Nuwayrī, *Nihāyat al-arab fī funūn al-ʿarab*, II, p. 150 and Ibn al-Jawzī, *Dhamm al-hawā*, p. 102. See also:

آلت لواحظه على أهل الهوى إن لا قتلًا بغر منهد

تسل سيوفها من لواحظ طرفها ولكن لها من عادة الجفون غامد

Both the verses are in Ibn Abī Ḥajala (d. 776/1375), *Dīwān al-Ṣabāba*, p. 78.

[45] Abū l-Muṭahhar, *Ḥikāya*, p. 51.

[46] 'Al-ʿAbbās b. al-Aḥnaf was an author of love poetry in early ʿAbbāsid Iraq: 'Al-ʿAbbās, as his Muslim biographers have noted, cultivated only one genre, the *ghazal*. [...] In his *ghazal*, al-ʿAbbās appears as a successor to the poets of Ḥijāz ʿUmar b. Abī Rabīʿa, (d. 93/712 or 103/721) and Jamīl b. Maʿmar al-ʿUdhrī (d. 82/701)'. S. Enderwitz, 'al-ʿAbbās b. al-Aḥnaf', *EI*[3], 2009–1, p. 2a and p. 3a.

[47] Al-Sarī l-Raffāʾ, *al-Muḥibb wa-l-maḥbūb wa-l-mashmūm wa-l-mashrūb*, I, p. 249.

[48] See for example in Taqī l-dīn al-Azrārī, *Khizānat al-adab wa-ghāyat al-arab*, II, p. 142:

أما والهوى لا حلت عن عطف أغيد ولا بت في رمان صدر مفرطًا

[49] Abū l-Muṭahhar, *Ḥikāya*, p. 52.

[50] Dāwūd al-Anṭākī, *Tazyīn al-aswāq*, p. 479.

[51] Al-Tawḥīdī, *al-Baṣāʾir wa-l-dhakhāʾir*, VI, p. 64.

[52] ʿUmar b. Abī Rabīʿa is a well known Umayyad poet of *ghazal*. The *Dīwān* of ʿUmar is the most remarkable and substantial example of Ḥijāzī *ghazal*. J.E. Montgomery, 'ʿUmar b. Abī Rabīʿa', *EI*[2], X, pp. 887b–888b.

قينة بيضاء كالفضّة سوداء القرون[53]

(6) Abū l-Qāsim makes use of animal imagery like the antelope (مهاة), and the partridge (قطاة) to describe the girl's way of walking, which is also extremely common in *ghazal* poetry.[54]

(7) Our *ṭufaylī* quotes as well another poem of Ibn al-Ḥajjāj's *ghazal* poetry, which contains the classical comparison of the girl with a fawn (شادن), so perfect that it can be considered as a proof of God the creator's power. She is like the sun in a dark obscure night and bends like a tree branch in the breeze.[55]

Al-Sarī l-Raffāʾ's *Kitāb al-muḥibb wa-maḥbūb wa-l-mashmūm wa-l-mashrūb* (d. 362/972–3)[56] contains, as far as I know, the most exhaustive collection of poetry describing women in terms of their physical features. Each chapter in the first volume of this book quotes poems dealing with one part of a woman's body. All the most classical poetic topoi of *ghazal* poetry appear in the pages of al-Sarī al-Raffāʾ's work. The consultation of *Kitāb al-muḥibb* confirms that the physical description that Abū l-Qāsim gives of the Baghdadi *qayna* is absolutely 'canonical', because the *Ḥikāya* reproduces exactly the same topoi.

Let us now consider the poetic terms Abū l-Qāsim uses to complain about the cruelty of the beloved and to recall the sufferings that his love for her causes.[57] He beseeches his beloved to give him back his heart (*ruddī fuʾādī*) and his life, but he declares he is ready to die for love of her if she will not agree to do this.[58] The poem is quoted from Ibn al-Ḥajjāj (d. 391/1001), a poet known in particular for his *sukhf* and *mujūn* poetry,[59] but it is reported as being an example of his *ghazal* poetry.[60] The same request to have his heart back, formulated with exactly the same words, can also be found in a verse attributed to Jarīr (d. 110/728–9).[61]

[53] Abū l-Muṭahhar, *Ḥikāya*, p. 52. The same verse is in the *Dīwān al-maʿānī* by Abū Hilāl al-ʿAskarī, I, p. 220.

[54] Abū l-Muṭahhar, *Ḥikāya*, p. 53.

[55] Abū l-Muṭahhar, *Ḥikāya*, p. 57.

[56] Al-Sarī al-Raffāʾ is an Arabic poet and anthologist known in particular for his descriptive poetry. His *al-Muḥibb wa-maḥbūb wa-l-mashmūm wa-l-mashrūb* is an anthology of *maʿānī*, a selection of poetic fragments classified according to their motifs and giving the description of the different elements of the beloved, of the spring, or of the wine. W.P. Heinrichs, 'Al-Sarī al-Raffāʾ', *EI*², IX, pp. 58a–59b.

[57] According to Teresa Garulo it is the extraordinary popular success which greeted love poetry that canonised the image of the woman as the ever-cruel and ungrateful object of love. T. Garulo, 'Women in Classical Arabic Poetry', p. 31.

[58] Abū l-Muṭahhar, *Ḥikāya*, p. 56.

[59] See D.S. Margoliouth [Ch. Pellat], 'Ibn Al-Ḥadjdjādj', *EI*², III, pp. 803b–804a.

[60] See: al-Khaṭīb al-Baghdādī, *Tārīkh Baghdād*, VIII, p. 14 and Ibn Khallikān, *Wafayāt al-aʿyān*, II, p. 169.

[61] ردي فؤادي وكوني بمنزلتي يا قبل نفسك لاقى نفسي التلف

A few lines below, Abū l-Qāsim recalls in a poem the classical motifs of the sick, wounded heart (*qalb majrūḥ ʿalīl*), and of the lack of patience when he is far away from his beloved:[62]

يا صحيح القلب قلبي   منك مجروح عليل
يا كثير الغدر صبري   عنك مذ غبت قليل

The theme of the wounded heart can be found for instance in this verse attributed to Ibn Isrāʾīl (d. 677/1278):[63]

فقال شهود ليس يقبل قولها   فدمعك مقذوف وقلبك مجروح

And the lack of patience in this one composed by Ibn Zaydūn (d. 463/1070):[64]

فديتك إن صبري عنك صبري   لدى عطشي عن الماء القراح

This list of motifs could be much longer but the examples I offer are sufficient to show my purpose. When he has finished with all these classical motifs, our orator suddenly changes the key of his talk to fire a singing slave present in the assembly he entered with his relentless eloquence.

A qayna from Isfahan

Abū l-Qāsim compares the *qayna* from Isfahan to a monkey and a *ghūl*.[65] She has white hair like coloured wool, a yellow face that makes her resemble an exhumed corpse. Her legs are green.[66] She is old. As for her facial and body features:

1) She has a big old mouth that spits noxious saliva that could kill a poisonous snake.[67]
2) She has a nose cut from the inside of her face like a protruding clitoris.[68]
3) Her eyes are so small that she cannot put kohl on them without smearing it all over her face.[69]

Jarīr is a famous Umayyad poet especially known for his satiric poems. A. Schaade-[H. Gätje], 'Djarīr', *EI²*,II, p. 492ab.

Ibn Qutayba, *ʿUyūn al-akhbār*, I, p. 50.

[62] Abū l-Muṭahhar, *Ḥikāya*, p. 56.

[63] Dāwūd al-Anṭākī, *Tazyīn al-aswāq*, p. 488.

[64] Al-Maqqarī al-Tilmisānī, *Nafḥ al-ṭīb min ghuṣn al-Andalus al-raṭīb*, III, 279. Ibn Zaydūn is Andalusian poet whose most important poems deal with his love for Wallāda. G. Lecomte, 'Ibn Zaydūn', *EI²*, III, pp. 998a–999a.

[65] The *ghūl* is a kind ogre that confuses the travellers and eats them starting from the feet. A. de B. Kazimirsky, *Dictionnaire Arabe-Français*. Abū l-Muṭahhar, *Ḥikāya*, p. 57.

[66] I take this as an allusion to her having a lot of varicose veins. Abū l-Muṭahhar, *Ḥikāya*, p. 57.

[67] Abū l-Muṭahhar, *Ḥikāya*, p. 57.

[68] Ibid., p. 57.

[69] Ibid., p. 58.

4) When she cuts her eyebrows, she can make baskets out of the hair.[70]
5) Her hair is like a bale of dusty reeds.[71]
6) One of her breasts is like an old leather bag and the other like the water seller's goatskin. One of them reaches her knee and the other her hip.[72]
7) Her posterior is constantly emitting farts and faeces.[73]
8) She has the legs of a spider and the neck of a beetle.[74]
9) Her armpits smell worse than white onion.[75]
10) Her waist is covered with rolls of fat, but her breast and her bottom are extremely skinny.[76]

These are only a few of the characteristics by which the *qayna* from Isfahan is described. Abū l-Qāsim's eloquence largely oversteps the limits of what we have mentioned. Nevertheless, it suffices to see that she is described in the most unpleasant way possible.

In the pages that follow the description of the old and ugly singer from Isfahan, exactly the same procedure is used to speak about a beardless young man (*ghulām*). First, Abū l-Qāsim gives a description of how he should be. He says for instance that a *ghulām* should have a forehead like a crescent moon and eyebrows like they have been traced with a pen.[77] His cheeks should be like roses whose beauty would be increased by a fine down like a fawn's, and his skin should be as soft as silk.[78] He should be perfumed by the most exquisite fragrances.[79]

If we compare the poems of the *Kitāb al-muḥibb* by al-Sarī al-Raffāʾ with the motifs that Abū l-Qāsim brings up in his description of the young man we can see that they are also very common topoi. A glance through the poems of this book in the chapter about cheeks shows that describing the cheeks like roses is very common.[80] The same can be said about the phrases used to describe the forehead and eyebrows.[81]

Instead of being like the ideal described by Abū l-Qāsim, the *ghulām* of Isfahan is compared to a stinking billy goat. He has a sullen face.[82] On his face nobody can tell the hairs of the nose from the ones of his moustache.[83] One could give many more examples, but further discussion would exceed the limits of this article.

---

[70] Ibid., p. 58.
[71] Ibid., p. 61.
[72] Ibid., p. 58.
[73] Ibid., p. 62.
[74] Ibid., p. 62.
[75] Ibid., p. 63.
[76] Ibid., p. 63.
[77] Ibid., p. 65.
[78] Abū l-Muṭahhar, *Ḥikāya*, p. 66.
[79] Abū l-Muṭahhar, *Ḥikāya.* p. 66.
[80] Al-Sarī l-Raffāʾ, *al-Muḥibb wa-l-maḥbūb*, I, pp. 66, 69, 70, 71, etc.
[81] Al-Sarī l-Raffāʾ, *al-Muḥibb wa-l-maḥbūb*, I, p. 87.
[82] Abū l-Muṭahhar, *al-Muḥibb wa-l-maḥbūb*, p. 67.
[83] Abū l-Muṭahhar, *al-Muḥibb wa-l-maḥbūb*, p. 68.

Mujūn Poetry about qiyān and ghilmān: Topoi of Ugliness

The description of the *qayna* and the *ghilman* are one of the most, if not the most, common topics of *ghazal* poetry. 'The image of women in *adab* literature was subject to literary convention, complicated by the presence of *topoi* which have the potential of substantially deforming reality'.[84] Her description in poetry follows a well known canon. This is true not only for the free women of the pre-Islamic era, but also for the *qayna*, that became, as al-Jāḥiẓ (d. 255/868) observes in his *Risālat al-qiyān*, the idealised lady that inspires love[85] when the concept of passionate love (*ʿishq*) was transferred from the desert to an urban location.

As the examples above illustrate, Abū l-Qāsim is perfectly aware of the conventions that rule the description of the women in *ghazal* poetry and he uses all the topoi characteristic of this kind of poetry in his description of the beauty of the Baghdadi slave girl. His perfect mastery of this kind of poetry allows him to build his description of the Persian singing slave starting from *ghazal* motifs. When he describes the *qayna* from Baghdad or the perfect young man, he creates a complete image of them involving all five senses. In the same way, he creates a new negative canon of ugliness and unpleasantness for both of them in which the five senses participate. In doing this, as the examples given show clearly, Abū l-Qāsim follows all the conventions of the genre and gives his public exactly what they would expect to hear.

This parallel between the themes is exceptionally surprising when Abū l-Qāsim passes from the *ghazal*'s motifs of beauty to the themes of ugliness and awfulness. It is my opinion that this reversal of classical motifs to cause such a surprise is one of the most prominent characteristics of *mujūn*.

CONCLUSION

I have examined here how the image of the *mājin* is built starting from the model of the refined man and how *mujūn* poetry was born out of *ghazal* patterns. This phenomenon has already been observed by Philip Kennedy concerning Abū Nuwās's wine song; '*Mujūn* is a counter-genre', he points out, 'which plays a literary game by inverting the conventions of 'normative' *ghazal*'.[86] It creates 'an entertaining dissonance between *nasīb* and *khamr*', he continues, producing 'a literary parody of the older poetry which simultaneously articulates *mujūn*'.[87] My paper shows that this statement can also be extended to other kinds of poetry and prose.

A further confirmation of the proximity between *ghazal* poetry, motifs of *ʿudhrī* love, and *mujūn* can be found, if needed, in the comparison between a verse of Abū Nuwās

---

[84] N.M. El-Cheikh, 'Women's History: A Study of al-Tanūkhī', p. 132.

[85] F. Sicard, 'L'amour dans la *Risālat al-qiyān* –essai sur les esclaves chanteuses – de Ǧāḥiẓ (m. 255/868)', p. 336.

[86] P. Kennedy, *The Wine Song in Classical Arabic Poetry*, p. 64.

[87] P. Kennedy, *Wine Song*, p. 52.

quoted by al-Nuwayrī in his *Nihāyat al-arab fī funūn al-ʿarab*, and three verses of love poetry found in *al-Wāḍiḥ al-mubīn fī dhikr man ustush'hida min al-muḥibbīn* by Mughulṭāy (d. 762/1361). In these verses, the same motif, told with the exactly same words, is used to express parallel and opposite meanings.

While Abū Nuwās expresses his ideal of a 'good' life in these terms:

لا خير في العيش إلا في المجون مع ال . . . أكفّاء والراح والريحان والآس[88]

Three authors of love poetry whose names are not mentioned say:

لا خير في الدنيا ولا في نعيمها وأنت وحيد مفرد غير عاشق[89]

and

لا خير في الدنيا بغير صبابة ولا في نعيم ليس فيه حبيب[90]

or

لا خير لي يا بدر في البقاء ما خير العيش بعد موت الحبيب.[91]

As we have seen, the *Ḥikāya* of Abū l-Qāsim al-Baghdādī, which can be considered a masterpiece of *mujūn*, could not exist without reference to earlier forms of prose and poetry, because its comic and parodic effect is entirely based on reference back to old models. Furthermore, there cannot be any *mujūn* without the effect of surprise created by deceiving the readers' expectations. This is particularly evident in the passages of the *Ḥikāya* in which Abū l-Qāsim describes the *qayna* or the *ghulām* according to normative 'standards' and then undertakes to destroy these models systematically.

Comedy is an important element of *mujūn*. This is caused by the gap that separates the expectations of the public and the distorted images of people that Abū l-Qāsim actually gives them. This unexpected comic effect allows the author of the *Ḥikāya* to draw a caricature of the people of his time and thus to criticise the political power, the costumes, and the lifestyle of the society he lives in.

[88] Al-Nuwayrī, *Nihāyat al-arab fī funūn al-ʿarab*, IV, p. 95.
[89] Mughulṭāy, *al-Wāḍiḥ al-mubīn fī dhikr man ustush'hida min al-muḥibbīn*, p. 64.
[90] Mughulṭāy, *al-Wāḍiḥ*, p. 64.
[91] Mughulṭāy, *al-Wāḍiḥ*, p. 378.

WORKS CITED

Abū Ḥayyān al-Tawḥīdī, al-Risāla al-Baghdādiyya, ed. ᶜA. al-Shālijī (Köln: al-Kamel Verlag, 1997).
Abū Ḥayyān al-Tawḥīdī, al-Baṣāʾir wa-l-dhakhāʾir (Beirut: Dār Ṣādir, 1988).
Abū Hilāl al-ᶜAskarī, Dīwān al-maᶜānī (Beirut: Dār al-Kutub al-ᶜIlmiyya, 1994).
Abū al-Mutahhar al-Azdī, Ḥikāyat Abī l-Qāsim, ed. A. Mez (Heidleberg: Carl Winter's Universitätbuchhandlung, 1902).
Abū al-Mutahhar al-Azdī, 24 heures de la vie d'une canaille, trans. R. Khawam (Paris: Phébus, 1998).
M. Balda, 'Genèse et essor d'un genre littéraire: les traités d'amour dans la littérature arabo-islamique médiéval (IIe/VIIIe–VIIIe/XIVe siècle)', Synergie Monde Arabe, 6 (2009), pp. 121–130.
M. Balda, 'Marginalité et éloquence contestataire: le personnage d'Abū al-Qāsim dans la Ḥikāyat Abī al-Qāsim d'Abū al-Mutahhar al-Azdī', in Cristina De la Puente (ed.), Identitades marginales (Madrid : Consejo Superior de Investigationes científicas, 2003), pp. 371–393.
R. Basset, 'Burda', EI2, I, pp. 1354b–1355a.
Th. Bauer, Liebe und Liebesdichtung in der arabischen Welt des 9. und 10. Jahrhunderts (Wiesbaden: Harrassowitz, 1998).
Th. Bauer and A. Neuwirth, Ghazal as World Literature I, Transformations of a Literary Genre (Beirut: Ergon-Verlag, 2005).
M.A.J. Beg, 'al-Khāṣṣa wa-l-ᶜāmma', EI2, IV, pp. 1128b–1130b.
R. Blachère, 'Dhū al-Rumma', EI2, II, pp. 252a–253a.
A.M. El-Cheikh, 'Women's History: A Study of al-Tanūkhī', in M. Marín and R. Deguilhem (eds.), Writing the Feminine: Women in Arab Sources (London/New York: I. B. Tauris, 2002), pp. 129–148.
Dāwūd al-Anṭākī, Tazyīn al-aswāq fī akhbār al-ᶜushshāq (Beirut: Dār Maktabat al-Hilāl, 1993).
Dhū al-Rumma, Dīwān (Beirut: Dār al-Kutub al-ᶜIlmiyya, 1995).
S. Enderwitz, 'al-ᶜAbbās b. al-Aḥnaf', EI3, 2009-1, 2a–4a.
B. Farès (ed.), 'Murūʾa', EI2, VII, pp. 636a-638a.
R. Farrin, Abundance from the Desert: Classical Arabic Poetry (Syracuse, NY: Syracuse University Press, 2011).
F. Gabrieli, 'Abū l-Muṭahhar al-Azdī', EI2, p. 31a.
T. Garulo 'Women in Medieval Classical Arabic Poetry', in M. Marín and R. Deguilhem (eds.), Writing the Feminine: Women in Arab Sources (London/New York: I. B. Tauris, 2002), pp. 25–40.
G.J. van Gelder, Of Dishes and Discourse: Classical Arabic Literary Representation of Food (Richmond: Curzon, 2000).
M.F. Ghazi, 'Un groupe social: "Les raffinés" (ẓurafāʾ)', Studia Islamica XI (1959), pp. 39–71.
W.P. Heinrichs, 'Al-Sarī al-Raffā', EI2, IX, pp. 58a–59b.
Ibn Abī Ḥajala, Dīwān al-Ṣabāba (Beirut: Dār Maktabat al-Hilāl, 1999).
Ibn al-Jawzī, Akhbār al-ẓirāf wa-l-mutāmajinīn (Beirut: Dār Ibn Ḥazm, 1997).
Ibn al-Jawzī, Dhamm al-hawā (Cairo: Dār al-Kutub al-Islāmiyya, 1962).
Ibn Khallikān, Wafayāt al-aᶜyān (Beirut: Dār Ṣādir, 1900).
Ibn Manẓūr, Lisān al-ᶜarab (Beirut: Dār Ṣādir, 1997).
Al-Khaṭīb al-Baghdādī, Tārīkh Baghdād (Beirut: Dār al-Kutub al-ᶜIlmiyya, 1997).
P.F. Kennedy, The Wine Song in Classical Arabic Poetry (Oxford: Clarendon Press, 1997).
G. Lecomte, 'Ibn Zaydūn', EI2, III, pp. 998a–999a.
Al-Maqqarī al-Tilmisānī, Nafḥ al-ṭīb min ghuṣn al-Andalus al-raṭīb (Beirut: Dār Ṣādir, 1968).
D.S. Margoliouth [Pellat Ch.], 'Ibn Al-Ḥadjdjādj', EI2,III, pp. 803b–804a.
J.E. Montgomery, 'ᶜUmar b. Abī Rabīᶜa', EI2, X, pp. 887b–888b.
J.E. Montgomery, 'ẓarīf', EI2, XI, pp. 497b–498b.

Mughulṭāy, al-Wāḍiḥ al-mubīn fī dhikr man ustushhida min al-muḥibbīn (Beirut: al-Intishār al-ʿArabī, 1997).
Al-Nuwayrī, Nihāyat al-arab fī funūn al-ʿarab (Beirut: Dār al-Kitāb al-ʿIlmiyya, 2004).
Papoutsakis, G.-N., Desert Travel as a Form of Boasting: a Study of Ḏū r-Rumma's poetry, Arabische studien 4 (Wiesbaden: Harrassowitz Verlag, 2009).
Ch. Pellat, 'Mudjūn', EI2, VII, p. 304a–b.
W. Raven, 'al-Washshāʾ', EI, XI, pp. 175b–176a.
E.K. Rowson, 'The Effeminates of Early Medina', Journal of the American Oriental Society 111.4 (1991), pp. 671–93.
S.M. Stern, 'Abū Ḥayyān al-Tawḥīdī', EI2, I, pp. 130a–131a.
Al-Sarī al-Raffāʾ, al-Muḥibb wa-l-maḥbūb wa-l-mashmūm wa-l-mashrūb (Damascus: Majmaʿ al-Lugha al-ʿArabiyya, 1986).
Al-Shayzarī, Rawḍat al-qulūb wa-nuzhat al-muḥibb wa-l-maḥbūb, eds. D. Semah and G. J. Kanazi (Wiesbaden: Harrassowitz Verlag, 2003).
F. Sicard, 'L'amour dans la Risālat al-qiyān –essai sur les esclaves chanteuses – de Ǧāḥiẓ (m. 255/868)', Arabica 34 (1984), pp. 326–38.
Taqī al-dīn al-Azrārī, Khizānat al-adab wa-ghāyat al-arab (Beirut: Dār Maktabat al-Hilāl, 1987).
Al-Washshāʾ, Kitāb al-Muwashshā or al-Ẓarf wa-ẓurafāʾ, ed. Kamāl Muṣṭafā (Cairo: Maktabat al-Khānijī, 1953).
K. Zakharia, 'Genèse et évolution de la prose littéraire: du kātib à l'adīb', in T. Bianquis, P. Guichard et M. Tillier (eds.), Les débuts du monde musulman, viie–xe siècles (Paris: Presses Universitaires de France, 2012), pp. 313–31.

APPENDIX 1: THE RULES OF *ADAB*, *MURŪʾA* AND *ẒARF*

The rules are drawn from al-Washshāʾ, *Kitāb al-Muwashshā*, pp. 6–11, 13–15, 19–25, 29, 32–37, 39–41, 51–52, 59, and 192.

Rules of *adab*	Rules of *murū'a*	Rules of *ẓarf*
To read books and to transmit poetry and prose (*akhbār*).	To have an open face (*ṭalāqat al-wajh*).	The pillars (*ʿimād*) of refinement are: to protect his nearest and dearest; to defend his honor; to stay away from opprobrium; to refrain from any fault.
Not to speak too much. To answer only when questioned. To stay silent is much better than to say wrong or bad words.	To like people (*al-tawaddud ilā l-nās*).	There is no *ẓarf* without clarity of speaking (*faṣāḥa*), eloquence (*balāgha*), chastity (*ʿiffa*) and honesty (*nazāha*).
The *adīb* will never be aggressive in speaking. He will always tell the truth and speak the words of his heart.	To satisfy the needs of people (*qaḍā ḥawāʾij al-nās*).	*Ẓarf* is self-restraint (*ẓulf al-nafs*), generosity (*sakhāʾ al-kaff*), and chastity.
He will not make jokes or say silly words, because jokes belittle people and destroy friendships.	To be upright in his faith, to live honestly, to have a generous mind, and to be compassionate.	*Ẓarf* is to have a sensible nature, to speak the truth, and to keep secrets. A *ẓarīf* should never interrupt somebody speaking or say something that would be better to leave unsaid.
He must associate with clever and well-dressed people.	Not to exceed in eating and drinking.	*Ẓarf* is based on four virtues: modesty, generosity, chastity, and abstinence.
He must love his friends and rarely contradict them.	To take care of his brothers.	*Ẓurafāʾ* are always neat and clean, graceful, gentle, elegant, and perfumed.
Not to exceed in loving his friends and in loathing his enemies.	To hide what is shameful to show and to chastise his tongue by his heart (*muwāṭaʾat al-qalb al-lisān*).	They have handsome faces and beautiful appearances.
Not to visit his friends too frequently.	There is no *murūʾa* without being patient, modest, not telling lies, being present, behaving properly, forgiving easily, doing good and keeping your promises when you are in a position of power.	They have desiring souls, loving hearts, eyes that look furtively, and passionate spirits.
The *adīb* should be in love because love opens the minds, broadens the hearts, gives courage to the coward, makes the miser generous, loosens the stammerer's tongue, and strengthens the resolution of the weak.		The qualities distinguishing them are gravity, humility, noble nature, good manners, and noble minds.

APPENDIX 2: REFINEMENT IN THE *MUWASHSHĀ* VS. CHARACTERIZATION IN THE *ḤIKĀYA*

Scope of comparison	Features of the refined man and lover according to the *Muwashshā*	Features of Abū l-Qāsim and of the characters in the *Ḥikāya*
Physical appearance	1) The *ẓarīf* is constantly affected by the malady of love, thus he has a thin delicate body and an unhealthily pale face. He must keep his face open and show humility by lowering his eyes.	1) Abū l-Qāsim has a purple-red face and darting eyes.
	2) He must be neat and properly perfumed.	2) Both Abū l-Qāsim and the members of the assembly are dirty and smell bad. Their hands are soiled. They fart incessantly.
	3) The *ẓurafāʾ* are graceful and beautiful, with handsome faces.	3) The members of the assembly are all extremely ugly. They are compared to dogs and monkeys in their ugliness.
Dress code	The refined man must be dressed in a discreet, elegant way that does not draw attention.	One of the assembly's members wears a big turban to brag about.
Manner of speech	1) The *ẓurafāʾ* are eloquent but they never speak too much.	1) Abū l-Qāsim's eloquence is inexhaustible.
	2) They never interrupt a speaker.	2) His verbosity is extremely aggressive.
	3) They never made bad jokes or say something that should be kept unsaid. Their words always come from their hearts.	3) He never speaks about anybody without attacking him with the most hurtful insults and the lewdest jokes.
Manner of eating	The refined man is moderate in eating or drinking. He follows a special diet.[92] He never speaks or laughs too much or too loudly when eating.	The people described by Abū l-Qāsim are greedy and can gulp down enormous quantities of food and drink.[93] They would do anything just to get a good meal. Abū l-Qāsim never stops talking during the meal.
Learning	The *ẓarīf* must read books and be able to transmit poetry and prose.	The people in the assembly in Isfahan are ignorant and stupid, but they pretend to think about big political and theological issues.
General behaviour	The *ẓurafāʾ* must always keep their promises, be generous, love people, and behave properly towards them.	Abū l-Qāsim is malignant and quarrelsome, malicious and hypocritical. The people he describes are the opposite of what they pretend to be. Some of them are described as misers.
Sexual habits	The *ẓurafāʾ* are chaste and do not love young men.[94]	Abū l-Qāsim is described as bawdy, homosexual, and willing to have sex with anyone at any time. Two members of the assembly are described as lovers of young men.

[92] Al- Washshāʾ, *Kitāb al-Muwashshā*, pp. 165–172.

[93] Zeal and immoderation in the consumption of food, also disregard for religious precepts. R. Farrin, *Abundance from the Desert*, p. 221.

[94] This specific point of *ẓarf*'s code is clearly pointed out by al-Shayzarī in the 8th chapter of his *Rawḍat al-qulūb wa-nuzhat al-muḥibb wa-l-maḥbūb*, 233–234.

8

Mujūn is a Crazy Game

Emily Selove

> 'Come!' cried old Omar. 'Let us drink, and break into new patterns the tedious roof of heaven!'
>
> F.V. Morley, *My One Contribution to Chess*

Ḥikāyat Abī al-Qāsim, probably written in the 11th century by Abū al-Muṭahhar Muḥammad ibn Aḥmad al-Azdī, tells the story of a Baghdadi party-crasher in Isfahan, and is introduced by its author as a microcosm of Baghdad. Indeed the protagonist Abū al-Qāsim seems to cover every topic imaginable as he dominates the conversation of the party that he is crashing. Late in the afternoon, Abū al-Qāsim challenges another guest to a game of chess, and for every chess-piece that is moved, he has a scabrous remark or a baffling poem to recite. During this game, the narrator repeatedly describes Abū al-Qāsim's speech as 'nonsense' (*hadhayān*). This paper will explore ideas of game-playing and its characteristically nonsensical creation of rules and use of language, comparing this episode of the *Ḥikāya* to a story in Al-Zubayr's 9th-century *al-Akhbār al-muwaffaqiyyāt* in which the head of a household, in an act described as kind of *mujūn*, arbitrarily demands that everybody stand on one foot until the servants come back from the market with some sugar. Thus I will read the chess game described in the *Ḥikāya* itself as a microcosm of the world of *mujūn*, often characterized not only by an inversion of the rules of everyday life, but by the establishment of another topsy-turvy set of temporary rules.

Despite this topsy-turvy atmosphere of the text, the *Ḥikāya* may invite readers to use it as an encyclopedia of material goods or otherwise as a source of historical and antiquarian interest for a number of reasons.[1] One of these reasons is its obscenity, or focus on 'low' topics not typically addressed in other forms of literature. The *Ḥikāya* often employs a literary style known as *mujūn*, distinguished by its focus on low topics and use of obscene vocabulary. In 'Arabic *Mujūn* poetry', Julie Meisami writes: 'Discussions by Arab scholars typically adopt historical, sociological, or biographical approaches' to *mujūn* literature.

[1] For examples of such usages of the *Ḥikāya*, see Aḥsan, *Social Life,* 11, and Dhū al-Nūn Ṭāhā, 'Mujtamaᶜ' 14–25.

Futhermore, 'the literary aspects of *mujūn* poetry have received little attention.'[2] In order to facilitate historical or antiquarian readings of the *Ḥikāya*, among other reasons, we should strive to understand the literary definition of *mujūn* itself. This is not easily done, and some ink has already been spilled trying.[3]

Here, in discussing the chess game played in the *Ḥikāya*, I will show that *mujūn* itself can be thought of as a kind of game, and that thus the style of language known as *mujūn* is by definition playful. In the introduction to his edition of the text, Adam Mez identifies the chess game as the only section comprised of entirely original material in the *Ḥikāya.*[4] However this essay (supplemented by a full translation in the appendix), argues that the chess game can be read as a synecdoche for the work as a whole. With its specific and familiar-sounding details, it tempts us to try to reconstruct the game exactly as described. Upon closer examination, however, we find that the events described are impossible to reconstruct because they are each presented only as hypothetical examples of events, as well as being couched in playfully disorienting language. But before exploring the chess game, I will begin with a further discussion of *mujūn* by examining a story from al-Zubayr ibn Bakkār's 9th-century *al-Akhbār al-muwaffaqiyyāt* that describes not a type of literature, but a type of behavior defined as *mujūn.*

THE RULES OF THE GAME

This story is about four sons who are accused before the caliph al-Maʾmūn of unseemly *mujūn.*[5] When the caliph confirms the accusation by discovering the silly statements engraved on their signet rings, one son explains that they learned this behavior from their father, a treasurer in al-Maʾmūn's court. By way of example he tells a story of the long and harrowing night in which his father discovered that there were no more cones of sugar in the house. In this story, his father angrily demands that his entire household stand on one foot until the servants can purchase more sugar in the middle of the night. While his tired family abides by his arbitrary command, he raves on a wide range of subjects such as property taxes, the improper behavior of women, and – when the servants finally do return with sugar – the minute details of lawful Islamic buying and selling practices.

Since this story is presented as evidence of their father's *mujūn,* we can look to it for

[2] Meisami, 'Arabic Mujūn Poetry: the literary dimension,' 9.

[3] Meisami reviews some of these attempts and ultimately defines it as 'bacchic and erotic, both taken to extremes...not merely anti-religious but also anti-heroic in outlook.' She later adds that *mujūn* is a 'counter-genre which inverts the conventions of "normative" *ghazal* and *waṣf al-khamr*' ('Arabic Mujūn Poetry', 8–9, 14). Geert Jan van Gelder points out that in distinguishing it from a different style, *hijāʾ*, or invective, 'the text alone is not enough to decide its nature: one needs to know the intention of the poet and his relationship with the victim' (*The Bad and the Ugly*, 51). He is distinguishing between invective (*hijāʾ*) which, in Everett Rowson's words, has 'defamatory intent', and *mujūn*'s 'essential lightheartedness'. Rowson later adds 'It is less the illicitness of the subject than the presence of explicit vocabulary and graphic description that sets off *mujūn*' ('Mujūn', 546–7).

[4] Azdī, *Sittenbild,* V.

[5] Bakkār, *Akhbār,* 69.

information on the defining characteristics of *mujūn* itself.[6] ʿAlī ibn Ṣāliḥ, the treasurer, in his night-long act of *mujūn*, establishes an alternative set of rules for his party to live by (that everyone must stand on one foot until he receives a cone of sugar). Meanwhile, as noted by Stefan Leder in his 'Prosa-Dichtung in der aḫbār Überlieferung', his absurd behavior undercuts any wisdom that may be found in his discussion of the laws that regulate daily life (such as property taxes and buying and selling practices). As for ʿAlī ibn Ṣāliḥ's speech, Leder writes, 'It shows that he considers the lack of sugar a disaster – itself already a laughable exaggeration of a really inconsequential problem – and that he goes from the particular to the general to the point that he seeks to integrate his subjective perception into the level of general truth – the truth of the revelation and the sunna.'[7] *Mujūn*, therefore, can describe behavior that follows a set of bizarre rules, whose enactment parodically echoes the logic of the daily laws under which we live (though this may sometimes have the effect of confirming the logic of these laws).[8]

In this sense, *mujūn* is like playing a game. Game-playing also demands that we abide by a set of arbitrary rules. Paradoxically, abiding by these rules constitutes a break from abiding by the rules of daily life. So to relax and have fun, instead of temporarily eschewing laws altogether, we sometimes prefer to adhere to a very strict regimen of separate rules. Leslie Kurke's *Coins, Bodies, Games, and Gold* shows that games as portrayed in certain Greek texts have a similarly contradictory status as at once mirroring the laws of life outside the game and representing a distraction from that life. In the *Odyssey*, she writes, Penelope's suitors (themselves party-crashers of a sort), pass the time away playing what sounds like a miniature bowling game in which, in this case, the pin is called 'Penelope'.[9] This is damning evidence of the suitors' lack of 'Greek manhood' because of their 'symbolic substitution' of game logic for life (the active courting of Penelope).[10] At the same time, however, Kurke describes how the game board is likened to a city, and by implication, life in a city is likened to a game, as, for example, in fragments of Herakleitos.[11] One such fragment ('Time is a boy playing, playing *pessoi*; kingship belongs to the boy,') portrays certain games, like the strategic board game *pessoi*, as reflecting the order of the cosmos. As Charles Kahn interprets, '...these moves follow a definite rule, so that after one side plays it is the other's turn, and after the victory is reached the play must start over from the beginning. The rules of the *pessoi*-game thus imitate the alternating measures of cosmic fire.'[12] As shown below, later texts, and some medieval Arabic texts, make similar analogies, especially with regard to the game of chess.

---

[6] Michael Cooperson first directed me to this story as an interesting subject of study for a student of *mujūn*, and we read it together in the summer of 2010 along with Stefan Leder's 'Prosa-Dichtung'.

[7] Stefan Leder, 'Prosa-Dichtung in der aḫbār Überlieferung Narrative', *Der Islam* 64 (1987): 16.

[8] Examples are found throughout Victor Turner, *The Ritual Process.*

[9] Kurke, *Coins*, 256.

[10] Ibid., 260.

[11] Ibid., 268–70.

[12] Ibid., 263.

A PLAYFUL MICROCOSM

Of all the games Abū al-Qāsim could have played, chess is certainly not the most absurd, or the one most readily likened to *mujūn*. Abū al-Qāsim in fact proposes that they play either chess or backgammon (Abū al-Jalab and Abū al-Ṣannāj, his nonsense jargon nicknames for the games).[13] Backgammon, according to medieval game lore, was thought to symbolize a more arbitrary, fate-driven universe, while chess symbolized the logical, careful choices of an agent with free will.[14] Indeed in his humorous work *My One Contribution to Chess*, F.V. Morley complains that by careful study of the patterns of chess, the game may cease to be a game altogether, and become something of a mathematical exercise, precluding a sporting match between two players of unequal experience or knowledge of, for example, opening moves.

Morley sees the game of chess as a 'dromenon', defined as 'a pattern of dynamic expression in which the performers express something larger than themselves...'[15] In other words, chess is a model for life, and is often considered, like Abū al-Qāsim, to be a microcosm with certain heuristic utilities. When working in a government office dedicated to the resolution of labor disputes (the War Labor Board), Morley found relief from the mixture of chaos and red tape that characterized his job in the relatively orderly representation of the universe provided by the game of chess.[16] Having lived through two world wars, he even recommends chess as an activity over which families may reconnect with returning veterans. Chess, long thought of as a representation of war, may provide a more orderly and socially pleasurable representation of real life which, though also played according to rules, can nevertheless seem senseless in comparison.[17]

Chess is similarly considered an orderly representation of the universe in Arabic sources contemporary with the *Ḥikāya*:

> Look, and you will see chess revolving like fate
> Day and night, misfortune and blessings.
> Its Mover remains, all the rest of it passes,
> And after annihilation, it is revived and its bones resurrected.[18]

In his *Gambling in Islam*, Franz Rosenthal writes that chess was praised by some for its 'usefulness for improving the mind and teaching military strategy.' On the other hand, however, it was criticized as 'too engrossing and causing neglect of.... religious duties.'[19] So despite its therapeutic orderliness and status as a dromenon, chess remained a distraction from real life. In an (almost certainly apocryphal) condemnation of the game,

---

[13] For a description of similar nicknames used for food in Arabic literature, see van Gelder, 'Edible Fathers and Mothers', 105–120.

[14] Masʿūdī, *Murūj*, I:161, V:3477–81.

[15] Morley, *My One Contribution*, 47, quoting Jane Harrison in *Ancient Art and Ritual.*

[16] Morley, *My One Contribution*, 78

[17] It may be of interest that Abū al-Qāsim, as a representative of Baghdad, once a center of empire, wins this metaphorical war against the Isfahani guest.

[18] This poem, by Badr al-Dīn ibn al-Ṣāḥib, is quoted by al-Ghuzūlī in *Maṭāliʿ al-budūr* and translated by Franz Rosenthal in his *Gambling in Islam*, 161.

[19] Rosenthal, *Gambling in Islam*, 89.

ʿAlī ibn Abī Ṭālib says, 'Chess-players are the biggest liars of all or among the biggest liars, saying "I killed", when they did not kill.'[20] This condemnation, like the narration of the chess-game in the *Ḥikāya*, links game-playing to a type of speech with a complex relationship to the truth.

Abū al-Qāsim's speech is wild, drunken, and self-contradictory, but nevertheless forms a kind of microcosm. Likewise, despite criticisms of chess in particular and game-playing in general as distractions from the realities of life, chess also represents a microcosm. For example, the 7th-century Pahlavi text by Meher-Awan Kai-khusru, *The Explanation of Chatrang*, explains that the thirty pieces are 'like the thirty days and nights' (presumably of a month), the 'turning of the board' is like 'the revolution of the stars and the rotation of the sky', and the 'progress in a circle of the pieces... resemble the movements of men in this world... who pass away from this earth [and] who become revived at the time of resurrection.'[21] This description of chess-as-microcosm closely resembles descriptions of man-as-microcosm found, for example, in the 34th *risāla* of the secret philosophical society known as the Brothers of Purity, or Ikhwān al-Safāʾ (10th/11th century), *Fī maʿnā qawl al-ḥukamāʾ anna al-ʿālam insān kabīr* (about the meaning of the wise men's saying that the world is a giant human).[22] In this epistle, the Ikhwān describe how the course of the planets, the different types of human personalities, and even the number of the days of the week are all reflected in the various organs and characteristics of the individual human beings.[23] Like chess, man (as well as the *Ḥikāya* itself) is represented as an intersection of disparate parts that together form a cosmic whole. But when these representations of the universe are presented as nonsensical or divorced from reality, they may cast doubt on man's perception of the universe itself, highlighting our capacity to live under nonsensical rules or to be convinced by eloquent and seductive but perhaps ultimately misleading speech.

WHAT KIND OF NONSENSE?

In the poem cited above, the reordering of the chess board after a game is imagined as a metaphor for the day of resurrection. At the end of the *Ḥikāya*, after Abū al-Qāsim has passed out in drunkenness along with his exhausted fellow guests, he wakes up in the morning and resumes his pious manner and appearance exactly as at the beginning of the book, as if none of his raving or drunken insults had ever been enunciated. Rather than providing a comfortingly orderly representation of the universe, however, this resurrection seems to cast doubt on the reality of anything – of his pious demeanor when entering or exiting the party, or of the whirlwind of verbosity that occupies the bulky middle section of the text.

The *Ḥikāya*, though representing the passing of time with almost unprecedented realism, inhabits a topsy-turvy time in which day and night themselves are reversed and confused.

[20] Ājurrī, *Taḥrīm al-nard*, 61.

[21] Translated by J.C. Tarapore. Kai-khusru. *The Explanation*, 13–14. Also see Murray, *History of Chess*, 209.

[22] G.J. van Gelder suggested the term 'macranthrope' in a private communication to me.

[23] This epistle and its relation to the *Ḥikāya* is explored in detail in E. Selove, *The Hikaya*, 132–160.

The night is the appropriate time for frivolous conversation (*samar*, or 'evening chat'), but the *Ḥikāya* begins its *samar* in the morning. Moreover, as Abū al-Qāsim and his fellow guests begin their game of chess, Abū al-Qāsim recites a nonsense poem expressive of this sense of topsy-turvy time:

> He would begin by advancing his pawns, and reciting some nonsense (*hadhayān*) by way of opening the game:
>
> We went out early late at night after the start of day,
> And hunted rabbits, jackals, wolves, but donkeys got away![24]

In *Nonsense,* Susan Stewart offers a list of five ways to fail to make sense. Though she emphasizes the fluidity and incompleteness of this list in her preface, we can nevertheless easily find the category 'discourse that denies itself', which best suits Abū al-Qāsim's poem.[25] As an example of this category of nonsense, she quotes a poem that begins: 'Ladies and jellyspoons: / I come before you / To stand behind you / To tell you something / I know nothing about. / Last Thursday / Which was Good Friday / There will be a mothers' meeting / For Fathers only...' Both Abū al-Qāsim's poem and this poem sound like they refer to a specific time with detailed language ('early late at night after the start of day' and 'Last Thursday / Which was Good Friday') but each added detail actually detracts from our information by rendering the date described impossible and contradictory. Stewart begins her description of 'discourse that denies itself' by saying:

> The metacommunication necessary for the message 'This is play' or 'This is a fiction' implicitly carries a denial and a criticism – a denial because of the status of the representation as an activity that is framed as both real and non real, and a criticism because the discourse has been framed, set off, and is examinable from many sides and able to be manipulated.[26]

Thus this type of nonsense in the *Ḥikāya* further contributes to the tension between literary representation and reality felt throughout the text. Stewart's nonsense category of 'discourse that denies itself' best suits not only Abū al-Qāsim's speech during the chess game, but nonsense in the *Ḥikāya* more generally.[27]

But as for the type of speech explicitly designated as nonsense in the chess game, aside from the familiar-sounding example quoted above, we also have the following: 'Umm Razīn, she shat in the bread, / "It helps it rise!" Umm Razīn said.'[28] Also: 'This is odd manners, gentlemen! This is the uncouth language of Baghdad's Bāb al-Ṭāq, and the strange whims of chance!'[29] The poem about Umm Razīn may be nonsense because it does not directly

---

[24] *Ḥ,* 279. Cf. Lewis Carroll's, 'The sun was shining on the sea, / Shining with all his might... /And this was odd, because it was / The middle of the night' (*Through the Looking-Glass,* 183).

[25] Stewart, *Nonsense,* viii, 72–7.

[26] Ibid.

[27] For example, in describing this category of nonsense Stewart also discusses unreliable narrators like Tristram Shandy, and parodies of didactic speech in Lewis Carroll's *Alice.* Both the concepts of unreliable narrators, and mockeries of the didactic in the *Ḥikāya* are discussed in E. Selove, *The Hikaya,* 52f., 97f.

[28] Umm Razīn's name means something like 'mother of the staid one'.

[29] *Ḥ,* 288, 289.

pertain to its context in the story, and also because it describes an absurd action justified with a 'logical' explanation (not unlike ᶜAlī ibn Ṣāliḥ's moralizing speeches made while standing on one foot waiting for sugar in the middle of the night). These two examples of 'nonsense' are nevertheless disturbing to me because they make about as much sense as does the rest of the *Ḥikāya*. In fact they make more sense than a good deal of Abū al-Qāsim's conversation. No doubt this is due in part to the specific references to time and place found in some of the vocabulary. Why, for example, he refers to the Bāb al-Ṭāq neighborhood of medieval Baghdad is now less than clear. Some of Abū al-Qāsim's conversation during the chess game in particular can be identified as popular sayings and are locatable in books of Arabic proverbs (see Appendix). One senses that most of his comments in this section are in fact similarly derived from idioms and sayings, and naturally many of these sayings are obscure to modern readers. However, as shown previously, much of the party-crasher's conversation throughout the day also seems to confuse his fellow guests and contemporaries. But by emphasizing the ideas of 'nonsensical' or 'raving' speech during the chess game, the narrative aligns game-playing with a particular kind of speech.

Though the *Ḥikāya* is generally brim-full of difficult language whose meaning often seems impossible to determine, the chess game is one of the most difficult passages to understand. Not only is it filled with forgotten sayings and nonsense-poetry, the chess moves described are rarely clear. Like the rest of the narrative, this game is presented in a kind of hypothetical grammatical construction, with each move described only as a possible example of a move that could be made.[30] This chess game itself is purely hypothetical, for when Abū al-Qāsim asks to play chess or backgammon, the narrator writes, 'They would bring out, for example, a chess game,' suggesting that they could have just as easily brought out a backgammon board.

For each hypothetical chess move, the narrator suggests that Abū al-Qāsim would have a quip or poem to recite. Given that there are more possible chess games than atoms in the observable universe, this would indeed render Abū al-Qāsim a man of microcosmic verbal ability.[31] As for the chess moves themselves, they often seem hastily described excuses for the production of creative taunts (or in other words, set-ups for a joke). Therefore, just as the portrait of Baghdad provided in the *Ḥikāya* is always ambiguous and unreliable, and the nature of its competition with the city of Isfahan flounders in a disorienting flow of words, the precise chess game played in the *Ḥikāya* is impossible to reconstruct.

---

[30] For example: 'And if his opponent would take up one of his pawns in his hand, and act as if he were going to move it, he would say, "If you see the chicken pecking the rooter's ass, you know that she's telling him 'fuck, fuck'!"' (*Ḥ*, 282).

[31] This fun fact has widely circulated among chess and math enthusiasts, and is explained in careful detail in Breslin, 'Number of Possible'.

RECONSTRUCTING A HYPOTHETICAL CHESS GAME

To demonstrate the futility of this endeavor, I will here attempt (and fail) to do exactly that. In doing so, I will show that two types of games are being played (as defined by Roger Caillois): *Agôn* (competition), the relatively orderly game of chess, and *Ilinx* (vertigo), the disorienting and dizzying game of *mujūn*. In the chess game here described, the raving quality of the discourse (*mujūn*) drowns out the orderly nature of the competition, which we find un-reconstructible.

According to H.J.R. Murray, the tradition of white (or red) playing first is a modern one, so we cannot determine the color of Abū al-Qāsim's pieces based on the fact that he plays first.[32] Abū al-Qāsim begins by advancing his pawns. His opponent likewise advances his pawns. Given that the pawns, unlike in the modern game, could advance only one square at a time on their opening move, Abū al-Qāsim's response to his opponent's seemingly modest and conservative opening sounds especially nonsensical:[33]

> Then his fellow player would advance his pawns, and he would say, 'Hey loser, bite by bite so you don't choke! Just two squares at a time, so you don't end in the black! Camel by camel or you'll break the *maḥāmil*![34] I say enough, but he's sneaking up! Your basket won't split, mister! Don't hurry, my lord, hurrying's for tom-cats. He gets two of my pawns for one pawn, now that's a good deal!'

This last comment seems to suggest that Abū al-Qāsim and his opponent have exchanged pawns, and Abū al-Qāsim in fact goes on to elaborate on this exchange, reciting: 'He traded a beard for my shiny asshole.' In terms of sexual value, a hairless asshole may prove more valuable than a beard, as bearded men were not typically considered attractive (to other men). So it seems that Abū al-Qāsim's opponent is slightly in the lead.

Abū al-Qāsim would then *yastaẓhir bi-firzān band* (perhaps 'advance the Queen protected by a pawn'). According to Reinhard Wieber, who cites this very line in his *Das Schachspiel in der arabischen Literatur*, this suggests that the queen's movement is protected by the pawn sitting in front of her.[35] The queen, then known as the *firzān* or adviser, could move only one diagonal space at a time.[36] Abū al-Qāsim, perhaps, advances his *firzān* behind a diagonal line of pawns who had already begun their advance.[37]

Having thus moved his queen in relation to his pawns, Abū al-Qāsim makes a baffling comment: *Iṣʿad bi-liḥāf wa-nzil bi-mirwaḥah*. Michael Cooperson suggested the reading 'Go

[32] Murray, *History of Chess*, 224.

[33] Ibid., 226.

[34] Litters for camel-back, which presumably could be become entangled and break if the camels walked side-by-side.

[35] Wieber, *Schachspiel*, 322.

[36] Murray, *History of Chess*, 225.

[37] Khawam translates: *Cette fois, c'est la Reine qu'il envoie en renfort sur le pion le plus menacé*, suggesting that Abū al-Qāsim moves a queen in order to defend a pawn, though this seems an unlikely strategy, even given the diminished value of the queen in medieval Arabic chess (al-Azdī, *24 heures*, 245). It is also tempting to consider this a reference to a set opening series of moves (see, for example, Murray's description of the *Queen's Pawn Opening* popular in the Medieval European game (*History of Chess*, 472–3).

up with a blanket and come back down with a fan', speculating that, given the pre-modern Arab habit of sleeping on the roof on warm evenings, to go up with a blanket to cool off would be counter-intuitive. Likewise to come back down, presumably to warm up, while carrying a fan, would also be counter-intuitive. This reading makes this comment another kind of 'discourse that denies itself', providing contradictory, self-cancelling advice. Mary St. Germain, citing a series of Arabic chess terms provided by Wieber, translates this comment as referring directly to the game, though her interpretation of these terms and the resulting translation ('back up a square to go around a piece') I find less than convincing.[38] Cooperson's interpretation seems to me the most likely, given the density of proverbs recited during the chess game, many of them locatable in Freytag's and others' dictionaries of Arabic proverbs.[39] This does not, however, mean that the chess-related double meaning of some of these words is without significance, especially considering that the verbs 'go up' and 'come down' were used specifically to describe the movement of the queen.[40] Ultimately the meaning is unclear. As with so much of Abū al-Qāsim's abundant and head-spinning speech, we must ask ourselves if even his opponent or the other guests watching the chess game know what he means. This impression is strengthened by the narrator's repeatedly describing Abū al-Qāsim's speech during the chess game as 'raving' (*hadhāyān*) or saying that he 'talks nonsense' (*yuhjir*).

The narrator goes on to say that Abū al-Qāsim would limit his opponent's play from the sides.[41] If the opponent broke out of this trap, he would recite an obscene poem. This move is clearly too vague and hypothetical to reconstruct precisely. The narrator continues with a blessedly clear description of the next move: 'His opponent would send his knight into the center after the advancing of the pawns.'[42] So despite all the talk and braggadocio, we appear still to be in a very early stage of a game, which is unfolding in a usual way with the advance of pawns and a knight.

Abū al-Qāsim then suggests that his opponent move 'the king's guard', probably the pawn in front of the king.[43] From this comment we can guess at least that this pawn has not yet moved. Little beyond this is clear. His opponent considers and rejects several moves and is duly mocked for his hesitation. Abū al-Qāsim then takes a pawn on the side of the board, remarking, 'if you can't find a rose, take a cyclamen.'[44] His opponent in turn takes one of his pawns. When the audience asks Abū al-Qāsim why he did not see the threat to his pawn, Abū al-Qāsim tells them to go to hell (in so many words) and takes his opponent's

38 St Germain, *Anomalous*, 328. Wieber, *Schachspiel*, 308, 333.

39 See Appendix for more detail. Adam Talib suggested in a private communication to me that this potential proverb be read as meaning 'cover all of your bases', or bring a blanket even if the weather is warm, and a fan even if it is cool.

40 Murray, *History of Chess*, 227.

41 St Germain interprets this line not as a move but as further commentary of Abū al-Qāsim (*Anomalous*, 328). It seems unlikely that Abū al-Qāsim is speaking here because this comment is *followed* by 'he would say', which throughout the game introduces Abū al-Qāsim's speech, while commentary of the audience is introduced by 'it would be said'.

42 *Ḥ*, 281.

43 Or perhaps a piece otherwise protecting the king from attack (see Wieber, *Schachspiel*, 300).

44 *Ḥ*, 283.

queen or knight. 'A blow of the stone hammer is better than a thousand strikes of the mallet', he says. The next several moves are described in only the most general terms, Abū al-Qāsim's opponent erring and hesitating and receiving due mockery, being forced to take one move he quickly regrets. The opponent moves the knight to the side of the board and is mocked for this by Abū al-Qāsim (it is indeed poor strategy to limit the knight's movement in this way). He then blocks Abū al-Qāsim, who screams (he screams and even neighs several times during the game). But he soon takes some of his opponents' pieces in retaliation. Beyond this, our picture of the state of the board is now wholly unclear. More hesitations and retractions are described than actual moves. At this point we know only that Abū al-Qāsim is dominating both the board and the conversation.

Several more hesitations and false starts follow, until suddenly Abū al-Qāsim's opponent simultaneously threatens his king and his bishop. It looks bad for our (anti-)hero, who screams again, but in a series of partially nonsensical but clearly threatening poems, indicates that his opponent has in fact fallen into a trap. Indeed his next described move threatens his opponent's rook and king with his bishop, 'an admirable, elegant move'.[45]

Abū al-Qāsim's opponent struggles for the rest of the game. The narrator tells us that his head is spinning, he curses, his king is in a tight spot, and his pawns are scattered. Or as Abū al-Qāsim puts it, 'He's in the shit up to his throat and the dogs are standing guard.'[46] He then moves in for the checkmate using his knight, and upsets the chessboard in raucous triumph, thus ending the game.[47]

CONCLUSION

Like so much of the *Ḥikāya*, this chess game is a mixture of tantalizingly specific-sounding details comprising a wholly hypothetical and historically un-reconstructible scene, couched in familiar but often incomprehensible conversation. In his work *The Most Human Human*, Brian Christian compares the game of chess to a conversation. In both chess and conversation, there are standard traditional openers and closers from which we rarely deviate. Computers can hold a conversation or play chess within these set parameters as well as humans can. As with life itself, he writes, which always starts with birth and ends with death, it is the variations in the middle that make each conversation or chess game uniquely human.[48] By entering and exiting the party dressed as an ascetic and reciting pious poetry, Abū al-Qāsim evokes the standard pious openings and endings of contemporary Arabic texts. The center of the *Ḥikāya*, however, casts jarring doubt on even these familiar signposts.

On January 27th, 2002, Bobby Fischer, former chess World Champion, declared the game of chess dead.[49] Entire games could now be played 'by the book', a phrase used to describe

---

45 *Ḥ*, 289.

46 Ibid., 291.

47 A chess-board at that time would probably have been made of soft patterned cloth (Murray, *History of Chess*, 220).

48 Christian, *Most Human Human*, 99–131.

49 This radio interview with a station in Reykjavik can be found on Chessbase News.

moves memorized in patterns, themselves repetitions of former games by past masters. Though filled with literary clichés – familiar tropes and poetic quotations – the *Ḥikāya* is nevertheless not a dead game, and not 'by the book'. Partly by virtue of its iterative mode, which leaves all events described hovering between the realms of truth and fiction, and partly by virtue of Abū al-Qāsim's refusal to adhere even to the outlandish norms of the buffoon (he will not let his audience laugh), the *Ḥikāya*, like the chess-game described within it, remains stubbornly anomalous – resembling those games recorded in 'the books', but not quite identifiable within these books. So *mujūn* may be a crazy game, but it may tend to occur within certain temporal and literary parameters in the game of daily life which it parodies and inhabits. *Ḥikāyat Abī al-Qāsim*, baffling, evading, and turning the very game-board on its face, does not play by the rules.

The chess game in Abū al-Qāsim is paradigmatic not only because it offers us an opportunity to explore the definition of *mujūn* as a type of playful language, but also because the game, like Abū al-Qāsim, is a microcosm. Playing a game, though a distraction from everyday life, can nevertheless teach us something about the universe.

APPENDIX: A TRANSLATION OF THE CHESS GAME

Then he would wash his hands and say, 'Where are Abū al-Jalab and Abū al-Ṣannāj?' (by which he meant the games of chess and backgammon). And they would bring out, for example, a chess set.

'Who's up for it?' he would say. 'Which poor sap wants to offer up his head?'

They would be reluctant to play. 'Yes, when the governor arrives,' he would say, 'Ruqayqīm hides!' until one would finally agree.[50] When he noticed him he would say, 'The pharmacist meets his medicine![51] Now isn't this Mr. Terrible about to become Mr. Terrified!'

'So how does the bum play?'[52] he would then ask.

'He's a good player!' they would say.

'Well an old mule isn't frightened by the tinkle of a bell,'[53] he would reply, and turn to him, saying:

---

[50] I have been unable to identify the meaning of this proverb. Mez renders this *raqīquhum* (their slaves (Azdī, *Sittenbild*, 93). In a private communication to me, A. Talib suggested reading the final *mīm* as the Persian possessive pronoun 'my'.

[51] Specifically *bizr qaṭūn* (or *quṭūn*), which, according to al-Shāljī are black seeds with multiple medicinal benefits, including the lowering of fevers, still in use in Baghdad today (*Ḥ*, 279). St. Germain, who identifies them as 'flea-bane seeds', adds the creation of erections to their medicinal utilities (*Anomalous*, 327).

[52] See al-Shāljī for a definition of this insulting term, Abū Mushkāḥal, which he claims is of Aramaic origins, derived from a word used to describe someone who employs trickery to obtain his daily bread (*Ḥ*, 279).

[53] A proverb. Mez refers us to Freytag, where we find it among 'more recent proverbs' translated thus: *Mulus decrepitus sono tintinnabuli non terretur* (*Proverbia*, I: 207).

You who challenged me, you've thrown a fire on dry sticks![54]
Now when this boxthorn sticks you, you're going to get a prick!

And he would begin by advancing his pawns, and reciting some nonsense by way of opening the game:

We went out early late at night after the start of day,
And hunted rabbits, jackals, wolves, but donkeys got away!

Then his fellow player would advance some pawns, and he would say, 'Hey bum, don't bite off more than you can chew! Just two squares at a time, so you don't end in the black![55] Camel by camel or you'll break the *maḥāmil.* I say enough, but he sneaks on up. Your basket won't split, mister! Don't hurry, my lord, hurrying's for tom-cats. He takes two of my pawns for one pawn – now that's a good deal!

Every time he sold his beard, I sold a hairless asshole.

An elegant man, by God!

I gave it to him good, and he found it rather thrilling.[56]
'Your beard up in my ass,' I said, and he was more than willing.

He would advance the Queen protected by a pawn,[57] and say 'Go up with a blanket and come down with a fan.'

He would constrain his opponent's play from the sides, and say, 'In Mrs. Curves' crack, for it's made of solid rock!

A gift from me sent into you, in myrtle, basil wrapped,
A peach on bottom, topped with knob of apple, pomegranate.[58]

But if his opponent broke out and escaped him, he would say:

He slept, but with a shitty shoe,
I slapped him and said 'wake up!'
Now look the veins show in his neck
Just how they liked the shake-up.

His opponent would send his knight into the center after the advancing of the pawns. 'Well done!' Abū al-Qāsim would say, 'Now we've moved on from playing jacks to spinning tops!' And he would say, 'The morning found me occupied with what I did all night, thus one keeps at a thing until mastering it. So, gentlemen, shit and play with it; that way you can do two things at the same time! Stand on the river-bank and tie up what washes up.'[59]

---

[54] Specifically *ʿarfaj*, a flammable plant.

[55] This translation is based on al-Shāljī's assertion that *tā* was a Baghdadi colloquial shortening of *ḥattā*, now pronounced *dā* (*Ḥ*, 280). Tā is also an abbreviation for ḥattā in Persian.

[56] The meaning of this line is unclear. A more literal translation might read, 'I moved him in love, and it, when it got power over him, he coughed.'

[57] See Wieber (*Schachspiel*, 322).

[58] Clearly an extended metaphor for a penis. Cf. Abū al-Qāsim's earlier taunt: 'That's right, honey, you want something planted at one end, with a nozzle at the other. It's not an eggplant, and it's not a gourd... I think you want something that starts with a truffle, ends with a cucumber, and has a nose-bag hanging on its neck. You'd like a good blow on the proverbial horn!' (*Ḥ*, 78).

[59] 'What washes up' is an educated guess for *mābāqāt*, used earlier in a similar context: 'It's as

'You could move the king's guard, dumbass,' he would suggest. 'Your bread is covered in fish paste.[60] If you weren't plotting over something you wouldn't be eating your bread in the corner.'

And if his opponent would take up one of his pawns in his hand, and act as if he were going to move it, he would say, 'If you see the chicken pecking the rooter's ass, you know that she's telling him, "fuck, fuck"!'

Then his opponent would stammer, his error apparent to him, and Abū al-Qāsim would say, 'So OK, the blind man shits on top of the roof and thinks that no one can see him.[61] You dumbass! The one who farted in your beard ate beans from my farm! Your hand is closer to heaven than to that piece, and one who strives to stomp on the wind is but farting in his mustache.'

Then he would say to one of the people there, 'Why don't you watch this game and see something really amazing?' This would garner a little interest among some of the crowd, who would begin cautioning and advising his opponent, much to the annoyance of Abū al-Qāsim.

'Gentlemen, I told you to watch,' he would say, 'I didn't tell you to get in the way! Leave him alone so he can get his finger jammed in the door, and then I'll show you how I slap him!'

But his opponent would be distracted. 'Damn you, what do you expect?' he would ask, 'For piping always distracts the piper from eating flower dry!'[62]

If he would groan out loud worrying over something, Abū al-Qāsim would say, 'He sings the song of a hornet in his clothes! He took a break from his work to cry about his mother-in law. How he raves, God bless him, like a Hindu divorcee!'[63]

If someone says to him, 'Take that pawn in exchange for one of your pawns,' and he saw that there wasn't any benefit in doing so, he would leave it and say, 'If it's a monkey for a monkey, better to take the monkey that's house-broken.'

Then he would take one of the pawns on the side of the board and say,

If you can't get a rose, take a cyclamen.

Many a thing you despise at first turns out to be worthless.'

His opponent would then take one of his pawns. 'Too bad Abū al-Qāsim!,' someone would say, 'Why did you sacrifice it without compensation?'

'Go to hell,' he would reply, 'And bring a bit of firewood!'

---

though he's the Grand High Treasurer of Chicken-shit, or the Trustee of the River Bank in charge of all the duck droppings, or the commissioner of the Tigris tying up the *mābāqāt* with palm fronds' (*Ḥ*, 61). Also see Steingass, *Dictionary,* 1136: '*mā bāqi*: the remainder, the rest...*mā bāqīya*: remaining over, rest, remainder, remnant; arrears, balance, surplus.'

[60] See *bunn* in Dozy, *Supplément,* 116. He provides a recipe for this fermented fish paste condiment.

[61] A proverb. St Germain (*Anomalous,* 328) refers us to Freytag *Proverbia,* II:169, where we find it translated thus: *Caecus super tecto cacat et ipsum homines non videre putat.*

[62] Meaning unclear. For an alternate reading of this line see Mez, who reads the piper with his pipe (*al-zāmir bi-zamrihi*) as al-Zāmir ibn Murrah, Ibn Murrah being a nickname for the devil (Azdī, *Sittenbild,* LI).

[63] Al-Shāljī recognizes this saying as one popular in 10th/11th-century Baghdad (*Ḥ*, 282).

Then he would take a queen or a knight on the opposite side.[64]

'Gentlemen,' he would say, 'a blow of the stone hammer is better than a thousand taps of the mallet.'

'Never mind,' his opponent would say.

'If you hear someone say "never mind" in a war, you know that the shit's above his head,' he would reply.

His opponent would err in his positioning, and then realize it and begin to catch up. 'After the fart, he tightened his ass,'[65] Abū al-Qāsim would say.

And his opponent would want to swerve to the side with his knight, but then would see that this was not possible for him, and Abū al-Qāsim would say, 'You dumbass! If they let you go on the hajj, take the straight path!'[66] So he would return it to its place.

'The seed rolls round and round, then returns to the mill,'[67] Abū al-Qāsim would say.

Then his opponent would softly mutter over something evincing worry, concern and vexation, and Abū al-Qāsim would say,

O you whose anger has led him to press
On the dregs of my ass with his fangs... [68]

How longwill you grieve? How long will you gripe? How long will you grow angry?' Then he would say, 'Poor thing. What's he doing? His flour fell in the thorn bushes and he can't get it back together again.'

He would play for something and his opponent would block him, and he would scream, 'Hey! He stopped me, by God, by sword and by flame! What do I do?'

But then his opponent would make a mistake in his play, and surrender some pieces to him, and he would say, 'Nice going, boneless doggy bag![69] Put the spoon of your face in my ass!'

Then his opponent would take a piece, and see his error and want to put it back, but Abū al-Qāsim would force him to take it and say, 'By God you'll take it even against your will!'

'And what should he do with it?' someone would say.

'What the slave-girl of al-Sukkarī did,' he would reply.

'What did she do?' they would ask.

'Take it in her hand and put it in her cunt,' he would reply.

Then he would turn to him and recite,

---

[64] Since the queen could only move one diagonal square at a time (Murray, *History of Chess,* 225), its loss would not be quite the devastating blow that it is in the modern game.

[65] A proverb meaning something like 'to shut the barn door after the horse has bolted', which according to al-Shāljī is still used in Baghdad today with a slight variation ('after he farted, he fell silent' [*ṣamat*] [*Ḥ,* 283]).

[66] Literally, 'the road of Ctesiphon' or al-Madāʾin, a city south of Baghdad and consequently between Baghdad and Mecca.

[67] A proverb. St Germain (*Anomalous,* 331) refers us to Freytag, *Proverbia,* I: 419 (where it is translated: *Granum circumvertitur et ad molam redit*).

[68] This and other poems were recently emended through my collaboration with van Gelder on a forthcoming translation of the *Ḥikāya*. Many further notes and emendations to this provisional translation are expected.

[69] The word for doggy-bag (*zallah*) also means mistake, and this is perhaps some kind of pun.

'Your cheek turns after the evening meal
To the black-hairy hole of my ass.'

So be content with the bitter truth,

Or otherwise, just let it pass.
And if you are angry, tomorrow
do like al-Sukkarī's lass.

Then he would say, 'This, by God, has been the way of the game since its invention, until it bore this fruit that it bore. Yes, for the donkey is on hire until death.[70] Free straw bursts the sacks.'

Then his opponent would tempt him to take a piece, and he would stretch out his hand to take it, thinking it was free. But the error of his thinking would appear to him, and he would neigh and scream and recite,

O son of whom my pickle jar penis
comes and goes in her ass's avenues...

Another:

Oh you who hurry towards destruction
visiting this place,
the rook of my hand is coming down
to slap the king of your face.

Dumbass! If you jump on two pegs, one of them is going up your butt.[71]

Then his opponent would turn to someone as if to ask advice. 'If the sea-turtle has need of a boat, he's finished,' Abū al-Qāsim would say.

But the person would advise him to do something, so Abū al-Qāsim would turn to him and say, 'Sure, take it from someone whose intellect fits in a fruit-basket. You grew so long, my cock, that you came out of my sleeve!' And he would recite:

'What dire time is this that they go trampling on my game?
At my expense I'll teach this stupid ass.
I don't play favorites to the beards a-rubbing in my ass,
Except my friend here, him I'll get to last.'

By whom he meant the host of the party. Then someone would say to him, 'Damn you, you can ask advice too if you like, just stop insulting people!'

And he would say, 'May the back be broken of the mother of the one who has to eat beans in order to fart!'

His opponent would strike at both his king and his bishop,[72] and he would scream and say, 'I'll give you some advice, sir, by God!'

'What advice?' he would ask.

And Abū al-Qāsim would reply:

---

[70] Al-Shāljī informs us that this saying is still in use today in Baghdad in much the same form (*Ḥ*, 286).

[71] This proverb is also found in al-Tawḥīdī, *Baṣāʾir* (ed. Wadād al-Qāḍī), Maydānī, *Majmaʿ*, 2:387, and al-Ābī, *Nathr al-durr*, 6:513.

[72] The bishop (*fīl* or elephant) could move only two squares diagonally (Murray, *History of Chess*, 225).

'Tie up your beard, for deep in an ocean of shit
you have now fallen down.
A sea from my anus which looks like it's drawn
With a compass, so perfectly round.'[73]

Then he would say in a sing-song voice:

'Father of Ḥusayn, son of al-Ḥasan,
Your head and your body grow wide!
Your beard too has grown and I wish that it would
Deep in mi culo *go hide.'*[74]

Then raving he would say,

'Umm Razīn shat in the bread,
"it helps it rise!" Umm Razīn said.'[75]

'What does this cuckold care about?' he would ask, 'A hard head and firm horn!', and he would recite: ...[76]

Another:

'O youth whose soft black beard hangs lank
Like long loose strands of silk...[77]
It's wrapped up in your mother's shit
and sealed up with a fart.'

Another:

'O vilest, lowest of mankind, in my view, without doubt,
I copied cutting verses with my shoe between his eyes.
His head's allowed for plundering, ears, shoulders blown about,
By power of my hands, now try my shoe-slap on for size.
Fear God, the cartilage of your ears, the weak veins of your snout!'[78]

Suddenly the king and rook would lie exposed to Abū al-Qāsim's bishop, an admirable elegant move, and his opponent would leap up in surprise. Abū al-Qāsim would talk nonsense in a sing-song voice, saying, 'This is odd manners, gentlemen! This is the uncouth language of Baghdad's Bāb al-Ṭāq,[79] and the strange whims of chance!'

---

[73] According to Mez, a poem by Ibn al-Ḥajjāj (Azdī, *Sittenbild,* LI).

[74] The Arabic poem includes the phrase 'in my ass' in Persian, *bikūne man*, here translated in Spanish.

[75] Van Gelder, who considered this translation to be excessively abbreviated, translated it: 'Umm Razīn shat in the flour one day. "Why so?"/We asked. She said, 'It is the leaven in the dough.'

[76] The meaning of the poem here omitted is too unclear to present a translation, and the beginning of the second line appears corrupt in the manuscript. A tentative translation would look something like this: 'O husband of she who sold her ass for an i.o.u./return my penis's semen with a lentil dish on top./Don't you see my shoe is curly-toed and Daybulī? (see *Ḥ*, 288 and Azdī, *Sittenbild,* LI)/With it I come to you and stuff your narrow collar.'

[77] Part of this line is missing in the manuscript.

[78] The last two lines of this translation indulge in poetic license. The second to last line in the Arabic plays on the similarity between the sound of the words 'hand' and 'power,' and 'sandal' and 'light' ('Under the hands (*ʾaydin*) by whose powers (*ʾaydun*) they freely administer sandals (*khifāf*) to the head not lightly (*khifāf*).' In the original poem 'snout' in the last line is actually 'neck'.

[79] A neighborhood in Baghdad (G. le Strange, *Baghdad,* 218).

Then he would say, 'A chess player on his death bed, as he was giving up the ghost, counseled his son thus: "Beware, my son, the side of the rook! Fear the pounce of the knight! Heed the leap of the bishop! For it is better to sit on the cock of a donkey than to sit in a square open to attack!" And then he died.'

'Sound advice, by God! A religious duty! He gave his son his due, and left him his legacy, may God not bless his carcass nor water his grave!'

This play would end with his opponent's head spinning. 'Alas for you!' Abū al-Qāsim would say, 'This young man, God bless him, came to my party today, but do you know what he ate?'

'No,' they would say.

'A thousand cocks in a loaf of bread!'

His opponent would respond with a curse, which he would tolerate. 'Poor you!' he would say, 'For the loser is allowed to mock and scorn, while the winner should be tolerant and kind. So I don't blame him, by God. At this knot the carpenter farted.'[80]

His opponent's king would be in a tight spot, and he would say, 'Too bad! You escaped into a corner.' And he would recite mockingly,

'He said "spin it," I said "in her cunt
Would that it would, good sir, spin..."'

Should his opponent's pawns be scattered, he would try to gather them together with crafty maneuvering, holding them back, and Abū al-Qāsim would say, 'When the shepherd dies, the sheep scatter.'

'And has the shepherd died, Abū al-Qāsim?' someone would ask.

'Half of him died,' he would say, 'and the other half is on its way.'

'How's he really doing, gentlemen?' someone would ask.

'He's in the shit up to his throat,' Abū al-Qāsim would reply, 'And the dogs are standing guard. He's doing about as well as beetroot in a hot pot. He shat in the pan, or rather on the chessboard. He shat in his own coffin. His juices are dry, and only the dregs remain.'

His opponent would rush to evade him with one of his pawns, and someone would say, 'How quickly he moves his pawn!' To which Abū al-Qāsim would reply, 'Someone said to a tent-peg, "How quickly you go in!" and it answered, "If you knew what was beating my behind, you'd understand!"[81] He moved faster than a half-inserted penis or a fleeing gazelle with his young running before him,' he would mockingly remark.

His opponent would be stumped, and Abū al-Qāsim would say, 'Night-blindness in the day-time is blindness all the time.'

And he would say, 'Gentlemen, we slapped that monkey until we went blind,' and he would recite,

---

[80] Mez adds only that 'this must be a saying', (Azdī, *Sittenbild,* LI). Given the density of sayings and proverbs used during this chess game, he is likely to be correct. He does not, however, suggest a possible interpretation.

[81] For this saying Mez (Azdī, *Sittenbild,* LII) refers us to Socin's *Arabische Sprichwörter* (203), where we find it translated: *Man fragte den Pflock: 'Warum gehst du in die Mauer hinein?" Er antwortete: "Weil Jemand, der hinter mir ist, Gewalt anwendet.'* ('Someone asked the stake, "Why do you go into the wall?" It answered, "Because someone who is behind me uses force"').

'Incense-like his shit did fall,
Oh what a transgression!'

'Abū al-Qāsim,' someone would say...
'Yes, there's nothing for it but a draw! As the poet once said,

The time comes for a truce when truce becomes the only way.
Not peace but poop and in your beard is what you get, I say!'[82]

He would be planning to checkmate his opponent with his knight, and then he would strike, saying, 'All right! Take a white thing for your coal-black, you scum!' And he would knock the chessboard over on his face.

Someone who was absent at the time of the victory would ask what had gone on between them. 'We were slapping one another,' he said, 'and now he's complaining of a weak constitution!'

Then he would look around at everybody and ask, 'Are we fasting today?'

BIBLIOGRAPHY

Muhammad Ahsan, *Social Life under the Abbasids* (London: Longman Group, 1979).
Muḥammad ibn al-Ḥusayn al-Ājurrī, *Taḥrīm al-nard wa-al-shaṭranj wa-al-malāhī* (Beirut: Dār al-Kutub al-ʿIlmiyyah, 1988).
Muḥammad ibn Aḥmad Abū al-Muṭahhar al-Azdī, *24 heures de la vie d'une canaille*, translated by R.C. Khawam (Paris: Phébus, 1998).
Muḥammad ibn Aḥmad Abū al-Muṭahhar al-Azdī, *Ḥikāyat Abī al-Qāsim al-Baghdādī al-Tamīmī*, British Library, Oriental and India Office Collections, manuscript number ADD 19, 913.
Muḥammad ibn Aḥmad Abū al-Muṭahhar al-Azdī, *Hikāyat Abī al-Qāsim al-Baghdādī/Abūlkāsim: ein bagdāder Sittenbild*, ed. Adam Mez (Heidelberg: Carl Winter, 1902).
Muḥammad ibn Aḥmad Abū al-Muṭahhar al-Azdī, *Hikāyat Abī al-Qāsim al-Baghdādī*, published as Abū Ḥayyān al-Tawḥīdī [attributed], *Al-Risālah al-Baghdādiyyah*, ed. ʿAbbūd al-Shāljī (Koln: Manshūrāt al-Jamal, 1980).
Andy Breslin, 'The Number of Possible Different Games of Chess,' in *Andy Rants*, accessed April 11, 2012, http://andyrantsandraves.blogspot.com/2009/10/number-of-possible-different-games-of.html.
Roger Caillois, *Man, Play and Games*, trans. Meyer Barash (Chicago: University of Chicago Press, 2001).
Lewis Carroll, *Through the Looking Glass*, in *The Annotated Alice*, ed. Martin Gardner (New York: W.W. Norton, 2000).
Chessbase News, accessed April 15th, 2012. http://www.chessbase.com/newsdetail.asp?newsid=153.
Brian Christian, *The Most Human Human: What Talking with Computers Teaches us about What It Means to Be Alive* (New York: Doubleday, 2011).
ʿAbd al-Wāḥid Dhū al-Nūn Ṭāhā, 'Mujtamaʿ Baghdād min khilāl Ḥikāyat Abī al-Qāsim al-Baghdādī', *Al-Mawrid* 3 (1974): 14–25.
Reinhart Peter Anne Dozy, *Supplément aux dictionnaires arabes* (Leiden: Brill, 1927).
G.W. Freytag, *Arabum Proverbia* (Bonnae: A. Marcum, 1838).

---

[82] The original poem uses a play on the words 'truce' and 'shit', which sound similar in Arabic. According to Mez this is an old joke found also, for example, in the poetry of Ibn Hajjāj (Azdī, *Sittenbild*, LII).

Geert Jan van Gelder, *The Bad and the Ugly: Attitudes Towards Invective Poetry* (Hijāʾ) *in Classical Arabic Literature* (Leiden: Brill, 1988).
Geert Jan van Gelder, 'Edible Fathers and Mothers: Arabic *Kunyas* used for Food', in Manuela Marín and Cristina de la Puente (eds.), *El banquete de las palabras: la alimentación de los textos árabes* (Madrid: Consejo Superior de Investigaciones Científicas, 2005), 105–120.
Al-Zubayr Ibn Bakkār, *Al-Akhbār al-muwaffaqiyyāt* (Qum: Manshūrāt al-Sharīf al-Raḍī, 1995).
Edward William Lane, *Arabic-English Lexicon*, reprint (Beirut: Librairie du Liban, 1968).
Leslie Kurke, *Coins, Bodies, Games, and Gold: The Politics of Meaning in Ancient Greece.* (Princeton: Princeton University Press: 1999).
Stefan Leder, 'Prosa-Dichtung in der aḫbār Überlieferung Narrative', *Der Islam* 64 (1987): 6–41.
Guy Le Strange *Baghdad during the Abbasid Caliphate* (Oxford: Clarendon Press, 1900).
Abū al-Ḥasan ʿAlī Masʿūdī, *Murūj al-dhahab wa-maʿādin al-jawhar*, 6 vols., ed. Charles Pellat (Beirut: Universite Libanaise: 1966–74).
Julie Scott Meisami, 'Arabic Mujūn Poetry: the literary dimension' in Frederich De Jong (ed.), *Verse and the Fair Sex* (Utrecht: M.Th. Houtsma Stichting, 1993), 8–30.
F.V. Morley, *My One Contribution to Chess* (New York: B.W. Huebsch, 1945).
H.J.R. Murray, *A History of Chess* (Northampton, Massachusetts: Benjamin Press, 1986).
Franz Rosenthal, *Gambling in Islam* (Leiden: Brill, 1975).
Everett Rowson, Review of *Live Theatre and Dramatic Literature in the Medieval Arabic World* by Shmuel Moreh, *Journal of the American Oriental Society* 114.3 (1994): 466–468.
Emily Selove, 'The Hikaya of Abu al-Qasim al-Baghdadi: The Comic Banquet in Greek, Latin, and Arabic', Ph.D. dissertation, University of California Los Angeles, 2012.
Albert Socin, *Arabische Sprichwörter und Redensarten* (Tübingen: Heinrich Laupp, 1878).
Francis Joseph Steingass, *A Comprehensive Persian-English Dictionary*, reprint (London/ Boston: Routledge & Keegan Paul, 1977).
Susan Stewart, *Nonsense: Aspects of Intertextuality in Folklore and Literature* (Baltimore: John Hopkins University Press, 1979).
Mary St. Germain, 'Al-Azdī's *Abī al-Qāsim al-Baghdādī*: Placing an anomalous text within the literary developments of its time', Ph.D. dissertation, University of Washington, 2006.
J.C. Tarapore (trans.), *The Explanation of Chatrang* (Bombay: Parsee Punchayet, 1932).
Victor Turner, *The Ritual Process: Structure and Anti-Structure* (Ithaca: Cornell University Press, 1969).
Reinhard Wieber, *Das Schachspiel in der arabischen Literatur von den Anfängen bis zur zweiten Hälfte des 16. Jahrhunderts.* (Walldorf-Hessen, Germany: Verlag für Orientkunde, 1972).
Yāqūt ibn ʿAbd Allāh al-Ḥamawī, *Muʿjam al-buldān*, vols. 1, 2 and 4 (Leipzig: F.A. Brockhaus, 1866).

9

Dignity at Stake: *Mujūn* epigrams by Ibn Nubāta (686–768/1287–1366) and his contemporaries

Thomas Bauer

PRELIMINARY NOTE

Between c. 720 and 760 AH four of the most important poets of the Mamluk period composed a large number of *mujūn* epigrams thus reviving a genre that had nearly died out after its first blossoming in the early and middle Abbasid periods. In the Mamluk period, however, *mujūn* was no longer the same as it was in the Abbasid period. The following is a very preliminary study of *mujūn* epigrams by Ibn Nubāta al-Miṣrī, who was generally considered the most important poet of the period and who set the standard in the *mujūn* chapter of his *dīwān* of epigrams entitled *al-Qaṭr an-Nubātī*. Epigrams by his contemporaries Ṣafī ad-Dīn al-Ḥillī (667–750/1278–1350) and Ṣalāḥ ad-Dīn aṣ-Ṣafadī (696–764/1297–1363) will be taken into account cursorily. Ibrāhīm al-Miʿmār (d. 749/1348) will be given somewhat more prominence in the following section.[1] Ibn Dāniyāl, who had died already in 710/1310 and is more interesting for his shadow plays and longer poems than his epigrams, and Ibn Sūdūn, a writer of the following century, will be disregarded.

Aṣ-Ṣafadī is the author of several books on literary subjects such as the comparison (*tashbīh*), the double entendre (*tawriya*), the topic 'eye' etc., which could be called 'studies-cum-anthologies'. They are divided like a syllogism into First *Muqaddima* 'premise I' and Second *Muqaddima* 'premise II', which comprise the study, and a final section, the *Natīja* or 'conclusion', comprising the anthology. With something similar in mind, I will adopt

[1] 750/1350 is the most probable dating of Ṣafī al-Dīn al-Ḥillī's death. See Thomas Bauer, 'Ibn Nubātah al-Miṣrī (686–768/1287–1366): Life and Works. Part I: The Life of Ibn Nubātah', *Mamlūk Studies Review* 12.1 (2008), pp. 1–35, p. 29 n154.

this pattern for the present article. *Muqaddima I* includes, in addition to general remarks, an attempt to classify the most important themes of Mamlūk *mujūn*, *Muqaddima II* gives an overview of the *mujūn* epigrams composed by the four poets mentioned above, and the final *Natīja* presents a selection of epigrams from the chapter *al-Mudāʿaba wa-l-mujūn* from Ibn Nubāta's still unedited *al-Qaṭr an-Nubātī.*[2]

MUQADDIMA I: CHARACTERISTICS AND THEMES OF 8TH/14TH CENTURY *MUJŪN*

The 7th and 8th /13th and 14th centuries saw a revival of genres that had once flourished during the early and middle Abbasid period (2nd to 4th/late 8th to 10th centuries) but left little traces in the centuries in between.[3] Hunting poetry is one example, *mujūn* is another.[4] The authors of the Ayyubid and Mamluk period were quite conscious about their Abbasid predecessors, but they did not copy them. Instead, they developed and transformed the genre and adopted it to their own needs. In the case of *mujūn*, Ibn al-Ḥajjāj (d. 391/1001) was a model to which the literati of the Mamluk period referred several times.[5] Aṣ-Ṣafadī described Ibn Dāniyāl as 'the Ibn al-Ḥajjāj of his age and the Ibn Sukkara of his city';[6] Ibn Nubāta al-Miṣrī (686–768/1287–1366) published a selection of Ibn al-Ḥajjāj's poetry under the title *Talṭīf al-mizāj min shiʿr Ibn al-Ḥajjāj*[7]; and Ṣafī ad-Dīn al-Ḥillī composed a *muʿāraḍa* on one of Ibn al-Ḥajjāj's poems.[8] Yet nearly all of these poets also composed *mujūn* poetry that had little in common with that of their Abbasid predecessors. They explored new subjects, used new forms such as the shadow play or the *zajal*, and even a new language as in the case of al-Miʿmār's *azjāl* (sing. *zajal*) in the Cairene colloquial.

The most widespread poetic form in the Ayyubid and Mamluk periods was the epigram, a short, pointed poem of mostly two or three lines. Epigrams were omnipresent at the time.[9] They are found in the *dīwāns* of poets, in anthologies, in books of *adab* and history and often enough even in religious texts. In addition to Ibn Nubāta's *al-Qaṭr an-*

---

[2] I would like to thank Adam Talib, not only for improving my English, but also for his comments and critical remarks.

[3] On genre in Arabic literature see Gregor Schoeler, 'The Genres of Classical Arabic Poetry: Classifications of Poetic Themes and Poems by Pre-Modern Critics and Redactors of Dīwāns', in *Quaderni di Studi Arabi, nuova serie* 5–6 (2010–2011), pp. 1–48.

[4] On Mamluk hunting poetry, see Thomas Bauer, 'The Dawādār's Hunting Party. A Mamluk *muzdawija ṭardiyya*, probably by Shihāb al-Dīn Ibn Faḍl Allāh', in A. Vrolijk, J.P. Hogendijk (eds.), *O ye Gentlemen: Arabic Studies on Science and Literary Culture in Honour of Remke Kruk* (Leiden: Brill, 2007), pp. 291–312.

[5] See the forthcoming study of this poet by Sinan Antoon (*The Poetics of the Obscene: Ibn al-Ḥajjāj and Sukhf*, Palgrave–Macmillan).

[6] E.K. Rowson, 'Ibn Dāniyāl', in EAL, p. 319.

[7] Ed. Najm ʿAbd Allāh Muṣṭafā, Tūnis 2001.

[8] See al-Ḥillī, *Dīwān*, pp. 561–563.

[9] See EI^3, s.v. 'Epigram 1. Classical Arabic' [Geert Jan van Gelder], as well as Adam Talib, 'Pseudo-Ṯaʿālibī's *Book of Youths*', *Arabica* 59.6 (2012), pp. 599–649, esp. pp. 609–18.

Nubātī, the first collection of epigrams by a single author, several poets compiled collections of their epigrams arranged according to genre. Three of these thematically arranged *dīwāns* of epigrams contain a chapter dedicated to *mujūn* and related topics. On the basis of these three *mujūn* chapters, which will be discussed in more detail in the *Muqaddima II*, we will try to elucidate what was considered *mujūn* poetry in the 8th/14th century. I will limit myself to ten examples to supplement the twenty-one epigrams given in the *Natīja* below. As an homage to the most important *mujūn* poet in the period between Ibn Dāniyāl and Ibn Sūdūn, I will take these examples from the *Dīwān* of Ibrāhīm al-Miᶜmār.[10]

The first thing to note is that Mamluk-era *mujūn* is a slippery genre. Comparing epigrams no. [1] and [13] in the *Natīja*, for example, one would hardly consider them to belong to the same genre, but they are nevertheless grouped together in the same chapter. It is also obvious that E.K. Rowson's definition of Abbasid-era *mujūn* is not applicable without modification. According to this definition, '[...] *mujūn* refers behaviourally to open and unabashed indulgence in prohibited pleasures, particularly the drinking of wine and, above all, sexual profligacy. *Mujūn* literature describes and celebrates this hedonistic way of life, frequently employing explicit sexual vocabulary, and almost invariably with primarily humorous intent.'[11] Though texts of this kind still account for a large part of Mamluk *mujūn*, it cannot be denied that a number of completely different themes were incorporated under the banner of *mujūn*.

Since it is obviously no longer possible to find a definition that encompasses all kinds of poems included in the *mujūn* category, the following classification into three major categories may be helpful:

Category A comprises poems in which *behavior of questionable appropriateness* is displayed, proclaimed, or reported. This category comes close to Rowson's definition of Abbāsid *mujūn*. A typical example is the following epigram by al-Miᶜmār:

يا لائمي في ذا العذار أَفْتِنِي هل يُركَبُ الجَحْشُ بلا مِقْوَدِهْ
أُحِبُّ أربابَ اللحى شَهوةً وكلَّ مَن لحيتُهُ في يَدِهْ

> You blame me for [desiring one] whose beard has sprouted. Tell me your verdict: Can a donkey foal be ridden without a rein?
> I go crazy for men with full beards; yeah, even those who can grip theirs with their hands![12]

In this epigram, the nature of *mujūn* as 'counter-genre' is clear.[13] Whereas the love of youths who have not yet grown a dense beard was tolerated according to social norms,

[10] *Dīwān Ibrāhīm al-Miᶜmār*, ed. Thomas Bauer, Anke Osigus, Hakan Özkan. In preparation. In the following quotations from the *Dīwān al-Miᶜmār* I will give the number according to this edition and additionally mention the folium of the Escorial manuscript, our main source.

[11] E.K. Rowson, '*mujūn*', in *EAL*, p. 546.

[12] al-Miᶜmār, *Dīwān* no. 176 [Sarīᶜ], MS El Escorial 463, f. 25b.

same-sex relations between fully grown men were not. Apologising for loving a youth who has already begun to grow a downy beard is one of the main topics of *ghazal* poetry. In al-Miʿmār's epigram, however, the poet confesses to loving grown men, even those with long beards. In addition, the speaker has not been struck by love for a particularly charming person, but rather admits to loving *all* bearded men; he is not the victim of the untamable force of love, but rather pure lust (*shahwa*). If the celebration of 'unabashed indulgence in prohibited pleasures' is the core of *mujūn*, this epigram can be reckoned a very typical representative of it.[14] This poem is an example of a sub-category of Category A, which I would call the 'ostentatious violation of norms' sub-category.

The epigram that immediately precedes the confession of love for bearded in al-Miʿmār's *Dīwān* is a different case. In it, al-Miʿmār uses one of his favourite word plays: the word *qāʿida* is the active participle of the verb *qaʿada* ('to sit') in the feminine gender. Besides 'sitting', it is also a noun that means 'base'. In the architectural lexicon, however, it did not designate the 'base' of a column or pillar, but rather the capital, which 'sits' atop the column.[15] Al-Miʿmār uses this double meaning to create the following beautiful *tawriya*:

يا ليلةً مرَّتْ بِنَا   فَهَلْ تَراها عائدَهْ
عَمُودُ أيري قائمٌ   وهْيَ عليهِ قاعدهْ

Oh what a night we spent together! Will it ever come once more?
My penis pillar stood upright as she was sitting upon it / *was a capital upon it.*[16]

In this epigram, a violation of social norms is much less visible. Pre-modern Islamic societies in general were not prudish, and it was not against social norms to have good sex. We are not told if the woman was the legitimate wife or concubine of the speaker, in which case the act described in the epigram would comply even with religious norms. In any case, boasting about a violation of norms is obviously not the poet's concern. If any norm is broken, it is the genre convention of the *ghazal*. In *ghazal*, the poet may very well allude to the sexual act, but he should not describe it as outspokenly and in such detail as in our epigram.[17] Since poems of this kind were never included in *ghazal*-chapters of anthologies at the time, but could crop up in *mujūn*-chapters, there can be no doubt that *mujūn* is the genre to which it belongs. Poems of this kind should, however, be distinguished from the ostentatious-violation-of-norms sub-category. One could call

---

[13] Julie Scott Meisami, 'Arabic *mujūn* Poetry: The Literary Dimension', in F. De Jong (ed.), *Verse and the Fair Sex: Studies in Arabic Poetry and in the Representation of Women in Arabic Literature* (Utrecht: M.Th. Houtsma Stichting, 1993), pp. 8–30, here p. 19.

[14] E.K. Rowson, '*mujūn*', in *EAL*, p. 546.

[15] This has already been suspected by William Popper, *The Cairo Nilometer*, Berkeley, Los Angeles: University of California Press, 1951, p. 43, and is corroborated by a number of al-Miʿmār's poems.

[16] Al-Miʿmār, *Dīwān* no. 175 [Rajaz], MS El Escorial 463, f. 25b.

[17] As in poems in which the beloved appears as *zāʾir* 'visitor', see Thomas Bauer, *Liebe und Liebesdichtung in der arabischen Welt des 9. und 10. Jahrhunderts* (Wiebaden: Harrassowitz, 1998), p. 506–512.

them the 'highly explicit' sub-category. Poems of this type talk about sex or other pleasures that are not principally prohibited in an affirmative way. It is only the way in which the subject is discussed that makes this poem transcend the borders of genres like *ghazal* or *khamriyya*. In cases like these, the inappropriateness lies in the presentation rather than what is presented.

Boasting about sexual conquests or reports about an attempt to seduce – irrespective of their religious permissiveness – is a major topic of category A poems. Since Ibn Nubāta does not have much to offer in this respect, I will give another example by al-Miʿmār. In the following epigram, the speaker tries to entice a *muqriʾ* (a Quran reciter), who holds a post in a *madrasa* (religious college), which is a *waqf*-endowment:

قُلتُ لِذَا المُقْرِي ٱستَمِعْ يا صَاحِبَ الوَظَائِفْ
أَصْبَحَ أيْرِي واقِفاً فَٱعْمَل بِشَرْطِ الوَاقِفْ

'Listen,' I said to the Quran reciter, 'You, who are employed here:'
'My penis is standing upright so do according to the condition of the upright / *waqf-donor*!"[18]

On the other hand, most poems about sex do not talk about good sex, but about bad sex; these will be treated in category B.

As for wine-poetry, the situation did not deviate much from the Abbasid pattern. Wine poetry continued to be produced in the form of the idyllic *khamriyya*, even by poets like al-Miʿmār. In such poems, the subject is treated without provocation and with hardly any reference to the religious prohibition. In addition to this, wine remained a topic in *mujūn* poetry (and, in the case of al-Miʿmār, hashish became a new topic), where it was often treated in the ostentatious-violation-of-norms sub-category, as in the following epigram by al-Miʿmār:

أَفْتَوا إذا غُصَّ شَخْصٌ بالخَمْرِ يَدْفَعُ رُخْصَهْ
فَٱدْفَعْ بِذٰلِكَ هَمِّي فَالهَمُّ أعْظَمُ غُصَّهْ

Legal scholars say that it is permitted to cure choking with wine.
So use it to dispel my sorrows, for sorrows are the worst form of suffocation![19]

Poems in category A are not necessarily about sex or drugs, though. In the following epigram, the builder al-Miʿmār boasts about his prodigal lifestyle, building himself a 'house of pleasure':

وَلائمٍ في المالِ أَفْسَدْتُهُ وذاكَ فيهِ عَيْنُ إصْلاحِي
وبَيْتُ مَالِي حِينَ خَرَّبْتُه عَمَّرْتُ مِنهُ بِيْتَ أفْراحِي

They criticise me for wasting all my money. This they think is how they'll set me right.

[18] al-Miʿmār, *Dīwān* no. 330 [Rajaz], MS El Escorial 463, f. 47a.

[19] al-Miʿmār, *Dīwān* no. 273 [Mujtathth], MS El Escorial 463, ff. 39b–40a; رخصه according to the majority of manuscripts; El Escorial has غصّه instead.

> But though I ruined the house of my fortune, I used it to build the house of my pleasures![20]

Building a 'house of pleasures' may of course lead to penury (*iflās*), which is an important subject in the poetry of al-Miʿmār and others. This leads us already to category B.

Category B includes poems about all different kinds of misfortune: Things do not work as they should; trouble and embarrassments of all kinds arise. These mishaps are depicted and confessed in an ironic tone. Poems of this kind are (or at least should be) characterised by a certain degree of self-deprecation (though, as aṣ-Ṣafadī shows, not all poets could manage that).

As I have already indicated, most *mujūn* poems about sex fall into this category. Instead of boasting about a spectacular conquest, a poet usually related the humiliating story of a spectacular rebuff. He confessed his impotence or, the other way around, his horniness at the most inappropriate times; Ṣafī ad-Dīn al-Ḥillī's epigrams about masturbation fall into this category. In other poems, the speaker complains about the size of his penis or, more often, the size of the potential place of penetration, which is either too big or too small. A single example by al-Miʿmār should suffice. It is a poem in which he makes use of still another meaning of the root *q-ʿ-d*. The word *qawāʿid* is not only a plural of *qāʿida* in its sense 'sitting (f.)', 'base', and 'capital', but is also the plural of *qāʿid*, meaning a 'woman who is too old to bear children'. This meaning is used in the following epigram:

صغيرةٌ كلَّفتُها أيْري فقالتْ وَيْكَ باعِدْ
ما ظنّ يحملُ ذا العمو د مِنَ النساء سِوَى القواعد

> I wanted to impose my penis upon a young girl, but 'you better keep away!' she said.
> 'This column cannot be expected to bear other women than old ones / *capitals*!'[21]

Occasionally poems on wine may also fall into category B rather than Category A; for example when the poet talks about the embarrassing consequences of drunkenness. The following example shows that *mujūn* poems need not be in the first person, which gives them a (pseudo-)-autobiographical touch. This poem is instead narrated in the third person about someone suffering the detrimental effects of mixing hashish and wine:

خَلَطَ الحَشِيشةَ بِالنَبِيــ ـذِ فمالَ سُكْراً واْخْتَلَطْ
وغَدَا يُعَرْبِدُ في المَقا مِ فَقُلْتُ ما هذا اللَغَطْ
فَأجابَنِي لمّا صَحَا سَامِحْ أخَاكَ إذا خلَطْ

> Having mixed hashish with wine, he became confused and staggered in his inebriation.
> He started to riot in the place, and I said: 'What's the turmoil?!'
> After he had sobered up, he answered: 'Have mercy with your brother when he mixes!'[22]

---

[20] al-Miʿmār, *Dīwān* no. 143 [Sarīʿ], MS El Escorial 463, f. 21b.
[21] al-Miʿmār, *Dīwān* no. 174 [Kāmil], MS El Escorial 463, f. 25b.

The nub of the poem is the fact that the last hemistich is a quote from al-Ḥarīrī's 23rd *maqāma* (*al-Maqāma ash-Shiʿriyya*), in which it is a response to an accusation of plagiarism.[23]

Excluding hashish, the topics of the preceding poems are all quite compatible with the Abbasid pattern of *mujūn*. It is striking, however, that a large number of epigrams about mishaps considered *mujūn* by the Mamluk period poets who wrote them have nothing to do with sex or drugs or the violation of any social norms. These poems are hardly compatible with common definitions of *mujūn*: things do not work properly; riding animals stumble, get lame or old; cloths are stolen in the bath; people or animals are bothersome; one cannot get rid of one's slave or wife; one cannot cope with extraordinarily hot or cold weather. Poems about the hardships of Ramadan are of this variety and they treat a religious matter in an ironic tone. The subject was quite popular in al-Miʿmār's work:

شَهرُ الصيامِ مُبارَكٌ إن لم يَكُن في شَهر آبِ
خِفْتُ العَذابَ فَصُمْتُهُ فَوَقَعْتُ في وَسَطِ العَذابِ

The month of fasting is a blessed month – as long as it doesn't come in August.
I feared the torments [of hell] so I observed the fast – and found myself already amidst hell![24]

It should be noted that a tone of irony regarding religious matters could appear in different genres in Mamluk times as, for example, in more or less frivolous quotations from the Quran and the Ḥadīth in *ghazal* and *madīḥ* poems.[25] Given this openness towards religious matters, I found nothing especially blasphemous among the *mujūn* poems in our corpus. Unlike as in the Abbasid period, blasphemy seems not to have been an agenda of *mujūn* any longer. Satire (*hijāʾ*) of religious figures such as Sufis or the holders of religious offices, on the other hand, is quite common, especially in al-Miʿmār's *Dīwān*.

A few poems, like the next one, may belong to both categories A and B. The complaint about annoying animals makes it a Category B-poem. The remedial measure that is proposed, however, falls into one of the sub-categories of Category A: the ostentatious violation of norms. Remarkable is the daring enjambment, which may suggest that the therapy has already started:

إنَّ البَرَاغِيثَ اللِئا مَ قَسَوْا عليَّ فَقُلْتُ ما لي
إلّا الخُمورُ إذا ٱخْتَمَر تُ وقَرَّضُوني ما أُبَالي

---

[22] al-Miʿmār, *Dīwān*, no. 291 [Kāmil], MS El Escorial 463, ff. 41a–41b, see also Franz Rosenthal, *The herb; hashish versus medieval Muslim society* (Leiden: Brill, 1971), p. 66.

[23] See ash-Sharīshī, *Sharḥ Maqāmāt al-Ḥarīrī*, ed. Muḥammad Abū l-Faḍl Ibrāhīm, 5 vols. (Beirut: 1413/1992), vol. 3, p. 158.

[24] al-Miʿmār, *Dīwān* no. 34 [Kāmil], MS El Escorial 463, f. 7a.

[25] See Geert Jan van Gelder, 'Forbidden Firebrands: Frivolous *Iqtibās* (Quotation from the Qurʾān) According to Arab Critics', *Quaderni di studi arabi* 20–21 (2002–2003), pp. 3–16.

When the wicked fleas have no mercy on me I say: No remedy against them
Besides wine. They keep on biting, but I don't care any longer when I'm drunk![26]

Category C comprises poems about troubled friendships. In these cases, it is a friendship or another close relationship that does not function properly. The poet expresses his disappointment about a friend, feels abandoned, forsaken or deceived, or complains about his loneliness or inability to make friends.

A large number of these poems deal with troubled communication between friends. A joke may be misunderstood; a present may be delayed or not live up to expectations. Poems in which friends (or ex-friends) are addressed can range from playful teasing to mild criticism to downright *hijāʾ* (invective). It should be noted that *mujūn* and *hijāʾ* were seen as related genres at the time. In the British Library manuscript of the *Dīwān* of al-Miʿmār, the only manuscript of the *Dīwān* that is arranged thematically, *mujūn* poems are included within the *hijāʾ* section.[27] Despite this, and despite the fact that the dedicatee of this article is a pioneer in the study of *hijāʾ*, I will not treat poems that belong to the genre of *hijāʾ* and focus rather on those that are *mujūn*.[28]

Another group of poems of this kind are poems in which the poet has not yet received a present but is asking for one. The act of begging may be seen as humiliating and so is dealt with in a humorous way. Here again it is self-mockery rather than criticism of perfidious friends that is in the focus.

It is quite obvious that Category C is actually a sub-category of B. In the case of Category C, the 'thing' that does not function properly is friendship. To make it a separate category is mainly justified by the fact that with Ibn Nubāta it seems to be the most important category in his chapter on *al-mudāʿaba wa-l-mujūn*. Ibn Nubāta must have been quite conscious of this fact as the chapter heading demonstrates. Unlike earlier instances, he added the word *mudāʿaba* ('teasing back and forth') and even put it before the word *mujūn*. This reference to communication with 'others' is characteristic of the more communicative nature of Mamluk literature as compared to earlier periods.[29] Obviously, this general trend can be noticed also in the case of *mujūn*.

Since a number of poems of this category can be found in the *Natīja*, a single example by al-Miʿmār may suffice. It is a complaint about being forsaken while ill. The epigram is most certainly an adaption of one of Ibn Nubāta's (see *Natīja* [13]). The rhyme is maintained, but the meter al-Miʿmār uses is shorter and Ibn Nubāta's reference to a single visitor is deleted, thus making it more generally applicable:

---

[26] al-Miʿmār, *Dīwān* no. 381 [Kāmil], MS El Escorial 463, f. 54a.

[27] *Dīwān al-Miʿmār*, MS British Museum 8054, f. 52b: *fīmā warada lahū mina l-hajw wa-mā yajrī majrāhu.*

[28] Geert Jan van Gelder, *The Bad and the Ugly: Attitudes Towards Invective Poetry (*Hijāʾ*) in Classical Arabic Literature* (Leiden: Brill, 1988).

[29] See Thomas Bauer, '"*Ayna hādhā min al-Mutanabbī*!" Toward an Aesthetics of Mamluk Literature', *Mamlūk Studies Review*, forthcoming, and id., 'Mamluk Literature as a Means of Communication', in S. Conermann (ed.), *Ubi sumus? Quo vademus? Mamluk Studies - State of the Art* (Göttingen: Bonn University Press, 2013), pp. 23–56.

لم يَعُودُوا بي بضُعْفي وبِفَرْطِ اللَّوْمِ عَادُوا
ثُمَّ قالوا هُوَ ماضٍ كلُّ ماضٍ لا يُعَادُ

> When I felt weak, nobody came to visit me. It was only severe rebuke that made them come to my sickbed.
> Then they said: 'He passes away, and what passes away will not come back again / be visited'[30]

It is obvious that wit, irony and (self-)mockery are indispensable qualities of *mujūn* poems. In the Mamluk period, this aspect is certainly more important than the celebration of prohibited pleasures. But humour is not exclusive to *mujūn*. Is there ultimately a common thread linking the three categories A, B, and C? I would say yes and venture the following characterization: *mujūn* poems from the period in question are characterized by an attitude of relaxation, of letting-go, of a loosening of discipline so that one could talk about things about which one could not talk – at least not in this manner – without the risk of violating one's dignity. By composing *mujūn*, the poet puts his dignity at stake, even if only playfully and ironically. An honourable and dignified man should not discuss his erectile dysfunction in public, nor boast about having sex with bearded men, nor talk about licit sex in a highly explicit way. Similarly it is undignified to fall from a mule, ride a lame donkey, be stuck with bothersome slaves, or be forced to beg for a coat or one's livelihood. Seen in this way, the subject of friendship fits the genre perfectly: a distinguished and dignified person should have friends – trustworthy friends. He should not need to bestow upon them the honour of a visit, rather he should be visited by them. In his chapter on 'the positive sides about being imprisoned', ath-Thaʿālibī quotes the poet ʿAlī ibn Jahm, who says that prison is the proper place for a noble (*karīm*) man because 'in [prison] he is the one who is visited and not the one who visits' (*yuzāru fīhi wa-lā yazūru*).[31] This piece of wisdom from Abbasid times was still valid in the Mamluk period. So long as one was not in prison for some abominable act, it was better to be visited in prison than to beg or to humble oneself or to have no friends at all.

'Dignity at stake' is, therefore, the common denominator in *mujūn* poems of the 8th/14th century and so it is interesting to see how authors indulge in the production of *mujūn* epigrams differently depending on the degree of dignity they stand to lose. This subject is the topic of *Muqaddima II*.

---

[30] al-Miʿmār, *Dīwān*, no. 187 [Ramal], MS El Escorial 463, f. 27a.

[31] See ath-Thaʿālibī, *Taḥsīn al-qabīḥ wa-taqbīḥ al-ḥasan*, ed. Shākir al-ʿĀshūr (Damascus: 2006), p. 46.

MUQADDIMA II: FOUR MAJOR AUTHORS OF *MUJŪN* EPIGRAMS IN THE 8TH/14TH CENTURY

Jamāl ad-Dīn Ibn Nubāta al-Miṣrī (686–768/1287–1366)[32] was the main representative of 'high' literature, including poetry and prose, in his day. Born into a family of scholars, he began his career as an intellectual and poet in Damascus, where he spent the greater part of his life. His style is characterized by a permanent striving for elegance and sophistication. He earned his greatest fame for his elaborate *madīḥ*-poems and his polished prose letters, but also for his epigrams. *Mujūn* is certainly not the first genre that comes to mind when Ibn Nubāta is mentioned, but, after all, his contribution to the genre is not entirely insignificant. I have already mentioned his comprehensive selection from the Dīwān of Ibn al-Ḥajjāj, *Talṭīf al-Mizāj*. In his own work, Ibn Nubāta treated *mujūn* exclusively in the form of epigrams. This is not surprising since the *zajal*, an important vehicle for *mujūn* for poets like al-Miʿmār, was not really Ibn Nubāta's style (he shunned dialect more than obscenity), and long *mujūn* poems (*qaṣāʾid*) in the style of Ibn al-Ḥajjāj were hardly composed at the time except by Ṣafī ad-Dīn al-Ḥillī.

Most of Ibn Nubāta's *mujūn* epigrams can be found in *al-Qaṭr an-Nubātī*, a pioneering work and one of his most popular. In all likelihood, Ibn Nubāta was the first poet to have the idea of compiling a *dīwān* of poetry made up exclusively of epigrams and arranged according to theme and genre. The work, the title of which will be explained in the commentary to poem 18b in the *Natīja*, was finished prior to the year 729 and dedicated to Abū l-Fidāʾ, a descendant of the Ayyubids.[33] Between 710/1310 and 732/1331, he ruled Ḥamāh as governor for the Mamluk sultan, who awarded him the title of al-Malik al-Muʾayyad. *Al-Qaṭr an-Nubātī* is preserved in several manuscripts, the most reliable of which was written in 732 by Ibn Nāhiḍ, a personal acquaintance of the author.[34] The fourth chapter (following chapters on *madḥ*, *ghazal*, and *rithāʾ*) is titled *al-mudāʿaba wa-l-mujūn* and comprises sixty-six epigrams, amounting to almost one quarter of the entire book. In a later recension, the number grows to seventy-seven despite the omission of several epigrams from the earlier version.[35] This proportion shows that Ibn Nubāta had no problem putting his dignity on the line. After all, he managed to get along without holding a major scholarly or administrative position until comparatively late in life. When circumstances finally forced him to enter the chancellery of Damascus at the age of 57 in 743, his fame as poet, prose writer and intellectual was beyond question. Most of his

---

[32] See Thomas Bauer, 'Ibn Nubātah al-Miṣrī (686–768/1287–1366): Life and Works. Part I: The Life of Ibn Nubātah', *Mamlūk Studies Review* 12.1 (2008), pp. 1–35; and *idem*, 'Ibn Nubātah al-Miṣrī (686–768/1287–1366): Life and Works. Part 2: The Dīwān of Ibn Nubātah', *Mamlūk Studies Review* 12.2 (2008), pp. 25–69.

[33] It is mentioned in the *ijāza* for which aṣ-Ṣafadī asked Ibn Nubāta in this year, see ibid., Part I, p. 5.

[34] MS Paris 2234, fol. 158–200, completed on 9 Rabīʿ II 732 by Taqī ad-Dīn Ibrāhīm ibn Muḥammad ibn Nāhiḍ al-Ḥalabī (on him see aṣ-Ṣafadī: *Aʿyān al-ʿaṣr wa-Aʿwān an-naṣr*, ed. ʿAlī Abū Zayd, 6 vols. [Beirut/Damascus: Dār al-Fikr al-Muʿāṣir, 1418–1419/1998], vol. 1, pp. 126–27).

[35] Ibn Nubāta, *al-Qaṭr an-Nubātī*, MS Florence, Laurenziana 521, ff. 65b–78b. This recension is not taken into account here.

mujūn epigrams, however, (including all those given in the *Natīja*) were composed earlier during his career as a 'freelance' intellectual.

In his *mujūn* epigrams, sex plays a comparatively minor role, as does the indulgence of any kind of violation of norms. More central is the self-deprecating treatment of misfortune. The most important topic, though, is friendship, as the examples chosen for the *Natīja* show.

Ibn Nubāta's *Qaṭr* set a precedent. The first to emulate this model was the Aleppan littérateur Badr ad-Dīn Ibn Ḥabīb (710–779/1310–1377). Ibn Ḥabīb composed his own *dīwān* of epigrams immediately after he encountered Ibn Nubāta's *Qaṭr*. It is his very first work, and he cannot have been much older than eighteen at the time of its composition. It is obvious that for a youngster at the very start of his career, before he had acquired any dignity to put at stake, *mujūn* was not an appropriate genre. No wonder then that of the four epigram collections in question, Ibn Ḥabīb's is the only one that does not include *mujūn*.[36]

The next to follow Ibn Nubāta's model was the poet Ṣafī ad-Dīn al-Ḥillī (667–750/1278–1350).[37] He was of Iraqi origin, but settled in Mārdīn, which was under the suzerainty of the Artuqid dynasty, and came to the Mamluk Empire only as a guest. There, at the court of the Ayyubids of Ḥamāh, he met Ibn Nubāta. They seem to have got along quite well, though later authors tried to play them against each other. In any case, their styles are conspicuously different. It was in Ḥamāh that al-Ḥillī got the inspiration to compile his own *dīwān* of epigrams. Al-Malik al-Afḍal, son of and successor to al-Malik al-Muʾayyad, suggested that he compile such a *dīwān* of epigrams – at least this is what al-Ḥillī says in his dedication to this patron.[38] Al-Afḍal reigned between 732/1332 and 742/1341, but as he quickly lost interest in poetry and turned to asceticism, his encouragement of al-Ḥillī must have come in 732 or only a few years later. At that time, more than ten years had elapsed since al-Ḥillī had compiled a *Dīwān* of poetry, comprising both long and short poems, including strophic poetry, 'at the suggestion of al-Nāṣir b. Ḳalāwūn, probably in 723/1322'.[39] Following al-Afḍal's spurring, al-Ḥillī did little more than excerpt existing poems or parts of existing poems and re-arrange them in twenty chapters (instead of the twelve chapters in his Dīwān). The result was a small book entitled *Dīwān al-Mathālith wa-l-mathānī fī l-maʿālī wa-l-maʿānī*, which includes only epigrams of two and three lines.[40] In this respect, al-Ḥillī was stricter than Ibn Nubāta, who included some longer pieces in his

---

[36] See Thomas Bauer, '"Was kann aus dem Jungen noch werden!" Das poetische Erstlingswerk des Historikers Ibn Ḥabīb im Spiegel seiner Zeitgenossen' in O. Jastrow, S. Talay, and H. Hafenrichter (eds.), *Studien zur Semitistik und Arabistik: Festschrift für Hartmut Bobzin zum 60. Geburtstag* (Wiesbaden: Harrassowitz, 2008), pp. 15–56.

[37] See Wolfhart Heinrichs, 'Ṣafī al-Dīn al-Ḥillī', in EI² 8:801–805.

[38] Ṣafī ad-Dīn al-Ḥillī, *Dīwān al-Mathālith wa-l-mathānī*, MS Paris 3341, ff. 1b–2a.

[39] W. Heinrichs, 'Ṣafī al-Dīn al-Ḥillī', p. 802b.

[40] The only edition so far (Muḥammad Ṭāhir al-Ḥimṣī, Damascus 1419/1998) is based on a single, not very good manuscript and contains an inacceptable number of mistakes. The one- and four-liners in this edition are, without exception, errors. A new edition, based on the Paris manuscript, is a strong desideratum.

al-Qaṭr an-Nubātī. On the other hand, al-Ḥillī's *Dīwān al-Mathālith wa-l-mathānī* contains very little (if any) material that had not already been included in his *Dīwān*.

In the long *Dīwān*, *mujūn* poems appear in sub-chapter (*faṣl*) three, *fī l-iḥmāḍ wa-l-mujūn*, of chapter (*bāb*) eleven, *fī l-mulaḥ wa-l-ahājī wa-l-iḥmāḍ fī t-tanājī* ('jocular verse, satirical poems, and obscene poems').[41] The *faṣl* contains thirty-five poems, some of them of considerable length. For the corresponding chapter in his *Dīwān al-Mathālith wa-l-mathānī*, al-Ḥillī chose eight two-liners and five three-liners from his *Dīwān*. None of the thirteen epigrams is a secondary epigram (i.e. an epigram that was created by excerpting two or three lines from an originally longer poem), nor did the author add a single line to the versions given in the *Dīwān*. There are, however, a number of textual variants the status of which can only be ascertained by a critical edition of both the *Dīwān* and the *Dīwān al-Mathālith wa-l-mathānī*. For the *mujūn*-chapters, we lack both. In both the latest editions of al-Ḥillī's *Dīwān* and the (very faulty) edition of his epigram collection, the *mujūn*-chapters have fallen victim to censorship and are omitted completely. For the *Dīwān*, readers may resort to the *editio princeps* of al-Ḥillī's *Dīwān* (Damascus 1297–1300/1879–1883), which is the only edition of the *Dīwān* to include the *mujūn*-chapter, though it is not in its proper place; it is included at the end so the user has the opportunity to remove it.[42] For *Dīwān al-Mathālith wa-l-mathānī*, the excellent manuscript Paris 3341 has to be used. Folio 20 is out of order, but this problem can easily be fixed. The *mujūn* chapter (chapter 19) here bears the headline *Fī l-hazl wa-l-iḥmāḍ li-ʿiddat aghrāḍ*.[43] Here is a concordance of the *mujūn*-epigrams in *Dīwān al-Mathālith wa-l-mathānī* and their counterparts in the Damascus edition of al-Ḥillī's *Dīwān:*

	Ms. Paris fol.	*Dīwān* (page/line)
1	49b	567/3–4
2	20a	567/6–7
3	20a	568/10–11
4	20a	569/4–5
5	20a–b	568/16–18
6	20b	563/13–14
7	20b	570/15–16
8	20b	571/5–6
9	50a	569/17–19
10	50a	563/16–18
11	50a	569/7–8
12	50b	569/21–570/2
13	50b	568/13–14

[41] Translation W. Heinrichs, 'Ṣafī al-Dīn al-Ḥillī', p. 802a.
[42] See W. Heinrichs, 'Ṣafī al-Dīn al-Ḥillī', p. 805a.
[43] MS Paris fol. 3b; the word *al-hazl* is omitted on fol. 49b.

It is remarkable that al-Ḥillī adopted the new form of an epigram *dīwān*, but did not adopt Ibn Nubāta's new approach to the genre of *mujūn*. Instead, all his *mujūn* epigrams are about masturbation, penetration, or farting. Like Ibn Nubāta, al-Ḥillī was not dependent on a prestigious position and consequently had no problems writing rather outspoken *mujūn*. Unlike Ibn Nubāta, the Iraqi al-Ḥillī was more firmly rooted in the Abbasid tradition and composed *mujūn* very much in the vein of his Abbasid predecessors.

Khalīl ibn Aybak aṣ-Ṣafadī (696–764/1297–1363) followed a few years later with his own *dīwān* of epigrams entitled *ar-Rawḍ al-bāsim wa-l-ʿarf an-nāsim*. The editor considers it one of aṣ-Ṣafadī's latest works, but it cannot be that late.[44] When aṣ-Ṣafadī met Ibn Nāhiḍ (who was incidentally also the copyist of the manuscript of *al-Qaṭr an-Nubātī* used for this study) in Aleppo in the year 756, he 'heard my book *ar-Rawḍ al-bāsim* and others'.[45] It is reasonable, therefore, to suspect that the book was compiled not too long before.

The book is arranged in 46 chapters. Almost all headlines denote a theme rather than a genre; the penultimate chapter '*Fī l-mujūn*' is an exception to that rule. It is made up of forty-five epigrams, which amounts to less than six per cent of the whole work. This comparatively low percentage corroborates the impression that aṣ-Ṣafadī did not feel comfortable writing in the genre of *mujūn*. Unlike the other authors dealt with here, aṣ-Ṣafadī pursued an official career as secretary, though because he was hard of hearing he never reached the position he deserved to on account of his talent. It seems plausible (though it remains speculation) that this social circumstance made him reluctant to indulge in *mujūn* too excessively and openly. Already at the beginning of the *mujūn* chapter, the author stresses that the following is fiction: *qawl bi-lā ʿamal*, and he repeats this phrase later on.[46] There is little self-mockery in his chapter; instead, several of aṣ-Ṣafadī's epigrams describe the mishaps of others, not his own. Strangely enough, aṣ-Ṣafadī explains the crux of his epigrams several times, saying that they contain a paronomasia (*jinās*), a double entendre (*tawriya*), or a quotation (*taḍmīn*). The last of these is the most common type deployed in the chapter. But whereas quotations that are taken out of context and given a completely new meaning were also popular with other authors of *mujūn* at the time, I did not encounter word-plays based on spelling (like in the following) in the works of the other four poets:

تَقُولُ إِذْ رَقَدَتْ في الفَرْشِ هَلْ لَكَ في كَأسٍ تُرَوِّي عِظَامَ المَيْتِ في الجَدَثِ
فَقُلْتُ – والقَصْدُ لا يَخْفَى على فَطِنٍ – إِنْ كانَ شَيْئاً فَكَأسٌ نَاقِصُ الثُلُثِ

Lying drowsy on the mat, she said: 'What about a cup of wine that can moisten the bones of a corpse in its grave?'

---

[44] See aṣ-Ṣafadī, *ar-Rawḍ al-Bāsim wa-l-ʿArf an-Nāsim*, ed. Muḥammad ʿAbd al-Mujīb Lāshīn (Cairo: Dār al-Āfāq al-ʿArabiyya, 1425/2005), p. 28.

[45] See aṣ-Ṣafadī, *Aʿyān al-ʿAṣr* 1:127.

[46] aṣ-Ṣafadī, *ar-Rawḍ al-Bāsim*, p. 246, 253.

> I answered – and smart people will understand what I mean – 'If anything, it's a "cup one-third empty".'[47]

The 'cup one-third empty' is, of course, the word *k-ʾ-s* without its middle letter, which thus gives *k-s* or '*kuss*' ('cunt'). What starts in a quite original way in picturesque decadence – a drowsy woman on her bed offering wine – is, at least to my mind, spoiled by the redundant filler 'smart people will understand' (in Arabic stylistics this would have been called *ḥashw* or 'stuffing') and the all too trivial word play that constitutes the point.

As for the themes treated in aṣ-Ṣafadī's *mujūn* chapter, sex clearly dominates, but the theme of non-sexual mishaps is also present. In this respect, aṣ-Ṣafadī follows Ibn Nubāta (though the subject of 'friendship' is absent from the *mujūn* chapter). Unfortunately, aṣ-Ṣafadī does not only follow Ibn Nubāta's scheme in his book and in his *mujūn* chapter, he actually plagiarizes him. The second epigram in aṣ-Ṣafadī's *mujūn* chapter is about the cloth for his turban that was stolen.[48] The whole idea (perhaps including the theft itself) is taken from Ibn Nubāta's *Qaṭr*, however.[49] Aṣ-Ṣafadī's chapter ends with another instance of plagiarism. Aṣ-Ṣafadī's last poem is almost identical to a well attested epigram by al-Miʿmār.[50]

Ibrāhīm al-Miʿmār (d. 749/1348) was a stonecutter and builder. His *Dīwān*, preserved in at least seven manuscripts, consists of epigrams and a *maqāma* in standard Arabic, and *mawāliyyā* and strophic poems mostly in dialectal Arabic. The *Dīwān*, which was not compiled by al-Miʿmār himself, is preserved in two recensions: one long and one short. In all three manuscripts of the long recension and three of the four manuscripts of the short recension, the non-strophic poems are arranged alphabetically according to rhyme-letter. In the thematically arranged (and rather deficient) manuscript from the British Library, *mujūn* is grouped together with invective (*hajw*).[51]

As a craftsman, al-Miʿmār did not have to worry about scholarly dignity and so he could indulge in *mujūn* as much as he liked; and liked it he did! The selections of al-Miʿmār's poems in anthologies and biographical dictionaries suggest that he owed his fame to his *mujūn* poems especially. This impression cannot be fully corroborated by his *Dīwān*, however. It is true that al-Miʿmār fancied *mujūn* of any kind and did not even shy away from the extraordinarily obscene. It is also true, however, that the proportion of *mujūn* poems among his epigrams is clearly lower than twenty percent. Nevertheless he remains the most important and original *mujūn* poet of the time, not only on account of his epigrams, but also for his *azjāl*. I would say that his series of three *azjāl on intoxicating substances* – on wine, beer, and hashish – are among the most impressive specimens of

---

[47] aṣ-Ṣafadī, *ar-Rawḍ al-Bāsim* no. 685 [Basīṭ], p. 249.

[48] aṣ-Ṣafadī, *ar-Rawḍ al-Bāsim* no. 678, p. 247.

[49] Ibn Nubāta, *al-Qaṭr an-Nubātī* no. 179, MS Paris 2234, fol. 184a.

[50] Compare aṣ-Ṣafadī, *ar-Rawḍ al-Bāsim* no. 721, p. 261 and al-Miʿmār, *Dīwān* no. 173, MS El Escorial 463, fol. 25a .

[51] MS British Museum 8054.

eastern *zajal* poetry and a conscious attempt by their author to open up new literary dimensions for this form of popular poetry.[52]

One of the fascinating things about literary life in the Mamluk period is the fact that almost all layers of society took part. This is, as we have seen, also the case for a genre as precarious as *mujūn*, to which such different characters as the sophisticated elite writer Ibn Nubāta, the touchy intellectual aṣ-Ṣafadī, the cosmopolitan tradesman al-Ḥillī, and the semi-educated craftsman al-Miʿmār contributed, each in his own conspicuously different way.

This article began with several epigrams by the popular poet al-Miʿmār. It is only fitting, therefore, that it should conclude with a selection of epigrams composed by the elite poet Ibn Nubāta, who was in many ways al-Miʿmār's exact opposite, thereby demonstrating the broad unity of Mamluk literature across all social boundaries.

NATĪJA: TWENTY-ONE *MUJŪN* EPIGRAMS BY IBN NUBĀTA AL-MIṢRĪ

[1]

Category A, the portrayal or description of behavior of questionable appropriateness is not a major subject in Ibn Nubāta's *mujūn* epigrams. Most epigrams of this kind are moderate confessions of hedonism, such as the epigram that concludes the *mujūn* chapter in the *Qaṭr*. The notion of a 'violation of norms' is barely present, if at all. If the following were an Abbasid poem (or one by Ṣafī ad-Dīn al-Ḥillī), it would have been included in a chapter on wine poetry (*khamriyyāt*). Ibn Nubāta himself composed a number of *khamriyyāt*, especially in the *muwashshaḥ* form, in which bacchic and erotic subjects are treated in much the same way as in this epigram. There is, however, no *khamriyyāt*-chapter in the *Qaṭr*, which is perhaps why this epigram was included in the *al-Mudāʿaba wa-l-mujūn* section. The point of the epigram revolves around a *tawriya*. The speaker craves the lad's *ḥadīth* 'talk' and his *ʿatīq* 'old, good wine'. This last word suggests the unintended sense of *ḥadīth* meaning 'new', thus giving the pair of opposites 'new and old'. Setting aside this typically post-Abbasid rhetorical device, this is one of the most Abbasid-style poems in the chapter:

إنّي إذا آنستُ همًّا طـارِقـاً   عجَّلتُ باللذّات قطع طريقِهِ
ودعَوتُ ألفاظ المليح وكأسه   فنَعِمتُ بين حديثه وعَتيقِهِ

> When sorrow seeks to join me in the night, I hasten toward pleasure so as to block its path.
> I ask the beautiful lad for his conversation and his cup, and relish in his *new and old* / talk and his old wine.[53]

---

[52] On the beer *zajal* see Hinrich Biesterfeldt, '*Mizr fī Miṣr*. Ein Preisgedicht auf das Bier aus dem Kairo des 14. Jahrhunderts', in Hinrich Biesterfeldt and Verena Klemm (eds.): *Differenz und Dynamik im Islam: Festschrift für Heinz Halm zum 70. Geburtstag* (Würzburg: Ergon, 2012), pp. 383–398.

[53] Ibn Nubāta, *al-Qaṭr an-Nubātī* no. 210 [Kāmil], MS Paris 2234, fol. 189b.

[2]

The following poem could also be subsumed under the category of *khamriyyāt*. This time, Ibn Nubāta's confession of hedonism is not a solipsistic declaration. Instead, an anonymous interlocutor is addressed. He is obviously a poet composing a hunting poem, in which he describes 'tall' and 'reddish-brown' horses. But hearing the words *nahd* and *kumayt* the poet cannot help but think about a girl's bosom and dark red wine, for which *kumayt* is one of the most common designations. The conversational nature of the poem together with its point – again relying on *double entendre* – makes it a clearly post-Abbasid epigram. Again, the notion of a violation of social norms is hardly present. The person being addressed is even expected to share in the poet's pleasures:

يا واصف الخيل بالكميتِ وبالـ   ـنَهد أرِحْني من طُول وسواسِ
لو كنتَ تحت الدجى تُشاهدني   لاُستحسنَتْ مقلتاك أفراسي
لا نَهْدَ إلّا من صدر غانيةٍ   ولا كميتاً إلّا من الكاسِ

You with your horses 'reddish-brown and lofty', would you give me a rest from this endless temptation!
If only you'd spied me, 'neath the cover of darkness, your eyes would have seen the beauty of my 'mares';
Nothing's so 'lofty' as a woman's full bosom and nothing so 'red' as the wine in my cup.[54]

[3]

The 'boasting about a violation of norms' is, however, not completely absent in Ibn Nubāta's *mujūn* chapter. One of the main topoi in *mujūn* is confessing love for a man who has already grown a dense beard. As already mentioned above, it is the density (or fullness) of the beloved's beard that divides *ghazal* and *mujūn*. As this example clearly demonstrates, it is not religious, but social norms that matter most. Ibn Nubāta's example:

وقالوا أحاطَت ذَقنُه بخدوده   ووجدك لا ينفكُّ يذكر حُسنَهُ
فقلتُ نعم ضَيفٌ بقلبِيَ نازل   أعظّم مثواه وأكرم ذقنَهُ

They said: A beard covers his cheeks, but in your passion you still praise his beauty!
Yes, I said. A guest has taken up residence in my heart so I exalt his abode and honour his beard![55]

The last hemistich seems to be a quotation or an idiom of some kind, but I could not verify it in the sources accessible to me. This is, by the way, one of the main obstacles in studying *mujūn* from the Mamluk period. All too often, the modern reader is quite aware of the fact that there is 'something' behind the last word(s) of the epigram – a quotation,

---

[54] Ibn Nubāta, *al-Qaṭr an-Nubātī* no. 149 [Munsariḥ], MS Paris 2234, fol. 180a.
[55] Ibn Nubāta, *al-Qaṭr an-Nubātī* no. 189 [Ṭawīl], MS Paris 2234, fol. 186a.

an allusion, a hidden double meaning – but cannot figure out what it is. For quite a number of epigrams, we may never be able to discern with certainty what exactly the point is.

[4]

A quotation or saying may also be the root of the point in the following epigram, but it is fully comprehensible regardless. It is an example of the narrative form of category A and one of the most sexually explicit epigrams in Ibn Nubāta's *mujūn* chapter.

يا رُبَّ ليلٍ بِتُّه متنعّماً   برشيقةٍ تعيَى بردفٍ مثقلِ
أيري بجانبِ كسّها في جُحْرِها   عرف المحلّ فبات دون المنزلِ

> How many a night did I enjoy with a slender girl who wearies of the burden of her heavy buttocks.
> My penis was in the burrow besides her cunt. He knew the proper place of alighting, but preferred to spend the night outside home.[56]

[5]

One of the rare epigrams in which Ibn Nubāta boasts of a sexual conquest is the following, which uses the terminology of the goldsmith's craft:

يا حبَّذا الظبي الذي   قد كان يعتمد النِفَارا
عاينتُ صَوْغ صِفاته   فجعلتُ خاتمَهُ سِوَارا

> There was a shy gazelle who always used to run away.
> But I learned how to mould his temperament and made his seal ring my bracelet.[57]

[6]

In the following epigram the poet addresses his slave girl *Shahd* ('Honey'). The final word *ʿusayla* is a diminutive of *ʿasal*, another word for 'honey', but also designates the sexual act. Since it is in complete accordance with both religious and social norms to have sex with one's slave girl, it is only the brazenness of the poem that makes it *mujūn*:

يا شهدُ لا والله أقـ   ـنَعُ أن أعاودَ قُبلَتكْ
ما أنتِ عندي شهدة   حتى أذوق عُسَيلتك

> By God, Honey, it's not enough for me to kiss you over and over.
> You won't be a real 'honey-comb' to me till I get to taste your 'honey'.[58]

[7]

---

[56] Ibn Nubāta, *al-Qaṭr an-Nubātī* no. 198 [Kāmil], MS Paris 2234, fol. 187b.
[57] Ibn Nubāta, *al-Qaṭr an-Nubātī* no. 192 [Kāmil], MS Paris 2234, fol. 186b.
[58] Ibn Nubāta, *al-Qaṭr an-Nubātī* no. 174 [Kāmil], MS Paris 2234, fol. 183b.

Slave girls do not only grant pleasure; they can also be annoying. This leads us to category B. The point of the following epigram rests on the use of *jinās* (paronomasia):

رامتْ زبيباً ولوزاً   ورُمتُ بَيناً ورِحلَه
فتلك تطلبُ نُقلاً   والقلبُ يطلبُ نَقله

> She wanted raisins and almonds, I wanted space and departure.
> She was asking for sweetmeats (*nuql*), while my heart was trying to get away (*naqla*).[59]

[8]

In the next epigram, the source of embarrassment is a mule. Again *jinās* (paronomasia) is used; this time between the rhyme words (*qaṣaṣā* - *qafaṣā*). The phrase *aṣbaḥat qafaṣan* is still today often used to mean 'it became like a prison'. Note the dialogic introduction:

أصبحتُ يا سيّدي ويا سَنَدي   أقُصُّ في أمرِ بغلَتي القصَصَا
بالأمس كانَت لفَرطِ سُرعتها   طيراً وفي اليوم أصبحتْ قَفَصا

> I've been reduced, my lord and my sustainer, to telling stories about my mule.
> Just yesterday it blazed so fast it was a bird, though today it's come to be a cage.[60]

[9]

In the following epigram Ibn Nubāta recycled an idea he had first used some years before in a letter to the Khaṭīb of Damascus, Jalāl ad-Dīn al-Qazwīnī, during one extraordinary cold and snowy winter in 716/1316–1317. Making use of several quotations from the Quran, he writes:

أمّا أنا فقد تحصّنتُ في هذه ﴿الواقعة﴾ [الواقعة : ١] بظلّ ﴿السماء ذات البروج﴾ [البروج : ١] *
ولبستُ السنجاب الأبلق إلا أنه من زرقة الجَسَدِ وبياض الثلوج *

> As far as I am concerned, to protect me from this 'terror' (Q 56:1), I have taken refuge in the shadow of 'the heaven with the fortresses / zodiac' (Q 85:1), | and I put on the fur of the white-spotted squirrel by combining the blue of the (skin of my) body with the white of the snow.[61]

Ibn Nubāta pretends to be clad in a coat made of the fur of a *sinjāb*, a sort of squirrel whose fur was imported from Russia or the Caucasus. Its colour is blue and white. But in fact, Ibn Nubāta could neither find shelter nor afford such a precious fur coat, and therefore had to rely on the white of the snow and the blue of his cold skin. The poet liked this idea quite a lot and not only did he use it in several of his collections of prose

---

[59] Ibn Nubāta, *al-Qaṭr an-Nubātī* no. 181 [Mujtathth], MS Paris 2234, fol. 184b.

[60] Ibn Nubāta, *al-Qaṭr an-Nubātī* no. 151 [Munsariḥ], MS Paris 2234, fol. 180a.

[61] The text here is according to the autograph manuscript *Min Tarassul Ibn Nubātah*, Escorial MS 548, fol. 91b.–92b. A full version is given in Thomas Bauer, '"Ayna hādhā min al-Mutanabbī!" Toward an Aesthetics of Mamluk Literature' (to appear in *Mamlūk Studies Review*).

texts, he also transformed it to an epigram, which he included in his *Qaṭr*. It came into the *mujūn* section because it is a confession of being impoverished and helpless in the face of cold weather, but also perhaps because – at least in the letter – the poet is pretending to beg for the gift of a fur coat. Since the idea was first used in a letter, a dialogic structure suggests itself:

يا سيّدي عَطفاً فإني ميّتٌ وفي دمشق اليوم بردٌ قد عَتَا
زرقةُ جسمي وبياض ثلجها سنجابي الأزرق في فَصل الشتا

Compassion, Sir, for I'm dying as the cold in Damascus is harsh beyond measure!
The blue of my (frozen) body and the whiteness of the snow are my coat of blue-squirrel fur this winter![62]

[10]

The genre *mujūn* intersects with the genres of love poetry (*ghazal*), wine poetry (*khamriyya*) and invective (*hijāʾ*), but it has hardly any connection to the genre of threnody (*rithāʾ*). The following epigram, however, is one such exception. It deals once again with a slave, but the trouble this slave causes is quite different from other annoyances commonly mentioned in *mujūn*: he is dead. At first glance, it is difficult to understand why this poem was placed in this chapter, but a comparison with other epigrams in the *mujūn* chapter provides an explanation. It shows that its main focus is less on the trouble created by the dead servant, but rather the subject of the poet's loneliness. This epigram takes us from category B to category C: trouble with friends, which is treated in a self-deprecating manner. Obviously this epigram falls under this latter category, although self-directed irony is not very prominent in it. The point here revolves around a *tawriya*: the word *faraj* means 'relief' and is also the servant's name:

كان لي عبدٌ تسمّى فَرَجاً نَصَبَ الدهرُ عليه الشبكا
وأنا اليومَ كما تبصرني لا أرى لي فَرَجاً إلا البُكا

I had a servant, Faraj / *relief* was his name. Fate cast its net upon him.
And now, as you see, I cannot find relief / *Faraj* except in tears.[63]

[11]

The next epigram is a rare combination of two different themes of Ibn Nubāta's *mujūn*: sex and friendship. Still, it does not sound very much like *mujūn* but rather a poem of advice and admonition. For a fuller understanding, it is helpful to know the variant reading in the printed *Dīwān* where the first words are: يا أير لا تركن لعلقٍ 'Oh penis, don't rely on a rent-boy'.[64] The headline says that the redactor 'copied this from the poet's autograph'. Given the fact that Ibn Nubāta constantly revised his own works and

[62] Ibn Nubāta, *al-Qaṭr an-Nubātī* no. 208 [Rajaz], MS Paris 2234, fol. 189a.
[63] Ibn Nubāta, *al-Qaṭr an-Nubātī* no. 207 [Ramal], MS Paris 2234, fol. 189a.
[64] Ibn Nubāta, *Dīwān*, p. 270.

compiled an entirely new version of his *Qaṭr* in later years, this statement is credible. Therefore it may be taken for granted that the 'beardless' young man (*amrad*) in the first version of the epigram is in fact a rent-boy. The epigram thus combines two *mujūn* themes. The first line is about trouble, in this case with rent boys (category B), while the second is about friendship (category C). The message of the poem is to warn against relationships that are based on money. They never lead to honesty and friendship; not those in which you are the one who pays nor those in which you receive remuneration:

لا تَبْغِ للأمرد عهداً ولا   تَثِقْ به واُتركه معْ نفسِهِ
ولا تُرَجِّ الودَّ ممن يرى   أنّك محتاجٌ إلى فلسه

Don't seek company with a beardless (rent-)boy; don't put your trust in him but leave him to himself.
And don't hope for love from one who thinks that you are in need of his money.[65]

[12]

One of the main topics Ibn Nubāta writes about is his disappointment with friends. The inclusion of epigrams of this kind in the chapter *al-Mudāʿaba wa-l-mujūn* is justified by a witty point, which gives the poems an air of self-deprecation. In the following epigram, the point is constituted by a *tawriya*. *Wadd* and *Sudāʿ* are the names of pre-Islamic Arabian gods, which also have another meaning that is the one primarily intended in the epigram:[66]

ألا يا رُبّ خِلٍّ أرتجيه   كما يُرجَى من الوَثَنِ اُنتفاعُ
رميت بودّه وصدفتُ عنه   فلا ودٌّ لديَّ ولا سُواع

On how many a friend have I pinned my hopes! It was as if I'd asked an idol for help!
So I tossed aside his friendship and turned away from him. And here am I: No *Wadd*/<u>friendship</u> and no *Suwāʿ*/<u>rest at night</u>.[67]

[13]

People in the pre-modern Middle East were horrified by the idea that they would die as a 'stranger' (*gharīb*) far from home, mourned by no one. To be sick and house bound, not visited or comforted by anyone, came close to that. It happened once to Ibn Nubāta. He was ill, and nobody visited him except for the famous scholar Kamāl ad-Dīn ibn az-Zamlakānī (667–727/1269–1327).[68] Ibn Nubāta memorialized this event in an epigram in which he made use of the double meaning of the verb *ʿāda* 'to return' and 'to visit (a sick person)'. Since both meanings are incorporated, the stylistic device here is not *tawriya*, but rather *istikhdām*:

---

[65] Ibn Nubāta, *al-Qaṭr an-Nubātī* no. 197 [Sarīʿ], MS Paris 2234, fol. 187a.
[66] See EI^2 svv.
[67] Ibn Nubāta, *al-Qaṭr an-Nubātī* no. 188 [Wāfir], MS Paris 2234, fol. 185b-186a.
[68] On him see aṣ-Ṣafadī, *Aʿyān al-ʿAṣr* 4:624–642.

مرضتُ فعادني أزكى البرايا وأغنى عن مراض الودّ حادوا
رأوا أنيّ إلى الأجداثِ ماضٍ فقالوا كلّ ماضٍ لا يُعادُ

When I was ill, the most righteous of all mankind visited me and I saw I had no need for any of those ill-loving people who'd shunned me.
They thought that I was on my way to the grave and said: 'What passes away will not come back again/be visited'[69]

As we have seen before, al-Miʿmār borrowed and popularised this idea.

[14]

In another epigram, Ibn Nubāta complains about Shihāb ad-Dīn al-Amshāṭī (d. 725/1325), who, in Ibn Nubāta's eyes, started to neglect him after he became successful.[70] This time it is the friend's name Shihāb (ad-Dīn), which provides the basis for another *istikhdām*:

ولي صاحبٌ قد غيّرتْه سَعَادةٌ فما كدتُ من بعدِ التواصُلِ ألقاهُ
أرى الشهب في الدنيا يؤثّر حكمها وهذا شهابٌ أثّرتْ فيه دنياه

I have a friend who's been changed by worldly bliss. I hardly see him anymore whereas before we were together all the time.
I always knew that stars had the power to change the world, but this one's a star/Shihāb whom the world has changed instead.[71]

[15]

Of all the troubled friendships in this period the most spectacular was certainly the friendship of Ibn Nubāta and aṣ-Ṣafadī, which left deeper traces in the work of Ibn Nubāta than in aṣ-Ṣafadī's. Ibn Nubāta repeatedly complained about aṣ-Ṣafadī's disloyalty as in the following epigram, in which an *istikhdām* is created with the word *al-khalīl*, which means 'friend' and was also aṣ-Ṣafadī's given name:

فديتُ من الخُلاّن قوماً سألْتُهمْ دَوامَ الوفا إنّ الوفا لقليلُ
وإنّ اُفتقادي واحداً بعد واحدٍ دليلٌ على أنْ لا يدوم خليلُ

I would do anything for those friends whom I asked for everlasting loyalty – though loyalty is rare.

[69] Ibn Nubāta, *al-Qaṭr an-Nubātī* no. 202 [Wāfir], MS Paris 2234, fol. 188a, see also Ibn Nubāta, *Dīwān*, p. 172

[70] On him see aṣ-Ṣafadī, *Aʿyān al-ʿAṣr* 1: 287–292.

[71] Ibn Nubāta, *al-Qaṭr an-Nubātī* no. 193 [Ṭawīl], MS Paris 2234, fol. 186b.

> And the fact that I lost them one after the other is proof that no friend/Khalīl lasts forever.[72]

[16]

The permanent cause of strife in Ibn Nubāta's and aṣ-Ṣafadī's friendship was the charge of plagiarism – an accusation that was all too justified as can be seen in the instances of plagiarism in aṣ-Ṣafadī's *mujūn* chapter. The following epigram was composed as a reaction to a dispute that arose when Ibn Nubāta recited a poem about a headache and aṣ-Ṣafadī claimed that he was not the author of the poem:

وصديقٍ أنشدتُه لِيَ بَيْتَيْـ ـنِ حَوَت في الصُداع معنىً بديعا
فادَّعاها لأجنبيٍّ ولو كا نَ ٱدّعاها لَخاف أمراً شَنِيعا
وغَدَتْ لا له ولا لِيَ تُعْزَى وٱسترحنا من الصُداعِ جميعا

> When I composed two brilliant and original verses about a headache and recited them to a friend,
> He pretended that a third person had invented the idea. If he'd claimed they were his own, he should've braced himself for something horrible!
> And so it was attributed neither to him nor to me – and we both were rid of the headache.[73]

In fact, Ibn Nubāta did not really give in; he included the headache-poem in his *Qaṭr.*[74]

[17]

The exchange of presents was an important means for people of all social layers to create, strengthen and consolidate social relations of any kind.[75] In the correspondence of Ibn Nubāta, aṣ-Ṣafadī and other contemporaries, presents play a central role. But gifts do not always turn out as expected. When Ibn Nubāta received a gift of dates sent by a friend, he inevitably noticed that the dates were not without blemish. He used the double meaning of *nawan* ('date pits', but also 'distance, remoteness') to create the following epigram:

يا صاحباً لي إن يغِبْ فعُهودُه لم تُنسَ حيثُ تناست الغُيَّابُ
أرسلتَ تمراً بل نَوىً فقَبِلتُه بيَدِ الوِداد فما عليك عتابُ
وإذا تباعدت الجسوم فودُّنا باقٍ ونحن على النَوَى أحْبابُ

[72] Ibn Nubāta, *al-Qaṭr an-Nubātī* no. 163 [Ṭawīl], MS Paris 2234, fol. 181b–182a.

[73] Ibn Nubāta, *al-Qaṭr an-Nubātī* no. 164 [Khafīf], MS Paris 2234, fol. 182a, see also Ibn Nubāta, Dīwān, pp. 311–312.

[74] Ibn Nubāta, *al-Qaṭr an-Nubātī* no. 8 [Wāfir], MS Paris 2234, fol. 160a, see also *Dīwān* p. 312.

[75] See Elias Muhanna, 'The Sultan's New Clothes: Ottoman-Mamluk Gift Exchange in the 15th Century', *Muqarnas* 27 (2010), pp. 189–207; as well as Jocelyn Sharlet, 'The Thought that Counts in Gift Exchange Poetry by Kushājim, al-Ṣanawbarī, and al-Sarī al-Raffāʾ', *Middle Eastern Literatures* 14.3 (2011), pp. 235–70; and idem, 'Tokens of Resentment: Medieval Arabic Stories about Gift Exchange and Social Conflict', *Journal of Arabic and Islamic Studies* 11 (2011), pp. 62–100.

When you are far, my comrade, I do not forget the time of our company though others forget one another when they are out of sight.
You sent me dates, nay: date pits. I received them with a hand of friendship – no blame on you!
Yet though our bodies be far apart, our affection abides and we love each other – despite the distance / date pits.[76]

[18a]

In another instance the donor had promised to send Ibn Nubāta a present of sugar, but it did not arrive. Ibn Nubāta complained of the delay:

كلّ فِعال العلاء تُعجِبُني كأنّني بالعَلاءِ مَفْتُونُ
يُحمِضُ بالمطْلِ حُلوَ مَوعدِه فوَعْدُه سُكّرٌ وليمونُ

All those deeds of magnanimity are my delight. It's as if I've fallen in love with magnanimity.
His sweet promise is soured by long delay, thus he made a promise of sugar and lemon.[77]

[18b]

The complaint worked and the gift arrived so, of course, Ibn Nubāta had to answer it with another epigram. This is based on a play on words using the term *al-qaṭr an-nubātī* (or, more correctly, though minus the pun: *al-qaṭr an-nabātī*). It is the designation for sugar molasses, which was cheaper than refined sugar. It also provides the title of his epigram anthology, where it could be interpreted in three different ways: as (1) sugar molasses, (2) Ibn Nubāta's drops, i.e. his epigrams, which are 'drops' compared to longer poems, and (3) it could refer to himself, who is the 'drop' = offspring of ʿAbd ar-Raḥīm Ibn Nubāta, the famous preacher. The epigram shows that he used this wordplay already before he compiled his anthology of epigrams:

حلا ثنائي على عليٍّ كما حَلا جُودهُ المواتي
فرُحتُ ذا سُكّرٍ بيَاضٍ وراح ذا سكّرٍ نبَاتي

Sweet is my praise of ʿAlī, and sweet is his favorable generosity.
Now I've got white, refined sugar, and he's got *sugar molasses* / Nubātian sugar.[78]

[19]

A present of roosters was faultless. Ibn Nubāta had nothing to criticize. Instead, he asked the donor to repeat his gift. It is certainly this dimension of 'begging' that made the

[76] Ibn Nubāta, *al-Qaṭr an-Nubātī* no. 165 [Kāmil], MS Paris 2234, fol. 182a.
[77] Ibn Nubāta, *al-Qaṭr an-Nubātī* no. 183 [Munsariḥ], MS Paris 2234, fol. 185a.
[78] Ibn Nubāta, *al-Qaṭr an-Nubātī* no. 184 [Majzūʾ al-Basīṭ], MS Paris 2234, fol. 185a.

epigram shift from the *madīḥ* section to the *al-Mudāʿaba wa-l-mujūn* chapter. A *tawriya* is created by the double meaning of the word *ʿurf*:

وصلتنا ديوك برِّك تُزهي   بوجوهٍ جميلةٍ مستجادَهْ
كلّ عُرفٍ يروق حسناً وإنيّ   أرتجي أن يكون عُرفا وعاده

The roosters, presents of your kindness, have arrived and shine with their beautiful appreciated faces.
Each rooster's comb excites admiration for its beauty, and I can only hope that it will be *a rooster's comb* / <u>custom</u> and habit.[79]

[20]

The notion of begging is also present in the following epigram, with which Ibn Nubāta claims his reward for a panegyric poem. The poem's *rawī* (rhyme-letter) was the rare consonant *zāy*, one of the most difficult consonants to rhyme in Arabic:

نظمتُ للصاحب المرجَّى   زائيّةً كالجمان تُلقَطْ
تروم من بِرِّه نُقُوطاً   والحُكْم للزاي أن تُنقَّطْ

For the friend on whom I put my hopes I composed a poem rhyming in *zāy*, as beautiful as collected pearls.
It asks [in turn] for a kind wedding gift (*nuqūṭ*) for it is a rule that the *zāy* should have a <u>dot</u> / <u>present</u>.[80]

[21]

A few epigrams in the chapter are simply jokes with friends. They are not self-deprecating, but the victim of the sarcasm is the friend, such as in the following two-liner in which the friend's son is addressed with common expressions from love poetry, but the poem takes a surprising turn:

سَلَبتْ محاسنُكَ الغزال صفاته   حتى تحيّر كلّ ظبي فيكا
لك جِيدُه ولحاظُه ونِفارُه   وغدا تصير قُرونُه لأبيكا

Your beauties have stolen the gazelle's properties so that all gazelles are baffled when they see you.
You've got the gazelle's neck, its glances and its shyness, and soon your father will get its horns.[81]

---

[79] Ibn Nubāta, *al-Qaṭr an-Nubātī* no. 199 [Khafīf], MS Paris 2234, fol. 187b.
[80] Ibn Nubāta, *al-Qaṭr an-Nubātī* no. 201 [Basīṭ], MS Paris 2234, fol. 188a.
[81] Ibn Nubāta, *al-Qaṭr an-Nubātī* no. 180 [Kāmil], MS Paris 2234, fol. 184b.

WORKS CITED

Sinan Antoon, *The Poetics of the Obscene: Ibn al-Ḥajjāj and Sukhf*, Palgrave–Macmillan (forthcoming).

Thomas Bauer, '"Ayna hādhā min al-Mutanabbī!" Toward an Aesthetics of Mamluk Literature', *Mamlūk Studies Review* (forthcoming).

Thomas Bauer, 'The Dawādār's Hunting Party: a Mamluk *muzdawija ṭardiyya*, probably by Shihāb al-Dīn Ibn Faḍl Allāh', in A. Vrolijk and J.P. Hogendijk (eds.), *O ye Gentlemen: Arabic Studies on Science and Literary Culture in Honour of Remke Kruk* (Leiden: Brill, 2007), pp. 291–312.

Thomas Bauer, 'Ibn Nubātah al-Miṣrī (686–768/1287–1366): Life and Works. Part I: The Life of Ibn Nubātah', *Mamlūk Studies Review* 12.1 (2008), pp. 1–35.

Thomas Bauer, 'Ibn Nubātah al-Miṣrī (686–768/1287–1366): Life and Works. Part 2: The Dīwān of Ibn Nubātah', *Mamlūk Studies Review* 12.2 (2008), pp. 25–69.

Thomas Bauer, *Liebe und Liebesdichtung in der arabischen Welt des 9. und 10. Jahrhunderts* (Wiebaden: Harrassowitz, 1998).

Thomas Bauer, 'Mamluk Literature as a Means of Communication', in S. Conermann (ed.), *Ubi sumus? Quo vademus? Mamluk Studies - State of the Art* (Göttingen: Bonn University Press, 2013), pp. 23–56.

Thomas Bauer, '"Was kann aus dem Jungen noch werden!" Das poetische Erstlingswerk des Historikers Ibn Ḥabīb im Spiegel seiner Zeitgenossen' in O. Jastrow, S. Talay, and H. Hafenrichter (eds.), *Studien zur Semitistik und Arabistik: Festschrift für Hartmut Bobzin zum 60. Geburtstag* (Wiesbaden: Harrassowitz, 2008), pp. 15–56.

Hinrich Biesterfeldt, "*Mizr fī Miṣr.* Ein Preisgedicht auf das Bier aus dem Kairo des 14. Jahrhunderts," in Hinrich Biesterfeldt and Verena Klemm (eds.), *Differenz und Dynamik im Islam: Festschrift für Heinz Halm zum 70. Geburtstag* (Würzburg: Ergon, 2012), pp. 383–398.

Geert Jan van Gelder, *The Bad and the Ugly: Attitudes Towards Invective Poetry* (Hijāʾ) *in Classical Arabic Literature* (Leiden: Brill, 1988).

Geert Jan van Gelder, 'Epigram 1: Classical Arabic' in *Encyclopaedia of Islam, Third Edition*, Part 2012–1, pp. 131–133.

Geert Jan van Gelder, 'Forbidden Firebrands: Frivolous *Iqtibās* (Quotation from the Qurʾān) According to Arab Critics', *Quaderni di studi arabi* 20–21 (2002–2003), pp. 3–16.

Wolfhart Heinrichs, 'Ṣafī al-Dīn al-Ḥillī', in *Encyclopaedia of Islam*, Second Edition, 8:801–805.

Ṣāfī ad-Dīn al-Ḥillī, *Dīwān al-Mathālith wa-l-mathānī*, ed. Muḥammad Ṭāhir al-Ḥimṣī (Damascus: Dār Saʿd ad Dīn, 1419/1998).

Ṣāfī ad-Dīn al-Ḥillī, *Dīwān al-Mathālith wa-l-mathānī*, MS Paris 3341.

Ibn Nubāta, *al-Qaṭr an-Nubātī*, MS Florence, Lauenziana 521.

Ibn Nubāta, *al-Qaṭr an-Nubātī*, MS Paris 2234.

Ibn Nubāta, *Min Tarassul Ibn Nubātah*, Escorial MS 548.

Ibn Nubāta, *Talṭīf al-mizāj min shiʿr Ibn al-Ḥajjāj*, ed. Najm ʿAbd Allāh Muṣṭafā (Tūnis, 2001).

Ibrāhīm al-Miʿmār, *Dīwān*, MS British Museum 8054.

Ibrāhīm al-Miʿmār, *Dīwān*, MS El Escorial 463.

Ibrāhīm al-Miʿmār, *Dīwān Ibrāhīm al-Miʿmār*, ed. Thomas Bauer, Anke Osigus, Hakan Özkan (in preparation).

Julie Scott Meisami, 'Arabic *mujūn* Poetry: The Literary Dimension', in F. De Jong (ed.), *Verse and the Fair Sex: Studies in Arabic Poetry and in the Representation of Women in Arabic Literature* (Utrecht: M.Th. Houtsma Stichting, 1993), pp. 8–30.

Elias Muhanna, 'The Sultan's New Clothes: Ottoman-Mamluk Gift Exchange in the 15th Century', *Muqarnas* 27 (2010), pp. 189–207.

William Popper, *The Cairo Nilometer* (Berkeley/Los Angeles: University of California Press, 1951).

Franz Rosenthal, *The Herb: hashish versus medieval Muslim society* (Leiden: Brill, 1971).

E.K. Rowson, 'Ibn Dāniyāl', in *Encyclopedia of Arabic Literature*, p. 319.

E.K. Rowson, '*mujūn*', in *Encyclopedia of Arabic Literature*, p. 546.

aṣ-Ṣafadī, *Aʿyān al-ʿaṣr wa-Aʿwān an-naṣr*, ed. ʿAlī Abū Zayd, 6 vols. (Beirut/Damascus: Dār al-Fikr al-Muʿāṣir, 1418–1419/1998).
aṣ-Ṣafadī, *ar-Rawḍ al-Bāsim wa-l-ʿArf an-Nāsim*, ed. Muḥammad ʿAbd al-Mujīb Lāshīn (Cairo: Dār al-Āfāq al-ʿArabiyya 1425/2005).
Gregor Schoeler, 'The Genres of Classical Arabic Poetry: Classifications of Poetic Themes and Poems by Pre-Modern Critics and Redactors of Dīwāns', in *Qaderni di Studi Arabi, nuova serie* 5–6 (2010–2011), pp. 1–48.
ash-Sharīshī, *Sharḥ Maqāmāt al-Ḥarīrī*, ed. Muḥammad Abū l-Faḍl Ibrāhīm, 5 vols. (Beirut: 1413/1992).
Jocelyn Sharlet, 'The Thought that Counts in Gift Exchange Poetry by Kushājim, al-Ṣanawbarī, and al-Sarī al-Raffāʾ', *Middle Eastern Literatures* 14.3 (2011), pp. 235–70.
Jocelyn Sharlet, 'Tokens of Resentment: Medieval Arabic Stories about Gift Exchange and Social Conflict', *Journal of Arabic and Islamic Studies* 11 (2011), pp. 62–100.
Adam Talib, 'Pseudo-Ṯaʿālibī's *Book of Youths*', *Arabica* 59.6 (2012), pp. 599–649.
ath-Thaʿālibī, *Taḥsīn al-qabīḥ wa-taqbīḥ al-ḥasan*, ed. Shākir al-ʿĀshūr (Damascus: 2006).

10

Lyrics on a Fart

Ewald Wagner

While working on my article 'Verse über Abū Nuwās', I came across the following verses by Ibn al-Rūmī (d. 896) (*mutaqārib*):[1]

> 1. *wa-ḍarṭatu Wahbin mina l-ḥādithā- * -ti ʾidh*[2] *dhukirat ḥādithātu z-zaman*
>
> ....
>
> *a-yā Āla Wahbin la-qad ruʿtumū * ʿiẓāma n-Nuwāsīyi aʿnī l-Ḥasan*
> *fa-uqsimu: law kāna ḥayyan bakā * bi-mā ṣanaʿat rīḥukum bi-d-diman.*
>
> 1. That fart of Wahb's was one of the (major) events when the events of history are recalled.
>
> ....
>
> Oh, people of Wahb, you excited the bones of al-Nuwāsī, I mean al-Ḥasan.
> I swear: If he were alive today, he'd be in tears because of what your wind has done to the remaining ruins of the abodes.

Curious to learn a little bit more about this *ḥādithat al-zaman* (historical event), I searched for further information and found it in al-Thaʿālibī's *Thimār al-qulūb* under the heading *ḍarṭatu Wahbin.*[3] According to al-Thaʿālibī, Wahb b. Sulaymān b. Wahb b. Saʿīd was a postmaster. He let out an inadvertent fart while in the assembly of the vizier ʿUbayd Allāh b. Yaḥyā Ibn Khāqān in front of a crowd of people.[4] Ḥasan Kāmil al-Ṣayrafī in his edition of al-Buḥturī's *Dīwān* tries to date the event. He thinks that it happened during ʿUbayd Allāh's second vizierate under al-Muʿtamid, in about the year 260 H. = 873/4.[5] However, in

---

[1] E. Wagner, 'Verse über Abū Nuwās', *Orientalistische Studien zu Sprache und Literatur: Festgabe zum 65. Geburtstag von Werner Diem* (Wiesbaden: Harrassowitz, 2011), 343–56, here 349 = No. 17. The poem comes from Ibn al-Rūmī, *Dīwān*, ed. Ḥusayn Naṣṣār, pts. 1–6 (Cairo: Maṭbaʿat Dār al-Kutub, 1973–81), VI, 2562 = No 1439, verse 1; 4; 5 of 5 verses.

[2] The *idhā* of the printed edition does not fit the metre.

[3] Abū Manṣūr ʿAbd al-Malik b. Muḥammad al-Thaʿālibī, *Thimār al-qulūb fī al-muḍāf wa-al-mansūb* (Cairo: Maṭbaʿat al-Ẓāhir, 1326 H. = 1908), 164–166.

[4] For ʿUbayd Allāh cf. Dominique Sourdel, 'Ibn Khāḳān', EI², III, 824.

[5] Al-Buḥturī, *Dīwān*, ed. Ḥusayn Kāmil al-Ṣayrafī, vols. 1–3, Dhakhāʾir al-ʿArab. 34 (Cairo: Dār al-Maʿārif, 1963–64), I, 348.

one of his poems on the fart (no. 11), Ibn al-Rūmī mentions the earthquake in al-Ṣaymara, which happened in 258 H. = 872, which would put the fart a little farther back in time.[6] As al-Thaᶜālibī tells us, 'the news of this (i.e. the fart) flew over the horizons and fell on the tongues of the poets. It also became a proverb for fame so that people began to say: "More famous than the fart of Wahb" and "More scandalous than the fart of Wahb". Aḥmad b. Abī Ṭāhir Ṭayfūr (d. 893) wrote a book [all] about stories of the fart and excuses for it.[7] That was after much had already been said about it.'

Wahb's fart inspired more than thirty poems, mostly by Ibn al-Rūmī and al-Buḥturī, but also by some other poets whom al-Thaᶜālibī quotes. The fact that a tiny event – whether indecent or not – was treated so often in poetry seems to me a characteristic feature of Arabic poetry. There are several similar examples: let me mention only the verses on the *ṭaylasān* of Ibn Ḥarb[8] and all the poets who composed poems which included Abū Nuwās' *miṣrāᶜ* (hemistich) *'kalāmu l-layli yamḥūhu l-nahārū'* as *taḍmīn.*[9] In all three cases, I do not think western poets would have exploited these unimportant topics so extensively. For the Arabic poet however, it is a challenge to connect a commonly treated topic with a new *maᶜnā* or a new rhetorical device. If they are able to do this with a bit of wit, they can be sure that the audience will appreciate it. It is my hope that the celebrant of this Festschrift will also appreciate the different ways in which Arabic poets lyricized the fart of Wahb b. Sulaymān.

Most of the poems I will treat here are short epigrams intended to satirize the producer of the fart. That means that they belong to the genre of *hijāʾ*. In *hijāʾ*, one of the effective methods for slandering someone is by exaggeration. *Mubālagha* (hyperbole), therefore, is most often the rhetorical device used in these poems, and, it is most often applied to the windy character of the fart. Such is also the case in the verses quoted above. What is surprising, however, is that Ibn al-Rūmī chose the bones of Abū Nuwās, in particular, as the object that would be riled by the damage of the abandoned abodes. Abū Nuwās was well known for his anti-*aṭlāl nasīb*s so he would hardly have minded the *aṭlāl*'s destruction. Or did Ibn al-Rūmī intend to say that the destruction was so heavy that even an enemy of the *aṭlāl* would weep out of pity? That of course would enhance the exaggeration.

---

6 Professor Gregor Schoeler called my attention to Said Boustany, *Ibn ar-Rūmī, sa vie et son oeuvre* 1: Ibn ar-Rūmī dans son milieu (Beirut: Université libanaise, 1967), (Publications de l'Université libanaise. Section des études littéraires. 2.), 172–173, where the incident is also dated 258 H. = 872 on the basis of an increase in prices which happened in this year, and was mentioned by Ibn al-Rūmī in connection with Wahb's fart. (Ibn al-Rūmī, cf. n. 1, IV, 1444 = No. 1103).

7 Cf. Shawkat M. Toorawa, *Ibn Abī Ṭāhir Ṭayfūr and Arabic writerly culture: a ninth-century bookman in Baghdad* (London and New York: RoutledgeCurzon, 2005) (RoutledgeCurzon studies in Arabic and Middle-Eastern literatures 7.), p. 69 and n. 140 on p. 156 with further references. The title of Ibn Abī Ṭāhir's pamphlet was either: *K. Iᶜtidhār Wahb min ḥabqatihī* or *K. Iᶜtidhār Wahb min ḍarṭatihī.* For this reference, I am also indebted to Prof. G. Schoeler.

8 Cf. Josef van Ess, *Der Ṭailasān des Ibn Ḥarb: 'Mantelgedichte' in arabischer Sprache* (Heidelberg: Winter, 1979). (Sitzungsberichte der Heidelberger Akademie der Wissenschaften. Philosophisch-historische Klasse. 1979, 4.)

9 Ewald Wagner, 'Abū Nuwās-Verse als taḍmīn', *Asiatische Studien* 64 (2010), 707–726, here 721–724 = No. 44–51.

The destructive nature of this special wind is also elaborated in some other poems by Ibn al-Rūmī (*ramal*):[10]

> 2. *inna Wahba bna Sulaymā- * -na bni Wahbi bni Saʿīdī*
> *hatakat ḍarṭatuhū sit- * ra abīhī min baʿīdī*
> *inna kashfa l-khabari l-mas- * -tūri min shaʾni barīdī.*
>
> 2. From far away the fart of Wahb b. Sulaymān b. Wahb b. Saʿīd
> tore his father's veil to pieces.
> Unveiling veiled news, however, is just what postmen do.

In the last verse Ibn al-Rūmī alludes to Wahb's profession as a postmaster. This provides the opportunity for another insult: He accuses postmen of not respecting the privacy of letters. Ibn al-Rūmī connects the two topics (fart and post) through the rhetorical device of *ishtiqāq*, using two different derivatives of the same root *s-t-r*, one in its original sense (*sitr*) and one in a figurative sense (*mastūr*). The poem is further adorned by the *muṭābaqa* (antithesis) between the roots *k-sh-f* ('to expose') and *s-t-r* ('to cover').

A long *hijāʾ* of Ibn al-Rūmī on Wahb begins with the verses (*kāmil*):[11]

> 3. *habbat li-Wahbin rīḥu sūʾin ʿāṣifin * bārā bihā shahra r-riyāḥi shubāṭā*
> *min faqḥatin ḥaqqa -ttisāʿu ḥitārihā * idh lā tufāriqu dahrahā miswāṭā*
> *law annahā habbat khilāla muʿaskarin * lam yubqi fīhi ḥafīfuhā fusṭāṭā*
> *marrat ʿalā ādhāninā wa-unūfinā * fa-asāʾati l-asmāʿa wal-asʿāṭā.*
>
> 3. A disastrous stormy wind of Wahb's blew. With it he rivaled the windy month February.
> (It came from an) arsehole of ample width as such was always with a pestle.
> Should it blow through an army's camp, its rustle wouldn't leave a single tent intact.
> It passed our ears and noses and damaged the hearing and snuffing organs.

The poem starts with a *tajnīs* between the words *habbat* and *Wahb*, followed by an *ishtiqāq* between *rīḥ* and its plural *riyāḥ*. In the *istiʿāra* (metaphor) in line 2, pestle stands for penis.

Before Ibn al-Rūmī mentions in line 3 and 4 the negative effects of the fart, he tells us in line 2 why the fart could be so effective: Wahb's arse is wide as a consequence of continuously playing the passive part in sodomy (*ubna*). Wahb is accused of *ubna* in other poems on his fart as well, but in those the causal chain is missing.[12] Both topics appear quite disconnected. Line 4 refers to the noise and smell of the fart. The latter appears only here, the former in several poems. In the following verses by Ibn al-Rūmī, the noise and destructive power of the wind are combined (*mutaqārib*):[13]

---

[10] Ibn al-Rūmī (cf. n. 1), II, 735 = No. 568; in full. Translated into German by Manfred Ullmann, *Zur Geschichte des Wortes barīd "Post"* (Munich: Verlag der Bayerischen Akademie der Wissenschaften, Beck in Komm., 1997). (Beiträge zur Lexikographie des Klassischen Arabisch. Nr. 13.) (Bayerische Akademie der Wissenschaften. Philosophisch-historische Klasse. Sitzungsberichte. 1997, H. 1.), 20 = No. 24.

[11] Ibn al-Rūmī (cf. n. 1), IV, 1441–1442 = No. 1102; verse 1–4 of 38 verses.

[12] Cf. no 24 and no 27. Cf. also Ibn al-Rūmī (cf. n. 1) IV, 1444 = no. 1103; verse 4 of 6 verses, and al-Buḥturī (cf. n. 5), II, 1087 = no. 427; last verse of 4 verses. Both poems I do not translate, because the context is not quite clear to me.

[13] Ibn al-Rūmī (cf. n. 1), II, 749 = No. 581; in full. German translation by Ullmann (cf. n. 10), 48 =

*4. atat min barīdiyyinā ḍarṭatun * taʿallamahā min bighāli l-barīdī*
*wa-kāna abūhu ʿalā shuqqatin * fa-ṣakka bihā udhnahū min baʿīdī*
*la-qad hatakat mā atā dūnahū * bi-ḥaddin ḥadīdin wa-baʾsin shadīdī.*

4. Our postmaster let out a fart which he'd learned from the post-mules.
And (though) his father was far away, even then he (Wahb) kept his (his father's) ears burning with it over the long distance.
It tore to pieces whatever came its way, with much courage and a sharp edge.

The last line contains an *ishtiqāq* (*ḥaddin ḥadīdin*) and a *tarṣīʿ* (internal rhyme). The first line again connects the fart with Wahb's profession and gives another reason for his perfection in farting.

Another poem by Ibn al-Rūmī runs as follows (*munsariḥ*):[14]

*5. yā ḍarṭatan yukhliqu z-zamānu wa-mā * tabraḥu iḥdā ṭ-ṭarāʾifi l-jududī*
*arsalahā ṣāḥibu l-barīdi kamā * quwwiḍa baʿḍu l-hiḍābi min Uḥudī*
*sārat bilā kulfatin wa-lā taʿabin * sayra l-qawāfī l-awābidi sh-shurudī*
*kaʾannamā ṭārati r-riyāḥu bihā * fa-alḥaqathā bi-kulli dhī buʿudī*
*law anna akhbārahū ka-ḍarṭatihī * idhan kafathū maʾūnata l-burudī.*

5. Oh, what a fart – time wears things out, but one strange novelty lasts forever –
what the postmaster sent out, (so noisy) as if some hills of Uḥud crashed down.
Untroubled and tireless it runs, (as quick as) fleeing beasts trying to hide.
As if the winds flew with it and passed it on to everybody distant.
If his news were (flying) like his fart, it would save him annoying the couriers.

Ullmann translates the second hemistich of the third line entirely differently: "so wie Verse, die sich überall hin verbreiten, ausschwärmen" (or: 'Like verses of poetry that roam here and there'). Perhaps Ibn al-Rūmī succeeded in inventing a good *tawriya* (double entendre); the nearer meaning (*maʿnā qarīb*) may be that translated by Ullmann, since *qawāfī* allows one to think at first of rhyme and verse. Only a second thought would reveal the farther meaning (*maʿnā baʿīd*) of *qafā* 'to hide oneself' and *awābid* 'wild beasts', which I chose for my translation. The poem contains three similes (*tashbīh*) partly introduced by a comparative particle, partly constructed with an inner object.

Al-Buḥturī said (*mutaqārib*):[15]

*6. taḥaqqarta yā Wahbu fī ḍarṭatin * fa-aḍḥat aḥādīthuhā shāʾiʿah*
*wa-mā sumiʿat qablahā mithluhā * wa-qad rāʿahum ṣawtuhā rāʾiʿah*
*fa-qālū wa-mā abʿadū innahū * yufarriṭu min faqḥatin wāsiʿah.*

6. Oh, Wahb! You became despised because of a fart, since the news about it spread all around.
Something like that had never been heard before. Its sound, dreadful as it was, scared everyone.
They said – and they were not far from truth – : 'He farted out of a loose arse.'

---

no. 155.

[14] Ibn al-Rūmī (cf. n. 1), II, 735 = No. 569.; in full. German translation by Ullmann (cf. n. 10), 35–36 = no. 102. The poem is also quoted by Ibn al-Shajarī, *Kitāb al-Ḥamāsah* (Hyderabad: Dāʾirat al-maʿārif al-ʿUthmāniyya, 1345 H. =1926), 270–271.

[15] Al-Buḥturī (cf. n. 5), II, 1339 = No. 534; in full.

In addition to the sound-motif, the poem contains two other motifs that are also found in Ibn al-Rūmī's poem: the spread of the news in no. 5 and the size of the arse in no. 3. In line 2 we find an *ishtiqāq* (*rāʿa* and *rāʾiʿah*).

The sound of Wahb's fart not only gives zest to invectives on him, but also on other persons. A certain ʿĪsā al-Qāshānī uses the fart of Wahb to ridicule a female singer (*sarīʿ*):[16]

7. *idhā tughannīnā ḥakā ṣawtuhā * ḍarṭata Wahbi -bni Sulaymānī.*

7. When she sings for us, her voice resembles the fart of Wahb b. Sulaymān.

Again in another context the sound was mentioned by the well known historian Aḥmad b. Yaḥyā al-Balādhurī (d. 892)[17] (*sarīʿ*):[18]

8. *layta ṭubūla l-ʿīdi taḥkī lanā * ḍarṭata Wahbi -bni Sulaymānī*
*fa-innahā kānat tarūʿu l-ʿidā * mā bayna Miṣra wa-Khurāsānī*
*yā ḍarṭatan law annahā sharraqat * awdat bi-Ṣanʿā wa-Sijistānī.*[19]

8. I wish the drums of the festival would sound to us like the fart of Wahb b. Sulaymān!
It used to frighten the enemies between Egypt and Khurāsān.
Oh, what a fart! If it goes eastward, it would destroy Ṣanʿāʾ and Sijistān.

Ibn al-Rūmī compares the fart with thunder (*kāmil*):[20]

9. *law kunta ghaythan ṣāʾiban * lam yuhja raʿduka bal mudiḥ.*

9. If you were a rain-spending cloud, your thunder would not be scoffed at, but praised.

Yuhja and *mudiḥ* form a *muṭābaqa* (antithetical pair).

Ibn al-Rūmī again uses the same comparison in another poem (*basīṭ*):[21]

10. *yā Wahbu lā taktarith li-l-ʿāʾibīka bihā! * fa-innamā anta ghaythun rubbamā raʿadā.*

10. O Wahb, do not be worried by those who blame you for it! You are a rain cloud which sometimes thunders.

Ibn al-Rūmī describes the destructive effect of the fart also without mentioning its noise (*ramal*):[22]

---

[16] Al-Thaʿālibī (cf. n. 3), 165; verse 5 of 5 verses.

[17] Cf. Fuat Sezgin, *Geschichte des arabischen Schrifttums*, Bd. 2: Poesie bis ca. 430 H. (Leiden: Brill, 1975), II, 614.

[18] Al-Thaʿālibī (cf. n. 3), 165; in full (?). Another lampoon on Wahb's fart by al-Balādhurī is quoted by Ibn al-Nadīm, *Kitāb al-Fihrist*, ed. Riḍā Tajaddud (Tehran, 1350 H. Sh. = 1971), 126, translated by Bayard Dodge, *The Fihrist of al-Nadīm: a tenth-century survey of Muslim culture* (New York & London: Columbia University Press, 1979). (Records of civilization: Sources and studies, No. 83.), I, 247–248, and Yāqūt b. ʿAbdallah al-Rūmī, *Muʿjam al-udabāʾ*, (Miṣr: Maktabat ʿĪsā al-Bābī al-Ḥalabī, 1936–38), V, 93, in the biography of al-Balādhurī.

[19] All three *qāfiyas* could be read correctly as diptotes without disturbing rhyme or metre. In the edition however, the *alif* is missing. Perhaps, the three verses are part of a longer poem ending in *-ānī*. On the other hand, the author is also not so correct in locating Ṣanʿāʾ.

[20] Ibn al-Rūmī (cf. n. 1), II, 557 = no. 411; last verse of 9 verses.

[21] Ibn al-Rūmī (cf. n. 1), II, 736 = no. 570; verse 5 of 8 verses.

[22] Ibn al-Rūmī (cf. n. 1), III, 1075 = no. 825; in full.

11. *zalzalat ḍarṭatuhū bi-ṣ-Ṣaymarah * fa-aʿādat kulla dārin maqburah*
*wa-amā lawlā muḥābātu l-fatā * li-abīhī kāna fī-man dammarah*
*ḍarṭatun ḥābat abā ḍāriṭihā * athbitūhā fī l-banīna l-bararah!*
*wa-ḥdharū ḍarṭata Wahbin baʿdahā! * innahā rīḥun ʿaqīmun munkarah.*

11. His fart caused an earthquake in al-Ṣaymara.[23] Afterwards every house was a tomb.
Really, had the lad not respected his father, the latter would have also been among those he annihilated.
Record a fart, which respected the farter's father, in (the list) of respectful sons!
Beware of Wahb's fart, which may follow! It could be a distressing abominable wind.

Abū ʿAlī b. Jaʿfar al-Baṣīr (d. after 866)[24] does the same (*khafīf*):[25]

12. *qul li-Wahba l-baghīḍi: yā waḥsha l-khil- * -qati yā nāṭiqan bi-ghayri lisānī:*
*kānati ḍ-ḍarṭatu l-mashūmatu nāran * aḍramat fī jawānibi l-buldānī*
akhbati n-nufūsa wa-kānat la-ʿamrī [26] ʿuddatan fī l-ḥurūbi li-ṣ-sulṭānī.*

12. Say to the hated Wahb: 'Oh, you wild character, you speaker without tongue!
The disastrous fart became a fire that burnt in all regions of the country.
It extinguished the souls and became – by my life! – a tool of war for the sultan."

In the first line the fart is interpreted as speech, an idea which is expressed by several poets, for instance by Ibn al-Rūmī (*sarīʿ*):[27]

13. *yā Wahbu dhū ḍ-ḍarṭati lā tabtaʾis! * fa-inna li-l-astāhi anfāsā*
*qad tanṭuqu l-astāhu fī majlisin * wa-tumlaʾu l-afwāhu ikhrāsā*
*fa-ḍriṭ lanā ukhrā bilā ḥishmatin! * ka-annamā kharraqta qirṭāsā*
*li-tuʾnisa l-ūlā bihā muḥsinan * fa-innahā taṭlubu īnāsā.*

13 O Wahb of the fart! Do not be sad! All arses breathe.
Sometimes the arses speak in the assembly, while the mouths are filled with dumbness.
So fart for us another time, without self-restraint, noisily, as if you rip a paper,
so that the first one will have a good companion since it longs for comradeship!

Al-Buḥturī composed the following three lines (*ramal*):[28]

14. *yā -sta Wahbi bni Sulaymā- * -na bni Wahbi bni Saʿīdī!*
*qad taḥaddathti bi-raghmin * minhu ʿan amrin rashīdī*
*anti fī maghnāki dhā ab- * -laghu min ʿAbdi l-Ḥamīdī.*

14. Oh arse of Wahb b. Sulaymān b. Saʿīd,
you spoke against his will, and you talked sense.
In this abode of yours, you are more eloquent than ʿAbd al-Ḥamīd.[29]

---

[23] Ṣaymara was a town in Luristān, which was destroyed by an earthquake in 872, cf. C.E. Bosworth, 'Ṣaymara', *EI*², IX, 113–114.

[24] Cf. Sezgin (cf. n. 17), II, 536.

[25] Al-Thaʿālibī (cf. n. 3), 164; in full.

[26] This hemistich does not fit the metre.

[27] Ibn al-Rūmī (cf. n. 1), III, 1219 = no. 991; verse 5–8 of 8 verses.

[28] Al-Buḥturī (cf. n. 5), II, 784 = no. 306; in full.

[29] ʿAbd al-Ḥamīd b. Yaḥyā al-Kātib (d. 750), the famous secretary of the last Umayyads and the founder of Arabic epistolary style, cf. H.A.R. Gibb, 'ʿAbd al-Ḥamīd', in EI², I, 65–66.

An anonymous poem combines the speaking-motif with allusions to Wahb's profession and to the incident in the vizier's assembly (*ramal*):[30]

15. *inna Wahba bna Sulaymā- * -na bni Wahbi bni Saʿīdī*
*ḥamala ḍ-ḍarṭata li-r-Ray- * -yi ʿalā ẓahri l-barīdī*
*istuhū tanṭuqu yawma l- * ḥafli bi-l-qawli r-rashīdī*
*lam yajid fī l-qawli fa-ḥtā- * -ja ilā dubrin majīdī.*

15. Wahb b. Sulaymān b. Wahb b. Saʿīd
transported the fart to Rayy on the back of a post horse.
His arse spoke sense on the day of the festival.
He (Wahb) could not find the right word so he needed an excellent arse.

In the last line *yajid* and *majīd* form a *tajnīs.*

Al-Buḥturī first goes into details on the width of the arse (cf. no. 3 and no. 6) and touches upon its speaking faculties only in the last verse. Here, he disagrees with al-Baṣīr (cf. no. 12) on the number of necessary tongues (*sarīʿ*):[31]

16. *man yaʾmanu l-balwā! wa-baynā fatan * min Āli Wahbin baynanā idh ḥabaq*
*saʾaltu ʿan dhāka fa-qīla: -stuhū * makshūfatun laysa ʿalayhā ṭabaq*
*law ʿaṣarat ʿunqa ẓalīmin wa-qad * adkhala fīhā raʾsahū mā -khtanaq*
*qulnā wa-qad anṭaqahā baʿdahū * yā dhā l-lisānayni idhā mā naṭaq.*

16. Who is safe from misfortune! While the lad of the Wahb family was staying with us, he suddenly broke wind.
I asked about that (how it happened) and it was said: 'His arse is open. It has no cover.
Should it squeeze the neck of an ostrich that has poked its head inside of it, its throat won't get strangled.'
We said – and he (Wahb) made it (the arse) speak afterwards, too – : 'Oh, you owner of two tongues! (How exciting is it) when you speak!'

The first line contains twelve labials and eleven nasals – whether this is intended or not, I do not know. In the last line *anṭaqahā* and *naṭaq* form an *ishtiqāq.*

Ibn al-Rūmī combines the eloquent arse with another theme that is also treated more than once: the fame of the fart (cf. no. 1 and 5) and its power to inspire the poets (*mutaqārib*):[32]

17. *atat min barīdiyyinā ḍarṭatun * fa-arsalahā mathalan sāʾirā*
*kadhā Ālu Wahbin lahum faḍluhum * yuwarrithuhū awwalun ākharā*
*maḍaw bulaghāʾa bi-afwāhihim * wa-astāhihim kābiran kābirā*
*wa-abqaw lanā khalafan ṣāliḥan * fa-lam yulfa ʿan qaṣdihim jāʾirā*
*Abā Ḥasanin yā lahā ḍarṭatan * tarakta s-samīra bihā sāmirā*
*wa-zidta bihā shāʿiran fiṭnatan * wa-anbaghta man lam yakun shāʿirā.*

17. A fart came from our postmaster. He sent it out as a circulating proverb.
Such is the family of Wahb: They have their merit, which one bequeathes to the other:
(From generation to generation) they became more and more eloquent with their mouths and their arses.
They left with us a righteous successor. He was never found deviating from their aims.

30 Al-Thaʿālibī (cf. n. 3), 165; in full.

31 Al-Buḥturī (cf. n. 5), III, 1559 = no. 609; in full.

32 Ibn al-Rūmī (cf. n. 1), III, 1074–1075 = no. 823; in full.

O Abū Ḥasan! What a fart! By it you kept the nocturnal travelers gossiping.
You added to the creativity of the poets and made people who couldn't have rhymed into good poets.

The following two lines were also composed by Ibn al-Rūmī (*khafīf*):[33]

18. *mā laqīnā min ẓarfi ḍarṭati Wahbin * ṣayyarat ahla dahrinā shuʿarāʾā*
*hiya ʿindī ka-jūdi Faḍli bni Yaḥyā * ghayra an laysa tanʿashu l-fuqarāʾā.*

18. The elegance we were granted by Wahb's fart made the people of our time poets.
In my opinion, the fart equals the generosity of Faḍl b. Yaḥyā,[34] except it does not bring the poor happiness.

Its ability to inspire poets is also mentioned by an anonymous author (*kāmil*):[35]

19. *fa-ghadā wa-ḍarṭatuhū shanārun shāʾiʿun * shaghalat bihā ʿan ghayrihā l-ashʿārū.*

19. His fart became a shame, spreading all around. With it the poems deviated from all other topics.

While the preceeding verse considered the fart a reason to be ashamed, Ibn al-Rūmī saw it as the reason for Wahb's fame. What the poets who always insisted on the same theme produced became boring, however, and so their fame decreased. In his words there might have been a bit of self-irony, since he was the one who contributed the most to making the story hackneyed (*basīṭ*):[36]

20. *mā ḍarṭatun badarat Wahban bi-wāhibatin * li-man hajāhu ka-ḥaẓẓin nālahū abadā*
*yā laytanī niltu mimmā nāla ṭāʾifatan * wa-annanī ḍāriṭun ʿinda l-wazīri ghadā!*
*qad akthara n-nāsu fī Wahbin wa-ḍarṭatihī * ḥattā la-qad mulla mā qālū wa-qad baradā*
*lā taʿlu ḍarṭatu hājīhī ka-ḍarṭatihī * fī dh-dhākirīna wa-lā yuḥsad kamā ḥusidā!*

20. The fart that took Wahb by surprise was not a gift for those who mocked him; not like the stroke of luck it was for him (Wahb); a gift that kept on giving.
Oh, that I might partake of the phantom-roamer he (i. e. Wahb) attained. Oh, that I were farting at the vizier's tomorrow!
People talked at such length about Wahb and his fart that what they said became boring and frosty.
The farting of those who mock Wahb will never be as highly esteemed by the raconteurs as Wahb's fart, and the satirizers will never be envied as much as Wahb!

The poem contains several *ishtiqāq*s, the first one, using Wahb's own name, is clearly intended.

In the preceeding poem the fame of the fart was considered positive for its producer. The same is true of the two poems by al-Buḥturī, though, of course, this may be ironic. Ibn al-Rūmī also speaks about the negative effect of the fame. Here are the verses of al-Buḥturī (*wāfir*):[37]

---

[33] Ibn al-Rūmī (cf. n. 1), I, 101–102 = no. 41; Al-Thaʿālibī (cf. n. 3), 164; in full. The couplet is also quoted by Ibn al-Shajarī (cf. n. 14), 270.

[34] Al-Faḍl b. Yaḥyā al-Barmakī (d. 808), son of the famous vizier of Hārūn al-Rashīd, Yaḥyā al-Barmakī, cf. Dominique Sourdel, 'Al-Faḍl b. Yaḥyā al-Barmakī', EI^2, II, 723.

[35] Al-Thaʿālibī (cf. n. 3), 166; verse 2 of 3 verses.

[36] Ibn al-Rūmī (cf. n. 1), II, 735–736 = no. 570; verses 1–4 of 8 verses.

[37] Al-Buḥturī (cf. n. 5), I, 348 = no. 134; in full.

*21. taʿālā -llāhu yajzī kulla amrin * wa-in kariha l-ʿibādu bi-mā aḥabbā*
*barā sūqan wa-amlākan ʿalayhim * wa-qaddara minhumū ʿabdan wa-rabbā*
*wa-faḍḍala fī l-kitābati Āla Wahbin * wa-qaddama baynahum bi-ḍ-ḍarṭi Wahbā*
*akabba ʿalā l-wazīri yurīdu qawlan * fa-arsala ḍarṭatan lammā akabbā*
*fa-yā laki ḍarṭatan ḥallat makānan * wa-sāra ḥadīthuhā sharqan wa-gharbā.*

21. God, the exalted, requites everything according to His will, even if His servants do not like it.
He created ordinary people and kings over them, He determined who of them should become servant and who, master.
Among the scribes He preferred the family of Wahb, and in farting He put Wahb above them all.
He bowed before the vizier, intending to speak. And while bowing, he sent out a fart.
What a fart! It kept a high rank and its fame spread east and west.

In the first line *kariha* and *aḥabba* form a *muṭābaqa* (antithesis), as do *sharq* and *gharb* in the last line. In the second line we find in *barā* and *rabbā* a *tajnīs al-qalb*, in which the two consonants are reversed. In the fourth line the rhyming word is anticipated by the first word (*akabba*); a device that goes under the term *radd al-ʿajuz ʿalā l-ṣadr* or *taṣdīr*. Also *qaddara* and *qaddama* may be an intended *tajnīs*.

And (*sarīʿ*):[38]

*22. a-laysa ṭabʿan fī banī Ādamin * an yakhjala ḍ-ḍāriṭu min ḍarṭatih?*
*qad nāla Wahbun ʿindahā rifʿatan * wa-zulfatan fa-zdāda fī saṭwatih.*

22. Is it not natural among the children of Adam, that a farter feels ashamed because of his fart?
By it, however, Wahb won rank and dignity, and his authority increased.

As in poem no. 17, Ibn al-Rūmī mentions the proverbiability of the fart. He also refers to the event in the vizier's assembly (*basīṭ*):[39]

*23. ḥayyā Abū Ḥasanin Wahbun Abā Ḥasanin * bi-ḍarṭatin ṭayyarat ʿuthnūnahū khuṣalā*
*thumma -stamarrat fa-ṣārat fī l-bilādi lahū * kaʾannahā arsalat min dubrihī mathalā*
*biʾsa t-taḥiyyatu ḥayyāhā l-wazīra ḍuḥan * wal-ḥaflu min sarawāti l-qawmi qad ḥafalā*
*yā layta shiʿriya ʿan Wahbin wa-faqḥatihī * wa-kayfa ʿātabahā fī l-ḥushshi ḥīna khalā!*

23. Abū l-Ḥasan Wahb greeted Abū l-Ḥasan[40] with a fart, which made his beard fly tuftwise.
Then it carried on and pervaded his lands. So, it was as if it sent out from his arse a saying.
What a bad greeting with which he greeted the vizier in the morning, when the assembly of high society had just gathered!
Oh, would that I knew about Wahb and his arse, how much he would scold it, when he withdrew to the privy!

And (*khafīf*):[41]

---

[38] Al-Buḥturī (cf. n. 5), I, 391 = no. 159; verses 1 and 2 of 3 verses.

[39] Ibn al-Rūmī (cf. n. 1), V, 2038 = no. 1585; in full.

[40] Wahb and the vizier must have had the same *kunya*. That of Wahb is attested in another poem (no. 17); I cannot find that of the vizier in a second source.

[41] Ibn al-Rūmī (cf. n. 1), V, 2038 = no. 1586; in full.

*24. lumta yā Wahbu ahla dahrika fīmā * anta awjadtahum ilayhi s-sabīlā*
*wa-taghaḍḍabta min kalāmi unāsin * aktharū idh ḍaraṭta qālan wa-qīlā*
*lā talumhum! fa-inna lawmaka lā yan- * -faʿu wa-rfuq bi-aklika ṭ-ṭafshīlā!*
*wa-ttakhidh ḥushwatan wa-aʿfi jiʿirrā- * -ka mina ṭ-ṭaʿni bi-l-uyūri qalīlā!*

24. O Wahb, you reproached your contemporaries for a matter, for which you yourself paved the way
You became angry about the talk of the people who gossipped profusely when you farted.
Do not reproach them, because your reproach will not help! (Better) be careful when eating *ṭafshīl*![42]
Look at (your) bowels and give your arse a bit of leave from being pierced by the pricks!

Ibn al-Rūmī composed two long invectives on Wahb and his family respectively, in which juxtaposed stinginess with spending to generosity with farting. Such verses, of course, must be based on a *muṭābaqa*. In the first *hijāʾ* the following verses are relevant (*ṭawīl*):[43]

*25. wa-law anna Wahban kāna aʿdā akuffakum * ʿalā l-bukhli min jūdi -stihī bi-l-awābidī*
*la-ẓallat ʿalā l-ʿāfina asmaḥa bi-n-nadā * mina l-hāṭilāti l-bāriqāti r-rawāʿidī.*

25. If Wahb miraculously infected your stingy hands with the generosity of his arse,
they could have stayed more generous to guests than flashing, thundering rainclouds.

I left *bi-l-nadā* untranslated, though it has an important rhetorical function as a *tawriya*, which may be included either in the semantical field of the primum comparationis: 'more generous in generosity' or in that of the secundum comparationis: 'more generous in rain than the rain-spending clouds'. *Rawāʿid* alludes to the fart.

The following verses by Ibn al-Rūmī are part of the same poem as no. 3 (*kāmil*):[44]

*26. mā bālu ḍarṭatikum yuḥallu ribāṭuhā * ʿafwan wa-dirhamukum yushaddu ribāṭā?*
*ṣurrū ḍurāṭakumu l-mubadhdhara ṣarrakum * ʿinda s-suʾāli l-falsa wal-qīrāṭā!*
*aw fa-smuḥū bi-ḍurāṭikum wa-nawālikum! * haihāta! lastum li-n-nawāli nishāṭā*
*law judtumū bi-himā maʿan la-wajadtumū * farashan lakum ʿinda r-rijāli bisāṭā*
*lākinnakum farraṭtumū fī wāḥidin * wa-hwa ḍ-ḍurāṭu fa-ʿaddilū l-ifrāṭā!*

26. How is it that your fart string is willingly loosened, while your money-belt is securely tied?
Place your spendthrift fart into the collection-bag, when small change is asked for!
Or be generous with your fart and your gifts! But alas, you are not active in giving!
Were you generous with both together, you'd find a carpet spread for you among men.
You are however, exaggerating in only one.....in farting. Balance out the excess!

In the first line, the *muṭābaqa* (antithesis) 'generosity' versus 'stinginess' is transferred to 'loosen' versus 'tie'. In the fourth line we find the *tajnīs* between *judtumū* and *wajadtumū*, and in the fifth line, between *ḍurāṭ* and *ifrāṭ*.

I add here three verses of a certain Ibn Bassām, which also criticize the Wahb's family lack of generosity (*wāfir*):[45]

---

[42] A food containing beans.
[43] Ibn al-Rūmī (cf. n. 1), II, 762 = no. 592; verses 17–18 of 19 verses.
[44] Ibn al-Rūmī (cf. n. 1), IV, 1443 = no. 1102; verses 28–32 of 38 verses. The verses are also quoted by al-Thaʿālibī (cf. n. 3), 164. In line 4 I preferred his reading.
[45] Al-Thaʿālibī (cf. n. 3), 166.

*27. sa-adhkuru ʿan Banī Wahbin umūrā * wa- laysa l-ghamru ka-r-rajuli l-khabīrī*
*wa-akhlāqu l-bighāli idhā -stumīḥū * wa-ḍarṭun fī l-majālisi ka-l-ḥamīrī*
*wujūhun lā tahishshu ilā l-maʿālī * wa-astāhun tahishshu ilā l-uyūrī.*

27. I will mention some things about the Banū Wahb – and the inexperienced man is not like the expert:
Mulish in [their manners], when asked for a favour; farting in the assembly like donkeys;
[With] faces, indisposed to noble deeds, and arses well disposed to pricks.

The last line shows a *parallelismus membrorum*, called *tarṣīʿ* by some Arabic literary critics.[46]

A last group of poems excuses Wahb on the grounds that farting is natural. The first one is by Ibn al-Rūmī (*sarīʿ*):[47]

*28. laysa ʿalā ḍ-ḍāriṭi taʿyīrū * wa-lā ʿalā ḍ-ḍāḥiki taghyīrū*
kilāhumā ajrāhu maqdūruhū[48] * *karhan wa-hal tuʿṣā l-maqādīrū?*
*kam ḍarṭatin tatbaʿuhū ḍaḥkatun! * wa-mā ʿalā th-thintaini tankīrū*
*kilāhumā in qīsatā faltatun * ḥānat wa-li-llāhi tadābīrū.*

28. There is no need to shame the farter, and no need to change one who laughs.
In both cases, his fate makes it happen by force. And can predestination be disobeyed?
How many farts are followed by laughter! Neither can be suppressed.
Put into perspective, they are unexpected events; they just happen, and management is with God.

The last verse does not occur in all manuscripts, perhaps because the scribes hesitated to make God responsible for a fart. The first line shows a *tarṣīʿ* and at the same time it contains a *tajnīs muṣaḥḥaf* (*taʿyīr* and *taghyīr*), in which the two words differ only in the pointing of the letters.

Two other apologetic poems are written by anonymous poets (*ṭawīl*):[49]

*29. ayā Wahbu lā tajzaʿ li-iflāti ḍarṭatin! * naʿāhā ʿalayka l-ʿāʾibūna wa-afraṭū*
*wa-lā taʿtadhir minhā wa-in jalla amruhū * fa-qad yaghlaṭu l-ḥurru l-karīmu fa-yaḍriṭū.*

29. O Wahb! Do not be sad over the escape of a fart for which the faultfinders reproached you excessively.
Do not apologize for it, though it was a big thing! Sometimes the noble free man makes a mistake and farts.

And (*ṭawīl*):[50]

*30. la-qad qāla Wahbun idh raʾā n-nāsa ashrafū * li-ḍarṭatihī qawla -mriʾin ghayri dhī jahlī:*
*ayā ʿajaban li-n-nāsi yastashrifūnanī * kaʾan lam yaraw baʿdī ḍarūṭan wa-lā qablī.*

30. When Wahb saw people looking down on him because of his fart, he said, not unintelligently:
'How amazing that people look down on me (especially)! As if they never observed a farter before me or after me!'

---

[46] For the different definitions of *tarṣīʿ* in the Arab rhetoric cf. Gregor Schoeler, 'Tarṣīʿ', EI², X, 304–306.

[47] Ibn al-Rūmī (cf. n. 1), III, 996 = no. 755; in full.

[48] The text reads *miqdāruhū*.

[49] Al-Thaʿālibī (cf. n. 3), 165.

[50] Al-Thaʿālibī (cf. n. 3), 165.

I hope this panorama of poems has shown how many aspects Arabic poets can wrest from a tiny event and how they embellished their products with at least some rhetorical adornments. I will close my collection with three short verses by Aḥmad Ibn Abī Ṭāhir. He disguises the fart in the metaphor of a she-camel and, in a *metaphora continuata*, he sustains the illusion till the end of the poem. It is only in the last line that a *tawriya* hints at the real meaning (*sarī*ᶜ):[51]

31. *yā Wahbu inna nāqatan * aẓʾamtahā fa-waradat*
*wa-nafarat shāridatan * fa-abraqat wa-arᶜadat*
*law kunta lammā waradat * ᶜaqaltahā mā sharadat.*

31. O Wahb! You made a she-camel thirsty. So she went down to the watering-place.
She broke loose to flee, causing terror.
Had you tied her legs, when she descended to the water, she wouldn't have fled.

The verb *ᶜaqala* means 'to tie the legs of a camel' and 'to confine the bowels'.[52]

WORKS CITED

C.E. Bosworth, 'Ṣaymara', EI², IX, 113–114.

Said Boustany, *Ibn ar-Rūmī, sa vie et son oeuvre* 1: Ibn ar-Rūmī dans son milieu (Beirut: Université libanaise, 1967).

Al-Buḥturī, *Dīwān*, ed. Ḥusayn Kāmil al-Ṣayrafī, vols. 1–3, Dhakhāʾir al-ᶜArab. 34 (Cairo: Dār al-Maᶜārif, 1963–64).

Bayard Dodge, *The Fihrist of al-Nadīm: a tenth-century survey of Muslim culture* (New York & London: Columbia University Press, 1979).

Josef van Ess, *Der Ṭailasān des Ibn Ḥarb: 'Mantelgedichte' in arabischer Sprache* (Heidelberg: Winter, 1979).

H.A.R. Gibb, 'ᶜAbd al-Ḥamīd', in EI², I, 65–66.

Ibn al-Nadīm, *Kitāb al-Fihrist*, ed. Riḍā Tajaddud (Tehran, 1350 H. Sh. = 1971).

Ibn al-Rūmī, *Dīwān*, ed. Ḥusayn Naṣṣār, pts. 1–6 (Cairo: Maṭbaᶜat Dār al-Kutub, 1973–81).

Ibn al-Shajarī, *Kitāb al-Ḥamāsah.* (Hyderabad: Dāʾirat al-maᶜārif al-ᶜUthmāniyya, 1345 H. =1926).

Fuat Sezgin, *Geschichte des arabischen Schrifttums*, Bd. 2: Poesie bis ca. 430 H. (Leiden: Brill, 1975).

Dominique Sourdel, 'Ibn K͟hāḳān', EI², III, 824.

Abū Manṣūr ᶜAbd al-Malik b. Muḥammad al-Thaᶜālibī, *Thimār al-qulūb fī al-muḍāf wa-al-mansūb* (Cairo: Maṭbaᶜat al-Ẓāhir, 1326 H. = 1908).

Shawkat M. Toorawa, *Ibn Abī Ṭāhir Ṭayfūr and Arabic writerly culture: a ninth-century bookman in Baghdad* (London and New York: RoutledgeCurzon, 2005).

Manfred Ullmann, *Zur Geschichte des Wortes barīd "Post"* (Munich: Verlag der Bayerischen Akademie der Wissenschaften, Beck in Komm., 1997).

Ewald Wagner, 'Abū Nuwās-Verse als taḍmīn', *Asiatische Studien* 64 (2010), 707–726.

Ewald Wagner, 'Verse über Abū Nuwās', *Orientalistische Studien zu Sprache und Literatur: Festgabe zum 65. Geburtstag von Werner Diem* (Wiesbaden: Harrassowitz, 2011).

[51] Al-Thaᶜālibī (cf. n. 3), p. 166.

[52] Those who would like to read more poems about farting may wish to consult: al-Rāghib al-Iṣbahānī, *Muḥāḍarāt al-udabāʾ wa-muḥāwarāt al-shuᶜarāʾ wa-l-bulaghāʾ*, parts 1–2 (Cairo: al-Maṭbaᶜah al-ᶜĀmirah al-Sharafiyyah, 1326 H. = 1908), II, 124–127.

11

Two fart jokes in Ibn ᶜArabī's *Muḥāḍarat al-abrār*

Denis E. McAuley

'The international baseline of all humour: farts'
Stewart Lee

Muḥyī l-Dīn Ibn ᶜArabī (1165–1240) is not the most obvious author to turn to for obscene material.[1] The dominant theme in his writing is what has been termed Sufi metaphysics, a daring fusion of experiential mysticism with the concepts and categories of philosophy.[2] His vast output, which has yet to be fully explored despite growing scholarly interest, includes Sufism, *fiqh*, *kalām*, poetry and even a work of *adab*, but not – as far as I know – any *mujūn*. Readers might therefore be taken aback on finding that the *adab* work in question, entitled *Muḥāḍarat al-abrār wa-musāmarat al-akhyār*, includes, for no apparent reason, two fart jokes.

Ibn ᶜArabī's propriety probably has to do with his overwhelming sense of purpose. Born to a well-to-do family in Murcia, in al-Andalus, he had his first mystical experience in his teens. A series of visions convinced him that he was the Seal of Muhammadan Sainthood, and he states in several places that his writing is directly inspired by God.[3] His understanding of the nature and scope of literature is a highly moral one. In line with many mainstream Sunni scholars, he argues that poetry is licit or illicit depending on the use to which it is put.[4] That view rescues poetry from the apparent condemnation expressed in Qur'an 26:224–7, but it also leaves little space for bacchic, panegyric and, of course, *mujūn* poetry.[5]

---

[1] I am grateful to Adam Talib for some very valuable comments regarding translation; my father and late grandfather for information on Bird Flanagan; and Stephen Hirtenstein for giving me access to a digitised manuscript of the *Muḥāḍarat al-abrār*.

[2] For a succinct introduction to his ideas and the concept of 'Sufi metaphysics' see Ronald Nettler, *Sufi Metaphysics and Qur'anic Prophets* (Cambridge: Islamic Texts Society, 2003), Chapter 1.

[3] Michel Chodkiewicz, *Seal of the Saints: prophethood and sainthood in the doctrine of Ibn Arabi*, trans. Liadain Sherrard (Cambridge: Islamic Texts Society, 1993), pp. 17–19.

[4] Denis McAuley, *Ibn ᶜArabī's Mystical Poetics* (Oxford: Oxford University Press, 2012), pp. 37–9.

[5] Ibn ᶜArabī is suspicious of panegyrics that 'praise those who do not deserve it.' See Muḥyī l-Dīn Ibn ᶜArabī, *al-Futūḥāt al-Makkiyya*, 4 vols. (Beirut: Dar Ṣādir, n.d.), vol. 3, p. 562; McAuley, *Mystical Poetics*, p. 52.

His own verse can occasionally be racy. One lyric in his best-known collection of poems, the *Tarjumān al-ashwāq*, refers to the beloved thus:

> *Tawrātuhā lawḥu sāqayhā sanan wa-anā * atlū wa-adrusuhā kaʾannanī Mūsā*
>
> Her Torah is the marble slabs of her legs in brightness, and I declaim and study them like Moses.[6]

Yet even at his most risqué, Ibn ʿArabī does not come close to *mujūn*. The most graphic poem of his that I have come across depicts a dream sequence in which Ibn ʿArabī has sex with a woman (*jāriya*), but even here the treatment is disconcertingly clinical rather than obscene:

> *nakaḥtu farjan lahā ʿan ruʾyatin wa-ʾatat * naḥwī li-aqḍiya fī ḍammī lahā waṭarī*
> *wa-ʿammati l-ladhdhatu l-aʿḍāʾa ajmaʿahā * fa-lam ajid ʿindamā -stayqaẓtu min atharī*
>
> I entered her in the vision, and she came towards me, for me to gain my desire in embracing her
> Pleasure spread over my limbs, and on waking, I did not find any trace.[7]

Ibn ʿArabī's only known work of *adab*, the *Muḥāḍarat al-abrār*, is consistent with that perspective. It is a large and varied work, which seems to have been put together gradually as a side-project between AH 611 and 627 (around 1215–1230).[8] As in any book of *adab*, there is some light-hearted material, but Ibn ʿArabī makes it clear that it is intended as good clean fun:

> I have included comical, distracting stories so long as they do not corrupt the faith: stories that make the souls repose when they hear them, and that bring about neither reward nor burden. I have kept the book free from any invective or blame (*hijāʾ*, *mathlaba*), and included all approval and praise (*thanāʾ*, *manqaba*). Where a comical story is about a well-known and well-regarded man of faith or scholarship, and involves an unintentional action or a slip that made those around him laugh, I have mentioned it because it gives the soul repose. I have not, however, named the person referred to, so that his dignity is intact and his reputation does not suffer after he has reached fame and honour.[9]

This is hardly the voice of a dangerous topical comedian, and the prevailing tone in the book is one of piety. Ibn ʿArabī's wariness of invective reflects the attitude of many (though by no means all) religious scholars.[10] Moreover, as the celebrant of this volume has shown,

---

[6] Muhyi l-Dīn Ibn ʿArabī, *The Tarjumán al-Ashwáq: A Collection of Mystical Odes*, trans. Reynold A. Nicholson (London: Theosophical Publishing House, 1911), p. 15.

[7] MS Veliyuddin 1681, folio 80 a; McAuley, *Mystical Poetics*, p. 124.

[8] Claude Addas, *Quest for the Red Sulphur: The Life of Ibn ʿArabī* (Tr. Peter Kingsley, Cambridge: Islamic Texts Society, 1993), p. 96. Osman Yahya registers some doubt as to the authenticity of the *Muḥāḍarat al-abrār* (Osman Yahya, *Histoire et classification de l'œuvre d'Ibn ʿArabī*, 2 vols. [Damascus: Institut francais de Damas, 1964], vol. II, p. 397). However, Addas' overview makes it clear that apart from a few later interpolations, the book is genuine. As regards the fart jokes, an apparent reference to Ibn ʿArabī's time in Fez suggests that we are on safe ground.

[9] Muḥyī l-Dīn Ibn ʿArabī, *Muḥāḍarat al-abrār wa-musāmarat al-akhyār*, 2 vols. (Beirut: Dar Ṣādir, 1968), vol. I, pp. 5–6.

[10] G.J.H. van Gelder, *The Bad and the Ugly: Attitudes towards invective poetry* (hijāʾ) *in classical Arabic*

literary anthologists were often ambivalent about quoting coarse material – although they were often stricter in theory than in practice – and critics in Ibn ʿArabī's native al-Andalus were perhaps more negative than elsewhere.[11]

Unusually for Ibn ʿArabī, the *Muḥāḍarat al-abrār* contains little of his distinctive metaphysics. As Addas suggests, his aim is probably to reach out to a wider audience of non-initiates.[12] The book begins with an encomium on books and *adab* that quotes various *shuyūkh*, but also the *adab* writer (*adīb*) al-Jāḥiẓ.[13] In addition to stories that he witnessed or heard personally, his list of sources includes conventional *adab* writers (*udabāʾ*), such as Abū Ḥayyān al-Tawḥīdī, Ibrāhīm al-Ḥuṣrī and al-Jāḥiẓ; Sufi teachers, such as Abū ʿAbd al-Raḥmān al-Sulamī and Abū l-Qāsim al-Qushayrī; and the standard hadith collections.[14]

The book is divided into sections, each of which begins with a fresh *basmala*.[15] They mostly do not appear to be thematically linked. Most of the material consists of edifying stories with a broader appeal or, at most, what could be called 'Sufism-lite'. The topics include almanac-type information, such as the Prophet Muhammad's vital statistics (vol. I, pp. 25–48); the reigns of the Rāshidūn (i.e. rightly-guided), Umayyad and Abbasid caliphs (vol. I, pp. 63–87); information about the prophets (vol. I, pp. 123–38); various sermons, proverbs[16] and snippets of history; sections on such topics as the praiseworthy qualities of women and men, consisting of poetry with lexical glosses (pp. 383–86); and some anecdotes, including the story of a wolf who bore witness to the prophecy of Muhammad (p. 395), a bird that circled the Kaʿba (p. 407) and some snakes that did the same (vol. II, pp. 59; 62). At the more specifically Sufi end of things, there are several stories in which the Sufi master Abū Madyan of Tunis appears in a vision to various protagonists.[17] As one might expect, there is plenty of poetry, both secular and religious, and much of it by the author.[18]

Comparatively less frequent is pure comic relief. In one place, there are some lines of poetry making fun of a man with a lisp and a man who pronounces the letter *rāʾ* as *ghayn* (vol. II, p. 105). There are two anecdotes featuring the idiot Habannaqah, a figure similar to Juḥā (vol. I, p. 308). These are followed by two stories about Jumʿa, a bread seller whom Ibn ʿArabī used to know in Seville, and who was famous for acting as a mediator and delivering wacky but wise verdicts. In the first story, for instance, Jumʿa is asked to arbitrate between two men, one of whom claims that the other slept with his wife. When it emerges

literature (Leiden, New York, Copenhagen and Cologne: EJ Brill, 1988), pp. 24–35.

[11] Ibid., pp. 90–5.

[12] Addas, *Quest*, p. 101. For further context, including some information on Ibn ʿArabī's sources, see ibid., pp. 128–130.

[13] Ibn ʿArabī, *Muḥāḍarat*, pp. 6–10.

[14] Ibid., vol. I, pp. 11–12.

[15] The distinction is less clear in the Beirut edition than in the manuscript I have consulted (MS Esad Efendi 1897), in which each segment ends with the words *intahā l-samar*.

[16] Not all of these are Islamic: some are ascribed to such figures as Buzurgmihr, Ānushīrvān, Azdashīr, Plato, Aristotle, Pythagoras and Socrates (vol. II, pp. 424–5).

[17] E.g. ibid., vol. I, pp. 257–58, 300–1, 326–27, 343, 370–71.

[18] Most of the poems by Ibn ʿArabī come from the collection *Tarjumān al-ashwāq*. Unlike much of his other, more abstruse poems, they consist of straight love lyrics that might appeal to a non-initiate. Ibn ʿArabī does, however, make it clear that the poems are not to be taken literally. For example, one piece is introduced as 'an allusion to the Highest Station (*ishāra lil-maqām al-aʿlā*)' (vol. II, p. 59).

that the adultery only took place in the perpetrator's dream, Jumʿa rules that he should be taken outdoors and his shadow given one hundred lashes (vol. I, pp. 308–9).

The fart gags, too, are intended as comic relief. They occur at the very end of one section (vol. II, pp. 162–3), after some stories about the caliphs and before the text of a letter from the Prophet Muhammad to Chosroes. The first runs as follows:

> It is said that there was a teacher called Abū ʿĀṣim who used to teach boys. One day, when he was standing in front of three young Bedouin (*ʿarab*) boys teaching them, he farted.[19]
>
> One of the boys said:
>
> *wa-ḍarṭatin jāʾat ʿan ghaflatin * min mafliqi l-shaykhi Abī ʿĀṣimī*
>
> In a moment of inattention, there came a fart from the arse of Shaykh Abū ʿĀṣim.
>
> The second said:
>
> *fa-ʾayqaẓat man kāna min nāʾimin * wa-ʾaqʿadat man kāna min qāʾimī*
>
> Those who were asleep were jolted; those who were standing were floored.[20]
>
> The third said:
>
> *wa-nhaddati l-arḍu wa-ajbāluhā * wa-ltazama l-maẓlūmu bil-ẓālimī*
>
> The land and its mountains crumbled; the oppressed cowered with the oppressor.[21]

The three boys improvise on the same metre and rhyme, besting one another with increasingly hyperbolic and apocalyptic descriptions of the fart. In so doing, they carry on the tradition of Ibn al-Rūmī's poems: one such piece, which Professor Wagner has described in this volume, depicts the fart of Wahb causing an earthquake in al-Ṣaymara. The occurrence of similar motifs over three centuries later testifies to their enduring popularity. In this case, the crumbling of the mountain also recalls Qur'anic accounts of the Day of Judgment:

> When the mountains crumble (56:5)
> When (...) the mountains are crushed with a single blow (69:14)
> When (...) the mountains become a slipping heap of sand (73:14)
> When the mountains are scattered (77:10)
> When the mountains are set in motion (78:20, 81:3)
> And the mountains will be like plucked wool-tufts (101:5)[22]

The connotation is apt, in that the unfortunate Shaykh's teaching would have focused on the Qur'an. The joke therefore lies at least partly in the way the pupils turn their coursework on its head.

---

[19] This was a noisy *ḍarṭa* rather than a silent *faswa*.

[20] Reading *man kāna min nāʾimi* and *man kāna min qāʾimi* in line with MS Esad Efendi 1897, folio 188a.

[21] The two fart jokes are separated by another mildly indecent anecdote, in which a poet is hauled before the *muḥtasib* and begs for mercy, swearing by various parts of the *muḥtasib*'s mother's anatomy until he exclaims, 'Release him before he goes any lower!'

[22] In translating these verses, I have referred to Arberry's version: A.J. Arberry, *The Koran Interpreted*, 2 vols. (London: George Allen & Unwin Ltd., 1955).

The second joke follows the same model of frame narrative and poem:

> A *muḥtasib* [official responsible for public order] that we had in Fez[23] once brought in a poet who had committed some crime and ordered that he be beaten. The man kept asking the *muḥtasib* for clemency, making him angry. The *muḥtasib* shouted to the man with the whip, 'Get him!' and, in mid-shout, farted repeatedly. While being whipped, the poet said:
>
> *ismaᶜūnī wa-ᶜjabū * ḍaraṭa l-muḥtasibū*
> *ḍarṭatan ṣāfiyatan * ṭāra minhā l-ᶜatabū*
> *sahilat ḥalqa Salā * wa-ᶜarat Wādī Sabū*
> *sabᶜatan fī nasaqin * bu bu bubbū bu bu bū*
>
> Listen to me and stand amazed: the *muḥtasib* farted!
> It was a pure fart, bearing even its shame away.
> It descended the gorge of Salā and headed for valley of Sabū.[24]
> Seven in a row: *bu bu bubbū bu bu bū.*

Here too, the poem elicits a comparison with the pieces in Professor Wagner's contribution. Ibn al-Rūmī and his peers portray the fart of Wahb as travelling to various far-flung places. In the same way, the *muḥtasib*'s fart wafts over a distinctly Moroccan landscape. The last line works the sound of the fart into the verse, playing on the metre in a truly inspired manner. The truncated *sarīᶜ* metre allows the first and fifth syllables to be long or short. The line can thus be scanned in other ways, such as *bubbu bubbū bubbu bū*, depending on the reader's preference.

As in the anecdote about Abū ᶜĀṣim, the person in charge is shown up. Although the poet does not escape punishment, he wins the day by using the power of words to humiliate the *muḥtasib* in front of the onlookers. In this sense, the stories build on two comedic tropes that appeal in any place and time, and to people of any age: first, the fart, and second, the upstaging of a figure of authority. Yet while the hierarchies in the stories are subverted, neither story has a moral. There is no suggestion that Abū ᶜĀṣim is a malicious or incompetent teacher, or that the *muḥtasib* was wrong to arrest the poet. The *muḥtasib* loses his temper unprofessionally, but the poet had indeed committed 'some crime'. The fart causes a loss of face and ritual purity, but it is not a sin.

The lack of a moral makes these anecdotes unusual for Ibn ᶜArabī's work, which is overwhelmingly concerned with imparting a message. A comparison with Ibn ᶜArabī's near-contemporary Jalāl al-Dīn Rūmī (1207–1273) will make this point clearer. These two giants of thirteenth-century Sufism have often been compared stylistically and doctrinally but not, as far as I know, scatologically. The contrast in the way they deploy their material

---

[23] Ibn ᶜArabī was in Fez in AH 591 (1195), 593–94 (1196–8) and 597 (1200–1) (Addas, *Quest*, pp. 299–301).

[24] Wādī Sabū is located to the north of Fez. Salā is a coastal town in Morocco, but is located on a flat stretch of land. The place name is often confused with the nearby Shalla, which is on a height and is therefore a better fit (*EI*² s.v. 'Salā' and 'Shalla', both articles by Halima Ferhat). However, neither is on the way from Fez to Wādī Sabū. It therefore seems likely that the poet was referring to a different Salā, although it is also possible that some of the farts travelled north and others west.

is illuminating. Ibn ʿArabī's attitude in the preface to the *Muḥāḍarat al-abrār* might give the impression that he was taking sides in a confrontation between purveyors of indecent material on the one hand and frowning religious teachers on the other. This case is not necessarily typical. Rūmī reportedly made generous use of foul language in his daily life and had no qualms about using obscene verse to lampoon an enemy:

> A hundred donkey dicks up his ass!
> A hundred dog farts in his beard![25]

Rūmī's masterpiece, the *Mathnavī-yi maʿnavī* is full of scabrous tales, and the following episode about a fart is a case in point. A man shoots a wolf in the dark, and the animal passes wind on falling to the ground. A peasant who was with him accuses him of killing his donkey:

> The wind from his arse
> I would know like wine from water! (...)
> Among twenty other winds, I would know that wind
> Like a traveller knows his bags![26]

The story does not end here; there follows a lengthy argument, which turns into an excursus about hypocrisy:

> The wine of God is truth, and does not lie –
> You've been drinking yoghurt! Yoghurt! Yoghurt! (...)
> You set yourself up as Manṣūr al-Ḥallāj,
> Setting the cotton of the lovers ablaze,
> But you couldn't tell ʿUmar from Abū Lahab,
> Though you recognise your donkey's fart in the dead of night![27]

In this story, the comical anecdote and the teaching are intertwined: Rūmī moves back and forth between the fart and the moral of the tale. Indeed, he often appears to be playing a game with his readers, leading with an outrageously obscene story before pulling back to a moral. In one case, a wife walks in unexpectedly to find the servant girl in evident disarray and her husband deep in prayer:

> Shamelessly she pulled back his robe;
> His scrotum and penis were covered in semen.
> The last drop of semen was dripping from his penis;
> His thigh and knee were wet and soiled.
> She slapped his face, saying, 'You wretch,
> Are those the testicles of a man who prays?
> Is that penis (*dhakar*) in a fit state for prayers and remembrance (*dhikr*)?
> Or those soiled thighs and groin?'[28]

---

[25] Franklin Lewis, *Rumi: Past and Present, East and West* (Oxford: Oneworld, 2000), p. 316. The translation is Lewis's.

[26] Jalāl al-Dīn Rūmī, *Mathnavī-yi Maʿnawī*, ed. Tawfīq Ṣubḥānī (Tehran: Vizārat-i Farhang ū ʿIlm-i Islāmī, 1373/1994–5), p. 360 (Book 3, vv .656, 662).

[27] Ibid., p. 361 (Book 3, vv. 659, 692–3).

[28] Ibid., p.761 (Book 5, vv. 2201–4).

Again, Rūmī launches into a denunciation of hypocrisy:

> On the Day of Gathering, everything hidden will be known;
> Every wrongdoer will be disgraced.
> Hand and foot will bear witness plainly
> To their own corruption before their Judge.
> The hand will say, 'I stole such-and-such,'
> The lips will say, 'I asked for such and such,'
> The foot will say, 'I went after my desires,'
> The genitals will say, 'I screwed a woman.'[29]

In what must surely be the most infamous and astonishing of these stories, Rūmī tells us about a lady who secretly watches her servant girl being pleasured by a donkey. Eager to follow suit, she sends her servant girl on a spurious errand and takes her place. However, she does not realise that the servant girl was using a gourd to protect herself from the full force of the donkey's substantial member:

> The donkey did as he was told, pressing balls-deep
> Into the lady, who died on the spot.
> Thrusting, the donkey's dick ripped open her liver,
> And her guts were torn apart.[30]

Sure enough, the matter does not end here. There are two, apparently mutually exclusive, lessons to be learned. First, the donkey stands for base passions:

> Know that the animal soul is that donkey stud:
> To be under it is uglier even than that.
> If you die for the lower soul (*nafs*), out of desire,
> Then know the truth that you are like that woman.[31]

Second, a good Sufi should never dispense with a teacher, or confuse the exoteric with the esoteric:

> If you want to act without a master (*ustād*)
> You are ignorantly giving away your life (...)
> You saw the external form (*ẓāhir*), but the secret (*sirr*) was hidden.
> Did you open shop without being a master?
> You saw the dick, like honey or dates in butter,
> But how could you miss the gourd, you eager one?
> You were submerged in passion for the donkey,
> But the gourd was hidden from your sight.
> You learned the externals of the craft from a teacher,
> Then blithely walked off with that knowledge.
> Many a rogue, heedless fool,
> Sees nothing of the way of true men but their wool (*ṣūf*).[32]

---

[29] Ibid., p. 761 (Book 3, vv. 2211–14).

[30] Ibid., p. 728 (Book 5, vv. 1386–87).

[31] Ibid., p. 728 (Book 5, vv. 1392–93). Rūmī may be hinting at a pun: *munā* means desire, *manā* death or fate and *manī* semen.

[32] Ibid., p. 729 (Book 5, vv. 1404, 1439–23).

One wonders if there is an element of self-parody here. Does the story genuinely pave the way for the moral, or are the morals proffered tongue-in-cheek as pretext for some raunchy material? Either way, unlike Ibn ʿArabī's material, this episode relies on an unstable mixture of *jidd* (earnest) and *hazl* (jest), a combination that has been perceptively explored by the celebrant of this volume.[33] Quite apart from the fact that Ibn ʿArabī would almost certainly not have told a joke about bestiality to begin with, it is also difficult to imagine him connecting such a story with a higher purpose. The fart jokes in the *Muḥāḍarat al-abrār* are offered completely for their own sake. Conversely, when Ibn ʿArabī tells a story involving bodily functions in order to prove a point, he shrinks from making any jokes. An example is the following anecdote about a talking chamber pot:

> In the year 603 (1206–7), in Fusṭāṭ (*Miṣr*),[34]Abū l-ʿAbbās al-Ḥarīrī told me that he was once walking with Abū ʿAbd Allāh al-Qurbāqī[35] in the small market of Wardān. Al-Qurbāqī had bought a small chamber pot for a young son of his to urinate in (...). There were righteous men with them, and they felt like eating something, so they looked for something to use as a dip with bread. They agreed to buy some treacle, saying, 'This chamber pot has not been soiled, and it is brand new.' They filled it and sat down to eat until they had finished and everybody left. The owner of the chamber pot left with it, walking with Abū l-ʿAbbas.
>
> Abū l-ʿAbbas told [me], 'By God, I heard with my own ears, and so did Abū ʿAbd Allāh al-Qurbāqī, that the chamber pot said, "After friends of God (*awliyāʾ*) have eaten from me, am I to be the container of filth! God forbid!", whereupon it slipped out of his hand, fell to the ground and broke. We were both gripped by a mystical state (*ḥāl*) because of what it had said.'
>
> After he told me the story, I said, 'You[36] have missed the lesson which the chamber pot taught you. The matter is not as you claimed. How many chamber pots have been eaten from by better people than you, then used for filth! No, what it said to you was, "Brethren, after God has made your hearts a container for His knowledge and manifestation, you should not use it for anything else (*aghyār*). But God has not forbidden that your hearts should be a container for him". Then it broke. In other words, be like that with God!'
>
> [Abū l-ʿAbbās] said to me, 'What you have just told us had not occurred to us.'[37]

It is tempting to see implicit humour in the contrast between the nature and medium of the message. The very image of respected holy men eating from a chamber pot appears

[33] Geert Jan van Gelder, 'Arabic debates of jest and earnest', in G.J. Reinink and H.L.J. van Stiphout (eds.), *Dispute poems and dialogues in the Ancient and Mediaeval Near East* (Louvain: Peeters, 1991), pp. 199–212.

[34] The *samāʿ* of another work by Ibn ʿArabī places him in nearby Cairo on 19 Shaʿbān 603 (1207) (Addas, *Quest*, p. 305). According to Denis Gril, *Miṣr* in this context would have meant Fusṭāṭ rather than the newer city of Cairo. See Denis Gril, 'Ibn ʿArabī in Egypt or the Speech of Things – "The Cosmos"(*al-ʿālam*)', *Journal of the Muhyiddin Ibn Arabi Society* 53 (2013), pp. 25–36, on p. 28.

[35] On these two Andalusian Sufis, see Ralph Austin, *Sufis of Andalusia* (Berkeley and Los Angeles: University of California Press, 1971), pp. 91–5.

[36] Ibn ʿArabī uses the plural form rather than the dual, suggesting a more colloquial register.

[37] Ibn ʿArabī, *al-Futūḥāt al-Makkiyya*, 4 vols. (Beirut: Dār Ṣādir, n.d.), vol. I, p. 410. For more background on this story and the lesson behind it see Gril, 'Ibn ʿArabī in Egypt.'

to cry out for a joke.[38] However, if there is any humour here, it is deadpan. Yet one feels certain that had the story been told by Rūmī, the stench of excrement would rise from the page.

The fart jokes and the story about the chamber pot suggest that unlike Rūmī, Ibn ʿArabī was loath to work his off-colour material into the thread of an argument. This is uncharacteristic of an author who usually seems able to spin a symbolic meaning out of almost anything. To that extent, the two jokes – minor though they are in the grand scheme of things – are a slight corrective to the idea that Ibn ʿArabī

> only took an interest in *adab* or made use of it either to the extent that this literature invariably contains a moral and is therefore the expression of a kind of universal wisdom, or because it represents an excellent educational tool.[39]

By and large, the *Muḥāḍarat al-abrār* is clearly intended to be an improving work, but it has space for the odd story that is a little indecent, though not sinful. These anecdotes, at least, are given purely for the hell of it. And it is perhaps fitting that this most universalist of writers should have left a universal, if unsophisticated, brand of humour: the fart joke.

WORKS CITED

Claude Addas, *Quest for the Red Sulphur: the life of Ibn ʿArabī*, trans. Peter Kingsley (Cambridge: Islamic Texts Society, 1993).

A.J. Arberry, *The Koran Interpreted*, 2 vols. (London: George Allen & Unwin Ltd., 1955).

Ralph Austin, *Sufis of Andalusia* (Berkeley and Los Angeles: University of California Press, 1971).

Michel Chodkiewicz, *Seal of the Saints: prophethood and sainthood in the doctrine of Ibn Arabi*, trans. Liadain Sherrard (Cambridge: Islamic Texts Society, 1993).

Halima Ferhat, 'Salā' and 'Shalla', *Encyclopaedia of Islam*, 2nd edition, eds P. Bearman, Th. Bianquis, C.E. Bosworth, E. van Donzel, and W.P. Heinrichs (Leiden: Brill Online, 2013). School of Oriental and African Studies (SOAS), 13 July 2013.

Geert Jan van Gelder, 'Arabic debates of jest and earnest', in G.J. Reinink and H.L.J. van Stiphout (eds.), *Dispute poems and dialogues in the Ancient and Mediaeval Near East* (Louvain: Peeters, 1991),

Geert Jan van Gelder, *The Bad and the Ugly: Attitudes towards invective poetry* (hijāʾ) *in classical Arabic literature* (Leiden: Brill, 1988).

Denis Gril, 'Ibn ʿArabī in Egypt or the Speech of Things – "The Cosmos" (*al-ʿālam*)', *Journal of the Muhyiddin Ibn Arabi Society* 53 (2013), pp. 25–36.

Muḥyī l-Dīn Ibn ʿArabī, *Dīwān*, MS Veliyuddin 1681.

Muḥyī l-Dīn Ibn ʿArabī, *al-Futūḥāt al-Makkiyya*, 4 vols. (Beirut: Dar Ṣādir, n.d.).

Muḥyī l-Dīn Ibn ʿArabī, *Muḥāḍarat al-abrār wa-musāmarat al-akhyār*, 2 vols. (Beirut: Dar Ṣādir, 1968).

Muḥyī l-Dīn Ibn ʿArabī, *Muḥāḍarat al-abrār wa-musāmarat al-akhyār*, MS Esad Efendi 1897.

[38] There is in fact an anecdote in Dublin lore about a man who used to walk around Woolworth's department store eating crumbled chocolate cake and lemonade from a chamber pot. My grandfather said that the man was the practical joker William 'Bird' Flanagan (1867–1925), but I have not been able to corroborate that version, and at least some of the pranks attributed to Flanagan are clearly apocryphal. (On Flanagan, see further http://humphrysfamilytree.com/Flanagan/the.bird.html, last accessed 27 September 2012).

[39] Addas, *Quest*, p. 101.

Muḥyī l-Dīn Ibn ʿArabī, *The Tarjumán al-Ashwáq: A Collection of Mystical Odes*, trans. Reynold A. Nicholson (London: Theosophical Publishing House, 1911).
Franklin Lewis, *Rumi: Past and Present, East and West* (Oxford: Oneworld, 2000).
Denis McAuley, *Ibn ʿArabī's Mystical Poetics* (Oxford: Oxford University Press, 2012).
Ronald Nettler, *Sufi Metaphysics and Qur'anic Prophets* (Cambridge: Islamic Texts Society, 2003).
Jalāl al-Dīn Rūmī, *Mathnavī-yi Maʿnawī*, ed. Tawfīq Ṣubḥānī (Tehran: Vizārat-i Farhang ū ʿIlm-i Islāmī, 1373/1994–5).
Osman Yahya, *Histoire et classification de l'œuvre d'Ibn ʿArabī*, 2 vols. (Damascus: Institut français de Damas, 1964).

12

Love Or Lust: Sexual relationships between humans and jinns in the *Thousand And One Nights* and the *Nightingale's Eye*

Richard van Leeuwen

Among the main incentives for telling, writing and reading fictional stories is the possibility they provide to explore events that can be imagined but not easily experienced. Fictional narrative penetrates into realms that lay hidden inside our everyday reality and that contain forces, creatures and worlds which can normally only be fathomed in our imagination. That does not necessarily mean that these realms do not exist; they are conjectural, but they derive their reality from the effects they have on us through our imagination. And perhaps some of the strange elements in the world of the unseen are more real than we think. Reality has always contained a potential which cannot be grasped by the rational mind alone and whose workings can only be examined by wandering outside the realm of rationality and by venturing into worlds dominated by unknown forces and filled with unexpected encounters.

The world of stories, therefore, is always a world of adventure, since its laws are essentially unpredictable and it is filled with surprising phenomena. It contains the promise of bliss and happiness, but also the threat of doom and ultimate horror. It may offer a reward in the end, but also severe punishment. Moreover, it may evoke not only encounters with peculiar forces and creatures, but also with parts of the reader himself, which remain hidden in everyday life. This instability of fictional narration is perhaps most vigorously symbolized by the appearance of demons of various kinds, such as fairies, ghosts, ogres and jinns. It is creatures such as these that inhabit the diffuse zone between the realms of reality and unreality and which use the human imagination to cross the boundaries between the two. They represent the forces of the unknown, the unseen, and the ungraspable, but they 'embody' their manifestation in reality, thus bringing humans in touch with what lays hidden inside their experience of reality.

According to some, the occurrence of fairies and ghosts in fictional stories should be seen as the sudden expression of drives and desires which are lumbering in the human psyche, waiting to reveal themselves. In this Freudian view, demons represent the 'return of the repressed' or the impulsive interruption of rationally conceived and projected courses of action. Demons are first of all sudden interventions which change the perception of the situation in which the hero finds himself, and which, presumably, are caused by urges hidden inside the hero himself, as an uncontrollable force. They represent secret wishes and fears, suppressed desires, irrational impulses or intuitive choices. They are, perhaps, the Id, the uncontrollable counterpart of the Ego. They are also the force defying discipline, authority, and all forms of organized systems and codes. They are the essence of fictionality, as a force imposing on the reader, as it were, an encounter with the world of the unseen.

Apart from these psychological aspects, ghosts and demons fulfil very specific narrative functions. They are not only emissaries of the realm of the unseen; they also typically emerge at junctures in the sequence of stories. Their appearance usually interrupts the course of events, inserts a new plot element, and steers the adventure of the hero into new directions. They represent the unexpected intervention of the outside in the experience of the hero, the strangeness of the world in which he roams, and the supernatural forces, which – at least partly – govern his life. Therefore, they are the manifestation of the narrative forces that direct the story toward its plot and lead the hero toward his destiny. Thus, demons and ghosts are often instruments of Fate, a typical example of how the incomprehensibility of such an enormous force can be transformed, through the imagination, into an, admittedly extraordinary, phenomenon integrated into a vision of the world.

What the two proposed functions of demons and ghosts – psychological and narratological – have in common is a sense of transgression. The Freudian Id does not care about the codes of propriety, and the narratalogical demon disrupts narrative logic and effuses boundaries between the rational and the irrational. This is indicative of the potentially subversive power possessed by fictional narration. By appealing to the imagination, fictional stories tend to question social conventions, moral discipline and all kinds of order. They defy well-established visions of life and society by imbuing them with alternative visions, potential worlds, and a destabilization of commonly accepted values. This potential disruptiveness of narration should be contained, and therefore stories are usually bound to conventions of various kinds. They often, in spite of their essential boundlessness – or perhaps through it – are connected to reality and present a moral lesson, which confirms established values and attitudes. They tend to use the potential disruptiveness of narration not to destroy social conventions, but rather to reaffirm them more convincingly, by exposing threats and accentuating their significance.

In this essay I will examine two examples of the abovementioned incursions of the imagined world into the real world in fictional narratives, focusing on the way in which they represent forms of transgression with regard to both moral propriety and the laws of narrative plausibility. They show how storytelling conjures up disruptive forces, but contains them at the same time, and how demons fail to heed accepted values, but are still submitted to them. The two examples relate more specifically to sexual relationships between humans and jinns (genies), a type of demon that has become known in the West especially through the stories of the *Thousand and One Nights*. We will first discuss a modern story by the British author A.S. Byatt, in which the middle-aged heroine has an invigorating experience with a jinn (also djinn), and subsequently a story from the *Thousand and One Nights*, in which human-jinn relationships play an essential role. Both stories explore the extent to which the forces of fantasy are allowed to interfere in human affairs, and, especially in the first case, the extent to which sexual relationships between representatives of the two realms are possible and allowed. But first of all some remarks about the nature of jinns and their relations with humans should be made.

ON THE NATURE OF JINNS

Whereas in the West demons and ghosts have gradually been marginalized over the centuries, being relegated to the world of fantasy only, in some parts of the Arab world jinns have always remained part of the visions of life and the world. The Qurʾan mentions jinns in several verses, which means that they are acknowledged as creatures living in the real world as a part of creation, among the various natural phenomena. Their nature is more elaborately described in narrative literature, ranging from eschatological texts to entertainment stories. They are usually considered creatures made of fire and a thin skin, able to fly, and endowed with magic powers and the ability to take on all kinds of shapes. These qualities make them elusive and hard to control since they allow them a grip on the material world which greatly surpasses human capabilities, for instance they can cover huge distances in a wink of the eye, change shape in a second, cast spells on spaces, persons or objects. On the other hand, jinns are usually not very bright and this allows humans to outsmart them.

In his handbook about the legal implications of social intercourse between humans and djinns, the 14th-century scholar Badr al-Dīn al-Shiblī dedicates a special chapter to the subject of sexual relations between the two species.[1] He first investigates whether sexual intercourse between humans and jinns is possible at all. On the one hand, humans and jinns do not appear to be compatible; for jinns are made of fire, while humans consist of the four elements. The womb of a female jinn (*jinniyya*) would thus be too hot to fruitfully receive the semen of a human male. On the other hand, jinns can take any shape, including the shape of a human so a man may not even be aware that he is having intercourse with a demon. Therefore, despite their incompatibility, intercourse between a human and a jinn is not impossible.

This is confirmed by the Prophet Muhammad's denunciation of precisely this kind of relationship, which is an implicit acknowledgment of its potentiality. According to al-Shiblī, scholars, referring to the prophet, agree that sexual relationships between jinns and humans are prohibited. Men and women were created as a pair from one soul (*nafs*) with

---

[1] Badr al-Dīn al-Shiblī, *Kitāb Ākām al-marjān fī aḥkām al-jānn* (s.l. 1326H), pp. 66–72; see also: Fred Leemhuis, 'Épouser un djinn? Passé et présent,' *Quaderni di Studi Arabi* 11 (1993), pp. 179–192.

affection (*mawadda*) between them, whereas jinns were created from fire. Jinns have therefore no affinity with the human soul and belong to a different species. Because of this a relationship between man and jinn cannot serve the aim for which sexual relationships and affection are intended: to provide trust and reassurance. By this reasoning it follows, too, that irresistible passion or being abducted by force does not negate the prohibition of illicit intercourse, since it will not result in the desired aim of mutual trust. Thus, in all cases sexual intercourse between humans and djinns is reprehensible.[2]

Al-Shiblī's arguments are supplemented, remarkably, by three anecdotes that seem to exemplify the possibility of sexual intercourse with jinns rather than its reprehensibility. First, he mentions the example of a traveller who slept in a cave and was approached by a female jinn with a 'split eye', who, officially, married her daughter to him, to which he conceded out of fear. Second, reference is made to the story of Solomon, who took Bilqīs the queen of Sheba as his wife. She herself was the daughter of a human mother and a jinn (and as a result had hairy legs). Third, the anecdote is told of a traveller, who after being shipwrecked washed up on an uninhabited island where one day nymph-like girls emerged from the sea carrying brilliant pearls. He captured one of the girls, impregnated her, and returned to the human world with a half-human son. These stories do not exactly condemn relationships with jinns, but they relegate them to the realm of strange adventures, distant regions, and ancient history and legends. The association with Solomon is of course not coincidental since according to the religious tradition he is the king and master of the jinns.[3]

In Arabic storytelling, in its various forms, the negative and the positive implications of the existence of jinns are eagerly exploited. Jinns are staged either as the evil force which has to be defeated in the name of Fate or love, or as a *deus ex machina*, which helps an unfortunate hero escape from his predicament. In general, sexual relationships between man and jinn are not a common theme, although they may occur, usually to show how difficult and extraordinary they are. In the *Thousand and One Nights* we find several stories which contain this element, either as an incidental motif or as a structural theme. In the frame story, for instance, King Shahriyār and his brother meet a girl who has been captured by a jinn and kept imprisoned in a chest. She forces the two unfortunate kings to have intercourse with her. A more general motif is the human girl who is held imprisoned by a jinn in a cave (story of the 'Third Qalander') or through an enchantment ('Muhammad Lazybones'). In these cases it is human ingenuity that is needed to rescue the girl, although in the first case the hero may not always succeed in saving her.[4]

These examples indicate that relationships between male jinns and human women are more often than not involuntary and compelled by the jinn. It is different when a human male is enraptured by the beauty of a female jinn, as in the stories of 'Ḥasan of Basra' and 'Jānshāh'. Ḥasan first enjoys the pleasures of a number of jinn-princesses, before he conquers his beloved by stealing her coat of feathers, preventing her from flying away. In

---

[2] Al-Shiblī, p. 68.

[3] Ibid., pp. 71–72.

[4] References are to the Būlāq edition; summaries of the stories can be found in: U. Marzolph and R. van Leeuwen (eds.), *The Arabian Nights Encyclopedia*, 2 vols. (Santa Barbara: ABC-CLIO, 2004).

this example, what is especially stressed is how difficult it is to realize a harmonious union between a man and a jinn, how many obstacles have to be overcome, how determined the hero has to be, and how precarious the relationship will remain. In the case of Ḥasan, it is debatable whether the marriage is entered into voluntarily or if Ḥasan imposes it on the female jinn. It also demonstrates that love itself is not enough to secure a stable marriage. Thus, the stories tend to emphasize the incompatibility of the two lovers, although they do not exclude union. There are three factors determining the outcome: true love, the tenacity of the hero, and, of course, Fate.

THE BENEVOLENT DJINN

A.S. Byatt's fairytale *The Djinn in the Nightingale's Eye* is about Gillian Perholt, an Englishwoman in her fifties and an internationally respected narratologist, who, after divorcing her husband, has the feeling that her life is meaningless and empty.[5] In a rather depressed mood she attends a conference in Ankara about 'stories of women's lives' where she will give a presentation about the story of patient Griselda in the Canterbury tales. A Turkish colleague and friend Orhan Rifat will speak about 'Powers and powerlessness: djinns and women in the *Arabian Nights*'. During her lecture Gillian is suddenly petrified by the apparition of a 'cavernous female form', which, in its repugnancy, seems to embody her sense of decay, ugliness and mortality. After her presentation, Orhan speaks about the misogyny of pre-modern story-collections, the role of Fate in the *Thousand and One Nights* and the nature of fictionality in the tales. He concludes that in the story of Qamar al-Zamān a 'djinn brings about a satisfactory adjustment to the normal human destiny in the recalcitrant prince'.[6]

This brief summary indicates the main themes of the story. First, the story is about the powers and, especially, powerlessness of women, symbolized by the patient Griselda, who refuses to disobey her husband Walter, although he tests her servility to cruel and even absurd extremes. In this story all freedom is withheld from Griselda because Walter monopolizes all the roles in the story: 'the hero, the villain, destiny, God and narrator'.[7] This is of course compared to the frame tale of the *Thousand and One Nights* in which Shahriyār personifies the husband and destiny combined. The counterparts of Griselda can be found in the women and goddesses in ancient stories and myths, such as Siduri in the epic of Gilgamesh, Cybele, Astarte, Artemis, and all kinds of priestesses who represent the power of femininity within the great cultural traditions, filling them with a sense of awe and mystery.

Second, the situation of women, their relationships with men, and their power as symbols are embedded in stories, myths and narratives of various kinds, and it is through these narratives that their symbolic content becomes activated within reality. Fictional narratives and myths function as channels between fictional realms in which representations are constructed, and the real world, in which the reader is entangled with other human

---

[5] A.S. Byatt, 'The Djinn in the Nightingale's Eye' in *The Djinn in the Nightingale's Eye: five fairy stories* (London: Chatto & Windus, 1994), pp. 93–277.

[6] Byatt, p. 127.

[7] Ibid., p. 120.

beings and her material surroundings. This implies, third, that storytelling is an act of power, an effort to control the destinies of others, often to the disadvantage of women. Finally, it is within this 'narrative zone' that not only struggles for emancipation and self-fulfilment are situated, but that also Fate is enabled to manifest itself in the lives of the protagonists and even of the readers.

These thematic elements are not only reflected upon in the tale, they are also integrated into the course of events. While visiting Istanbul with Orhan, after the conference, Gillian relates how she experiences what she calls 'encounters with Fate', which makes her ponder the issues discussed in her and Orhan's presentations and the way in which they are present in her own life, her own fate. Then, in a bazaar, which she compares to Aladdin's cave, she buys a strange flask that is more than a hundred years old. In her hotel room she cleans the bottle – made of a kind of glass called 'the nightingale's eye' – and suddenly a huge jinn appears and offers to fulfil her three wishes. After having recovered from her initial shock, Gillian decides to be modest and wishes only for her body to return to the shape she was in when she last liked it. The jinn now tells her his story: he had served the Queen of Sheba, an Ottoman princess, and the concubine of a merchant in Smyrna. According to his story he comes across as a supporter and liberator of women, helping them to develop their abilities and knowledge. Nevertheless during all that time he failed to escape from his imprisonment in the bottle.

Gillian subsequently tells her life-story, which will not be recapitulated here, but which is also related to the theme of men exerting power over women and the consequences for women's feelings about their own body image. Now she wishes for the jinn to become her lover and he not only reveals himself to be proficient in lovemaking, but also turns out to be an amiable, helpful, and caring companion. In the end Gillian uses her third wish to set him free, but he promises to come and visit her from time to time.

Before commenting on this story, we will first discuss a 'true' story from the *Thousand and One Nights.*

ENTERING THE REALM OF THE JINNS

Like many other stories in *The Thousand and One Nights*, the story of 'Sayf al-Mulūk and Badīʿ al-Jamāl'[8] begins with the looming fall of a dynasty and empire: the elderly king has no offspring to succeed him. His vizier travels to the court of King Solomon, who instructs him to kill two snakes at a certain place, boil their flesh and give it to the wives of the king and the vizier to eat. They should have intercourse with them that same night. He also gives him presents for the sons that will be born from these unions. The vizier acts accordingly: the snakes are boiled in a 'delicious onion sauce' and after a while the prince Sayf al-Mulūk and Saʿīd, the son of the vizier, are born. When they reach adolescence, they are given the presents from Solomon, a robe and a ring for Sayf, and a seal and a sword for Saʿīd. When Sayf unfolds the robe, he discovers sewn into it the portrait of a beautiful girl, embroidered with pearls, bearing the following words: 'This is Badīʿ al-Jamāl, daughter

[8] Nights 758–778.

of one of the believing jinns (*al-jānn al-muʾminīn*) living in the town of Bābil and the Garden of Iram ibn ʿĀd the Great.'[9]

Sayf immediately falls in love with the girl, but not even the travelling merchants have heard of Bābil and the Garden of Iram. They advise him to go to China, but when he arrives there they tell him to continue on his journey to the islands of Hind. Crossing the seas for four months, Sayf suffers storm and shipwreck, meets vicious demons and man-eating ghouls, is imprisoned in cages and attacked by monkeys. He journeys overland through mountains and deserts until he reaches a black castle. Here he enters a magnificent hall where a girl is seated on a golden throne. She turns out to be Dawlat Khātūn, the daughter of the king of Hind who lives on the island of Sarandīb. One day, while she was bathing with her slave-girls, she was captured by a jinn, who approached her 'like a cloud'. The jinn changed himself into a handsome prince and said that he was the son of the blue jinn-king. The palace in which he holds her imprisoned is a journey of 120 years from Hind. Dawlat Khātūn always rejected his advances and has remained a virgin, since the jinn-prince only kisses and embraces her chastely. Dawlat Khātūn tells Sayf that Badīʿ al-Jamāl is her foster-sister.

Sayf bravely announces that he will kill the jinn-suitor, who has hidden his soul in the craw of a bird, stored in a box that is preserved in fifteen chests in a marble sarcophagus, at the other end of the ocean. Fortunately, Sayf possesses Solomon's ring, which allows him to order the coffin to come to him and to destroy the jinn's soul just when he arrives at the castle. Sayf and Dawlat now set out on a raft and sail many days – Sayf sleeping with his back turned to her and a sword between them – until they arrive in a harbour and continue their journey to Sarandīb. The father of Dawlat Khātūn offers Sayf his throne as a reward for saving his daughter. As soon as Badīʿ al-Jamāl hears that Dawlat Khātūn has returned, she visits her and is told about Sayf's infatuation. Badīʿ explains that the whole affair has sprung out of coincidence: her mother had given the robe to Solomon as a present, hoping that the mighty king would be enticed to marry Badīʿ on seeing her portrait, but apparently Solomon had given it away without unfolding it.

When Badīʿ meets Sayf, she is enraptured, but she considers a union totally impossible, since humans and djinns are incompatible and humans are unfaithful. To Sayf she says: 'Prince, I fear that I will not find love and affection with you when I surrender to you completely because humans possess little good and are usually volatile. Know that our lord Solomon, son of David, was in love with Bilqīs, but when he saw another woman who was more beautiful than she, he deserted her.'[10] In spite of these objections the two swear loyalty to each other. Then suddenly, Sayf is kidnapped by a jinn and taken away to be punished for killing the jinn-prince. Badīʿ al-Jamāl's grandmother admits that there will never be harmony between humans and jinns, but she nevertheless persuades her son to set out and rescue Sayf, although it is considered unfitting for jinns to fight one another for the sake of a human. In the end, Sayf is liberated and united with Badīʿ. Two wedding parties are celebrated, one for Sayf and Badīʿ and one for Saʿīd and Dawlat Khātūn.

---

[9] Night 762.

[10] Night 775.

JINNS AND NARRATIVE

The summary of the story of 'Sayf al-Mulūk and Badīᶜ al-Jamāl' shows that the narrator broadly follows the pattern that is common for jinn-stories in the *Thousand and One Nights* and, more generally, the lore concerning jinns. Immediately in the beginning the diegetic reality of the story is linked to the realm of magic, through the delegation of the vizier to Solomon, the magical snake-recipe and, importantly, Solomon's gift. The two realms are now no longer juxtaposed; they are interconnected through the birth of Sayf al-Mulūk and the presents he receives. Now his destiny is interwoven with other lives and destinies that link the worlds of humans and jinns, the realms of everyday reality, and the overarching realm of Solomon, who governs the hidden forces and creatures of nature. It is this spilling over of realms into each other that provides the incongruence from which the narrative potential and dynamism are derived.

The incongruence is partly caused by the impenetrable nature of the boundaries between the two realms, at least for human beings. Whereas the delegation of Sayf's father to Solomon could apparently reach Solomon's court without difficulty, Sayf has to conquer enormous obstacles and distances to reach the habitat of his beloved. It would seem that the ability to cross the boundary is related to the purpose of the journey and the destiny of the traveller. The king's destiny has more or less reached its completion; it has only to be linked to a new, prospective destiny, which still has to be lived and 'acquired' by Sayf. Thus, while the vizier has no trouble travelling to Solomon's court, the young hero is obliged to travel great distances, be exposed to all kinds of dangers and, especially, venture into a diffuse zone in which nobody knows the way, in which there are no certainties, no laws known to humans. Sayf enters a world from which there may be no return and in which he can easily perish.

The unpredictability of the boundary and the diffuse zone related to it link the story to the conventions of the love romance. They represent the narrative space in which love manifests itself in its full force, throwing the hero into the realm of emotions, irrationality, insecurity, and destiny. The hero has to show his determination, his courage, and his ingenuity to be worthy to appropriate his destiny, in the shape of his beloved. Love is unsettling and perilous; it represents the precarious phase in which the continuity of life, and of society and the kingship, should be secured, while at the same time it is fundamentally endangered. Love is the force making the continuation of the life-cycle possible, but it is also its greatest threat because it is unstable and unpredictable. It is therefore at the same time both an aim to strive for and a danger to be neutralized.

The mingling of the jinn-story and the love romance strengthen the impact of both components. Since in love stories the conquest of the beloved should preferably be as difficult as possible, and deferred as much as possible, since it is the effort of the hero that constitutes the story, rather than the plot, the jinn-element adds a wide range of possibilities. On the one hand it enhances the attractiveness of the beloved, through the jinns' magic properties in general, combined with the 'magic' of love, while on the other hand it also emphasizes the potential incompatibility of the envisioned pair and the improbability of their union. Thus, the essential components of a love story are multiplied as a result of the linking of the two realms. This is narratologically symbolized by the arduous journey taken by the hero across mountains, deserts, and seas, his battles with monstrous enemies, and the puzzle of finding his way out of the labyrinth with nothing more than a belief in his destiny to support him.

The component of love is also conducive to a narrative exploration of the realm of the jinns. It is only the force of love which propels the heroes into the dangerous world of magic and demons, and through their adventures the readers come to know about the dispositions of jinns, their powers, the objects related to their magic, and their manners and customs. If there is one force capable of forcing an exploration of the compatibility of jinns and humans, it is passionate love, in all its devious and often unfathomable ways. Thus, the hero in love sacrifices himself to take the readers to far-off places, to show them the beauty, the ugliness, the strangeness, and powers of the jinns, but, significantly, also their stubbornness and stupidity. Still, in spite of the enchantment effused by the jinns, love relationships between humans and jinns remain precarious and are often only of brief duration, either because other humans envy the hero his beautiful demon wife, or because the female jinn returns to her homeland, or, of course, because death intervenes.

In the story of Sayf al-Mulūk the patterns of the love romance and the jinn-adventure are combined to structure the narrative elements and the plot lines. Spatial and temporal elements are imbued by the narrative potential of both themes, which ultimately come together in a notion of destiny and Fate. After all, the whole adventure is intended in the first place to enable Fate to take its course to 'realize' itself through the heroes. Love and the intervention of the djinns have made the course of destiny uncertain, but the character of the hero has enabled it to preserve its grip on the course of events. It seems that even the antagonism between humans and jinns is used by Fate as an instrument to neutralize the possible danger of deviance from the projected course: jinns can set humans in motion in the right direction, while humans can thwart inappropriate interventions by the jinn, for instance, in Sayf al-Mulūk's case, the abduction of Dawlat Khātūn. Fate can lean back relieved when the 'brothers' Saᶜīd and Sayf al-Mulūk are united with the 'sisters' Dawlat Khātūn and Badīᶜ al-Jamāl.

Although 'The Nightingale's Eye' does not follow the same patterns as the story of Sayf al-Mulūk, some elements are quite prominently the same. For instance, the heroine finds herself in a kind of diffuse zone, not because she is in the prime of her life and bound to be initiated into love, but rather because she seems to have ended up in an impasse in a life that is narrowing down and appears rather anti-heroic, and, which moreover has been marked by a traumatic experience in her youth. This diffuse zone is made more diffuse by her occupation and her interest in storytelling. In addition, she travels to an exotic country, where remnants can be found of an enchanted vision of the world, in which it is not an anomaly to encounter manifestations of the supernatural. As in the story of Sayf al-Mulūk, this context furnishes a setting susceptible to miraculous intervention, which gradually unleashes its narrative potential. Finally, there is the element of – apparent – incompatibility, manifested in the jinn's 'physical' size which can hardly be contained by the hotel room, by his smell, by his adventures and long history – as compared to Gillian's uneventful life – and by his aversion to the modern world.

The similarities with the *Thousand and One Nights* are repeatedly emphasized in the story itself. The modern age is presented as an age of marvels, the protagonists reflect on the nature of storytelling, stories are inserted in the main narrative, an atmosphere of magic is evoked, and the relationship between dominant men and narrating women is a major theme. And of course the references to the *Nights*, Aladdin's cave, the jinn's flask, and Orhan's lecture indicate a strong intertextual relationship. The relationship is crucial, since in 'The Nightingale's Eye' it is storytelling in general, and the *Thousand and One Nights* in particular, which is instrumental in shifting from one realm to the other. It is through storytelling that the boundaries between fiction and real life become blurred and can be crossed. It is storytelling, which provides the corridor through which communication between the two realms becomes possible.

In contrast to the story of 'Sayf al-Mulūk', in 'The Nightingale's Eye' the passages between the realms of magic and normality are not explored in a structural way, as two worlds existing next to each other and from time to time interfering with each other. The jinn and his peculiar context are not an elementary force structuring the story, like the 'force' of storytelling, which by weaving its intricate worlds and illusions destabilizes diegetic reality. It is rather, in the style of the fairytale, a force miraculously intervening, as in the *Thousand and One Nights* tale of 'The Fisherman and the Jinn' in which the life of the protagonist changes suddenly. Whereas the jinn-component in the story of Sayf al-Mulūk fulfils the role of the 'narratological' jinn (i.e. a marvellous element which determines the narrative pattern of the story), the jinn in 'The Nightingale's Eye' seems rather to represent the 'fairytale' jinn (i.e. the 'embodiment' of inner drives, irrationality, mental breakthrough, and unpredictable phenomena in the dusk between fantasy and reality). But how do these two types of jinn relate to our main topic, their erotic encounter with humans?

CONCLUSION: JINNS AND EROTICISM

The stories of 'Sayf al-Mulūk' and 'The Nightingale's Eye' each provoke specific anticipations in the reader. In the case of Sayf al-Mulūk, the reader expects to witness, in the end, an actual sexual union between the hero and the female jinn; in the case of Gillian, the reader hopes to be informed, through Orhan Rifat's lecture, about the relationship between jinns and women in the *Thousand and One Nights*. We can be brief about this hope: the summary of Orhan's lecture is not about the announced subject, but rather about the role of djinn in bringing lovers together in the story of Qamar al-Zamān. What we come to know about the relations between women and jinns is limited to the jinn's life-story. But to what extent is the other 'desire' satisfied?

As in other stories of the *Thousand and One Nights*, the protagonists of the story of Sayf al-Mulūk are extraordinarily beautiful. Their love is passionate and fuelled by physical attraction. We should expect, therefore, that the encounter between the two would be consummated, especially after the perilous journeys required to realize the union. Moreover, it would seem that the imaginative inventors of the *Nights* stories would be inclined to exploit fully the narrative potential of the jinns in this respect: the ability to assume all forms and substances, to take on all sizes and appearances, to become invisible, to move swiftly and change environments in the wink of an eye, etc. If jinns are indeed manifestations of repressed human drives and desires, we would expect that this would be exemplified in the story. Which storyteller would forfeit such a chance to display his narrative ingenuity and proficiency?

It is rather disappointing, therefore, that the actual encounters are rather restrained. It is understandable that the storyteller holds himself in check in the case of Dawlat Khātūn. It is explicitly stated that the jinn who abducted her has not touched her in an indecent way and has only kissed and embraced her. It can be condoned that he did not invoke the help of his other charms, either because he was not very resourceful, or because Dawlat Khātūn's virginity and honour could be preserved for Saᶜīd at the story's final denouement. For this reason it is also mentioned that Sayf al-Mulūk did not touch her while they were wandering across the ocean on a raft. Dawlat Khātūn has to be delivered to Saᶜīd intact.

This prudency is less excusable, however, in the case of Badīᶜ al-Jamāl. To the dismay of the reader, when she hears about Sayf al-Mulūk's infatuation for her, she starts philosophizing about the incompatibility of humans and djinns, stating that a union between them is completely impossible. Even after she has seen Sayf al-Mulūk's beauty, she remains reluctant because, according to her, humans are not faithful. She cites the example of Solomon: 'Son of a king, I fear that I will not find love and affection with you when I give myself completely to you, because man possesses little good and is often volatile. Know that our Lord Solomon, son of David, once loved Bilqīs, but when he saw another woman more beautiful than she, he left her.'[11] Her grandmother adds bitterly: 'How could there ever be harmony between humans and jinns?'[12]

These statements are somewhat ironic, of course, because, from the perspective of humans, it is rather the jinn who are volatile. Moreover, the whole story was set in motion by Badīᶜ al-Jamāl's grandmother sending the robe with her granddaughter's image sewn into it to Solomon, hoping that he would be inclined to marry her. This same Solomon, a potential, no, ideal, son-in-law has now become the paragon of infidelity. Apparently, all those involved in the end acknowledge the futility of these arguments and the couple swear loyalty to each other. A double wedding takes place, but after all the deliberations there is no energy left to muster for a passionate closing scene. In contrast to the story of Sayf al-Mulūk, 'The Nightingale's Eye' contains a passionate scene between Gillian and her jinn, possibly the only detailed description of a sexual encounter between a jinn and a woman in decent literature. Although the description shows some ingenuity, it is still limited in space and passion, but it makes up for the other unfulfilled expectations. At least the reader has a glimpse of how such a union can take place, and she can be reassured that it is indeed possible.

It is ironic, perhaps, that whereas sexuality is such an important motif in both stories, its occurrence is rather subdued. As suggested above, this is caused by several kinds of restrictions. The first restriction is, of course, propriety. Since in the pre-modern Arabic-Islamic imagination the phenomenon of the jinn was a potential reality, it had to be treated with care. Encounters between humans and jinns had moral and even legal implications. It is remarkable in this respect that while the marriage of Saᶜīd and Dawlat Khātūn – both

[11] Night 775.

[12] Night 776.

human – is confirmed by witnesses and a contract, the bond between Sayf al-Mulūk and Badīᶜ al-Jamāl is not established legally. Propriety not only prevents a description of a physical union between the two lovers, it even eliminates the suggestion that a legal matrimony between jinns and humans is admissible, possible, or imaginable at all. From the beginning to the end, the storyteller is aware of his limitations: he uses his imagination not to cross moral and social boundaries, but to reconfirm them.

The second restriction is imposed by narrative conventions. When dealing with jinns, especially in relation to women, the space for fantasizing seems boundless. The storyteller has to show his proficiency by evading the trap of exuberance and extravagance, and finding the right balance between the strange and the plausible. It is his task to fit the potentially unlimited material into narrative conventions that will enable him to convey his message. As Gillian astutely realizes, she should respond mindfully and sensibly to the offer of three wishes by the jinn. They should be wishes that will not radically alter her life, but rather make her present life more bearable. This may be a symptom of modesty, but it is also a law of narration that the potential forces evoked by the narrator should be used to serve his aim. After all, although sexuality and eroticism are so central in the two stories, they are not the main theme. The stories are not about indulgence in fantasy and bliss, but about people who enter a new phase of their lives with a little help from jinns and their imagination.

EPILOGUE

Some time after finishing this article I, quite accidentally, came across the translation by Aditya Behl of a Hindavī Sufi romance entitled the *Mirigāvatī*, which was written in 1503 by the Chishtī mystical poet Qutban Suhravardī.[13] The story is about a prince who falls in love with a magic doe, the symbol of a divine spirit. The prince conquers her, but she leaves him, and he has to set out to a faraway city in search of her. Although Behl discusses the parallels between this romance and the well-known cycle of Sindbād in the *Thousand and one Nights* extensively in his study accompanying the translation,[14] he apparently failed to notice the striking resemblance to the story of 'Sayf al-Mulūk'. In the romance, as in 'Sayf al-Mulūk', the prince rescues a princess captured by a demon and held imprisoned in a distant palace; he burns out the eyes of a man-eating giant; and he has to flee from an island with serpents. Moreover, the romance contains several motifs that are reminiscent of other stories from the *Thousand and One Nights*, such as the prohibition against opening a specific door in the palace.

Although this is not the place to speculate about the philological relationship between the stories of Sayf al-Mulūk and the *Mirigāvatī*, it seems relevant to supplement our discussion of 'Sayf al-Mulūk' with the observation that, intriguingly, in the *Mirigāvatī* the union between the prince and his demon-wife is elaborately and poetically described, in

[13] Aditya Behl (tr.), *The magic doe; Qutban Suhravardī's* Mirogâvatî, edited by Wendy Doniger, Oxford University Press, Oxford 2012.

[14] Aditya Behl, *Love's subtle magic; an Indian Islamic literary tradition 1379-1545*, edited by Wendy Doniger, Oxford University Press, Oxford 2012.

a quite explicit fashion. Perhaps disappointingly, it is the princess who relates her euphoric experience to her friends, and we learn nothing about the erotic proficiency of the princess. Of course, this makes the reader wonder how the difference between the two stories should be explained. Is 'Sayf al-Mulūk' a bowdlerized version of an Indian predecessor? Is the *Mirigāvatī* based on 'Sayf al-Mulūk' and re-shaped in accordance with the new cultural/ social environment? Does the Indian context allow a larger measure of erotic frankness?

WORKS CITED

Aditya Behl, *Love's Subtle Magic; an Indian Islamic literary tradition 1379–1545*, ed.Wendy Doniger (Oxford: Oxford University Press, 2012).

Aditya Behl (trans.), *The Magic Doe; Qutban Suhravardî's* Mirigâvatî, ed. Wendy Doniger (Oxford: Oxford University Press, 2012).

A.S. Byatt, 'The Djinn in the Nightingale's Eye,' in: *The Djinn in the Nightingale's Eye: five fairy stories*, (London: Chatto & Windus 1994), pp. 93–277.

Fred Leemhuis, 'Épouser un djinn? Passé et présent,' *Quaderni di Studi Arabi*, vol. 11 (1993), pp. 179–192.

Ulrich Marzolph and Richard van Leeuwen (eds.), *The Arabian Nights Encyclopedia*, 2 vols. (Santa Barbara, CA: ABC-CLIO, 2004).

Badr al-Dīn al-Shiblī, *Kitāb ākām al-marjān fī aḥkām al-jānn*, s.l. 1326H, pp. 66–72.

13

The Obscenity of Sexual Torture

Roger Allen

The theme of '*mujūn*' that has been selected for this volume in honour of a pre-eminent scholar in Arabic literature is one that has been critically applied in the main to the creative writings of Arabic of littérateurs in the pre-modern era and indeed – following the predominant trends in literature recorded in textual form over the course of those centuries – primarily to modes of poetic expression. That is not to say, of course, that the theme is not to be found in other forms and genres of literary expression and, at least potentially, in modern and contemporary works as well, but rather that the lion's share of critical attention seems to have focused on pre-modern poetry. Whence my personal difficulty, at least initially, in identifying a topic that I might contribute to this volume as a specialist in modern Arabic narrative genres.

All that said however, Everett Rowson draws attention (in his article on '*mujūn*' in the *Encyclopedia of Arabic Literature*) to the term's connection to profligacy, particularly in matters of wine-drinking and sex, but it is his reference to '*sukhf*', a word whose semantic field he describes as 'upsetting the squeamish', that provides me with the link to my own topic here, the issue of sexual perversion and its use as a method of torture as exemplified in the recent novel, *Muʿadhdhibatī*, by the Moroccan novelist (and Minister of Culture), BenSalim Himmich.[1] However, before I consider this specific work of fiction, I will place the topic – albeit briefly – within the broader context of prison literature within modern Arabic fiction.[2]

[1] BenSalim Himmich, *Muʿadhdhibatī*, Cairo: Dar al-Shurūq, 2010. The novel was short-listed for the Arab Booker Prize in 2011, but the award was shared between another Moroccan littérateur (and former Minister of Culture), Muḥammad al-Ashʿarī, and Rajāʾ ʿĀlam from Saudi Arabia. For Rowson's article on '*mujūn*', see *Encyclopedia of Arabic Literature,* eds. Julie Scott Meisami and Paul Starkey (London: Routledge, 1998), vol. 2, pp. 546–8. I should also note that 'Himmich' is the author's preferred spelling of his name, although the normal transliteration of Arabic into Anglophone alphabets would require 'Himmīsh'.

[2] I have in fact discussed this topic in a previous article, 'Arabic Fiction and the Quest for Freedom', in 'The Quest for Freedom in Modern Arabic Literature', Essays in Honour of Mustafa Badawi, *Journal of Arabic Literature* 26.1–2 (1995): pp. 37–49.

The use of prisons and torture by the security forces of the newly independent Arab nations in the 1950s and '60s has been well documented; indeed details of the phenomenon have more recently been amplified by the comments and memories of those involved in the movements of change in the region in 2011. Incarceration and torture have also served as topics for a number of novels and indeed of a small library of critical works that have analysed them. In the article mentioned above (note 2) I commented in some detail on the work of the Syrian writer, Nabīl Sulaymān, both his novel, *Al-Sijn* (1972) and his article, 'Naḥwa adab al-sujūn',[3] before analysing in greater detail two novels that are much concerned with the subject: Sunʿallāh Ibrāhīm's *Tilka al-rāʾiḥa*[4] and ʿAbd al-Raḥmān Munīf's *Sharq al-mutawassiṭ*.[5] In a chapter of Jean Fontaine's study on the modern Arabic novel that is devoted to the central and lively novelistic tradition to be found in Egypt, he provides a list of the novelists who have themselves spent significant amounts of time in prison.[6] Najīb Maḥfūẓ (d. 2006) would appear to have been an exception, although reports suggest that it was only the intervention of the then Egyptian Minister of Culture, Tharwat ʿUkāsha, that prevented him from suffering the same fate as a result of governmental dissatisfaction with his commentary on Egyptian society, and especially its cultural sector, in the novel, *Tharthara fawq al-Nīl*, in 1966.[7] In fact, Maḥfūẓ was to address himself to the issues of prison and torture in more specific detail in two separate works, *Al-Marāyā* and *Al-Karnak*, both of which reflect the recriminatory atmosphere that characterized Egypt in the aftermath of President ʿAbd al-Nāṣir's (Nasser's) death in 1970 – a process that in Maḥfūẓ case might be termed one of 'looking back in anger'.[8] The dates of publication of these two works might suggest that *Al-Marāyā* (1972) was composed first, and yet, as far as I am aware, *Al-Karnak* is the only novel by Maḥfūẓ that specifically notes on its final page the date when it was completed (Dec. 1971). The fact that the novel was not to appear in book form until 1974 – a highly lengthy and thus unusual time-period where the publication of his novels in book form is concerned – suggests that the contents of the novel may well have been subjected to adverse censorial scrutiny. Indeed, the fact that the novel recounts the experiences of young students in prison during the 1960s and their gruesome torture at the hands of the Secret Police is narrated through a series of sections named after each of them in turn (and furthermore that the one who dies under torture – Ismāʿīl al-Shaykh – has no section of his own) raises the possibility that the published version of this short novel may not in fact be in its complete original form.[9] It is thus, it would appear, at exactly

[3] *Al-Mawqif al-adabī* 3.1–2 (1973): pp. 137–41. See also Samar Rūḥī Fayṣal, *Al-Sijn al-siyāsī fī al-riwāyah al-ʿArabiyyah*, Damascus: Manshūrāt Ittiḥād al-Kuttāb al-ʿArab, 1983.

[4] Cairo: Maktabat al-Anglo-Miṣriyyah, 1971 (English trans., *The Smell of It*, London: Heinemann, 1971).

[5] Beirut: Al-Muʾassasa al-ʿArabiyya li-al-Dirāsāt wa-al-Nashr, 1979.

[6] *Romans arabes modernes*, Tunis: IBLA, 1992, p. 12.

[7] Cairo: Maktabat Miṣr, 1966 (English trans. *Adrift on the Nile*, Cairo: AUC Press, 1993).

[8] *Al-Marāyā*, Cairo: Maktabat Miṣr, 1972 (English trans.., *Mirrors*, Minneapolis: Bibliotheca Islamica, 1977, 2nd illustrated ed., Cairo: AUC Press, 1999); *Al-Karnak*, Cairo: Maktabat Miṣr, 1974 (English trans., *Karnak Café*, Cairo: AUC Press, 2007).

[9] *Al-Karnak* was made into a highly exploitative film in 1975, directed by ʿAlī Badrkhān and starring the renowned film-actress, Suʿād Ḥusnī, whose rape in prison is graphically portrayed in the film

the same time-period that Maḥfūẓ is also composing the set of fifty-five vignettes of Egyptians that make up the contents of *Al-Marāyā*. In the case of both 'Aḥmad Qadrī' and 'ʿAshmāwī Galāl', however, we are only presented with the narrator's comments on these two Egyptians accused of torture, the former a childhood friend who claims that he was only doing his job ('We tortured like you fill out a form or write a report to the minister – only a job with its scale of excellence in performing public duties'),[10] and the latter an almost legendary figure from the era of the 1919 Revolution and its aftermath ('News of him ran like tales of horror: that he killed with no mercy, that he tortured his victims, tying students to his horse and galloping away, his victim dragged behind, mangled by stones and asphalt until dead').[11]

The modern Arabic novel is thus no stranger to the theme of imprisonment and torture, and throughout the various phases of the genre's development. Many of the phenomena depicted in the works cited above (and many others as well) find a direct reflection in the famous study, *Surveiller et punir* (1975; English trans., *Discipline and Punish*, 1977) by Michel Foucault. In that work he provides a valuable historical and theoretical background to this particular subgenre of fiction and the critical modes of its analysis and, above all, the way in which prison creates its own kind of society and societal norms, both of them mirrors of the society and age in which prisons exist and function. He explores the ways in which incarceration has moved from earlier ideals of humanitarian reform to a system involving the exercise of power, and particularly power over the body, as expressed through the categories of torture, punishment and discipline and the institution of the prison. In earlier times torture itself had been applied through public display, exemplified by such institutions as the Inquisition. The aim of such spectacles was to show the power of the Church as exercised through the will of the sovereign and, needless to say, to serve as a warning to those adherents of other faiths who would thereby be persuaded, or, more accurately, terrorized, to convert. The practice of public hangings, beheadings and corporal punishment, now abolished in most Western nations but still in practice in certain Middle Eastern countries, is presumably based on the same logic. However, the very process of removing such public acts from view and, more recently, of attempting to redefine what torture actually is can be regarded in many ways as not only a more sinister but also a more cogent exercise of power, in that precise details concerning its performance are thereby mostly restricted to the enforcement arms of the authorities involved.

Foucault's discussion, briefly described above, concerning the transfer of punishment procedures from the public domain to the highly controlled environment of prison and the role of torture in the process is, needless to say, of direct relevance to any discussion of BenSalim Himmich's novel, *Muʿadhdhibatī*, that is my primary focus here, in that the novel takes as its context and major theme the practice of what has been termed 'extraordinary rendition'. In particular, Foucault's emphasis on power being exercised over the human body through imprisonment is illustrated in graphic form within the novel's

– leading some commentators to term it the symbolic rape of Egypt by security forces during the 1960s.

[10] *Al-Marāyā*, p. 27; *Mirrors* [1999 ed.], p. 22.

[11] *Al-Marāyā*, p. 304; *Mirrors* [1999 ed.], p. 140.

narrative. The basic definition of this procedure, one about which there is – once again, needless to say – a good deal that remains unknown, has involved the transfer of citizens of one country or region to another for the purpose of interrogation.[12] In the wake of the attack on the World Trade Center in New York in September 2001 ('9/11'), the United States security agencies (and notably the Central Intelligence Agency) instituted a program whereby suspected 'terrorists' were abducted from their places of residence, wherever that happened to be, and transported by air to other countries (often via so-called 'black sites') where they were often liable to be tortured. Here is not the place to discuss in detail the lengthy and elaborate discussions concerning the widely acknowledged illegality of this procedure and the consequences of debates over its implementation within the legal frameworks of both the United States and Europe, but merely to point out that such a case of 'extraordinary rendition' forms the starting point for Himmich's novel.

It is the novel's narrator who, following extraordinary rendition, is to suffer at the hands – and other parts of the body – of the novel's title figure, a woman of apparently French origins nicknamed "Mama Ghūla" (Mother Ghoul). I have rendered the title of the novel into what may well be an English neologism, namely 'torturess', in order both to underline the feminine gender of the original Arabic and to accentuate the highly unusual circumstance, it would appear, of utilizing a woman and especially a woman's body in the exercise of torture involving male internees.[13] The narrator's name is Ḥammūda, we learn, and he hails from the Eastern Moroccan city of Oujda, where he operates a bookstore. His own statements throughout the narrative and his regular invocations and prayers make it clear that he is a devout Muslim; indeed, at one point during his lengthy incarceration (the exact length of which we only discover at the conclusion of the narrative) he is appointed as the prisoners' *muftī*.[14] However it is the activities of his cousin, al-Ḥusayn al-Masmūdī, a member – we later learn – of a jihadist group operating in the Atlas Mountains, that appear to arouse the interest of the security forces who subject Ḥammūda to 'rendition'. As he himself notes about the process involved:

> I have no real memory of what happened or how I came to find myself in this detention center...All I can recall is that three masked men who said they were from the secret police dragged me out of my book-store... and led me to a grimy car with dirty number-plates. Shoving me inside, they blindfolded me, then gave me an injection of some kind that made me lose consciousness very quickly. When I came round, I could sense that there were other people around me along with a loud noise that may well have been the sound of a helicopter.[15]

Needless to say, the exact location of this 'detention center' and indeed the precise

[12] To cite an editorial from the *New York Times* (Dec. 16th, 2011, p. A38) that comments on the procedure in retrospect, the American President claimed – in the aftermath of the September 2001 attack on the World Trade Center – 'the inherent power to detain anyone he chose, for as long as he chose, without a trial; to authorize the torture of prisoners; and to spy on Americans without a warrant'.

[13] As I compose this essay [early 2012], my translation of Himmich's novel into English, from which the extracts below are taken, is under consideration for publication.

[14] *Muᶜadhdhibatī*, p. 189.

[15] *Muᶜadhdhibatī*, p. 17.

nationalities of its personnel are initially unknown and undisclosed. However, the overall context of the system soon becomes clear to Ḥammūda:

> What was now completely clear and not subject to the slightest doubt was that this secret prison of undefined location was being directed by unknown foreign agencies. The policies were being implemented by people from a variety of nationalities (and I had encountered Arabs up close). Within that system I had been programmed to go through a variety of trials and examinations, duly labeled torture, mistreatment and brain-washing. Once I had managed to survive the worst of these dreadful processes through my own endurance, I would then be a candidate for one of a number of disgusting positions that were in hot demand from the spy agencies that were clearly in charge. Those positions included agents who would infiltrate opposition groups, others who would collect valuable information, others who would become hired assassins, and still others whose functions I neither knew nor could conceive.[16]

Among the variety of 'trials and examinations' that Ḥammūda is forced to endure are exposure to the treatment of a variety of guards in different segments of the prison,[17] cell-blocks subjected to intense noise, the placement of 'plants' – other 'prisoners' who actually are not in that category – in Hamūda's cell itself and both the exercise-yard and cafeteria (when and if he is allowed access to them), and fake firing-squads.[18] However, the most direct method takes the form of cross-examinations involving two primary figures. The first is the Investigating Judge, a fellow-Arab, it would appear from his lengthy discussions of the pedantries of correct Arabic language-use and his delight in debates on literature and style, who, in justifying the methods of torture employed by the second figure, Mama Ghūla (the 'torturess'), reveals to Hammūda and the reader exactly who those 'foreign agencies' are:

> She should be punished not merely for what she's done to you but also because, when it comes to monstrous conduct and illicit behavior, she has no peer; when it comes to terror and violence, no one else comes even close. But how can I be blamed when Uncle Sam has written her a blank cheque? What am I supposed to do? The Yankees have given her a green light – in fact, it's so green that there's nothing fresher and greener. And, if you've never heard of the Yankees and Uncle Sam, then let me tell you that it's the Americans..."[19]

It is only when the efforts of this Judge to persuade Ḥammūda (and other prisoners) to reveal information about themselves, their 'terrorist activities', and, in Ḥammūda's case, the whereabouts and activities of his cousin, fail to produce the needed results that they are consigned to Mama Ghūla's ministrations. The sequence of the narrative manages to provide a terrifying accumulative picture of this fiendish woman, but the narrator's first

---

16 *Muʿadhdhibatī*, p. 133.

17 In the narrator's own words: 'What curs they are! Worse than children with no faith or creator!' *Muʿadhdhibatī*, p. 181.

18 *Muʿadhdhibatī*, pg. 255.

19 *Muʿadhdhibatī*, p. 125. The presence of Americans at the detention center is confirmed later when Ḥammūda the narrator finds himself waiting in a bar where the majority of the clientele are Americans (p. 238). In the final 'scenario' of the narrative, an evening entertainment at the prison, an American 'expert' on Islam is brought in to give a lecture (pp. 264–5).

actual view of her occurs when he participates in a vicious soccer game that she is supposedly refereeing between the prisoners and a set of thugs who essentially flatten their opposition.[20] Soon afterwards however it is his turn in the torture chamber about which he has already heard so much. As one of the narrator's cell-mates has warned him:

> They'll hand you over to the professional torturess who's an expert in all kinds of degradation and torture. The worst of them she's learned in specialized foreign centers, but she's also invented others of her own that she delights in testing on imprisoned suspects like you and me. Compared with the torture she inflicts, the torments of the grave are a joke, kid's play. I don't want you to fall prey to the woman they call Mama Ghūla – and may God protect you from her barbaric madness![21]

Once again, the reader's attention is drawn here to the 'specialized foreign centers' where Mama Ghūla has received training, but it is the 'other' methods of torture that inject into the narrative aspects of sexual perversion that are indeed more than liable to 'upset the squeamish'. Indeed they involve 'degrading' practices that are so extreme as not only to cause maximum harm and offense to those prisoners who adhere to beliefs of Islam and the norms of Arab society, but also to replicate in the reader's mind the general outrage generated by the release of the photographs taken inside the Abu Ghraib Prison in Iraq and the debates over the practice and very legitimacy of 'water-boarding'.[22] At least with the narrator Ḥammūda, the sexual nature of the torture could hardly be more explicit:

> Pulling me towards her with a laugh, she started squeezing me in her tattooed arms and her ample bosom, just like a mother with her suckling child. I felt completely helpless and stunned as I found myself compulsorily rubbing up against her vile body, confronting her lewd and distracted expression, and smelling her body-sweat with its cheap and nasty perfume... 'Listen, cheri,' she told me, 'this breast isn't the last piece of bandage. What do you think of it? Do you like it? Tell me the truth. It's yours; you're going to suckle from it and kiss it. But if you bite it, like that dog who came before you, then I'll castrate you with no mercy. You can still ejaculate, I trust...' With one hand she thrust her breast into my mouth, and with the other she grabbed my penis as though it were a piece of dough. She started feeling and squeezing it as though to measure and weigh it. I started moaning, and that led to her to interpret things in her own debauched and perverted fashion. 'Not bad,' she yelled, 'not bad.' [23]

It is only when these procedures fail to achieve their goals that the torturess resorts to other means of physical abuse – stubbing out lighted cigarettes on his body, hanging him upside down, thrusting a bottle into his anus, and then ruing the fact that he is too thin

[20] *Muʿadhdhibatī*, pp. 88–93.

[21] *Muʿadhdhibatī*, p. 49.

[22] A detailed investigation of the Abu Ghraib Prison is: Seymour M. Hersh, *Chain of Command: The Road from 9/11 to Abu Ghraib*. New York: HarperCollins, 2004. The literature on water-boarding – particularly following revelations in 2007 of its use by the American Central Intelligence Agency, its lengthy history as a form of torture, and its (il-)legality, is enormous. The narrator is 'water-boarded' during a second torture session: *Muʿadhdhibatī*, pp. 149–50.

[23] *Muʿadhdhibatī*, pp. 97–8.

to scrape off parts of his flesh as she has done with other victims.[24] At a later session aimed at forcing Ḥammūda to talk, she makes still more egregious use of her female body as a torture device, a process termed 'hot suffocation':

> The female ghoul now came over and sat cross-legged on my face. I could feel her press one of her orifices over my nose which prevented me from breathing and forced me to smell her foul gases and disgusting body odors. She only relaxed her revolting grip a little in order to ask if I was ready to cooperate. Yet once she realized that I was still maintaining my stance, she simply resumed her position.[25]

Even with this, Mama Ghūla is still not finished with her attempts at using forms of sexual torture in order to extract 'information' from this particular victim. In a truly grotesque scene, Ḥammūda later finds himself in bed with his torturess. She claims that they are married and even brings in 'witnesses' to corroborate her story. As if that is not enough, she enlivens the events of the night by summoning her 'court-jester', a midget who specializes in telling dirty jokes. In spite of the utterly gruesome context of its narration within the novel in question, the following anecdote from the midget's repertoire may even be deemed an appropriate contribution in the context of this volume devoted to the topic of '*mujūn*':

> He told another story about an Egyptian from the South who took his wife to the gynecologist. When the doctor was alone with her and told her to take her undergarment off, she ran out to her husband in the waiting-room screaming and complaining. He scolded her and told her to do as the doctor asked. When she went back inside and the doctor asked her again to remove her undergarment, she replied flirtatiously: 'Take yours off first.' On the way home, the husband told his wife that the doctor clearly had a big brain, as big as this...To which his wife responded: 'Yes, and his penis is that big too!' 'Did you do it with him?' he asked her. 'You told me to,' she said. 'As of tomorrow, you're divorced,' he replied.[26]

Bearing in mind the vicious and perverted ways in which Mama Ghūla has utilized sexual perversion as a means of assaulting the unfortunate inmates of this detention center, it is hardly surprising, indeed perhaps fitting, that her own demise should result from violent confrontation. At a grotesque evening entertainment organized for the prisoners by the 'administration' – all of whose principals are present, an enormous, deaf-mute black guard is invited to play his drum. As his expert performance works his audience up into a frenzy of action and movement, Mama Ghūla gets to her feet and rides on the black drummer's back, noting, as she does so, that she has previously been a wild-animal tamer. Suddenly the drummer throws her to the ground and delivers a series of deadly blows before he is shot dead by guards. With that the entertainment is brought to a rapid and chaotic close.[27]

The narrator's 're-rendition' is brought about through the intervention of the medical authorities at the center and with the tacit support of Naʿīma, one of the succession of

[24] *Muʿadhdhibatī*, pp. 108–9.
[25] *Muʿadhdhibatī*, pp. 148–9.
[26] *Muʿadhdhibatī*, pp. 216–7.
[27] *Muʿadhdhibatī*, pp. 273–4.

secretaries to the Investigating Judge, she being a fellow Moroccan to whom the entire narrative is addressed at its beginning and end.[28] She provides Ḥammūda with a vial of blood so that he can replicate the symptoms of tuberculosis in yet another interview with the Judge. However the circumstances of his release and return to his homeland are as obscure as those of his arrival:

> They must have re-injected me with a powerful, long-lasting sedative several times during my transfer; I had not the slightest sense of its mode, method, or duration. I woke up to find myself in the shade of a palm tree with a bag containing some conserved food, bottles of water, and Moroccan money. I was able to confirm that I was back in my beloved homeland when a camel driver came up and asked me in the purest Moroccan colloquial if I needed any help. After thanking him for his offer, I asked him what the date was. He told me it was Wednesday in the Muslim month, Rabiᶜ ath-thani 1425; in the Western calendar the 17th of May, 2006. So, I muttered to myself, I've been in prison for five years.[29]

As the narrative reaches its conclusion, Ḥammūda has begun the process of resuming something approaching a normal life in the Oujda region. In fact, thanks to the good offices of a local shaykh, he is now residing in the plains outside the city at the house of an elderly widow whose daughter, Zaynab, he has married. It is in such quiet rural surroundings that he can begin his life afresh and write a record of his horrendous experiences.

****

Himmich's novel, *Muᶜadhdhibatī*, certainly provides its readers with disconcertingly convincing testimony as to the efficacy of the institution of incarceration and in particular its effects on the body as outlined in the work of Michel Foucault cited earlier. The seemingly endless months of confinement in a variety of cell-blocks, the modes of 'discipline' imposed by guards and custodians of different nationalities and temperaments, and the utterly disconcerting ignorance of the location of place and the passage of time (the last, as just noted, only discovered by the narrator at the time of his release), all these factors combine to render the victims of the process both mentally and physically weakened as they confront their interrogators. It is in such a context that the rugged resistance of the narrator is all the more remarkable, particularly in view of the appalling sexual taunts and assaults to which he is subjected by the title character. However, while the very levels of violence, intimidation and sheer debauchery practiced in this particular detention center – albeit depicted via the traditionally effective critical armament of fiction – suggest that a very particular kind of 'society' has been created, they raise a whole series of issues as to the values of that broader society that, according to Foucault, such an institution is supposed to reflect.

The sheer brutality and sexual perversion depicted in Himmich's novel, examples of which have been cited above, are clearly sufficient to 'upset the squeamish', to cite Rowson's criteria for '*sukhf*'. Beyond that however, it clearly presents in its fictional guise a more than implicit challenge to society (or perhaps societies) to consider the ways in which

---

[28] *Muᶜadhdhibatī*, pp. 9 and 286.

[29] *Muᶜadhdhibatī*, pp. 276–7.

its/their values have been and still are reflected in the very existence of such institutions (and the prisons of Abu Ghraib, Guantanimo, and, no doubt, others elsewhere – unknown or unacknowledged).

This article is dedicated to my academic colleague, co-editor, and fellow-musician, Geert Jan van Gelder, as a small tribute to his enormously important career, his immense erudition, and his wonderful sense of humor – all of which will be missed by his colleagues. I wish him well as he joins me in retirement.

WORKS CITED

Roger Allen, 'Arabic Fiction and the Quest for Freedom', in 'The Quest for Freedom in Modern Arabic Literature', Essays in Honour of Mustafa Badawi, *Journal of Arabic Literature* 26.1–2 (1995): pp. 37–49.

Samar Rūḥī Fayṣal, *Al-Sijn al-siyāsī fī al-riwāya al-ʿArabiyya* (Damascus: Manshūrāt Ittiḥād al-Kuttāb al-ʿArab, 1983).

Jean Fontaine, *Romans arabes moderns* (Tunis: IBLA, 1992).

Michel Foucault, *Surveiller et punir* ([Paris]: Gallimard, 1975); English trans., *Discipline and Punish* (London: Allen Lane, 1977).

Seymour M. Hersh, *Chain of Command: the road from 9/11 to Abu Ghraib* (New York: HarperCollins, 2004).

BenSalim Himmich, *Muʿadhdhibatī* (Cairo: Dār al-Shurūq, 2010).

Sunʿallāh Ibrāhīm, *Tilka al-rāʾiḥa* (Cairo: Maktabat al-Anglo-Miṣriyya, 1971); English trans., *The Smell of It* (London: Heinemann, 1971).

Najīb Maḥfūẓ, *Al-Karnak* (Cairo: Maktabat Miṣr, 1974); English trans., *Karnak Café* (Cairo: AUC Press, 2007).

Najīb Maḥfūẓ, *Al-Marāyā* (Cairo: Maktabat Miṣr, 1972); English trans., *Mirrors* (Minneapolis: Bibliotheca Islamica, 1977, 2nd illustrated ed./Cairo: AUC Press, 1999).

Najīb Maḥfūẓ, *Tharthara fawq al-Nīl* (Cairo: Maktabat Miṣr, 1966); English trans., *Adrift on the Nile* (Cairo: AUC Press, 1993).

ʿAbd al-Rahmān Munīf, *Sharq al-mutawassiṭ* (Beirut: Al-Muʾassasa al-ʿArabiyya li-al-Dirāsāt wa-al-Nashr, 1979).

Everett Rowson, '*Mujūn*', *Encyclopedia of Arabic Literature,* eds. Julie Scott Meisami and Paul Starkey (London: Routledge, 1998), vol. 2, pp. 546–8.

Nabīl Sulaymān, 'Naḥwa adab al-sujūn', *Al-Mawqif al-adabī* 3.1–2 (1973): pp. 137–41.

14

Modern Arabic Literature and the Disappearance of *Mujūn*: Same-Sex Rape as a Case Study

Frédéric Lagrange

Sexuality is no longer a discursive taboo in modern Arabic fiction, as has been amply proved by many recent novels and novellas.[1] Homosexual behaviours and/or identities in particular have now become almost as regularly alluded to as they were in pre-modern texts, after the long colonial-era parenthesis. But the humorous element so pervasive in mediaeval texts is now absent: 'deviant' sexualities are mostly perceived in terms of individual suffering, as a metaphor for political oppression, as a 'trope of national decline,'[2] or as a social issue caused by gender segregation. *Mujūn* (ribaldry, debauchery and shamelessness),[3] a topos of pre-modern Islamicate literatures essentially linked to laughter

---

[1] See Hanadi Al-Samman, 'Out of the Closet: Representation of Homosexuals and Lesbians in Modern Arabic Literature', *Journal of Arabic Literature* 39 (2008), 270–310. This does not mean that novels cannot be forbidden at times because of explicit sexual contents, even in relatively 'liberal' countries in the Arab world: from ʿAbduh Wāzin's *Ḥadīqat al-ḥawāss* (1993) banned by the Lebanese law courts to Muḥammad Shukrī's 1973 novel *Al-Khubz al-ḥāfī*, infamously suspended from the American University in Cairo's Arabic curriculum in 1999 following a violent press campaign against Prof. Samia Mehrez, then the inexplicable banning of Ḥaydar Ḥaydar's 1983 *Walīma li-aʿshāb al-baḥr* when it was reprinted in Cairo in 2000, there are numerous examples of State censorship under the pretence of the prosecution of pornography. What I argue is that what gets actually printed and distributed in bookshops (or exchanged in scanned copies on the internet) and escapes censorship is much more important that what sporadically gets blocked for moral/political reasons. I also mean that including sexually explicit passages, whether to shock, arouse or raise the consciousness of the reader, is now quite common, not limited to male authors, and does not endanger one's position in the literary establishment: see Saudi authors Zaynab Ḥifnī and Warda ʿAbd al-Mālik's graphic descriptions of intercourse in their novels (although one suspects these aliases may hide a male author).

[2] See Joseph A. Massad, *Desiring Arabs* (Chicago: The University of Chicago Press, 2007), 310.

[3] E.K. Rowson's definition is particularly concise: 'A term used to describe both a mode of behaviour and a genre of medieval poetry and prose. Closely related [...] to the throwing off of societal restraints, *mujūn* refers behaviourally to open and unabashed indulgence in prohibited pleasures, particularly the drinking of wine and, above all, sexual profligacy. *Mujūn* literature describes and celebrates this hedonistic way of life, frequently employing explicit sexual vocabulary, and almost invariably with

and comedy in which homoeroticism,[4] in its outrageous and transgressive declensions, was a major element, hardly exists anymore, at least in fiction. The ways in which same-sex relations are depicted in contemporary fiction are at odds with the pre-modern literary tradition. Graphic descriptions of intercourse, heterosexual or homosexual, may have become more common in the last decade, some authors may even celebrate the pleasures of the body and seek to arouse their readers, as the Syrian Salwa al-Nuʿaymi does in her acclaimed erotic novel *Burhān al-ʿasal*,[5] which attempts to link modern Arabic literature and Arab identity with the exaltation of desire and pleasure found in mediaeval erotica; but more often than not, the function of crude descriptions of sexual acts is to provide an occasion for the denunciation and condemnation of social dysfunction.[6]

If sexuality is obviously much less linked to humour in modern literature than it was in mediaeval *adab* and poetry, 'revivalist' currents[7] would see this as the sorry consequence of modern rigourism and the untimely adoption by contemporary Islamicate societies of those very Victorian moral values that Western cultures, after centuries of supposed Christian denial of the body, have learnt to forget and have replaced with an open attitude towards sexuality. But is the case so clear-cut? The motif of homosexual rape could be taken as a case study for a comparison between its treatment in the mediaeval sources and in contemporary fiction. The homosexual *dabīb*, i.e. the rape of a male adolescent in his sleep, or the tricks used to lure a young man and abuse him, appear in various forms in a number of mediaeval texts and forced sex between males was one of the most common humorous and erotic scripts of *mujūn* in pre-modern literature and verse; it is still very present in contemporary fiction, although cast in a different light, neither comical, nor (voluntarily) erotic. Forced and non-consensual sex, which was deemed a frivolous but

primarily humorous intent.' *Encyclopedia of Arabic Literature* (London/New York: Routledge, 2010 [1st ed. 1998]), 2: 546.

[4] I will avoid the use of the term homosexuality when dealing with pre-modern literature, see Khaled El-Rouayheb, *Before Homosexuality in the Arab-Islamic World, 1500–1800* (Chicago: The University of Chicago Press, 2005), and Frédéric Lagrange, *Islam d'interdits, Islam de jouissance* (Paris: Téraèdre, 2008). When used, it is not intended as an essentialist concept.

[5] Salwa al-Nuʿaymī, *Burhān al-ʿasal* (Beirut: Riyāḍ al-Rayyis, 2008). English translation: *The Proof of the Honey*, trans. Cal Perkins (New York: Europa Editions, 2009).

[6] This is particularly true of same-sex intercourse, which hardly aims at arousing the reader, see examples analysed by Massad, *Desiring Arabs*, chapter 'Deviant Fictions', 269–334.

[7] By 'revivalist currents' a term I coin here, I mean authors and intellectuals such as René Khawam, Malek Chebel, Abdelwahab Meddeb in France, Hafid Bouazza in Holland, western publishers of mediaeval Arabic erotica (translated or not), such as Manshūrat al-Jamal / Kamel Verlag in Germany, that constitute, consciously or not, an editorial current presenting mediaeval Arab-Islamic societies as cultures allowing pleasure, celebrating the body, and tolerating various irregularities that are presently condemned in contemporary Arab-Islamic societies. This discourse aims at 'rehabilitating' Islamic cultures, both for Western opinion and the liberal readership in Arab-Islamic societies, through this 'uncovering' of a pleasure-tolerant past. As generous and perhaps even necessary as this endeavour might be, in the light of the common negative perception of Islamic cultures, this trend seldom questions what mediaeval texts really say, and in the end proves no less essentialist than the opposite current denouncing Arab-Islamic societies as cultures of eternal repression, see Lagrange, *Islam d'interdits*, 9–28. (In French).

immensely amusing and arousing subject in *adab*, is hardly considered a laughing matter nowadays and forces us to take a closer look at 'the rapist's laugh' of mediaeval lore as opposed to the insistence on the victim's (or the torturer's) shame of contemporary fiction. A clarification: only 'actual' rape as a social phenomenon will be examined here, and the article will not deal with forced homosexual penetration as a political metaphor or allegory denouncing the Arab man's loss of honour, identity or virility when submitted to violence, direct or symbolic, exerted by the State, or the West, or globalization. The political economy of (homo)sexuality, common in many Egyptian and Levantine novels, has already been analysed in depth by Joseph Massad.[8]

MUJŪN AND ITS DISAPPEARANCE

Mujūn, in both its heteroerotic and homoerotic dimensions, remained a legitimate mode of discourse in Arabic prose and poetry until the 19th century. Indeed, the word 'mode' could almost be replaced by 'mood,' in its grammatical sense, for modals alter reality and *mujūn*, likewise, is a ritual discourse that does not necessarily describe something that takes place, but expresses a wish, an accusation, or a fantasy of highly coded forbidden desires. Pre-modern *mujūn* poetry and mediaeval and post-mediaeval *adab* prose that deal with *mujūn* please readers by arousing and/or making them laugh with accounts of transgression – for *mujūn* is not presented as a serious matter and remains linked to humour and jest (*hazl, lahw*). However, this discourse on transgression is not a transgression *per se*, as long as it is enunciated in the right form and at the right time and place. In prose, *mujūn* is a mood because the author seldom takes responsibility for it: anecdotes dealt with are usually attributed to an informant and present a character who is neither the informant nor the author. Even if the author should mention his own experience, his account is not necessarily to be taken for granted and acknowledged as a reality, precisely because his discourse falls within the realm of *mujūn* or *sukhf*[9] (obscenity), where exaggeration and outrage are expected. With regard to verse, it is accepted that *khayr al-shiʿr akdhabuhu* (the best poetry is the most insincere);[10] thus poets do not have to account for the reality of their claims (unless the State or the Prince has some harsh example to set[11]). The

[8] Massad, *Desiring Arabs*. See in particular his analysis of Ṣunʿallāh Ibrāhīm's *Sharaf*, 376–386.

[9] 'Obscenity and scatology, particularly as used in poetry for its shock value and humorous effect [...] Although often paired with *mujūn* in later literature, *sukhf* is distinguished from it in referring less to hedonistic behaviour offensive to the prudish than to gross language and comportment upsetting to the squeamish.' E.K. Rowson, 'sukhf,' *The Routledge Encyclopedia of Arabic Literature*, 743.

[10] Ibn Rashīq al-Qayrawānī, *Al-ʿumda fi maḥāsin al-shiʿr wa-adabih*. In the electronic version downloadable from www.al-mostafa.com, 248. All translations in the article are the author's, unless stated otherwise.

[11] According to the pseudo-biographical elements on Bashshār b. Burd in the *Aghānī*, or on Abū Nuwās in Ibn Manẓūr's *Akhbār Abī Nuwās*, the former's flogging by order of al-Mahdī and the latter's banishment to Egypt under the reign of al-Rashīd had more to do with political reasons than their supposed *zandaqa* or misbehaviours. As a general rule, a poet's *mujūn* doesn't expose him to the ruler's wrath unless it is coupled with political satire or a close relationship with the enemies of the State.

transgression of social or sacred norms is in itself normed: the anomic deeds or sayings alluded to in *mujūn* literature are highly ritualistic and pertain to a closed list of socially and/or sexually transgressive attitudes, usually intertwined and alluded to in clusters: wine-drinking, utterance of crude words referring to sexual organs, sexual intercourse and bodily functions, boasting by men of illicit intercourse with women, of anal penetration of boys, of rape, expression by women of inextinguishable desire in the coarsest terms, hyperbolic description of sexual organs, etc. If pre-modern *mujūn* is often a satire or a subversion of religious lore and sacred laws, it is nevertheless quite conservative on the level of social hierarchies and it confirms male domination: the phallus remains almighty, the free Muslim male, preferably of the *khāṣṣa* (elite), dominates the scene, and marginalized groups remain marginalized when laughter recedes. Poets and prose writers might very well 'successfully deconstruct textual, theological, and social-hierarchical barriers dominating Arabic literature, politics and society',[12] but this Bakhtinian perspective on mediaeval laughter, as we shall argue, underestimates comedy's aptitude at reinforcing the norms that it simultaneously subverts.

One of *mujūn*'s last expressions in pre-modern Arabic literature is probably Fāris al-Shidyāq's *Al-sāq ʿalā al-sāq* (*Crossing Legs*, 1855),[13] which operates, unusually, in a purely heteroerotic declension. This fictional travelogue favours allusive and peculiar vocabulary when dealing with sexuality, whereas mediaeval works preferred to call a spade a spade, and therefore an *ayr* (penis) an *ayr.* But Shidyāq also opens the gates to 'new perversions,' unknown to classical mediaeval *mujūn* and *sukhf* discourse: for instance, he describes with a daunting profusion of details the sexual specialties practised by Parisian women of the mid-nineteenth century (or perhaps French prostitutes; this is not clearly stated, since all Parisian women are believed to have loose morals), and he particularly mentions oral sex, in highly refined and lexically cryptic – though extremely obscene – images:[14] '*fa-minhum man turīd ʿalā ṣifāt al-mudqim, al-ṣifa al-latī dhakarahā Abū Nuwās fī l-hamziyya, wa-minhunna man yuʾthir al-tajaḍḍum al-kamarī ʾaw al-imtilāj al-qunubī*' (Among them some should be qualified as *mudqim*,[15] in the sense Abū Nuwās mentioned in his poem rhyming in *hamza*,[16] while others prefer penile absorption or clitoral mastication). It must be noted that our translation hardly reflects the lexical inventiveness and the utter rarity of those terms and roots, which is such that no educated reader of the 19th century could have been expected to understand precisely the sexual innuendo without an intensive search through its mediaeval lexicon. Oral sex is indeed hardly ever alluded to in classical sources, as E.K.

[12] J.W. Wright, Jr., 'Masculine Allusion and the Structure of Satire,' *Homoeroticism in Classical Arabic Literature* (New York: Columbia University Press, 1997), 16–17.

[13] Translation by Humphrey Davies, *Leg over Leg* (New York: NYU Press, 2013).

[14] Fāris al-Shidyāq, *Al-sāq ʿala al-sāq* (Beirut: Dar al-Raʾid al-ʿArabi, 1982), 626.

[15] According to *Lisān al-ʿArab*, root *d/q/m*: 'The *mudqima* among women is the one whose vagina devours anything, and it has been said that it even makes sound during intercourse.'

[16] Presumably Abu Nuwās's verse '*min yadi dhāti ḥirrin fī ziyyi dhī dhakarin / lahā muḥibbāni lūṭiyyun wa-zannāʾu*' ([wine] served by one with a vagina in the attire of one with a penis / who has two lovers: an active sodomite and a philandering adulterer), i.e. a woman who is seeking both vaginal and anal intercourse.

Rowson rightly remarks.[17] This is another clue that should arouse caution: the mere fact that a fairly common sexual act such as fellatio[18] is virtually unknown to pre-modern Arabic sources suggests how ritual and modal the discourse of *mujūn* is in classical sources.

At the turn of the 20th century though, Shidyāq's *al-Sāq ʿalā al-sāq* had become unbearably obscene for Jurjī Zaydān, who explains in his *Encyclopaedia of Famous Men* (*Mashāhir al-Sharq*):[19]

> [Shidyāq] included in his book words and expressions by which he intended *mujūn*, but it passed the limits to the point that a man of education would never consider uttering them, and one certainly wishes they had never passed through our shaykh's mind and had never been written in his book, for writers' pens should avoid phrases that would make a young man blush, not to mention a maid.

At the same time that this classical work of *adab*[20] was suddenly judged inadequate for a new generation of readers fifty years after its first publication, Muḥammad ʿAbduh decided to castrate Hamadhānī's *Maqāmāt* in his famous edition, still used in schools, for young women were now included in the virtual readership and unmediated silent reading had become the norm. In the *Maqāma mawṣiliyya*, for instance, when the anti-hero Abu al-Fatḥ al-Iskandarī outrageously pretends that a corpse is still alive by putting his finger up its warm anus (*istuhu*), ʿAbduh's edition reads 'under his armpit' (*ibṭuhu*), a lexical alteration which obviously does not fit with the original rhyme (*sajʿ*) of the text (*lamastuhu/istuhu*) but is certainly close enough to take in an inattentive reader.[21] *Adab*, not *muʾaddab* enough, now needed to be *muhadhdhab* (refined).[22]

Khalid El-Rouayheb, in his monograph *Before homosexuality in the Arab-Islamic World 1500–1800* has also shown how the homoerotic contents of Mamluk and Ottoman poetry were gradually erased from literary memory.[23] Not only would new editions of the classics

---

[17] See Everett K. Rowson, 'The Categorization of Gender and Sexual Irregularity in Medieval Arabic Vice Lists' in *Body Guards, The Cultural Politics of Gender Ambiguity*, ed. J. Epstein, K. Straub (New York: Routledge, 1991), 50–79.

[18] Making assumptions about sexual practices of pre-modern Arab societies is certainly problematical, but fellatio is documented in Ancient Egypt (the myth of Isis reviving Osiris through fellatio), Ancient Greece, Mesopotamia, the Roman Empire and the *Kama Sutra*. See Thierry Leguay, *Histoire raisonnée de la fellation* (Paris: Le Cercle, 1999). We believe it is highly improbable that fellatio was unknown to the classic Islamic world, an heir to those civilizations.

[19] Jurjī Zaydān, *Mashāhīr al-Sharq*, 2 vols. (Beirut: Dar Maktabat al-Ḥayāt, n.d.), 2:112.

[20] *Al-Sāq ʿala al-Sāq* is a pivotal text, considered both as one of the last monuments of *adab* in the mediaeval sense of the word, and one of the founding works of modern Arabic literature, see Sabry Hafez, *The Genesis of Arabic Narrative Discourse* (London: Saqi Books, 1993); M. Peled, 'Al-Sāq ʿalā l-sāq, A Generic Definition', *Arabica* 32 (1985), 31–46.

[21] See Badīʿ al-Zamān al-Hamadhānī, *al-Maqāmāt*, ed. Muḥammad ʿAbduh (Algiers: Mufam, 1988), 152, compare with Muhammad Muḥyi al-Dīn ʿAbd al-Ḥamīd, *Sharḥ Maqāmāt al-Hamadhānī* (Beirut: Dar al-Kutub al-ʿIlmiyya, 1979) 113–120, a reprint of Hamadhānī, *al-Maqāmāt*, ed. Muḥammad Muḥyi l-Din ʿAbd al-Ḥamīd (Cairo: Al-Maktaba al-azhariyya, 1324/1923), 108–114.

[22] On the suppression and/or condemnation of the *mujūn* and homoerotic dimension in classical Islamicate literatures, also see Paul Sprachman, *Suppressed Persian* (Costa Mesa: Mazda Publishers, 1995), El-Rouayheb, *Before Homosexuality*, 156–161, Massad, *Desiring Arabs*, 290–301.

[23] El-Rouayheb, *Before Homosexuality*, 63.

of Arabic literary lore be emptied of any material deemed unsuitable for the new reading public created by the development of public education, but no modern *adīb,* at the turn of the twentieth century, would consider dealing with bodily functions, with desire, with sexualities, and with transgressions of social and religious norms as crudely as pre-modern authors. The 'space of transgression' (and specifically of verbal transgression) allowed within the realm of classical *adab* had disappeared in prose fiction.

However, the vanishing of *mujūn* cannot be analysed simply as a sorry consequence of Arabic literature's confrontation with European criteria of decency during the colonial age and its resulting self-censorship, and it cannot be dismissed as the progressive imposition of prudish norms seen as tokens of modernity. The gradual relegation of the crudest forms of *mujūn* to the field of the 'unspoken' or the 'unpublished' is not merely a loss of freedom or a moral restriction imposed upon Arab societies by modernity and the extension of the reading public. It is precisely *because* of its outrageously misogynistic tone, of its celebration of homosociality, of its homoerotic flavour, that this whole corpus of Arabic literature became, during the 19th century, at odds with the evolution of Arab societies as they aimed at redefining the role of 'woman' (*al-marʾa*), an essentialized and abstract entity that was to be the only legitimate object of male desire.

When a previously strictly homosocial world opened itself to (limited) mixing of the sexes in the public space, the norms of literary production had to be modified. This 'new refusal' of obscenity and awkwardness regarding the excesses of the desiring body may be explained by changes in the ways in which literature, along with other cultural productions, was consumed: written works now circulated freely, without the long schooling in textual consumption formerly provided by the shaykh to his pupil. The progress of women's status and rights in Arab societies throughout the 19th and 20th centuries imposed new rules and conventions for a literature now available and legible to a large audience.[24]

One century later, now that the heteronormalization of most Arab urban societies has been gradually achieved, can *mujūn* resurface in new forms of Arabic fiction, and can its homoerotic dimension be brought back to life? In other words, can Arabic literature present same-sex love/sexuality as a fact of life that can be viewed with a smile instead of a frown or a sigh? Thus worded, the question suggests that the reappearance of *mujūn* would enable a desirable rejuvenation of a humorous dimension absent in contemporary literature, where the essential link between sexuality and laughter seems lost. However, this revivalist perspective makes sense only if the mediaeval laugh is suitable for the modern world, which is what I shall next examine.

[24] On heteronormalization in society, Afsaneh Najmabadi's perspective on Iranian society in *Women with Mustaches and Men without Beards, Gender and sexual anxieties of Iranian Modernity* (Berkeley: University of California Press, 2005) can be applied to Arab societies. For literature, in addition to Massad, *op. cit.*, see Lagrange, *Islam d'interdits.* On women's image and essentialization, see Fedwa Malti-Douglas' classic *Woman's body, Woman's word, Gender and Discourse in Arabo-Islamic Writing* (Princeton: Princeton University Press, 1991). The relationship between the expansion of female readership in the Arab world and the heteronormalization of literature still needs to be closely studied.

DABĪB GONE WRONG? THE RAPIST'S LAUGHTER IN MEDIAEVAL *ADAB*

Dabīb in early Umayyad poetry is a common motif of erotic poetry (*ghazal*): the lover 'crawls' (*dabba*) around his lady-love's tent, and surprises her in the middle of the night; she feigns outrage and asks him to leave but ultimately gives in and grants him a whole night of poetry, a kiss, or more. A semantic change occurs in early Abbasid poetry, when *dabīb* comes to mean a form of scenarized rape, usually of homosexual nature, although sometimes heterosexual.[25] 'Consensual *dabīb*' was the original behavioural script, in the sense developed by J. Gagnon;[26] later, 'forced *dabīb*,' i.e., rape, developed as another script. Desire for the narrative's pretty boy and arousal of the reader were triggered by the latter's identification of familiar elements and the unfolding of an oft-repeated scenario. This script includes: a reluctant (or supposedly reluctant) boy, a cunning hero, wine-drinking and induced sleep, the difficulty of undoing the drawstrings of the victim's trousers, penetration, the victim's awakening either during the act or the next morning, the traces of the evil deed, and the final confrontation.

This new form of *dabīb* became a topos in 10th-century *adab*, a change that culminated in entire chapters of mediaeval erotica being given over to *dabīb*.[27] It appeared as a standard episode in folk-tales and the rapist (the *dābb*) developed into a stock-character in the anecdotes of high-literature and poetry, as well as in popular narratives.[28] No more is the enamoured knight given a secret rendezvous by his Bedouin or Umayyad princess; now the *dābb* has become the lascivious lover of adolescents, whether slaves ready to surrender themselves for a few silver coins or free *fityān* (young lads) ready to kill for their honour, and the 'rapist' deploys the most malicious tricks to make them fall into his clutches and penetrate them against their (avowed) will.

The reason for this semantic evolution is probably twofold: in poetry, the 'new' *dabīb* is obviously a parody of Umayyad courtly *dabīb*, as the cunning tricks used to penetrate the desired lad mimic ʿUmar b. Abī Rabīʿa's tricks to enter the lady's tent unnoticed by her tribe. The courtly warrior becomes a rascal, in poems that are an ironical wink at this common motif of 'old' poetry, just as *khamriyya* poetry can include a parody of the *wuqūf ʿalā l-aṭlāl* section of the *qaṣīda* or subvert images of *ʿudhrī* love-poems. The parodic nature of *dabīb* narratives, which speak nonchalantly and jokingly of rape and always seemingly take the rapist's side, laughing with him and rejoicing at his victories, certainly reduces

[25] The 'rape' meaning of *dabīb* is certainly already present at an early period, and the line between surprise and forced sex already crossed: see *Akhbār Sukayna bt. al-Ḥusayn* in Iṣfahānī's *Aghānī*, in which the verb *dabb ʿala* is used by the author when the Umayyad poet al-Farazdaq is caught by a Bedouin whose maid he tried to sleep with at night, betraying his host's hospitality. Jarīr naturally blamed him for this shameful act. But *dabīb* in poetry, at this early exclusively heteroerotic stage, has not yet undergone its mutation.

[26] See John Gagnon, 'The Implicit and Explicit Use of the Scripting Perspective in Sex Research,' *The Annual Review of Sex Research* 1 (1990): 1–44.

[27] See Aḥmad al-Tīfāshī, *Nuzhat al-albāb*, ed. Jamāl Jumʿa (London: Riyad al-Rayyis, 1992), 207–221 and Aḥmad b. Muḥammad b. ʿAlī al-Yamanī [=Ibn Falīta], *Rushd al-labīb ʾilā muʿāsharat al-ḥabīb* (Al-Māya, Libya: Talā, 2006), 133–163.

[28] See for instance Everett K. Rowson analysis of Ibn Dāniyāl's *Lawʿat al-Shākī* in 'Two Homoerotic Narratives from Mamlūk Literature,' *Homoeroticism in Classical Arabic Literature*, 158–191.

their shockingness for a contemporary reader. The parody partly accounts for the fact that *dabīb* is necessarily associated with humour, jest and *hazl*. On the other hand, *dabīb* could not have become a literary script if it were entirely unrelated to social realities and practices. This scenario, narrated from the perspective of the rapist, is simply the other side of popular narratives of young heroes escaping rapists (by cunning or through violence), told from the virtual victim's point of view; both illustrate a fear of male-male rape, at the age when boys are moving toward manhood but have yet to achieve it, and allude to what must have been a reality of pre-modern societies.[29] As explained by Walter G. Andrews and Mehmet Kalpaklı in their book *The Age of the Beloveds, Love and The Beloved in Early-Modern Ottoman and European Culture and Society*:

> Beneath the surface violence of love rhetoric in the Age of the Beloveds – the language of war and self-defense, of swords and daggers, bows and arrows [...] lies a subtext of sexual violence. In both Europe and the Ottoman Empire, where it was common for mature men and youths to seek sexual relations with quite young boys and women, sexual violence was widespread [....] it is true that actual sexual violence (as opposed to the symbolic or displaced violence of the stories) was a problem in the Ottoman Empire as it was in the rest of Europe.[30]

The mediaeval scenario will be examined through two anecdotes (*akhbār*): Ibn Manẓūr's account of Abū Nuwās' adventure with 'The Three Egyptian Lads' and Iṣfahānī's account of the rape of Abū al-Aṣbagh's son in the *Kitāb al-Aghānī*.

The Three Egyptian lads

This anecdote is found in both Abū Hiffān's *Akhbār Abī Nuwās*[31] and Ibn Manẓūr's *Akhbār Abī Nuwās*.[32] The poetic verses upon which the anecdote is constructed are quoted additionally, although with significant variations, in Wagner's edition of Abū Nuwās's *Dīwān*, based on Ḥamza al-Iṣfahānī's collection,[33] and the anonymous collection *Al-fukāha wa-l-iʾtinas fī mujūn Abī Nuwās*.[34]

While walking through the markets of Fusṭāṭ (presently Old Cairo) after having fled Baghdad and joined al-Khaṣīb's court, Abū Nuwās spots three handsome lads, *kaʾannahum al-ṭawāwīs* (as beautiful as peacocks), all three *fityān* of noble origin or sons of rich merchants. He disguises himself as a street porter and proposes to help them take the merchandise they have bought to the house they are sharing. When he reaches their place, he cleans

[29] See for instance the story of Tāj al-Mulūk and Dunyā in the *Arabian Nights*.

[30] Walter G. Andrews and Mehmet Kalpaklı, *The Age of the Beloveds: Love and the Beloved in Early-Modern Ottoman and European Culture and Society* (Durham/London: Duke University Press, 2005), 256–257.

[31] Abu Hiffān, *Akhbār Abī Nuwās*, ed. ʿAbd al-Sattār Aḥmad Farrāj (Cairo: Maktabat Miṣr [ʿUyūn al-adab al-ʿarabī], 1954), 60–66.

[32] Ibn Manẓūr, *Akhbār Abī Nuwās*, ed. *Mulḥaq al-Aghānī* (Beirut: Dār al-Kutub al-ʿIlmiyya, 1992), 179–181.

[33] Abū Nuwās, *Diwān* ed. E. Wagner, 5 vols. (Beirut: Klaus Schwarz Verlag, 2003), 5: 22–23.

[34] *Al-fukāha wa-l-iʾtinās* = Abū Nuwās, *Al-nuṣūs al-muḥarrama*, ed. Jamāl Jumʿa (London: Riyāḍ al-Rayyis, 1998), 60–62.

their house, prepares a delicious dinner, and pours wine until they are so drunk that they fall asleep. He rapes the three of them while they are unconscious, then spreads some saliva between his own thighs, lets his pants down on his ankles, and falls asleep. When the three lads awaken on the next morning, he pretends they are all victims of an unknown rapist: 'Each one of us has become like a young virgin deflowered on her wedding night, so let's eat and drink and enjoy the pleasures of life as she would do with her husband' (an ambiguous sentence and *de facto* avowal of his crime they fail to decipher). They all decide to hush the story so their reputation will not be endangered. But the poet finally decides to change his clothes and reveal himself as the famous Abū Nuwās, by whom they were all afraid to be abused, for his reputation as a *lūṭī* (sodomite) has preceded him. While they are about to hit him, he argues that what is done is done and that they had better finish the remaining wine with him. They reluctantly accept, and he leaves them, reciting verses that tell the whole story.

The anecdote is obviously conceived as a prosaic expansion of elements found in the original verses, whether they are by Abū Nuwās himself or any *mājin* poet of his generation. The prosaic version adds to the poem some symbolically relevant elements and follows a script that involves key items: the well-known predator in disguise; young lads who take the risk of living out of the family cocoon and pay a dear price for it; wine-drinking and its dangers; the tricky opening of the drawstring of the sleeping victim's trousers (*tikkat al-sirwāl*), a challenge that will be turned into an art in Ibn Falīta's *Rushd al-Labīb* (14th century), an obscene parody of treaties on the art of war; abusing a lad while he has passed out; traces of saliva and semen on the thighs; the will to kill then the final surrender to escape dishonour; the public shame of poetry.

The narrative is constructed from the predator's point of view, never from the lads' perspective. Abū Nuwās's verses conclude the anecdote, and readers laugh with him, enjoying his victory and mocking the young men's naivety, for they got what they deserved. The lesson is twofold: (1) young men cannot be protected like girls through seclusion, even if self-imposed, and however hard they try to ward off predators using unnatural ways (living together locked up in their house, not interacting with strangers), their lack of knowledge of the outside world will lead to accident; (2) they failed in their mission of reaching adulthood with an unaltered body (i.e. un-penetrated anus) because they indulged in illicit worldly pleasures (wine). The narrative opens many ambiguous paths, though: Abū Nuwās the *lūṭī* doesn't object to being momentarily seen by the lads as a victim of rectal penetration and he feminizes himself along with them, admitting to have become a *ʿarūs*; the text seems to suggest that if being penetrated is a sorry accident on the path to manhood, it is not a permanent stigma as long as purely accidental and since no pleasure was felt or sought by the victim.[35] The final *coup de théâtre*, when Abū Nuwās identifies himself, seems unnecessary on the plot's level since it exposes him to the lads' desire to take their revenge. From the perspective of mediaeval comedy, though, this revelation is indispensable: without it the trick played on the three boys would be incomplete. They

[35] See the enlightening lines on the significance of feeling pleasure vs. the mere fact of being penetrated in David M. Halperin, *How to Do the History of Male Homosexuality* (Chicago: University of Chicago Press, 2002), 122.

need to know they were played, their arrogant beauty must be soiled, and they have to face their humiliation by drinking wine, however reluctantly, with their rapist. Laughter is triggered by two paradigmatic situations identified by Henri Bergson: repetition (of the *dabīb* scenario played anecdote after anecdote in Ibn Manẓūr's collection, so that the lads' defeat is expected with a smile), and inversion (the shameless *lūṭī* is the one teaching a lesson instead of being punished; the victims are invited to drink and rejoice with their torturer in their own house instead of throwing him out and cannot but accept). This confirms Bergson's hypothesis that 'any arrangement of acts and events is comic which gives us, in a single combination, the illusion of life and the distinct impression of a mechanical arrangement.'[36] The inclusion of this narrative in a series of anecdotes on the devious schemes of the lustful *lūṭī*, in which Abū Nuwās himself is depicted as having once been a *muʾājar* (male prostitute) assuming the passive role and in which other desirable lads (*fityān*) are simultaneously seekers of boys, negates the trauma of rape and laughs it off as a fact of life, certainly better avoided but quite common. Male pleasure is linked to coercion: while Abū Nuwās could have paid some pretty *muʾājar* for sex, it was much more enjoyable for him to trick free, Muslim, rich, reputable, handsome *fityān*, who are *not* supposed to be available for penetration (although they can legitimately be objects of chaste passion). He expresses this conception of desire in these verses, also quoted in Ibn Manẓūr's *Akhbār*: '*Aladhdhu n-nayki mā kāna -ghtiṣābā / bi-manʿi l-ḥibbi ʾaw bi-manʿi r-raqībi*' (*The sweetest fuck is that obtained by coercion / Whether the lover refuses or the censor does).* This conception of pleasure should certainly not be considered a unique social norm or the standard attitude towards pleasure expressed in the realm of mediaeval Islamicate cultures; indeed, a considerable number of erotic treatises advocate that pleasure should be felt by both partners – although such a conception is only to be expressed in the case of heterosexual intercourse. But the *lūṭī* as a literary comic figure must ritualistically defend a posture of aggressive masculinity. Abū Nuwās's argument, shocking by modern standards, should not be taken too seriously: *mujūn* is a parodic mode that subverts the narratives of epic victory and applies its principals to sexuality; it seeks to provoke laughter and pleasant outrage. But the mere fact that this conception of pleasure is seen as amusing in mediaeval literature in the form of *hazl* or *mujūn* or *sukhf*, is in itself indicative of an elitist conception of society. The free Muslim grown-up man is the only dominant element and can deal with bodies other than his own as he wishes, whereas bodies of not-yet-adult males, such as our *fityān*, that are still desirable, may fail to reach maturity and the stage of masculinity without incident.

Mediaeval Arabo-Islamic *adab*, a repository of Aristotelian philosophy, certainly expresses the opinion that 'jesting is witty contumely,' that contumely consisting of 'the disgracing of another for one's own amusement' for those who are chiefly risible are 'those who are in some way inferior, especially morally inferior, although not wholly vicious in character.'[37]

[36] Henri Bergson, *Le rire* (Paris: Quadrige/PUF, 1989 [5th ed]), 53. English translation by C. Brereton, F. Rothwell, available on http://www.authorama.com/laughter-1.html.

[37] Aristotle, *Poetics* ed. and trans. by Stephen Halliwell (London: Loeb 1995), 44, quoted and analysed by Quentin Skinner, 'Hobbes and the Classical Theory of Laughter,' *Visions of Politics*, vol. III Hobbes and Civil Science (Cambridge: Cambridge University Press, 2002), 143.

Laughter is primarily an expression of power and superiority and no mercy is shown for the weak. The surprising ambiguity of such anecdotes is that the laughing man is himself a dubious figure, much more so than his victims. There are two ways to interpret this apparent contradiction: on the one hand, we can argue that the only absolute norm expressed by *mujūn* literature is that of hegemonic masculinity, a norm the *lūṭī* reinforces in his own dissolute and unethical way; he is therefore the only one entitled to laugh, and the reader/consumer of these anecdotes is brought to side with him by the deployment of narrative perspective. On the other hand, *mujūn* is a ritualized subversion of norms, particularly religious and moral ones. Its legitimacy in high literature makes it more akin to what Mikhail Bakhtin characterized, for French literature, as the Renaissance attitude towards laughter than to the mediaeval banning of comedy from 'serious' literature (in spite or because of its 'exceptional radicalism, freedom and ruthlessness'[38]) and the later conceptualization according to which laughter 'can only refer to individual and individually typical phenomena of social life.' During the Renaissance, explains Bakhtin, 'Laughter has a deep philosophical meaning, it is one of the essential forms of the truth concerning the world as a whole, concerning history and man.'[39] It is a cosmic satire inherited from mediaeval laughter transposed into literature, for laughter is an interior form of liberation, that frees man not only from exterior censorship but, and above all, from the 'great interior censor,'[40] – the fear of sacred and authoritarian prohibitions. Bakhtin's take on Renaissance laughter certainly is in keeping with the nature of laughter in mediaeval Arabic literature. Even a seemingly untouchable social norm, the 'classic' construction of masculinity by sexual roles, is partly ridiculed in anecdotes where ambiguity and gender blurring are extreme. I would argue that the two conceptualizations, i.e. of 'laughter as expression of power' and of 'laughter as expression of liberation,' are opposing forces present at the core of mediaeval *mujūn*. In that genre, laughter confirms social norms (while mocking the sacred ones) as a condition for its legitimacy and its collective consumption, whereas it also subverts them for individual reading. The great ambiguity of *mujūn*, the fact that it is never possible to decide whether it finally strengthens or mocks conventions, may well be the ultimate reason for its unsuitability for modern times, as we shall see.

Also to be noticed is the fact that physical pleasure is secondary in this narrative, and clearly second to literary pleasure. Neither the verses nor the accompanying anecdote dwell very long on Abū Nuwās's sexual enjoyment: his pleasure is derived from domination and from poetry; it is primarily an intellectual enjoyment. As for the passive partners' pleasure, it is simply unsaid and unthinkable. The three Egyptian lads literally feel *nothing* during the act (improbable as this may sound); only the next morning's pain can be, for them, a legitimate feeling. Pleasure would turn them into *maʾbūn-s* (catamites), a physical condition and a position of infamy, whereas being the accidental victim of a pleasureless rape is a mere stain that will go away with time, washed away by adulthood like those conspicuous traces of saliva or semen on their thighs that are highlighted by the narrative.

---

[38] Mikhail M. Bakhtin, *Rabelais and his world*, (Bloomington: Indiana University Press, 1984), 71.

[39] Ibid., 66–67.

[40] Ibid., 93.

Aṣbagh's son

This anecdote is found in many *adab* collections. The version translated here is taken from Al-Shābushtī's famous *Kitāb al-Diyārāt*[41] (10th century):

> There was in Kufa a man called Abū al-Aṣbagh, who traded in singing slaves,[42] and whose son Aṣbagh had the most beautiful face ever seen. Muṭīᶜ b. Iyās, Yaḥyā b. Ziyād, and Ḥammād ᶜAjrad were regular visitors to his household, for they had fallen for his son, but they could obtain nothing from him. One day, Abū al-Aṣbagh decided to invite Yaḥyā b. Ziyād for a morning draught. The preceding evening, Yaḥyā sent him goat meat, hens, chickens, fruit, and wine. Abū al-Aṣbagh said to his female servants: 'Yaḥyā b. Ziyād will be our guest, prepare for him what he likes most.' When he was done with ordering the food, he couldn't find any messenger to send [to tell Yaḥyā was expecting him] but his own son Aṣbagh, to whom he said, 'Do not leave Yaḥyā's place without him!' When Aṣbagh arrived there, Yaḥyā told his servant: 'Let the boy in, then step aside and lock the door, and prevent him from getting out in case he attempts an escape.' When Aṣbagh entered and delivered [his father's] message, Yaḥyā tried to seduce him, to no avail. Then he fought with the boy, threw him on the ground, and went to open his trousers' waistband. As the cord resisted, he cut it. When he was done with the boy, he gave him forty dinars that were under his prayer rug, and the lad took them. Yaḥyā then told him: 'Go ahead, I'll be behind you.' Aṣbagh left his house and Yaḥyā went to wash. Then he sat down to spruce up his appearance[43] and perfume himself with incense. [His friend] Muṭīᶜ stepped in at that moment and saw Yaḥyā smartening up. 'What's come over you?' he asked, but Yaḥyā didn't answer: he merely raised his nose contemptuously, and furrowed his brow. Muṭīᶜ asked again: 'I see that you are dressing up and putting on perfume, where are you going?' But the other wouldn't answer. 'Woe on you!' said Muṭīᶜ, 'What's happened to you? Has a divine revelation fallen down on you? Did the angels speak to you? Have you been acknowledged as the new caliph?' But Yaḥyā kept shaking his head in denial. Then Muṭīᶜ said : 'I see that you are too proud to deign answering, as if you had fucked Aṣbagh, the son of Abu al-Aṣbagh, in person.' 'In fact, that's what I just did,' answered Yaḥyā, 'and I gave him forty dinars.'
>
> 'And where are you going now?' asked Muṭīᶜ.
>
> 'His father's invited me.'
>
> 'May he repudiate his wife if you don't let me kiss your cock!' Yaḥyā showed it to him and Muṭīᶜ kissed it indeed. Then he asked: 'How did you manage to do it?'
>
> Yaḥyā explained the whole story, then went to Abū al-Aṣbagh's house. Muṭīᶜ followed him and waited for an hour [at the door], then knocked and asked to be received. A messenger told him that the master was busy today, that he had no time to meet him and was sorry for this. Muṭīᶜ asked for a roll of paper and some ink, and wrote those verses to Abū al-Aṣbagh:
>
> Abū al-Aṣbagh, may you always remain in the unreachable skies!

---

[41] Al-Shābushtī, *Al-Diyārāt*, ed. Kurkis ᶜAwwād (Beirut: Dar al-Rāʾid al-ᶜArabī, 1986 [reprint of Baghdad, 1951]), 254–256.

[42] This is the most probable meaning of *muqayyin*, generally used in the feminine form *muqayyina*, lady's maid. The version of this anecdote in the *Kitāb al-Aghānī* uses *lahu qiyān*, 'who owns (or deals in) singing slaves.'

[43] The meaning of *yatazayyanu* is both 'to shave' and 'embellish oneself.' The mention of perfume (used by both males and females) and Yaḥyā's boastful banter however suggest more than shaving (one's head, for the beard is a necessity for the male) and contribute to a subtle feminization of his character.

> But do not betray our friendship like he who ignominiously cut the cord
> And did what he'd been craving for, unstopped by fear or respect for a lost right.
> Had you seen Aṣbagh thrown under him, humbled by shame, yielding
> To his hasty and lustful urge, how would you have hated his deed!
> Call Aṣbagh, and ask him: you will discover a ghastly truth.

> Abū al-Aṣbagh said to Yaḥyā [upon seeing the note]: 'You did it, son of an adulteress!'
>
> 'I didn't', protested Yaḥyā, but Abū al-Aṣbagh checked his son's trousers with his hand, found the waistband had been cut, and was convinced the scandal had taken place. Yaḥyā told him:
>
> 'What happened happened, and Muṭīᶜ, this son of an adulteress, has come to tell you everything. Take my son, he is prettier than yours, we're both Arabs born of an Arab woman, while you and your son are Nabateans born of a Nabatean. Fuck my son ten times for the one time I fucked yours, and you'll keep the money as well, ten times what I paid your son.'
>
> Abū al-Aṣbagh burst with laughter and told his son: give me the dinars, you son of a whore! The boy handed the money and went away in shame, while Yaḥyā said: 'By God, may you never receive Muṭīᶜ again, that son of an adulteress!' But Abū al-Aṣbagh and his singing girls argued: 'He should be received immediately; he has cast disgrace upon us!' So Muṭīᶜ was ushered in, and sat down to drink with them, while Yaḥyā insulted him with all the words his tongue could speak. He kept on laughing the whole time.'

This anecdote amply illustrates the differences of perception between what was felt as humorous in a distant past, and what is nowadays an unacceptable object of laughter. There is no doubt that this story was felt to be immensely comical, while today it would certainly provoke bewilderment, for the desecration of an adolescent's body is hardly considered an acceptable laughing matter. The anecdote is the narrative of a rape. It not only confirms that the summit of the social pyramid is the adult ethnically Arab male, but also reveals that this adult Arab male is the only subject, while others are merely objects. Like Abū Nuwās in the former anecdote, Muṭīᶜ b. Iyās and Yaḥyā b. Ziyād are famous *mujjān* (rakes) whom the reader is primarily supposed to laugh with, not at – although the narrative opens a door for ambiguity with Yaḥyā's conceited ways and Muṭīᶜ's parody of homage to the king. The text calls indeed for a distinction between the character mocked by the actors (the boy) and those who are derided by the narrative (all of them). Laughter is here again based on repetition and inversion: the predictable penetration of Aṣbagh, who will be (literally) the butt of the joke, and the inversed scale of punishments accorded to wrongful acts: all the actors are heavy sinners, a parade of transgressors (drinkers of wine in the morning, a homosexual rapist, a boy accepting a bribe for his silence, a man kissing another one's penis, a father pimping his own son after pimping slave singers, another father offering his own son for penetration as compensation, girls laughing off an adolescent's rape in wine) but the only character being laughed at by all the actors is the least of the sinners, the boy. We can hear both laughter as expression of power and laughter at the reversal of the cosmic order ordained by God. But the one voice that is not heard is the victim's voice, for such *nawādir* (piquant and rare anecdotes) never allow the victim to trick his aggressor.

Such jokes, short of reflecting actual behaviours, express at least common representations. The 'pimping father' is a topos of *khamriyya* (wine-drinking) poetry and *shiᶜr al-diyārāt* (evocation of the pleasures lived in Christian monasteries) as the Christian or Jewish tavern owner customarily looks away while his son pleases his patrons, as in Abū Nuwās's poetry[44]. The father here is a Nabatean, that is of peasant origin (*anbāṭ al-ʿIrāq*) as opposed to tribal Arab aristocracy; it is not specified whether he is a Muslim or not, but he might not be. Although the term *muqayyin* is ambiguous, it probably designates a dealer in *qiyān* (female slave singers) and as such someone who is already a kind of pimp. Those loose girls are present when he finally decides to receive Muṭīʿ and they argue in favour of letting him in (to hush the scandal). But the immensely transgressive detail is that the other father, Yaḥyā the *lūṭī*, also appears as a pimping father, offering his son to the insulted father in a parody of *diya* (the bloodprice). Is his proposal 'sincere' (in terms of the fiction) or is it nothing but another joke, the forty dinars being an acceptable compensation the father is quick to pocket? The text will not answer this point.

Also remarkable is the reversal of the paradigmatic preparation for sexual intercourse (which, in real life, culminates in wedding ceremonies) in this anecdote: Yaḥyā takes a bath, shaves and perfumes himself after intercourse has occurred. Whereas the passive partner should be the one making himself desirable before intercourse, the active partner here makes himself desirable *post coitum*.[45]

The wording used in the course of Aṣbagh's seduction/rape scene, '*rāwadahu ʿan nafsihi*', is obviously reminiscent of the Koranic scene in which Potiphar's wife tries to seduce Joseph.[46] She is struck with young Joseph's handsome looks, as is Yaḥyā with Aṣbagh's – as if he were a female charmed by early manhood. Although Yaḥyā (a successful version of Zulaykha) rapes the boy, it is remarkable that he is as cunning as a lecherous woman in this section of the episode, as witnessed by the fact that he pampers himself, perfumes himself with incense, and acts with mock haughtiness, as a woman would be supposed to; today we might say he behaves like a 'bitchy queen.' The active *lūṭī* in this anecdote and elsewhere is slightly different from an über-male who dominates both male and female partners and simply fails to tame his sexual urges, for there are puzzling traces of 'feminization' in his portrait, and although he stands for maleness (*dhukūra*), he never embodies the true values of virility (*murūʾa*). The *lūṭī* of *adab* literature is not the *fāʿil fiʿl qawm lūṭ* of Islamic jurisprudence: the sexual preference implied by the word also goes with a hint of slight effeminacy, as Tawḥidi perfidiously remarked of the vizier Ibn ʿAbbād.

As for the penis kissing scene, it is clearly a parodic echo of the *mubāyaʿa* (allegiance) ceremony, jokingly alluded to by Muṭīʿ's question '*aw būyiʿa laka bi-l-khilāfa*' (have you been recognized as caliph?): Yaḥyā is, by this outrageous act, metaphorically crowned 'Caliph of the sodomites.' At the same time, the kissing of the penis is also a parody of oral sex.

---

44 See *Dīwān Abī Nuwās*, ed. Ewald Wagner, vol. 3 (references here are made to the reprint edition, Damascus: Dār al-Madā, 2003), piece 62 (pp. 96–97), mention of father of the boy accepting *dabīb* on line 17; piece 84 (pp. 115–117) no mention of the father in Wagner's edition, but the same poem has an additional line in Ilīya al-Ḥāwī's edition (Beirut: Al-sharika al-ʿālamiyya lil-kitāb, 1987): '*lammā raʾānī abūhu qad qaʿudtu lahū / ḥayyā wa-ʾayqana ʾannī mutlifun ṣafadī*'; piece 101, p. 133, the female tavern owner offers a boy (her son?); piece 108 (pp. 148–49) the young *dhimmī* is penetrated by all the drinkers at the end of the poem, is the father unaware?

45 One would ritually perform ablution after intercourse, but Yaḥyā's grooming of his body is typically a women's expected attitude before intercourse, especially the wedding night.

46 Qurʾān 12:30 *imraʾtu l-ʿazīzi turāwidu fatāhā ʿan nafsihi*, see also 12:32 and 12:51.

Muṭīᶜ had already jumped to kiss a female servant's vagina in the same chapter of Shābushtī's book, so we discover him as a worshipper of both male and female genitalia. The whole anecdote certainly suggests that the dividing line between various categories of *mujjān* is a very thin one, and mediaeval humour, in its Bakhtinian dimension, particularly mocks – between lines – the *lūṭī*'s contention that his manhood cannot be affected by repeated intercourse with other males: to be aroused by a handsome adolescent is normal for any man, but preferring adolescents to maidens is a dangerous slope that may lead to some behavioural ambiguities, warns the anecdote.[47]

In both narratives, the mediaeval conception of humour considers forced sex imposed on male adolescents an acceptable subject of laughter. The narrative takes into account the predator's point of view, watches his triumph with a tone combining feigned shock, weak disapproval, utter amusement and slight arousal. But if mediaeval *mujūn* walks a tightrope between the laughter of the almighty shameless male and the subversive laughter that mocks religion, social norms, and even the construction of masculinity, the absence of the victim's perspective, unnecessary in an *adab* text since his torment is considered to be of no account, might be one of the reasons for this mode of writing's disappearance in modern literature.

FROM *DABĪB* TO HOMOSEXUAL RAPE: THE PERSPECTIVE OF MODERN FICTION

Dabīb hardly exists as such in modern Arab fiction: indeed the word itself has disappeared. The scripted approach leading to the prey, the cunning devices used to induce a boy or a young man's sleep, the final boast of victory, and most of all, the boisterous laugh associated with this victory are not to be found. Since modern literature does not necessarily converse with *turāth*, and particularly not with *mujūn*, this comes as no surprise. However, the elements at the heart of *dabīb* that make this script plausible, i.e. the desirability of male adolescents to slightly or considerably older males, the difficulty of reaching manhood with an unaltered body, the notion that public space is dangerous for boys and young men, particularly if they are good looking and have a fair complexion, the fact that older adolescents will try to force themselves on younger boys and that this is an accepted fact of life, none of these have receded, according to literature, from twentieth century societies. The way to manhood is paved with sexual ambushes and dangers, whether embodied in the shape of an older man, slightly older friends from school or the neighbourhood, or fellow prisoners, just as in the narratives of *Alf layla wa-layla*. However, it took a long time for these representations to be clearly expressed in modern fiction. The danger of

[47] On the normalcy of being attracted to handsome adolescents, see El-Rouayheb, *Before Homosexuality*, 13–51; also see Dror Ze'evi's introduction in *Producing Desire, Changing Sexual Discourse in the Ottoman Middle East 1500–1900* (Berkeley/Los Angeles: University of California Press, 2006). On Ibn ᶜAbbād and the accidental construction of the 'homosexual' in Tawḥīdī's libel, negating the distinction between active and passive partners, see Lagrange, 'The Obscenity of the Vizier', in K. Babayan and A. Najmabadi (eds.), *Islamicate Sexualities, Translations across Temporal Geographies of Desire* (Cambridge: Harvard University Press, 2008), 161–203.

homosexual rape appeared in Muḥammad Shukrī's classic *Al-Khubz al-ḥāfī* (*For Bread Alone*) in a flimsy hotel, on the beach, and in a cemetery where the narrator sleeps and has to beware of older teenagers who want to abuse him;[48] in the same author's *Al-Shuṭṭār* (1994), the narrator has become a 20-year-old man and now constitutes in his turn a danger for younger boys, following in the footsteps of Abū Nuwās.[49] In Abdellah Taia's *Une mélancolie arabe* (in French, 2008),[50] the 12-year-old openly gay narrator is almost raped by an older boy in the Moroccan town of Salé (Salā). Ali, the horny older boy, calls the narrator Layla, refusing to grant him a male identity. The gay narrator will accept penetration only if Ali recognizes him as a boy and kisses him. But Ali is not interested in consensual sex: the whole game is meaningful and acceptable only if it appears as a rape. Otherwise Ali's desire would enter a grey zone and turn him into what he cannot be – a partner for the narrator. This is why he calls four other friends to abuse the boy with him, this 'young boy in the red swimming trunks on a blue mattress, shutting his eyes as if plunging into a blue pool.' Only exterior elements will save him: the call for prayer and Ali's mother climbing up the stairs. Rape and/or group sex in this novel fortuitously appear as variations on Abū Nuwās's claim that *aladhdhu n-nayki mā kāna-ghtiṣābā*. *Dabīb*, or its modern counterpart same-sex rape, are means to escape the danger of same-sex sexuality's ambiguities. Ali's partners in crime are not called to the scene to indulge in pleasure but to witness that this pleasure is taken by force and that the penetrative role is played without hesitation.

One obvious difference between the mediaeval narrative of *dabīb* and modern literature is the narrative point of view. In classical *adab*, the perspective is always that of the *dābb*, the rapist, with the victim's perception being either ignored or hastily alluded to with only one ritual feeling – shame – allowed; that, and the will to cover up the deed so as not to be stigmatized or the readiness to accept money as a compensation. The modern narrative, however, dwells on the victims' feelings, and even, in this rare instance, allows for sexual arousal at the prospect of homosexual intercourse.

Non-metaphorical male-male rape is not a rare subject in contemporary fictions. It is alluded to in at least four novels published in 2009: in the Jordanian ᶜAbdallāh Riḍwān's *Ghiwāyat al-zanzalakht* (Temptation of the Chinaberry Tree); in two Saudi novels: *Shāriᶜ al-ᶜAṭāyif* (Atayif Road) by ᶜAbdallāh bin Bakhīt and ᶜAbduh Khāl's *Tarmī bi-sharar* (It Throws Off Sparks); and in the Iraqi Ṣalāḥ Ṣalāḥ's *Būhīmyā al-kharāb* (The Bohemia of Devastation). It is a 'common' danger, whether as a consequence of gender segregation (as mid-century Orientalists[51] and these Saudi novelists alike would have it), or because male-male desire is traditionally constructed as natural and masculinity as a social gender is a matter of sexual role regardless of the partner's gender, as contemporary research in gender studies would advocate. This unexpectedly common theme of rape suggests that non-consensual sex between men and adolescents or among adolescents is perceived by authors as an important issue of contemporary Arab societies that has to be dealt with, in the frame of

---

48 Muhammad Shukri, *Al-Khubz al-ḥāfī* (London: Dar al-Saqi, 1982), 110–115.

49 Muhammad Shukri, *Al-Shuṭṭār* (London: Dar al-Saqi, 1994). See J. Massad *Desiring Arabs*, 314–319, for a discussion of *Al-khubz al-ḥāfī*.

50 Abdellah Taia, *Une mélancolie arabe* (Paris: Seuil, 2008), 15–32.

51 See Charles Pellat's unsigned article 'Liwāṭ,' *Encyclopaedia of Islam* II.

the 'realist-reformist paradigm' of fiction.[52] The fact that homosexual rape is so commonly alluded to shows that modern novels deem it necessary to denounce what they perceive as an unfortunate consequence of the failure to achieve mixing of the sexes and the heteronormalization of desire, leading to violence, sexuality by proxy, and deeply hurt souls and bodies. There is no doubt that one of the dominant images of 'homosexuality' in contemporary Arab fiction is forced intercourse, a fact that partly explains the continuing use of '*shādhdh*' (pervert, abnormal, queer) rather than the more politically correct '*mithlī*' in present-day novels that mention same-sex intercourse: what is dealt with is presented as substitution sexuality and unrequited attraction.

Another obvious difference between mediaeval and modern narratives is that in the latter non-consensual sex, far from being a comical matter and a legitimate field for the expression of wit, is viewed as a personal tragedy and/or a social scandal to be denounced. The most obvious resemblance, on the other hand, is that physical pleasure, whether for the active or the passive partner, is in most cases an irrelevant issue: homosexual rape is an assertion of one's domination before being an easy satisfaction of bodily needs and a substitute for heterosexual sex.

Ṣalāḥ Ṣalāḥ's novel on an aborted bohemia in 1980s Baghdad in the days of the Iran-Iraq war mentions a culture of organized pederasty, with the *farakhjiyya* (literally, 'chicken-hawks') boasting their deeds and conquests. The narrator mentions his own rape while spending a night in jail for disorderly behaviour. Coincidentally in accordance with mediaeval accounts of *dabīb*, the narrator inadvertently takes tablets of Tafranil that put him to sleep:[53] 'They were handed over to me by a guy. Then I lost in this place my first virginity. I've never considered honour had anything to do with preserving your anus' chastity. That is, as far as my first rape was concerned.'

This rather light attitude to forced penetration and the uncommon refusal of the standard definition of masculinity is perhaps dictated by the relativity of horrors in the Baghdad of the 1980s. But it is noteworthy that it still takes no account of the possibility of pleasure felt during intercourse.

This 'light attitude' is quite different from that found in ʿAbdallāh Riḍwān's novel, in which the narrator regrets having been the silent accomplice of a rape scene. While playing on a mountain overlooking their refugee camp, two Palestinian adolescents are suddenly surrounded by four men in their early twenties, also children of refugees, who threaten them with knives:[54]

> Yūsuf asked:
> – What do you want from us?
> – Take off your clothes, answered Ḥasan, self-confidently.
> – What? We cried in unison.

[52] See Richard Jacquemond, *Entre scribes et écrivains, le champ littéraire dans l'Egypte contemporaine* (Paris/Arles: Actes Sud, 2003).

[53] Ṣalāḥ Ṣalāḥ, *Būhīmyā l-kharāb* (Beirut: Dār al-Tanwīr, 2009), 26. Farakhjiyya, 49–51. Prison rape, 56.

[54] ʿAbdallāh Riḍwān, *Ghiwāyat al-zanzalakht* (Amman: Durūb/Al-Yazūrī, 2009), 36–37. Same-sex pleasure is also alluded to in the novel (25–26), while all the Palestinian boys of a same class escape school for a session of collective masturbation, the winner being the first one to ejaculate.

– I said take off your clothes, or else... he added, brandishing his knife in our faces.
We all started wriggling and squirming like snakes. No way to escape. I looked Ḥasan in the eye. I knew he was a distant relative of mine, on my mother's side. It was as if I was begging for this kinship. Ḥasan suddenly yelled at me: 'Ali, go to the top of the valley and watch. If anybody comes, if you hear anything, call me. Understood? I'll cut your throat if you run away or if you let anybody approach. Got it?'

I quickly answered: 'Understood.' The guy holding my wrist was surprised by Ḥasan's decision. 'Let him go', he told him, 'he's a relative of mine, he won't tell anything'. He freed my hand and I fled, slowly at first, almost crawling, then running faster and faster. I don't know from where I gathered the ability to run, like a madman, without stopping, I passed the valley, the mountain, the plain, the camp, our house's courtyard, and I did not stop until I reached the corner of the inner room. My mother looked at me wondering: 'What got you so scared?' My sisters stared at me in awe. Mama cried: 'Let him drink from the "fright cup", who knows what the boy's been through? What's up, lad?' I didn't say a word. I was just panting. My heart was about to burst. [...] Yūsuf became everybody's mount. All us boys rode him. His look changed. A broken, sad soul. He wasn't the Yūsuf we used to know anymore, everybody rode him now, including me. From here on out, [I] decided [I] was never going to submit to anyone, for the broken look of submission in Yūsuf's eyes never went away.

This is a story of guilt, an avowal of the rapist's shame. The narrator escapes rape and becomes an 'unbending male' (*alladhī lā yankasir*) while reducing another male to an ever-bended one, *al-munkasir*, a status that cannot be changed with time, an indelible stain, in contrast to the mediaeval narratives' take on rape.[55] Easy physical pleasure can be the only reason why the narrator becomes one of Yūsuf's 'users,' for girls were unavailable in a refugee camp in 1965 (the scene takes place during Habib Bourguiba's visit to the West Bank). Even if the narrator admits having practiced it, male-male sexuality can only be alluded to in terms of substitutive sexuality, and not as a matter of taste.[56] Pleasure, however, is not the topic of this text, and remains irrelevant. The comparison between the textual surface of the original incident (two pages) and the mention of the narrator's use of Yusuf (3 lines) – a narrative surface that is completely at variance with the actual facts and their duration, for the use of Yusuf must have continued for months if not years – show that the original trauma is the only fact the narrator is ready to deal with. Guilt, shame and cowardice can be avowed, but not pleasure. The main reason for this suppression is that many modern narratives are denunciatory and reformist in intent. Same-sex intercourse

[55] Unless Yūsuf enjoys intercourse with other boys, a question the self-centered narrator is not interested in investigating. In this case, mediaeval as well as mid-twentieth social norms would construct him as deviant, but only modern fiction would see him as suffering and self-loathing, while he would be laughing stock for mediaeval *mujūn*.

[56] In Rabʿī al-Madhūn's *Al-Sayyida min Tall Abīb* (Beirut: Al-Muʾassasa al-ʿArabiyya lil-Tawzīʿ wal-Nashr, 2009), the main character, Walīd Dahmān, is embarrassed to cross paths in Gaza with the camp's effeminate, ʿAbd al-Ḥamīd, nicknamed Munā by everybody. He had once had sex with him, and felt like prey: 'Why is this cocksucker [*manyak*] always determined to hurt my honor? It happened only once, by mistake. What does he want from me?' (20). Consensual sex with a recognized passive homosexual (the narrator interestingly uses *mithlī*) is apparently more dangerous than rape; the passive partner is constructed by the narrative as the chaser, i.e. the one with the socially active role, even if not in the actual intercourse. The perspective is here quite different from that found in mediaeval literature.

is not about enjoyment, not about human sexuality, but is an index of underdevelopment, of out-dated gender separation, of ubiquitous violence (generated, in this example's case, by the Palestinian tragedy).

ᶜAbdallāh bin Bakhīt's novel *Shāriᶜ al-ᶜAṭāyif* also takes place in the 1960s, in an imaginary town very reminiscent of the Saudi capital, Riyadh. Its graphic mention of various anomic behaviours in Saudi Arabia some forty years ago led to tepid reviews in Gulf media, which deemed this work a 'novel to forget.'[57] The first part of the novel deals with a character strangely called Faḥīj (wide-open legs), until we later learn his real name, Nāṣir (Victor), an irony of fate that does not go unnoticed by the character. The narration starts as Nāṣir's dead mother is being washed by women of the family before being buried in the very same cemetery in which the character was repeatedly raped during his teen years. While the whole family is busy, Nāṣir seizes this occasion to brutally murder one of his two regular abusers, cuts off his genitals and stuffs them in the man's anus. Later, as an old man on his deathbed, he tells his secret to his wife and asks her to kill his second tormentor. Faḥīj's social agony is described in detail. A plump adolescent, he was ambushed by his two tormentors, the wine of mediaeval narratives being replaced by a dizzying first cigarette: on the slippery slope of transgression, a first mistake, however mild it might seem, is perhaps necessary for the ultimate fall:[58]

> When he lies down under a man, he looks at his body and sees himself lying on the ground as if it were someone else. He observes his bare ass as the stallion is about to assail him. The first time he gave in to other males, he felt disgusted and insulted. He was approximately sixteen. Suwaylam and Faṭīs had dragged him to the old deserted cemetery of the ᶜAjliyya, under the pretense of smoking cigarettes. [...] They took him to an abandoned hut, built of clay, covered by a tin roof [...] He entered the room with Faṭīs, who lit up a cigarette and handed it over to him. He took it with utter pleasure. It was his very first. He puffed twice, felt some dizziness and the pleasure of discovery. When he regained his balance, he noticed Suwaylam hadn't come inside with them. He wondered about it, and Faṭīs told him 'he's making sure no one will catch us.' He thought the guy meant about the cigarettes, and kept silent. Faṭīs made it clearer:
>
> 'Next time, I'll bring a mattress, this time we'll just do it standing.' [...]
>
> Faṭīs and Suwaylam had betrayed him. They had made him think he was one of them, they had even mentioned young boys in front of him, and boasted about their sexual talents. Eventually, he had imagined he was part of their gang. Faṭīs got closer to him and put his hand on his thigh. He stood up, getting away from him.
>
> 'Man, put out your cigarette, let's get done with it.'
>
> He tried to flee, but Faṭīs seized him by the collar and pushed him hard up against the wall. [...]
>
> After this day, the only thing he wished for was that this incident would remain a secret between the three of them. They swore, on condition that he would submit to their demands whenever they wished. Over time he became their intimate friend, and the cemetery his second home. As time passed, the number of his 'intimate friends' going with him to the cemetery to have sex grew. But he remained faithful to Suwaylam and Faṭīs, who both owned his body.

---

57 Saᶜd Muḥārib al-Muḥārib, 'Shāriᶜ al-ᶜAṭāyif, riwāya li-l-nisyān,' *al-ᶜArabiyya* 07/03/2009, http://www.alarabiya.net/views/2009/03/07/67899.html (accessed 24 may 2010).

58 ᶜAbdallah Bin Bakhīt, *Shāriᶜ al-ᶜAṭāyif* (London/Beirut: Dar al-Sāqī, 2009), 60 and sqq.

As the chapter develops, Faḥīj becomes the neighbourhood ride. The seven players of the local soccer team, older men, even boys from other neighbourhoods: 'He heard them whispering and laughing, describing him as 'wide open' because he didn't feel pain anymore during penetration, as before. He heard Abū Munīf describing him as '*afḥaj*' [open hole].'[59] As they grow up, the two hoodlums, who have a long history of rape cases and almost faced public scandal after abusing a schoolboy, whose father was 'wise enough to shut up so that his son wouldn't be dishonoured,' finally lose interest in Nāṣir. Their very last intercourse, while he is in his twenties, is a pathetic scene where everybody is embarrassed and pretends to joke about it. As an adult, Nāṣir is still called Faḥīj behind his back by people, and tries to keep his head down for an insult recalling his shameful past (*al-tārīkh al-mushīn*) can always be thrown at him: when a friend of his is made fun of and Nāṣir laughs too eagerly, he is reminded of his position:[60] 'Even queers laugh at us now!' The stigma of passive sodomy is never erased. Even in old age, a married man, Nāṣir remains Faḥīj, and even the assassination of his tormentor, as it remains unacknowledged, does not wash away the sins of his shattered adolescence.

Bin Bakhīt's novel obviously aims at shocking the Saudi readership with his detailed account of a man sexually broken by other men, in a society driven by what he qualifies as 'abnormal desires' (*raghabāt shādhdha*). Although he does not specifically say so, it is quite clear that mixing of the sexes is in his mind the only cure for such an illness (each of the three intertwining plots of the novel insists on the tragic consequences of women's inaccessibility). Once again, however, pleasure is never alluded to in Bin Bakhīt's narrative. Faḥīj feels no pain at being penetrated, but it is never once suggested that he might actually enjoy it. His assailants' preference for boys makes them *shādhdh*, but Nāṣir's repeatedly forced role as passive partner never suggests, for the narrative authority (unlike the neighbourhood), that identity derives from repeated acts. Why have other boys escaped Nāṣir/Faḥīj's fate? Could the narrator be 'in denial'?

The language of sex used in the novel, even if mainly metaphorical, never suggests eye contact between both partners: Fahij is always *under* another man (*taḥt rajul*). His only derisory victory, during his very last intercourse with Suwaylam, is that he refuses, for once, to be totally under him:[61] 'He twisted his body so that Suwaylam could reach his goal without him lying on his belly. Suwaylam didn't hesitate and didn't ask for more. It seemed that he also wanted to walk half the way so that they could end this thing. He cuddled on his side and shook him a few times, in a half-hearted effort that could not lead to climax.'

Sexual intercourse remains 'this thing' for the rapist, a sick desire for domination, which is actually more important than reaching climax.

ʿAbduh Khāl's *Tarmī bi-Sharar*[62] offers rich material for a comparison with mediaeval

[59] Ibid., 62.

[60] Ibid., 81.

[61] Ibid., 77–78.

[62] This novel won the International Prize for Arabic Fiction 2010. English translation: *Throwing Sparks*, trans. Maia Tabet and Michael K. Scott (London/Doha: Bloomsbury Qatar Foundation Publishing, 2014).

Arabic literature. The novel's title is an intertextual play alluding to a Qurʾanic description of hell's fire as 'throwing sparks as big as a castle' (77–32). The action takes place in a palace, set on the coast of Jeddah, owned by an incarnation of evil. The inhabitants of the popular district called Hell's Quarter (*ḥayy al-nār*) dream of working in it and take it for heaven, whereas those who entered it know it is the true Gehenna. The narrator, Ṭāriq Fāḍil, works as a torturer and a pimp for the Master of the Palace (in a bold allegory of the Saudi kingdom). Known as a rough guy and a chaser of adolescents in his neighbourhood, and renowned among bored widows and housewives for his 'third leg,' he flees home after having deflowered the street's belle, Tahānī, and indirectly caused her death, as he discovers many years later. He has no choice but to work as a professional rapist for the Master, who films him as he repeatedly sodomizes his enemies in order to humiliate them: 'a he-goat fecundating he-goats' (*tays yulaqqiḥ tuyūsan*),[63] the ultimate image of uselessness in a society in which status is achieved through family. Ṭāriq is forbidden to masturbate or to have intercourse with women: his penis and his body are the property of the Master, whose wild parties with women and forbidden alcohol turn out to be far from the Abbasid pleasures they evoke. The transgression of all rules and disrespect of all sacred laws prove to be more pathetic than flamboyant, and even the early morning drunken prayer (*ṣalāt al-sukārā*), a clear reminiscence of comparable *mujūn* scenes in mediaeval *adab*, shows none of the joy of rule-breaking felt by Muṭīʿ b. Iyās or Bashshār b. Burd. The Master's boon companions are worthless businessmen, whose fortune depends on the Master's whims and goodwill and who can only copulate hastily and sadly with shattered prostitutes while the Master is asleep, for everybody's body is under control. On a superficial level, Ṭāriq's narrative could appear as the torturer's voice, mimicking the mediaeval perspective in which the only angle ever given is the rapist's. But not only does the rapist here not laugh, he also immediately understands that ever since he was hired for his phallus, he has become a victim as well. This realization comes with regrets: 'I destroyed many boys, without ever paying attention to the feeling of defeat and subjugation engendered inside them. And here I am, tasting an inverted defeat myself.'[64] With the loss of ownership over the body, sexual roles cease to bear meaning: 'This night, I grasped the horror of what I was doing in dark streets. What I did tonight, I did many times before. But now I feel I'm the one being raped, that I call for mercy and no one answers.'[65] In his monologue of self-hatred, Ṭāriq defines himself as *lūṭi* and *shādhdh* (deviant), and the whole system he lives in as producing this corruption: words like *ithm* (sin), *danas* (pollution), *lawath* (filth), *suqūṭ* (fall) are repeated page after page. The narrator obviously does not define himself as homosexual. *Lūṭī* means (to him) a rider of boys, not a man seeking another as a sexual and romantic partner: 'Having sex with other males was not true homosexuality/perversion (*shudhūdh mutaʾaṣṣil*). It was the thing to do in order to escape the claws of boy-seekers, this social habit which appears as a way to show off (*istiwjāh*), because you have to be either a hunter,

---

[63] ʿAbduh Khāl, *Tarmī bi-sharar* (Baghdad/Beirut/Freiberg: Al-Kamel Verlag [=Manshūrāt al-Jamal], 2009), 117.

[64] Ibid., 132

[65] Ibid., 136.

or a prey. This perversion became a job [...],'[66] The rehabilitation of the homoerotic dimension *of mujūn* is not on ᶜAbduh Khāl's agenda. However, one should not hastily conclude from his character's vocabulary and attempted atonement for homosexual acts that this Saudi novel presents homosexuality *per se* as deviance. What it denounces, along with Bin Bakhīt in *Shariᶜ al-ᶜAṭāyif*, is a political, religious and social system in which individuals have no rights over their own bodies.

****

If one can regret that modern Arabic fiction does not deal with same-sex sexuality with the same pleasure and laughter-oriented freedom that is witnessed in mediaeval literature,[67] the ambiguous nature of humour found in *mujūn* narratives and verses explains much of its present-day unacceptability. The laughter we hear in *adab* anecdotes, while subtly undermining the foundations of social and sacred norms, primarily appears as the laughter of the powerful, of the dominant figure, of the predator whose prey will be humiliated in fact and in poetry. This laughter is a collective peal sent to the universe, for texts are seldom the expression of an individual's vision. Physical pleasure is only a pretence in the game of *dabīb*: it is in the first place a race for domination, and, on a second and more hidden level, a deconstruction of traditional masculinity the contradictions of which it exposes through the stock character of the *lūṭī*. Social mores are a given that satirical literature can mock but does not seriously seek to reform. The modern writer, on the other hand, is responsible for his voice; his take on the body, on intimacy, on pleasure is an intellectual's discourse.[68] If forced same-sex intercourse is an 'issue' and a 'disgrace,' not merely an unavoidable social phenomenon, then it cannot be laughed at. The rape scene embodies 'what is wrong' with society as a whole: 'unhealthy' desires, whether in refugee camps or an out-dated homosocial society such as Saudi Arabia. But equal partners remain unseen, uninteresting, and unmentioned.

WORKS CITED

Abu Hiffān, *Akhbār Abī Nuwās*, ed. ᶜAbd al-Sattār Aḥmad Farrāj (Cairo: Maktabat Miṣr, 1954).
Abū Nuwās, *Dīwān*, ed. E. Wagner, 5 vols. (Beirut: Klaus Schwarz Verlag, 2003).
Abū Nuwās, *Dīwān*, ed. Īlīya Ḥāwī (Beirut: Al-Sharika al-ᶜĀlamiyya lil-Kitāb, 1987).
Abū Nuwās, *Al-Nuṣūs al-muḥarrama*, ed. Jamāl Jumᶜa (London: Riyāḍ al-Rayyis, 1998).
Samira Aghacy, *Masculine Identity in the Fiction of the Arab East since 1967* (Syracuse: Syracuse University Press, 2009).

---

66 Ibid., 204.

67 At least male-male sexuality, for lesbianism seems much less of an issue in contemporary novels, see ᶜAlawiyya Ṣubḥ's recent *Ismuhu l-gharām* (Beirut: Dar al-Adab, 2009). Lesbianism is out of the scope of this essay and needs further elaboration, both for contemporary fiction (no study until today) and pre-modern sources, for which the only and insufficient reference is Sahar Amer, *Crossing Borders, Love between Women in Medieval French and Arabic Literatures* (Philadelphia: University of Pennsylvania Press, 2008).

68 See the conclusion of Samira Aghacy's essay *Masculine Identity in the Fiction of the Arab East since 1967* (Syracuse: Syracuse University Press, 2009).

Sahar Amer, *Crossing Borders: love between women in medieval French and Arabic literatures* (Philadelphia: University of Pennsylvania Press, 2008).
Walter G. Andrews and Mehmet Kalpaklı, *The Age of the Beloveds: Love and the Beloved in Early-Modern Ottoman and European Culture and Society* (Durham/London: Duke University Press, 2005).
Mikhail M. Bakhtin, *Rabelais and his world*, (Bloomington: Indiana University Press, 1984).
Henri Bergson, *Le rire*, 5th ed. (Paris: Quadrige/PUF, 1989); English translation by C. Brereton, F. Rothwell, available on http://www.authorama.com/laughter-1.html.
ʿAbdallah Bin Bakhīt, *Shāriʿ al-ʿAṭāyif* (London/Beirut: Dār al-Sāqī, 2009).
Khaled El-Rouayheb, *Before Homosexuality in the Arab-Islamic World, 1500–1800* (Chicago: The University of Chicago Press, 2005).
John Gagnon, 'The Implicit and Explicit Use of the Scripting Perspective in Sex Research', *The Annual Review of Sex Research* 1 (1990): 1–44.
Sabry Hafez, *The Genesis of Arabic Narrative Discourse* (London: Saqi Books, 1993).
David M. Halperin, *How to Do the History of Male Homosexuality* (Chicago: University of Chicago Press, 2002).
Badīʿ al-Zamān al-Hamadhānī, *al-Maqāmāt*, ed. Muḥammad ʿAbduh (Algiers: Mufam, 1988).
Badīʿ al-Zamān al-Hamadhānī, *Sharḥ Maqāmāt al-Hamadhānī*, ed. Muḥammad Muḥyi al-Dīn ʿAbd al-Ḥamīd (Beirut: Dār al-Kutub al-ʿIlmiyya, 1979), a reprint of Hamadhānī, *al-Maqāmāt*, ed. Muḥammad Muḥyi l-Din ʿAbd al-Ḥamīd (Cairo: Al-Maktaba al-Azhariyya, 1324/1923).
Ibn Falīta [Aḥmad b. Muḥammad b. ʿAlī al-Yamanī], *Rushd al-labīb ʾilā muʿāsharat al-ḥabīb* (Al-Māya, Libya: Talā, 2006).
Ibn Manẓūr, *Akhbār Abī Nuwās*, ed. *Mulḥaq al-Aghānī* (Beirut: Dār al-Kutub al-ʿIlmiyya, 1992).
Ibn Rashīq al-Qayrawānī, *Al-ʿumda fi maḥāsin al-shiʿr wa-adabih*, electronic version downloadable from www.al-mostafa.com.
Richard Jacquemond, *Entre scribes et écrivains: le champ littéraire dans l'Egypte contemporaine* (Paris/Arles: Actes Sud, 2003).
ʿAbduh Khāl, *Tarmī bi-sharar* (Baghdad/Beirut/Freiberg: Al-Kamel Verlag [=Manshūrāt al-Jamal], 2009).
Frédéric Lagrange, *Islam d'interdits, Islam de jouissance* (Paris: Téraèdre, 2008).
Frédéric Lagrange, 'The Obscenity of the Vizier', in K. Babayan and A, Najmabadi (eds.), *Islamicate Sexualities: translations across temporal geographies of desire* (Cambridge: Harvard University Press, 2008), 161–203.
Thierry Leguay, *Histoire raisonnée de la fellation* (Paris: Le Cercle, 1999).
Rabʿī al-Madhūn, *Al-Sayyida min Tall Abīb* (Beirut: Al-Muʾassasa al-ʿArabiyya lil-Tawzīʿ wal-Nashr, 2009).
Fedwa Malti-Douglas, *Woman's Body, Woman's Word: gender and discourse in Arabo-Islamic writing* (Princeton: Princeton University Press, 1991).
Joseph A. Massad, *Desiring Arabs* (Chicago: The University of Chicago Press, 2007).
Saʿd Muḥārib al-Muḥārib, 'Shāriʿ al-ʿAṭāyif, riwāya li-l-nisyān,' *al-ʿArabiyya* 07/03/2009, http://www.alarabiya.net/views/2009/03/07/67899.html (accessed 24 may 2010).
Afsaneh Najmabadi, *Women with Mustaches and Men without Beards: gender and sexual anxieties of Iranian modernity* (Berkeley: University of California Press, 2005).
Salwa al-Nuʿaymī, *Burhān al-ʿasal* (Beirut: Riyāḍ al-Rayyis, 2008); English translation: *The Proof of the Honey*, trans. Cal Perkins (New York: Europa Editions, 2009).
M. Peled, 'Al-Sāq ʿalā l-sāq, A Generic Definition', *Arabica* 32 (1985), 31–46.
[Charles Pellat] Ed., 'Liwāṭ' *Encyclopaedia of Islam*, 2nd ed., eds. P. Bearman, Th. Bianquis, C.E. Bosworth, E. van Donzel, W.P. Heinrichs (Brill Online, 2013), School of Oriental and African Studies (SOAS), 14 July 2013.
ʿAbdallāh Riḍwān, *Ghiwāyat al-zanzalakht* (Amman: Durūb/Al-Yazūrī, 2009).

Everett Rowson, 'The Categorization of Gender and Sexual Irregularity in Medieval Arabic Vice Lists' in J. Epstein and K. Straub (eds.), *Body Guards: the cultural politics of gender ambiguity* (New York: Routledge, 1991), 50–79.
Everett Rowson, 'Two Homoerotic Narratives from Mamlūk Literature,' in J.W. Wright, Jr. and Everett K. Rowson (eds.), *Homoeroticism in Classical Arabic Literature* (New York: Columbia University Press, 1997), 158–91.
Everett Rowson, '*Mujūn*', in Julie Scott Meisami and Paul Starkey (eds.), *Encyclopedia of Arabic Literature* (London/New York: Routledge, 1998), 2: 546–8.
Everett Rowson, '*Sukhf*,' in Julie Scott Meisami and Paul Starkey (eds.), *Encyclopedia of Arabic Literature* (London/New York: Routledge, 1998), 2: 743.
Ṣalāḥ Ṣalāḥ, *Būhīmyā l-kharāb* (Beirut: Dār al-Tanwīr, 2009).
Hanadi Al-Samman, 'Out of the Closet: Representation of Homosexuals and Lesbians in Modern Arabic Literature', *Journal of Arabic Literature* 39 (2008), 270–31.
Al-Shābushtī, *Al-Diyārāt*, ed. Kurkis ʿAwwād (Beirut: Dār al-Rāʾid al-ʿArabī, 1986 [reprint of Baghdad, 1951]).
Fāris al-Shidyāq, *Al-sāq ʿala al-sāq* (Beirut: Dār al-Raʾid al-ʿArabi, 1982); English translation by Humphrey Davies, *Leg over Leg* (New York: NYU Press, 2013).
Muhammad Shukri, *Al-Khubz al-ḥāfī* (London: Dar al-Saqi, 1982).
Muhammad Shukri, *Al-Shuṭṭār* (London: Dar al-Saqi, 1994).
Quentin Skinner, 'Hobbes and the Classical Theory of Laughter', *Visions of Politics*, vol. III: Hobbes and Civil Science (Cambridge: Cambridge University Press, 2002).
Paul Sprachman, *Suppressed Persian* (Costa Mesa: Mazda Publishers, 1995).
ʿAlawiyya Ṣubḥ, *Ismuhu l-gharām* (Beirut: Dār al-Ādāb, 2009).
Abdellah Taia, *Une mélancolie arabe* (Paris: Seuil, 2008).
Aḥmad al-Tīfāshī, *Nuzhat al-albāb*, ed. Jamāl Jumʿa (London: Riyad al-Rayyis, 1992).
J.W. Wright, Jr., 'Masculine Allusion and the Structure of Satire', in J.W. Wright, Jr. and Everett Rowson (eds.), *Homoeroticism in Classical Arabic Literature* (New York: Columbia University Press, 1997), 1–23.
Jurjī Zaydān, *Mashāhīr al-Sharq*, 2 vols. (Beirut: Dār Maktabat al-Ḥayāt, n.d.).
Dror Ze'evi, *Producing Desire: changing sexual discourse in the Ottoman Middle East 1500–1900* (Berkeley/Los Angeles: University of California Press, 2006).

15

The Foul-Mouthed *Faḥla*: Obscenity and Amplification in Early Women's Invective

Marlé Hammond

> A woman, when she writes, wants to become a *faḥl* ([a stallion] like a stallion of the poets, for example), but the language instead turns her into a *faḥla*, and we must not be deceived by this 'sound' etymological declination. For *faḥla* in the dictionaries is a sharp-tongued one (*al-Qāmūs al-Muḥīṭ*): she who uses her tongue as a sword. Hence the derivation (from *faḥl* to *faḥla*) does not preserve the meaning of the (of course masculine) origin. The derivation is irregular.[1]
>
> ʿAbd al-Majīd Jaḥfa

> Le dérivé d'un genre deviant péjorative quand il désigne l'autre genre.[2]
> A word derived from one gender becomes pejorative when it designates the other.
>
> Tahar Labib Djedidi

Elsewhere I have argued that the use of sexually explicit or obscene language and imagery is a tacit if often unacknowledged criterion of *fuḥūla* – that quality of poetic 'prowess' or 'machismo' that in the Arabic tradition distinguishes the outstanding poets from those who are merely accomplished.[3] Another criterion, and one which is widely recognised, is that the poets should excel in the genre of *hijāʾ* (invective or satire) and be

[1] ʿAbd al-Majīd Jaḥfa, *Saṭwat al-nahār wa-siḥr al-layl: al-fuḥūla wa-mā yuwāzīhā fī l-taṣawwur al-ʿArabī* (Casablanca: Dār Tūbqāl, 1996), 38.

[2] Tahar Labib Djedidi, *La poésie amoureuse des Arabes: le cas des ʿUḏrites* (Algiers: Société Nationale d'Edition et de Diffusion, 1974), 17. Jaḥfa's annotations led me to this source.

[3] See 'On Stallions, Viragos, and Tears', Chapter 1 of my monograph *Beyond Elegy: Classical Arabic Women's Poetry in Context* (Oxford: Oxford University Press, 2010), 29–58.

able to defeat their rivals in versified slinging matches.[4] There would appear to be a link, then, between the *faḥla*, or 'sharp-tongued' woman, and the celebrated male poet, even if there is no 'stallionette' in the classical Arabic poetic canon.[5]

There are accounts of women poets defeating their male counterparts in rounds of flyting,[6] and their poetic aptitude was judged accordingly, but far more common in female-authored literature are poetic jibes recounted as if they are addressed to husbands and lovers, men of whom the poets would have had intimate knowledge. Large swathes of Ibn Abī Ṭāhir Ṭayfūr's *Balāghāt al-Nisāʾ*, a ninth-century treatise on women's eloquence,[7] are devoted to what women have had to say in prose or verse about the merits and inadequacies of their husbands. A great deal of this material is patently folkloric, unattributed to any particular individuals and/or highly formulaic in its presentation, and much of it contains material that is either erotic or obscene.[8] The formulaic presentation manifests itself in a kind of escalation, whereby there is a tendency to move from the trivial to the egregious, in the case of faults, and from the mildly admirable to the sublime, in case of merits. Insults get worse and worse, compliments get better in better, and in both cases there may be a tendency for the traits described to become increasingly sexual.

THE FORMULA

This kind of momentum can be found in the longer folkloric anecdotes where unnamed figures speak in turn, such as in the version of the *ḥadīth* of Abū Zarᶜ that occurs in Ibn Ṭayfūr's *Balāghāt al-Nisāʾ*. ᶜĀʾisha reports that one day the Prophet said to her, 'To you, I am like Abū Zarᶜ'. 'O Messenger of God', she replies, 'who is this Abū Zarᶜ'? Muḥammad

[4] See, for example, Adonis, *al-Thābit wa-l-mutaḥawwil*, vol. 2: 'Taʾṣīl al-uṣūl' (Beirut: Dār al-ᶜAwda, 1977), 37–46.

[5] Al-Khansāʾ famously ranks among the most celebrated poets and appears in Ibn Sallām al-Jumaḥī's *Ṭabaqāt fuḥūl al-shuᶜarāʾ*, but the class to which she belongs is called '*ṭabaqat aṣḥāb al-marāthī*' ('masters of elegies' rather than 'stallions of elegies'). See Hammond, *Beyond Elegy*, 36.

[6] One such famous exchange of invective between a man and a woman where the latter was judged (at least retrospectively by the critics) to be the winner occurred between Laylā l-Akhyaliyya and al-Nābigha l-Jaᶜdī. See Muḥammad ᶜAbd al-Qādir Aḥmad (ed.), *Fuḥūlat al-shuᶜarāʾ li-Abī Ḥātim al-Sijistānī: taḥqīq wa-dirāsa* (Cairo: Maktabat al-Nahḍa l-Miṣriyya, 1991), 125.

[7] The treatise is one of three surviving parts of a much longer work on prose and verse called *Kitāb al-Manthūr wa-l-manẓūm*. See the introduction to Muḥsin Ghayyāḍ (ed.), *al-Manthūr wa-l-manẓūm: al-Qaṣāʾid al-mufradāt allatī lā mathal lahā* by Abī l-Faḍl Aḥmad b. Abī Ṭāhir Ṭayfūr (Beirut: Turāth ᶜUwaydāt, 1977), 23.

[8] I should note here that there is an entirely separate section dedicated to the anecdotes about the *mawājin*. This section, which is even more heavily folkloric, contains humorous, titillating and disturbing reports about illicit sexual encounters between women and various other entities. Most reports involve completely anonymous figures, but there is a collection of *akhbār* featuring the legendary Ḥubbā of Medina. For a discussion of this notorious *mājina*, see Fedwa Malti-Douglas, *Woman's Body, Woman's Word: gender and discourse in Arabo-Islamic writing* (Princeton: Princeton University Press, 1991), 45–8.

then told the story of eleven women in the pre-Islamic period, five of whom denigrated their spouses and six of whom praised theirs. The first of the censurers complains that hers is skinny; the second that hers is sickly and impotent; the third that hers is a ravenous eater and shuns physical contact; the fourth that hers is gangly and keeps her suspended in a state of limbo between marriage and divorce; the fifth then reveals that her husband's faults are so numerous that she fears her words would be too long. The six admirers of their husbands then speak: the first says hers is neither hot nor cold, neither fearsome nor boring; the second that hers smells nice; the third that hers has an excellent physique; the fourth that hers is brave and has a healthy libido; the fifth that her husband, Abū Mālik, has lots of camels and is very generous with them; and finally the sixth says that her husband, Abū Zarᶜ, found her among herders of camels and made her a keeper of horses, and she then goes on to explain at great length how her husband fulfilled her every need. One day Abū Zarᶜ divorces her, and when she remarries a wealthy nobleman she declares that the latter could never measure up to the former. ᶜĀʾisha then seals the narrative, quoting Muḥammad as saying that to her he was like Abū Zarᶜ to Umm Zarᶜ.

This pattern of escalation in degree of intensity and especially in intensity of physicality that occurs in the above anecdote and is particularly noticeable with the first three responses of each category of wife also manifests itself in the shorter *akhbār* related by Ibn Ṭayfūr. Consider, for example the following statement, uttered by a woman whose husband pleads for her to praise/deride[9] the qualities she knows in him, as she has done to a previous husband. Much to his regret, she publically pronounces the following:

اعلمك اذا اكلت احتففت واذا شربت اشتففت واذا اشتملت التففت واعلمك تشبع ليلة تضاف وتنام ليلة تخاف واعلم عينك نؤمة واستك يقظة وعصاك خشبة ومشيك لبجة[10]

> I know you to gobble up when you eat and gulp down when you drink, and you get twisted up when you cover up. I know that you fill up on a guest night and you sleep on a fright night. I know that your eye dozes while your anus stays awake, and that your cane is rigid though your walk is limp.

These formulaic patterns seem to predominate in the more anonymous, more folkloric *akhbār*, but their impressions are also felt in the anecdotes related about historical figures such as the narratives embedding the verses of Ḥumayda, daughter of the Companion to the Prophet, al-Nuᶜmān b. Bashīr (d. 684 CE). I have chosen Ḥumayda because she epitomises, perhaps, the *faḥla*, or the sharp-tongued woman who, like the *faḥl* or 'stallion

---

[9] The expression 'athnā ᶜalā' (أثنى على) means either to praise or to deride someone for a certain quality, and it comes up in some of these anecdotes especially in the imperative uttered by the husband and addressed to the wife. One can read these commands in two ways: either the husband is expecting to be praised and instead is ridiculed; or the husband enjoys his spouse's invectives and eggs her on. The latter reading is often reinforced by the fact that the husband often responds in kind to the jibes.

[10] Ibn Ṭayfūr, *Balāghāt al-Nisāʾ*, 87–8.

poet', is celebrated for her scathing invective. Ḥumayda is said to have married three men and satirised each in turn. Drawing primarily on the content of Ibn Ṭayfūr's *Balāghāt al-Nisāʾ* and al-Iṣfahānī's *Kitāb al-Aghānī*, works dating from the 3rd/9th and 4th/10th centuries respectively, in the following exploration of the 'obscene' or at least 'scatological' content of her *hijāʾ*, I will attempt to locate echoes of this folkloric pattern of escalation and ask whether the historical 'chronological' narrative surrounding the stories either reinforces or obstructs these patterns.

ḤUMAYDA BT. AL-NUʿMĀN: SATIRICAL MONOGAMIST

Abū l-Faraj al-Iṣfahānī sums up Ḥumayda's character as follows:

كانت شاعرة ذات لسان وعارضة وشرّ، فكانت تهجو أزواجها[11]

'She was a poet with tongue, contrariness, and evil, and she would satirise her spouses.'[12] Hence she seems a fine candidate for the *faḥla* sobriquet. When one reconstructs her marital career from the various anecdotes circulating about her interactions with her husbands, one finds an escalation in the fierceness of the invective, particularly with regard to its scatological content and humour derived from bodily functions and sexual drives. This escalation would seem to represent a folkloric impulse, a folkloric impulse which is not necessarily unhistorical or ahistorical, but rather reflects a mode of representation which was either resisted or de-prioritised by the scholars who were recording the anecdotes in writing; husbands 1, 2 and 3 retain their chronological positions, but this chronology loses control of the sequencing of the written narrative.[13] In these books of belles-lettres, Husband #2, who as a one-time governor of Palestine is the most historically prominent of the three, comes to the fore, and the main story becomes one about Ḥumayda's marriage to him rather than about the escalation of tension in a series of marriages.[14] The positions of husbands 1 and 3 are either

[11] Abū l-Faraj al-Iṣfahānī, *Kitāb al-Aghānī*, ed. Iḥsān ʿAbbās et al (Beirut: Dār Ṣādir, 2004), 16:38.

[12] Arie Schippers refers to this same passage in his piece 'The Role of Women in Medieval Abdalusian Arabic Story-Telling', in Frederick de Jong (ed.), *Verse and the Fair Sex: Studies in Arabic Poetry and in the Representation of Women in Arabic Literature* (Utrecht: M.Th. Housma Stichting, 1993), 140.

[13] Vladimir Propp argues that early literature, or what is often termed 'belles-lettres' is almost entirely 'reflected and refracted folklore'. See *Theory and History of Folklore*, trans. Ariadna Y. Martin and Richard P. Martin, ed. Anatoly Liberman (Minneapolis: University of Minnesota Press, 1984), 13. One definitely gets that sense here; for even though Ḥumayda is a 'historical' figure, it could be that her persona was inserted into a pre-existing narrative.

[14] According to their respective entries in the second edition of the *Encyclopaedia of Islam*, Rawḥ b. Zinbāʿ was 'especially prominent in upholding the Umayyad cause against the Zubayrids in the second civil war' while al-Nuʿmān b. Bashīr 'declared openly for ʿAbd Allāh b. al-Zubayr' after Yazīd b. Muʿāwiya's death in 683. See G.R. Hawting, 'Rawḥ b. Zinbāʿ', *Encyclopaedia of Islam*, 2nd edition, Brill Online, 2012, School of Oriental and African Studies (SOAS), 29 December 2012, and K.V. Zettersteén, 'al-Nuʿmān b. Bas̲h̲īr', *Encyclopaedia of Islam*, 2nd edition, Brill Online, 2012, School of

destabilised or deemphasised in the narrative sequencing, and the folkloric pattern is somewhat repressed.

Husband #1

The first husband whom she is said to have satirised is identified as either al-Ḥārith b. Khālid b. al-ʿĀṣī b. Hishām b. al-Mughīra or Khālid b. al-Muhājir b. Khālid b. al-Walīd b. al-Mughīra:[15]

نكحت المدينيّ إذ جاءني فيالك من نكحة غاوية
كهول دمشق وشبّانها أحبّ إلينا من الجالية
صنانٌ لهم كصنان التيو س أعيا على المسك والغالية[16]

I married the Medinan when he came to me
O what a misguided marriage
The men of Damascus, old as well as young
Are preferable to me than the émigrés
They have the body odour of billy-goats
A smell that defies all musk and ambergris

And so her first husband, we learn, was smelly. This is not, on the face of it, a particularly stinging or obscene smear. Yet an investigation of the word *ṣunān* reveals a certain sexual innuendo. While its basic meaning, according to Lane is a 'stink or stench whether of the armpit or otherwise', it is often applied to 'the odour of the he-goat when excited by lust'.[17] Since the word for male goats (*tuyūs*) appears alongside *ṣunān* the implication is clear: the husband smells bad when he is horny. In the *Aghānī*, the husband's supposed response, insinuating that Damascene ladies smell like rotten hides although they smear their *ṣunān* with musk, is set as a song.[18] Thus, I suppose the feeling was mutual.

Husband #2

If husband number one smelled like a randy goat, husband number two, Rawḥ b. Zinbāʿ (d. 703), had even more repulsive traits. At least one of these traits is rather transparently a poetic conceit, as it is based on a double entendre involving the name of her husband's tribe: Judhām – the name means 'leprosy'.

Oriental and African Studies (SOAS), 29 December 2012. It may be that political tensions between the pro-Umayyad husband and the pro-Zubayrid father fed into the folklorization of the fractiousness of Ḥumayda's marriage to Rawḥ.

15 Al-Iṣfahānī, *Aghānī*, 9:168.

16 Al-Iṣfahānī, *Aghānī*, 9:168.

17 Edward William Lane, *Arabic-English Lexicon* (London: Williams and Norgate, 1863–7), *ṣ – n – n*.

18 Al-Iṣfahānī, *Aghānī*, 9:168.

بكى الخز من روح وأنكر جلده وعجت عجيجاً من جذام المطارف[19]

The Silk whined about Rūḥ and disdained his skin
Whilst the Shawls clamoured about the Judhām

Leprosy is not the only trait she impugns in him, for it turns out that Rawḥ, much like her first husband, reeked. Consider the following exchange of insults Rawḥ initiates with Ḥumayda:

أثْني عليّ بما علمت فإنني مثن عليك بنتن ريح الجورب[20]

Deride me for what you know, for I
Deride you for the stink of your socks

فثناؤك شرّ الثناء عليكم أسوى وأنتن من سلاح الثعلب[21]

Your derision is the vilest of you all
Worse and more noxious than the thin dung of a fox

Notice that much as was the case with the first husband, Ḥumayda associates him with a bad odour emitted by an animal. Yet it is not simply a case of repetition but of escalation: she complains not of the smell of an effusion (body odour) but rather of the smell of an emission (excrement). Another poetic utterance by Ḥumayda makes a further link between the undesirability of the husbands:

وهل أنا إلّا مُهرةٌ عربيةٌ سليلةُ أفراسٍ تجلّلها بَغلُ
فإنْ نُتِجَت مُهراً كريماً فَبالحَرَى وإنْ يَكُ إقرافٌ فَمِن قِبَلِ الفَحْلِ[22]

Am I nought but an Arab filly,
the offspring of horses, who has been mounted by a mule?
If she gives birth to a noble colt, then that's only fitting
But if it's a hybrid, that's down to the male.[23]

In the above poem Ḥumayda ridicules her husband for his inferior breeding; after all, as a daughter of a Companion to the Prophet, one imagines it would be difficult for a spouse to compete with her pedigree. But there is also a sense in which she ridicules him sexually – the idea of a mule 'mounting' a filly is counterintuitive since a mule is the

[19] Ibn Ṭayfūr, *Balāghāt*, 95.

[20] Ibn Ṭayfūr, *Balāghāt*, 96.

[21] Ibn Ṭayfūr, *Balāghāt*, 96. Al-Iṣfahānī, *Aghānī*, 9: 170.

[22] Al-Jāḥiẓ, *Kitāb al-qawl fī l-bighāl* (Cairo: Muṣṭafā l-Bābī l-Ḥalabī, 1955), 121. Ibn Ṭayfūr, *Balāghāt*, 96, has 'taḥallalahā' instead of 'tajallalahā'.

[23] Al-Zamakhsharī cites this line as evidence that the word *iqrāf*, which here refers to miscegenation, is used specifically in those cases where it is the father who is non-Arab, as opposed to *hujna*, which would refer to cases where it is the mother who is non-Arab. See *Asās al-Balāgha* (Beirut: Maktabat Lubnān, 1996), *q-r-f*. He does not attribute the line to Ḥumayda.

barren offspring of a horse and a donkey. One wonders if she is not also asserting her poetic supremacy when she calls herself a *muhra*, and strips the word *faḥl* of any positive association with male prowess or fecundity.[24] Indeed, one could say that she divests it from all connotations apart from anatomical masculinity and imbues it with negativity through its association with *baghl*, that is both its parallel positioning as a rhyme word and the fact that it too refers directly to the object of her satire. This contention that Ḥumayda is in effect claiming for herself the poetic status of *muhra* as a linguistically viable parallel to *faḥl* could be countered by the observation that there is a fault in the prosody of the couplet, a fault known as *iqwāʾ* whereby a rhyme word is in the wrong grammatical case, forcing either a syntactical error or a discordant vocalisation of the rhyme. This particular *iqwāʾ*, however, strikes me as exquisite, especially if we read *baghlū* as the rhyme carrying the fault. The *baghl*, quite simply, is out of place: it should be the offspring of a filly not the mate of one. As al-Jāḥiẓ remarks in *Kitāb al-Qawl fī-l-bighāl*, the poet has used the term outside its usual context (*fa-waḍaʿat al-baghl fī ghayri mawḍiʿih*); the mule is wrong, the rhyme is wrong, the husband is wrong.

Husband #3

If husband number one smelled like a randy goat, and husband number two was leprous, had loose stools, and was an inadequate mate, husband number three, who, incidentally, we are told was very handsome, turned out to be the most disgusting of them all. Here again there is wordplay: the name of her third husband, Fayḍ, which has a basic meaning of 'overflowing' and is associated with generosity, has enormous scatological and sexual potential, and most of the jibes Ḥumayda directs against Fayḍ feature his name and test the boundaries of its associations, as in the examples below:

سميت فيضاً ولا شيء تفيض به   إلا بجعرك بين الباب والدار[25]

Your name is Fayḍ but you overflow with nothing
Save your excrement between door and dwelling

الا يا فيض كنت أراك فيضاً   فلا فيضاً وجدت ولا فراتا[26]

Did I not think of you Fayḍ as overflowing?
But no water did I find, neither flowing nor sweet

[24] Something similar occurs in an invective by Nazhūn addressed to a male satirist. There, the rhyme word is *mudhakkar*. As an attribute of the poem's addressee, namely his masculinity, the word accrues a lot of negativity through its association with negative rhyme words. As an attribute of the poet Nazhūn's verse, it takes on the positive meaning of 'mentioned'. See *Beyond Elegy*, 144, or my original article 'He Said "She said": Narrations of Women's Verse in Classical Arabic Literature – a case study: Nazhūn's *hijāʾ* of Abū Bakr al-Makhzūmī,' *Middle Eastern Literatures* 6.1 (2003), 11.

[25] Ibn Ṭayfūr, *Balāghāt*, 97.

[26] Ibn Ṭayfūr, *Balāghāt*, 97.

While the first verse above makes a very explicit association between Fayḍ and an identifiable bodily emission, the second is rather cryptic; the *fayḍ* of the second hemistich would seem to me to refer to semen, and Fayḍ's lack thereof. An insistence on interpreting the image as a bodily emission is, I think, justified, both because of all the other verses that refer to these emissions explicitly, and because of the framing narratives, which describe Fayḍ as an alcoholic who would vomit in Ḥumayda's lap.[27] A third invective directed against Fayḍ represents the climax of Ḥumayda's scatological verbal abuse.

وليس فيض بفياض العطاء لنا   لكن فيضا لنا بالسلح فياض

ليث الليوث علينا باسل شرس   وفي الحروب هيوب الصدر حياض[28]

Fayḍ does not overflow with gifts for us
    Rather he is overflowing [*fayyāḍ*] with loose stool for us
A scowling ill-tempered lion when he sets on us
    Yet in wars he is timid of bosom and [*ḥayyāḍ*]

I leave *ḥayyāḍ* untranslated for the moment, both because among all the versions of the poem I have consulted the word occurs uniquely in Ibn Ṭayfūr, and also because it is such a provocative image that it resists 'fluid' translation and my rendering of this image into English would at least initially be dismissed by the reader as unlikely, as it must have been by all those redactors who no doubt thought that they were correcting an error in transcription when they rendered *ḥayyāḍ* '*jayyāḍ*', meaning 'cowardly' or 'fleeing'.[29] *Ḥayyāḍ*, however, yields a much more forceful indictment of the husband's character, and one which fits into the trajectory of her imagery of bodily emissions. It translates as 'menstruating' or 'overflowing with menstrual blood'. Talk about unsound etymological derivations! If a woman cannot be a 'stallion', surely a man cannot menstruate, and yet this is precisely the force, the viciousness, and the ingenuity of Ḥumayda's verse. Apart from the fact that one of the basic meanings of the verb *ḥāḍa*, which is nearly always conjugated in the feminine, is 'to menstruate', as noted by the editor of the *Balāghāt* in connection with this image,[30] my substantiating evidence for this reading is threefold.

First, the context in which the couplet appears, that is both the neighbouring verses and the narrative framework, suggests, as I have demonstrated, a preoccupation with bodily fluids and emissions. Not only do we have numerous references to these (to body

[27] Ibn Ṭayfūr, *Balāghāt*, 97; Al-Iṣfahānī, *Aghānī*, 9: 172 and 16:38.

[28] Ibn Ṭayfūr, *Balāghāt*, 98.

[29] Al-Iṣfahānī, *Aghānī*, 9:172. This word is also found in Ibn ʿAsākir, *Tārīkh Madīnat Dimashq*, ed. ʿUmar Ibn Gharāma al-ʿAmrāwī (Beirut: Dār al-Fikr, 1995–1998), 69:100. *Jayyāḍ* means 'fleeing from the enemy' (al-Zamakhsharī, *Asās al-Balāgha*, *j-y-ḍ*), and certainly makes sense in the context of the line. Curiously, this word, too, may be said to evoke menstruation, albeit indirectly. According to al-Zamakhsharī (*Asās al-Balāgha*, *ḥ-y-ḍ*), one says of a man whose habit is to flee and run away that he nearly menstruates:

فلان ديدنه أن يحيص ويجيض ويوشك أن يحيض

[30] Ibn Ṭayfūr, *Balāghāt*, 98, note 2.

odour, to excrement, to vomit, [to semen]) but we also see a progressive escalation from least to most offensive, from least to most repulsive. Second, the words *fayyāḍ* and *ḥayyād*, *fayḍ* and *ḥayḍ*, are semantically linked, as they are both associated with water and its abundant flowing. Third, menstrual imagery is not uncommon in women's poetry – or men's for that matter – and is associated in particular with the battlefield, which is precisely where Ḥumayda places Fayḍ in this hemistich. The association stems mainly from images of menstruation in early elegies and blood-vengeance poetry; both the corpse of the deceased and his surviving kinsmen are sometimes portrayed as 'polluted' or 'defiled' by menstrual blood, as Suzanne Stetkevych has shown.[31] One also finds a lexical connection between menstruation and war in words derived from the root ᶜ – *r*- *k*, although no such word is used here.[32]

It would seem that Ḥumayda's whole literary and marital career was all building up to this, the ultimate of put-downs. Earlier, and in verses not cited here, she had cast feminizing aspersions on her second husband, Rawḥ,[33] but she saves the best for last, so-to-speak, and targets Fayḍ for this particular jibe, associating him with what is perhaps perceived as the most repugnant bodily emission, and one that is normally confined to the female of the species, one which, in its non-intensive form, *ḥā*ʾ*iḍ*, does not normally take the feminine marker when applied to a woman, since only women bleed in this way.

SEQUENCING AND THE SERIAL MONOGAMIST

The pattern of amplification is discernible in the sources but diluted somewhat due to the scholarly interventions of the redactors of Ḥumayda's corpus. As I mentioned earlier, as the most historically significant husband, Rawḥ is privileged, occupying more of the narrative's attention. In Ibn Ṭayfūr her marriage to Rawḥ, their versified exchanges as husband and wife, and Ḥumayda's exchanges relating to this marriage with third parties come first and consist of some forty lines of text. Fayḍ enters in to the narrative in the context of her marriage to Rawḥ; her marriage to Rawḥ ends with the latter predicting that she will find a husband who will slap her and vomit in her lap.[34] This third marriage, her verses devoted to her third husband, and the story of an exchange she had with al-Ḥajjāj b. Yūsuf after their daughter married him consume only about seventeen lines of text. Finally the first husband comes last and consumes about fourteen lines. The sequencing of the narrative thus upsets the pattern of escalation; however Ibn Ṭayfūr's redaction of her poetry perhaps best preserves the amplification inherent in what I think

[31] See Suzanne Pinckney Stetkevych's book, *The Mute Immortals Speak: Pre-Islamic Poetry and the Poetics of Ritual* (Ithaca: Cornell University Press, 1993), 66–7, 172–5, 194–6, 227, as well as her article 'Sarah and the Hyena: Laughter, Menstruation, and the Genesis of a Double Entendre,' *History of Religions* 35.5 (1996), 13–41.

[32] See Stetkevych, *Mute Immortals*, 172–4.

[33] See Ibn Ṭayfūr, *Balāghāt*, 97, and al-Iṣfahānī, *Aghānī*, 9:171, where she accuses Rawḥ of lining his eyes with kohl like an adulterous prostitute (مومسة زانية).

[34] Ibn Ṭayfūr, *Balāghāt*, 97.

of as the 'original' folkloric narrative through the retention of at least one key item of vocabulary: *ḥayyāḍ*. Two accounts of Ḥumayda's marital career are found in the *Aghānī*, once in the chapter on al-Ḥārith b. Khālid, who is sometimes identified as Ḥumayda's first husband, and once in the chapter on her father al-Nuᶜmān b. Bashīr and his progeny.[35] In both of these accounts, the chronology of the marriages is retained in the narrative sequencing, thus the potential for the amplification is formally unperturbed. However, in the second account, which is very short, there are no references to bodily emissions in the verses addressed to Rawḥ, so the sense of escalation is muted somewhat. The first account, which resembles the narrative of Ibn Ṭayfūr quite a bit, apart from its repositioning of the first husband of the start of the narrative, does contain a reference to Rawḥ's bowel movements, so the sense of escalation created by the sequencing of odour→excrement→vomit is maintained. However, the sense of escalation here too is diluted in part by the unequal attention to the husbands – once again Rawḥ predominates – as well as the fact that *jayyāḍ*, 'fleeing', is substituted for *ḥayyāḍ*, 'menstruating'. By the time the narrative appears in Ibn ᶜAsākir's twelfth-century *Tārīkh Madīnat Dimashq*,[36] the momentum of escalation is almost entirely lost; although the chronology of the husbands is maintained, the insults directed against them do not really relate to one another. No bodily emissions are evoked, except in the verses about Fayḍ. She does not address any poetry to Rawḥ at all, although she does insult his tribe in prose. What seems to take the place of that section of the narrative that would normally be devoted to her exchanges of insults with Rawḥ are a couple of elegiac fragments mourning the passing of her father.

CONCLUSION

Ḥumayda's verses and their narrative embedding thus offer us insights into two questions that beset aficionados of Arabic women's writing, one being a question of literary history, the other of grammar. Regarding what we perceive as the diminishment of women as poets after the coming of Islam, and especially after the Umayyad era, a diminishment that would seem to coincide with the transition of verbal culture from an oral phase to a written one, the folkloric pattern inherent in both her words and their narration and the way in which the redactors of her story interfered with this patterning captures an intriguing moment of literary history. This moment has implications for men's verse as well as women's, obviously, but it may also help to explain how the eventual predominance of the written over the oral affected or distorted the images, innuendos and structures which may have characterised women's poetry in particular, since the males recording women's words in writing were not necessarily privy or attentive to their nuances.

On the question of grammar, Ḥumayda's verses demonstrate the flexibility of gender division in the Arabic language, which, in my opinion is too often seen as inherently rigid,

---

[35] Al-Iṣfahānī, *Aghānī*, 9:168–73 and 16:38–9.

[36] Ibn ᶜAsākir, *Tārīkh madīnat Dimashq*, ed. ᶜUmar Ibn Gharāma al-ᶜAmrāwī (Beirut: Dār al-Fikr, 1995–1998), 69: 98–101.

sexist, and therefore oppressive for its female if not also its male users. Too often the grammatical markings of femininity are understood as diminutive, while the masculine, the *faḥl*, is thought to reign supreme. One never seems to consider the possibility that Arabic, with its absence of 'neuter' – that is with its categorisation of all nouns and all verb conjugations as either masculine or feminine – may provide more opportunities for meaningful subversions than a language that does have the category of 'neuter'. To my mind there are two instances of such subversions in the verses cited above. When Ḥumayda calls herself a *muhra*, she is acknowledging that one may not add a *tāʾ marbūṭa* to the *faḥl*, since its basic meaning is 'male'. Yet one may add a *tāʾ marbūṭa* to *muhr*, since its basic meaning is 'horse'. She cannot be a 'stallionette', but she can be a 'filly'. Meanwhile, by associating the *faḥl* (stallion) with the *baghl* (mule), she divests the former of its connotations of sexual procreativity and good breeding, and links masculinity with sexual inadequacy. The other subversion is, of course, *ḥayyāḍ*. I do not think this intensive adjective is a common way of expressing 'menstruating', and therefore I cannot comment on the absence of a feminine marker, but the active participle *ḥāʾiḍ* does not need to take one. By describing her husband as 'menstruating', she clearly subverts the lexicon at the same time that she conforms to grammar.

On a final note, I would like to revisit a claim I made at the opening of this essay, that the best poets are often assumed to be those (men) who excel at sexually explicit satire. Not everyone would agree with this generalization; for it seems that some preferred invective of an innocent and dainty variety. As Geert Jan van Gelder relates in his book *The Bad and the Ugly*, the eighth-century *qāriʾ* Abū ʿAmr b. al-ʿAlāʾ is often quoted as saying, 'the best *hijāʾ* is what a virgin may recite in her private room without impertinence'.[37]

WORKS CITED

Adonis, *al-Thābit wa-l-mutaḥawwil*, vol. 2: 'Taʾṣīl al-uṣūl' (Beirut: Dār al ʿAwda, 1977).

Geert Jan van Gelder, *The Bad and the Ugly: attitudes towards invective poetry (hijāʾ) in classical Arabic literature* (Leiden: Brill, 1988).

Marlé Hammond, *Beyond Elegy: Classical Arabic Women's Poetry in Context* (Oxford: Oxford University Press, 2010).

Marlé Hammond, 'He Said "She said": Narrations of Women's Verse in Classical Arabic Literature – a case study: Nazhūn's *hijāʾ* of Abū Bakr al-Makhzūmī,' *Middle Eastern Literatures* 6.1 (2003)

G.R. Hawting, 'Rawḥ b. Zinbāʿ', *Encyclopaedia of Islam*, 2nd edition, Brill Online , 2012, School of Oriental and African Studies (SOAS), 29 December 2012.

Ibn ʿAsākir, *Tārīkh madīnat Dimashq*, ed. ʿUmar Ibn Gharāma al-ʿAmrāwī (Beirut: Dār al-Fikr, 1995–1998).

Ibn Ṭayfūr, *Balāghāt al-Nisāʾ* (Cairo: Maṭbaʿat Madrasat Wālidat ʿAbbās al-Awwal, 1908).

Abū l-Faraj al-Iṣfahānī, *Kitāb al-Aghānī*, ed. Iḥsān ʿAbbās et al (Beirut: Dār Ṣādir, 2004).

---

37 Geert Jan van Gelder, *The Bad and the Ugly: Attitudes towards invective poetry (hijāʾ) in classical Arabic literature* (Leiden: Brill, 1988), 43.

ʿAbd al-Majīd Jaḥfa, *Saṭwat al-nahār wa-siḥr al-layl: al-fuḥūla wa-mā yuwāzīhā fī l-taṣawwur al-ʿArabī* (Casablanca: Dār Tūbqāl, 1996).
al-Jāḥiẓ, *Kitāb al-qawl fī l-baghl* (Cairo: Muṣṭafā l-Bābī l-Ḥalabī, 1955).
Fedwa Malti-Douglas, *Woman's Body, Woman's Word: Gender and Discourse in Arabo-Islamic Writing* (Princeton: Princeton University Press, 1991).
Vladimir Propp, *Theory and History of Folklore*, trans. Ariadna Y. Martin and Richard P. Martin, ed. Anatoly Liberman (Minneapolis: University of Minnesota Press, 1984).
Arie Schippers, 'The Role of Women in Medieval Andalusian Arabic Story-Telling', in Frederick de Jong (ed.), *Verse and the Fair Sex: Studies in Arabic Poetry and in the Representation of Women in Arabic Literature* (Utrecht: M.Th. Housma Stichting, 1993), 140.
Suzanne Pinckney Stetkevych, *The Mute Immortals Speak: Pre-Islamic Poetry and the Poetics of* Ritual (Ithaca: Cornell University Press, 1993).
Suzanne Pinckney Stetkevych, 'Sarah and the Hyena: Laughter, Menstruation, and the Genesis of a Double Entendre,' *History of Religions* 35.5 (1996), 13–41.
al-Zamakhsharī, *Asās al-balāgha* (Beirut: Maktabat Lubnān, 1996).
K.V. Zetterstéen, 'al-Nuʿmān b. Bas̲h̲īr', *Encyclopaedia of Islam*, 2nd edition, Brill Online , 2012, School of Oriental and African Studies (SOAS), 29 December 2012.

16

A Saudi 'housewife' goes to War: الفتاوي الشريرة or 'the evil *fatwas*'

Clive Holes

BACKGROUND

Poetry as a vehicle for invective and dissenting opinion – even the lampooning of public figures – has a very long history in Arabic literature, going back at least as far as the *naqāʾiḍ* ('flytings') of Jarīr and Farazdaq in 7th-century Iraq. In the modern Arab World, satirical verse in colloquial Arabic has been the weapon of choice for taking to task colonialists and other political undesirables for at least a century, and more recently for criticizing the interventions of foreign governments in Arab and Middle Eastern affairs.[1] It has also been extensively used to comment on controversial local social issues, from the education of girls to the fashion for marrying foreign wives to the consumerism of the modern Gulf.[2] This paper looks at a recent example of this type, which was played out in a glare of publicity initially on satellite television, subsequently on internet bulletin boards and forums, and eventually even in the Western press. The bone of contention on this occasion was the acceptability of the mixing of the sexes (*ikhtilāṭ*) at work and in educational contexts in Saudi Arabia, notably at KAUST, the brand new King Abdallah University of Science and Technology. The issue of men and women mixing in public places has generated much debate in Saudi Arabia in recent years owing to the liberal stance of the present king on social matters compared with his royal predecessors and many prominent figures in the religious establishment.

---

[1] See C.D. Holes and S.S. Abu Athera, *Poetry and Politics in Contemporary Arab Society* (Reading: Ithaca, 2009), which covers international and domestic political issues in the period from 1956 to 2006 in 41 poems by five poets from Sinai and Jordan, and C.D. Holes, 'Letter to Obama' in the journal *Middle Eastern Literatures* 14.2 (2011) pp. 183–193 for the analysis of a recent long poem by an Iraqi colloquial poet on the American-led intervention in Iraq of 2003.

[2] See C.D. Holes and S.S. Abu Athera, *The Nabati Poetry of the UAE* (Reading: Ithaca, 2011), which presents poems and verse translations of 53 poems by 25 poets, many of them on social issues of the moment.

The story is as follows

In March 2010, the poem presented below was awarded third prize (a considerable amount of money) in the final of the 4th season of the colloquial poetry talent competition 'Poet in a Million' produced and broadcast by Abu Dhabi satellite TV.[3] This is a very popular show in which poets aged between 18 and 45 compete against each other for large cash prizes. The show is dedicated to so-called 'nabaṭī' poetry, that is, the traditional colloquial poetry of the Bedouin of Arabia. This fact guarantees that the contestants come overwhelmingly from the countries of the GCC where this tradition is still very much alive. The format of the show, with its panel of expert judges and audience phone-in voting, seems to have been borrowed from British and American singing and dancing talent competitions like 'The X-Factor', 'American Idol', and the BBC's 'Strictly Come Dancing'. The composer and performer of the poem, a 43 year-old Saudi woman, later predictably depicted in the Western media that picked up the story as a 'housewife and mother-of-four'[4] is Ḥiṣṣa Hilāl, whose nom-de-plume is *rīmiyya* ('little gazelle'). In fact she is much more than a housewife and mother: a professional journalist who speaks fluent English[5] and has published critical studies of 'nabaṭī' poetry in Arabic and at least one collection of her own verse.[6] In the show, Ḥiṣṣa recited her poem fully veiled on a stage before a judging panel of four male experts, a mixed, live theatre audience of several thousand men and women, and millions watching at home on TV. If that scenario was not shocking enough to conservative opinion in Saudi Arabia, the poem takes issue – though obliquely – with a thorny issue: the tendency of Saudi clerics to issue *fatwas* in line with their own particular interpretations of Islam. This is described in indirect but at the same time graphic imagery: a monster has appeared from beneath its protective covers – a savage, intolerant fanaticism that is blind to all other points of view. The poem goes on to lament both the loss of traditional societal values (hospitality and the acceptance of outsiders), which, the poet implies, has been one of the results of increased Islamist bigotry, and the 'sale' of Saudi Arabia to unnamed forces and their vested interests.[7] But in the end, the poem concludes, the religious fanatics and corrupt

---

[3] The Arabic title of the show ‹‹شاعر المليون›› can be interpreted in various ways. In the first series, the first prize was a million UAE dirhams (it is now much more), and the show's title seemed to allude to that fact. But the Arabic can also mean 'Poet of the Million' or 'Poet in a Million' respectively, highlighting either the popular nature of the colloquial poetry it celebrates, or the transcendent talent of the winning poet.

[4] http://www.independent.co.uk/news/world/middle-east/saudi-woman-poet-lashes-out-at-clerics-in-arabic-idol-1926176.html.

[5] See her interview with the BBC: http://news.bbc.co.uk/1/hi/8587185.stm.

[6] e.g. ‹‹الطلاق والخلع شعرا›› ('Divorce of women by men and men by women, expressed through poetry'), (Abu Dhabi: Abu Dhani Culture and Heritage Academy of Poetry, 2009). A collection of her poems was recently published under the title ‹‹تنوير›› ('Enlightenment'), (Abu Dhabi: Abu Dhabi Culture and Heritage Academy of Poetry, 2011).

[7] The poet is quoted in the Saudi Gazette as saying that she wrote the poem to 'announce my rejection of the fatwa chaos which has got worse in recent times and which legitimizes bloodshed, and some of which are made out of personal interests'. See http://www.saudigazette.com.sa

politicians will be shown up for the liars and cheats they are. Strong stuff!

Not surprisingly, the poem caused a violent reaction in Saudi Arabia. Some, using the anonymity of internet message boards, expressed admiration for the poet's outspoken courage; but to religious conservatives the poem and its author are anathema. The poem has been interpreted as a personal attack on one particular cleric, highly respected in their circles, the blind 77 year-old Sheikh ʿAbd ar-Raḥmān bin Nāṣir al-Barrāk. At the end of February 2010, two weeks before the show in which Ḥiṣṣa recited her poem, Sheikh ʿAbd ar-Raḥmān had issued a *fatwa*, condemning the mixing of the sexes even in the workplace and educational establishments because this was, according to him, 'against Islam', and recommending that those who went against his ruling, if they did not recant, be killed.[8] Ḥiṣṣa Hilāl has repeatedly denied that her poem was ever intended as a reply to Sheikh ʿAbd ar-Raḥmān, still less a personal attack on him, but, she claims, simply draws attention to the chaotic and confusing situation that has arisen for ordinary Muslims as a consequence of the contradictory rulings of many *fatwas*. However, her denials have not prevented death threats being issued against her. Most interestingly, and following an age-old nabaṭī literary tradition, her poem has attracted a number of poetic rebuttals, attacking her and defending the *status quo*, as we shall see later on.

Here is Ḥiṣṣa's poem as she performed it on the show.[9] The English verse translation I have provided rhymes and is therefore somewhat liberal, though not in any way which is inconsistent with the literal meaning of the original. The rhyme scheme is a common one in nabaṭī poetry, double mono-rhyme, with all the first hemistiches in one rhyme (here -*āwī*), and all the second hemistiches in another (here -*ām*). The metre is a common nabaṭī one, a member of the metrical class known as *hjēnī* that is, sung while riding a camel (*hijin*). It does not correspond exactly to any of the Classical metres. The scansion of each hemistich follows the following pattern, with (/) indicating the division into feet:

$$- \cup - / - \cup - - / - \cup - / - \cup - (-)$$

The bracketed final long syllable occurs only in the first hemistich of each verse. In nabaṭī poetry, the hemistich is best conceived of as a syllabic matrix which completely ignores word boundaries.[10] Thus the first verse scans as follows:

/index.cfm?method=home.regcon&contentID=2010030965714.

[8] The key passage in the fatwa is:

«ومن استحلَّ هذا الاختلاط ـ وإن أدى إلى هذه المحرَّمات ـ فهو مستحلٌّ لهذه المحرَّمات، ومن استحلَّها فهو كافرٌ، ومعنى ذلك أنه يصير مرتدًّا، فيُعرَّف وتقام الحجَّة عليه فإن رجع وإلا وجب قتله»

'Whoever declares this mixing to be permissible – and should this mixing lead to those forbidden things – that person has thereby declared those forbidden things permissible, and whosoever declares them to be so is an un-believer. This means that he has become an apostate, and he should be identified as such and condemned. If he recants, (all well and good); if he does not, he must be killed'.

[9] It can be viewed and listened to at: https://www.youtube.com/watch?v=DXbT3skBjeg. A written version appears in a recently published collection of the poet's work (see fn. 6 above), which differs slightly from the version performed on the programme and available on the internet.

[10] For more details on scansion, see S. Sowayan, *Nabati Poetry* (Berkeley: University of California

–	∪	–/	–	∪	–	– /	–	∪	– /	–	∪	–	(-)
shif	*t*	*shar*	*riy*	*t*	*wā*	*yag*	*min*	*ʿu*	*yū*	*nal*	*fa*	*tā*	*wī*
fī	*za*	*mā*	*nin*	*ḥa*	*lā*	*lah*	*mil*	*g*	*ḥī*	*nah*	*ḥa*	*rām*	

الفتاوي الشريرة

by Ḥiṣṣa Hilāl

1	In the eyes of opinions I saw evil glinting:	شفت شر يتوايق من عيون الفتاوى
	What once was permitted's no longer allowed;	فى زمانٍ حلاله ملقحينه حرام
2	From the facades of truth, when the covers were lifted	عن وجوه الحقايق لارفعت الغطاوى
	A monster emerged from beneath its head shroud.	بان مسخ تخفى تحت ستر اللثام
3	Savage, resentful, purblind and barbaric,	وحشى الفكر ساخط بربرى عماوى
	Wearing death's robes and a suicide belt,	لابس الموت لبس وشد فوقه حزام[11]
4	A jackal howls loud from political hill tops,	فى حزوم السياسة يرعب الناس عاوى
	And preys on the peaceful whose terror's heartfelt.	يفترس كل نفس طامحة للسلام
5	The voices of truth fled the scene and were cornered:	لاذ صوت الحقيقة وانزوى الحق ثاوى
	For free speech takes cover when self-interest speaks;	يوم عند المصالح ذل حر الكلام
6	O nation, corralled by wild beasts and attackers,	أمتى لاغديتى بين عاوى وهاوى
	I see you entrapped in a gorge dark and bleak.	كن عينى تشوفك فى شعيب الظلام
7	You don't any more kindle fire for the stranger,	لا تشبين نار ولا حميتى جلاوى
	Ignoring your duties, you hide all alone,	ملبدة ما رفعتى بالمواجيب هام
8	Midst a gang that spreads fear with no human compassion,	بين قوم مخيفه مابها حى ياوى
	Men like wild dogs that tear flesh from the bone.	ما بها إلا ضوارى قضمها بالعظام
9	You are the bowl that sates all creatures' hunger,	أنتى القصعه اللى تشبعين المقاوى
	The predatory bird's and the scavenging beast's;	كل جارح وضارى فيك يلقى طعام
10	Friends starve to death – unconcerned, you ignore them,	يوم طاوى محبك بالهفا كل طاوى
	Whilst at banqueting tables fat hypocrites feast.	فيك ألذ الولايم لـ المنافق تقام
11	The shepherd boy's scared and the camel-herd's cowering;	هاب راعى البعير وذل ولد الشواوى
	You parade round the ring, the crowd bids up the price;	جالبك كل جالب يوم سايمك سام

Press, 1985), pp. 156–160.

[11] In the published written version, an extra line is inserted here which is missing from the performed version:

He wants to leave life, and on top of that, (he has) a desire	يبى فرقا الحياة وفوق هذا شفاوى
To take the lives of others on (his) path to death	ياخذ اعمار غيره فى سبيل العدام

12 How long you have suffered: a prize slaughter-camel,	آه يا طول ضيمك يا جزورالشفاوى
Led off by the nose by a man steeped in vice.	يوم الأسحم يقودك لأبرقِ بالخطام
13 In the conjuror's bag there's a trick for each trickster,	بالجراب المصرصر غاية لكل حاوى
Their murky intentions round white doves are coiled;	حيث رقط النوايا لاويه بالحمام
14 Your stock in the politics market's rock-bottom,	نزلوا سهمك اللى ياكلون الرشاوى
Broken to bits, and by bribery soiled.	وسط سوق السياسة لين عود حطام
15 To too many friends, when they plead for assistance,	كم محبٍ ومخلص لو يزج النخاوى
You turn up your nose, in disgust turn away;	عند عينك تغطرس قل شوفك وشام
16 But the time, it will come, when true friends show their colours,	يجى يوم يبين فيه صدق الهواوى
And the traitors all hide on the Lord's Judgement Day.	لا بجد كل خاين فى نهار الزحام

Commentary

Ḥiṣṣa is from Najd, and her poem contains certain linguistic forms and vocabulary particular to that region, which make it difficult for non-Saudis to understand so some help will be given here. First, a couple of phonological observations. The pronunciation is that of ordinary Najdi speech: *g*, as throughout central and eastern Arabic, is the reflex of CLA *q* and the 2nd feminine singular enclitic pronoun is pronounced as a dental affricate *ts* (different from the alveolar affricate *ch* used on the Gulf coast), e.g. l.10 *muḥibbits* 'the one who loves you', and *fīts* 'in you' and l. 11 *jālbits* 'who brings you'. The dialectal form of *tanwīn*, if that is the correct way to describe it, is always -*in*. It is common in traditional poetry and occurs a number of times here: *zamān-in* (l.1), *gōm-in* (l.8), *abrag-in*[12] (l.12), *muḥibb-in* (l.15), *yōm-in* (l.16). Glosses are given below of Bedouin lexical items and allusions. It will be noted that many of these are related to CLA words and senses not used in MSA or in other dialects of Arabic.

l. 1 ‹‹عيون الفتاوي›› 'the eyes of opinions'. The 'eyes' here are meant in the sense of the authoritative 'sources' of legal opinions or the 'springs' from which they emanate. The verb يتوايق has the sense in Bedouin Arabic of 'emerge / peep out furtively'.[13] The second

---

[12] Both in ordinary speech and poetry, dialectal *tanwīn* occurs freely on many word-types, like this one, whose CLA equivalents never carried *tanwīn*. This suggests that dialectal *tanwīn* is not a residue of the Classical system, but may be a development of it. But this assumes – and this is a moot point – that any historical relationship at all existed between them. The survival of 'dialectal *tanwīn*' in very similar forms in the early Arabic dialects for which we have textual evidence, such as Andalusian, and in others, such as those of central Asia, which date from even earlier (c. 9th century CE) and became 'frozen' by being completely cut-off from main-stream Arabic at an early date, suggests that this form of *tanwīn* is extremely old.

[13] P.M. Kurpershoek, *Oral Poetry and Narratives from Central Arabia,* Vol. 5: Glossary (Brill: Leiden, 2005), p. 357 notes *wāg*, *yiwīǵ* 'to see, look, examine, peek, pry, steal a glance' and *wāyag* with similar meanings. NB: here (ǵ) stands for the dental affricate (IPA [dz]), a realization of [q] (*qāf*) in

hemistich suggests that 'what is prohibited' is being clandestinely grafted onto 'what is permitted' thereby changing its nature to 'prohibited'. The sense is of an insidious take-over of public morals by opportunist clerics who see a chance to impose their views.
l. 2 The implication is that the 'faces of truth' of some religious sheikhs are no more than a facade: under them lurks an extremist Islamist agenda, which is the 'monster' ‹‹مسخ›› the poet depicts as emerging from under a headcloth bound around the lower face (which is one of the preferred styles of Islamist activists in video clips). The verb رفعت (*rifᶜat*) 'are lifted' is a dialectal passive form – passive verbs are part and parcel of spoken Najdi, as in many other Arabian Arabic dialects. لا is a variant of الا (*ila*) 'if / when'.
l. 3 The use of the word ‹‹عماوي›› has outraged some religious conservatives, as they take it as a slighting reference to Sheikh ᶜAbd ar-Raḥmān al-Barrāk's blindness (he lost his sight at the age of nine). But this word does not refer here to physical blindness (which would be ‹‹عمى›› *ᶜamay*), but rather to figurative 'blindness', e.g. a tunnel vision that is 'blind' to the points of view of others. The picture in the second hemistich is of a bomber (‹‹لابس الموت لبس›› 'dressed up as death') complete with a suicide belt.
l. 4 ‹‹حزوم السياسة›› lit. 'the hills of politics': sing ‹‹حزم›› 'hill', a Najdi term.[14] The sense of the line is that the Islamists are like jackals or wolves howling their political message from the desert hill-tops.
l. 5 ‹‹ثاوي›› : the truth hides itself and is (lit.) 'buried'.[15] The point of the line is that people who normally tell the truth keep quiet to protect themselves when faced with Islamists who are pushing their personal agendas (مصالح): free-speech (حر الكلام) is thereby 'abased' (ذل).
l. 6 ‹‹أمتي›› 'my nation'. From this line onwards, the poet is addressing the Saudi nation as a whole. ‹‹لا غديتي بين عاوي وهاوي›› lit. 'When you are between a howler (= a wolf) and an attacker'. The rhyming idiom is equivalent to 'between a rock and a hard place'/'between the devil and the deep blue sea'.
l. 7 The reference here – 'lighting a fire and protecting strangers' – is to the Bedouin tradition of offering hospitality and protection to unknown visitors from outside one's tribe, a mind-set which the poet sees as having been trumped by religious bigotry. ‹‹جلاوي›› is a Bedouin term which refers to a member of another tribe who has been outlawed and seeks refuge and protection with another.[16] The second hemistich literally means '(you're) hidden, and you haven't raised your head (above the parapet to carry out) your duties'.
l. 8 ‹‹مابها حي ياوي›› : 'among whom there is no living being who gives refuge'. The ‹‹ها›› and the feminine adjective ‹‹مخيفة›› refer back to ‹‹قوم››, in Bedouin parlance 'an army of warriors' (i.e. here, the Islamists). Human collectives (another example is ‹‹ناس››) usually require feminine singular concord.

---

contiguity with (usually high) front vowels found in Central Arabian dialects. In Gulf Arabian dialects, this is realized as (j) (IPA [ʤ]).

[14] Kurpershoek, *Oral Poetry*, p. 55: *ḥazim*, pl *ḥzūm* 'an elevation, rather low, but long and dotted with many small hillocks'.

[15] Cf. CLA *thuwiya* 'to be buried'.

[16] Kurpershoek, *Oral Poetry*, p. 40.

l. 9 ‹‹قصعة›› is a wooden eating bowl. ‹‹المقاوي›› 'the starving', pl of ‹‹مقوي››.[17]
l. 10 Lit: 'When those who love you are hungry (طاوي), (you say) "death (الهفا) to the hungry", but in you (= in your land) the most delicious banquets are prepared for hypocrites'.
ll. 11–12 In these two lines, Saudi Arabia is depicted as an animal which has been all but abandoned by its traditional protectors, the camel-herd and the shepherd, who represent the two types of Arabian pastoralists, those who raise camels (راعي البعير), that is, the Bedouin of the inner desert, and those who live on the desert edge and raise sheep (الشواوي). The second hemistich of l. 11 literally means 'Every bringer brought you (to market) when the bargainer for you bargained.' The sense is that the Saudi government has allowed the nation to be sold off to the highest bidder. It is being led to the slaughter (l. 12) as if it were a ‹‹جزورالشفاوي››, a Bedouin expression for 'prize slaughter-camel',[18] by an unspecified evil man (الأسحم) (lit. 'the black one').‹‹ابرق›› is a topographical term for a dark coloured desert mountain partly covered with sand. It is unclear what the significance of this term is in the context – perhaps it is a favoured spot for slaughter.
l. 13 ‹‹جراب›› is a bag, here of a conjuror or snake-charmer (حاوي).[19] ‹‹مصرصر›› means 'tightly closed'.[20] ‹‹حيث رقط النوايا لاويه بالحمام›› lit. 'in which spotted (i.e. dishonest) intentions are coiled around doves'. The adjective ‹‹رقط›› (here a plural form) 'spotted', 'speckled' is often applied to animals, especially lizards and snakes. The sense of this line is that the Islamists are like the conjurors who produce live doves from a bag, but their real intentions are evil, coiled like snakes around these 'doves', which stand for their ostensibly peaceful intentions.
l. 14 لين عود حطام (= *lēn ʿawwad ḥiṭām*) lit. 'until it became broken in pieces'. The sense is that Saudi politicians' credibility and reputation have been irrevocably devalued by their bribe-taking and corruption.
l. 15 Lit. 'Many a one who loves you and is faithful, when he directs his calls for help (نخاوي) to your eye, you behave haughtily (تغطرس) and your helping (lit: 'looking at') (him) is little (شوفك قل)[21] and turns in disgust away (from him) (شام).[22]
l. 16 ‹‹صدق الهواوي›› 'the constancy of those who love (you)'.[23] ‹‹بجد›› (*bijad*) 'is concealed / conceals himself' – the verb is passive.[24] The last hemistich is literally 'when every traitor hides himself when bright day comes to the crowded place'

It had been anticipated that Ḥiṣṣa Hilāl would win the competition with this poem, as it gained very high praise from the members of the judging panel and a mark of 47 out of

[17] Cf. CLA *qawiya* 'to be hungry'.
[18] Kurpershoek, *Oral Poetry*, p. 162: *shifāwī* 'longing, desiring'.
[19] Cf. the Egyptian proverb: ‹‹ياما في الجراب يا حاوي›› lit. 'how much you have in your bag, conjuror!' = 'the world is full of surprises!'
[20] ‹‹صرصر›› is reduplicative verb < صر 'to tie, bind' signifying 'to tie tightly'.
[21] In the published version, the verb ‹‹قصر›› 'falls short' is substituted for ‹‹قل›› 'is little'.
[22] Kurpershoek, *Oral Poetry*, p. 171: *shām* 'to loathe, get fed up with'.
[23] ‹‹هواوي››: A. Socin *Dīwān aus Centrarabien* (Leipzig: Teubner, 1900–1), vol. 3, p. 319 gives the meaning as 'verliebt', and Kurpershoek, *Oral Poetry*, Vol V, p. 341 gives 'lover, fancier, love-stricken'.
[24] Le C. de Landberg, *Glossaire Dathînois* (Brill: Leiden, 1920–42), p. 135.

50, the highest score they awarded in the final round of the competition. However, 40% of the result depended on the viewing public who voted via their mobile phones, and what is thought to have been mass voting by the members of tribes larger than Ḥiṣṣa's gave victory to a Kuwaiti (male) contestant.

Rebuttal

Ḥiṣṣa's poem sparked a number of furious replies. One of the most widely quoted on internet forums, by the well-known Saudi nabaṭī poet Fayṣal ibn Jazāʾ al-Dōsarī, is given below, again with my versified translation. At about the same time, he wrote disparagingly in a Saudi newspaper that the show was just about distributing money, not encouraging poetic talent, and accused the chairman of the judging panel, a UAE-based Jordanian who is a leading expert in nabaṭī poetry, of 'not knowing our [= Najdi] language'.[25]

The reply follows time-honoured tradition by imitating the metre and rhyme scheme of the original poem. As we shall see there are numerous allusions to and echoes of the original poem, sometimes by the switching around of the radical consonants of words so that an opposite meaning is given. The tone throughout is direct, outraged and scurrilous bordering on the slanderous, opening with a description of Ḥiṣṣa as 'a hyena who's howling' and a 'foolish old hag'. As before, the poem is followed by notes on the language.

A reply, by Fayṣal ibn Jazāʾ al-Dōsarī

1	God strike her dumb, that hyena who's howling!	اخرس الله لسان الضبعه اللى تعاوى!
	That foolish old hag on the 'Seashore of Trash',	العجوز السفيهه وسط شاطى الخمام
2	In this age when each shameless, immoral, lewd scoundrel,	في زمانٍ تجرى كل فاجر وغوي
	Dares to mouth off, Sheikh Barrak to abash.	بالتطاول على البراك عالى المقام
3	His opinions hurt those such as you who oppose them,	الفتاوى تضرك ياعدو الفتاوى
	They don't suit your whims nor permit what's harām	ماتوافق هواك وماتحلل حرام
4	Husaysa, your poem is full of vile slanders,	ياحصيصه سجلك حافل بالمساوى
	You don't know a rogue from a sheikh and imām.	فرق بين الوضيع وبين شيخ وامام
5	Your nickname, 'gazelle-like', you should be ashamed of;	وصمة العار ريميه مع اسمك تخاوى
	Your mouth is polluted, your mind is unplugged;	دامه لسانك ملوث دام تفكيرك ظلام

[25] See http://www.7ail.net/vb/thread28592.html for the full text of the article.

6	If you washed your brain out with strong disinfectant	ولو غسلتى دماغك بالمبيد الكيماوى
	What good would it do? You're all filth and bugs!	وش ينظف قذوراتٍ بوسط الدرام
7	You love liberation, the chaos of mixing,	تعشقين التحرر واختلاط وبلاوى
	The proof's that you stood facing that motley crowd,	والدلايل وقوفك وسط ذيك الزحام
8	Strutting the stage as if you're on a dance-floor,	فوق مسرح شبيهٍ بالمراقص وخاوى
	The ostriches led by a low-life who's cowed.	من يديره وضيع وقايد لنعام
9	The judges lack morals and follow their fancy,	ولجنةٍ محتويها كل ساقط هواوى
	How hateful their faces, so sombre and grim;	كره ذيك الوجيه ومعتريها جهام
10	But men of real mettle protect the Shari'a,	حوزة الدين محميه وراها عزاوى
	Our government and people will never give in.	الحكومه وشعبٍ لشريعه حزام

Commentary

l. 1 In the first line of the original, Ḥiṣṣa describes herself as 'seeing' evil glinting in the 'eyes of opinions'; the first line of the reply exhorts the Almighty to destroy another of her senses, speech, by 'stilling her tongue', which 'howls' (تعاوي) like a 'hyena', or ‹‹عاوي››, echoing the word she had used to describe the Islamists howling from the hill-tops. In the second hemistich, ‹‹شاطي الخمام››: lit. 'the beach of trash' is a mocking allusion to the name of the theatre in Abu Dhabi where the 'Poet of the Million' programme is recorded ‹‹شاطئ الراحة›› 'the beach of relaxation' (or 'Pleasure Beach').

l. 2 The first hemistich echoes the syntax of the second hemistich of line 1 of the original: ‹‹في زمانٍ ...›› = *fī zamān-in...* 'at a time when...', but here the poet is accusing the poet of daring

(تجرى = *tajarra*) to attack Sheikh ʿAbd al-Raḥmān al-Barrāk.

l. 3 The poet turns the poet's accusation on its head, saying that the Sheikh's legal opinions do not suit her fancy and declare permissible what is prohibited (she had accused him of declaring prohibited what had been permissible).

l. 4 The poet addresses the poet using the diminutive form of her name ‹‹يا حصيصه›› in order to belittle her.

l. 5 Lit. 'The imprint of shame, o little gazelle, accompanies (تخاوي) your name; as long as it, your tongue, is polluted, your mind will be in the dark'.

l. 6 Lit. 'Were you to wash your brain with chemical insecticide, what would it clean (= what good would it do)? The filth is inside the rubbish bin (= your brain)'. ‹‹درام›› < Eng. '(oil) drum', used throughout the Gulf as a rubbish bin when empty.

l. 7 ‹‹زحام›› 'crowd', here used negatively to refer to the mixed audience ('motley crowd'), but echoing its use in the last line of the original poem, where cowards take cover in the crowd to protect themselves from being discovered.

l. 8 The first hemistich describes the stage as being 'like dance-floors', a negative for any religious conservative, and understood as floors on which men and women might mix. ‹‹خاوي›› means 'empty', i.e. the stage was empty apart from the poetess herself. The second hemistich means 'the one directing it (= the show) is a wretch and leads the ostriches (= the contestants) (onto the stage)'. Ostriches in traditional poetry are paradigms of timidity who copy each other's behaviour without thinking, rather like 'mindless' or 'timid' sheep in English.

l. 9 The members of the judging panel (لجنة, or as it is formally known in the programme لجنة التحكيم) are described as 'morally disreputable' (ساقط) and at the same time 'mindless, given to whimsy' ‹‹هواوي›› (*hawāwī*): This last word can have a positive or a negative sense. Ḥiṣṣa Hilāl uses it in her poem (l. 16) positively to mean 'lover (of the nation)'. But in the riposte the word is used in the sense of 'foolish, irrational'.[26] The second hemistich literally means 'Those faces covered with black clouds (جهام) (i.e. having a stern, sombre demeanour) are repugnant'.

l. 10 ‹‹حوزة الدين محمية وراها عزاوي›› lit. 'the realm of religion is protected, behind it (= supporting it) are men on the father's side'. ‹‹عزاوي›› or ‹‹عزوات›› (pl of عزوة) in Bedouin parlance has the extended sense of 'supporters / helpers in a time of need'. The last word of the final hemistich, ‹‹حزام›› (*ḥizām*), is here used as the pl of حازم meaning 'resolute, determined', a word with positive connotations. It is a deliberate metathesis of the radicals of the last word of the original poem, ‹‹زحام›› (*ziḥām*), which can carry the negative sense of 'chaotic crowd, mass of people, rabble'. The poet is saying that 'valiant men', 'the 'government' and 'the people' (شعب) are better protectors of what is right in Islam than a random, mixed throng such as that which assembled at the 'Pleasure Beach' theatre in Abu Dhabi to hear Ḥiṣṣa Hilāl's poem.

WORKS CITED

Ḥiṣṣa Hilāl ‹‹الطلاق والخلع شعرا›› ('Divorce of women by men and men by women, expressed through poetry'), (Abu Dhabi: Abu Dhabi Culture and Heritage Academy of Poetry, 2009).

‹‹تنوير›› ('Enlightenment'), (Abu Dhabi: Abu Dhabi Culture and Heritage Academy of Poetry, 2011).

C.D. Holes, 'Letter to Obama', *Middle Eastern Literatures* 14.2 (2011) pp. 183–193.

C.D. Holes and S.S. Abu Athera, *The Nabati Poetry of the UAE* (Reading: Ithaca, 2011),

C.D. Holes and S.S. Abu Athera,*Poetry and Politics in Contemporary Arab Society* (Reading: Ithaca Press, 2009).

P.M. Kurpershoek, *Oral Poetry and Narratives from Central Arabia,* Vol. 5: Glossary (Brill: Leiden, 2005).

Le C. de Landberg, *Glossaire Dathînois* (Brill: Leiden, 1920–42).

C. Reinhardt, *Ein arabischer Dialekt gesprochen in Oman und Zanzibar*, reprint of the 1894 original (Amsterdam: Philo Press, 1972).

A. Socin *Dīwān aus Centrarabien* (Leipzig: Teubner, 1900–1).

S. Sowayan, *Nabati Poetry* (Berkeley: University of California Press, 1985).

[26] C. Reinhardt, *Ein arabischer Dialekt gesprochen in Oman und Zanzibar*, 1894, reprint (Amsterdam, Philo Press, 1972), p. 54 gives 'leichtsinnig' for the sense of this word in Omani Arabic, which is how it is being used here. The use of the word in this sense reflects the poet's view that the panel of judges is not serious. His negative comment on the linguistic knowledge of the chairman of the judges was noted earlier.

17

Caricature and Obscenity in *Mujūn* Poetry and African-American Women's Hip Hop

Adam Talib

> To see gangsta rap as a reflection of dominant values in our culture rather than as an aberrant pathological standpoint does not mean that a rigorous feminist critique and interrogation of the sexist [*sic*] and misogyny expressed in this music is not needed. Without a doubt black males, young and old, must be held politically accountable for their sexism. Yet this critique must always be contextualized or we risk making it appear that the problems of misogyny, sexism, and all the behaviors this thinking supports and condones, including rape, male violence against women, is a black male thing. And this is what is happening. Young black males are forced to take the heat for encouraging via their music the hatred of and violence against women that is a central core of patriarchy.
>
> bell hooks[1]

Hip hop is simultaneously one of the most successful and despised musical genres in the United States and the wider, globe-spanning American cultural sphere. In its celebration of violence against the state and criminality (e.g. N.W.A.'s 'Fuck tha police', 1988), it can be juxtaposed to country music's hymns to the nation (e.g. Toby Keith's 'Courtesy of the Red, White, and Blue', 2002). On the other hand, the rap ethos is supremely conservative – indeed, reactionary – in its frequent recourse to misogyny and homophobia, its objectification of women and glamorization of violence against them, its celebration of materialism and bling, etc.[2] Kimberle Crenshaw has written specifically about the descriptions of women in 2 Live Crew's infamous 1989 album *As Nasty as They Wanna Be*.

> The first time I listened to 2 Live Crew, I was stunned. The issue had been distorted by descriptions of 'As Nasty as They Wanna Be' as simply 'sexually explicit.' 'Nasty' is much more: it is virulently misogynist, sometimes violently so. Black women are cunts, 'ho's',

[1] bell hooks, *Outlaw Culture: resisting representations*, New York: Routledge, 2006, pp. 135–36.

[2] See, *inter alia*, Edward G. Armstrong, 'Gangsta Misogyny: a content analysis of the portrayals of violence against women in rap music, 1987–1993', *Journal of Criminal Justice and Popular Culture*, 8:2, 2001, pp. 96–126.

> and all-purpose bitches: raggedy bitches, sorry-ass bitches, lowdown slimy-ass bitches. Good sex is often portrayed as painful and humiliating for women.[3]

In her piece, Crenshaw refers ambivalently to Henry Louis Gates, Jr.'s public defence of 2 Live Crew when they were tried in Florida for obscenity in 1990, but the analysis, which Gates submitted at the time, is still informative more than two decades later. Writing in *The New York Times* on 19 June 1990, Gates argued that 2 Live Crew's lyrics were coded as are many products of African-American literature and that their true meaning was indeed subversive:

> 2 Live Crew is engaged in heavy-handed parody, turning the stereotypes of black and white American culture on their heads. These young artists are acting out, to lively dance music, a parodic exaggeration of the age-old stereotypes of the oversexed black female and male. Their exuberant use of hyperbole (phantasmagoric sexual organs, for example) undermines – for anyone fluent in black cultural codes – a too literal-minded hearing of the lyrics.[4]

For Gates, 2 Live Crew's lyrics are a further development of the vernacular African-American verbal art called 'the dozens' (compare the Arabic genres *naqāʾiḍ, ridḥ*, and of course *hijāʾ*), which Gates himself famously brought to wider attention in his seminal *The Signifying Monkey: a theory of African-American literary criticism* (published in 1988). In Gates' view, '2 Live Crew, like many "hip-hop" groups, is engaged in sexual carnivalesque.'[5] This sexual carnivalesque – which, according to Gates, is devoid of the 'euphemism' or 'subterfuge' found in mainstream pop and rock music – is so extreme as to be parodic: '[m]uch more troubling than its so-called obscenity is the group's overt sexism. Their sexism is so flagrant, however, that it almost cancels itself out in a hyperbolic war between the sexes. [...] Still, many of us look toward the emergence of more female rappers to redress sexual stereotypes.'[6] We will return to the figure of the female rapper shortly. Robin Kelley has defended rap as a compelling and sincere form of literary resistance against the background of a horrific and misunderstood economic, social, and political reality in the ghetto. Kelley argues that:[7]

> Gangsta rappers construct a variety of first-person narratives to illustrate how social and economic realities in late capitalist L. A. affect young black men. Although the use of first-person narratives is rooted in a long tradition of black aesthetic practices, the

[3] Kimberle Crenshaw, 'Beyond Racism and Misogyny: Black Feminism and 2 Live Crew', *Boston Review* 16 (December 1991) [accessed online at <http://bostonreview.net/BR16.6/crenshaw.html>]. On the obscenity case, see also Jon Pareles, 'Rap: Slick, Violent, Nasty and, maybe, Hopeful', *The New York Times*, 17 June 1990, pp. E1–E5.

[4] Henry Louis Gates Jr., '2 Live Crew, Decoded', *The New York Times*, 19 June 1990, A23.

[5] Ibid.

[6] Ibid.

[7] Robin Kelley, 'Kickin' Reality, Kickin' Ballistics: "Gangsta Rap" and Postindustrial Los Angeles' in *idem*, *Race Rebels: Culture, Politics, and the Black Working Class*, New York, NY: Free Press, 1994, pp. 183–227, p. 194; see also Michael Eric Dyson, 'Gangsta Rap and American Culture' in *idem*, *The Michael Eric Dyson Reader*, New York, NY: Basic Civitas, 2004, pp. 411–17; as well as many of the contributions in the excellent collection *That's the Joint! The Hip-Hop Studies Reader*, edited by Murray Forman and Mark Anthony Neal, New York, NY: Routledge, 2004.

> use of 'I' to signify both personal and collective experiences also enables gangsta rappers to navigate a complicated course between what social scientists call 'structure' and 'agency.' In gangsta rap there is almost always a relationship between the conditions in which these characters live and the decisions they make.

In this way, gangsta rap's distasteful rhetoric reflects a bleak economic and social reality. Moreover the goal of putting such rhetoric into the mouth of the protagonist is psychological verisimilitude. There is clearly some tension between interpretations of gangsta rap as exaggerated, carnivalesque, and parodic and as realist, resistant, and fatalist, and, though it may seem implausible at first, it is likely that this tension is embedded already in the generic code itself. A similar sort of tension attends the case of *mujūn* (ribaldry, obscenity) in classical Arabic literature. On the one hand, the texts that have come down to us are written from a highly specific, and surprisingly uniform, authorial perspective that purports to mobilize parody and caricature for comic effect. At the same time, however, much of the content that is presented humorously is appalling when read in earnest, irrespective of moral anachronism.

Classical Arabic literature was written in a context no less patriarchal (male supremacist) than that of hip hop, and indeed some Arabic *mujūn* poetry could give gangsta rap a run for its money in celebrating the sexual assault of women and young men; this is amply borne out by examples in many of the articles presented in this volume. I often ask myself why I find classical Arabic poetry so edifying despite the fact that it is clear to me (and almost instantly to my students) that Arabic literary production is, in the main, steeped in misogyny.[8] That is not to say that every work of Arabic literature treats the subject of women in a disparaging way, nor is it to say that coeval cultures in Europe, Asia, or Africa were more enlightened, but it strikes me that the preponderance of mean, nymphomaniac, and deceitful female characters in classical Arabic literature (despite many notable exceptions including Shahrzād, the narrator of *The 1001 Nights*) signals something; something unsavoury to the modern reader. That a similar social sensitivity impedes many people from enjoying hip hop – or even considering it art in the first place – makes for a potentially instructive comparison.

---

[8] It is interesting to note that the celebrant of this volume, Geert Jan van Gelder, poses a closely related question in a forthcoming article on 'Sexual Violence in Verse: the case of Jiʿthin, al-Farazdaq's sister', which he was kind enough to share with me as I prepared this article. My thinking on this and related issues has benefited from the work of Marlé Hammond (*Beyond Elegy: classical Arabic women's poetry in context*, Oxford: Oxford University Press, 2010); Abdelfattah Kilito (*The Author and His Doubles: essays on classical Arabic culture*, trans. Michael Cooperson, Syracuse, NY: Syracuse University Press, 2001); Andras Hamori, (*On the Art of Medieval Arabic Literature*, Princeton, NJ: Princeton University Press, 1974); Joseph Sadan, (Yūsuf Sadān, *al-Adab al-ʿarabī al-hāzil wa-nawādir al-thuqalāʾ: al-ʿāhāt wa-l-masāwiʾ al-insāniyyah wa-makānatuhā fī al-adab al-ʿarabī*, Cologne; Baghdad: Manshūrāt al-Jamal, 2007); Boaz Shoshan (*Popular Culture in medieval Cairo*, Cambridge: Cambridge University Press, 1993); and others.

EXPLICIT LYRICS AND SEXUAL OBJECTIFICATION

> Much speech is full of tropes, and even layers of tropes, which to varying degrees remove tokens from the sphere of literal, direct interpretation. By token, I mean specific instances of speech said in specific social situations by and to specific interlocutors with specific social identities, histories, motivations, and goals. [...] Consequently, speech does not always reflect beliefs, attitudes, and behavior in a direct way.[9]

> Bitches ain't shit but hos and tricks[10]

Language is, of course, one of the primary grievances of those who object to hip hop and *mujūn* poetry and attempt to distance or exclude these genres from the category of artistic expression. Language here comprises the semantics, pragmatics, and syntax of the expression. Both genres deal explicitly with the prurient in a (to borrow Pieter Smoor's description) frank and often humorous way, with frequent recourse to slang, non-standard, or allusive diction. To deriders, however, all of this amounts to nothing more than '"pornographic filth"'.[11] The prejudicial appraisal of hip hop is compounded by a centuries-old bias against African-American (or Black) English. Although vernacular Arabic (*ʿāmmiyah*, 'the popular language') has often been considered to be sub-literary, historically there has been no comparable bias against it. Regardless, comparing the case of Arabic linguistic registers to the issue of American English sociolects sheds light on their deployment in specific genre settings. African-American English is, not unlike *ʿāmmiyah*, an oft vilified dialect of spoken and written language that remains extremely popular, innovative, and artistically productive:

> Powerfully influential on our popular culture, spoken by a group widely distributed across the country, existing in an ever-challenging relationship with mainstream society, and adopted by an increasing number of members of other minority groups, Black English is the nonstandard dialect all Americans have the most immediate, edgy, and electric relationship with.[12]

The adjectives John McWhorter uses to describe mainstream America's relationship with African-American English seem to me apt to describe the place of *ʿāmmiyah* in contemporary and historical Arab societies as well. Much has been written about the sophisticated space of online social networking and audio-visual media in today's Arab political discourse, generally misunderstood as a purely youth phenomenon, but little attention has been paid to the crucial – and no doubt catalytic – expansion of written and spoken *ʿāmmiyah* in

---

[9] Arthur K. Spears, 'African-American Language Use: ideology and so-called obscenity' in S.S. Mufwene, J. Rickford, G. Bailey, and J. Baugh, (eds.), *African-American English: structure, history and use*, New York: Routledge, 1998, pp. 226–50 at p. 245.

[10] Dr. Dre, 'Bitches Ain't Shit', *The Chronic*, Death Row, 1992; 2001 (re-release).

[11] This was the opinion of Civil Rights and 'anti-Rap' activist C. Delores Tucker. See Yvonne Shinhoster Lamb, 'C. Delores Tucker Dies at 78; Rights and Anti-Rap Activist' [obituary], *The Washington Post*, 13 October 2005, accessed online at <http://www.washingtonpost.com>.

[12] John McWhorter, *Word on the Street: debunking the myth of "pure" standard English*, Cambridge, MA: Perseus, 1998, p. 128.

these new political arenas.[13] As with any textual discourse, the characteristics of a given sociolect or dialect become touchstones when that register becomes the code of a specific literary genre (its mode). In the art of Egyptian facebook and twitter, for example, the code is a sarcastic, highly literate *ʿāmmiyah* written in either the Arabic script or with modified Roman alphanumerics; the language of *a7a* (*aḥḥā*).[14] In *mujūn*, the language can either be Classical Arabic (*al-ʿarabiyyah*) or *ʿāmmiyah*, but it should always be uncensored (i.e. obscene or explicit), ribald, scatological, etc. Both these codes share African-American English's characteristic of directness, which is amplified greatly in the rap mode.[15]

The modal affinities between *mujūn* and hip hop can be illustrated satisfactorily by comparing a canonical and highly explicit rap song to a Mamluk-era Syrian *bullayq* poem (i.e. a ribald *zajal*). 2 Live Crew's 1991 single 'Pop that Pussy' describes women's bodies, sex work, and sexual intercourse in some of the raunchiest language imaginable.[16] The song describes a trip to a strip club '[t]o see freaky hoes doin' shows' where the women, who exist exclusively to give the men pleasure, are said to '[...] do anything to turn us on'. The title, which is also the song's frequent refrain, refers to a style of dancing known most commonly as 'twerking', but it also functions as a constant reminder of the women's instrumentality in the world of the song.[17] The women in the song never speak, yet even more significantly their agency is constrained to the point of non-existence by two factors: (1) they are present only to '[bring] to the men more satisfaction' and (2) the constant stream of imperatives (e.g. 'pop that pussy', 'bend over backwards, make me shout', 'bend over and spread 'em', 'rub that ass and play with that clit', etc.) make it clear that these women are nothing but tools to serve and be manipulated by their male conductors. Hip hop is by definition a highly verbal art, akin to poetry, and thus language is the element that most determines the narrative tone, especially in the case of 2 Live Crew whose beats are somewhat rudimentary. The same may also be said of the following Arabic *bullayq* poem that deals with women's bodies and sexual interaction in uncannily similar terms.

The *bullayq* poem, rhyming in *-bah*, was written by Sharaf al-Dīn Ibn Rayyān (b. Shawwāl 702/1303 in Aleppo, d. in 769 or 770/1367–8 or 1368–9), the most outstanding *bullayq* poet of his day according to Ṣalāḥ al-Dīn al-Ṣafadī, who includes it in his biographical entry on

[13] See Ivan Panović, *Literacies in Contemporary Egypt: everyday writing and political change* (forthcoming from Routledge in 2014) as well as Ursula Lindsey, 'The Arab World's Tangled Linguistic Landscape', *al-Fanar* <http://www.al-fanar.org>, 19 April 2013. Arabic hip hop has also attracted a great deal of attention of late and the interested reader would do well to begin with the work of University of Arkansas anthropologist Ted Swedenburg.

[14] A7a-culture can also be compared profitably to hip hop's 'caustic' tone: 'With regard to rap specifically, it must be mentioned that most types of rap have a caustic turn, one that touches all the topics it considers. Rap comments and discourses on women, people of same-sex orientation, government social policy, the police, capitalism, rival rap groups, and alienation tend all to be equally caustic.' (Arthur K. Spears, 'African-American Language Use', p. 231).

[15] See Arthur K. Spears, 'Directness in the use of African-American English' in Sonja Lanehart (ed.), *Sociocultural and Historical Contexts of African American English*, Amsterdam; Philadelphia, PA: John Benjamins, 2001, pp. 239–59.

[16] 2 Live Crew, 'Pop that Pussy', *Sports Weekend: As Nasty as They Wanna Be, Pt. 2*, Luke Records, 1991.

[17] See Wikipedia, s.v. 'Twerking' <http://en.wikipedia.org/wiki/Twerking>.

the poet.[18] Al-Ṣafadī introduces the poem, saying, 'I chose the following from his *bullayq* poems although its eloquent description of indecency is like a rose in a thorny bush'.[19]

ومما اخترته له من البُلَّيْق وإن كان لفظه العذب فى فحش المعنى كالورد فى العُلَّيْق قوله:

[١] والِكْ قَحْبَهْ   ديري اَلثُّقْبَهْ
[٢] رِيحى نَفْسِكْ   ماْ رِيدْ كُسِّكْ   ديري فِلْسِكْ   واَثْنى اَلرُّكْبَهْ
[٣] شيلى قَعْرِكْ   وارخى ظَهْرِكْ   يبقى جُحْرِكْ   مثل اَلقُبَّهْ
[٤] عندي سِفار   يهْوى اَلأبعارْ   عمري جَحَّارْ   نَيَّاكْ ثُقْبَهْ
[٥] أركبْ قَصِّكْ   واَكثرْ بَعْصِكْ   واَخرجْ جَعْصِكْ   باير كُبَّهْ
[٦] إيري قد فازْ   بالزِّيجْ حينْ حازْ   كِنُّو عُكَّاز   راسُو حَرْبَهْ
[٧] فى الزِّيجْ يغطَسْ   ما يهْوَى اَلكُسّ   لَوْ بالْ تُرْمُسْ   فَسَّى حُلْبَهْ
[٨] قُمتْ أتْرَكِّبْ   واَيري اَوَكِّبْ   ما زِلْتْ أسْحَبْ   أَلفَيْنْ سَحْبَهْ
[٩] واَرجع أرجعْ   لاوَّلْ واَدفعْ   حتّى تسمعْ   للنِّيكْ هَبَّهْ
[١٠] صارتْ ستّى   تبكى تحتى   دقْنَك فى اَستى   تهذي اَلقَحْبَهْ
[١١] هذي اَلفَصْعَهْ[20]   نيك من حِقَّهْ   ما هْيَ نَزْقَهْ   فى اَوّل جَذْبَهْ
[١٢] عندي جرَّهْ   خيرْ مِنْ دُرَّهْ   لى فى كبرَه   فى اَلزِّيجْ طَرْبَهْ
[١٣] ربّى غافرْ   ذنبَ اَلكافرْ   إيشْ هُوْ اَلشاعرْ   يكذبْ كَذْبَهْ
[١٤] أرجو ربّى   ما زالْ حسبى   واَيْشْ هُوْ ذنبى   ما لُو نِسْبَهْ
[١٥] لمّا يشفعْ   أحمدْ ينفعْ   ما زالْ يدفعْ   عنّا اَلكُرْبَهْ
[١٦] اصغوُا يا اَصْحابْ   هذي اَلآدابْ   تحكى اَلجُلَّاب   حلوهْ عذبهْ

1. Come on, you slut
show me that ass![21]

2. Don't you worry
I don't want your pussy

---

[18] On the poet, see al-Ṣafadī, *al-Wāfī bi-l-Wafāyāt*, 30 vols., ed. Hellmut Ritter, et al. 2nd edition, Wiesbaden: Franz Steiner Verlag, 1931–2007, vol. 12, pp. 369–77; Ibn Ḥajar al-ʿAsqalānī, *al-Durar al-kāminah*, 6 vols., ed. Fritz Krenkow and Sharaf al-Dīn Aḥmad, Hyderabad: Maṭbaʿat Majlis Dāʾirat al-Maʿārif, 1929–31, vol. 2, pp. 55–6, no. 1589. *Bullayq*: on this ribald version of *zajal*, see Ṣafī al-Dīn al-Ḥillī, *al-ʿĀṭil al-ḥālī wa-l-murakhkhaṣ al-ghālī*, ed. Ḥusayn Naṣṣār, Cairo: al-Hayʾah al-Miṣriyyah al-ʿĀmmah li-l-Kitāb, 1981, p. 6. The poem appears in al-Ṣafadī, *al-Wāfī*, vol. 12, pp. 376–77. I have modified the layout of the *bullayq* (*zajal*) poem to better represent the strophic structure. I have also occasionally modified the voweling and orthography to better fit the metre and better represent features of dialectal Arabic. Metre: each line is made up of four feet of four long syllables, except for the opening line (*maṭlaʿ*), which consists of two feet of four long syllables (LLXL). Rhyme scheme: AA, bbbA, cccA, etc.

[19] al-Ṣafadī, *al-Wāfī*, vol. 12, p. 376.

[20] In the edited text of al-Ṣafadī's *al-Wāfī* this word is written *f-s-ʿ-h* without any explanation as to its meaning. The possible meanings and my interpretation are given in the notes to the translation below. Here I have emended the spelling to *faṣʿah*, though it could equally be written *faṣʿā* (or in standard Arabic, *faṣʿāʾ*).

[21] lit. 'turn your anus around'.

turn your butthole 'round
and bend your knees.

3. Pull your bottom up
and relax your back,
make your pelvis
[curve] like a dome.

4. I've got a nose-bit
that loves [rooting out] shit.
All my life I've been an orifice-diving (*jaḥḥār*),
butthole fucker.

5. I straddle your chest
and trouble you more,
I force you to sit up
with my bell-end.

6. My dick hit the jackpot
in the conjugal [game][22] when it won out,
as if it were a staff
with a spear at the tip.

7. It plunges when it fucks[23],
but it doesn't like pussy.
When it pees, it's lupin beans,
and when it farts, it's fenugreek!

8. I got up to get on
and made my dick go slow,
I was still thrusting[24]
two thousand strokes [later].

9. I withdraw almost the whole way
and then I slam forward
so you can hear
the whoosh of my fucking.

10. My lady began crying out
when I was on top,[25]
'Your beard's in my asshole!'
The bitch was just raving.

11. Take this slut,[26]

---

[22] lit. 'marriage'.

[23] lit. 'marriage'.

[24] lit. 'I was still pulling (out)'.

[25] lit. 'from underneath me'.

[26] I have emended the text of the edition of al-Ṣafadī's work above for the sake of meaning. The printed edition has the word *f-s-ʿ-h*, which seems to me likely to represent dialectal pronunciations of words derived from roots *f-ṣ-ʿ* or *f-s-ḥ*, for which both consonantal shifts have been attested. I have preferred the reading of *fuṣʿā* (lit. uncircumcised woman), a slur analogous to American 'slut' or British 'slag', though I would not rule out the following two alternatives: *faṣʿah* ('foreskin', here

and fuck her right.
She's no headstrong mare,
once attraction's there.

12. I've got moves[27]
smoother than pearl.
And when it comes to size
for sex, I've got a wide one (*ṭarbah*)

13. My God forgives
The infidel's sins.
So what if a poet should
tell some lies?

14. I beg God's forgiveness
for He's still enough for me.
In any case, what's my sin?
This is hardly a big deal.

15. When he intercedes for us,
Aḥmad always comes through.[28]
He still always frees us
from distress.

16. Listen up, friends,
living like this
is just like rose-water,
it's sweet and it's smooth.

DRAG KING MCS

> As a masculinist form with masculinist aesthetics, hip hop, and the art form's masculinist ideals of excellence and competitiveness, have often forced women to occupy roles gendered male.[29]
>
> Black women rappers resist patterns of sexual objectification and cultural invisibility, and they also resist academic reification and mainstream, hegemonic, white feminist discourse.[30]

Setting aside the issue of obscenity in gangsta rap proper, I would like to pick up from Gates' wish, uttered in passing, for the emergence of more female rappers in order to 'redress sexual stereotypes'. Only a few years after the 2 Live Crew obscenity case, Missy

as a synecdoche for penis) and *fusḥah* ('void', here as an epithet for a woman's vaginal or rectal orifice).

27 lit. 'I have a stroke (or pulling motion; or trace)'.

28 Aḥmad is one of the names of the Prophet Muḥammad.

29 Imani Perry, *Prophets of the Hood: Politics and Poetics in Hip Hop*, Durham, NC: Duke University Press, 2004, p. 156.

30 Tricia Rose, 'Never Trust a Big Butt and a Smile' in *That's the Joint!*, ed. M. Forman and M.A. Neal, pp. 291–306 at p. 303.

Elliott, a producer who would go on to become the most successful female rapper in history, released her debut album *Supa Dupa Fly* (1997); it went platinum. Gates seems to suggest at one point that while 2 Live Crew's 'overt sexism' is an exaggerated, and ultimately parodic, discursive mode intended to destabilize 'stereotypes of the oversexed black female and male', female rappers will inevitably be more earnest lyricists and will be preoccupied with 'redressing sexual stereotypes'. This is not immediately obvious. In gangsta rap and hip hop culture more broadly, women are often characterized as 'gold-diggers', 'bitches' and 'hos', i.e. deceitful, vapid sex objects, and, as Mark Anthony Neal has noted, '[...] many female raps [*sic*] artists are less concerned with challenging the circulation of sexism and misogyny (Sarah Jones' "Your Revolution" notwithstanding) than they are with simply being recognized as peers alongside male rappers.'[31] Although hip-hop has lately entered a period of, what one might call, self-conscious reform led by artists such as Kanye West and Frank Ocean – bolstered no doubt by Barack Obama's deliberate projection of bourgeois African-American values – rap written and performed by women is not necessarily more politically correct.[32] Nor is it necessarily less parodic or raunchy.

For example, Lil' Kim (b. 1974) begins her 2000 single 'How Many Licks?' by boasting about her promiscuity: 'I've been a lot of places, seen a lot of faces / Ah hell I even fuck with different races'.[33] This verse continues by listing five of the rapper's sexual partners whom she identifies and describes, often with reference to racial stereotypes. There is the wealthy and conventional 'white dude', who offers a version of suburban idyll: 'He asked me if I'd be his date for the prom / And he'd buy me a horse, a Porsche, and a farm'. This character is then immediately juxtaposed to his polar opposite, the hypervirile, antebellum black 'buck': 'Dan my nigga from down south'. In an interesting twist, though, the woman narrating her sexual adventures assumes the role of sexual dominant inverting hip hop's conventional sexual paradigm: 'Used to like me to spank him and cum in his mouth.' Indeed for Lil' Kim, receiving oral sex from a subordinate male partner is the ultimate sexual boast (e.g. the lines 'He ate my pussy from dark till the mornin', 'But now he be sucking me off on the weekend', 'Lick it right the first time or you gotta do it over').[34] Even when she

[31] Mark Anthony Neal, 'I'll be Nina Simone Defecating on Your Microphone: Hip-Hop and Gender', introduction to part four of, *That's the Joint!*, ed. M. Forman and M.A. Neal, pp. 247–50 at p. 247. See in addition to part four of the book mentioned previously, Imani Perry, *Prophets of the Hood*, ch. 5.

[32] This recent reform movement in hip-hop bears the mark of commercial interests (see Imani Perry, *Prophets of the Hood*, ch. 7) and is not at all related to the much older tradition of politically engaged rap, in which female rappers, notably Queen Latifah (b. 1970), have been active.

[33] Lil' Kim, feat. Sisqó, 'How Many Licks?', *The Notorious K.I.M.*, Atlantic Records, 2000.

[34] In this regard, Lil' Kim has much in common with Roman sexual mores: '[i]n [Latin] invective literature, the worst possible insult is to accuse a man of fellating another man, and the worst possible threat against a man is that of forcing him to fellate someone.' (John R. Clarke, 'Look who's laughing at sex: Men and Women Viewers in the *Apodyterium* of the Suburban Baths' in David Frederick (ed.), *The Roman Gaze: Vision, Power, and the Body*, Baltimore, MD: Johns Hopkins Press, 2002, p. 162; see also Craig Williams, *Roman Homosexuality: Ideologies of Masculinity in Classical Antiquity*, Oxford: Oxford University Press, 1999). Romans in fact made the helpful distinction between *fellatio* and *irrumatio* (forced oral sex), and it is usually the latter that is being described in sexual invective across languages and centuries. In the case of Lil' Kim, however, she is actually channelling a mainstream view in hip hop culture that views oral sex, whether consensual or rape, as a highly

mentions that one of her partners is very well endowed, she gives the same weight to the familiar phallocentric totem as she does to his ability to please her orally: 'He had a big-ass dick and a hurricane tongue'. This can be seen, too, in the song's title (an allusion to a famous candy commercial) and in the title of another song from the same album called 'Suck My Dick'.[35] To me, this pose is pure 'drag'; indeed Imani Perry has called Lil' Kim 'a male player inverted'.[36] In the latter song, Lil' Kim adopts a masculinized, sexually aggressive voice with the same focus on dominance and subordination in sexual exchange as seen in lyrics like the following: 'Imagine if I was a dude hittin' cats from the back / with no strings attached. Yeah, nigga, picture that. / I'd treat y'all niggas like y'all treat us, no doubt.' This form of sexual invective has clear parallels in the Arabic tradition.[37]

Other female rappers who rap about sex also engage in a similar sort of sexual boasting or invective. As with Lil' Kim's adoption of a masculine 'gangsta' voice, and indeed the vocabulary of male sexual anatomy, female rappers often channel a hypersexualized, aggressive, drag persona when discussing sex as if to imitate, or more likely caricature the hypermasculinized characters put forward by their male counterparts. I do not want to suggest that the female artists discussed here are wholly representative of mainstream women's hip-hop, but these are the voices who contrast most profitably with the Arabic *mujūn* tradition. Davarian L. Baldwin has argued that these female artists do not attempt to parody their male counterparts but rather adopt and adapt the gangsta value system:

> Female identity in these musical texts becomes performance by coupling highly materialistic and aesthetically violent and excessive personas with infectious beats and rhymes.
>
> The rhymes make it obvious that the relentless pursuit of status, power, and sexual satisfaction is not gender-specific, and thus reverse the objectification of women as sexual objects by viewing men as accesses to pleasure and capital accumulation, if necessary, through sexual exchange.[38]

In either analysis, however, it holds that in the sphere of women's hip hop, some female performers, working in an originally underground artistic context that, for all its commercial success and mainstreaming, has retained an ethos of outlaw marginality including a quintessential misogyny and in whose masterworks women are dehumanized,

---

demeaning act. The most extreme example of this attitude known to me is the song 'Blowjob Betty' by the rapper Too $hort in which the title character chokes to death on the rapper-persona's semen. (Too $hort, 'Blowjob Betty', *Get in where you fit in*, Jive Records, 1993).

[35] Lil' Kim, 'Suck my dick', *The Notorious K.I.M.*, Atlantic Records, 2000.

[36] Imani Perry, *Prophets of the Hood*, p. 158.

[37] See, *inter alia*, Geert Jan van Gelder, *The Bad and the Ugly: attitudes towards invective poetry* (hijāʾ) *in classical Arabic literature* (Leiden: Brill, 1988) as well as *idem*, 'Sexual Violence in Verse: the case of Jiʿthin, al-Farazdaq's sister' (forthcoming) in which van Gelder notes the case of Umm Jaʿd, a woman who boasted in verse of raping the poet Aws b. Ḥajar.

[38] Davarian L. Baldwin, 'Black Empires, White Desires: The Spatial Politics of Identity in the Age of Hip-Hop' in *That's the Joint!*, ed. M. Forman and M.A. Neal, pp. 159–76 at p. 171. This type of female rapper corresponds to Cheryl L. Keyes' category of 'Sista with Attitude', one of four types of female rap artist she identifies. The other categories are 'Queen Mother', 'Fly Girl', and 'Lesbian'. See Cheryl L. Keyes, 'Empowering Self, Making Choices, Creating Spaces: Black Female Identity via Rap Music Performance' in *That's the Joint!*, ed. M. Forman and M.A. Neal, pp. 265–76.

objectified, and instrumentalized, often choose to ape their male counterparts, to adopt their voice, register, dominant pose, and sexual values.[39] But why?

CARICATURE + PLAY = CAMP

Satire is an efficient and plausible mode of resistance to any system of entrenched and self-justifying authority including social codes. By caricaturing the sources (textual, institutional, traditional, individual, etc.) of authority, marginal voices are able to ridicule power (cultural, political, social, religious, etc.) indirectly by parodying it and using its own discourse against it. Hypersexual women's hip hop and certain categories of classical Arabic *mujūn* poetry may operate in this fashion. To Tricia Rose, 'Black women rappers' public displays of physical and sexual freedom challenge male notions of female sexuality and pleasure.'[40] The voice which certain female hip hop artists and Arabic poets adopt in these parodies combines caricature with irreverence to destabilize generic codes and social mores. In hip hop culture, this irreverence is known as *play*; in classical Arabic culture, this is classed as *mujūn*.[41] As Kyra D. Gaunt explains, 'Play is considered an experience or an act that is performed for its own sake, for pleasure or reward known as *flow*. The rewards for flow experience are said to be intrinsic, often marked by imaginative creativity, improvisation, and adventurousness – unbounded and fearless exploration.'[42] Flow clearly has much in common with the notion of *ṭarab* familiar from Arab musical culture.[43] As for *play* and *mujūn*, they are ultimately camp modes in which artists and performers indulge in the furthest excesses of the parodic mode.

Consider, for example, what a non-parodic reading of the explicit description of sexual violence in the following excerpt from a poem by Abū Nuwās would mean for both reader and author.[44]

---

[39] Kyra Gaunt has argued that rap as a muscial form appears male when in fact it incorporates a great deal of African-American women's spoken culture, which needs unearthing so that women who participate in the art form are not seen as somehow out of place. She explains that:

> 'It is the ideological power of maleness in a mass-mediated hip-hop culture that makes it so difficult to fully appreciate African-American women's creative and expressive participation as anything other than subsidiary to men's. From such a distorted viewpoint, women are simply perceived as acting out myths and stereotypes. Girls and women play and live out their lives through a complex form of identity politics that questions prevailing constructions of maleness and femaleness.
>
> This masculinized view of rap places female participants in rap and hip-hop culture in the precarious position of being attracted to a musical expression that is apparently "bad" for them, that "talks bad" about them, and therefore diminishes their social capacity and respectability as African-American women.' (Kyra D. Gaunt, 'Translating Double-Dutch to Hip-Hop: The Musical Vernacular of Black Girls' Play' in *That's the Joint!*, ed. M. Forman and M.A. Neal, pp. 251–63 at p. 261.)

[40] Tricia Rose, 'Never Trust a Big Butt and a Smile', p. 301.

[41] See further Wen-Chin Ouyang's contribution to this volume.

[42] Kyra D. Gaunt, 'Translating Double-Dutch to Hip-Hop', p. 252.

[43] See further Ali Jihad Racy, *Making Music in the Arab World: the culture and artistry of Ṭarab*, Cambridge, Cambridge University Press, 2003.

[44] Abū Nuwās, *Dīwān Abī Nuwās*, 7 vols., ed. E. Wagner and G. Schoeler, Wiesbaden: Franz Steiner

[من الوافر]

[١٤] فخاتَلْنا فأسكرْنا فنِمْنا إلى أنْ همَّ ديكٌ بالصِّياحِ
[١٥] فقُمْتُ إليهِ أرفُلُ مستقيماً وقد هيّأْتُ كَبْشي للنِّطاحِ
[١٦] فلمّا أنْ ركزتُ ٱلرُّمْحَ فيهِ تَنَبَّهَ كالوقيذِ من ٱلجَراحِ
[١٧] فقُلْتُ لَهُ : بِحَقِّ أبيكَ سَهِّلْ ولا تُحْوِجْ إلى سَفَهِ ٱلتَّلاحي
[١٨] قالَ : لقد ظَفِرْتَ فَنِكْ هَنيئاً بإسعافٍ وبَذْلٍ مستماحِ
[١٩] فلمّا أنْ وضعتُ عليه رَحْلي تبدَّى مُنْشِداً شِعْرَ ٱمتِداحِ :
[٢٠] «أَلَسْتُمْ خَيْرَ من رَكِبَ ٱلمَطايا وأندَى ٱلعالِمِينَ بُطونَ راحِ»

14. So we stalked him, and got drunk, and we slept
    until a cock began to crow.
15. Then I rose and went straight for him, my garment trailing;
    I'd already prepared my ram to butt.
16. Then when I planted my spear inside him
    he woke as if dazed from a wound.
17. 'By your father's (life)', I said, 'don't fight it,
    'and don't make (me) curse you in anger'.
18. 'You've bested me', he replied, 'so fuck away happily!
    'with my help and my precious permission.'
19. Then when I slung my saddle-bags astride him,
    he began reciting a poem of praise:
20. 'Aren't you the greatest to ever mount a steed
    and the most generous man the world's ever seen!'[45]

Here, even if one is concedes that the male-male sexual pairing might be read as customary, the rape that Abū Nuwās is describing is not an instance of sexual assault but rather the absurd consequent of the *ghazal* (courtly love poetry) paradigm in which daring lovers pursue reluctant beloveds by all manner of tricks, charms, and wiles. Julie Scott Meisami has highlighted this dimension of *Mujūn* poetry exactly:

> [The] persona of such poetry [*mujūn*] is typically a self-deprecating *eiron* (to use the late Northrop Frye's term) who emerges as the antithesis both of the courtly or ʿUdhrī lover of *ghazal* and of the heroic persona characteristic of *fakhr* [...] [what] logically follows, is that *mujūn* is a counter-genre which inverts the conventions of 'normative' *ghazal* and *waṣf al-khamr*.[46]

Verlag, 1958–2006) vol. 3, ed. E. Wagner, pp. 90–1, no. 62.

[45] Geert Jan van Gelder pointed out to me that this concluding line is a quotation (*taḍmīn*) of a famous verse by Jarīr (d. c. 110/728–9) (see *Dīwān Jarīr bi-sharḥ Muḥammad b. Ḥabīb*, edited by Nuʿmān Muḥammad Amīn Ṭāhā, 2 vols., Cairo: Dār al-Maʿārif, 1969–71, vol. 1, p. 89, l. 15).

[46] Julie Scott Meisami, 'Arabic *Mujūn* Poetry: the literary dimension' in *Verse and the Fair Sex: studies in Arabic poetry and in the representation of women in Arabic literature*, edited by Frederick de Jong, Utrecht: M.Th. Houtsma Stichting, 1993, pp. 8–30 at p. 19.

My analysis of *mujūn* as a camp and parodic mode differs only in that whereas Meisami finds *mujūn* poets adopting a 'self-deprecating' persona, which Andras Hamori in connection with Abū Nuwās once called the 'ritual clown', I find them adopting a pose of conscious taboo-breaking. I agree, therefore, with John Mattock, who in an important article on the poetry of Abū Nuwās, notes the poet's '[...] pervasive emphasis on the "wickedness" of his behaviour'.[47] Some female rap artists likewise caricature the hypermasculine and misogynistic tone of much hip hop by adopting a provocative, over-the-top camp persona, acting out the part of 'pimp'.

Khia's 2002 breakthrough hit 'My Neck, My Back (Lick it)' from the *Thug Misses* album is a perfect distillation of the phenomenon.[48] Khia begins her song by exhorting women to 'pop their pussy', a likely intertextual reference to 2 Live Crew's notorious hit, and then quickly transitions to addressing heterosexual men (the implied addressees of the song). The song, like those by Lil' Kim mentioned above, is an extended discussion of oral sex from the perspective of a dominant woman; the female equivalent of male rappers' 'blowjob ballads' (i.e. Akinyele's 'Put it in your mouth', Too $hort's 'Blowjob Betty', or the live fellatio recorded at the end of Notorious B.I.G.'s 'Respect').[49] Khia orders her male interlocutor to 'Suck this pussy just like you should / My neck, my back / Lick my pussy and my crack'. Here analingus serves as a symbol for both woman's confident assertion of her sexual desires and her dominance over the subordinate man. Khia leaves no doubt as to her estimation of gangsta males' boasting and her primacy in the sexual exchange: 'You might roll dubs / You might have G's / But fuck that, nigga / Get on your knees'. This same hypersexual tone can be seen in the personas of women working in a similarly male-dominated work atmosphere: stand-up comedy. The Queens of Comedy, a group of four African-American female stand-up comedians, were formed after the success of the male *The Original Kings of Comedy* concert film and tour. The four women, Laura Hayes, Adele Givens, Sommore, and Mo'Nique, deliver frank and unabashed commentary on sex and sexual relationships for a primarily African-American audience in an explicit tone that mirrors the hypersexual caricatures deployed by the female rap artists discussed above. When *Glamour* magazine asked the comedians for their '10 Commandments of Sex', the magazine found the women's responses too explicit for print.[50] The following exchange between Sommore and Mo'Nique demonstrates the extent to which these women have repurposed the masculine register familiar from hip hop culture to articulate their own sexual desires.

---

[47] John Mattock, 'Description and Genre in Abu Nuwas' in *Atti del XIII Congresso dell'Union Européenne d'Arabisants et d'Islamisants (Venezia 29 settembre – 4 ottobre 1986), Quaderni di Studi Arabi*, 5–6, Venice: Università degli studi di Venezia, 1987, pp. 528–40 at p. 533. See Andras Hamori, *On the Art of Medieval Arabic Literature*, p. 50: '[...] in Abū Nuwās the borrowing of heroic language is of the brandy-is-for-heroes kind, and the borrower gives the cold shoulder to such heroism as might be sought outside the wine garden and the upstairs room.'

[48] Khia, 'My Neck, My Back (Lick it)', *Thug Misses*, Artemis, 2002.

[49] Akinyele, 'Put it in Your Mouth', *Put it in Your Mouth*, BMG Records, 1996; Too $hort's 'Blowjob Betty' (see above); Notorious B.I.G., 'Respect', *Ready to Die*, Bad Boy, 1994.

[50] Margeaux Rawson, 'The Queens of Comedy on the Commandments of Sex', *Jezebel*. <http://www.jezebel.com>, 16 April 2012.

> SOMMORE: Noise is a must. You gotta make some noise.
> MO'NIQUE: Yes! And you gotta talk the nastiest, filthiest shit you can imagine. Call me a bitch! Call me all kinds of bitches and hoes and sluts. Oooh! I like that! Call me a dirty bitch, nasty bitch, stanky bitch.... And you gotta be a little rough. Hit a bitch in the back of her head. Pow! Smack my hair up. Kick a bitch in her back. Bam!
> SOMMORE: Grab a bitch's ass and spread her cheeks open. Do something surprising.

To say that these women have adopted a macho (or thug) register to describe their sexual preferences is not to say that these preferences are insincere or deviant, it is simply to underline the fact that one dimension of their performance intends to parody the mainstream, hypermasculine sexual paradigm reflected in hip hop and wider culture. In her discussion of female rap artists, Tricia Rose has argued that '[t]he distinctly black, physical and sexual pride that these women [AT: rap duo Salt-N-Pepa] (and other black female rappers) exude serves as a rejection of the aesthetic hierarchy in American culture that marginalizes black women.'[51] This kind of ribald play in women's hip hop culture and classical Arabic *mujūn* should be read as a burlesque of the hypermasculine sexuality found in the mainstream of both cultures respectively. These female rap artists and *mujūn* poets are parodying the severe – and often misogynistic and homophobic – obscenity employed by rappers like Eazy-E, Slick Rick, and Eminem and poets like Ibn al-Ḥajjāj, Jarīr, and Ibn al-Rūmī, which we might better describe as *sukhf* (obscenity).[52] In the following long poem by Sharaf al-Dīn Abū al-Ṭayyib Ibn al-Ḥalāwī al-Mawṣilī (born 603/1206–7, died 656/1258), the playful and camp dimension of parody – sexual and otherwise – that I have identified as a key constituent of the *mujūn* genre is critical to understanding how the poem makes meaning.[53]

[من مخلّع البسيط]

[١] أرثَّ صرفُ ٱلزمانِ حالي   فما لدهري تُرى وما لي
[٢] حتّى كأنّي لهُ عدوٌّ   يرشُقُني منه بالنِّبالِ
[٣] وطالَما كنتُ وَهْوَ عنّي   وعن أخلّايَ في ٱشتغالِ
[٤] ولو أتاني لَصُلْتُ فيهِ   أمراً ونهْياً ولا أُبالي
[٥] أينَ زَماني ٱلّذي تَقَضَّى   وأينَ جاهي وأينَ مالي
[٦] وأينَ خُفّي وطَيْلَساني   وأينَ قيلي وأينَ قالي
[٧] وأينَ عَيْشي وأينَ طَيْشي   وأينَ حُسْني وحُسْنُ حالي
[٨] ونحنُ في فِتيَةٍ كِرام   نُجارُهُمْ في ٱلفَخارِ عالِ
[٩] قدْ جَعَلوا ٱللَّهْوَ رأسَ مالٍ   فَدَتْهُ نَفْسي من رأسِ مالِ
[١٠] قَدْ دَرَسوا ٱلفِسقَ مِنْ قَديم   فَكَمْ لَهُمْ فيهِ مِنْ جِدالِ

---

51 Tricia Rose, 'Never Trust a Big Butt and a Smile', p. 302.

52 I have not had the chance to read Sinan Antoon's new book on Ibn al-Ḥajjāj, though I have read the dissertation on which it was based. See S. Antoon, *The Poetics of the Obscene: Ibn al-Ḥajjāj and Sukhf*, Palgrave–Macmillan, 2013.

53 On this poet see, al-Ṣafadī, *al-Wāfī*, vol. 8, pp. 102–8; David Morray, *An Ayyubid Notable and His World. Ibn al-ʿAdīm and Aleppo as portrayed in his biographical dictionary of people associated with the city*, Leiden: Brill, 1994, pp. 37–9.

[١١] مِنْ أرْغَبِ ٱلنَّاسِ في ٱلفِقاحِ ٱلـــ ـــلذيذةِ ٱلمَنْيَكِ ٱلثِّقالِ
[١٢] مُخَنَّثٌ عِنْدَهُمْ لِنَيْكٍ أحسَنُ مِنْ زِيْنَةٍ ومالِ
[١٣] فَما لَهُمْ قَطُّ مِنْ حَديثٍ فيهِ سِوَى ٱلنَّيْكِ والبِدالِ
[١٤] فَقائِلٌ ناكَني فُلانٌ ونِكْتُهُ لا لَهُ ولا لي
[١٥] وقائِلٌ حينَ طاحَ سُكْراً وراحَ يَحْبُو إلى ٱلبُزالِ
[١٦] شَوارِبي فَقْحَتي سِبالي مَقْعَدَتي قِمَّتي نِعالي
[١٧] ونَحْنُ في مجلِسٍ بديعٍ جَلَّ عَنِ ٱلوَصْفِ والمِثالِ
[١٨] جُمِّعَ فيهِ من كلِّ شيءٍ فتَمَّ في غايةِ ٱلكَمالِ
[١٩] فالرَّاحُ في ٱلرَّاحِ والمَلاهي في ٱللَّهْوِ والنُّقْلُ في ٱلنِّقالِ
[٢٠] وللمَلاهي بِهِ ضَجيجٌ وللرَّواويقِ والمقالي
[٢١] فالدُّفُّ دُفْ دُفْ دُدُفْ دُدُفْ دُفْ والزَّمْرُ تَلَّى تَلَلْ تَلالي
[٢٢] والجَنْكُ دَنْ دَنْ دَدَنْ دَدَنْ دَنْ تُصْلِحُهُ رَبَّةُ ٱلحِجالِ
[٢٣] خَريدةٌ رُؤْدَةٌ رَداحٌ سَبَحْلَةٌ عَذْبَةُ ٱلمَقالِ
[٢٤] تَفْتِنُ بالدَّلِّ والتَّجَنِّي والحُسْنِ والتِّيْهِ والدَّلالِ
[٢٥] غَنَّتْ فَهامَ ٱلفؤادُ منّي وَجْداً إلى سِحْرِها ٱلحَلالِ
[٢٦] وَبَيْنَنا قَهْوَةٌ كَتِبْرٍ رَصَّعَها ٱلمَزْجُ باللّآلي
[٢٧] حَديدةُ ٱلطَّعمِ عَتَّقَتْها ألفاً فألفاً يَدُ ٱللَّيالي
[٢٨] صفراءُ كالنَّارِ بل تراها مذْ شابَها ٱلماءُ ذا ٱشتغالِ
[٢٩] يَسْعَى بِها شادِنٌ رشيقٌ مُهَفْهَفُ ٱلقَدِّ ذو ٱعتدالِ
[٣٠] مُوَرَّدُ ٱلوَجْنَتَيْنِ حُلْوٌ سِواهُ في ٱلنَّاسِ ما حَلا لي
[٣١] قُلْتُ لَهُ إذْ أطالَ وَعْدي ولَجَّ في ٱلعَذْلِ والمِطالِ
[٣٢] دَعِ ٱلتَّجَنّي فَلَسْتُ أسلو أخْ أخْ أخ يا مُحالي
[٣٣] لمّا بَدا وَهْيَ في يَدَيْهِ كالشَّمْسِ في راحَةِ ٱلهِلالِ
[٣٤] فطَبَّ طُرْطُبَّ فَوْقَ رأسي وطاقَ طِرطاقَ في قَذالي
[٣٥] وتُفَّ تَخْ تُفَّ وَسْطَ وَجْهي وقاعَ قَعْ قاعَ في سِبالي
[٣٦] وَبَظْرِ أمّي وَرَحْمِ أختي ولِحْيَتي في خَرا عَيالي
[٣٧] ونَعْلِ عَمّي بلا ٱمتِراءٍ مُدَحْرَجٌ في قذالِ خالي
[٣٨] إن كنتُ عاينتُ قطُّ غُصْناً مَرَّتْ بِهِ نَسْمَةُ ٱلشَّمالِ
[٣٩] أحْسَنَ منهُ إذا تَثَنَّى تُميلُهُ نَشْوَةُ ٱلدَّلالِ

1. The vicissitudes of time have worn me out.
   There's nothing left to see, not of my life, nor of me.
2. It's as if Fate sees me as an enemy;
   it hurls arrows at me to drive me away.
3. To think back on all that time when it
   was too busy to vex me and my friends.
4. If it had come to me then, I'd have taken it down,
   with power and might, without batting an eyelid.
5. What's happened to the life I lived?

What of my station? What of my wealth?
6. What's come of the boots I once wore? Of my mantle?
The chats and discussions I once had?
7. What of my life? What of my elation?
What of my beauty and my beautiful station?
8. [When] we [were] with those princely young men
whose noble lineages have long been lofty.
9. They'd made pleasure their stock-in-trade (*raʾs māl*)
for which my soul ransomed my every penny (*raʾs māl*).
10. They'd long been students of the ways of dissolution,
and Oh! How they debated the finer points!
11. They were some of the greatest fans of
nice-for-fucking, well seasoned assholes.
12. They had a nancy boy they kept for fucking
who was better than any adornments or mere money.[54]
13. The only subjects they spoke of
in relation to him were fucking and taking turns.
14. One of them says, 'So-and-so fucked me
and then I fucked him'. Though he hadn't the right, nor had I!
15. And one of them said, when he was plastered
and creeping toward the bung-hole of the wine cask:
16. My mustache! My asshole! My whiskers!
My bottom! My head! My heels!
17. We were in exquisite (*badīʿ*) company
too lush to be described (*waṣf*) or compared (*mithāl*).[55]
18. It had everything that could be desired
and so it was as perfectly complete as could be.
19. There was joy (*rāḥ*) in wine (*rāḥ*), and diversions
in pleasure, and sweet treats in passing round the cups.
20. The musical instruments make a great clamor,
as do the wine-strainers and the skillets.
21. And the *duff* goes *duf duf duduf duduf duf*,[56]
And the oboe (*zamr*) follows (*tallā*) *talal talālī*
22. And the harp (*jank*) [hums] *dan dan dadan dadan dan*,
it's set right by a lady's hand.[57]
23. A delicate and plump virgin maiden,
an [excuse] to say 'Glory be!', which rolls off the tongue.
24. She enchants with her flirtation and trickery,
and her beauty, self-satisfaction, and coquetry.
25. When she sang, my heart was in raptures

---

54 Compare Quran 18:46.

55 There is a pun in this line on the word *badīʿ*, which means 'amazing' and is also a technical literary term for uncommon or original imagery in poetic description (*waṣf*).

56 The *duff* (known today also as *daff*) is a large, circular frame drum.

57 Compare Turkish *çengi* (female dancers at the Ottoman court). Lines 20–22 are included with an annotated translation in S.A. Bonebakker and M. Fishbein (eds), *A Reader of Classical Arabic Literature*, Ser. Quaderni di Studi Arabi. Studi e testi, vol. 1, Venice: Cafoscarina, Università Ca'Foscari di Venezia, 1995 [repr. Ser. Resources in Arabic and Islamic Studies, Atlanta, GA: Lockwood Press, 2012], pp. 219–21.

of love for her licit magic.
26. The wine we [were drinking] was like gold
studded, from mixing, with pearls.
27. A robust wine aged
by a thousand, and yet a thousand more, nights
28. Golden like fire, which you can actually see
now that troubled water has made it hoary.
29. Taken round by a lithe gazelle fawn,
slender and well proportioned.
30. Rosy-cheeked, handsome.
Out of everyone, only he is pleasing to me.
31. I told him – should he be slow to [give me] what he'd promised –
and be stubborn, and blame, and put it off,
32. 'Put an end to this cruelty. I won't be made to forget.
[Cheering,] "Joy! Joyous Joy!" (*akh akh akh*)! That's beyond me!'
33. When he appeared, carrying it (i. e. the wine),
it looked like the sun cradled in the crescent moon's palm.
34. The liquid murmured (*fa-ṭabba ṭurṭubba*) in the jug above my head,[58]
and in the back of my mind, the millstone began to turn (*ṭāqa ṭirṭāqa*).
35. And he spit sour spit (*wa-taffa takh taffa*) in my face,[59]
followed by bitter water (*qāʿa qaʿ qāʿa*) at my mustache.
36. By my mother's clitoris, and my sister's womb,
and by my own beard in my children's shit,
37. And by my uncle's shoe, which – without a doubt –
runs back and forth against the back of my other uncle's head.
38. I know I've never seen a pliant branch before
swaying in a northward breeze.
39. More beautiful than him when he saunters past,
bending to the ecstasy of coquetry.

This poem combines a number of strange and outlandish images with playful, and occasionally onomatopoeic, vulgar language to conjure up a decidedly debauched atmosphere. The poem begins conventionally enough with a lamentation on the vicissitudes of time (ll. 1–5), though this nostalgic overture soon presages the farcical realm that forms the poem's core when the poet recites a litany of rhyming questions (ll. 5–7). Line 8 begins the run up to the long party (*majlis*) sequence (ll. 17–39) that makes this *mujūn* poem most like a *ghazal* (love poem) or *khamriyyah* (wine-poem). The poet recounts spending his salad days with other noble young men who were expert libertines (l. 10: '*qad darasū l-fisq*') and sexual deviants. The sexual practices of these young men is encapsulated in lines 11 and 12 in which the poet explains that the men were avid sodomites and that they kept a catamite (*mukhannath*) as a sort of sex slave. Much has been written about the acceptability (legal, religious, moral, social, etc.) of male-male sex in the pre-modern Islamicate world, and there is not sufficient space to discuss the issue here, but it is clear from the tone and

[58] This line is not entirely clear, but the recorded meaning of *ṭurṭubb* as 'big and flabby breast' (see G.J. van Gelder, *Sound and Sense*, p. 222) does not seem to fit here.

[59] *takh*: compare the contemporary Cairene onomatopoeia *ṭakhkh* or *ṭākh* ('whack!') (see in Martin Hinds and El-Said Badawi, *A Dictionary of Egyptian Arabic*, Beirut: Librairie du Liban, 1986).

content of lines 11 and 12 that the poet does not mean to represent this sort of sexual behaviour as normative or licit. Indeed the word '*bidāl*' in line 13 may mean, in addition to 'taking turns', what is known in some gay slang today as 'flipping', i.e. engaging in both roles in anal sex. Equally eyebrow-raising is the implication in Line 14 that the men also enjoy having sex with one another. Lines 17–25 describe the party (*majlis*) and specifically the musical accompaniment. In this sequence, we find the poet first deploying the rhetorical devices and onomatopoeia that define the poem's playful voice. Among the rhetorical devices, we find *tawriyah* (line 17), *jinās* (line 19), and in lines 21–22, a wonderful and rare example of Arabic poetic onomatopoeia.[60] It is not easy to represent the complete effect of this sequence in translation as there is an underlying semantic dimension to the words used to describe the sounds of the musical instruments; this is also the case in lines 34–35. Nevertheless it is clear from the Arabic as well as the English translation that the poet intends to exceed the bounds of direct meaning and grammar so as to embellish the description of licentiousness and corruption.

The poet continues in his description of the party setting by describing two erotic characters: the female musician (ll. 22–25) and the male wine-bearer (29–39). In contrast to the previously mentioned character of the *mukhannath* (catamite), who was more an object of ridicule than desire, the young woman and man described here are unavailable, out-of-reach. The woman is 'virginal' (l. 23) and they are both described as being coquettish (l. 24 and l. 39 respectively). The woman receives about as much ekphrastic attention in the poem as the wine does (ll. 26–28; 33) before the young man – the love interest – arrives on the scene in line 29. The Ganymede is described in conventional terms as being lithe (l. 29), rosy-cheeked (l. 30), and stingy with affection (l. 31). Where he deviates from the stock beloved type familiar from *ghazal* poetry – and where this poem re-enters the realm of *mujūn* after a relatively polite interlude – is when the poet confronts the young man for being slow to fulfil his promise (presumably of sexual union). Here again the poet uses onomatopoeia and wordplay when describing the sexually charged, but humiliating exchange between the persona and the beloved. The connection between this style of indirect, playful *mujūn* and the African-American literary mode known as 'Signifying' made famous by Henry Louis Gates Jr. clearly deserves more attention. In the climax of the poem when the lover complains to the beloved, as lovers in Arabic *ghazal* often do, the beloved attacks him in the most humiliating fashion. The language here is not entirely clear, but it seems that the beloved pours wine on the lover's head (l. 34), slaps him on the back of the neck (l. 34), and then spits in his face (l. 35). The poet reacts by swearing in a markedly ironic way (i.e. l. 36: on his mother's clitoris, his sister's womb, and his own beard which he says is covered in his children's faeces) and this parody is made farce by the two lines that close the poem. After this ludicrous – and vulgar – oath, the poet tells us what it is he is testifying to: the beauty of the cruel beloved! What could be more camp than that?

[60] On Onomatopoeia (and sound patterns more generally) in classical Arabic poetry, see Geert Jan van Gelder, *Sound and Sense in Classical Arabic Poetry*, Ser. Arabische Studien, vol. 10, Wiesbaden: Harrassowitz, 2012, ch. 4, esp pp. 269–89.

THE BODY AS BASE

> Historically, it has been black people's responsibility to link pleasure or freedom with the non-material. [...] If moral and cultural correctness is seen as denial, then open representations of sexuality and grotesque and carnivalesque characterizations/ eroticizations of violence can be understood as potentially liberating.[61]

In her magisterial study of 'gender and discourse in Arabo-Islamic writing', Fedwa Malti-Douglas identifies the three axes of the female character type in classical Arabic *adab* works as:

1. woman's eloquence
2. woman's ruse
3. woman's sexuality[62]

These three qualities, the first of which Marlé Hammond discusses in her contribution to this volume, locate the role of literary women in a narrowly defined characterological rubric that is owed fundamentally to a crude and misogynistic psychological interpolation from a corporeal basis. Women's bodies determine their psychology. These three qualities are thus logical corollaries to the fact (scil. phenomenon) of the female body: a woman's eloquence is rooted in her dishonesty (ruse), which is itself a manifestation of her manipulative sexual cunning (sexuality), which is the only reasonable consequent of her status as sex object. In Malti-Douglas' words, '[...] her speech remains tied to the seductive power of her body.'[63] Borrowing from Martha Nussbaum's analysis of the forms of objectification, we can say that this typology does not necessarily deny woman's autonomy and subjectivity, nor does it stipulate that a woman is violable, fungible, or inert, though she may occasionally be ownable, but it is ultimately instrumentalist.[64] The woman character could be an autonomous agent possessed of subjectivity and liberty who enjoys bodily integrity and is unique, but she is always, despite the above, fundamentally a manifestation of her sexual role. In practice, however, she is usually characterized as a sex object who is also inert, or violable, or enslaved, or supine. The situation is slightly more complicated when speaking of subordinate males who are characterized as sex objects because the absolving element in this sort of pairing is fundamentally the subordinate male's status as always inferior as regards age and often as regards class, social station, ethnicity, religion, etc.[65]

---

[61] Davarian L. Baldwin, 'Black Empires, White Desires', p. 168.

[62] Fedwa Malti-Douglas, *Woman's Body, Woman's Word: gender and discourse in Arabo-Islamic Writing*, Princeton, NJ: Princeton University Press, 1991, p. 31.

[63] Ibid., p. 110.

[64] See Martha Nussbaum, *Sex and Social Justice*, Oxford; New York, NY: Oxford University Press, 1999, pp. 213–39, esp. p. 218.

[65] See, *inter alia*, especially James E. Montgomery, 'For the Love of a Christian Boy: a song by Abū Nuwās', *Journal of Arabic Literature*, 27:2, 1996, pp. 115–24; and Franklin Lewis, 'Sexual Occidentation: The Politics of Conversion, Christian-Love and Boy-Love in ʿAttār', *Iranian Studies*, 42:5, December

In the United States, African-American male bodies have been subject to extreme scrutiny, as well as state and social violence, throughout centuries of bondage, lynching, Jim Crow, and mass incarceration, and continue to serve as a cultural lightning rod. One need only think of the prominence of African-American male bodies in pornography and team sports – two of contemporary white America's most popular spectacles – and the ways in which they are presented simultaneously as inherently dangerous and as objects of lust to complicate the reductive notion of hip hop culture as uniquely hypermasculine, priapic, misogynistic, and homophobic.

> The consumption of black male bodies has proven a popular feature of North American culture. If one thinks of the athlete, the thug, the kinetic entertainer, the idea of inherent physical ability and intellectual inability, and the hypersexual threat, there emerges an obsession with and the observation, parody, and mutilation of black male bodies.[66]

Much of white America's ancient angst about African-American men and their bodies is brought out in the hip hop characters created by African-American male artists, though it is not yet clear to what extent this can also be understood as self-parody. Clearly when female artists adopt the gangsta, thug, or pimp persona, they are seen to be poking fun at it and the image of hypermasculinity it projects. Likewise, female rap artists like Lil' Kim and Khia invert the normative sexual paradigm of most hip hop by casting themselves as the dominant partner in sexual relationships: receiving oral sex, boasting of multiple partners, etc. Here the African-American male is cast once again as sex object; this time by African-American women.

What the figure of the African-American male and the character of woman in classical Arabic literature have in common is that they are both ultimately determined by what their societies imagine to be their bodily imperatives. On the other hand, African-American women are characterized psychologically – by mainstream American culture as well as male African-American rap artists – as being venal, deceitful, and nymphomaniac.[67] This is true, too, of classical Arabic queers, i.e. the debauched hedonists portrayed in *mujūn* poems and tales, whose proclivities and perversions are rooted in their behaviours and their psychology rather than in their bodies, which are indistinguishably male. We have seen how certain female rap artists have turned this slander on its head by mimicking a male persona, which – according to social and generic codes – can boast of the equivalent, masculine personality attributes with impunity (i.e. being a 'baller' and 'player'). Whether

---

2009, pp. 693–724.

[66] Imani Perry, *Prophets of the Hood*, p. 120.

[67] The role of mainstream culture (institutions and consumers) in this dynamic should not be underestimated: 'The white male consumer, who accounts for the greatest consumption of hip hop today, not only exploits, fuels, and exemplifies the social conditions leading to hypermasculinity in hip hop in the sense that record companies encourage images from artists that are appealing to consumers, but he also exists as a voyeur to the sexual politics between black men and women as they are presented in hip hop. Black male hip hop artists do not simply assert power over women's bodies in a kind of effort to create imaginative patriarchy; they also use black women as a kind of commodity expression of wealth and sexual power in the face of racialized economic powerlessness.' (Imani Perry, *Prophets of the Hood*, p. 127; note too Davarian L. Baldwin, 'Black Empires, White Desires', p. 166).

the caricature of hypersexual, misogynistic masculinity put forth by male rap artists is already itself a parody remains to be seen, but it is likely that cultural and social prejudices against African-American language, culture, and artistic expression have precluded any sensitivity to irony on the part of the listening audience.

Similarly the overlap between varieties of obscene expression in classical Arabic literature has hindered a critical awareness of *mujūn*'s specifically satirical generic intention. Much more than *sukhf*, classical Arabic *mujūn* poets should be read as caricaturing and ridiculing a moralistic system, often by locating their transgressions in the world of the body. They often rebel, for example, against a simplistic and reified understanding of sexual codes (including manifestations of heterosexual and same-sex desire, behaviour, exchange, power dynamics, and taste). That they do so by exaggerating *ad absurdum* what mainstream society stipulates is inevitable, and in consciously obscene language no less, demonstrates how *mujūn* functions primarily on a parodic level. If in the past *mujūn* has not been sufficiently appreciated as a culturally resistant and socially marginal discourse, it is perhaps a victim of its own success and popularity. As this volume shows, a variety of elite and popular authors and poets from a wide range of ethnic, religious, and class backgrounds wrote obscene literature in Arabic, and it is this prevalence that has likely diminished the chance of one specific subset of this literature, i.e. *mujūn*, to be taken seriously. Now more than ever *mujūn*, like hip hop, deserves a critical, open-minded, and sensitive audience who will appreciate the artistry and profound social criticism that lies in obscenity.

WORKS CITED

I. Publications

Sinan Antoon, *The Poetics of the Obscene: Ibn al-Ḥajjāj and Sukhf.* Palgrave–Macmillan, 2013.

Edward G. Armstrong, 'Gangsta Misogyny: a content analysis of the portrayals of violence against women in rap music, 1987–1993'. *Journal of Criminal Justice and Popular Culture*, 8:2, 2001, pp. 96–126.

Davarian L. Baldwin, 'Black Empires, White Desires: The Spatial Politics of Identity in the Age of Hip Hop' in M. Forman and M.A. Neal (eds.), *That's the Joint!*, pp. 159–76.

John R. Clarke, 'Look who's laughing at sex: Men and Women Viewers in the *Apodyterium* of the Suburban Baths' in David Frederick (ed.), *The Roman Gaze: Vision, Power, and the Body*, Baltimore, MD: Johns Hopkins Press, 2002.

Kimberle Crenshaw, 'Beyond Racism and Misogyny: Black Feminism and 2 Live Crew'. *Boston Review*, 16, December 1991 [<http://bostonreview.net/BR16.6/crenshaw.html>].

Michael Eric Dyson, 'Gangsta Rap and American Culture' in M.E. Dyson, *The Michael Eric Dyson Reader*. New York, NY: Basic Civitas, 2004.

Murray Forman and Mark Anthony Neal (eds.), *That's the Joint! The Hip-Hop Studies Reader*. New York, NY: Routledge, 2004.

Henry Louis Gates Jr., '2 Live Crew, Decoded'. *The New York Times*. 19 June 1990, A23.

Kyra D. Gaunt, 'Translating Double-Dutch to Hip-Hop: The Musical Vernacular of Black Girls' Play' in M. Forman and M.A. Neal (eds.), *That's the Joint!*, pp. 251–63.

Geert Jan van Gelder, *Sound and Sense in Classical Arabic Poetry.* Ser. Arabische Studien, vol. 10. Wiesbaden: Harrassowitz, 2012.

Geert Jan van Gelder, 'Sexual Violence in Verse: the case of Jiʿthin, al-Farazdaq's sister'. Forthcoming.

Geert Jan van Gelder, *The Bad and the Ugly: attitudes towards invective poetry* (hijāʾ) *in classical Arabic literature*. Leiden: Brill, 1988.

Ibn Ḥajar al-ʿAsqalānī, *al-Durar al-kāminah*. 6 vols. ed. Fritz Krenkow and Sharaf al-Dīn Aḥmad. Hyderabad: Maṭbaʿat Majlis Dāʾirat al-Maʿārif, 1929–31.

Marlé Hammond, *Beyond Elegy: classical Arabic women's poetry in context*. Oxford: Oxford University Press, 2010.

Andras Hamori, *On the Art of Medieval Arabic Literature*. Princeton, NJ: Princeton University Press, 1974.

Ṣafī al-Dīn al-Ḥillī, *al-ʿĀṭil al-ḥālī wa-l-murakhkhaṣ al-ghālī*. ed. Ḥusayn Naṣṣār. Cairo: al-Hayʾah al-Miṣriyyah al-ʿĀmmah li-l-Kitāb, 1981.

bell hooks, *Outlaw Culture: resisting representations*. New York: Routledge, 2006.

Jarīr, *Dīwān Jarīr bi-sharḥ Muḥammad b. Ḥabīb*. ed. Nuʿmān Muḥammad Amīn Ṭāhā. 2 vols. Cairo: Dār al-Maʿārif, 1969–71.

Robin Kelley, 'Kickin' Reality, Kickin' Ballistics: "Gangsta Rap" and Postindustrial Los Angeles' in *idem*, *Race Rebels: Culture, Politics, and the Black Working Class*, New York, NY: Free Press, 1994, pp. 183–227.

Cheryl L. Keyes, 'Empowering Self, Making Choices, Creating Spaces: Black Female Identity via Rap Music Performance' in M. Forman and M.A. Neal (eds.), *That's the Joint!*, pp. 265–76.

Abdelfattah Kilito, *The Author and His Doubles: essays on classical Arabic culture*. trans. Michael Cooperson. Syracuse, NY: Syracuse University Press, 2001.

Yvonne Shinhoster Lamb, 'C. Delores Tucker Dies at 78; Rights and Anti-Rap Activist' [obituary]. *The Washington Post*. 13 October 2005. <http://www.washingtonpost.com>.

Franklin Lewis, 'Sexual Occidentation: The Politics of Conversion, Christian-Love and Boy-Love in ʿAttār'. *Iranian Studies*. 42:5. December 2009. pp. 693–724.

Ursula Lindsey, 'The Arab World's Tangled Linguistic Landscape'. *al-Fanar*. 19 April 2013. <http://www.al-fanar.org>.

Fedwa Malti-Douglas, *Woman's Body, Woman's Word: gender and discourse in Arabo-Islamic Writing*. Princeton, NJ: Princeton University Press, 1991.

John Mattock, 'Description and Genre in Abu Nuwas' in *Atti del XIII Congresso dell'Union Européenne d'Arabisants et d'Islamisants (Venezia 29 settembre–4 ottobre 1986)*. *Quaderni di Studi Arabi*. 5–6. Venice: Università degli studi di Venezia, 1987. pp. 528–40.

John McWhorter, *Word on the Street: debunking the myth of "pure" standard English*. Cambridge, MA: Perseus, 1998.

Julie Scott Meisami, 'Arabic *Mujūn* Poetry: the literary dimension' in F. de Jong (ed.), *Verse and the Fair Sex: studies in Arabic poetry and in the representation of women in Arabic literature*. Utrecht: M.Th. Houtsma Stichting, 1993. pp. 8–30.

James E. Montgomery. 'For the Love of a Christian Boy: a song by Abū Nuwās'. *Journal of Arabic Literature*. 27:2. 1996. pp. 115–24.

David Morray. *An Ayyubid Notable and His World. Ibn al-ʿAdīm and Aleppo as portrayed in his biographical dictionary of people associated with the city*. Leiden: Brill, 1994.

Martha Nussbaum, *Sex and Social Justice*. Oxford; New York, NY: Oxford University Press, 1999.

Abū Nuwās, *Dīwān Abī Nuwās*. 7 vols. ed. E. Wagner and G. Schoeler. Wiesbaden: Franz Steiner Verlag, 1958–2006.

Ivan Panović, *Literacies in Contemporary Egypt: everyday writing and political change*. Routledge, 2014 (forthcoming).

Jon Pareles, 'Rap: Slick, Violent, Nasty and, maybe, Hopeful'. *The New York Times*. 17 June 1990, pp. E1–E5.

Imani Perry, *Prophets of the Hood: Politics and Poetics in Hip Hop*. Durham, NC: Duke University Press, 2004.

Margeaux Rawson, 'The Queens of Comedy on the Commandments of Sex'. *Jezebel.* 16 April 2012. <http://www.jezebel.com>.
Tricia Rose, 'Never Trust a Big Butt and a Smile' in M. Forman and M.A. Neal (eds.), *That's the Joint!*, pp. 291–306.
Joseph Sadan (Yūsuf Sadān), *al-Adab al-ʿarabī al-hāzil wa-nawādir al-thuqalāʾ: al-ʿāhāt wa-l-masāwiʾ al-insāniyyah wa-makānatuhā fī al-adab al-ʿarabī.* Cologne; Baghdad: Manshūrāt al-Jamal, 2007.
Ṣalāḥ al-Dīn al-Ṣafadī, *al-Wāfī bi-l-Wafāyāt.* 30 vols. ed. Hellmut Ritter, et al. 2nd edition. Wiesbaden: Franz Steiner Verlag, 1931–2007.
Boaz Shoshan, *Popular Culture in medieval Cairo.* Cambridge: Cambridge University Press, 1993.
Arthur K. Spears, 'Directness in the use of African-American English' in Sonja Lanehart (ed.), *Sociocultural and Historical Contexts of African American English*, Amsterdam; Philadelphia, PA: John Benjamins, 2001, pp. 239–59.
Arthur K. Spears, 'African-American Language Use: ideology and so-called obscenity' in S.S. Mufwene, J. Rickford, G. Bailey, and J. Baugh, (eds.), *African-American English: structure, history and use*, New York: Routledge, 1998, pp. 226–50.
Craig Williams, *Roman Homosexuality: Ideologies of Masculinity in Classical Antiquity.* Oxford: Oxford University Press, 1999.

II. Recordings

2 Live Crew, 'Pop that Pussy'. *Sports Weekend: As Nasty as They Wanna Be, Pt. 2.* Luke Records, 1991.
Akinyele, 'Put it in Your Mouth'. *Put it in Your Mouth.* BMG Records, 1996.
Dr. Dre, 'Bitches Ain't Shit'. *The Chronic.* Death Row, 1992; 2001 (re-release).
Khia, 'My Neck, My Back (Lick it)'. *Thug Misses.* Artemis, 2002.
Lil' Kim (feat. Sisqó), 'How Many Licks?' *The Notorious K.I.M.* Atlantic Records, 2000.
Lil' Kim, 'Suck my dick'. *The Notorious K.I.M.* Atlantic Records, 2000.
Notorious B.I.G., 'Respect'. *Ready to Die.* Bad Boy, 1994.
Too $hort, 'Blowjob Betty'. *Get in where you fit in.* Jive Records, 1993.

18

Love and Sex among the Ottomans (1500–1800)

Jan Schmidt

As is well known, love and sex belong, together with eating and drinking, to the primary instinct-driven activities of man and woman. Without them, mankind simply cannot survive. So why should one study them in particular in the context of the early-modern Ottomans, or for that matter of any particular culture, historical or contemporary? The answer is clearly that there is a historical aspect to these phenomena: the way in which early-modern Ottomans indulged in these activities was, at least to a certain extent, different from the way that was done among modern, but also among other early-modern people, in particular early-modern Europeans. Like eating and drinking, love and sex, although they are essentially biological/psychological phenomena, are at the same time cultural ones in that their realization is up to a certain point ruled by the shared values, customs and practices that dominate a culture. Ottomans who were living before, roughly, 1800, did fall in love and did practice sex like we do, but – and this is an aspect on which I want to focus this contribution – the object of their amorous and sexual attention was often different from that of a contemporary European. By Ottomans here I mean men. Although we may like to know what early-modern Ottoman women thought, felt and did in this field, this is impossible, or almost impossible, because our sources, particularly more intimate literary sources, are mostly silent on this point. Sources on the feelings, attitudes and activities of men, however abound, so we can pay quite some attention to them here. The difference I just mentioned is that, in our sources, we find that the main object of Ottoman male attention was not a girl or a woman but a boy. That is not to say that men did not fall in love with girls or women or did not marry and beget children – the Ottoman Empire would not have lasted for 600 years if this had been the case – but our sources only exceptionally describe heterosexual love and sex.

In Ottoman sources, then, particularly in literary works, the infatuation of men for young boys is a recurring theme. As I will try to show here, the phenomenon was considered a normal variation in the sexual orientation of men at the time, even by orthodox moralists. Despite this fact, until recently not much attention was paid to this phenomenon. From the 1980s onward, it has been studied and discussed among Western orientalists – I say 'orientalists' and not: turcologists, because the phenomenon was not restricted to Turks or the Ottoman Empire – and the reason I come to speak of it is inspired by a number of important books published in Europe and the US during the last decade. In a way, you could consider this contribution as some sort of elaborate review article. I said 'Western orientalists', because the subject is still largely taboo, or wilfully explained away, in Arab countries and Turkey. İsmet Zeki Eyuboğlu in a well-known book on Ottoman 'classical' (*divan*) poetry published in 1968 – and reprinted in 1991 – did not deny that 'perverted love' – the words (*sapık sevgi*) occur in the title – was a dominant theme in that poetry, but maintains that it was an alien theme, a subject imported into Turkish literature by foreigners and not suitable to the historical, originally Central Asian Turkish 'realities', 'customs' and the Turkish 'way of life'; it clashed with historical Turkish culture in short.[1] Eyuboğlu was, until today, almost the only Turkish scholar working in Turkey, who addressed the phenomenon at all.[2] (Curiously, this reasoning, which presupposes that certain 'nations', 'ethnicities' or even 'races' are too 'healthy' to be effected by corrupt [or 'decadent'] morals, is also found in a famous book by Hellmut Ritter, in which he maintained that the love for young boys [*Knabenliebe*] was a phenomenon that had its origin among the Iranians, from whom the Indo-Germanic peoples inherited it, but that it had been unknown in Semitic culture.[3] (Ritter himself, by the way, was a homosexual who spent most of his life in Turkey.) Alien or not to certain people, the phenomenon was, as I said, widely spread, and not restricted to the Ottoman world, not even to the wider Islamic world. Despite the, to a certain extent, commonness of the phenomenon in pre-modern days, it is all the same puzzling to me for reasons I will explain at the end of this paper.

Let me now first turn to the aforementioned books in which the phenomenon is discussed. They are: (1) *The Age of Beloveds: love and the beloved in early-modern Ottoman and European culture and society* by Walter Andrews and Mehmet Kalpaklı (Durham and London 2005); (2) *Before Homosexuality in the Arab-Islamic World, 1500–1800* by Khaled El-Rouayheb (Chicago and London 2005); and (3) *Producing Desire: changing sexual discourse in the Ottoman Middle East, 1500–1900* by Dror Ze'evi (Berkeley, Los Angeles and London, 2006). Ze'evi, as is clear from his book, was not yet aware of the two earlier mentioned studies. The authors of the first study, Andrews and Kalpaklı, try to prove, quoting from a great number of Ottoman, mostly literary, sources that there flourished an 'Age of Beloveds' in the Ottoman Empire between 1450 and 1620, which it shared, in a way, with contemporary Renaissance Europe. In it, same-sex eroticism and love play an important role. The impression that one gets from the book is that it must have been pleasant to have lived in the world of the Istanbul and provincial courts where loving friendships played an important role and the elite had a good time partaking of rich banquets at which poems were quoted, wine flew copiously and flirting with boys was a main pastime.

This rosy picture is somewhat dimmed in the second book, the one by El-Rouayheb, in which the author tries in a rather detached, matter-of-fact manner, to get grip on our

[1] İsmet Zeki Eyuboğlu, *Divan Şiirinde Sapık Sevgi*, 2nd impr., ([Turkey]: Broy Yayınları, 1991), p. 203.

[2] See Kemal Silay, *Nedim and the Poetics of the Ottoman Court; medieval inheritance and the need for change* (Bloomington: Indiana University Turkish Studies, 1994), pp. 102–3.

[3] *Das Meer der Seele: Mensch, Welt und Gott in den Geschichten des Farīduddīn 'Attār* (Leiden: Brill, 1955), pp. 364, 501.

phenomenon. The study is based not only on literary, but also on legal and medical texts written in Arabic but within the confines of the Ottoman lands during the period between, roughly, 1500 and 1800. Ze'evi's book is, by and large, the most encompassing of the three studies, being based on legal, medical and travel texts as well as books on dream interpretation and the shadow theatre ('Karagöz'), written, as far as indigenous sources are referred to, in both Arabic and Turkish. His book also covers a longer period than either of its two predecessors by including the nineteenth century, when a 'hetero-normalized culture', as it existed in Europe and the US at the time, became dominant in the Ottoman Empire. El-Rouayheb and Ze'evi's findings, as far as our theme is concerned, are similar, so in what follows I will, for practical reasons, follow the argument as it is presented most comprehensively in El-Rouayheb's book.

El-Rouayheb distinguishes between two broad genres, namely (1) texts that discuss or describe or refer to sex and (2) texts that treat of platonic love. In view of El-Rouayheb's findings – and this is also true for Ze'evi – the time limit of about 1620, which according to Andrews and Kalpaklı marked the onset of the decline of the 'Age of Love', must be considered untenable. In fact, documentation, literary and otherwise, of the phenomenon only begins to decline in the course of the nineteenth century under the growing influence of Western culture, although even today, and particularly in the Arab world outside large urban areas, certain aspects of male to male bonding and sex as described in the older sources are still being (secretly) practiced.

Texts on sex between two male persons (the first category), El-Rouayheb points out, invariably sketch or refer to a stereotypic situation whereby a healthy (bearded) man has anal intercourse with a (beardless) teenage boy. The roles between penetrator [the one who commits *livat*, 'active sodomy'] and penetrated [the one who suffers from *ubna*, 'passive sodomy'] are strictly separated. The penetrator belongs to the rich, dominating, upper, literate class and the penetrated to the poor, dominated, lower, illiterate class. The boy either indulges in the activity because he likes it (and 'his arse itches', as medical texts have it), but more often because he earns protection, prestige or money by it. Of the active party it is often said that he was married and had children. This form of sex was strictly forbidden by jurists, in particular because it went against the divinely sanctioned obligation of procreation – it was, curiously, only allowed in Paradise although the jurists disagreed among themselves whether the 'immortal boys' [*wildān mukhalladūn*] there, mentioned in the Koran, were available for sex or only for contemplation. Despite this prohibition under the law, a majority of writers sympathised with the active party, whereas the passive party was always suspect, especially if the age limit of about eighteen years was exceeded and the first signs of down were making way for a full beard.

In texts of the second category, in which platonic love instead of carnal lust prevails, we find that literati, refined aesthetes and mystics are described as the active, albeit theoretically, involuntary (and therefore unblameworthy) party, because they could not help falling in love. The age gap and the social gap here were the same as in the first category. This love [*'ışk*] for, again, the beardless boy was not supposed to lead to any corporeal 'union', perhaps not even to fondling and kissing, and consequently, the lover suffered. Mystics and mystically inclined literati went further and associated physical beauty of the beloved with the divine. Because the infatuation was involuntary and there was no consummation, the jurists did not object to it. The same was true, on the whole, for the literary activities which surrounded the fruitless longing, like, for instance, the composing of *ghazels* (short, lyrical poems) in which the poet's passion for a beautiful boy was expressed. This was deemed legitimate by most jurists if not altogether commendable. The idea that physical beauty was an attribute of God, by contrast, found less acceptance among jurists because it reeked of pantheism.

Although the sources quoted in El-Rouayheb's book are exclusively drawn from Arabic literature, it is easy to find comparable Turkish texts. As a good example of the first category, we may mention Deli Birader's 'The Expeller of Sorrows and Remover of Worries' (*Dafiʿu l-gumum ve Rafiʿu l-humum*), composed sometime between 1483 and 1511, a work which is dedicated to sexual depravity. The hitherto obscure work was recently analysed by Selim Kuru.[4] An important aspect of the work is – and this seems in general also to be true of comparable texts or text fragments, as they, for instance, occur in the genres of the *mufahara* and *şehr-engiz* – is that of punning, playing with risqué metaphors referring to sex, particularly the act of penetration, and sexual organs as well as slander and satire. Far more serious are works of the second category. We may mention here the memoirs of the dervish 'Aşçı Dede' İbrahim Halil (1820–c.1910), published in transcription a few years ago. In it, the author described, among many other things, a number of platonic love affairs. While working at the Ministry of War (at the *ordular ruznamçe kalemi*) in Istanbul, İbrahim, who must have then have been in his late twenties, was struck by the appearance of an office boy called Osman. Cleverly playing with military metaphors, he described what happened:

> Osman during a period of five to six months had suddenly grown up, his stature had become vigorous and a different kind of beauty manifested itself. One day one of our colleagues said to me: 'My dear, haven't you ever thrown a glance at Osman Bey, look how the child has changed.' I was struck by his words and when I threw a lovable glance at him, it was as if I saw a second Yusuf. [...] Through this glance, I saw that he was at ease within the climate zone of his body and was completely certain of himself and I felt a secret movement among the soldiers of love [*ʿışk*] as if preparations for war were made and I witnessed secret proclamations issued to various parts. 'For heavens' sake, what is this and why such preparations?', I asked my brain that is the commander of love. In answer it said: 'Nothing is the matter as yet. But because the weapons in the hands of the soldiers have lately become rusty and they have not cleaned them, and because the army has not left its barracks for some time now and has not exercised on the field of love, you had this experience [...]'. When evening approached, I went home. The image of Osman began to turn around before my eyes. In order to drive it away I immediately took my books and busied myself with my homework. But when demonstrative pronouns like a pronoun or the word 'likewise' began to relate themselves to Osman Bey, this proved to be impossible.[5]

---

[4] Selim S. Kuru, 'Sex in the Text: Deli Birader's *Dâfiʿü 'l-gumûm ve Râfiʿü 'l-humûm* and the Ottoman Literary Canon', in *Middle Eastern Literatures* [incorporating *Edebiyât*] 10.2 (2007), pp. 157–74.

[5] '*... Osman Bey, beş altı ay zarfında maşallah birden bire serpildi, boy pos ve bir başka hüsn peyda etti. Bir gün arkadaşlarımızdan birisi fakire dedi ki "Azizim, Osman bey'e hiç nazar buyurmuyorsunuz, baksanıza çocuk başkalaştı" demesiyle, onun tarafından kulağıma gelen sözden bir tesir peyda olup şöyle bir âşıkane*

The author tried to find distraction by visiting some friends. But the next day, his first thought was of Osman. He went to morning prayers, but could not concentrate because he felt that 'Osman Bey's cotton of love [*muhabbet*] blocked his ears'.[6] When he arrived in the office later, 'I saw him like a moon rising in my room.'[7] He realized that he had fallen in love and had become a passive instrument in the boy's hands, his king who was like a second Yusuf seated on his elevated throne. What should he do? On the advice of his colleagues, whom his enamored state had not escaped, he joined the Mevlevi order of dervishes. His mother quickly arranged a marriage for him in order to distract his attention. From İbrahim Dede's further commentary it is clear that his love for the boy would remain platonic because only then could it function as a bridge to true, divine love.

One could reason that the example is atypical, because it is set in the world of dervishes and mysticism. But the phenomenon was much wider spread than that. Of the famous polymath Mustafa Âli (d. 1600), about whose life we are relatively well informed, it is known, as he himself states in one of his many works, that as a young man he was both attracted to 'pretty girls' and 'handsome boys'. Later he married and had a son. His collected correspondence, 'published' when he was 44 years of age, contains a letter in which he asks for the hand of a gentleman's daughter but also a 'letter of longing' to an (anonymous) young man or boy.[8] He could perhaps be compared to literary figures such as Lord Byron and Oscar Wilde, who had romantic or not so romantic affairs with boys but were also married and had children.

The combination of an adoration of boys with a strong urge to have sex with them is found in Aşık Chelebi's *Meşaʿiru ş-şuʾara*, one of the most famous Ottoman *tezkire*s (biographical dictionaries) ever written, which describes how the poet Meʾali (d. 942/1535–6) becomes the victim of a boy. This supposedly happened when Meʾali was kadi in the town of Mihaliç near Bursa, and must have been between 23 and 31 years old, perhaps even somewhat older.[9] Meʾali, we are told, was in the possession of a rather striking

---

nazar ettiğimde sahîhen bir Yûsuf-ı sânî gibi gördüm... İşte bu nazardan dolayı onu gördüm ki bir hayli zamandan beri iklîm-i vücûdda asayiş ve emn ü emân ber-kemâl iken bir tedârükât-ı harbiyye var gibi asâkir-i aşkta hafî bir hareket hissettim ve sırren etrâf u eknâfa ilânât müşahede eyledim. "Aman nedir bu ahval ve bu tedârükât?" diye kumandan-ı aşk olan akla sual ettim. Dedi ki "Evet şimdilik daha bir şey yoktur. Ancak askerin elinde bulunan silâhlar bir hayli zamandır paslanmış olduğundan, onların tathîrine ve bir de asker çoktan beri kışlalarından çıkıp meydân-ı aşkta talim ve taallümlerinde bulunmadıklarından... böyle bir şey müşahedeniz olmuştur... O gün akşamı ettik, eve geldim. Osman Bey'in hayali başladı gözümün önünde dolaşmaya. Defetmek için derakab kitapları alıp ders bakmaya meşgul olup lâkin kitaplarda olan "zamir" ve "kezalik" gibi esmâ-yı işâretler Osman Bey'e raci olmaya başladığından, o da olmadı.', Mustafa Koç and Eyyüp Tanrıverdi, eds., *Aşçı İbrahim Dede. Çok Yönlü Bir Sufinin Gözüyle Son Dönem Osmanlı Hayatı Aşçı Dede'nin Hatıraları* I, Istanbul 2006, pp. 186–7. (My translation.)

6 *'Osman Bey'in muhabbet pamuğu kulağımı tıkamış olduğunu [hissettim]'*, ibid., p. 187.

7 *'... ay doğar gibi odaya tulû etmesiyle... onu gördüm...'*, ibid.

8 Jan Schmidt, 'Mustafa Âli of Gallipoli on Friendship' (forthcoming). For (rare) examples documented in 19th-century Ottoman literature, see Selim S. Kuru, 'Yaşanan, Söylenen ve Yazılan: Erkekler Arasında Tutkusal İlişkiler', *Cogito* 65–6 (2011), pp. 263–77.

9 Me'ali was born before 1490; he was kadi of Mihaliç during the reign of Selim I (1512–20), cf. Edith Ambros, *Candid Penstrokes: the Lyrics of Meʾālī, an Ottoman Poet of the 16th century* (Berlin: K. Schwarz, 1982), pp. 12, 23.

physiognomy: a huge, aubergine-like nose dominated his face and a very sparse beard consisting of little more than two or three hairs adorned his chin. He suffered moreover from bad health, had weak sight and was addicted to opium. The boy by contrast is described as a 'saucy-eyed and sweet-faced'[10] street urchin (*şehiroğlan*) of doubtful repute, endowed with – what else could we expect? – curly ambergris-perfumed hair. Street urchin or not, he is also said to be the son of a Janissary and an 'efendi', which means that he was not really 'lower-class', as Andrews and Kalpaklı seem to suggest in their discussion of the passage.[11] This is the more unlikely, because the boy, at least according to the story, wrote his beloved a letter in complicated rhymed prose. Me'ali began to court him (the terms *ʿışk* and *muhabbet* are used here), particularly by looking intently at him and smiling at him. The boy played the ogling game with him, responding in a sly, playful manner. Later Me'ali began to send him poems and love letters. The boy sent him an encouraging letter back, telling him that he looked forward to his company, serving him and profiting from his conversation and wisdom, and more than that ('If only... the cash of my beauty be spent and the merchandise of my love ['*ışk*] find favour!'[12]). More encouraging messages continued to be exchanged – Me'ali emphasizes that he is not interested in what is termed *şahid-bazlık* [traditionally translated with 'sodomy', but more literally meaning 'frolicking with catamites'] for which his kind [*bizüm ta'ife*] is often accused – until they agree to gather in a tumbledown farm not far from the town. To make a long story short, the boy led the kadi, caught unawares, to a lepers' colony, and while the boy pretended that he stood at the point of yielding to the kadi's wish of kissing him and laying together in corporal union [*visal*], 'to mingle soul with soul',[13] he disappeared under the pretext of fetching some wine. Soon afterwards, to Me'ali's horror, the lepers appeared, 'people with pustules on their faces, sores on their hands, [and] with scrofulous feet,'[14] who insisted sharing their food with him, celebrate 'union' with him and enjoy his company. In the end, having broken down and confessed that he, indeed, was a miserable 'catamite worshipper [*şahid-perest*] and pederast [*gulambare*]', he was saved by his steward [*kethüda*] and court summoners [*muhzırlar*]. Having fallen ill and suffering from terrible nightmares, he eventually asked God's forgiveness for his 'inebriation with the cup of lust and for his devotion to sensuality'.[15]

The story must have been fascinating to ʿAşık Chelebi's readers/audience, not in the least because it avoids many of the clichés of both the treatises on sex and the literature on platonic love. The protagonist, Me'ali, wants sex but is forced to remain abstinent although he had, while dismounting his horse, fallen on top of the boy and later tried to grab him by the long hair that flowed down his back.[16] Typical, also here, is the age-difference

[10] '*şuh-çeşm ü hoş-nüma*'. Quotations of the original text are based on the transcription as edited by Filiz Kılıç in her dissertation of 2007; for the English version, I follow Ambros's translation, *Candid Penstrokes*, pp. 44–60.

[11] Andrews and Kalpaklı, *The Age of the Beloveds*, p. 217.

[12] '*kaşki... nakd-ı hüsnümüz yirine harc olaydı ve mata-ı ışkumuz revac bulaydı*'.

[13] '*canı cana... katalum*'

[14] '*yüzleri abileler elleri yareler ayakları hun-abelerdür*'

[15] '*cam-ı şehvet ile mestligine ve heva-perestligine istigfarına [sebeb oldı]*'.

[16] The edition has *muy-ı miyan*, but it should be read as *muy-miyan*, cf. Steingass, *Persian-English Dictionary* (p. 1350): 'long hair flowing down the back (reaching the waist)' – these words have

between lover and beloved – the boy had not yet grown a beard (it is said of him that he was *sade-ru*) and must have been a young adolescent – but a-typical is the relatively high social status of the boy who, despite being described as a 'street urchin', must have been of, what we would nowadays call, middle class background and was anything but illiterate. The text clearly is a moralizing fable as well as a story of revenge whereby the potential victim of unwarranted sex turns the tables on an unattractive would-be master.

The question raised by the literature so far discussed is, and has been in the recent past, whether this longing for and lusting after small boys was in any way realistic. Or are we talking here about literary fantasy which could flourish – the texts were clearly addressed at a male audience/readership – because, as some have reasoned, girls and women were simply not available in the public sphere and that it was a taboo to write about them in any disrespectful way? Or is it because, as Ze'evi suggests, men were simply considered to belong to the more perfect gender?[17] El-Rouayheb rejects this view, rightly so I think, on the simple grounds that the theme of sex with and love for boys would not have occurred if it had not struck a cord among audiences and must therefore have been related to genuine feelings and tastes among them. To transpose the situation to a modern Western setting, as El-Rouayheb does: one can hardly imagine that heterosexuals like Frank Sinatra or Tom Jones had sung about their love for a downy-cheeked boy of fourteen![18] In other words: pre-modern Islamic audiences expected and wanted to hear poems and songs idealising boys as do modern Western audiences about the love of men for girls and women. This is also clear from a quotation in El-Rouayheb's book of the Egyptian scholar Rifāʿa aṭ-Ṭahṭāwī. When the latter visited Paris in the early nineteenth century he was surprised that the French were not permitted 'the saying of *ghazal* of someone of the same sex, so in the French language a man cannot say: I loved a boy, for that would be unacceptable'; in translations of such texts therefore, aṭ-Ṭahṭāwī noticed, the boy was replaced by a young girl or, simply, 'a person'.[19]

The realism of our texts is enhanced if we take a look at the environment where men were said to look for and actually met boys: we find mentioned, both in indigenous sources as in travellers' accounts, that of the street, the school, the *tekke*, the coffeehouse, the bath, the taverns of Galata (where dancing boys offered their amorous services to customers), the home in case the boy was a household slave, and, as in the case of our İbrahim Halil, the office of a ministry.

At a higher level, one may add, the Ottoman court stands out as the environment *par excellence* where love, 'courtly love' indeed, flourished. This is already in an abstract way, reflected in an often recurring set of special metaphors ('king', 'padişah', Yusuf, 'slave', 'beggar', 'gate', 'palace', 'edict', 'the realm of love' etc.) which occurs in *ghazel*s but also, as we saw in the case of İbrahim Halil, in prose. In the long introductory part to Ahmed Hamdi Tanpınar's book on nineteenth-century Ottoman literature (originally of 1949) this is sketched in detail. The author mentions that the court-related metaphors all point to

---

remained untranslated in Andrews and Kalpaklı, cf. *The Age of the Beloveds*, p. 222.

17 Ze'evi, *Producing Desire*, p. 83.

18 El-Rouauyheb, *Before Homosexuality*, p. 77.

19 El-Rouayheb, *Before Homosexuality*, p. 62.

love (*ışk*), but he avoids, typically, to make explicit that this, of course, was all about passion and vain yearning between males transposed to the longing of courtiers, or rather, young page boys, for their capricious and cruel sultan.[20] That this was not simply about word play but rather reflected reality is clear from both Western and Ottoman sources. Bertrandon de la Brocquière, a French (Burgundian) envoy who passed through Ottoman Edirne provides a sober account of a meeting with Sultan Murad II (ruled roughly 1421–51) and a description of the palace in Edirne, not found in any other travel book. Bertrandon saw the sultan ('Grand Turk') when the latter was hunting in the surroundings of Edirne:

> His dress was a robe of crimson velvet, lined with sable, and on his hat he wore, like the Turks, a red hat; to save himself from the rain, he had thrown over this robe another, in the manner of a mantle, after the fashion of the country. [...] I heard him speak to his attendants, and he seemed to have a deep-toned voice. He is about twenty-eight or thirty years old, and is already very fat. [...] [He is] a little, short, thick man, with the physiognomy of a Tatar. He has a broad and brown face, high cheek bones, a round beard, a great and crooked nose, with little eyes; but they say he is kind, good, generous, and willingly gives away lands and money [...] His favourite pleasures are hunting and hawking; and he has, as they say, upwards of a thousand hounds, and two thousand trained hawks of different sorts, of which I have seen very many. He loves liquor and those who drink hard; as for himself, he can easily quaff from ten to twelve gondils of wine, which amount to six or seven quarts [...] He unites to his love for women a taste for boys, and has three hundred of the former and about thirty of the latter, which he prefers, and when they are grown up he recompenses them with rich presents and lordships...

After some days, the ambassador and Bertrandon himself were received by the sultan, and the curious ceremonies of the audience are described in great detail.[21]

Both wine drinking and the enjoyment of boys were activities associated with the eternal life in Paradise. The sultan, as God's shadow on earth, already allowed himself these pleasures on earth. In a more subtle way, this courtly environment is described in great detail in one of the introductory chapters of Evliya Çelebi's famous *Book of Travels*, where he, Evliya, describes how he is first received by Sultan Murad IV in 1636 and taken on by him as his boon companion. The sultan, again, was drinking wine and amusing himself in the company of pageboys, when Evliya, showing off his skills, mentioned the various *makams* ('modes') in which he could sing his verses. Among them, he mentioned the *buselik* ('kissing'), the *gerdaniye* ('hugging'), the *zengule* ('rattle' or 'penis') and the *rast* ('erect').

> At this last bit, I winked to [...] the cupbearer Ali Can. The sultan broke out laughing, as did the other royal companions. He looked around at the pageboys, all decked out in gold brocade and jewel-studded belts, and said, 'Which of you wants to listen to Evliya's *zengule* makam?' 'My Emperor', I said, 'they want the *uşşak* [lovers] makam. But your servant Mingune's favourite makam is Isfahani, which includes *büzürg* [big], so if I perform a *zengule* piece he will relax his tension and get pleasure from it.' [...] 'The

---

[20] Ahmet Hamdi Tanpınar, *XIX. Asır Türk Edebiyatı Tarihi*, ed. Abdullah Uçman, 6th impr. (Istanbul, 2009), pp. 23–7.

[21] Thomas Wright (ed.), *Early Travels in Palestine, Comprising the Narratives of Arculf, Willibald, Bernard* etc., reprint of the 1848 original (New York, 1968), pp. 346–54. The book contains a translation of the original *Voyage d'outremer et retour de Jérusalem en France.*

> rascal', cried the sultan. 'Every other word is either a pun or a double-entendre. Evliya,' he continued, '[...] Hence forth you are my royal companion' [...][22]

Evidence from Western travel literature, again, as in the case of Bertrandon de la Brocquière for the Ottoman court, confirms that much of what was going on at a lower social level as described in oriental sources must have been quite realistic. In this literature the perverse predilection of 'the Turks' for boys and 'sodomy' is a recurring topic. Dutch travellers observed that members of the ruling elite often entertained pageboys with whom they, obviously, also had sex. Janus Dousa (who travelled in the Ottoman Empire in 1597–8), saw on board the ship that brought him along the Danube and Black Sea to Istanbul, a slave trader who had purchased two women and a boy in Moldavia. When a monk and fellow traveller made so bold as to caress the boy, the Turk intervened and beat the monk half dead with his stick.[23] In another passage, he remarks that the Turks are mad about boys. They go as far as to sometimes offer a hundred or two hundred gold crowns for them. They tend to keep them in their homes until their beards begin to grow, the which, in their eyes, spoils their beauty.[24] Gerard Hinlopen (travelled in the Empire in 1670–1) became very angry with the captain who was supposed to steer him safely from Istanbul to Izmir. The 'beastly Turk', instead of doing his job, he wrote, spent most of his time drinking and buggering a slave boy.[25] Cornelis de Bruyn, author of what is perhaps the most famous Dutch travel book covering the Ottoman Empire, too writes that the sin of sodomy is widespread among the Turks. It was, apart from wine, the main theme of their songs. 'Herewith they demonstrate that they find pleasure in this bestial and unnatural desire, like [we in the West do] by wanting to mix with women,' he concludes.[26] De Bruyn also discusses public dancing girls, '*singis*' (*çengi*'s) with whom the Turks use to amuse themselves for hours on end. These were often Jewish or Armenian slave girls, but they could also be cross-dressed Jewish boys. While dancing, they used to manipulate 'small elongated bones' with their hands, holding them over their heads and producing rhythmic sounds. The Dutch ambassador at the time, Justinus Colyer, was wont to invite a troupe of these dancers to his residence on evenings when he received the French and Venetian envoys.[27] Pieter van Woensel (who travelled through the Empire in 1784–9) was also struck by the phenomenon. In certain houses in Galata, he writes, where the devotees go to eat, drink and dance, 'one finds also young gentlemen, all dressed up in women's clothes, and whose hair hangs in long tresses along their backs. When business is slack, they sit or walk about outside the front door, not only with the purpose of taking a breath of fresh air. In these houses, which one could compare with our *musico*'s [music halls], they take the place of

---

[22] Cf. Robert Dankoff, *An Ottoman Mentality: the world of Evliya Çelebi* (Leiden/Boston: Brill, 2006), p. 37, 152.

[23] *Verscheyde Voyagien, ofte Reysen: Gedaen door Jr. Joris vander Does na Constantinopolen* etc., (Dordrecht, 1652), pp. 17–8.

[24] Ibidem, pp. 24–5.

[25] Joris Oddens (ed.), *Een vorstelijk voorland: Gerard Hinlopen op reis naar Istanbul (1670–1671)* (Zutphen, 2009), p. 210.

[26] Cornelis de Bruyn, *Reizen van Cornelis de Bruyn, door de vermaardste deelen van Klein Asia* etc. (Delft, 1698), p. 141.

[27] Ibidem, p. 137.

frivolous woman folk. *De gustibus non est disputandum*,' [one can't argue about taste]. He adds that these houses were exploited as good money spinners by the local *voyvoda*.[28]

The phenomenon of the predilection for sex with and love for boys was not something that only existed in the Islamic world. It also existed among ancient Greeks and Romans[29] and in, for instance, pre-modern China. That it existed among the Ottomans is, therefore, perhaps less surprising than this was the case among the Chinese. Ottoman culture was, after all, at least partly rooted in that of the ancient world. It has been pointed out by various scholars, for instance, that the figure of the wine-pouring boy or catamite that figures in the Koran – earlier I mentioned the 'immortal boys' – and in countless Arabic, Persian and Ottoman-Turkish *ghazel*s, clearly had its ancestor in Ganymede, the wine pourer and catamite of the Greek god Zeus.[30] Such a connection did not exist in China. A recent study by Wu Cuncun[31] on the literature of late imperial China shows, nevertheless, striking parallels. Literary sources produced during the Ming and Qing dynasties (1368–1911) seem to suggest an elaborate cultivation of amorous relations between, mostly, upper class men and young boys aged between twelve and twenty, particularly in the urban milieu of Beijing. Here, too, there is corroboration from Western travel literature. The men were often wealthy literati, again, as in the case of the Ottomans, mostly married and in the possession of offspring, and the boys were often servants, actors, opera singers and/or catamites. As in the Ottoman Empire, male favourites were cultivated at the imperial court. The older men, also here, were the active sexual partners, the boys were supposed to submit to them passively. The aesthetic contemplation of beauty and the romantic idealizing of the relation between the lover and the beloved were here an important element as well; coarse sex was considered to be of poor taste (and reserved for women). The age limit, however, seems to have been less stringently maintained: there are cases known in which patrons did not discard their beloveds after they turned into adolescents, even after the boys had married and produced children. Otherwise, the fate of the, by origin lower class boys, was bleak; there is some documentation that suggests that the young men who lost their patronage lapsed into poverty or even committed suicide. (A parallel can, perhaps, be drawn with the Islamic world, although I have not come across documentation on this matter.) Different compared to the Islamic world was the non-existence of a religious taboo or a legal prohibition of same-sex relations, although moralizing puritans might now and then raise objections against impropriety and excesses (but not against pederasty as such).

What was abhorred and condemned in all these cultures were same-sex relations between two consenting adults. That is of course not to say that these did not exist, but documentation is almost non-existent.

---

[28] Pieter van Woensel, *Aanteekeningen gehouden op eene reize door Turkijen, Natoliën, de Krim en Rusland, in de jaaren 1784–89* (Constantinople, 1206–9), I, p. 75.

[29] For a recent discussion of the topic, see G.W. Bowersock, 'Men and Boys', in *The New York Review of Books* Vol. LVI/14 (2009), pp. 10–4.

[30] See, e.g., James T. Monroe (quoting Suzanne Stetkevych), '*The Striptease That Was Blamed on Abū Bakr's Naughty Son: Was Father Being Shamed, or Was the Poet Having Fun? (Ibn Quzmān's* Zajal No. 133)', in J.W. Wright, Jr. and Everett K. Rowson (eds.), *Homoeroticism in Classical Arabic Literature* (New York: Columbia University Press, 1997), pp. 94–139, p. 124.

[31] *Homoerotic Sensibilities in Late Imperial China* (London/New York: RoutledgeCurzon, 2004).

The question now rises: how can we explain this phenomenon? Was the cultivation of boys a matter of culture, was it, to use the words of Michel Foucault who is often quoted in this context, a 'construct' and not something 'essential'? (In the same way, some scholars following his lead have argued that homosexuality as it exists in the modern Western world is also a 'construct', because a 'homosexual identity' as we know it did not exist, or at least was not documented before c. 1850 and was more or less invented around that time.) Could the inclination to pederasty be explained as an aspect of outspoken patriarchal cultures that at the same time had a misogynistic character? But why only young boys? What was wrong with men of the same age? Was it because young boys looked like girls? There must, surely, have been men who were not particularly attracted to young boys. The word 'involuntary', which I earlier used in connection with falling in love, is crucial here – and makes our phenomenon even more puzzling. One's sexual orientation, as ongoing scientific research now seems to show, is caused by a combination of one's genes and the hormonal influences to which one is subjected as a fetus.[32] At least one group of Ottoman medical scholars were of a similar opinion, being convinced that the origin of sexual urges was biological.[33] Sexual attraction, therefore, is ultimately not dependent on cultural fashion, although its paraphernalia to a certain, even sometimes to a great extent, are. 'We live as if we are creatures of pure free will when philosophers and evolutionary biologists tell us this is largely a fiction... We live as if nature and nurture were equal parents when the evidence suggests that nature has both the whip hand and the whip', as Julian Barnes has it in one of his books.[34] Modern studies have also shown that between 5% and 10% of modern Western (European and American) males fall exclusively in love with boys and/or grown-up men and do not want sex with girls or women; a much smaller percentage considers itself bisexual and an unknown, but probably even smaller percentage of the population, has pedophiliac leanings.[35] This means that only a small minority of the male population in general is and, therefore, was, naturally attracted to young boys. We get the impression from our texts, however, that more than a tiny minority of literate Ottoman gentlemen indulged either in sex with or the platonic cult of young boys, certainly more than the 3% or so of the population that had a natural inclination for pedophilia. We can only conclude from this that the pressure of culture and convention, that shied away from openly courting either women or adult men, was so strong in certain areas of the pre-modern world that it was able to force certain 'constructed' forms of sex into dominance, thereby suppressing biological inclination. Such a construct, if it existed, could then perhaps be compared to 'ritualized forms' of homosexuality as we know them from anthropological studies of people in New Guinea and Melanesia.[36]

---

32 For a detailed treatment of this subject, see Simon LeVay, *Gay, Straight, and the Reason Why: the science of sexual orientation* (Oxford: Oxford University Press, 2011).

33 Ze'evi, *Producing Desire*, p. 38.

34 Julian Barnes, *Nothing to be Frightened of* (London: Vintage, 2009), p. 119.

35 See the Wikipedia website 'Pedophilia'.

36 Barry D. Adam, 'Age, Structure, and Sexuality: Reflections on the Anthropological Evidence on Homosexual Relations', in Evelyn Blackwood (ed.), *Anthropology and Homosexual Behaviour* (London, 1986), pp. 19–33, esp. p. 26.

WORKS CITED

Barry D. Adam, 'Age, Structure, and Sexuality: Reflections on the Anthropological Evidence on Homosexual Relations', in Evelyn Blackwood (ed.), *Anthropology and Homosexual Behaviour* (London, 1986), pp. 19–33.

Edith Ambros, *Candid Penstrokes: the Lyrics of Meʾālī, an Ottoman Poet of the 16th century* (Berlin: K. Schwarz, 1982).

Walter Andrews and Mehmet Kalpaklı, *The Age of Beloveds: love and the beloved in early-modern Ottoman and European culture and society* (Durham & London: Duke University Press, 2005).

Julian Barnes, *Nothing to be Frightened of* (London: Vintage, 2009).

G.W. Bowersock, 'Men and Boys', in *The New York Review of Books* Vol. LVI/14 (2009).

Cornelis de Bruyn, *Reizen van Cornelis de Bruyn, door de vermaardste deelen van Klein Asia* etc. (Delft, 1698).

Wu Cuncun, *Homoerotic Sensibilities in Late Imperial China* (London/New York: RoutledgeCurzon, 2004).

Robert Dankoff, *An Ottoman Mentality: the world of Evliya Çelebi* (Leiden/Boston: Brill, 2006).

Khaled El-Rouayheb, *Before Homosexuality in the Arab-Islamic World, 1500–1800* (Chicago/London: University of Chicago Press, 2005).

İsmet Zeki Eyuboğlu, *Divan Şiirinde Sapık Sevgi*, 2nd impr., ([Turkey]: Broy Yayınları, 1991).

Selim S. Kuru, 'Sex in the Text: Deli Birader's *Dâfi'ü 'l-gumûm ve Râfi'ü 'l-humûm* and the Ottoman Literary Canon', *Middle Eastern Literatures* [incorporating *Edebiyât*] 10.2 (2007), pp. 157–74.

Selim S. Kuru, 'Yaşanan, Söylenen ve Yazılan: Erkekler Arasında Tutkusal İlişkiler', *Cogito* 65–6 (2011), pp. 263–77.

Simon LeVay, *Gay, Straight, and the Reason Why: the science of sexual orientation* (Oxford: Oxford University Press, 2011).

James T. Monroe, '*The Striptease That Was Blamed on Abū Bakr's Naughty Son: was father being shamed, or was the poet having fun? (Ibn Quzmān's* Zajal No. 133)', in J.W. Wright, Jr. and Everett K. Rowson (eds.), *Homoeroticism in Classical Arabic Literature* (New York: Columbia University Press, 1997), pp. 94–139.

Joris Oddens (ed.), *Een vorstelijk voorland: Gerard Hinlopen op reis naar Istanbul (1670–1671)* (Zutphen, 2009).

Hellmut Ritter, *Das Meer der Seele: Mensch, Welt und Gott in den Geschichten des Farīduddīn 'Attār* (Leiden: Brill, 1955).

Jan Schmidt, 'Mustafa Âli of Gallipoli on Friendship' (forthcoming).

Kemal Silay, *Nedim and the Poetics of the Ottoman Court: medieval inheritance and the need for change* (Bloomington: Indiana University Turkish Studies, 1994).

Ahmet Hamdi Tanpınar, *XIX. Asır Türk Edebiyatı Tarihi*, ed. Abdullah Uçman, 6th impr. (Istanbul, 2009).

Verscheyde Voyagien, ofte Reysen: Gedaen door Jr. Joris vander Does na Constantinopolen etc. (Dordrecht, 1652).

Pieter van Woensel, *Aanteekeningen gehouden op eene reize door Turkijen, Natoliën, de Krim en Rusland, in de jaaren 1784–89* (Constantinople, 1206–9).

Thomas Wright (ed.), *Early Travels in Palestine, Comprising the Narratives of Arculf, Willibald, Bernard* etc., reprint of the 1848 original (New York, 1968).

Dror Ze'evi, *Producing Desire: changing sexual discourse in the Ottoman Middle East, 1500–1900* (Berkeley, Los Angeles & London, 2006).

Geert Jan van Gelder's List of Publications

BOOKS (AS AUTHOR, CO-AUTHOR, EDITOR, CO-EDITOR)

Abū l-ʿAlāʾ al-Maʿarrī (d. 449/1057), *The Epistle of Forgiveness*, Vol. 1, *with the Epistle of Ibn al-Qāriḥ*, and Vol. 2, ed. and trans. G.J. van Gelder and Gregor Schoeler, New York: NYU Press (Ser. Library of Arabic Literature). In Preparation.

Classical Arabic Literature: A Library of Arabic Literature Anthology, New York: NYU Press, 2013 (Ser. Library of Arabic Literature).

Sound and Sense in Classical Arabic Poetry, Wiesbaden: Harrassowitz, 2013 (Ser. Arabische Studien, Band 10).

Arabic Poetry: Studies and Perspectives of Research. Guest Editor. *Quaderni di Studi Arabi*, n.s. 5–6 (2010–2011).

Takhyīl*: The Imaginary in Classical Arabic Poetics*. Part 1: Texts, selected, translated and annotated by G.J. van Gelder and Marlé Hammond, Part 2: Studies, edited by G.J. van Gelder and Marlé Hammond, [Cambridge:] Gibb Memorial Trust, 2008.

New Perspectives on Arabian Nights: Ideological Variation and Narrative Horizons, ed. Wen-chin Ouyang and G.J. van Gelder, London & New York: Routledge, 2005.

Close Relationships: Incest and Inbreeding in Classical Arabic Literature, London: I.B. Tauris, 2005.

Een Arabische tuin: klassieke Arabische poëzie. Ingeleid, uitgekozen, uit het Arabisch vertaald en geannoteerd, Amsterdam: Bulaaq, 2000; 2nd printing 2008.

Of Dishes and Discourse: Classical Arabic Literary Representations of Food, Richmond, Surrey: Curzon, 2000 (Ser. Curzon Studies in Arabic and Middle Eastern Literatures) [also published New York: Columbia University Press as *God's Banquet: Food in Classical Arabic Literature*].

Poetry, Politics and Polemics: Cultural Transfer between the Iberian Peninsula and North Africa, ed. Otto Zwartjes, G.J. van Gelder and Ed de Moor, Amsterdam: Rodopi, 1997 (*Orientations*, vol. IV).

Het badhuis tussen hemel en hel, with Marjo Buitelaar, Amsterdam: Bulaaq, 1996.

Eet van de goede dingen: Culinaire culturen in het Midden-Oosten en de Islam, ed. Marjo Buitelaar and G.J. van Gelder, Bussum: Coutinho, 1995 (*MOI-publikaties, Nieuwe Reeks*, Nr. 14).

Eastward Bound: Dutch Ventures and Adventures in the Middle East, ed. G.J. van Gelder and Ed de Moor, Amsterdam: Rodopi, 1994 (*Orientations*, vol. II).

The Middle East and Europe: Encounters and Exchanges, ed. G.J. van Gelder and Ed de Moor, Amsterdam: Rodopi, 1992 [1993] (*Orientations*, vol. I).

The Bad and the Ugly: Attitudes Towards Invective Poetry (Hijāʾ) *in Classical Arabic Literature*, Leiden: Brill, 1988 (ser. Publications of the 'De Goeje Fund', no. 26).

De Pen en het Zwaard: literatuur en politiek in het Midden-Oosten, ed. Geert Jan van Gelder and Ed de Moor, Muiderberg: Coutinho, 1988 (*MOI-publicaties, Nieuwe Reeks*, Nr. 6).

Two Arabic Treatises on Stylistics: al-Marghīnānī's al-Maḥāsin fī 'l-naẓm wa-'l-nathr, *and Ibn Aflaḥ's* Muqaddima, *formerly ascribed to al-Marghīnānī, ed. from the MS Escorial 264, with an introduction*, Leiden–Istanbul, 1987. (Ser. Uitgaven van het Nederlands-Archaeologisch Instituut te Istanbul, vol. 60).

The Arabic Text of the Apocalypse of Baruch. Edited and translated, with a parallel translation of the Syriac text, with F. Leemhuis and A.F.J. Klijn, Leiden: Brill, 1986.

Beyond the Line: Classical Arabic Literary Critics on the Coherence and Unity of the Poem, Leiden: Brill, 1982 (Ser. *Studies in Arabic Literature, Supplements to the Journal of Arabic Literature*, vol. 8). [appeared also as Ph.D. Thesis, University of Leiden, 1982, with Dutch summary].

JOURNAL ARTICLES AND BOOK CHAPTERS

'Amphigory and Other Nonsense in Classical Arabic Literature', in Dominic Parviz Brookshaw (ed.), *Ruse and Wit: The Humorous in Arabic, Persian, and Turkish Narrative*, Boston, Massachusetts: Ilex Foundation, and Washington, D.C.: Center for Hellenic Studies, 2012 (Ser. Ilex Foundation Series, 8), pp. 7–32.

'On Coincidence: The Twenty-Seventh and Twenty-Eighth Nights of al-Tawḥīdī's *al-Imtāʿ wa-l-muʾānasa*. An Annotated Translation', in *Medieval Arabic Thought: Essays in Honour of Fritz Zimmermann*, ed. by Rotraud Hansberger, M. Afifi al-Akiti, and Charles Burnett, London–Turin: The Warburg Institute – Nino Aragno Editore, 2012 (Ser. Warburg Institute Studies and Texts, 4), pp. 209–220.

'Introduction' and 'Poets Against Ramadan' in *Arabic Poetry: Studies and Perspectives of Research* (special issue), *Quaderni di Studi Arabi*, n.s. 5–6 (2010–2011) pp. iii–ix; 103–19.

'Against the Arabic Grammarians: Some Poems' in Bilal Orfali (ed.), *In the Shadow of Arabic: The Centrality of Arabic to Arabic Culture. Studies presented to Ramzi Baalbaki on the occasion of his sixtieth birthday*, Leiden, Brill, 2011, pp. 249–263.

'Poetry in Historiography: The Case of *al-Fakhrī* by Ibn al-Ṭiqṭaqā' in Ramzi Baalbaki, Saleh Said Agha and Tarif Khalidi (eds.), *Poetry and History: The Value of Poetry in Reconstructing Arab History*, Beirut: American University of Beirut Press, 2011, pp. 61–94.

'Goede en slechte tafelmanieren, Arabisch en Europees: al-Ibsjiehi (1388–ca. 1446) en Erasmus (1466–1536)', *De Gids*, 2010 no. 6, pp. 628–638 (special issue: *Aan Tafel!*, ed. Roel Bentz van den Berg, Louise O. Fresco, Edzard Mik).

'Literary Criticism as Literature' in Lale Behzadi and Vahid Behmardi (eds.),*The Weaving of Words: Approaches to Classical Arabic Prose,* Beirut [Würzburg]: Orient-Institut [Ergon Verlag], 2009 (Ser. Beiruter Texte und Studien, 112), pp. 55–75.

'Shihāb al-Dīn al-Khafājī' in Joseph E. Lowry and Devin J. Stewart (eds.), *Essays in Arabic Literary Biography, 1350–1850*, Wiesbaden: Harrassowitz, 2009 (Ser. Mîzân: Studien zur Literatur in der islamischen Welt, 17: Essays in Arabic Literary Biography, 2), pp. 251–262.

'Kitāb al-Burṣhān: Al-Jāḥiẓ on Right- and Left-Handedness' in Arnim Heinemann, John L. Meloy, Tarif Khalidi, Manfred Kropp (eds.), *Al-Jāḥiẓ: A Muslim Humanist for our Time*, Beirut [Würzburg]: Orient-Institut [Ergon Verlag], 2009 (Ser. Beiruter Texte und Studien, 119), pp. 239–252.

'Traditional Literary Theory: The Arabic Background' in J.T.P. de Bruijn (ed.), *General Introduction to Persian Literature*, London: I.B. Tauris, 2009 (Ser. A History of Persian Literature, vol. I), ch. 5, pp. 121–138.

'The *Ḥammām*: A Space between Heaven and Hell', *Quaderni di Studi Arabi*, n.s. 3, special issue: *Luoghi e immaginario nella letteratura araba*, ed. Antonella Ghersetti, (2008 [2009]) pp. 9–24.

'Fools and Rogues in Discourse and Disguise: Two Studies' in Robin Ostle (ed.) *Sensibilities of the Islamic Mediterranean: Self-Expression in a Muslim Culture from Post-Classical Times to the Present Day*, London: I.B. Tauris, 2008 (Ser. The Islamic Mediterranean, vol. 7), pp. 27–58 (first study: 'Buffoons High and Low, or Marginal People at the Centre', pp. 27–36, second study: 'Disguises in the *Maqamat* of Ibn Naqiya (410–485/1020–1092)', pp. 37–51).

'"A Good Cause": Fantastic Etiology (*ḥusn al-taʿlīl*) in Arabic Poetics' and 'The Lamp and its Mirror Image: Ḥāzim al-Qarṭājannī's Poetry in the Light of his *Path of the Eloquent and Lamp of the Lettered*' in G.J. van Gelder and Marlé Hammond (eds.), Takhyīl*: The Imaginary in Classical Arabic Poetics* (see above), pp. 221–237; 265–73.

'The Hostage, or Who was Who? A Story from Pre-Islamic Arabia', *Middle Eastern Literatures* vol. 11, no. 2 (special issue: *Arabic Literature before al-Muwayliḥī: Studies in Honour of Roger Allen*, ed. by Devin J. Stewart and Shawkat M. Toorawa) (2008) pp. 127–137.

(with Hilary Kilpatrick) 'Recent Publications on Arabic Literature', *Middle Eastern Literatures*, vol. 11, no. 1 (2008) pp. 1–30.

'*Qaṣīda ghazaliyya-khamriyya*: Two Lyrical Poems by Ḥāzim al-Qarṭājannī (d. 684/1285)' in Beatrice Gruendler (ed. with Michael Cooperson), *Classical Arabic Humanities in Their Own Terms: Festschrift for Wolfhart Heinrichs on his 65th Birthday Presented by his Students and Colleagues*, Leiden: Brill, 2008, pp. 390–406.

'The Antithesis of *Urjūza* and *Badīʿiyya*: Two Forms of Arabic Versified Stylistics' in Annette Harder, Alasdair A. MacDonald and Gerrit J. Reinink (eds.), *Calliope's Classroom: Studies in Didactic Poetry from Antiquity to the Renaissance*, Leuven: Peeters, 2007, pp. 153–172.

'Precious Stones, Precious Words: al-Suyūṭī's "*al-Maqāma al-yāqūtiyya*", Translated and Annotated' in Arnoud Vrolijk and Jan P. Hogendijk (eds.), *O ye Gentlemen: Arabic Studies on Science and Literary Culture, in Honour of Remke Kruk*. Leiden: Brill, 2007, pp. 313–332.

'An Experiment with Beeston, Labīd and Baššār: On Translating Classical Arabic Verse', *Proceedings of the Seminar for Arabian Studies*, vol. 36 (2006), pp. 7–15.

'The Anatomy of Anonymity: The poet Anon. and his reception in Classical Arabic literature' in Angelika Neuwirth and Andreas Christian Islebe (eds.), *Reflections on Reflections: Near Eastern writers reading literature; dedicated to Renate Jacobi*, Wiesbaden: Reichert Verlag, 2006 (Ser. literaturen im kontext, vol. 23), pp. 17–34.

'Incidental Arabic Poetry' in Emilie Savage-Smith, *A Descriptive Catalogue of Oriental Manuscripts at St John's College, Oxford*, Oxford: Oxford University Press, 2005, pp. 129–146.

'Bashshar b. Burd' and 'Dhu al-Rummah (Abu al-Harith Ghaylan ibn 'Uqbah)' in Shawkat M. Toorawa and Michael Cooperson (eds.), *Arabic Literary Culture, 500-925*, Detroit, 2005 (Ser. Dictionary of Literary Biography, vol. 311), pp. 91–97; 108–113.

'Edible Fathers and Mothers: Arabic *kunyas* used for Food' in Manuela Marín and Cristina de la Puente (eds.), *El banquete de las palabras: La alimentación de los textos árabes*, Madrid: Consejo Superior de Investigaciones Científicas, 2005 (Ser. Estudios árabes e islámicos, Monografías, 10), pp. 105–120.

'*Mawālī* and Arabic Poetry: Some Observations' in Monique Bernards and John Nawas (eds.), *Patronate and Patronage in Early and Classical Islam*, Leiden: Brill, 2005 (Ser. Islamic History and Civilization: Studies and Texts, 61), pp. 349–369.

'Slave-Girl Lost and Regained: Transformations of a Story' in *Marvels and Tales: Journal of Fairy-Tale Studies*, vol. 18, no. 2 (2004), pp. 201–217 [A lightly revised version was published in Ulrich Marzolph (ed.), *The Arabian Nights in Transnational Perspective*, Detroit: Wayne State University Press, 2007, pp. 65–81].

'Poetry in Historiography: Some Observations' in Miklós Maróth (ed.), *Problems in Arabic Literature*, Piliscsaba, 2004, pp. 1–13.

'Poetry and the Arabian Nights' in Ulrich Marzolph and Richard van Leeuwen (eds.), *The Arabian Nights Encyclopedia*, Santa Barbara, CA: ABC-Clio, 2004, pp. 13–17.

'Poetry for Easy Listening: *insijām* and Related Concepts in Ibn Ḥijjah's Khizānat al-adab', *Mamlūk Studies Review*, vol. 7 (2003 [2002]) pp. 31–48.

'A conversation on contemporary politics in the twelfth century: "*al-Maqāma al-Baghdādiyya*" by al-Wahrānī (d. 575/1179)' in Chase F. Robinson (ed.), *Texts, Documents and Artefacts: Islamic Studies in Honour of D. S. Richards*, Leiden: Brill, 2003, pp. 103–119.

'Beautifying the Ugly and Uglifying the Beautiful: The Paradox in Classical Arabic Literature', *Journal of Semitic Studies*, vol. 48, no. 2 (2003) pp. 321–51.

'To Eat or Not to Eat Elephant: A Travelling Story in Arabic and Persian Literature', *Bulletin of the School of Oriental and African Studies*, vol. 66, no. 3 (2003) pp. 419–430.

'The Classical Arabic Canon of Polite (and Impolite) Literature' in Gillis J. Dorleijn and Herman L.J. Vanstiphout (eds.), *Cultural Repertoires: Structure, Function and Dynamics*, Leuven: Peeters, 2003, pp. 45–57.

'Forbidden Firebrands: Frivolous *iqtibās* (Quotation from the Qurʾān)', *Quaderni di Studi Arabi*, vol. 20–21 (2002–2003) pp. 3–16.

'Inspiration and "Writer's Block" in Classical Arabic Poetry' in Paolo Bagni and Maurizio Pistoso (eds.), *Poetica medievale tra oriente e occidente*, Roma: Carocci, 2003 (Ser. Biblioteca Medievale, Saggi, 11), pp. 61–71.

'al-Mutahhar ibn Tahir al-Maqdisi (ca. 966): Het boek van de schepping en de geschiedenis. De godsdiensten en sekten der wereldbewoners' (pp. 140–160); 'Abu Hayyan ʿAli ibn Muhammad al-Tawhidi (922 of 932 - na 1010), Genotsverschaffing en gezellige onderhouding: Over de superioriteit van de Arabieren' (pp. 161–70); 'Ahmad ibn al-Husayn Badiʿ al-Zaman al-Hamadhani (968–1008), Maqamat: Sterke verhalen (fragmenten)' (pp. 437–48); 'Abu al-ʿAlaʾ Ahmad ibn ʿAbd Allah al-Maʿarri (973–1058), De vergeving: Tocht naar hemel en hel' (pp. 449–68) [translations into Dutch] in Arnoud Vrolijk (ed.), *De taal der engelen: 1250 jaar klassiek Arabisch proza*, Amsterdam-Antwerpen: Uitgeverij Contact, 2002.

'*The Nodding Noddles*, or *Jolting the Yokels*: A Composition for Marginal Voices by al-Shirbīnī (fl. 1687)' in Robin Ostle (ed.), *Marginal Voices in Literature and Society*, Aix-en-Provence: Maison Méditerranéenne des Sciences de l'Homme, 2000 [2001] (Coll. Individual and Society in the Mediterranean Muslim World, a programme of the European Science Foundation), pp. 49–67.

'The Apposite Request: A Small Chapter in Persian and Arabic Rhetoric', *Edebiyât*, N.S. vol. 12, no. 1 (2001) pp. 1–13.

'Mirror for Princes or Vizor for Viziers: The Twelfth-Century Arabic Popular Encyclopedia *Mufīd al-ʿulūm* and its Relationship with the Anonymous Persian *Baḥr al-fawāʾid*', *Bulletin of the School of Oriental and African Studies*, vol. 64, no. 3 (2001) pp. 313–338.

'Mudrik al-Shaybānī's Poem on a Christian Boy: Bad Taste or Harmless Wit?' in Gert Borg and Ed de Moor (eds.), *Representations of the Divine in Arabic Poetry*, Amsterdam/Atlanta: Rodopi, 2001 (Orientations, vol. V), pp. 49–70.

'De verfraaiing van het lelijke en de verlelijking van het fraaie', *Sharqiyyât*, vol. 13. no. 2 (2001 [2002]) pp. 107–124.

'al-Mutanabbī's Encumbering Trifles', *Arabic and Middle Eastern Literatures* vol. 2, no. 1 (1999) pp. 5–19.

'Four Perfumes of Arabia: A translation of al-Suyūṭī's *al-Maqāma al-miskiyya*', *Res Orientales*, vol. 11, 1999, pp. 203–212.

'Rhyme in *Maqāmāt*, or, Too Many Exceptions Do Not Prove a Rule', *Journal of Semitic Studies*, vol. 44, no. 1 (1999) pp. 75–82.

'Persons as Texts / Texts as Persons in Classical Arabic Literature' in Stephan Guth, Priska Furrer and Johann Christoph Bürgel (eds.), *Conscious Voices: Concepts of Writing in the Middle East*, Beirut; Stuttgart: Franz Steiner Verlag, 1999 (Ser. Beiruter Texte und Studien, 72), pp. 237–253.

'Some Brave Attempts at Generic Classification in Premodern Arabic Literature' in Bert Roest and Herman Vanstiphout (eds.), *Aspects of Genre and Type in Pre-Modern Literary Cultures*, Groningen: Styx Publications, 1999 (Ser. COMERS/ICOG Communications, 1), pp. 15–31. [A Turkish translation by Hatice Aynur appeared as 'Modern öncesi Arap edebiyatında tür sınıflamasına yönelik cesur bir deneme' in Hatice Aynur et al. (eds.), *Nazımdan nesire edebî türler*, İstanbul: Turkuaz, 2009, pp. 212–230].

'*Diyāf*: for Camels, Swords and Nabataeans. A Nabataean Centre in Arabic Sources' in H.L.J. Vanstiphout (ed. with the assistance of W.J. van Bekkum, G.J. van Gelder and G.J. Reinink), *All Those Nations ...: Cultural Encounters within and with the Near East (Studies presented to Han Drijvers at the occasion of his sixty-fifth birthday by colleagues and students)*, Groningen: Styx Publications, 1999 (Ser. COMERS/ICOG Communications, 2), pp. 51–60.

'Dream Towns of Islam: Geography in Arabic Oneirocritical Works' in Angelika Neuwirth, Birgit Embaló, Sebastian Günther, and Maher Jarrar (eds.), *Myths, Historical Archetypes and Symbolic Figures in Arabic Literature: Towards a New Hermeneutic Approach. Proceedings of the International Symposium in Beirut, June 25th–June 30th, 1996)*, Beirut; Stuttgart: Franz Steiner Verlag, 1999 [2000] (Ser. Beiruter Texte und Studien, 64), pp. 507–520.

'145 Topics for Arabic School Essays in 1901 from Aḥmad al-Hāshimī's *Jawāhir al-adab fī ṣināʿat inshāʾ al-ʿarab*' in U. Vermeulen and J.M.F. van Reeth (eds.), *Law, Christianity & Modernism in Islamic Society (Proceedings of the 18th Congress of the UEAI, held at Leuven, September 3–9, 1996)*, Leuven: Peeters, 1998 (Ser. Orientalia Lovaniensia Analecta, 86), pp. 291–99.

'Dubious Genres: On some poems of Abū Nuwās', *Arabica*, vol. 44 (1997) pp. 268–83 [Translated into Arabic as '*Tadākhul al-aghrāḍ (Dirāsah fī baʿḍ qaṣāʾid Abī Nuwās)*' in Ilhām ʿAbd al-Wahhāb al-Muftī (introd. and tr.), *Fī l-qaṣīdah al-ʿAbbāsiyyah: Dirāsāt gharbiyyah muʿāṣirah*, Cairo: ʿĀlam al-Kutub, 2002, pp. 17–44].

'Compleat Men, Women and Books: On Medieval Arabic Encyclopaedism' in Peter Binkley (ed.), *Pre-Modern Encyclopaedic Texts: Proceedings of the Second COMERS Congress, Groningen, 1–4 July 1996*, Leiden: Brill, 1997, pp. 241–259.

'Tussen genot en verbod: drugs en islam in de middeleeuwen', *Groniek*, vol. 138 (September 1997), pp. 14–22.

'Informatie, misinformatie and vermaak: twee middeleeuwse reisverhalen', *Kleio (Tijdschrift van de vereniging van docenten in geschiedenis en staatsinrichting in Nederland)*, vol. 38, no. 8 (dec. 1997) pp. 2–8.

'Salman' in Maarten Asscher et al. (eds.), *Het woordenboek van* De Duivelsverzen, Amsterdam, 1996, pp. 83–84.

'Najīb al-Ḥaddād's Essay on the Comparison of Arabic and European Poetry' in J.R. Smart (ed.), *Tradition and Modernity in Arabic Language and Literature*, Richmond, Surrey, 1996, pp. 144–152.

'The Terrified Traveller: Ibn al-Rūmī's Anti-*Raḥīl*', *Journal of Arabic Literature*, vol. 27, no. 1 (special issue: *The Era of Abū Tammām and Ibn al-Rūmī: Proceedings of the Seventh Symposium on Classical Arabic Poetry [Cambridge, July 1993]*, ed. James E. Montgomery) (1996) pp. 37–48.

'Oosterse schatten voor de Academie: de collectie Christmann' in Jos. M.M. Hermans and Gerda Huisman (eds.), *Aan de Ketting: Boek en bibliotheek in Groningen voor 1669*, Groningen: Universiteitsmuseum/Universiteitsbibliotheek, 1996, pp. 76–80.

'Kufa vs Basra: The Literary Debate', *Asiatische Studien / Études Asiatiques*, vol. 50, no. 2 (1996) pp. 339–62 [in proceedings of 'Littérature et réalités dans le monde musulman' symposium (Crêt-Bérard, Switzerland, May 1995)].

'Recent Articles on Arabic Literature', *Journal of Arabic Literature*, vol. 27, no. 3 (1996) pp. 227–62.

'Waspish Verses: Abū Nuwās's Lampoons on Zunbūr Ibn Abī Ḥammād', *Annali di Ca' Foscari* (Venezia), vol. 35, no. 3 (1996) pp. 447–55.

'Arabic Poetics and Stylistics According to the Introduction of *al-Durr al-farīd* by Muḥammad Ibn Aydamir (d. 710/1310)', *Zeitschrift der Deutschen Morgenländischen Gesellschaft*, vol. 146,no. 2 (1996) pp. 381–414.

'Arabic Didactic Verse' in Jan Willem Drijvers and Alasdair A. MacDonald (eds.), *Centres of Learning: Learning and Location in Pre-Modern Europe and the Near East*, Leiden: Brill, 1995, pp. 103–17.

'A Muslim Encomium on Wine: *The Racecourse of the Bay (Ḥalbat al-Kumayt)* by al-Nawāǧī (d. 859/1455) as a Post-Classical Arabic Work', *Arabica*, vol. 42, no. 2 (1995) pp. 222–34.

'Bleke barbaren en agressieve ongelovigen: Middeleeuwse westerlingen in moslimse ogen', *Groniek*, vol. 129 (juli 1995) pp. 379–91.

"Heb je soms een kameel gevraagd?" in Angeline van Achterberg and Arita Baaijens (eds.), *De geur van kamelen*, Amsterdam, 1995, pp. 93–101.

'Eten, etiquette, ethiek: Voedsel in de klassiek-Arabische literatuur' in Marjo Buitelaar and G.J. van

Gelder (eds.), *Eet van de goede dingen: Culinaire culturen in het Midden-Oosten en de Islam* (see above), pp. 59–78.
'The Joking Doctor: Abū l-Ḥakam ʿUbayd Allāh Ibn al-Muẓaffar (d. 549/1155)' in Concepción Vázquez de Benito and Miguel Ángel Manzano Rodríguez (eds.), *Actas XVI Congreso UEAI [Salamanca, Aug–Sept. 1992.]*, Salamanca, 1995, pp. 217–28.
'*al-Anwāʿ fī taʿāruḍihā: al-nasīb wa-l-fakhr*', *Fuṣūl*, vol. 14, no. 2 (1995) pp. 204–13 [unauthorized translation of 'Genres in Collision: *Nasīb* and *hijāʾ*' (see below)]
'Street-Arabs, Satire, and the Status of Poetry' in A. Fodor (ed.), *Proceedings of the 14th Congress of the Union Européenne des Arabisants et Islamisants, Budapest, 29th August–3rd September 1988*, Budapest, 1995, vol. 2, pp. 121–32 (*The Arabist 15–16*).
'Pointed and Well-Rounded: Arabic Encomiastic and Elegiac Epigrams', *Orientalia Lovaniensia Periodica*, vol. 26 (1995) pp. 101–40.
'From Horwood to the Greenwood: A round and its origin in rondellus', *Leading Notes* (Cambridge), vol. 9, no. 1 (1995) pp. 5–6.
'A Cotton Shirt: an "unparalleled" poem by Ibn Abī Karīma (early 9th century)' in Wolfhart Heinrichs and Gregor Schoeler (eds.), *Festschrift Ewald Wagner zum 65. Geburtstag. Band 2: Studien zur arabischen Dichtung*, Beirut, 1994, pp. 283–96.
(with J. E. Montgomery, J.N. Mattock and R. Jacobi) 'Revelry and Remorse: a Poem of Abū Nuwās', *Journal of Arabic Literature*, vol. 25, no. 2 (1994) pp. 116–34.
(with Andrew Palmer) 'Syriac and Arabic Inscriptions at the Monastery of St Mark's in Jerusalem', *Oriens Christianus*, vol. 78 (1994) pp. 33–63.
'Troost je met een flinke kamelin. De kameel in de Arabische literatuur', *Sahara Berichten*, vol. 1, no. 4 (1993) pp. 4–6; vol. 2, no. 5 (1994) pp. 2–4.
'Groningen in een Arabische geografie uit de twaalfde eeuw', *Groningse Volksalmanak*, 1990 [1993] pp. 9–16.
'Rābiʿa's Poem on the Two Kinds of Love: a Mystification?' in Frederick De Jong (ed.), *Verse and the Fair Sex. Studies in Arabic poetry and in the representation of women in Arabic literature. A collection of papers presented at the 15th Congress of the Union Européenne des Arabisants et Islamisants (Utrecht/Driebergen, September 13–19, 1990)*, Utrecht: Publications of the M.Th. Houtsma Stichting, 1993, pp. 66–76.
'Satanische Versies: de Arabisch-islamitische achtergrond van *De duivelsverzen*', *Bzzlletin*, vol. 23, no. 210, nov. 1993, pp. 5–17.
'Articles on Arabic Literature Published in 1992', *Journal of Arabic Literature*, vol. 24, no. 3 (1993) pp. 258–70.
'Some Types of Ambiguity: a poem by Abū Nuwās on al-Faḍl al-Raqāšī', *Quaderni di Studi Arabi*, vol. 10 (1992 [1993]) pp. 75–92.
'Birds of Battle: Old English and Arabic', *File: A Literary Journal* (Groningen, Dept. of English), vol. 6 (1993) pp. 9–16.
'Musāwir al-Warrāq and the Beginnings of Arabic Gastronomic Poetry', *Journal of Semitic Studies*, vol. 36 (1991 [1992]) pp. 309–27.
'Arabic Banqueters: Literature, Lexicography, and Reality' in Rika Gyselen (ed.), *Banquets d'Orient* (special issue), *Res Orientales*, vol. 4, 1992, pp. 85–93.
'Mixtures of Jest and Earnest in Classical Arabic Literature', *Journal of Arabic Literature*, Part 1, vol. 23, no. 2 (1992) pp. 83–108; Part 2, vol. 23, no. 3 (1992 [1993]) pp. 169–90.
'Arabische tafelmanieren: literatuur, lexicografie, werkelijkheid', *Sharqiyyât*, vol. 3. no. 2 (1991) pp. 1–15.
'Arabic Debates of Jest and Earnest' in G.J. Reinink and H.L.J. Vanstiphout (eds.), *Dispute Poems and Dialogues in the Ancient and Mediaeval Near East. Forms and Types of Literary Debates in Semitic and Related Literatures*, Leuven: Peeters, 1991 (Ser. *Orientalia Lovaniensia Analecta*, 42), pp. 199–211.

'Genres in Collision: *Nasīb* and *hijā*ʾ', *Journal of Arabic Literature*, vol. 21, no. 1 (1990) pp. 14–25.

'Camels on Eyelids and the Bafflement of an Emperor: a Line of al-Mutanabbī translated into Greek', *Proceedings of the XIIth Congress of the International Comparative Literature Association, München, 1988. vol. 3: Space and Boundaries of Literature*, Munich, 1990, pp. 446–51.

'The Poem as a Message: 'Say to X...' and Related Formulas in Arabic Poetry', *Orientalia Lovaniensia Periodica*, vol. 20 (1989) pp. 195–211.

'"The Most Natural Poem of the Arabs": An Addition to the *Dīwān* of al-Kumayt Ibn Zayd', *Journal of Arabic Literature*, vol. 19, no. 2 (1988) pp. 95–107.

'De Pen en het Zwaard: dichters en machthebbers in de klassieke Arabische literatuur' in G.J. van Gelder and Ed de Moor (eds.), *De Pen en het Zwaard: literatuur en politiek in het Midden-Oosten* (see above), pp. 9–20.

'The Conceit of Pen and Sword: On an Arabic Literary Debate', *Journal of Semitic Studies*, vol. 32, no. 2 (1987) pp. 329–60.

'*Bidāyāt al-naẓar fī l-qaṣīda*', *Fuṣūl*, vol. 6, no. 2 (1986) pp. 11–33 [unauthorized translation of Chapter Two of *Beyond the Line* (see above)].

'Man of Letters *v.* Man of Figures: The Seventh Night from al-Tawḥīdī's *al-Imtā*ʿ *wa-l-mu*ʾ*ānasa*' in H.L.J. Vanstiphout et al. (eds.), *Signa Scripta Vocis: Studies about Scripts, Scriptures, Scribes and Languages in the Near East, presented to J. H. Hospers . . .*, Groningen: Egbert Forsten, 1986, pp. 53–63.

'Against Women, and Other Pleasantries: The Last Chapter of Abū Tammām's *Ḥamāsa*', *Journal of Arabic Literature*, vol. 16 (1985) pp. 61–72.

'Ibn Aflaḥ: Author of *Kitab al-Badī*ʿ attributed to al-Marġīnānī', *Arabica*, vol. 32 (1985) pp. 360–61.

'A Note on the Article by G. Kunaziʿ, *JSAI*, 2 (1980)', *Jerusalem Studies in Arabic and Islam*, vol. 6 (1985) p. 480.

'The Abstracted Self in Arabic Poetry', *Journal of Arabic Literature*, vol. 14 (1983) pp. 22–30.

'Nomadische heroïek en steedse retoriek: kunst en kunstigheid in de Arabische poetica' in W.L. Idema (ed.), *De vorsten van het woord. Teksten over dichterschap en poëzie uit Oosterse tradities: studies en vertalingen*, Amsterdam: Meulenhoff, 1983, pp. 11–29.

'The Poet as a Body-Builder: On a Passage from al-Ḥātimī's *Ḥilyat al-muḥāḍara*', *Journal of Arabic Literature*, vol. 13 (1982) pp. 58–65.

'Breaking Rules For Fun: Making Lines That Run / On: on Enjambment in Classical Arabic Poetry' in I.A. El-Sheikh, C.A. van de Koppel, R. Peters (eds.), *The Challenge of the Middle East: Middle Eastern Studies at the University of Amsterdam*, Amsterdam, Institute for Modern Near Eastern Studies, 1982, pp. 25–31, 184–186.

'Ḥâzim al-Qarṭâğannî en de structuur van de *qaṣīda*' in Hilary Kilpatrick et al. (eds.) *Aspekten van de arabische letterkunde*, Nijmegen, 1981 (Ser. *MOI-publikatie* No. 6), pp. 62–82.

'Brevity: the Long and the Short of it in Classical Arabic Literary Theory' in Rudolph Peters (ed.), *Proceedings of the Ninth Congress of the Union Européenne des Arabisants et Islamisants, Amsterdam, 1st to 7th September 1978*, Leiden: Brill, 1981, pp. 78–88.

'Arabisch, I. bn., II. zn. o.', *De Gids*, vol. 143, nos 9–10 (1980) pp. 606–15.

'Het Adab-complex', *De Gids*, vol. 143, nos 9–10 (1980) pp. 673–82.

'Critic and Craftsman: al-Qarṭājannī and the Structure of the Poem', *Journal of Arabic Literature*, vol. 10 (1979) pp. 26–48.

(with Rudolph Peters) 'A Bibliography of Dutch Publications on the Middle East and Islam (1945–75)', Amsterdam, University of Amsterdam, Institute for Modern Eastern Studies, 1976.

ENCYCLOPAEDIA ENTRIES

Encyclopaedia of Islam, Three, Gudrun Krämer, Denis Matringe, John Nawas, Everett Rowson (executive eds.), Leiden: Brill, 2007–, s.vv. 'Epigram 1. Classical Arabic' (2012); 'Banquet', 'Canon and canonisation in classical Arabic literature', 'City panegyric, in classical Arabic', 'Didactic poetry, Arabic' (2011); 'Badīᶜ', 'Badīᶜiyyah', 'al-Badīᶜī, Yūsuf', 'al-Badrī, Abū l-Tuqā' (2009); 'al-ᶜAbbāsī', 'Abū Riyāsh', 'Abū Saᶜd al-Makhzūmī' (2008); 'al-Abīwardī', 'ᶜAlī b. Khalaf', 'Ancients and Moderns', 'Apology', 'al-Arrajānī' (2007).

Encyclopedia of Arabic Language and Linguistics, Kees Versteegh (general ed.), 4 vols Leiden; Boston: Brill, 2006–2009, s.v. 'Poetic License', vol. 3 (2008), pp. 647b–652b.

Medieval Islamic Civilization: An Encyclopedia, ed. Josef W. Meri, 2 vols, New York; London: Routledge, 2006, s.vv. 'Beverages' (vol. 1, p. 106); 'Desserts and Confectionery' (vol. 1, pp. 204–5); 'Rosewater' (vol. 2, pp. 683–84); 'Spices' (vol. 2, pp. 767–68).

The Chicago On-Line Encyclopedia of Mamluk Studies [<http://www.lib-uchicago.edu/e/su/mideast/encyclopedia/>], s.vv. 'Ibn Ḥijjah al-Ḥamawī' (2006); 'al-Nawājī' (2007).

Encyclopaedia of Islam, New Edition, Edited by P. Bearman , Th. Bianquis , C.E. Bosworth, E. van Donzel and W.P. Heinrichs, 11 vols, Leiden: Brill, 1960–2009, s.vv. 'Muḥammad b. Sayf al-Dīn, Ibn Aydamir', 'Muḥdat͟hūn', 'Naẓm. 1. In metrical speech' (2004); 'al-Warrāḳ, Maḥmūd b. (al-)Ḥasan', 'al-Wāsānī', 'al-Waʾwāʾ' (2001); 'Tas͟hbīh (in rhetoric)' (1999); 'Ṭaᶜām (Food etiquette)', 'Taḍmīn (quotation, enjambment, implication)', 'Taᶜad͟jd͟jub', 'Tamt͟hīl (in rhetoric)', 'Tak͟halluṣ (in literary form)' (1998); 'S͟hamᶜa' (1996); 'Salm al-K͟hāsir', 'Sarāb. In poetry' (1995); 'Musāwir al-Warrāḳ', 'Naḳāʾid' (1992).

Encyclopaedia Iranica, ed. Ehsan Yarshater, New York: Columbia University Center for Iranian Studies, 1996–, s.vv. 'Incest and Inbreeding in Islam' (2004); 'Rāgeb Eṣfahāni' (2010).

Encyclopaedia of the Qurʾān, Jane Dammen McAuliffe (general ed.), 6 vols, Leiden: Brill, 2005, s.v. 'Hearing and Deafness', vol. 2, pp. 405b–406b.

Encyclopedia of Literary Critics and Criticism, ed. Christopher Murray, London: Fitzroy Dearborn, 1999, s.vv. 'ᶜAbd al-Qāhir al-Jurjānī' (pp. 1–3); 'Arabic Literary Theory' (pp. 40–45); 'Ḥāzim al-Qartājannī' (pp. 499–501); 'Qudāma Ibn Jaᶜfar' (pp. 905–906).

Encyclopedia of Arabic Literature, ed. Julie Scott Meisami and Paul Starkey, London: Routledge, 1998, s.vv. 'al-ᶜAbbās Ibn Mirdās', 'ᶜAbd Allāh ibn Rawāḥa', 'ᶜAbd al-Laṭīf al-Baghdādī', 'Abū l-ᶜAlāʾ al-Maᶜarrī', 'Abū ᶜAlī al-Baṣīr', 'Abū a-ᶜAynāʾ', 'Abū ᶜUbayda', 'al-Akhṭal', 'ᶜAlī ibn Jabala al-ᶜAkawwak', 'al-Āmidī', 'Aᶜshā Hamdān', 'al-Ashᶜath Ibn Qays', 'al-Babbaghāʾ', 'Basra', 'chronogram', 'commentaries', 'debate literature', 'Diᶜbil ibn ᶜAlī', 'didactic literature', 'Dīk al-Jinn', 'epigram', 'al-Farazdaq', 'figural poetry', 'Ḥammād ᶜAjrad', 'Ḥassān Ibn Thābit', 'al-Ḥātimī', 'hijāʾ', 'Hijaz', 'Ibn Abī al-Iṣbaᶜ', 'Ibn Ḥayyūs', 'Ibn Ḥijja al-Ḥamawī', 'Ibn al-Kattānī', 'Ibn Lankak', 'Ibn Maᶜṣūm', 'Ibn al-Muᶜadhdhal', 'Ibn Qutayba', 'Ibn Rashīq al-Qayrawānī', 'Ibn al-Rūmī', 'Ibn Sallām al-Jumaḥī', 'Ibn Sinān al-Khafājī', 'Ibn Ṭabāṭabā', 'Ibn ᶜUnayn', 'Ibn Wahb (Isḥāq ibn Ibrāhīm)', '*ījāz*', 'improvisation (in poetry)', 'inspiration', '*iqtibās*', '*ishāra*', 'Jarīr', 'al-Jurjānī (al-Qāḍī ᶜAlī ibn ᶜAbd a-ᶜAzīz)', 'al-Kalāᶜī', 'Khalaf al-Aḥmar', 'Khālid ibn Yazīd al-kātib', 'al-Khālidiyyān', 'al-Khansāʾ', 'al-Khaṭīb al-Tibrīzī', 'al-Khaṭṭābī', 'al-Khirniq', '*lughz*', 'al-Marghīnānī', 'Marwān Ibn Abī l-Janūb', 'al-Marzubānī (Muḥammad ibn ᶜImrān)', 'Mirbad 1. Medieval', '*muᶜammā*', '*muᶜāraḍa*', 'al-Mubarrad', 'Muḥammad al-Salāmī', '*mulammaᶜa*', 'al-Muṭarrizī', 'al-Mutawakkil al-Laythī', 'al-Najāshī', 'al-Nāmī (Abū al-ᶜAbbās)', '*naqāʾiḍ*', 'al-Nāshiʾ al-Akbar', 'al-Nāshiʾ al-Aṣghar', 'al-Nawājī', 'poetic contests', 'poetry vs. prose', 'al-Qālī', 'Ruʾba ibn al-ᶜAjjāj', 'al-Rummānī', 'al-Sakkākī', 'Ṣāliḥ Ibn ᶜAbd a-Quddūs', 'Salm al-Khāsir', 'satire 1. Classical', 'al-Shanfarā', 'al-Shantamarī', 'al-Sukkarī', 'al-Ṣūlī (Abū Bakr)', 'Taʾabbaṭa Sharran', 'al-Tihāmī', 'ᶜUkāẓ', 'ᶜUrwa Ibn al-Ward', 'al-Wāsānī', 'al-Waʾwāʾ al-Dimashqī', 'al-Yazīdī (Yaḥyā Ibn al-Mubārak)', 'al-Zafayān', 'al-Zawzanī', 'al-Zibriqān'.

BOOK REVIEWS

Rev. of Suzanne Pinckney Stetkevych, *The Mantle Odes: Arabic Praise Poems to the Prophet Muḥammad*, Bloomington & Indianopolis, 2010, in *Speculum*, forthcoming.

Rev. of Li Guo, The Performing Arts in Medieval Islam: Shadow Play and Popular Poetry in Ibn Dāniyāl's Mamlūk Cairo, Leiden/Boston: Brill, 2012, *Journal of the American Oriental Society*, forthcoming.

Rev. of *Emanations of Grace: Mystical Poems* by ʿĀʾishah al-Bāʿūnīyah (d. 923/1517), ed. and tr. with an Introd. by Th. Emil Homerin, Louisville, KY: Fons Vitae, 2011, *Der Islam*, forthcoming.

Rev. of Raymond Farrin, *Abundance from the Desert: Classical Arabic Poetry*, New York: Syracuse University Press, 2011, in *Speculum*, vol. 87, no. 4 (2012) pp. 1190–91.

Rev. of Khalid Sindawi, A Poet of the Abbasid Period: Abū al-Qāsim al-Zāhī (ʿAlī b. Isḥāq b. Khalaf al-Zāhī), 313–352 AH/*925–963 CE. His Life and Poetry, Annotated, edited with an introduction*, Wiesbaden: Harrassowitz Verlag, 2010, in *Journal of Islamic Studies*, vol. 23, no. 1 (2012) pp. 92–4.

Rev. of Ali Ahmad Hussein, *The Lightning-Scene in Ancient Arabic Poetry: Function, Narration and Idiosyncrasy in Pre-Islamic and Early Islamic Poetry*, Wiesbaden: Harrassowitz, 2009, in *Journal of the American Oriental Society*, vol. 131, no. 4 (2011) pp. 641–43.

Rev. of Kirill Dmitriev, *Das poetische Werk des Abū Ṣaḫr al-Huḏalī. Eine literaturanthropologische Studie*. Wiesbaden: Harrassowitz Verlag, 2008, in *Speculum*, vol. 86 (2011) pp. 742–43.

Rev. of Samer M. Ali, *Arabic Literary Salons in the Islamic Middle Ages: Poetry, Performance, and the Presentation of the Past*, Notre Dame, IN: University of Notre Dame Press, 2010, in *The Times Literary Supplement*, 25 February 2011 (No. 5630), p. 27.

rev. of ʿAbd al-Muʿīn b. Aḥmad al-Balkhi Ibn al-Bakkāʾ, Ghawānī al-ashwāq fī maʿānī al-ʿUshshāq / *A Treatise on the Concept of Love in Classical and Medieval Arabic Heritage*, ed. George Kanazi, Wiesbaden: Harrassowitz, 2008, in *Journal of Islamic Studies*, vol. 22, no. 1 (2010), pp. 72–4.

Rev. of The Brethren of Purity, *The case of the animals versus man before the king of the Jinn: An Arabic critical edition and English translation of Epistle 22*, ed. and transl. by Lenn E. Goodman and Richard McGregor, Oxford: Oxford University Press, in *The Times Literary Supplement*, 5 November 2010 (No. 5614), pp. 12–13.

Rev. of Martin Jagonak, *Das Bild der Liebe im Werk des Dichters* Ǧamīl ibn Maʿmar: Eine Studie zur *ʿuḏritischen Lyrik in der arabischen Literatur des späten 7. Jahrhunderts*. Wiesbaden: Harrassowitz, 2008 (Ser. Diskurse der Arabistik, vol. 13), in *Speculum* vol. 84, no. 4 (2009) pp. 1064–65.

Rev. of Shams al-Dīn Muḥammad b. Ḥasan al-Nawājī, *Taʾhīl al-Gharīb*, ed. Aḥmad Muḥammad ʿAṭā, Cairo: Maktabat al-Ādāb, 1425/2005, in *Mamlūk Studies Review* vol. 13, no. 2 (2009) pp. 174–76.

Rev. of Thomas Bauer and Angelika Neuwirth (eds.), *Ghazal as World Literature. I: Transformations of a Literary Genre*, Beirut [Würzburg]: Orient-Institut Beirut [Ergon Verlag] (Ser. Beiruter Texte und Studien, vol. 89), 2005; and Angelika Neuwirth, Michael Hess, Judith Pfeiffer and Börte Sagaster (eds.), *Ghazal as World Literature. II: From a Literary Genre to a Great Tradition. The Ottoman Gazel in Context*. Würzburg: Orient-Institut Istanbul [Ergon Verlag] (Ser. Istanbuler Texte und Studien, vol. 4), 2006, in *Middle Eastern Literatures*, vol. 12, no. 2 (2009) pp. 180–84.

Rev. of Robert C. McKinney, *The Case of Rhyme versus Reason: Ibn al-Rūmī and his Poetics in Context*, Leiden: Brill, 2004, in *Middle Eastern Literatures*, vol. 12, no. 2 (2009) pp. 185–87.

Rev. of Thomas Hoffmann, *The Poetic Qurʾān: Studies on Qurʾānic Poeticity*, Wiesbaden: Harrassowitz Verlag, 2007 (Ser. Diskurse der Arabistik, vol. 12), *Journal of Islamic Studies*, vol. 20, no. 3 (2009) pp. 408–11.

Rev. of *The Arabian Nights: Tales of 1001 Nights*. Translated by Malcolm C. Lyons, with Ursula Lyons. Introduced and annotated by Robert Irwin. 3 vols. London: Penguin Classics, 2008, in *The Times Literary Supplement*, Jan. 23 2009 (No. 5521), pp. 7–8.

Rev. of Shams al-Dīn Muḥammad b. Ḥasan al-Nawājī, *Kitāb al-Shifāʾ fī Badīʿ al-Iktifāʾ*, ed. Ḥasan

Muḥammad ʿAbd al-Hādī, Amman: Dār al-Yanābīʿ li-l-Nashr wa-al-Tawzīʿ, 2004, in *Mamlūk Studies Review*, vol. 11, no. 1 (2007) pp. 233–35.

Rev. of Shawkat M. Toorawa, *Ibn Abī Ṭāhir Ṭayfūr and Arabic Writerly Culture: A ninth-century bookman in Baghdad*, London: RoutledgeCurzon, 2005, in *Times Literary Supplement*, May 26 2006, p. 30.

Rev. of Suzanne Pinckney Stetkevych, *The Poetics of Islamic Legitimacy: Myth, Gender, and Ceremony in the Classical Arabic Ode*, Bloomington, IN: Indiana University Press, 2002, in *Journal of Islamic Studies*, vol. 16, no. 1 (2005) pp. 123–25.

Rev. of Ibrahim Kh. Geries (Ibrāhīm Khalīl Jiryis), *A Literary and Gastronomical Conceit:* Mufāḵẖarat al-Ruzz wa ʾl-Ḥabb Rummān, *The Boasting Debate Between Rice And Pomegranate Seeds, Or* al-Maḵāma al-Simāṭiyya *(The Tablecloth Maḵāma)*, Wiesbaden: Harrassowitz, 2002 (Codices Arabici Antiqui, vol. 7), in *Middle Eastern Literatures*, vol. 7, no. 1 (2004) pp. 87–90.

Rev. of Niloofar Haeri, *Sacred Language, Ordinary People: Dilemmas of Culture and Politics in Egypt*, London: Palgrave Macmillan, 2003, in *Times Literary Supplement*, Jan. 30 2004, p. 24.

Rev. of Akiko Motoyoshi Sumi, *Description in Classical Arabic Poetry: Waṣf, Ekphrasis, and Interarts Theory*, Leiden: Brill, 2004, in *Bulletin of the School of Oriental and African Studies*, vol. 67, no. 3 (2004) pp. 393–95.

Rev. of Abū l-Ṭāhir Muḥammad ibn Yūsuf al-Tamīmī al-Saraqusṭī Ibn al-Aštarkuwī, *Al-Maqāmāt al-luzūmīyah*, translated with a preliminary study by James T. Monroe, Leiden, 2002, in *Journal of Islamic Studies*, vol. 15, no. 3 (2004) pp. 352–54.

Rev. of Pierre Cachia, *Arabic Literature: An Overview*, London: RoutledgeCurzon, 2002, in *Times Literary Supplement*, Feb 21 2003 (no. 5212), p. 25.

Rev. of Dwight F. Reynolds et al., *Interpreting the Self: Autobiography in the Arabic Literary Tradition*, Berkeley: University of California Press, 2001, in *Journal of Islamic Studies*, vol. 13, no. 2 (2002) pp. 187–90.

Rev. of Maxime Rodinson, A.J. Arberry and Charles Perry, *Medieval Arab Cookery: Essays and Translations*, Blackawton, Totnes, Devon: Prospect Books, 2001, in *Journal of Islamic Studies*, vol. 13, no. 2 (2002), pp. 248–51.

Rev. of Kathryn Kueny, *The Rhetoric of Sobriety: Wine in Early Islam*, Albany, NY: SUNY Press, 2001, in *International Journal of Middle Eastern Studies*, vol. 34, no. 4 (2002) pp. 773–75.

Rev. of Herbjørn Jenssen, *The Subtleties and Secrets of the Arabic Language: Preliminary Investigations into al-Qazwīnī's* Talkḥīṣ al-Miftāḥ, Bergen, 1998, in *Edebiyât*, vol. 12 (2001) pp. 123–28.

Rev. of Thomas Bauer, *Liebe und Liebesdichtung in der arabischen Welt des 9. und 10. Jahrhunderts: Eine literatur- und mentalitätsgeschichtliche Studie des arabischen Ġazal*, Wiesbaden: Harrassowitz, 1998, in *Arabic and Middle Eastern Literatures*, vol. 4, no. 2 (2001) pp. 197–201.

Rev. of María Rosa Menocal, Raymond P. Scheindlin and Michael Sells (eds.), *The Literature of Al-Andalus*, Cambridge: Cambridge University Press, 2000 (Ser. The Cambridge History of Arabic Literature), in *Times Literary Supplement*, June 1 2001 (no. 5122), p. 7.

Rev. of Manfred Ullmann, *Das Motiv der Kreuzigung in der arabischen Poesie des Mittelalters*, Wiesbaden: Harrassowitz, 1995, in *Arabic and Middle Eastern Literatures* vol. 3, no. 1 (2000) pp. 98–100.

Rev. of *The Book of Strangers: Mediaeval Arabic graffiti on the theme of nostalgia.* Tr. by Patricia Crone and Shmuel Moreh, Princeton, NJ: Markus Wiener, 2000, in *Times Literary Supplement*, March 31 2000, (no. 5061), p. 11.

Rev. of Stefan Leder (ed.), *Story-telling in the framework of non-fictional Arabic literature*, Wiesbaden: Harrassowitz, 1998, in *Bibliotheca Orientalis* vol. 57, nos 1–2 (2000) col. 203–208.

Rev. of Eva Sallis, *Sheherazade Through the Looking-Glass: The Metamorphosis of the* Thousand and One Nights, Richmond, Surrey: Curzon, 1999, in *Journal of the Royal Asiatic Society*, 3rd Ser., vol. 10, no. 2 (2000) pp. 230–32.

Rev. of Wen-chin Ouyang, *Literary Criticism in Medieval Arabic-Islamic Culture: The Making of a Tradition*, Edinburgh: Edinburgh University Press, 1997, in *Bibliotheca Orientalis*, vol. 55, nos 5–6 (1998 [1999]) col. 927–931.

Rev. of Pierre Cachia, *The Arch Rhetorician, or The Schemer's Skimmer: A Handbook of Late Arabic badīᶜ drawn from ᶜAbd al-Ghanī an-Nābulsī's* Nafaḥāt al-Azhār ᶜalā Nasamāt al-Asḥār, Wiesbaden: Harrassowitz, 1998, in *Bibliotheca Orientalis*, vol. 56, nos 5–6 (1999) col. 798–801.

Rev. of Kathrin Müller, *Der Beduine und die Regenwolke. Ein Beiträg zur Erforschung der altarabischen Anekdote* (Ser. Beiträge zur Lexikographie des Klassischen Arabisch, Nr. 12; Bayerische Akad. der Wiss., Phil.-hist. Kl., Sitzungsberichte, Jrg. 1994, Heft 2), Munich, 1994, in *Bibliotheca Orientalis*, vol. 54, nos 1–2 (1997) col. 252–254.

Rev. of Ulrich Marzolph, *Arabia Ridens. Die humoristische Kurzprosa der frühen adab-Literatur im internationalen Traditionsgeflecht*. 2 vols, Frankfurt am Main, 1992, in *Bibliotheca Orientalis*, vol. 52, nos 1–2 (1995) col. 196–199.

Rev. of Adnan Abbas, *The band as a new form of poetry in Iraq, 17th century*, Poznań, 1994, in *Orientalistische Literaturzeitung*, vol. 91, no. 2 (1996) col. 193–195.

Rev. of Th. Emil Homerin, *From Arab Poet to Muslim Saint: Ibn al-Fāriḍ, His Verse, and His Shrine*, Columbia, SC, 1994, in *Bibiotheca Orientalis*, vol. 53, nos 3–4 (1996) col. 563–565.

Rev. of Ludwig Ammann, *Vorbild und Vernunft: Die Regelung von Lachen und Scherzen im mittelalterlichen Islam* (Ser. Arabistische Texte und Studien, vol. 5). Georg Olms Verlag, 1993, in *Bibliotheca Orientalis*, vol. 53, nos 5–6 (1996) col. 861–864.

Rev. of Kathrin Müller,*'Und der Kalif lachte, bis er auf den Rücken fiel'. Ein Beitrag zur Phraseologie und Stilkunde des klassische Arabisch.* (Ser. Beiträge zur Lexikographie des Klassischen Arabisch Nr. 10; Bayerische Akademie der Wissenschaften Philosophisch-historische Klasse / Sitzungsberichte. Jrg. 1993, Heft 2). Munich, 1993, in *Bibliotheca Orientalis*, vol. 53, nos 5–6 (1996) col. 864–865.

Rev. of *Sultan Osman (1623) & Bedroge Bedriegers (1646): Turkse tragedies van Kemp en Kroes*, Uitgegeven door C.G. Brouwer, Amsterdam: De Fluyte Rarob, 1994, (Ser. *De Oostersche Schouburgh*, vol. 1), in *Turcica*, vol. 28 (1996) pp. 385–87.

Rev. of Thomas Bauer, *Altarabische Dichtkunst: Eine Untersuchung ihrer Struktur und Entwicklung am Beispiel der Onagerepisode*, 2 vols, Wiesbaden: Harrasowitz, 1992, in *Bibliotheca Orientalis*, vol. 52, nos 1–2 (1995) col. 189–192.

Rev. of Paul Kunitzsch and Manfred Ullmann, *Die Plejaden in den Vergleichen der arabischen Dichtung*, Munich, 1992, in *Journal of Arabic Literature*, vol. 26, no. 3 (1995) pp. 282–84.

Rev. of Jaroslav Stetkevych, *The Zephyrs of Najd: The Poetics of Nostalgia in the Classical Arabic* Nasīb, Chicago, 1993, in *Journal of the American Oriental Society*, vol. 115, no. 2 (1995) p. 335.

Rev. of Mahmoud Darabseh, *Die Kritik der Prosa bei den Arabern (vom 3./9. Jahrhundert bis zum Ende des 5./11. Jahrhunderts)*, Berlin, 1990, in *Die Welt des Islams*, vol. 33 (1993) pp. 138–40.

Rev. of Sasson Somekh (ed.), *Studies in Medieval Arabic and Hebrew Poetics*, Leiden: Brill, 1991, (Ser. Israel Oriental Studies, vol. 11), in *Die Welt des Islams*, vol. 33 (1993) pp. 327–29.

Rev. of Avner Gilᶜadi, *Children of Islam: Concepts of Childhood in Medieval Muslim Society*, Basingstoke; London, 1992, in *The Times Literary Supplement*, Jan 15 1993, p. 8.

Rev. of ᶜAbdalqādir Ibn ᶜUmar al-Baġdādī, *Glossen zu Ibn Hišāms Kommentar zu dem Gedicht Bānat Suᶜād*, hrsg. von Nazif Hoca, Teil 2 I, II, Stuttgart, 1990, in *Bibliotheca Orientalis*, vol. 50, nos 5–6 (1993) col. 772–773.

Rev. of Mohamed Attahiri, *Kriegsgedichte zur Zeit der Almohaden*, Frankfurt am Main, 1992, in *Bibliotheca Orientalis*, vol. 50, nos 5–6 (1993) col. 771–772.

Rev. of Wolfhart Heinrichs (ed.), *Orientalisches Mittelalter*, (Ser. Neues Handbuch der Literaturwisschenschaft, vol. 5), Wiesbaden, 1991, in *Journal of the American Oriental Society*, vol. 113, no. 1 (1993) pp. 120–22.

Rev. of Julia Ashtiany et al. (eds.), *ᶜAbbasid Belles-Lettres* (Ser. The Cambridge History of Arabic Literature), Cambridge: Cambridge University Press, 1990, and Suzanne P. Stetkevych, *Abū Tammām and the Poetics of the ᶜAbbāsid Age*, Leiden: Brill, 1991, in *The Times Literary Supplement*, Jan 24, 1992, p. 12.

Rev. of George J. Kanazi, *Studies in the* Kitāb aṣ-Ṣināʿatayn *of Abū Hilāl al-ʿAskarī*, Leiden, 1989, in *Bibliotheca Orientalis*, vol. 48, nos 5–6 (1991) [1992] col. 938–940.

Rev. of George Makdisi, *The Rise of Humanism in Classical Islam and the Christian West, with special reference to scholasticism*, Edinburgh, 1990, in *Bibliotheca Orientalis*, vol. 49, nos 3–4 (1992), col. 538–540.

Rev. of Tilman Seidensticker, *Die Gedichte des Šamardal Ibn Šarīk. Neuedition, Übersetzung, Kommentar*, Wiesbaden, 1983, in *Bibliotheca Orientalis*, vol. 49, nos 3–4 (1992) col. 537–538.

Rev. of Salem M. H. al-Hadrusi, *Al-Muntahā fī l-kamāl des Muḥammad Ibn Sahl Ibn al-Marzubān al-Karḫī (gest. ca. 345/956). Untersuchung und kritische Edition von Bd 4-5 und 9-10*, Berlin, 1988, in *Bibliotheca Orientalis*, vol. 49, nos 3–4 (1992) col. 530–531.

Rev. of Mohamed Ait El Ferrane, *Die Maʿnā-Theorie bei ʿAbdalqāhir al-Ǧurǧānī (gestorben 471/1079). Versuch einer Analyse der poetischen Sprache*, Frankfurt am Main, 1990, in *Bibliotheca Orientalis*, vol. 49, nos 3–4 (1992) col. 528–530.

Rev. of Mansour Ajami, *The Alchemy of Glory: the dialectic of truthfulness and untruthfulness in medieval Arabic literary criticism*, Washington, 1988, in *Die Welt des Islams*, vol. 31 (1991) pp. 256–58.

Rev. of Stefan Sperl, *Mannerism in Arabic poetry: a structural analysis of selected texts (3rd century A.H./9th century A.D.-5th century A.H./11th century A.D.)*, Cambridge: Cambridge University Press, 1989), in *Bulletin of the School of Oriental and African Studies*, vol. 53, no. 2 (1990) pp. 343–44.

Rev. of Ziyad al-Ramadan az-Zuʿbī, *Das Verhältnis von Poesie und Prosa in der arabischen Literaturtheorie des Mittelalters*, Berlin, 1987, in *Die Welt des Islams*, vol. 30 (1990) pp. 257–58.

Rev. of Ewald Wagner, *Grundzüge der klassischen arabischen Dichtung*, 2 vols, Darmstadt, 1987–88, in *Bibliotheca Orientalis*, vol. 47, nos 3–4 (1990) col. 499–501.

Rev. of Mansour Ajami, *The Neckveins of Winter: the Controversy over Natural and Artificial Poetry in Medieval Arabic Literary Criticism*, Leiden: Brill, 1984, in *Die Welt des Islams*, vol. 226 (1986) pp. 172–75.

Rev. of Pieter Smoor, *Kings and Bedouins in the Palace of Aleppo as reflected in Maʿarrī's works*, Leiden; Manchester, 1985, in *MOI-publicatie*, vol. 13 (1986) pp. 76–9.

Rev. of Abu Bakr Muhammad ibn Tufayl, *Wat geen oog heeft gezien...: de geschiedenis van Hayy ibn Yaqzan*. Uit het Arabisch vertaald en ingeleid door Remke Kruk, Amsterdam, 1985, in *MOI-publicatie*, vol. 13 (1986) pp. 85–7.

Rev. of ʿAbd al-Qādir al-Baghdādī, *Ḥāshiya ʿalā Sharḥ Bānat Suʿād li-Ibn Hishām / Glossen zu dem Gedicht Bānat Suʿād*, Hrsg. von Nazif Hoca, Teil I, Wiesbaden, 1980, in *Bibliotheca Orientalis*, vol. 42, nos 1–2 (1985) col. 223–225.

Rev. of Muḥammad al-Tanasī, *Naẓm al-durr wa 'l-ʿiqyān, al-qism al-rābiʿ: fī maḥāsin al-kalām / Westarabische Tropik: Naẓm IV des Tanasī*, Hrsg. u. erl. von Nuri Soudan, Beirut; Wiesbaden, 1980, in *Bibliotheca Orientalis*, vol. 39, nos 3–4 (1982), col. 456–459.

Rev. of P. Knightley and C. Simpson, *The Secret Lives of Lawrence of Arabia*, London, 1969, in *Internationale Spectator: Tijdschrift voor internationale politiek*, vol. 24, no. 12 (1970) pp. 1126–31.

OBITUARIES

'Seeger A. Bonebakker in memoriam', *Quaderni di Studi Arabi*, n.s. 1 (2006) pp. 5–6.

'Seeger Adrianus Bonebakker', in *Levensberichten en herdenkingen 2007*, Amsterdam: Koninklijke Nederlandse Akademie van Wetenschappen, 2007, pp. 18–21.